THE LINDBERGH CASE

THE LINDBERGH CASE

J I M   F I S H E R

RUTGERS UNIVERSITY PRESS   NEW BRUNSWICK AND LONDON

FRONTISPIECE The baby a few months before the kidnapping. Courtesy New Jersey State Police.

Second paperback printing, 1998
Copyright © 1987 by Jim Fisher
All rights reserved
Manufactured in the United States of America

Designed by Liz Waite

Library of Congress Cataloging-in-Publication Data
Fisher, Jim, 1939–
The Lindbergh case.
Bibliography: p.
Includes index.
1. Lindbergh, Charles Augustus, 1930–1932.
2. Hauptmann, Bruno Richard, 1899–1936.   3. Kidnapping—New Jersey.   I. Title.
HV6603.L5F57   1987   364.1′54′0924 [B] 86-28023
ISBN 0-8135-1233-6 (cloth)
ISBN 0-8135-2147-5 (pbk.)

British Cataloging-in-Publication
information available

To my wife,
S U S A N

CONTENTS

*Illustrations appear on pages
231–246.*

PREFACE TO THE PAPERBACK EDITION

This paperback edition of *The Lindbergh Case* has given me an opportunity to correct minor errors, to expand and update the bibliography, and to chronicle new developments in the Lindbergh debate, including Mrs. Hauptmann's ongoing quest to clear her husband's name.

When *The Lindbergh Case* came out in the fall of 1987, many people believed the man electrocuted for the 1932 murder of the Lindbergh baby was innocent. Of those who still considered Hauptmann guilty, only a handful thought he had committed the crime alone. At the time of Hauptmann's execution in 1936, a vast majority accepted his guilt in the face of what seemed to be overwhelming, albeit circumstantial evidence. Few would have guessed that fifty years later a book confirming Hauptmann's guilt would be controversial.

In the interim, revisionists had captured the Lindbergh case, and in the process had rewritten history to achieve their own political and ideological goals. The revisionists have turned the Lindbergh case into a symbol of heavy-handed law enforcement and criminal injustice. Taking a position on Hauptmann's guilt or innocence has less to do with evaluating the evidence than with making a political statement.

Patterson Smith, an antiquarian bookseller from Montclair, New Jersey, specializing in books on crime and criminal justice, understands why "wrong man" books are published:

> Of all crime books published, those posing revisionist theories tend to attract the greatest media attention. They are "news." Far from merely adding to our knowledge of a past event or re-embellishing a tale previously grown stale in the retelling, they say to us, "you've been wrong about this case." And if someone is thought to have been unjustly convicted and executed, the news value is all the stronger.
>
> It has, after all, been observed that Americans have a greater sense of injustice than of justice. When a revisionist account reaches reviewers, the arguments put forth by its author can seem extraordinarily compelling, for very often the book does not aim for balance but selects only those facts that support its divergent thesis.
>
> Moreover—and this is very important—the reviewer of a book on crime written for the general public often has little or no background in the case which could help him weigh the author's novel contentions against countervailing evidence. The reviewer sees only one side of the story, and it usually looks good.[1]

In 1976 *New York Newsday* reporter Anthony Scaduto published a book called *Scapegoat* in which he alleged that every piece of physical evidence against Hauptmann was fabricated or distorted, and that all of the key prosecution witnesses took the stand and lied. Scaduto also recycled Burlington County detective Ellis Parker's old claim that the Lindbergh baby hadn't been killed. Parker had pointed to the discrepancy in the length of the corpse found in the woods—33½"—and the Lindbergh baby's height—

29"—as published on his wanted poster. Scaduto took Detective Parker's idea one step further by suggesting that Harold Olson, a businessman from Hartford, Connecticut, might be the living Lindbergh son. This height differential, a factor that has produced at least fourteen other Lindbergh baby claimants, was nothing more than a typographical error on the posters that were supposed to read 2 feet, 9 inches—33 inches.[2]

Scaduto fails to prove his allegations of perjury, evidence suppression, police coercion, and evidence tampering, but manages, through misdirection, the selective use of evidence, faulty analysis, character assassination, and rhetoric, to make a convincing case for Hauptmann. Ignoring overwhelming evidence to the contrary, Scaduto portrays Hauptmann as a decent, hard-working, and loving family man. Some reviewers of *Scapegoat* were taken in. According to *The New York Times*: "'Scapegoat' should be compulsory reading for those who fear that post-war rulings by the Supreme Court, protecting the rights of the accused, have tied the hands of justice. . . . The book also should be read by defenders of capital punishment."[3]

Scaduto didn't fool all the reviewers, however. Francis Russell, the respected Harvard historian and author, said this about *Scapegoat*:

> Mr. Scaduto started off with his conclusions intact, having been persuaded of Hauptmann's innocence by a dubious underworld figure, Murray Bleefeld, who had once helped kidnap the disbarred Trenton lawyer, Paul Wendel, and got him to confess to the Lindbergh kidnapping. Wendel, a former mental patient, later repudiated his confession, one that Bleefeld revived a generation later for Scaduto, hoping to make money out of it.[4]

On October 14, 1981, five years following the publication of Scaduto's book, San Francisco attorney Robert R. Bryan filed, on Mrs. Hauptmann's behalf, a $100 million lawsuit in which he asked the federal court to vacate Bruno Hauptmann's 1935 murder conviction.

In deciding who to sue for this travesty of justice, Bryan left no stone unturned. He sued David T. Wilentz, the Lindbergh case prosecutor; former New Jersey State Police officers Lewis J. Bornmann, John B. Wallace, Joseph A. Wolf, and Hugo Stockburger; former New Jersey governor Brendan T. Byrne; New Jersey State Police Superintendent Clinton J. Pagano; ex-FBI agent Thomas H. Sisk; and the Hearst Corporation, the money behind defense attorney Edward J. Reilly. After filing the initial suit, Bryan followed up with four amended complaints, the last being filed on March 7, 1983.

Attorney Bryan was not new to the Lindbergh case. In the mid-1970s he brought suit against Colonel Lindbergh's estate on behalf of a man named Kenneth Kerwin who, like Harold Olson and others, claimed to be the kidnapped Lindbergh heir. Bryan lost.

In answering Bryan's complaints, the other side asserted that the legal issues raised by Mrs. Hauptmann's suit had been addressed and resolved pursuant to Hauptmann's appeals following his conviction. Mrs. Hauptmann, they answered, had failed to produce any new evidence; all of her claims were merely recycled allegations. The defendants also objected to the suit on the grounds it had not been filed within the five-year statute of limitations—that Mrs. Hauptmann had learned of the so-called frame-up in 1976 when she read Scaduto's *Scapegoat*.

Arguing that she had not been put on notice by *Scapegoat* five years before bringing the action, Mrs. Hauptmann, in 1984, signed an affidavit that must have astounded Anthony Scaduto. Her affidavit read:

> I gave virtually no credibility to *Scapegoat*, since the author completely breached a written agreement with me entered several years before the book was published. In effect he lied to me, making it hard for me to believe anything he wrote. Also, the portion of the book I read seemed inaccurate with little new other than theories. He did not reveal to me in his interviews or book any new significant evidence, only theories.
> . . . Mr. Scaduto convinced me originally that he could be trusted. . . . After Mr. Scaduto broke his word with me, I felt I could place no value on what he had written. Since he misrepresented things to me, it was not reasonable to place any reliance on anything he said or wrote. This is the main reason why I did not read but a portion of the book after it was published. Additionally, I was elderly, not in good health, and had no money. And as stated in my earlier affidavit, what I did read seemed to contain theories, but no new facts.[5]

It is ironic that Mrs. Hauptmann would trash the book that had opened the door for her lawsuit, had led to the release of the Lindbergh case files, and had paved the way for the clearing of her husband's name. Because of Scaduto's book and the publicity that surrounded it, many people developed serious doubts that her husband was guilty. All of a sudden, it wasn't Hauptmann but the police and the courts who were the villains in the crime of the century. Mrs. Hauptmann could thank Scaduto for that.

In the winter of 1982, public television aired a one-hour BBC film called *Who Killed the Lindbergh Baby?* Written and narrated by the British television personality and true-crime writer Ludovic Kennedy, this shameful piece of propaganda cleverly disguised as a documentary made a moving if not factual case for Hauptmann. This program, *Scapegoat* set to pictures and music, turned Mrs. Hauptmann into a made-for-TV victim, transformed her husband into a dead hero, and painted the men who had solved the Lindbergh crime and brought a murderer to justice as a bunch of malicious, headline-grabbing persecutors. *Who Killed the Lindbergh Baby?* is television sophistry at its best, and history at its worst.

Attorney Bryan's lawsuit was dismissed in 1983. In throwing out the case, Federal Judge Frederick B. Lacey wrote: "Plaintiff's allegations of conspiracy are deficient as conclusory and nonspecific. . . ."[6] Bryan appealed Judge Lacey's decision and lost. He lost again when the Unted States Supreme Court denied his petition for further review.

Ludovic Kennedy, in 1985, came out with his own vindication of Hauptmann in a book called *The Airman and the Carpenter*. Although Kennedy ridiculed the idea the Lindbergh baby hadn't been killed, or that Violet Sharpe had anything to do with the crime, he repeated Scaduto's general thesis of manufactured evidence and perjured testimony.[7] Like Scaduto, Kennedy had his way with the critics. The reviewer for *The New*

York Times Book Review wrote: "One puts down 'The Airman and the Carpenter' troubled, and certain that what was billed as the trial of the century was an awful miscarriage of justice."[8] Even the conservative book critic for the *National Review* was taken in: "The jury convicted him, and he went expeditiously to the chair. But *was* he guilty? The answer seems to be almost certainly not."[9]

In Ludovic Kennedy's autobiography, published in 1989, the author, referring to his earlier book on the Lindbergh case, says: "Not a single critic of my book in America or Britain disagreed fundamentally with my findings."[10]

This is not true. Although Kennedy had fooled general readers, there were criminal justice practitioners and scholars all over the country who knew better. One of these was Judge John F. Keenan. Writing in the *Michigan Law Review*, Kennan observed:

> Where there is no confession, no apprehension at the scene with the smoking gun, no video or audio tape, no ultimate acknowledgment of guilt, then books abound. . . . The author . . . cannot acknowledge the guilt of the victim/martyr. Rather the investigators, the prosecutors, the witnesses, the judges, and even the defense counsel involved must become the villians. They are second-guessed. Their motives, their personalities, their techniques, their rulings are all put under a retrospective microscope. That is what *The Airman and the Carpenter* really is—a series of second guesses and hindsight criticisms, many of them awfully bitter and very vicious.[11]

Patterson Smith, the antiquarian bookseller and crime historian who has written extensively on the literature of the Lindbergh case, wrote:

> Kennedy's effort to overcome the massive evidence against Hauptmann is a failure. That evidence was entirely circumstantial—the strongest kind of evidence, since it does not rely directly on the accuracy of human observation or the memory or veracity of witnesses. Those elements of it that Kennedy cannot dismiss as irrelevant or concocted he attempts to explain away. But there's too much of it, and the logic with which he deals with it is badly flawed.[12]

In 1985, shortly after Ludovic Kennedy's book came out, 23,000 Lindbergh case documents were discovered in a South Amboy, New Jersey, garage. These papers had been gathered by Governor Harold G. Hoffman who, in 1935 following Hauptmann's conviction, launched his own investigation into the case. Hoffman gambled his political career on the chance that Hauptmann was either innocent or had accomplices. The so-called Hoffman Papers consist of hundreds of documents from the investigative files of the New Jersey State Police, and the reports, memos, and letters generated by a dozen or so private investigators working for the governor.[13]

One of these investigators, George H. Foster, had volunteered his services in the hopes of getting on the New Jersey State Police after the governor fired H. Norman Schwarzkopf.[14] The governor's investigation went nowhere, he was ruined politically, and although he fired Schwarzkopf, George H. Foster didn't get a job with the New Jersey State Police. Hoffman's so-called reinvestigation was a bust, but that didn't stop attorney Robert Bryan, fifty years later, from using the historically interesting but generally irrelevant and redundant Hoffman Papers to justify another lawsuit. This suit was dismissed in 1986 by Federal Judge Garrett E. Brown, Jr., who wrote: "Mrs. Hauptmann's suit is based upon broad and conclusory allegations . . . with no attempt to tie those allegations to the 'evidence' contained in the recently discovered documents."[15]

Having lost once again in a real court of law, Bryan arranged, as a publicity gimmick, a hearing before the San Francisco Court of Historical Review and Appeals, a nonjudicial forum where historical controversies such as the origin of the martini could be resolved once and for all.[16] The one-hour and fifteen-minute hearing before "Judge" George Choppelas, attended by a hundred supportive spectators and a handful of reporters, featured Mrs. Hauptmann's tearful declaration of her husband's innocence. Bryan addressed the group and announced that the Lindbergh kidnapping had been an "inside job" that resulted from an intimate relationship between a member of the Lindbergh family and a servant.[17] Those familiar with the case immediately thought of Colonel Lindbergh and the young and beautiful Betty Gow. To no one's surprise, Mr. Choppelas did what two U.S. District Court judges had refused to do: He recommended that the Lindbergh case be reopened. There was a historical need for this, he held.

Flushed with victory, Bryan said this to reporters: "I know who did it [the kidnapping] and how many people were involved. But I do not want to reveal all the details yet. I want to make sure we can tie down all the loose ends. We're 99% certain of what happened, who did it, why, and why such a samall ransom was demanded."[18]

Following the San Francisco hearing, this Wopneresque court of California kitch, Attorney Bryan presented Mrs. Hauptmann, who had just turned eighty-eight, a birthday cake with a single candle. While Mrs. Hauptmann sobbed, everybody—including the judge—sang "Happy Birthday."[19]

In November 1987, Bryan appealed Judge Garret E. Brown's dismissal of his federal suit, and the following month, in a newspaper interview, promised to reveal the real identity of the Lindbergh kidnapper.[20] The Third Circuit Court of Appeals on July 7, 1988, turned down Bryan's appeal, thus ending eight years of legal grandstanding and frivolous suing. Just hours after the Federal Appeals Court in Philadelphia rejected Bryan's case, David T. Wilentz died in his sleep at his summer home in Long Branch, New Jersey. Although the ninety-three-year-old former attorney general had been a dominant figure in New Jersey's Democratic party for thirty years, he would be remembered as the man who had sent Bruno Hauptmann to the electric chair.

Having exhausted his legal remedies, Robert Bryan turned to the New Jersey legislature, sending letters to the forty state senators and eighty assembly members, asking them for permission to appear before the legislature or its appropriate committee to plead Hauptmann's case. "I am prepared," he wrote, "to present credible evidence pertaining to the massive fraud spanning the entire spectrum of the case perpetrated by the New Jersey officials, which proves the unfairness of the trial and Mr. Hauptmann's lack of culpability." Bryan added that "newly discovered evidence unequivocally demonstrates Mr. Hauptmann was not involved in the crime and that a mistake of outrageous proportions occurred."[21] John F. Russo, the president of the New Jersey Senate, replied: "We're not a court of last resort. We will not get involved."[22]

Mrs. Hauptmann had lost in the courts, but she had won the hearts of the American people. She had won by staying alive into the 1980s, a time when ordinary citizens found it reasonable to believe that the New Jersey State Police, the FBI, and the New York City Police had joined forces to orchestrate a massive conspiracy of lies and fake evidence. Perhaps her less zealous supporters would have been a bit skeptical had they known that to accomplish this frameup, forty prosecution witnesses would have had to committed perjury with the knowledge of at least two hundred others. As for the physical evidence, the prosecution had presented over three hundred exhibits. If the police had tampered with or fabricated a large number of these items, someone would have spilled the beans. Moreover, it's a fact that faking physical evidence is easier said than done.

The pro-Hauptmann revisionists, unchallenged for so long, were caught off guard in 1987 when *The Lindbergh Case* came out. A month after its publication, Francis Russell's comparative review of *The Lindbergh Case*, *The Airman and the Carpenter*, and *Scapegoat* appeared in *The New York Review of Books*.[23] Under the title, "The Case That Will Not Close," Russell wrote:

> Both he [Scaduto] and Ludovic Kennedy had formed their conclusions in advance and worked backward. For them Hauptmann had to be innocent. Facts that suggested otherwise could and must be explained away. . . . Kennedy's belief was fixed from the start. Jim Fisher started with no fixed beliefs but rather with the intent of finding out what happened. . . . This gives him the advantage of being able to explore as well as to explain. I find his explanations of the three primary points [the ransom money in Hauptmann's garage, the handwriting on the extortion notes, and the identification of the kidnap ladder] more logical than those of the Hauptmann advocates.[24]

Incensed by Russell's analysis, Scaduto and Kennedy fired off a pair of angry letters. Scaduto, repeating his main theme, declared:

> All the witnesses who testified against Hauptmann lied; their original descriptions of the man they had seen at various stages of the Lindbergh crime did not match Hauptmann, and they tailored their testimony to help convict the man. . . . All the physical evidence against Hauptmann—including the kidnap ladder and the handwriting in the ransom letter—was either manufactured by police or distorted in the testimony of expert witnesses.[25]

In answering Scaduto's letter, Francis Russell noted that in researching *Scapegoat*, Scaduto had relied on the opinion of a man named Albert Hamilton who in 1934 declared that Hauptmann had not written the ransom notes. Russell, an expert on the Sacco-Vanzetti case, had run across Albert Hamilton before, and knew that he was a notorious charlatan who was ultimately banned from testifying in court. After bringing this to Scaduto's attention, Russell wrote: "When Mr. Scaduto . . . substantiates his thesis with a Doctor Hamilton, he is on very slippery ground indeed."[26]

While Scaduto and Kennedy were assuring everyone that *The Lindbergh Case* was nothing more than a propaganda book for the New Jersey State Police, Robert Bryan, with Mrs. Hauptmann at his side, was holding a press conference in Trenton. Although Mrs. Hauptmann said she hadn't read this awful new book, she could say with great authority that it was filled with lies.[27] Robert Bryan also had important news—he had discovered a fingerprint taken off one of the ransom notes. And guess what—it didn't belong to Hauptmann![28] How could anyone deny that this spectacular discovery proved, once and for all, that Mrs. Hauptmann's husband was innocent? Apparently none of the journalists who had gathered to report this news event bothered to ask how Bryan was able to identify the ransom note latent as the kidnapper's print.

In May of 1990, Mrs. Hauptmann, in a letter to New Jersey Governor Jim Florio, asked if they could meet to discuss some kind of formal recognition of her husband's innocence. The governor, with enough problems of his own, wasn't interested in hers. Refusing to take no for an answer, Bryan flew to New Jersey to hold another press conference in Trenton across the street from the State Capitol. Mrs. Hauptmann, ninety-one and still fighting for her husband, was there with him. "She shouldn't have to beg like this," Bryan told reporters. Mrs. Hauptmann said she could not understand why Governor Florio was ignoring her. After all, Anthony Hopkins, the actor who had played Hauptmann in a made-for-TV docudrama, had written a letter to the governor. Having portrayed Hauptmann in the 1976 movie, the British actor was convinced of his innocence, and was adding his voice to the multitudes of concerned people who demanded a review.[29]

Later that day, Governor Florio announced that he would talk to his attorney general about legal options in the case. He suggested that Mrs. Hauptmann write him another, more detailed letter, setting out exactly what she wanted.[30] Something had softened up the governor.

Bryan, in October 1991, was back in New Jersey, this time in Flemington where a local theater group was reenacting the Hauptmann trial in the original courtroom. Although Mrs. Hauptmann wasn't up to seeing the performance, she did meet with reporters afterward at the Union Hotel across the street from the Hunterdon County Courthouse.[31] Governor Florio had said that his attorney general was reviewing the material Bryan had sent him, but could see no reason to meet with Mrs. Hauptmann. Mrs. Hauptmann, however, wanted to see the governor, and once again she begged for a meeting. The governor did not respond.

The following spring, Governor Florio announced through a spokesperson that the material Robert Bryan had sent failed to justify a reopening of the case.[32] It seemed that Florio was in no mood to follow in the footsteps of Massachusetts's Governor Michael S. Dukakis who, on August 23, 1977, on "Sacco and Vanzetti Memorial Day," had issued a proclamation that the 1921 murder trial of Nicola Sacco and Bartolomeo Vanzetti had been "permeated with unfairness."

Robert Bryan was still telling reporters he knew the identity of the real kidnapper, but when pressed said only that he believes the culprit is no longer alive.[33] Regarding his promise to unmask the true kidnapper, Bryan had a problem. He could name, for example, Isador Fisch, everybody's favorite patsy. He could also finger John Condon, Betty Gow, Violet Sharpe, Paul Wendel—or even Al Capone. His problem is this: these people have all been fingerprinted, and their prints do not match the latents on the ransom note identified by Bryan as the kidnapper's. Bryan has painted himself into a corner.

Rebuffed by the governor's office (Bryan says "stonewalled") the so-called "F. Lee Bailey of the South" petitioned the New Jersey State Parole Board in March of 1992 for a posthumous pardon. The matter is still pending.

After ten years of lawsuits, newspaper interviews, TV appearances, and press conferences with Mrs. Hauptmann at his side, people were starting to catch on to Robert Bryan. In September 1991, two of Mrs. Hauptmann's closest friends publicly criticized Bryan for using Mrs. Hauptmann to generate publicity for himself and his anti–death penalty movement.[34] They also accused him of holding back the identity of the true kidnapper, saving that bombshell for a book, or a lucrative movie deal.[35] Bryan said he was not writing a book, and reminded his critics that he had not charged Mrs. Hauptmann a dime for his services, and has incurred, on her behalf, expenses that have come out of his own pocket.

Ludovic Kennedy, the man behind the biassed television documentary and the author of *The Airman and the Carpenter*, published, in 1989, an autobiography called *On My Way to the Club*. Published in England where Kennedy is a television celebrity, the memoir includes a chapter chronicling Kennedy's relentless pursuit of justice in the Lindbergh case.[36] Apparently still smarting over the publication of a book that challenges Hauptmann's innocence, Kennedy takes aim at the author, the publisher, *The New York Times*, and the New Jersey State Police:

> Indeed so concerned were the New Jersey authorities by Mrs. Hauptmann's suit and the books by Tony Scaduto and myself that they gave their backing to a recent book on the affair, *The Lindbergh Case* by Jim Fisher (1987); and the police officer in charge of the Lindbergh Archive Room at police headquarters became consultant to the project. Mr. Fisher is described as an associate professor of criminal justice at Edinboro University in Pennsylvania, and if that is so, I shudder to think of the standards of scholarship prevailing there. Nor will it enhance the reputation of the Rutgers University Press who published it; for in reaffirming the *status quo ante*, that Hauptmann was rightly convicted and executed, Mr. Fisher has, unbelievably, omitted almost all the information made available in recent years and used by Mrs. Hauptmann's lawyer, Tony Scaduto and myself to prove the exact opposite. His object doubtless was to pull the wool over the eyes of those beginning to be awakened to the fact of an injustice as great if not greater than those suffered by Dreyfus or Sacco and Vanzetti, and because the case is so complex that only those who have spent years studying it are familiar with all its ramifications, it may well have partly succeeded. The critics of *The New York Times* and *The New York Review of Books* were clearly baffled by it, and although Tony Scaduto and I write corrective letters in their correspondence columns, the bafflement was not entirely dispelled.[37]

Britain's Jonathan Goodman, the author or more than thirty true-crime books, took exception to the nature of Kennedy's attack on a rival book, calling it "irrelevant, hysterical, and sickening." Goodman also points out that Kennedy's assertions about the book and its author are not true.[38]

The second major television documentary on the Lindbergh case, produced by New Jersey Network, and featuring narrator Edwin Newman, old film clips, and just about everybody who has ever had the slightest brush with the case, was aired in New Jersey in March of 1989. The producers of *Reliving the Lindbergh Case* had the opportunity, and perhaps the obligation, to make an honest attempt to present an accurate historical account of the crime. But they just couldn't resist Mrs. Hauptmann and her tale of woe, which produced one of those "you be the judge" programs. The one-hour show was telecast nationally over PBS on October 17, 1989, just as the big earthquake hit San Francisco. A few months later it aired again in America, and for the first time in Britain.

Fiction writers occasionally use celebrated crimes as a basis for their novels. Agatha Christie, for example, used the Lindbergh kidnapping as a plot device in her 1934 mystery, *Murder on the Orient Express*. In 1991, Max Allan Collins published a book called *Stolen Away: A Novel of the Lindbergh Kidnapping*.[39] Collins mixes historical happenings and real people with characters, dialogue, and events he has made up. His narrator-protagonist, a salty private eye named Nate Heller, has an affair with Evalyn McLean, gets his pal Colonel Lindbergh to admit privately that he lied under oath when he identified Hauptmann's voice in the cemetery, repeatedly makes a fool out of Colonel Schwarzkopf, ridicules Hoover's FBI agents as a bunch of law school flunkies, and proves that Al Capone was the brains behind the kidnapping.

On June 5, 1991, Max Allan Collins appeared on "Geraldo." The 30-minute segment, called "Investigating the Lindbergh Murder," also featured attorney Robert Bryan and myself. When Collins is challenged regarding a particular fact in the Lindbergh case, or his thesis that Al Capone was involved, he can simply point out that his book is a work of fiction. When he's not challenged, Collins can masquerade as an expert on the case. The reviewer for *Publisher's Weekly* illustrates this point perfectly: "Veteran author Collins's reconstruction of the Lindbergh case is so believable, one forgets that this is fiction."[40] This is precisely the problem.

Perhaps an even worse problem is nonfiction books so unbelievable they ought to be classified as fiction. Such a book came out in 1993. Written by a small-town police chief from Goffstown, New Hampshire, and a lawyer from the same area, *Crime of the Century: The Lindbergh Kidnapping Hoax*, advances the authors' belief that Colonel Lindbergh accidentally killed his son while carrying the baby down from the homemade ladder as a practical joke on his wife.[41] That night, Lindbergh buried his son in a shallow grave along the Princeton-Hopewell Road where it was found ten weeks later. To cover his tracks, Lindbergh reported the baby as kidnapped. He then sat by quietly as Bruno Richard Hauptmann, a mere extortionist in the case, was tried, convicted, and executed for his son's murder.

The authors, Gregory Ahlgren and Steven Monier, told a reporter they had worked on the book "for three years, studying trial transcripts and more than two hundred thousand pages of reports in the archives of the New Jersey State Police."[42] But according to Lieutenant C. Thomas DeFeo, curator of the New Jersey Police Museum and Learning Center in West Trenton, the home of the Lindbergh collection, neither author set foot in the place. According to Lieutenant DeFeo, the authors had seen photographs in other books and requested some of these prints from the archives. They did not ask for any documents, material DeFeo would gladly have sent them upon request.[43]

Ahlgren and Monier became interested in the Lindbergh case after Ahlgren had read Alan Hynd's 1949 article, "Everyone Wanted to Get Into the Act."[44] The Hynd article, a heavy-handed rehabilitation of Hauptmann and his dismal defense, coupled with Ellis Parker's absurd theory that the Lindbergh baby wasn't dead, caused Mr. Ahlgren "concern," and "raised his suspicions."[45] Alan Hynd's entertaining, tongue-in-cheek piece, a classic example of the old pulp style, convinced Ahlgren and Monier that something was very wrong in the Lindbergh case.[46]

In the 1930s, Alan Hynd pounded out hundreds of true-crime articles for the monthly pulp magazine market. Between 1932 and 1937 he wrote twenty or so articles for *True Detective Mysteries* in which he glorified the work of the crime busters in the Lindbergh case. In 1938, after having painted Hauptmann as a cold-blooded baby killer, Hynd helped Governor Harold G. Hoffman write his sixteen-part article for *Liberty Magazine* called "What Was Wrong with the Lindbergh Case? The Crime, The Case, The Challenge."[47] That year Hynd also ghost-wrote a ten-piece *Liberty* article for the notorious flake, Evalyn McLean, the woman Gaston Means had bilked out of $104,000. Called "Why I Am Still Investigating the Lindbergh Case," McLean's article, notwithstanding Hynd's considerable talent for creating excitement out of absolutely nothing, is one of the silliest excesses in the history of Lindbergh case publishing.

Alan Hynd made his living writing what the people who paid him wanted him to write. He was, in that sense, the perfect hack. It is therefore revealing, and perhaps fitting, that the Ahlgren-Monier book was inspired by such a writer. One could argue that Hynd, when he wrote "Everyone Wanted to Get Into the Act," had people like Ahlgren and Monier clearly in mind.[48]

Alan Hynd would have admired a 1993 book called *Lindbergh, The Crime* by Noel Behn, a New York City novelist who retells the case, then at the end of the book suggests that the baby was murdered by Elisabeth Morrow, Anne Lindbergh's oldest sister. Behn, admitting that he has no evidence to prove his theory, asserts that Elisabeth threw the child out the nursery window on Saturday, February 27, three days before Colonel Lindbergh and his lawyer Henry Breckinridge staged the kidnapping to cover up the murder. According to Behn, Elisabeth, insanely in love with Colonel Lindbergh, killed the child out of jealousy. If this is true, then Colonel Lindbergh, his wife, Anne, Henry Breckinridge, and the two Lindbergh servants committed perjury at the Hauptmann trial. It is hard to imagine Anne Morrow Lindbergh lying under oath to protect her sister. Colonel Lindbergh and Henry Breckinridge would have also been guilty of evidence tampering.

Elisabeth Morrow never confessed to this crime, no one saw her do it, and there is no physical evidence linking her to the murder. The source of Behn's theory is a ninety-three-year-old man named Harry Green who had a brush with the Lindbergh case through Governor Harold G. Hoffman. Just before he died, Green said that a chauffeur for the Morrow family told him he suspected that Elisabeth may have had something to do with the baby's death. From this piece of third- or fourth-hand information comes a 464-page book on the Lindbergh case.

Given the publishing record of the Lindbergh case, the odds are even that the next book on the crime will have the baby snatched by an alien—not from Germany, but from space.

———

Mrs. Hauptmann made her final television appeal on January 10, 1992. She was featured, along with Bryan, in a "Current Affair" segment called "A Half-Century of Heartache."[49] Old, frail, and pathetic, she appeared on national television one last time as the victim-widow who had spent nearly sixty years trying to convince the world her husband was not a baby killer. Now she was making, out of sheer desperation, an incredible request. She wanted Mrs. Lindbergh, herself very old and frail, to set the record straight before it was too late. How Mrs. Lindbergh was to do this was not made clear, but the mere asking carried an unsavory, and unfounded, implication, the kind of thing that has been plaguing the Lindbergh family—the true victims of the crime—since the baby's murder. First it had been rumors that the Lindberghs had disposed of the child because he was somehow defective, then the crackpots claiming to be the Lindbergh baby couldn't understand why Mrs. Lindbergh wouldn't submit to a DNA test so they could prove they were her sons, and now, sixty years after the crime, two guys from New Hampshire were saying that the Lindbergh baby had been killed by his father. If that wasn't bizarre enough, the wife of the real killer now wanted the dead baby's mother to help clear her husband's name.

"A Half-Century of Heartache" also featured scenes from a two-act play called *Hauptmann* that appeared at the Victory Gardens Theatre in Chicago and was moving to New York. Written by John Logan, and starring Dennis O'Hare as Hauptmann, the play begins in prison just before Hauptmann's execution, flashes back to the crime, then moves to the trial in Flemington.[50] The trial is depicted as a circus, and the play is really about capital punishment and how innocent souls—like Hauptmann—can be executed.

Mrs. Hauptmann hasn't had much luck, over the years, with judges, criminal justice practitioners, criminalists, and forensic scientists who have given the case serious study. She does a lot better with TV hosts, book reviewers, liberals, people who watch shows like "Current Affair," and anti–death penalty crusaders.

Alan M. Dershowitz, the celebrated defense attorney, recognizes how a celebrated case can be put to good purpose by campaigners against capital punishment. In his Introduction to a 1989 reprint of Sidney B. Whipple's 1937 book, *The Trial of Bruno Richard Hauptmann,* Dershowitz writes:

> Indeed, one of the most powerful arguments offered by opponents of the death penalty is the assertion that innocent defendants—some say a few, others claim many—have been executed for crimes committed by others.
>
> The execution of Bruno Richard Hauptmann on April 3, 1936, is frequently cited as an instance of the capital punishment of an innocent defendant.[51]

It is probably not a coincidence that people opposed to capital punishment believe a lot of innocent defendants—including famous ones like Hauptmann—have been executed. Of course there is no way to disprove this proposition, but that doesn't make it true. It comes down to what one wants to believe. When the anti–death penalty activists, cop-haters, hack writers, and sob-sisters capture a celebrated case, the first thing to go is the truth. The invaders, if the evidence doesn't suit them, provide their own experts, create their own science, and argue their own logic. Now that the Lindbergh case is firmly in the grip of the idealogues, junk historians, victim mongers, and anti-establishment zealots, a rational debate is impossible.

I would like to thank the following who have contributed to this revised and expanded edition:

Margery Aklin, Jan Beck, Bill Blakefield, Michael Busichio, Oscar Collier, Dr. David A. Crown, Lt. C. Thomas DeFeo, Wendy Dellett, Donald Doud, Mark W. Falzini, Robert J. Felicito, Dr. Alan Filby, Armen Fisher, James D. Fisher, Susan G. Fisher, Jo Astrid Glading, Jonathan Goodman, Ray Hagen, Pat Hipko, James J. Horan, John T. Huddleson, Thomas J. Irey, Harry Kazman, Reva Kazman, Dr. John Kelly, Gus R. Lesnevich, Doris Lessig, Greg Lessig, Sean Maloney, Thelma Miller, Frank Pizzichillo, Robert W. Radley, Delores Raisch, Stephen Romeo, Chester G. Rose, Richard Schlesinger, Ross H. Spencer, Glenn Swift, Raymond Vanden Berghe, Albert L. Weeks, Virginia Wengel, and Robert J. Whelan.

NOTES TO PREFACE

1 Patterson Smith, "Puzzles of True Crime Literature: The Lindbergh Case," *AB Bookmans Weekly*, April 25, 1983.

2 Three other Lindbergh baby claimants are Don A. Staser, Kenneth Kerwin, and Bill Simons.

3 John L. Hess, "A Kidnapping and a Railroading?" *The New York Times*, November 14, 1976.

4 *The New York Review of Books*, February 18, 1988. Francis Russell, the biographer of Warren G. Harding and the author of many historical books and articles, also wrote articles and books on the Sacco-Vanzetti case. See *Tragedy in Dedham* (New York: McGraw-Hill, 1962) and *Sacco & Vanzetti: The Case Resolved* (New York: Harper & Row, 1986). Mr. Russell died on March 22, 1989, at the age of seventy-nine.

5 Mrs. Hauptmann's three-page affidavit, No. 84-5454, entitled "Plaintiff's Affidavit Concerning Statute of Limitations," was presented to the U.S. Court of Appeals for the Third Circuit in the case of *Anna Hauptmann et al. v. David T. Wilentz et al.*, 1984.

6 *Hauptmann v. Wilentz*, 570 F. Supp. 351 at 395 (1983).

7 In *The Airman and the Carpenter* (New York: Viking, 1985), Ludovic Kennedy writes: "Supporters of the Kerwin/Olson theory have never faced up to the consequences of their own logic, which necessitates a belief not in one kidnapping but two. . . . Does anyone think such a bizarre scenario likely?" (p. 416).

8 Ronald Goldfarb, "He had to Be Guilty," *The New York Times Book Review*, June 1985.

9 Jeffrey Hart, *National Review*, September 6, 1985. It's interesting to note that three years later, in reviewing my book, Hart had this to say about Hauptmann's conviction: "Professor Fisher is right, and so was the jury" (*National Review*, September 2, 1988).

10 *On My Way to the Club* (London: Collins, 1989), p. 393.

11 John F. Keenan, "The Lindbergh Kidnapping Revisited," *Michigan Law Review*, February–April 1986. Judge Keenan also wrote: "The fact is that very little of what Mr. Kennedy urges is new or has not been argued before. The Court of Errors and Appeals of New Jersey unanimously affirmed Hauptmann's conviction of October 9, 1935. All the major points raised by Mr. Kennedy were considered by the court on the appeal and addressed in its decision" (p. 821).

12 Patterson Smith, "The Literature of Ransom Kidnapping in America," *AB Bookmans Weekly*, April 23, 1990.

13 Some of these private investigators were George H. Foster, Leon Ho-Age, Robert W. Hicks, Julius B. Braun, Winslow P. Humphrey, Leo F. Meade, and Harold C. Keyes (Hoffman Papers, Lindbergh Collection, New Jersey State Police Museum and Learning Center).

14 George H. Foster letter to Harold G. Hoffman, June 4, 1936 (Hoffman Papers).

15 *Hauptmann v. Bornmann et al.* (1986). See Lee Seglem, "Judge Rejects Effort by Hauptmann Widow to Clear Her Husband," Gannett News Service, September 24, 1987.

16 Steve Wilstein, Associated Press, November 20, 1986.

17 Ibid.

18 Ibid.

19 Ibid.

20 *Philadelphia Inquirer*, December 13, 1987.

21 Associated Press, September 12, 1986.

22 Ibid.

23 Francis Russell, "The Case That Will Not Close," *The New York Review of Books*, November 5, 1987.

24 Ibid.

25 *The New York Review of Books*, February 18, 1988.

26 Ibid. Following the publication of *The Lindbergh Case*, Anthony Scaduto, the author of *Scapegoat* and a reporter for *New York Newsday*, was allowed to review the book for the Sunday edition of his paper. Calling his piece "A Lopsided Rehash of the Lindbergh Case," the kindest thing he said about the book, Scaduto, in what has to be one of the greatest understatements in book review history, wrote: "I admit I cannot be totally objective" (November 29, 1987).

Scaduto and I debated the Lindbergh case on April 14, 1988, at the University of Delaware. The debate was arranged and moderated by Dr. John Kelly, a criminal justice professor and Lindbergh case expert with the university. A video of the debate can be viewed at the New Jersey State Police Museum and Learning Center.

27 Associated Press, November 17, 1987.

28 Ibid.

29 See Associated Press story, June 13, 1990; *The Philadelphia Inquirer*, June 13, 1990; and Tony Scaduto, "The Lindbergh Case," *Crime Beat*, April 1993, p. 51. J. P. Miller's docudrama "The Lindbergh Case: Is History's Verdict Wrong?" starring Anthony Hopkins as Hauptmann, Clifford DeYoung as Colonel Lindbergh, and Joseph Cotton as "Jafsie," was aired on NBC in 1976. It is available on video.

30 Michael Vitez, *The Philadelphia Inquirer*, June 13, 1990.

31 Lee McDonald, *Courier-News*, October 5, 1991. See also *The New York Times*, October 5, 1991.

In 1990, a Flemington, New Jersey, playwright, Harry Kazman, wrote a play called *Lindbergh and Hauptmann: The Trial of the Century*. Directed and produced by Kazman and his wife, Reva, the play, drawn from the Hauptmann trial transcripts, is essentially an edited re-enactment of the trial. Kazman and a cast of talented actors from the New Jersey area performed twelve shows each fall in 1990, 1991, and 1992.

32 Leslie Gutman, "Attorney Battles History's Verdict," *San Francisco Chronicle*, March 29, 1992. Christopher Florentz, a spokesman for the New Jersey Attorney General's Office, said there was "no evidence raised in those papers [Bryan's] that would indicate that the conviction . . . of Mr. Hauptmann was anything other than appropriate and correct."

33 Ibid., p. 3.

34 Michael Vitez, "Widow of the Century," *The Philadelphia Inquirer*, January 19, 1992. Robert Bryan was national chairman of the Coalition Against the Death Penalty.

35   Ibid.

36   Kennedy, *On My Way to the Club.*

37   Ibid., p. 394.

38   In an unpublished manuscript, Jonathan Goodman said this regarding Kennedy's comments about *The Lindbergh Case* and its author: "If one were not sure that Kennedy has never suffered from paranoia, one might suspect that he may have been afflicted by some such ailment both when he wrote the despicable page and when he read the proof of it."

39   New York: Bantam, 1991.

40   *Publishers Weekly,* April 5, 1991, p. 139.

41   Gregory Ahlgren and Stephen Monier, *Crime of the Century: The Lindbergh Kidnapping Hoax* (Boston: Branden Books, 1993).

42   Gloria Negri, "New Hampshire Writers Say Lindbergh Responsible in Kidnapping," *The Boston Globe,* March 17, 1993, pp. 25, 26.

42   Lieutenant C. Thomas DeFeo was interviewed July 14, 1993. His assistant, Mark Falzini, was also asked about authors Ahlgren and Monier. Falzini said he has had no contact with either writer.

44   *True Magazine,* March 1949. Hynd's article was later reprinted, under a variety of titles, in numerous true-crime anthologies.

45   Ahlgren and Monier, *Crime of the Century,* p. 264.

46   Negri, "New Hampshire Writers," p. 26.

47   Fulton Oursler, editor-in-chief of *Liberty Magazine,* referred to Alan Hynd as Governor Hoffman's "editorial secretary" (Oursler letter to Harold G. Hoffman, November 24, 1937, Hoffman Papers).

48   Alan Hynd lived in Westport, Connecticut. The prolific and talented stylist died in 1974.

49   "A Half-Century of Heartache" was produced by David Lee Miller.

50   *Hauptmann,* directed by Terry McCabe, opened in New York in May 1992 at the Cherry Lane Theater in Greenwich Village. For a review of the play, see *The New York Times,* May 29, 1992. See also *Playbill,* June 1992.

51   Sidney B. Whipple, *The Trial of Bruno Richard Hauptmann* (1937; reprint, The Notable Trials Library, 1989).

THE LINDBERGH CASE

INTRODUCTION

ON APRIL 3, 1936, about four years after the twenty-month-old son of Charles and Anne Morrow Lindbergh was snatched from his crib near Hopewell, New Jersey, Bruno Richard Hauptmann, the man convicted of the crime, was led to the death chamber and electrocuted. During the months preceding his death, the governor of New Jersey told the thirty-six-year-old German-born carpenter from the Bronx that if he confessed to the crime his life would be spared. The nation and the world awaited the confession while prison authorities in Trenton, New Jersey, prepared for Hauptmann's execution. But instead of confessing, Hauptmann shuffled into the death chamber and sat down on the electric chair. A few seconds later he was dead.

In 1981, forty-five years after Hauptmann's execution, his eighty-three-year-old widow sued the state of New Jersey and others, alleging that her husband had been "Wrongfully, Corruptly, and Unjustly" executed. Anna Hauptmann's hundred-million-dollar claim was laid to rest four years later when a federal appeals court upheld the lower court's dismissal of her case. A few months later Mrs. Hauptmann was back in court, this time alleging that twenty-one thousand Lindbergh case documents recently discovered among the effects of the governor who had stayed her husband's execution contained new and startling evidence that her husband was innocent.

As a criminal justice professor, lawyer, and former FBI agent, I was vaguely familiar with the Lindbergh case, and like most people, unaware that there was any doubt regarding Hauptmann's guilt. In fact, because several famous handwriting experts had testified that Hauptmann had written all of the ransom notes, I had considered the case a milestone in the history of scientific crime detection.

My interest in the case was heightened in the winter of 1982 when I viewed a one-hour documentary aired on public television. Titled *Who Killed the Lindbergh Baby?*, it was based in part on the earlier research of Anthony Scaduto, a reporter who had published a book on the case five years before. The film seemed to document the theory that Hauptmann had been maliciously framed and railroaded. According to Scaduto, every

4   piece of physical evidence against Hauptmann had been fabricated, distorted or tampered with. He further asserted that all of the key prosecution witnesses had committed perjury, and that evidence proving Hauptmann's innocence had been suppressed. Even more shocking, Scaduto claimed that the Lindbergh baby hadn't been murdered, and that the infant corpse found two miles from the Lindbergh home was not Colonel Lindbergh's son.

Surprised by Mrs. Hauptmann's suit, the allegations in the television documentary, and the realization that several middle-aged men were publicly claiming to be Colonel Lindbergh's long-lost son (one had even sued the Colonel's estate as a legitimate heir following Lindbergh's death in 1974), I decided to look into the case myself. I was not particularly interested, at this time, in whether Hauptmann had received a fair trial: I was simply curious to know if he had kidnapped and murdered young Charles Lindbergh. Like so many before me, once I got into the case I was hooked. As a result, there is no aspect of the case I haven't explored.

My research began with a careful reading of the edited transcript of Hauptmann's trial. I then studied four books that had been written in the 1930's by people who had been directly involved in the case. I also read thirty or so articles that had been published during this period by several principals in the case.

By using the *New York Times Index* and the microfilm facilities at the university where I teach, I was able to read the entire *Times* reportage of the case from 1932 to 1937—an estimated three million words. By this time I had become a collector of Lindbergh case literature and had acquired, through a dealer in true-crime material, several large scrapbooks containing hundreds of old Lindbergh case clippings from a dozen New York City papers.

Having familiarized myself generally with the case, I read Scaduto's book and two others that were published after it and contained similar findings regarding Hauptmann's innocence. Although many of the theories and conclusions put forth by Scaduto and his counterparts seemed groundless and patently absurd to me, I couldn't ignore the specific allegations of wrongdoing by officers of the New Jersey State Police and the Lindbergh case prosecutors. According to Scaduto and his supporters, these charges were based upon newly discovered evidence. As a result, I couldn't dismiss Scaduto's and the other books as silly or exploitive until I had conducted my own investigation into these charges.

I had been studying the case for a year and a half when, in the spring of 1984, I learned that in November 1981, pursuant to an executive order issued by the governor of New Jersey, the Lindbergh case archives, in the possession and care of the New Jersey State Police, were opened to the public. It had taken Det. Sgt. Cornel Plebani, the official Lindbergh case archivist, and Lt. Tom Barna five years to catalogue, file, and index the two-hundred-thousand documents related to the case.

During the next two years I made four trips to the Lindbergh case archives, which were housed at the state police headquarters in West Trenton, New Jersey. On these occasions Detective Plebani made available, at my request, thousands of police reports, letters, memos, logs, affidavits, statements, photographs, press clippings, and trial exhibits. I also examined all of the physical evidence—the kidnap ladder, the fifteen ransom notes, Hauptmann's known handwriting, the baby's garments, and so on. In addition, I listened to several taped interviews of deceased Lindbergh case principals. At my request, the New Jersey State Police made photocopies of hundreds of documents, including large portions of the official 32-volume, 7,587-page transcript of the trial, Hauptmann's 190-page interrogation, and 224 pages of state police memos reporting Hauptmann's conversations and activities during his incarceration in the Flemington, New Jersey, jail. Thanks to Detective Plebani, I was able to examine hundreds of documents, material that no other researcher had studied. By taking advantage of all of this material, I was in a position to evaluate the soundness of Scaduto's theories and conclusions.

In April 1986, I spent three days looking through the Hoffman papers, the material discovered in the deceased governor's garage, documents Mrs. Hauptmann was relying upon to clear her husband's name.

After four years of studying considerably more Lindbergh case data than any previous researcher, I was able to draw, in great confidence, the following conclusions:

1 The New Jersey State Police conducted a thorough investigation under the most difficult circumstances, an investigation few modern law enforcement agencies could match if the crime were committed today. As in all investigations of celebrated crimes, the police in the Lindbergh case made mistakes and forgot to do certain things, but these errors were not major and turned out to be relatively harmless.

2 The Lindbergh case investigators and prosecutors did not fabricate any evidence of Hauptmann's guilt or suppress evidence of his innocence.

3 Hauptmann received as fair a trial as could be expected under the circumstances. The trial judge was unbiased, experienced, and competent, and the jury was made up of intelligent and rational people with a lot of common sense. Moreover, Hauptmann took advantage of a full range of appeals under the guidance of a competent and dedicated attorney.

4 There is no hard evidence to support the notion that Hauptmann was aided in the crime by accomplices.

5 The evidence clearly shows that the Lindbergh baby was in fact killed, and the corpse found near the Lindbergh estate ten weeks after the crime was his.

No one saw Bruno Richard Hauptmann snatch the baby from his crib, and no one, save the killer, witnessed the child's death. Since Hauptmann didn't confess, it will never be known exactly how and when the baby died. But in my opinion, based upon my understanding of Hauptmann's criminal record and personality as well as other evidence I have encountered, he murdered the baby in cold blood for the money.

I reach these conclusions with great confidence because this is the first book about the Lindbergh case based upon primary source materials.

Early on, I decided that I did not want to write a dry, academic analysis of the case. Instead, I have written the story of the Lindbergh kidnapping, using narrative techniques and dialogue.

6   The use of dialogue in a factual account requires additional comment. The dialogue used is of two types: direct quotes and conversation based on primary sources. Direct quotations and dialogue are taken from such sources as preliminary hearing and trial transcripts; published diaries, police memos reporting Hauptmann's jail conversations, the transcript of Hauptmann's interrogation, quotes and statements in newspapers, and quotes published in magazine articles and book-length accounts by a party to the conversation.

Conversations based on primary sources but not found verbatim in these sources actually took place at the time depicted and reflect accurately the information conveyed or emotion felt by the speakers. The dialogue reflects my idea as to what was said and by whom, based on my reading of the primary sources. Footnotes accompanying these conversations identify their origin in fact. For example, there is a scene in the book involving a private conversation between Hauptmann and an FBI agent in which Hauptmann indicated that if a deal can be struck he might confess:

"What kind of deal could I get?"

"Well, I'm not sure," the agent replied.

"Could the FBI guarantee an easy sentence?"

"The FBI couldn't do that."

The agent kills any chance for a confession by telling Hauptmann that such a deal can only be made by the New Jersey State Police:

". . . But you could possibly work something out with Schwarzkopf."

The dialogue in this scene is based upon two letters written by the FBI agent in 1977 in which he describes the circumstances under which Hauptmann almost confessed to him:

". . . he (Hauptmann) once asked me what leniency he would get if he would confess. I told him that I had no right to make such a promise to him, because it was not, at that time, a federal offense. However, I told him I would bring this to the attention of the state prosecutor and because of his confession he might receive leniency. That shut him up as tight as a clam. . . ."

There is no scene, conversation, or event in this book that did not happen. By presenting the story of this case in narrative form and in the words of the participants, I have attempted to re-create the circumstances and emotional climate in which the investigation of the Lindbergh baby's kidnapping was conducted. The story unfolds as the evidence available at this time dictates, providing what I believe is an accurate account of what took place. I began my research without prejudice. My conclusions, and the conclusions to which the narrative leads, are the logical ends of an investigation untarnished by preconceived notions. Although written for the general reader, the book is deeply rooted in the methods of scholarly research and professional criminalistics.

Readers interested in a detailed account of the research that went into this work, as well as the sources behind it, are referred to "Sources and Acknowledgments" at the end of the book.

Anne, they've stolen our baby!

— CHARLES LINDBERGH

1 THE CRIME

LIEUTENANT DUNN poured himself and Detective Bornmann a cup of coffee. It was 10:25 P.M., and in thirty minutes the lieutenant would be replaced by the swing-shift commander. Trooper Bornmann had just walked into the barracks after a busy night investigating minor traffic accidents on the rain-slick highways around Wilburtha.

"It's windy and getting cold out there," Bornmann said as he removed his raincoat. "March is coming in like a lion."

Lieutenant Dunn was about to say something when the telephone rang. He hated taking calls toward the end of his shift. Sometimes it meant a delay in getting home. "New Jersey State Police, Lieutenant Dunn speaking."

"This is Charles Lindbergh," the caller said. "My son has just been kidnapped."

Lieutenant Dunn looked at Bornmann then reached for a pencil. "What time was he taken?" he asked.

"Sometime between seven-thirty and ten o'clock. He's twenty months old and is wearing a one-piece sleeping suit." The caller hung up.

"What was that?" Bornmann asked.

"I don't know," Dunn replied. "Some guy said he was Lindbergh—said the baby was kidnapped. Jesus! Now what am I supposed to do? I mean, he's probably a nut. We get this shit all the time."

"What if he's not a nut?" Bornmann asked. "What if it's real?"

"I know, I know," the lieutenant said. He was agitated and worried; this was his responsibility—his decision.

"I got an idea," Bornmann said. "Call the Lindbergh house. If the Colonel answers and it's the same voice—it's legit. If he's not home or it's a different voice, forget it."

The lieutenant picked up the phone and spoke to the operator. "This is the police—I want the Lindbergh house." The call went through. "I can hear it ringing," Dunn said.

"Hello, this is Charles Lindbergh." It was the voice that had reported the kidnapping.

"This is Lieutenant Dunn, sir. Men are on their way."

"My butler has just called the Hopewell department," Lindbergh said. He then hung up.[1]

Before the lieutenant hung up the phone, Detective Bornmann was on another line notifying a nearby barracks. All of a sudden Dunn had a million things to do—men would have to be contacted and dispatched, the brass notified, and a teletype alarm prepared and sent to six hundred police departments in New Jersey, Pennsylvania, Delaware, and New York. Arrangements would also have to be made for roadblocks.

On this cold, rainy night of March 1, 1932, Lieutenant Dunn would be getting home a little late.

COL. CHARLES A. LINDBERGH was one of the most famous and revered men in the world. Although it had been five years since he had flown his small, single-engine plane across the Atlantic Ocean, he was still the most worshipped hero in the Western Hemisphere.

Born on February 4, 1902, Lindbergh grew up in the small town of Little Falls, Minnesota, where his father was a successful lawyer. In 1920, Charles enrolled as an engineering student at the University of Wisconsin. But college life didn't suit him. He wanted to fly airplanes. So, in March of 1922, he dropped out of school. Seven months later the young pilot was "Daredevil Lindbergh" on a midwestern barnstorming tour. Lindbergh spent the next several years barnstorming, taking on odd piloting jobs, and flying air mail between St. Louis and Chicago.

In May 1927, after his historic 3,610-mile flight across the Atlantic Ocean in the *Spirit of St. Louis,* the "Lone Eagle" received hundreds of medals, honorary memberships, and awards of every kind. His most prestigious honors included a commission as colonel in the U.S. Army, the Distinguished Flying Cross, and the Congressional Medal of Honor.

Besides making him a celebrity and an honored citizen, the flight made Lindbergh wealthy. He accepted a twenty-five hundred dollar-a-week salary from the Guggenheim Foundation for a series of goodwill tours throughout the Americas. He was given stock in TWA and American World Airways and wrote articles for *The New York Times* and *The Saturday Evening Post.*

Lindbergh's flight had come at a time when the American people needed a hero. The 1920's had been a period of moral decay, political corruption, and cynicism. Although Lindbergh's flight was a monument to the superiority of American technology, it was the pilot, not the airplane, that inspired the nation. Even though Lindbergh was quick to remind his worshippers that he would not have made it across the Atlantic Ocean without a reliable engine, it was the achievement of a self-reliant, courageous young American that people celebrated. Charles Lindbergh was a pioneer, and through him, the country was rediscovering its lost virtue.

In December 1927, shortly after he was awarded the Congressional Medal of Honor, Lindbergh flew *The Spirit of St. Louis* to Mexico City. The purpose of the trip was to improve America's relations with Mexico. Lindbergh was a guest at the home of Dwight D. Morrow, the U.S. ambassador to Mexico and one of the wealthiest men in America. The multimillionaire was a partner in the J. P. Morgan banking company.

In Mexico City, Lindbergh met and fell in love with the ambassador's daughter, Anne Spencer Morrow, a twenty-one-year-old honors graduate of Smith College. In many ways the two were opposites. She was dark-haired, small, and delicate and wanted to be a writer. He was tall, a college dropout, and interested in science and mechanics. They became engaged, and in May 1929 were married at the Morrow estate in Englewood, New Jersey. Because the couple was constantly being hounded by reporters and cameramen, the wedding ceremony was a small, private affair attended by a few friends and relatives.

On June 22, 1930, while the Lindberghs were living at the Morrow estate called Next Day Hill, Charles Augustus Lindbergh, Jr., was born. A real estate agent acting on Lindbergh's behalf had purchased thirteen small farms in East Amwell Township, New Jersey, a remote woodland area about two and a half miles north of Hopewell, a small farming community located in northern Mercer County. Mercer County, situated along the Jersey-Pennsylvania border, is in the middle section of the state. It is where the state capital, Trenton, is located.

Colonel Lindbergh and his wife had selected the 390-acre tract from the sky shortly after they were married. The terrain was too high for fog and faced what was then the busiest airline route in the world, the Newark-Camden Corridor.

About a hundred of Lindbergh's acres spread north into Hunterdon County, the site of the house itself. Construction of the fifty thousand-dollar, fourteen-room structure was started in the summer of 1930 while the Lindberghs were opening up new air routes in the Orient. While they were gone, the baby was kept in the Englewood, New Jersey, at the home of his grandparents, about sixty miles from Hopewell.

The new house, over seventy feet long and forty feet wide, was constructed of natural fieldstone. Covering the twenty-eight-inch thick boulders were several coats of sparkling whitewash. In addition to the living room, dining room, kitchen, four bathrooms, and five bedrooms, the house included two servants' bedrooms and a servants' sitting room. There was also a spacious pantry, a den, and a three-car garage. The front yard included a fifty-five-acre landing strip. Behind the house, beyond the area that had been cleared, were dense woods.

The fourteen- by twelve-foot nursery, situated at the southeast corner of the house directly above Colonel Lindbergh's den, had three shuttered windows. Two of the baby's windows faced south and the other east.

Except for landscaping and a few other odds and ends, the Lindbergh home was completed in 1931. When the Lindberghs returned from their expedition to the Orient in October 1931, they took up residence at the Morrow estate in Englewood.

In January and February of 1932, the Lindberghs and their baby began spending weekends at their newly built home. At this time they were served by three domestic employees. Residing at the Lindbergh estate were Oliver and Elsie Whately, a middle-

10 aged English couple who functioned as butler and cook. The Whatelys had been with the Lindberghs for two years. Oliver Whatley, called Ollie, was forty-seven years old, stocky and bald. He had come to America in March 1929. In England, Whately had worked as a jeweler, munitions worker, and machinist. His wife, Elsie, also forty-seven and a rather handsome woman, had arrived in America a year later. The Lindberghs had hired the Whatelys through an employment service. When the Lindberghs left for the Orient, the Whatelys were sent to the Morrow estate in Englewood. They had moved into the new Lindbergh home in December 1931.

The other servant, twenty-eight-year-old Betty Gow, the child's nursemaid, was from Glasgow, Scotland. She had been serving the Lindberghs since February 25, 1931. She had been hired on the recommendation of Mary Beattie, a lady's maid employed by Mrs. Morrow. Miss Gow had come to America in May 1929. Slender, dark-haired, and very pretty, Betty Gow was not in the habit of accompanying the Lindberghs and the baby on their weekend excursions to the estate at Hopewell.[2]

Colonel Lindbergh had built his new home in this rugged, remote area of New Jersey to get away from reporters, autograph hunters, and ordinary people who flocked to him at every chance. He was also hounded by cranks and mental cases. The Lindberghs felt endangered by these people and took every measure to avoid them.

There wasn't a major road to the Lindbergh estate. The only direct access to the house was a dirt lane. So it was here, in the Sourland Hills of New Jersey, that Lindbergh hoped to find peace and solitude.

On Monday, February 29, the Lindberghs decided not to follow their regular schedule of returning to Englewood on Monday morning. It was chilly, windy, and rainy, and the baby was still getting over a cold he had picked up on Saturday. On Sunday, Mrs. Lindbergh had kept the baby in his room all day. She had been giving him milk of magnesia and putting drops in his nose. At 11 Tuesday morning, Colonel Lindbergh telephoned the Morrow home and arranged to have Mrs. Morrow's chauffeur, Henry Ellison, drive the baby's nursemaid to Hopewell.

Mrs. Lindbergh, suffering from a cold herself, had periodically checked on the baby all night Sunday and Monday. After two nights of broken sleep, she was exhausted. Colonel Lindbergh thought his wife could use a little help in caring for the child.

Betty Gow arrived at the Lindbergh home at 1:30 on Tuesday. After eating her lunch, she went to the nursery, where she played with the baby while Mrs. Lindbergh, three months pregnant with her second child, strolled about the estate.

Outside the nursery the raw winds were damp and biting. At 3:30 Mrs. Lindbergh paused beneath the two nursery windows on the east side of the house. She picked up a handful of pebbles and tossed them, one by one, at the windows until a few of them bounced off the glass. Betty Gow appeared at the window with the baby in her arms. The pudgy, golden-haired child caught sight of his mother and smiled. The nursemaid helped him wave. Mrs. Lindbergh waved back, then continued her stroll.

At 6:00 the nursemaid carried the child to the nursery for his supper. While he was eating, Mrs. Lindbergh came into the room to help prepare him for bed.

Before tucking him into his crib, Betty gave the baby some milk of magnesia. He **11** resisted the medicine and some of it spilled on his nightclothes. When the nurse undressed him for a change of clothes, she decided to make him a little flannel shirt to wear next to his skin for protection against the cold. Betty asked Mrs. Lindbergh to watch the baby while she went for scissors and thread. When she returned she cut out a sleeveless shirt from a piece of flannel cloth. Betty rubbed Vicks Vaporub on the baby's chest, then pulled the homemade garment onto his body. She placed a second shirt, a store-bought one, over the one she had made. The baby now wore two shirts and a pair of diapers enclosed in a rubber covering. Next came the one-piece sleeping suit with enclosed feet and buttons in the back. It also had a flap in the seat. Betty hooked on the two metal guards that kept the baby from sucking his thumbs. She tied the strings securely around his wrists and over the sleeves of the sleeping suit. Lowering the crib rail, she laid him on the mattress. She covered him with a blanket and pulled it snugly across his shoulders, then hooked it to the mattress with two large safety pins.

After putting the baby to bed, Mrs. Lindbergh closed the window shutters. The ones to the French windows on the south wall and the window on the north side of the east wall were tightly closed and latched. But the shutters on the southeast window were warped and couldn't be brought together tight enough to be locked.

Mrs. Lindbergh walked out of the nursery and returned to the first floor. Betty sat in the little room until 8:00, then reported to Mrs. Lindbergh that the baby was sleeping peacefully. The nursemaid went to the sitting room and had supper with Mrs. Whately. Oliver Whately was working in the pantry.

At about 8:30, Mrs. Lindbergh heard Colonel Lindbergh's car pull into the garage at the west end of the house. He had been in New York City, where he was scheduled to attend a dinner at New York University. He had gotten his dates mixed up and instead of appearing at the dinner had driven home. The rain that had been falling all day had just stopped and it was turning cold. The Colonel climbed out of his Franklin sedan and entered the house through the kitchen. He greeted the servants, then joined Mrs. Lindbergh for dinner.

After supper, the Lindberghs walked into the living room and sat down on the sofa. It was 9:00. While sitting there, the Colonel heard a noise that made him think that slats of an orange crate had fallen off a chair in the kitchen. A few minutes later the Lindberghs retired to the bedroom. After a bath, the Colonel walked downstairs to his den, directly below the nursery. Mrs. Lindbergh remained upstairs and drew herself a bath.

At 10:00, Betty Gow decided that it was time for her to check on the baby. The only light in the nursery came from a small lamp in the hallway. She plugged in a small electric heater to take the chill out of the air, then placed her hand on the rail of the crib and peered into the bed. She couldn't see much because her eyes hadn't adjusted to the darkness. But she didn't hear the baby breathing. Startled, she ran her hands frantically over the bedclothes. He wasn't in his crib! The nursemaid rushed out of the nursery and into Mrs. Lindbergh's room.

"Mrs. Lindbergh, do you have the baby?"

12   "No," the mother replied. She had a startled look on her face. "I don't have him."

"Where is the Colonel?" Betty asked. "He may have him. Where is he?" she blurted, trying not to panic.

"He's downstairs in the den," Mrs. Lindbergh said. There was fear in her voice.

Betty ran to Colonel Lindbergh's den. He was still at his desk reading. "Colonel, do you have the baby? Please don't fool me," she cried.

"No," he said. "Isn't he in his crib?" The Colonel stood up.

"No!"

Lindbergh shot out of the room with Betty behind him. He climbed the stairs two at a time.

In the nursery, the side rail to the crib was up. The blanket was still pinned to the mattress. There was a pocket between the cover and the bed where the baby had been. It was clear to Colonel Lindbergh that the child had not gotten out of the crib by himself.

"Anne!" Lindbergh cried out, "They've stolen our baby!"

Colonel Lindbergh surveyed the nursery and saw that the right-hand shutter on the southeast window was standing open—and the window down. He felt the night air that had seeped into the room. The Colonel's eyes fell upon a small, white envelope on top of the radiator case that formed the window's sill. He assumed it contained the ransom demand and didn't pick it up for fear of ruining any fingerprints. The side of the envelope that he could see bore no writing.

Mrs. Lindbergh rushed into the room. She looked into the crib, then opened the baby's closet. The child was not under his bed or anywhere else in the room—he was gone! She ran back into her bedroom and threw open the windows. She leaned out over the sill. There was nothing to see, but she thought she heard something. It sounded like a cry, coming from the direction of the woodpile. Elsie Whately came up behind her. "That was the wind," she said.

Colonel Lindbergh said he was going outside, but before he left, he warned everybody not to touch the white envelope. With his rifle in hand, Lindbergh made his way a hundred feet or so along the road in front of the mansion before realizing his search was futile. He turned and walked back to the house, which now was ablaze with lights.

The first police to show up were Hopewell officers Harry Wolfe and Charles E. Williamson. They got there at 10:40 and were met at the door by Lindbergh, who took them directly to the nursery. Following a quick look into the baby's room where they noticed clumps of soil on the baby's leather suitcase beneath the southeast window, Lindbergh and the officers went outside. Beneath this window, the officers found two indentations in the mud, impressions made by a ladder. With the aid of a flashlight, they followed a set of footprints that led them from the house in a southeasterly direction. The footprints led them to a homemade ladder. The ladder was in two sections and lay about seventy-five feet from the house. It was the ladder the kidnapper had used to get up to the nursery window. Approximately ten feet away they found the wooden ladder's third, or top, section. The men returned to the house, where they waited for the New Jersey State Police. They left the ladder as they had found it.

In New York City police were being dispatched to the Holland Tunnel, the George Washington Bridge, and to all ferry terminals along the Hudson River. By 11:00 checkpoints at these locations were in full operation. Every vehicle coming into the city was searched and the occupants questioned. The license number of each car and truck was recorded.

In New Jersey, the police were setting up roadblocks and notifying every hospital in the state to report the admission of any child fitting the general description of the Lindbergh baby. Soon drifters, known criminals, and suspicious people all across the state would be rounded up and questioned.

There were people who fluttered around the flame of publicity, politicians who came and posed for pictures next to the kidnapper's ladder. There was one city official, acting as a self-appointed investigator, who woke me up in the middle of the night and asked me to re-enact his theory of the crime, which ended with the imaginary throwing of a baby into a furnace.

—A N N E   M O R R O W   L I N D B E R G H

2 THE CRIME SCENE

CPL. JOSEPH A. WOLF from Troop B in nearby Lambertville was the first member of the New Jersey State Police to arrive at the scene. When he arrived, he was greeted by Colonel Lindbergh and the two officers from Hopewell. It was 10:55 P.M.

Colonel Lindbergh gave Corporal Wolf a quick summary of events and stood by as Wolf relayed this information to headquarters. The officer on the desk said that the superintendent, H. Norman Schwarzkopf, had been notified and was on his way. When he hung up, Wolf informed Colonel Lindbergh that a squad of men from the Morristown Barracks were also en route.

Lindbergh took Corporal Wolf to the nursery and showed him the envelope on the radiator. Using a penknife so as not to touch the seven- by six and a half-inch container, Wolf moved it to the mantle over the fireplace. Colonel Lindbergh said the envelope should be left there for the fingerprint people. Corporal Wolf noticed that the southeast window was closed and that on the leather suitcase beneath it were clumps of yellow clay. Wolf and the Colonel returned to the living room, where the officer asked Lindbergh to identify all the people who had been in the house when Betty Gow discovered the baby missing. When he finished talking to Colonel Lindbergh, Wolf stepped outside to examine the muddy ground beneath the southeast nursery window, the kidnapper's point of entry. Under this window Wolf spotted a large footprint and several small impressions. With the aid of his flashlight, Wolf examined the large shoeprint closely. To get an idea of its size, he compared the print with his own shoe, a size nine, and found that the impression was larger than his. Under this window, Wolf also saw a pair of indentations that looked as though they had been made by the feet of a ladder. Wolf took no precise measurements of the ladder marks or the shoe impressions.

At 11:15 P.M., Dets. Lewis J. Bornmann and Nuncio De Gaetano, both assigned to the state police headquarters in West Trenton, reported to the scene. By this time, Corporal Wolf and the others had found a chisel in the mud below the baby's window. The wood-handled, three-quarter-inch tool, made by the Bucks Brothers Company, was nine and a

14

half inches long. The kidnapper must have planned to use the chisel to force open the nursery shutters.

Detective De Gaetano examined the large footprint beneath the nursery and noticed, within it, a textile pattern. He thought the kidnapper had covered his shoes with a sock or bag so he wouldn't leave telltale shoe impressions. Detective De Gaetano didn't have a ruler or a tape measure, so he gauged the size of the print by placing his fourteen-and-a-half-inch flashlight beside it. From this he estimated that the impression was twelve and a half inches long. He then matched the width of the shoeprint against the palm of his hand and concluded that it was about four and a quarter inches wide.

Detective Bornmann looked at the footprints and, like Wolf and De Gaetano, failed to measure them precisely. The officers assumed that the smaller prints near the large one had been made by Mrs. Lindbergh earlier in the day when she had stood beneath the window tossing pebbles at the baby's window.

No one at the scene made a plaster-of-paris cast of the shoe impressions. Although none of these footprints would have produced a plaster cast of any detail, the failure to cast them was an embarrassing oversight. The failure to measure the footprints was a more serious error.

At 11:25 P.M., two more state police officers, Troopers Cain and Sullivan from the Lambertville Barracks, arrived at the estate. Corporal Wolf immediately dispatched Sullivan to the main gate to direct the incoming police, arriving on motorcycles and in cars, to a place along Amwell Road about a mile southeast of the Lindbergh house. The idea was to keep the vehicles from obliterating tire tracks and other evidence that might have been left by the kidnappers. Trooper Cain was sent to the southeast corner of the house to keep people away from the shoe impressions.

A state trooper, canvassing the area around the estate, found a set of tire tracks on Featherbed Lane, a dirt road that ran north and south on the east side of the Lindbergh house. Since there was no discernable tread pattern in the tracks, the officer didn't preserve this evidence with plaster. And although he should have, he did not measure the distance between the tracks, the width of the tire, and the depth of the impression. Of course, he had no way of knowing if these tracks had anything to do with the crime.

Except for the ransom note, the most vital physical evidence was the three-piece homemade extension ladder. Weighing only thirty-eight pounds, the ladder extended to a maximum length of eighteen and a half feet. It was also tapered: The bottom of the first section was fourteen inches wide, the top of the third eleven inches across. The rungs were eighteen inches apart instead of the standard foot. Although crudely made, the ladder was functional and ingeniously designed. The rungs were cut into the side rails, and the three sections were made to fit on top of each other, compressing the ladder's overall length to slightly over eighty and a half inches. Three twelve-inch dowel pins, inserted through holes in the side rails of the adjoining sections, kept the ladder in the extended position. When the pins were slipped out and the three sections positioned into each other, the ladder could be easily carried, and fit into the back seat of a car.

A closer inspection of the ladder revealed that it was broken. The side rails of the middle section had split along the grain at the dowel-point where this section and the bottom part of the ladder came together. The officers speculated that the ladder had held the weight of the kidnapper going up, but when he descended with the extra weight of the baby, it had given way. The places where the ladder had split would have been about five feet off the ground. The officers concluded that the clumps of mud on some of the ladder rungs had come from the kidnapper's shoes.

About midnight, Col. H. Norman Schwarzkopf, the head of the New Jersey State Police, and his second-in-command, Maj. Charles Schoeffel, arrived at the Lindbergh house.

The thirty-seven-year-old Schwarzkopf, a second-generation German-American, was born in Newark, New Jersey, where his father had owned a jewelry store. In 1913, Schwarzkopf was appointed to the U.S. Military Academy at West Point; four years later he graduated eighty-eighth out of a class of 139. In 1917 he was sent overseas and a year later he was promoted to captain. As a battery commander in the Third Division fighting in France, he was gassed.

At the end of the war, Schwarzkopf was attached to the army of occupation in Germany. As a provost marshal, he gained valuable experience in law enforcement. He returned to the United States in 1919 and was assigned to the Seventh Cavalry which at that time was stationed in El Paso, Texas. Schwarzkopf was again assigned military police duties, this time along the Mexican border.

In July 1920, when his father became ill and was confined to a wheelchair, Schwarzkopf resigned his commission and returned to Newark to run the family business.

In 1921, the New Jersey legislature authorized the formation of a state police force. Gov. Teddy Edwards was looking for someone to head the new agency, and when the twenty-five-year-old Schwarzkopf heard of the opening, he applied for the job. He came highly recommended through his wartime friend, Capt. Irving Edwards, the governor's son. So, on July 1, 1921, Schwarzkopf was appointed as the first superintendent of the New Jersey State Police.

Schwarzkopf started his agency with a force of 120 carefully selected, highly motivated, and well-disciplined men. The organization was paramilitary; all ranking members had at least two years of commissioned military service. Troopers were not allowed to get married during their first tour of duty.[1]

Schwarzkopf and his men were smartly outfitted in blue uniform jackets, campaign hats, and yellow-striped riding breeches. Colonel Schwarzkopf, six feet tall and weighing 160 pounds, had short brown hair combed straight back, a tiny, neatly trimmed moustache, and a square, strong face. Known for his honesty and straightforwardness, he was a leader who had earned the respect of his men.

At the time of the kidnapping, Schwarzkopf was in the first year of his third five-year-term as superintendent. He lived with his wife and son in Lawrenceville, New Jersey, a small farming community five miles from Trenton. He and Colonel Lindbergh had never met.

Because his background was military rather than municipal or police, Schwarzkopf didn't have the patrol or investigative experience of most law enforcement heads, but he had overcome this lack of experience with common sense and an ability to select outstanding men. He was also a gifted administrator.

Accompanying Schwarzkopf and Schoeffel to the scene were Capt. John J. Lamb, the administrator in charge of the state's investigative services, and his subordinate, Lt. Arthur T. Keaten, the head of the local detective bureau. Once the initial investigative flurry subsided, Lieutenant Keaten would be supervising the Lindbergh investigation on a day-to-day basis.

Keaten, called "Buster" by his friends, joined the New Jersey State Police in October 1922 and became a member of the first police-training class. While at the police academy, Keaten fell off a horse and injured his shoulder. When his shoulder healed, Keaten rejoined the force as a member of the second class of trainees.

Keaten worked his way up to lieutenant through hard work and loyalty. He had investigated hundreds of crimes, including the celebrated Hall-Mills murder case in 1926. The solidly built detective was known as a patient but relentless investigator. Instead of force and physical intimidation, he got his confessions through persistence, psychology, and the softsell. Keaten was fiercely loyal to Colonel Schwarzkopf.[2]

One of Keaten's detectives, Nuncio De Gaetano, was already at the scene. Soon to follow were Det. S. J. Leon, Andrew Zapolsky, and E. A. Haussling.

Col. Henry C. Breckinridge, Lindbergh's friend and personal attorney, had also arrived at the house. Tall and distinguished, the Manhattan attorney had been Lindbergh's lawyer for five years. As a dashing young college student, Breckinridge had been a member of an international fencing team. Gray-haired, with a matching moustache, Breckinridge looked the part of a successful New York attorney. He and his wife had spent the previous weekend in Hopewell as the Lindberghs' guests. The well-spoken, well-dressed lawyer had Colonel Lindbergh's complete trust and confidence.

Shortly after his arrival, Colonel Breckinridge telephoned FBI Director J. Edgar Hoover. The two men had become friends when Breckinridge was in Washington, D.C., as the assistant secretary of war in the Harding cabinet. Hoover assured Breckinridge that his agents would be contacting their underworld sources to get a line on the people who had taken Colonel Lindbergh's son.

Cpl. Frank A. Kelly from the Morristown Barracks had arrived at the estate. Assigned to the Identification Bureau, Kelly performed duties as a fingerprint man and crime scene photographer. Like most fingerprint men of the time, Kelly had learned his trade on the job from an older, more experienced ID man. He had picked up the rest from books and his own cases.

Kelly was ushered into the nursery to process the room and the ransom note for fingerprints. Under the watchful eyes of the three Colonels, Lindbergh, Breckinridge, and Schwarzkopf, as well as Major Schoeffel and Officers Lamb, Keaten, Wolfe, De Gaetano, and Bornmann and the local police, Corporal Kelly prepared himself for the job. After putting on gloves, he gingerly carried the envelope from the mantle to the maple table in the center of the room. He took a small jar of fine black powder and tapped it lightly with his finger to sprinkle some of it onto the envelope. Using a fine-

18   haired brush at the end of a pencillike stick, he swept the excess powder off the envelope. The idea behind this procedure, called dusting for fingerprints, is this: The powder is supposed to stick to the dirt and oil on the spots that have been touched. When the excess powder is brushed away, the powder that remains shows up in the form of a ridge pattern or fingerprint.

Dusting for fingerprints is a hit-or-miss proposition. If the person who had handled the object doesn't touch it right, the prints will be smudged or smeared. If the handler placed his fingerprint on top of someone else's, his print is lost.

As for the envelope, Kelly had another problem. Certain surfaces do not take fingerprints very well. Fingerprint men are more likely to get results when they dust hard, shiny surfaces like glass. The most difficult and unrewarding material to process is paper, because it is porous and the fingerprint is absorbed. As a result, fingerprint men do not usually use powder on paper. A more effective method, one that was being used at the New York City Police Department at the time, involved exposing the paper to slightly heated iodine fumes. When this is done, the areas that have been touched turn purple. These purple stains quickly fade, but before they do, they can be photographed. Corporal Kelly's fingerprint kit did not include a crime scene iodine fumer: In 1932 such an instrument didn't exist. Iodine fuming had to be done in a crime laboratory.

Kelly brushed the excess powder off the envelope, but all that remained was a single smudge. Major Schoeffel picked up the envelope and slit it open with his penknife. He extracted and unfolded a single sheet of paper, and after a quick look, asked Colonel Lindbergh, "Now who do you want to see this note?" As he spoke, Schoeffel looked at Harry Wolfe, the local chief of police. Wolfe realized the state police didn't want him in the inner circles of the investigation. Before Colonel Lindbergh could answer, Chief Wolfe and his patrolman, Charles Williamson, walked out of the room.

Major Schoeffel handed the note to Lindbergh. The message on it was handwritten in blue ink. It read:

Dear Sir!

Have 50,000$ redy 2500$ in 20$ bills 15000$ in 10$ bills and 10000$ in 5$ bills. After 2–4 days we will inform you were to deliver the Mony.
    We warn you for making anyding public or for notify the polise the child is in gute care.
    Indication for all letters are singnature and 3 holes.

On the bottom right-hand corner of the note was a strange symbol, consisting of two interlocking circles each slightly larger than a quarter. In the oval formed where the circles overlapped was a solid red mark about the size of a nickel. Three small holes had been punched through the logo—one was in the center of the red mark and the other two were in line with it just outside the larger circles.

Corporal Kelly dusted the ransom note without producing even a smudge. Under tremendous pressure to get results, he was performing in the presence of an international hero whose son had just been kidnapped. He was nervous and working without the proper equipment. The success or failure of the crime scene investigation had been thrust into the hands of a corporal—a converted highway patrolman who, if given the choice, would have been chasing speeders.

The absence of prints suggested gloves—a common precaution even among amateurs. If the intruders had worn bags on their feet to prevent shoe impressions, they had probably worn gloves as well.

Kelly dusted the crib, the baby's sunlamp, the walls, both sides of the glass on the southeast window, and the leather suitcase. He brought out dozens of latents, but they were either smudged, smeared, or only partial prints.

Kelly photographed the yellow clay on the floor and on top of the leather suitcase, then took samples of it. With the immediate crime scene work in the nursery out of the way, the officers returned to the first floor, where they shifted their attention to the kidnap ladder.

Detective Bornmann had carried the three sections into the house. Ideally, the ladder would have been left outside as it had been found, but with the arrival of reporters and sightseers, the evidence could not be protected. The interior of the house also provided better working conditions for Corporal Kelly.

Kelly dusted the side rails, each rung, and the dowel pins for fingerprints. But because the ladder was made of wood, the process failed to produce any identifiable prints. Kelly gathered samples of the soil that had been deposited on the ladder rungs, noting that it was the same color and consistency as the dirt found in the nursery. When he was finished with the ladder, he marked the rungs and side rails with his initials.

The Bucks Brothers chisel had been brought into the house. Kelly dusted it, but once again, he was unable to bring out any pattern that could be identified.

Kelly was also the crime scene photographer. He took pictures of the ladder, the chisel, the large footprint beneath the southeast window, the tire tracks on Featherbed Lane, the ransom note, and, from many angles, the nursery itself. The ladder and chisel had been brought into the house before Kelly could photograph them in their original positions.

Kelly completed his crime scene duties by gathering additional soil samples from the base of the house beneath the southeast window and from Featherbed Lane in the area of the tire tracks.

At 1:00 A.M., Lieutenant Keaten, accompanied by Colonel Lindbergh, Sergeant Haussling, and Detective Horn, set out to interview Lindbergh's closest neighbors. They returned to the estate three and a half hours later—none of the neighbors they had questioned had seen anything suspicious.

Corporal Wolf's initial investigative report reflects the consensus regarding what had taken place that night:

> The kidnappers consisted apparently of a party of at least two or more persons. They are believed to have driven to the vicinity of the Lindbergh home in a car and parked the car as close as possible without being detected. Apparently two members of the party proceeded on foot to the east side of the Lindbergh residence and assembled a three piece home-made extension ladder which they brought along. The ladder was then placed in

position against the east side of the house so that one of the kidnapping party was able to enter a window of the victim's nursery which is located on the second floor in the southeast corner [of the building]. Apparently one person climbed the ladder, removed Charles Lindbergh, Jr. from his crib and left with the victim in the same manner. The ladder was then taken apart and thrown some distance southeast of the house, the kidnappers (then) proceeded to the waiting car and left with their victim for some place of hiding.[4]

By midnight, word of the crime had reached the news services. Radio stations all over the country were on the air all night broadcasting the latest developments in the case. By daybreak, the Lindbergh estate was swarming with reporters, cameramen, photographers, curious onlookers, and souvenir hunters. The stampeding mob overran the police, stomping over grounds where clues might have been found. Although the police eventually got control of the crowd, it was too late to save the crime scene. No one will ever know how much evidence was crushed.[5]

The Lindbergh house, rising majestically above the incoming cars, headlight beams, people, and confusion, was brilliantly lit. Inside, Lindbergh, Breckinridge, and Schwarzkopf were trying to figure out what to do next.

Early the next afternoon, Anne Lindbergh's mother and sister Elizabeth were driven to Hopewell to console her. Anne Lindbergh's father, Dwight Morrow, had died four months earlier, at the age of fifty-eight, from a stroke. Mrs. Morrow wanted her daughter to return to Englewood until the baby was back, but Mrs. Lindbergh insisted on staying with her husband in Hopewell.

Both Colonel Lindbergh and Colonel Schwarzkopf agreed that the crime was the work of criminals who knew what they were doing. They had custom-built a ladder for the job, had worn gloves, and had known that the Lindberghs would still be in Hopewell on Tuesday, a deviation from their normal routine.

Shortly after daybreak, Capt. John J. Lamb, Cpl. Joseph Wolf, and three troopers, Rutter, Jackson and Perry, tramped several miles through the woods west of the Lindbergh estate. They returned at 1:30 in the afternoon with nothing to report.

The Lindbergh house had been turned into a virtual police station. Officers were holding meetings in the bedroom and napping on the living room and dining room floors on mattresses, blankets, and newspapers. Policemen were sitting on the stairs, leaning against the kitchen appliances, and talking on the telephone. Amidst this bedlam, Oliver Whately served coffee to everyone.

The New Jersey State Police were already setting up a communications center in Lindbergh's three-car garage. A twenty-line telephone switchboard was being installed to handle all of the calls. While this was being done, forty telephone engineers were enlarging the phone facilities at the tiny telephone exchange in Hopewell.

Troopers were posted at all doors to the Lindbergh house, carefully screening everyone who entered. In front of the house, wandering about the courtyard and seated in cars, were thirty-five officers from the state, Jersey City, and Hunterdon, Mercer, and Bergen counties.

There were so many reporters in the area, a local railroad station was transformed into a news headquarters.

The next morning the kidnapping was front-page news all over the world. An extra edition *Pittsburgh Sun Telegram* screamed: "LINDBERGH BABY KIDNAPPED, ABDUCTORS DEMAND RANSOM." The *Sun Telegram's* coverage was typical. The entire front page was devoted to the kidnapping. The page one headline in *The New York Times* declared: "LINDBERGH BABY KIDNAPPED FROM HOME OF PARENTS ON FARM NEAR PRINCETON; TAKEN FROM HIS CRIB; WIDE SEARCH ON." News of the crime took up most of page one and all of page two. Shortly after the *Times* hit the street, 3,331 people called the paper for additional information.

Farther west, the headlines of the *Chicago Daily Tribune* blared: "LINDBERGH BABY IS STOLEN." This was the first time a crime other than the assassination of a national leader was front-page news on such a large scale. The story had driven the Sino-Japanese War and every other item of international and domestic importance right off the page.

Everybody wanted to help. Dr. John Grier Hibben, the president of Princeton University, said his students would form a human chain and search the woods around the Lindbergh estate. The Boy Scouts made a similar offer. Bloodhounds were readied and hundreds of state troopers from New York and Pennsylvania combed the forests along their states' New Jersey borders. An airplane club on Long Island contributed aircraft and pilots in an aerial search of New York, New Jersey, Pennsylvania, and Delaware.

President Herbert Hoover and Attorney General William D. Mitchell offered Colonel Schwarzkopf the full cooperation of the FBI, the Secret Service, the Postal Inspection Service, and the IRS.

The premiers of Great Britain, France, Japan, and China made public statements condemning the criminals who had taken the baby. Thousands of private letters and sympathy cards were mailed to the Lindberghs from all over the world.

On Wednesday morning, a description of the baby was released to the press and sent over the police teletype system. It was also broadcast on every radio station in the country.

Every police officer in America was looking for the Lindbergh baby, and law enforcement agencies everywhere were picking up information that the child was in their vicinity. Thousands of well-meaning citizens were calling their local police with stories of suspicious people they had seen carrying a twenty-month-old baby. In Chicago, members of the Secret Six, an elite squad of detectives who handled nothing but kidnapping cases, raided a rooming house on a tip that the Lindbergh baby was there.

The U.S. Coast Guard had notified all of its stations to be on the lookout for the Lindbergh baby, and the Department of Commerce had sent a similar message to all commercial airports. Federal immigration and customs authorities were put on alert, and every boat, car, and train entering Mexico from the U.S. was searched.

The hunt for the Lindbergh baby was so intense that a vacationing bank clerk from Trenton, New Jersey, motoring across the country in a car with New Jersey license plates, was stopped and questioned 107 times.

Late in the afternoon of March 2, three large sacks of mail were delivered to the Lindbergh estate. The letters were dumped into a large barrel and eight New Jersey state troopers were assigned the job of sorting them out. During the next month, a squad of officers, working eight hours a day, sat hunched over this barrel in an upstairs room of the Lindbergh house.

The Lindberghs would receive tons of mail. In addition to the sympathy letters, there were death threats, phony ransom demands, well-meaning suggestions, accounts of dreams, and the predictions of assorted spiritualists and soothsayers.[6]

The governor of New Jersey asked every city, state, and federal law enforcement agency in the country to search for the kidnappers. The governor placed the detective forces of Newark and Jersey City under Colonel Schwarzkopf's command and announced that the New Jersey legislature was about to make kidnapping a crime punishable by death. The state was also offering a twenty-five-thousand-dollar reward for information leading to the identity and capture of the kidnappers.

Colonel Lindbergh didn't want the state to change its kidnapping law, and he disapproved of the reward. He telephoned the governor and asked him to postpone these moves. Lindbergh was afraid these measures would endanger his child. Referring to the reward, he said, "I fear that the offer, generous though it is, might prove dangerous. It might seriously interfere with the effort to locate the baby. I must ask you to refrain from offering it."

The governor promptly withdrew the reward and set aside the proposed legislation. Kidnapping was already a serious crime in New Jersey, punishable by not less than thirty years. (In neighboring New York State, the crime only carried a ten- to fifteen-year sentence.)

On the morning after the crime, Lt. John J. Sweeney of the Newark Police Department began experimenting with the kidnap ladder. With the help of state troopers and Frank Kelly, who was there to take more photographs, Sweeney placed the feet of the ladder into the two indentations beneath the nursery window. He extended the three sections and leaned the ladder against the east wall of the house. Fully extended, the top section of the ladder reached well above the window. When Sweeney removed the top section, the ladder reached a spot thirty inches below the windowsill. It came to rest on the two places where the whitewash was rubbed off. Sweeney and the other officers concluded that these spots marked the place where the ladder had rested—the top section wasn't used. Corporal Kelly took photographs of the ladder in this position.

Through a magnifying glass, Sweeney examined the rubbed-off areas on the wall and found, sticking to the masonry, wood splinters from the kidnap ladder.

The kidnapper's ladder was taken down and replaced by a regular one from Colonel Lindbergh's garage. It was leaned against the house where the homemade one had been. Sweeney climbed up the ladder, set his left knee on the windowsill, then maneuvered his right leg and the rest of his 175-pound body through the nursery window. During the next hour or so, several troopers entered the Lindbergh house this way.

WHILE LIEUTENANT SWEENEY was experimenting with the ladder, Lieutenant Keaten and his detectives were chasing down false leads. For example, two elderly widows had reported hearing a conversation in which the words "Lindbergh," "kidnap," and "baby" had been spoken. The old women led several troopers through the woods, pointing out places the baby might have been hidden. Several Lindbergh neighbors and residents of nearby towns were recalling incidents involving strangers in cars asking directions to the Lindbergh estate. The butler, Oliver Whately, remembered that while talking to a shrub salesman, he saw a man and a woman in a green automobile drive up and take photographs of the house. Whately had sent the couple packing, but the salesman said he later saw the woman behind a bush focusing her camera on the nursery windows.

The police at Princeton received a tip that two men in a black or blue sedan with New York plates had asked directions to the Lindbergh estate. The description of the car was sent to police departments in New Jersey and New York. The automobile was subsequently identified by a resident of Brooklyn who reported that it had been stolen from him earlier that day.

A man named George Jennings who lived on one of the roads between Hopewell and the Lindbergh estate reported that on the night of the kidnapping a man and a woman in a dark-colored car had asked him directions to the Lindbergh place. A team of detectives were still trying to identify and locate these people.

A postcard sent from Newark contained the following hand-printed message: "Baby safe. Wait instructions later. Act accordingly." The card was addressed to "Col. Linberg, Princeton, N.J." The Newark police located the store where the postcard had been purchased. The store clerk described the buyer and, after visiting two hundred homes, the police identified the sender, a mentally disturbed boy. Two hundred Newark policemen had been assigned to this lead.

Hundreds of such messages were sent to the Lindberghs during the weeks following the crime. Another postcard writer told Colonel Lindbergh to "obey instructions or suffer consequences." The seventeen-year-old boy who had sent this message wanted to see if it would get reported in the newspapers.

In Trenton, the police were told that at midnight on the night of the kidnapping, a Pennsylvania Railroad brakeman had seen two men and a woman with a child in her arms on the train platform on Clinton Street. One of the men had nervously asked the brakeman when the next train to New York City was due. The railroad man described the suspects in great detail and the New York City Police Department sent out a general alarm based upon these descriptions. For the next few days thousands of New York City policemen looked for these people.

And so it went.

Captain Lamb of the New Jersey State Police and Jersey City Police Capt. Henry Gauthier strapped the kidnap ladder to the side of a patrol car and drove it to every contractor, carpenter, and hardware store within a twenty-mile radius of the Lindbergh estate. No one recognized or claimed the ladder, but those who saw it were struck by the cleverness of its construction. This led many to believe that it had been made by someone with carpentry skills. They noted that the nails were cleanly driven and the saw cuts straight and smooth. And the three sections fit into each other so well.

Lieutenant Keaten dispatched a pair of detectives to check the state home for epileptics at Skillman, New Jersey. (In 1932 epileptics suffered an undeserved stigma that fortunately does not exist today.) The institution was located about four miles from the Lindbergh estate. The detectives reported that all of the patients were accounted for on the night of the kidnapping.

A list of the workmen who had built the Lindbergh home was obtained from George Hullfish, the Lawrenceville, New Jersey, foreman employed by the company that had constructed the house. Every one of the workers, as well as their families and associates, would have to be investigated.

Lieutenant Keaten had to consider the possibility of an inside job. This called for an investigation of the backgrounds of the Whateleys and Betty Gow as well as the twenty-nine domestic employees of the Morrow home. This would tie up dozens of detectives and could be a waste of manpower, time, and money. But there was no other way—there could be no shortcuts.

The idea that a servant had either furnished the kidnappers inside information or had actually participated in the crime was not farfetched. It seemed the kidnappers had known that the Lindberghs weren't leaving Hopewell on Monday as usual. And the fact that the kidnapper had entered the nursery through the shutters that couldn't be locked might not have been coincidence. Moreover, the crime had been perfectly timed. If the ladder had been laid against the house during the period Colonel Lindbergh was at his desk, he would have seen it through his southeast window.

Lieutenant Keaten knew that the family dog Wahgoosh hadn't barked that night. Could it be that the intruder knew the pet? Maybe someone in the household had taken steps to see that the animal would not interfere with the kidnapping. There were other aspects of the crime that needed to be explained. For example, why didn't the kidnappers wait until later in the night to snatch the baby? Why didn't they wait until everyone in the Lindbergh house was asleep?

Keaten, like all experienced investigators, was keeping an open mind. Anything was possible and everyone was a suspect. It was also quite possible that the kidnapping had not been an inside job. The Lindbergh home and its construction had been featured, in great detail and with elaborate photographs, in newspapers and magazines all over the country. The house had also been the subject of several newsreel films. As for the Lindbergh baby, his birth had been a national event. The public had been kept informed almost daily of his health and activities. His photographs had appeared in hundreds of newspapers and magazines, and young Charles had also been the subject of several Movietone Newsreels, films shown in motion picture theaters throughout the country.

It was easy to observe the Lindbergh house from a hidden position in the surrounding woods. The land around the building had been cleared, but beyond the yard lay dense woods. Only one road led to the house, so movements of the family could have been monitored by anyone watching from the forest.

Maybe the kidnappers didn't know that the Lindberghs always returned to Englewood on Monday. People who read the newspaper would have known where the baby's nursery was. If they didn't know this beforehand, a surveillance of the house through a pair of fieldglasses would have told the story.

The kidnapper had brought a chisel to pry open the shutters. To Lieutenant Keaten this indicated that the kidnapper didn't know that the shutters to the baby's window were warped and couldn't be latched.

Wahgoosh hadn't barked that night, but the dog was old and slept at the other end of the house. And the howling winds would have drowned out any sounds of entry.

After mulling over the inside-job question, Keaten concluded that although it was a distinct possibility, the crime could have been done without inside help.

Everyone in the house had been on the first floor when the baby was taken. But even so, the kidnapper was taking a risk that the child would cry out. The intruder must have known that any commotion would bring the Lindberghs and the nursemaid running. The kidnapper was on the second floor, with a ladder his only escape. He would have been trapped! Schwarzkopf and Keaten had to think the unthinkable—maybe the baby had been killed in his sleep to keep him silent. There were no bloodstains on the baby's bedclothing or anywhere else in the room, so it was unlikely that he had been bludgeoned. But the child could have been throttled or suffocated. The kidnapper could have snuffed out the baby's life by pinching his nose and covering his mouth. This would have made things safer—and easier. With a dead baby there was no chance that halfway down the ladder he would wake up and start calling for his mother.

Lieutenant Keaten had noticed that the baby's blanket had not been turned back. It was still pinned to the mattress. This meant that the child had been pulled out of the crib by his neck or head, suggesting that the kidnapper had handled the child roughly—a bad sign.

Lieutenant Keaten had considered the possibility that the child had been chloroformed to stifle his cries. But there was no telltale odor in the room, and it is doubtful that the aroma would have followed the kidnapper out the window.

The Lindbergh investigators disagreed about how many people had committed the crime. Most of the investigators felt the kidnapping had been the work of two, three, or even four men. Only a few of the investigators believed the baby had been snatched by a lone wolf.

Regardless of how many people had been involved, the Lindbergh crime had the impact of a presidential assassination. The eyes of the world were on Colonel Schwarzkopf and his men. People everywhere hungered for the capture of the Lindbergh kidnappers.

His cold had gone to his chest a little bit and I made him a little flannel vest, rubbed his chest and got him fixed up and left him asleep peacefully.

—B E T T Y   G O W
in a letter to her mother

3 THE INITIAL INVESTIGATION

ON THE DAY FOLLOWING THE CRIME, Colonels Lindbergh, Breckinridge, and Schwarz-kopf were in the Lindbergh house planning their strategy and trying to figure out how to make contact with the kidnappers. Having made it perfectly clear that the first priority in the case was the safe return of his son, Colonel Lindbergh was in firm control of the investigation. The police were not to interfere in any way with his negotiations with the kidnappers. Colonel Schwarzkopf was not to authorize the arrest of anyone until the ransom had been paid and the baby was safely returned. The Lindberghs were pre-pared to meet any of the kidnappers' demands and, if necessary, to keep their identities confidential.

Late in the afternoon of March 2, Colonel Lindbergh announced that his old friend, Douglas G. Thompson, would serve as the intermediary between himself and the kid-nappers. Thompson, the former mayor of Englewood, was instructed to cooperate fully with the criminals.

Word had gotten out that Colonel Lindbergh was looking for some way to make con-tact with the underworld. A friend of a local racketeer named Morris ("Mickey") Rosner heard this rumor and urged Rosner to contact Lindbergh and offer his services. Rosner professed to know a great deal about the underworld and had identified a number of underworld characters for Insp. Harry Walsh of the Jersey City Police Department. In-spector Walsh had worked closely with Lieutenant Keaten of the New Jersey State Police on several cases in the past and was in Hopewell lending a hand on the Lindbergh investigation.

Wednesday afternoon, the day following the crime, Rosner talked to Colonel Breckin-ridge over the telephone and assured him that through his underworld contacts he would be able to determine who had taken the baby. Once this had been done, negotia-tions could be started that would lead to the child's return. Breckinridge passed this information on to Lindbergh, who agreed to meet with Rosner the following morning. Meanwhile, Lieutenant Keaten could run a check on the man.

Mickey Rosner was a small-time bootlegger and big-time swindler who operated out of New Jersey and New York City. He had been a police informant and often referred to himself as a former government agent. A small, dapper man, Rosner looked the part of a Prohibition Era racketeer. He liked to wear a gray felt hat with the right side brim turned down—an affectation inspired by Al Capone—and a three-piece suit with a white silk handkerchief bursting out of the breast pocket. Rosner was currently under indictment for grand larceny in connection with a stock-selling scam that had cost his "investors" two million dollars.

Schwarzkopf and Keaten advised Colonel Lindbergh not to bring Rosner into the case. They argued that a man like him couldn't be trusted. If he knew something about the kidnapping, he should come forward with this information, otherwise, he should not be brought into the inner circles of the investigation. Even if Rosner were well-meaning and on the level, he wasn't a cop and as such could foul up the investigation.

Colonel Breckinridge took the opposite view. At the moment, the police didn't have the foggiest idea who the kidnappers were, and the investigation was going off in a thousand directions. If the underworld did have something to do with the crime, it would be more likely to deal with someone like Rosner than with the police. Colonel Breckinridge reminded Schwarzkopf that this was not the ordinary case, that there were special circumstances. The purpose of the investigation was not to arrest anyone—the idea was to make contact with the criminals so that a deal could be made for the safe return of the baby. The police were not necessarily the best people to handle this kind of assignment.

Schwarzkopf and Keaten were angered and alarmed by Breckinridge's position. They argued that Rosner should not be brought into the case and made privy to confidential police information. As far as they were concerned it was an absurd and dangerous idea.

As Colonel Lindbergh's personal friend and trusted advisor, Henry Breckinridge prevailed. In the morning, he said, Mickey Rosner would come to Hopewell and be interviewed by Colonel Lindbergh. Of course, both he and Lindbergh wanted Colonel Schwarzkopf to be present. If it appeared that Rosner could accomplish what he said he could, the racketeer would be given the job. Colonel Schwarzkopf felt strongly that Lindbergh was getting bad advice, but he wasn't in a position to say so. He didn't want to jeopardize his own position in the case.

On the morning of Thursday, March 3, Mickey Rosner showed up at the Lindbergh estate. He was ushered into the library, where he was introduced to Colonels Lindbergh, Breckinridge, and Schwarzkopf. Lieutenant Keaten was also in the room. Rosner said that he was certain that the kidnapping was the work of professionals. He hinted that mobsters connected with the notorious Purple Gang of Detroit, hoodlums associated with the Al Capone people in Chicago, were behind the kidnapping. He said that his plan was to gain the confidence of underworld people by appointing low-level organized crime soldiers as official emissaries. Rosner said that the two men he had in mind for the job were Salvatore Spitale and Irving Bitz.

28   Colonel Schwarzkopf couldn't believe what he was hearing—Rosner wanted to bring two more crooks into the case. And that wasn't all, Rosner said he would operate right out of the Lindbergh home, where he would have direct and immediate access to everyone involved in the case. Rosner's two assistants, however, would set up headquarters in New York City.

Rosner made a favorable impression on Lindbergh and Breckinridge. He was confident and seemed to know what he was talking about. Schwarzkopf and Keaten weren't impressed, but there was nothing they could do: The decision had been made to engage the racketeer's services.

Rosner said he would need money to cover his expenses, so Breckinridge handed him twenty-five hundred dollars in cash. Rosner then asked to see the note the kidnapper had left in the baby's room. Someone fetched the original ransom message and handed it to Rosner, who read it and asked for a tracing of it to be made. This was done. Rosner needed one more thing, and he got it—a promise from Colonel Breckinridge that the police would not follow him as he made his underworld contacts.

Schwarzkopf and Keaten could do nothing but stand by and watch someone they believed to be a swindler and a thief walk out the door with a copy of the ransom note. That document was their only link to the kidnappers. The unique symbol of interlocking circles was the secret code that would distinguish the real abductors from the hundreds of extortionists who would try to capitalize on the crime. There was no telling who Rosner would show that secret symbol. When Schwarzkopf thought of all the schemers, thieves, and con men who would get a look at the nursery note, the most important and sensitive clue in the case, his blood boiled. How could Colonel Breckinridge have allowed this to happen?[1]

On the morning of Rosner's visit to the Lindbergh home, a message was broadcast over NBC radio to the kidnappers on behalf of the Lindberghs. The couple wanted the kidnappers to know that they were making every effort to contact them. They also promised to keep whatever arrangements they made with the kidnappers strictly confidential and to keep the police in the dark. The Lindberghs pledged their full cooperation. They made it clear that they were not interested in having anyone prosecuted for the crime: They simply wanted their baby back.

The Lindbergh message, with its implication of prosecutorial immunity, upset the law enforcement community, which felt that the Lindberghs were in no position to make such a promise. Many believed that by being so eager to keep the police away and pay the ransom money, the Lindberghs were encouraging other criminals to try their hands at kidnapping.

Schwarzkopf and some of his investigators were having second thoughts about whether the kidnappers were really professional. It seemed unlikely that real professionals would have stirred up a hornet's nest by abducting such a celebrated baby. And the phrasing of the ransom note didn't seem hard-boiled enough for professionals. For example, the note didn't contain any threats against the baby if the kidnappers' demands were not met.

Since the kidnappers were obviously familiar with the Lindbergh estate, Schwarzkopf believed the crime might have been committed by a local group. The fact that the ransom demand involved the relatively small sum of fifty thousand dollars made it somewhat unlikely that the kidnappers were part of a big-time, highly professional gang.

Schwarzkopf also thought things were getting hot for the kidnappers. Every cop and citizen in the country was on the lookout for the baby and his abductors. Time was working against the gang, and Schwarzkopf felt that if they didn't negotiate soon, they'd be frightened off by all of the attention.

Colonel Lindbergh was also worried that the kidnappers were afraid to negotiate, afraid that if they showed themselves they'd be caught. If that were so, what would happen to the baby? Because he didn't want to find out, Colonel Lindbergh was doing everything in his power to get the negotiations rolling.

Although Lindbergh couldn't accept the notion that his child was already dead, Schwarzkopf and his men believed that the baby's death was a distinct possibility—even a probability. But Schwarzkopf couldn't act on this assumption.

The Lindbergh estate was no longer crawling with reporters; they were now operating out of the old railroad station in Hopewell. Newsmen and photographers were still stationed, however, on Amwell Road and Featherbed Lane, where they could monitor the comings and goings of the Lindberghs, the police, and visitors to the house. But because journalists were no longer permitted on the grounds, Lindbergh and his wife could now stroll about their property without being molested.

Colonel Lindbergh had taken a nap Wednesday afternoon and had slept fairly well that night. Schwarzkopf, on the other hand, hadn't slept for forty-eight hours. He was struggling with the nearly impossible job of coordinating and controlling an investigation featuring hundreds of investigators, dozens of police agencies, thousands of leads, and more suspects than his men could investigate.

While Lindbergh and Breckinridge grappled with the problem of how to make contact and deal with the kidnappers, Lieutenant Keaten and his detectives, with the help of Captain Lamb and investigators from the Newark and Jersey City police departments, ran down the most immediate leads. Besides all of the mail and telephone calls coming directly to the Lindbergh house, Keaten and his men had to deal with the steady flow of information being passed on to them by the FBI and other law enforcement agencies all across the country.

On the day after the crime, New Jersey Governor A. Harry Moore had sent a telegram to every governor east of the Mississippi asking for assistance in the identification and apprehension of the kidnappers. Governor Moore had sent a similar message to President Herbert Hoover, asking for the cooperation and assistance of every federal law enforcement agency. Moore had also scheduled a conference in his office in Trenton and hoped that representatives of the various agencies would attend.

Governor Moore's conference was held at eleven o'clock Thursday morning. Hundreds of federal, state, county, and city law enforcement heads and investigators showed up for the meeting. Because so many policemen and private investigators had answered

30   Governor Moore's call, the meeting had to be held in a large assembly hall. Among those attending were big city chiefs of police, well-known private investigators, top police detectives, and J. Edgar Hoover. Also present was Elmer Irey, the head of the IRS Law Enforcement Division, the man who had put Al Capone behind bars.

Colonel Schwarzkopf spoke to the group for an hour, outlining the details of the crime, the nature of the evidence, and some of the theories regarding the kidnappers and how the crime had been planned and committed. Colonel Schwarzkopf did not divulge the fact that the kidnappers had demanded fifty thousand dollars. He kept the existence of the nursery note a secret.

After Schwarzkopf had finished his talk, he called for questions and suggestions. It became obvious that most of the investigators had come to the meeting with preconceived ideas and pet theories about the crime. What followed was a series of pointless quarrels and an occasional shouting match. The meeting accomplished little except to fuel rivalries. After the meeting, a few of the attendees visited the Lindbergh estate, where they examined the evidence and the overall crime scene. Before departing, most of the visiting investigators voiced their theory of the crime and offered Schwarzkopf their full cooperation.

After the last visitor had left the Lindbergh estate, Schwarzkopf, his head full of theories and suggestions, found a place to lie down in the Lindbergh house; he fell asleep.

Never far from Lieutenant Keaten's mind was the possibility that there was some connection, direct or indirect, between Colonel Lindbergh's domestic employees and the kidnappers. Since he had no proof of this, Keaten would have to tread very carefully. Right now, the lieutenant was most interested in Betty Gow, the nursemaid.

Miss Gow had been the last person in the household to see the baby. She was also one of the few people who had known of the family's last minute decision to stay in Hopewell, information that she could have passed on to her boyfriend, Henry ("Red") Johnson. Keaten was also thinking about Johnson's telephone call to the Lindbergh house at 8:30, thirty minutes before the crime. What connection, if any, did this call have to the kidnapping? And there was another nagging question bothering Keaten: It had to do with the sleeveless nightshirt Betty Gow had made for the baby. Could she have known that the child would be exposed to the forty-degree night?

Colonel Lindbergh had made it clear that he had total faith in his servants. If he learned that the police were grilling Betty Gow, he would be very upset. But Lieutenant Keaten was a courageous investigator with a strong sense of duty, and he knew that Betty Gow's background and her movements before and during the night in question would have to be checked. As for questioning the nursemaid, Keaten would keep things light and informal. But she had to be questioned and closely. So, on March 3, Keaten asked Betty Gow to give a straightforward account of her activities on the night of the kidnapping. When she got to the part about Henry Johnson's telephone call, Betty Gow said, "I tried to get Johnson on the telephone at Englewood before I left for Hopewell, but I couldn't reach him because he wasn't at his boardinghouse. So I left word for him to call me in the evening at Hopewell. We had intended seeing each other that evening.

He called me from Englewood between eight and nine that night and I told him how it happened that I wasn't at the Morrow house. I told him the baby had a cold."[2]

Betty had met the twenty-five-year-old Johnson in the summer of 1931 at North Haven, Maine. At the time she was taking care of the Lindbergh baby at the Morrow summer place. Johnson, a red-haired Norwegian, was working on a yacht owned by Thomas W. Lamont. When the summer was over and Johnson was no longer employed on the yacht, he continued the relationship by visiting Betty at the Morrow estate in Englewood. When he wasn't working, he stayed with his brother John in West Hartford, Connecticut. Betty Gow said that at the moment she didn't know where her boyfriend was.

Betty herself had been working as a domestic since she was fourteen. Her first job after coming to the United States was in Detroit. Six months later she was working for a Mrs. Sullivan in Englewood. She had two brothers, Alexander and James, both living in Scotland.

On March 3, Betty Gow wrote a letter to her mother in Scotland:

> Dear Mother:
>
> You will have heard long ago about this terrible thing that has happened to us. It is the most cruel thing I ever knew.
>
> I do not feel the least like writing, but I know you would be anxious to hear from me. I discovered that the baby had gone when I went to lift him at 10 o'clock as usual.
>
> The object is evidently ransom in a big way, and in that case they will take good care of him. I hope to goodness we have him back by the time you get this letter. I just feel numbed and terribly lost without that darling. I love him so.
>
> Reporters are just swarming around the house. The whole country is roused. Mrs. Lindbergh has been very brave about it. She's wonderful.[3]

On Wednesday, the morning after the crime, Mrs. Lindbergh, worried that the kidnappers were not caring for her baby, wrote out the baby's diet, a menu that appeared Thursday on the front page of every newspaper in America.

On March 4, the nation's newspapers carried a second message from the Lindberghs:

> Mrs. Lindbergh and I desire to make a personal contact with the kidnappers of our child.
>
> Our only interest is in his immediate and safe return and we feel certain that the kidnappers will realize that this interest is strong enough to justify them in having complete confidence and trust in any promises that we may make in connection with his return.
>
> We urge those who have the child to select any representatives of ours who will be suitable to them at any time and at any place that they may designate.
>
> If this is accepted, we promise that we will keep whatever arrangements that may be made by their representative and ours strictly confidential and we further pledge ourselves that we will not try to injure in any way those connected with the return of the child.
>
> Charles A. Lindbergh
> Anne Lindbergh

When Colonel Breckinridge handed reporters the press release containing that message, he felt obliged to explain why the Lindberghs were taking this action: "We are counting upon the personal statement to create a feeling of confidence in the minds of the persons who now have the baby, so they will feel free to establish a contact with us. Colonel Lindbergh is not afraid. Certainly the kidnappers cannot believe he would trifle with them in a matter of such extreme importance to him. He will meet with them anywhere, under any conditions they may wish to lay down, even to going into the underworld itself, to meet the men who have his baby and arrange for his return."[4]

After reading the Lindbergh's message, New Jersey Attorney General William A. Stevens issued a statement of his own. Although he understood the parents' concern, he wanted to make it clear that the Lindberghs were in no position to offer the kidnappers immunity. A serious crime had been committed and the state of New Jersey would do everything it could to bring the criminals to justice.

Throughout the day the Lindberghs' appeal was broadcast over every radio station in the country. Meanwhile, the Lindberghs could do nothing but wait. Three days had passed since the crime, and the ransom note had said that "After 2–4 days we will inform you where to deliver the mony."

The ordeal was taking its toll on Mrs. Lindbergh. She had only slept six hours since the baby had been stolen and was now suffering from a severe cold. There was concern that the stress, fatigue, and illness would threaten her pregnancy.

People continued to telephone the Lindbergh estate around the clock. Many of the callers said they had found the baby and he was alive and well. Colonel Lindbergh had insisted on taking all of these calls personally. He would patiently listen to each caller's story, then ask them to describe the baby. So far no one had described the child convincingly. Some people even showed up at the house. One such person was an impressive-looking man "with a secret he would tell no one but Anne Morrow Lindbergh." This man was taken to Mrs. Lindbergh's bedroom. Standing in the doorway before the child's distraught but hopeful parents, the man suddenly started reciting passages from Shakespeare. The visitor, obviously insane, was hauled off by the police.

On March 4, the Lindberghs finally received word from the kidnappers. The note had been mailed the night before in Brooklyn, New York. On the bottom right-hand corner of the single-page letter were the interlocking circles—the symbol on the ransom note left in the nursery. It was this unique symbol that convinced Schwarzkopf, Breckinridge, and the Lindberghs that the letter was legitimate. The message, handwritten in ink and scrawled on both sides of the paper, read:

> Dear Sir. We have warned you note to make anyding public also notify the police now you have to take consequences—means we will holt the baby until everyding is quite. We can note make any appointment just now. We know very well what it means to us. It is (is it) rely necessary to make a world affair out of this, or to get your baby back as sun as possible to settle those affair in a quick way will be better for both seits. Don't by afraid about the baby two ladys keeping care of its day and night. She also will fed him according to the diet. Singtuere on all letters

We are interested to send him back in gut health. And ransom was made aus for 50000 $ but now we have to take another person to it and probably have to keep the baby for a longer time as we expected. So the amount will be 70000 20000 in 50$ bills 25000 $ in 20$ bill 15000 $ in 10$ bills and 10000 in 5$ bills Don't mark any bills or take them from one serial nomer. We will form you latter were to deliver the mony. But we will note do so until the Police is out of the cace and the pappers are qute. The kidnaping we prepared for years so we are preparet for everyding.

Besides the symbol of interlocking circles, there were other similarities between the nursery note and the letter just received. The two notes contained many of the same misspelled words. For example, *signature* had been spelled "singtuere" and "singnature," *good* as "gut," and *money* as "mony." In the nursery note *anything* had been spelled "anyding," and in the letter *everything* was spelled "everyding." In both messages the writer had placed the dollar sign after rather than before the money figures. Although Lindbergh and the others weren't skilled documents examiners, they noticed a distinct similarity in the handwriting.

But it was the content of the letter, not its form or appearance, that most interested Colonel Lindbergh. The kidnappers said that the baby was in good health and that progress in the negotiations couldn't be made until the police were out of the case and the newspapers quieted. Mrs. Lindbergh was elated that the kidnappers had seen the diet she had published in the newspapers. No one seemed particularly disturbed that the kidnappers had raised the ransom another twenty thousand dollars.

The Lindberghs weren't the only ones eager to get the negotiations rolling. Governor Moore wanted the baby safely returned so that the police could nab the kidnappers and windup the investigation. On Friday the governor announced that the Lindbergh case was costing the state fifteen thousand dollars a day. Most of the added expenses were in the form of police salaries and increased telephone and telegram charges.

On the day the kidnappers' letter had been received by the Lindberghs, a man named Gaston Bullock Means paid a visit to the Washington, D.C., offices of Judge Marion DeVries. Means told the judge that the Lindbergh kidnappers had asked him to participate in the crime but that he had refused. Means added that he was in a unique position to locate the Lindbergh baby. Judge DeVries was impressed with Means and his story and suggested that he get in touch with the Lindberghs and obtain authority to work on the case.

Just before his meeting with the judge, Means had contacted several other influential people in New York City and Washington who knew the Lindberghs. He had also been in touch with Evalyn Walsh McLean, the estranged wife of the publisher of the *Washington Post*. Means had performed investigative work for Mrs. McLean, and when she heard that Means had an opportunity to recover the Lindbergh baby, she summoned him to her townhouse in Washington.

Chubby, bald and thirty-two years old, Gaston Means was an impressive talker who possessed a quick wit, an engaging smile, and the mind of a crook. In 1921, four years after he was acquitted in a murder case, Means joined the Bureau of Investigation headed by its fourth director, William J. Burns—the former private investigator and secret service agent who in 1909 started the nationally known detective and security guard company that bore his name. Burns had called Means one of the best investigators he had ever known.

When the assistant director of the Bureau of Investigation, J. Edgar Hoover, took over the agency in 1924, one of his first acts was to fire Agent Means. After that, Means was involved in a series of swindles and political scandals that sent him to federal penitentiary in Atlanta. Shortly after his release from prison, Means published an outlandish best-seller called *The Strange Death of President Harding.* In it Means claimed that the President had been poisoned by his wife. The book was a shameless collection of innuendoes and lies.[5]

Means told Mrs. McLean that he was in touch with the kidnappers and in a position to negotiate the return of the Lindbergh baby. "With your help," he said, "I can have the baby back to his mother in sight of two weeks." Means said that he had met the head of the kidnapping gang, a man known to the underworld as The Fox, when he was serving time in the Atlanta Penitentiary. The Fox wanted one hundred thousand dollars in exchange for the baby. When Mrs. McLean didn't flinch at the mention of the money, Means was encouraged. According to Means, the kidnappers had also insisted that the child be delivered to a Catholic priest who would swear that he would not describe or identify the men who turned the baby over to him. That was no problem, Mrs. McLean said. She knew a priest who could do the job.

The next day, Means met with Mrs. McLean, Capt. Emory Land—a Lindbergh in-law—and the Reverend J. Francis Hurney, pastor of the Church of the Immaculate Conception. Father Hurney was impressed with Means and agreed to help in any way he could. Means said that he had been in touch with The Fox, and this was the plan: The kidnappers would bring the baby to Mrs. McLean's summer home at Fairview, Maryland. Although the enormous house was closed for the winter, Mrs. McLean agreed to stay at the mansion with its only occupant, the caretaker. She would wait there until Means contacted her.

The meeting broke up with Captain Land agreeing to travel to Hopewell, where he would obtain Colonel Lindbergh's approval of the plan. If Lindbergh gave the green light, then Mrs. McLean would give Means the hundred thousand dollars.

On March 5, a letter from the kidnapper arrived in the mail at the Manhattan law offices of Colonel Henry Breckinridge. Along with this letter was a cover note directing the delivery of the message to Colonel Lindbergh. James Phelan, one of the attorneys in Breckinridge's law firm, delivered the letter to the Lindbergh estate. The message, hand-written on both sides in ink, bore the familiar symbol.

The March 5 letter contained nothing new in the way of negotiating terms and did not advance the ransom negotiations. The kidnappers seemed to be under the impression that the police had intercepted the first letter, so from now on, all of their messages would be sent through Colonel Breckinridge. The kidnappers assured the Lindberghs that the baby was in good health, then repeated the ransom demand. The letter read:

Dear Sir: Dit you receive ouer letter from March 4.we sent the mail on one off the letter—near Boro Hall, Brooklyn. We know Police interfer with your privatmail. How can we come to any arrangements this way. in the future we will send ouer letters to Mr. Breckenbridge at 25 Broadway. We believe polise captured our letter and let note forwarded to you. We will note accept any go-between from your seid. We will arrangh theas latter. There is no worry about the boy. He is very well and will be feed according to the diet. Best dank for information about it. We are interested to send your boy back in gut health.

It is necessary to make a world-affair out of it, or to get your boy back as soon as possible. Why did you ignore ouer letter which we left in the room the baby would be back long ago. You would not get any result from Polise becauce our kinaping was planet for a year allredy. But we were afraid the boy would not be strong enough.

Ouer ransom was made out for 50000 but now we have to put another to it as propperly have to hold the baby longer as we expected so it will be 70000$ 20000 in 50$ bills 25000 in 25$ bills 12000$ in 10$ bills and 10000 in 5$ bills. We warn you again not to mark any bills or take them for one ser.No. We will inform you latter how to deliver the mony but not before the polise is out of this cace and the pappers are quite.

Although there were several misspellings—"ouer" for *our,* "cace" for *case,* and "polise" for *police*—the writer of the note had correctly spelled words that were more difficult. Apparently the ransom note writer had used a dictionary to look up the tougher ones.

The March 5 letter was a legitimate communication from the kidnappers. There was the unique symbol and the writer had made reference to the message left in the nursery as well as the previous letter.

There was one sentence in the recent message that bothered Breckinridge. It read: "We will not accept any go-between from you sent." Breckinridge wasn't sure exactly what the kidnappers meant by that. Did they mean that they wouldn't deal with any negotiators picked by the Lindbergh people, or did they just object to dealing with the police or those closely associated with the Lindberghs?

Breckinridge didn't like the sound of this letter. Communications with the kidnappers seemed to be breaking down, and the ransom note writer seemed unwilling to negotiate with anyone directly representing the Lindberghs. Breckinridge, with these concerns in mind, obtained Colonel Lindbergh's permission to publish the following message in the press:

> If the kidnappers of our child are unwilling to deal direct we fully authorize 'Salvy' Spitale and Irving Bitz to act as our go-between. We will also follow any other methods suggested by the kidnappers that we can be sure will bring the return of our child.
>
> Charles Lindbergh
> Anne Lindbergh

When the Lindbergh message appeared in the press, Spitale and Bitz were working out of a Manhattan speakeasy on Forty-first Street. Their headquarters was in the rear of the building that housed the offices of the *New York Daily News.* Between the two of

36 them, they owned three Manhattan speakeasies, a couple of restaurants, and a place or two in Harlem.

Spitale was a flashy thirty-five-year-old who started out as a bouncer in a Williamsburg dance hall. Bitz had served time in Atlanta on a narcotics conviction and had worked as an enforcer for a small-time gangster named Jacob ("Little Augie") Organ.

About the time the Lindbergh message hit the papers, Spitale and Bitz were arrested by federal prohibition agents and charged with conspiracy. This charge had to do with their ownership of a shipload of bootleg liquor that had docked at Gerrittsen Beach in Brooklyn. Following a couple of frantic phone calls, the charges were dropped. The two bootleggers returned to their headquarters where they got back to the business of locating the Lindbergh baby.

Colonel Lindbergh's announcement that a pair of bootleggers had been authorized to deal with the kidnappers upset more than a few people. A well-known radio preacher with a large following was

> shocked to learn that Colonel Lindbergh had been driven to deal with underworld characters in an effort to regain his child . . . surely this is the most outrageous committal even seen by the American public. Do you know who these men are? They are unlawful. They are racketeers. They are the new almighty that we have in the United States. In all the history of civilization there was never such an admission made by any country. And that is what Prohibition has done for us—Prohibition that has not made the country safe for democracy but instead has made it safe for the bootleggers, the gangsters, and thugs. Such are the people Colonel Lindbergh felt it necessary to appoint.

Rosner, Bitz, and Spitale weren't the only underworld types interested in the Lindbergh case. Even Al Capone tried to get into the act. When the Lindbergh baby was stolen, Al Capone was in Chicago's Cook County Jail awaiting transfer to the federal penetentiary in Atlanta, where he was to serve an eleven-year sentence for tax evasion. Three days prior to the kidnapping, an appeals court had denied his bid for a new trial. When told of the Lindbergh crime, Capone was reported to have said, "It is the most outrageous thing I have ever heard of. I know how Mrs. Capone and I would feel if our son were kidnapped, and I sympathize with the Lindberghs. I'll give $10,000 for information that will lead to the recovery of the child unharmed." [7]

On March 5, Capone got in touch with Arthur Brisbane, a well-known columnist for the Hearst newspaper chain, and arranged for an exclusive interview.

"I can do as much as anybody alive in getting the baby back," Capone told Brisbane. "I've heard all the rumors about my connection with this case but the fact is I never dreamed the Lindbergh kid would be snatched and I had absolutely nothing to do with it. I think I can prove that. I'm pretty positive a mob did it; nobody else could get away with that job at a spot surrounded by bridges. If I'm right about it being a mob, any one knows that I ought to be able to turn up something in the case. Well, I'm willing. Let's get going." [8]

The next day, the front page of every newspaper in the country carried Brisbane's article containing Capone's offer to find out who had kidnapped the baby. There was one small catch—to achieve all of this, Capone would have to be released from jail. But with the baby's life hanging in the balance, who would deny Capone his freedom?

To assure the American public that he wouldn't leave the country, Capone said that he would put up $250,000 in bail and leave his brother Mitzi at the Cook County Jail in his place. Max Silverman, the Newark, New Jersey, bondsman who had arranged bail for Capone in the past, was standing by in Chicago ready to put up the $250,000 in case a deal could be worked out.

Brisbane's article touched off a national debate between those who wanted Capone freed and those who questioned his sincerity and/or disapproved of having gangsters doing the work of the police. A U.S. Senator from Connecticut publicly suggested that the Capone gang had committed the kidnapping in order to engineer Capone's release from jail.

When Colonel Lindbergh read Brisbane's article about Al Capone, he telephoned the secretary of the treasury, who sent Elmer Irey, head of the IRS Law Enforcement Branch, to Hopewell. Irey was the man who had built the tax evasion case against Capone that had resulted in Capone's conviction and eleven-year sentence. Nobody knew Alphonse Capone better than Elmer Irey.

Irey didn't mince words when he met with Lindbergh, Breckinridge, and Schwarzkopf at the Lindbergh estate. As far as he was concerned, Capone didn't have any idea where to look for the baby. Irey said that he doubted that a major crime organization had been responsible for the kidnapping. As a result, Capone was not in a position to find out who had stolen the child. Irey said that Capone had already tried to pin the kidnapping on a member of his own gang. IRS investigators had checked out this suspect and found that the man had been hundreds of miles from Hopewell when the crime was committed. Irey was sure that Al Capone was using the Lindbergh tragedy to get out of jail and flee the country.[9]

Although Irey didn't say so to Lindbergh, he disapproved of Rosner, Spitale, and Bitz being involved in the case. It was his opinion that they were taking advantage of the Lindberghs.

Elmer Irey impressed Lindbergh and Breckinridge. He convinced them that Al Capone was not in a position to get the baby back.

Before leaving Hopewell, Irey promised Lindbergh that his investigators would do everything they could to assist in the case. Lindbergh expressed his gratitude, then said that he had never intended, under any circumstances, to ask for Al Capone's release from jail.

Irey had convinced Breckinridge that Al Capone wasn't the answer, but Breckinridge still felt that the underworld held the key to the case. He persuaded Colonel Lindbergh to get in touch with Frank Costello, the acting boss of the Luciano family in New York City. Costello was eager to help, and a few days later reported back that no one in the underworld was responsible for the abduction. Costello told Breckinridge that in his opinion the baby was dead and that Lindbergh should be advised not to pay the ransom.[10]

On March 6, Capt. Emory Land reported to Mrs. McLean that Colonel Lindbergh and his advisor Colonel Breckinridge had approved of the plan to have Gaston Means make contact with the kidnappers. Lindbergh wanted it understood, however, that if the hundred-thousand-dollar ransom were paid, he would repay Mrs. McLean. Captain Land said that Lindbergh had insisted the plan be kept secret from the police, and, of course, the press.

The next day, Mrs. McLean went to her bank, and in the President's office, was handed one hundred thousand dollars in old, worn bills. She also withdrew another four thousand dollars—the sum Means had requested to cover his personal expenses.

Gaston Means accepted the one hundred thousand dollars with a grave expression. This was serious business, he said. But if he were right, this money would put the baby back into his mother's arms. And one other thing. If for some reason Father Hurney didn't get baby Lindbergh, the money would be returned to Mrs. McLean. Gaston Means then asked Mrs. McLean to solemnly pledge not to reveal any of this to anyone, not even to her friends, business advisors, or attorneys. Mrs. McLean promised.

At this point in the investigation, Colonel Lindbergh had mixed feelings about Schwarzkopf and the police. He opened his house to them and let them set up a communications headquarters in his garage. But his main concern was finding a way to make contact with the criminals who had his child, people who were obviously nervous about the police.

Lindbergh wanted desperately to let the kidnappers know that he had no intention of bringing the police into his dealings with them. He had made it clear to Schwarzkopf from the very beginning that the police were not to do anything that would endanger the life of his child. Schwarzkopf realized that Colonel Lindbergh was in charge— he and his men were merely guests in the Lindbergh home, serving at the Colonel's pleasure.

Three days had passed since Lindbergh had heard from the kidnappers. The baby had been away from his parents for over a week, and the strain on the Lindberghs was beginning to show.

Colonel Lindbergh had emphatically stated that he did not want the police to monitor his personal telephone line. He didn't want them listening when the kidnappers called. His discussions with the criminals had to be strictly confidential. Lindbergh was therefore enraged when he found out that a New Jersey State Police officer had been placed at the Hopewell telephone exchange to listen in on his calls. Lindbergh immediately drove to the Hopewell exchange and confronted the hapless trooper. With his boyish face drawn and gray, Lindbergh pointed a finger at the distraught officer: "Don't plug it in at all—not even halfway. Heed what I am saying!"

The officer shook his head in agreement as Lindbergh spoke. "It won't happen again," he said.

Colonel Lindbergh went home, and when he walked into his den he found Captain Lamb talking on his private telephone. "What are you doing on the telephone?" he shouted.

"It rang and I answered it," Captain Lamb explained.

"I want it understood very clearly and now," Lindbergh said coldly, "that neither you nor any other policeman is to touch that phone for any reason. You are here through my courtesy and I ask you not to interfere with my business." [11]

It had been eight days since the kidnapping, and the investigation was starting to flounder. The kidnappers were too timid to come forward and the police were being held at arm's length by Lindbergh and Breckinridge.

While Lindbergh and Breckinridge were holding secret meetings with mysterious and shadowy gangsters, con men, soothsayers, and others, the police, not totally convinced that the crime had been committed by professionals, ran down thousands of leads and looked into the backgrounds of anyone who had any connection to the Lindberghs or the Hopewell estate.

To compound matters, the news media, having run out of facts to report, were making up their own stories. No one was in control—not even the kidnappers.

I want to see that baby's arms around his mother's neck.
—DR. JOHN F. CONDON ("JAFSIE")

4 THE GO-BETWEENS

IN THE BRONX, NEW YORK, a recently retired seventy-two-year-old grade school teacher and principal named Dr. John F. Condon read in the newspaper that Colonel Lindbergh had authorized Salvatore Spitale and Irving Bitz to negotiate with the kidnappers.[1] The editorial page carried a political cartoon showing a baffled Uncle Sam admitting in frustration that he could not solve the Lindbergh case.

Dr. Condon was unabashedly patriotic, and he idolized Charles Lindbergh. To him, the kidnapping was more than a crime, it was a national disgrace. So, without conferring with the Lindberghs and over the objections of his daughter Myra and his two grown sons, Condon decided to offer his services as Lindbergh's intermediary. Using purple ink of his own manufacture, he penned the following letter, which appeared in the March 8 edition of his hometown paper, the *Bronx Home News:*

> I offer all I can scrape together so a loving mother may again have her child and Col. Lindbergh may know that the American people are grateful for the honor bestowed upon them by his pluck and daring.
>
> Let the kidnappers know that no testimony of mine, or information coming from me, will be used against them.
>
> I offer $1,000 which I have saved from my salary as additional to the suggested ransom of $50,000 which is said to have been demanded by Col. Lindbergh.
>
> I stand ready at my own expense to go anywhere, alone, to give the kidnapper the extra money and promise never to utter his name to any person.
>
> If this is not agreeable, then I ask the kidnappers to go to any Catholic priest and return the child unharmed, with the knowledge that any priest must hold inviolate any statement which may be made by the kidnappers.

Condon had been born and raised in the Bronx, a place he called "the most beautiful Borough in the world." In 1884 he earned a bachelor of arts degree from the College of the City of New York. A few years later he received a masters degree from Fordham University; at the time of the kidnapping he lectured part-time in the Education Department.

Condon had started his teaching career at P.S. 89 in Harlem, where he met his wife. When speaking of his fifty years of teaching, Condon would declare proudly that in all of those years he had missed only nineteen hours of class. America had been built, he said, by steady, hardworking men like himself.

The gray-haired schoolteacher with the neatly trimmed mustache lived with his wife on Decatur Avenue in the Bronx. His daughter Myra, also a teacher, was married to a young architect named Ralph Hacker. Myra and her husband had lived in the Condon house until they could afford a place of their own. They were now living across the Hudson in Englewood, New Jersey. Condon's two sons, John and Lawrence, were New York City attorneys.

The Condon house, a modest two-story affair with a comfortable front porch, was situated on a quiet, tree-lined residential street in the Bedford Park section of the Bronx, just west of Webster Avenue and the Bronx Park.

No matter where he was or what he was doing, Condon wore a dark, three-piece suit and a black derby hat. Having instructed schoolboys in swimming and boxing, Condon still thought of himself as a scholar-athlete. In his younger days he had excelled in football and baseball.

The *Bronx Home News,* with a circulation of one hundred thousand, was Condon's favorite newspaper. He had known the paper's owner and publisher, James O'Flaherty, since boyhood. Over the years Condon had contributed numerous little poems and essays extolling the virtues of God and country. Many of these pieces were signed P. A. Triot (patriot); L. O. Nestar (Lone Star); J. U. Stice (justice); and L. O. Nehand (Lone Hand). Once, in a special contest sponsored by the newspaper, Condon had won a twenty-dollar gold piece for the best New Year's resolution: "That I shall, to the best of my ability and at all times, help anyone in distress."

That was Condon—intelligent, athletic, romantic, patriotic, religious, hardworking and sentimental. But he was also a ham, overbearing, boastful, and at times an insufferable bore. Those who did not like him, and there were many, considered him a flag-waving know-it-all.

Outside the Bronx, Condon's letter to the editor went unnoticed. None of the people associated with the Lindbergh investigation had seen it. It created quite a stir in the Bronx, however. Total strangers telephoned Condon wanting to know who he thought he was sticking his nose into the Lindbergh case. Surely he didn't think the kidnappers read the *Bronx Home News?* Couldn't he see that he was making a fool of himself?

Even Condon's acquaintances believed that the old man was behaving like a busybody. He had no right to interfere with something as important as the Lindbergh case. But Condon's closest friend, Al Reich, thought that Condon had done the right thing. Reich admired Condon for his willingness to serve the Lindberghs. A former heavyweight boxer, Reich had won the New York State amateur boxing championship in 1913. The former prizefighter told Condon that he was willing to help him in any way he could.

The day after Condon's letter appeared in the *Home News,* Colonel Schwarzkopf made a nationwide radio address. Schwarzkopf stated that he had every reason to believe that the Lindbergh baby was safe and well. He said that whatever arrangements the Lindberghs were willing to make with the kidnappers were their own business. "The main purpose of all of us is the recovery of the Lindbergh baby alive and as quickly as possible," he said. "We are here as the police authority and are bending every effort to that end. We will make no predictions and we will make no guesses."[2] The past few days several New York city newspapers had been hinting of a rift between the Lindberghs and the police. Schwarzkopf, by his statement, was trying to put an end to these rumors.

On Wednesday, March 9, Dr. Condon was away from his house all day. He came home at ten that night and gathered the day's mail that had been put on the mantel beneath the bronze Tiffany clock. Shuffling through the twenty or so letters, he came upon one that stood out from the rest. The writing on the envelope was hand-printed and child-like. It was addressed to:

Mr. Dr. John Condon

2974 Decatur Ave.

New York, NY

The blood rushed to Condon's face as he tore open the envelope. Inside he found the following one-page, handwritten letter:

dear Sir: If you are willing to act as go-between in the Lindbergh case please follow strictly instruction. Handel incloced letter *personaly* to Mr. Lindbergh. It will explain everyding. don't tell anyone about it as soon we find out the press or Police is notifyd everyding are cancell and it will be a further delay. Affter you gett the mony from Mr. Lindbergh put these 3 words in the *New-York American*

Mony is redy After notise we will give you further instruction. don't be affraid we are not out fore your 1000$ keep it. Only act stricly. Be at home every night between 6–12 by this time you will hear from us.

The envelope was postmarked Station T, New York City, noon March 9. It also contained a smaller envelope and the following note:

dear Sir. please handel incloced letter to Col. Lindbergh. It is in Mr. Lindbergh interest not to notify the Police.

All of the writing visible to Condon was in ink.

Doctor Condon stuffed the two envelopes and the notes into his pocket. He would have to go to Hopewell to see Colonel Lindbergh. Although Condon didn't have a car, his friend Al Reich did.

Condon caught a trolley near his house and rode to Max Rosenhain's restaurant at 188th street and the Grand Concourse. His friend Al was usually in the restaurant at this time of night having a snack. When he got to the restaurant Max Rosenhain said that Al wasn't around. The old prizefighter was probably working late on a real estate deal, a business that Condon dabbled in himself.

Condon was so excited he couldn't resist showing the kidnapper's note to Rosenhain. Convinced that this was the real thing, Rosenhain suggested that he and Condon confide in their mutual friend Milton Gaglio. Gaglio, a clothing salesman, was in the restaurant—and he owned a car.

Gaglio agreed to drive Condon and Rosenhain to Hopewell. But before heading west, Condon said he would telephone Colonel Lindbergh and tell him the news.

Condon squeezed into a telephone booth and dialed the number to the Lindbergh estate. A man came on the line and switched the call to another voice who told Condon that he was the one who took all of the Colonel's calls. Condon replied that he had an important message and that he would only speak to Colonel Lindbergh. The man speaking to Condon was Robert Thayer, the Colonel's personal secretary. When Thayer asked Condon to identify himself, Condon said that he was Dr. John F. Condon, professor of education at Fordham University. Condon then recited his degrees and his other academic credentials. There was a pause then a voice Condon recognized came on the line: "This is Colonel Lindbergh, what is it?"

In a voice trembling with excitement, Condon said, "I have just received a letter, Colonel, which may be of importance to you. Shall I read it?"

Lindbergh said yes. When Condon had finished, he added, "Accompanying this letter, Colonel, is an enclosure which I did not open. It is addressed to you."

"Kindly open it and read it to me."

Condon ripped open the smaller envelope and pulled out another single-page note. It was hand written and in ink. He read it to Colonel Lindbergh:

> dear Sir, Mr. Condon may act as go-between. You may give him the 70000$. make one packet the size will bee about. . .

Condon paused to study the drawing the kidnapper had made. "There is a sketch of a box here," Condon said. "Its dimensions are seven by six by fourteen inches. Shall I continue reading the letter?"

"Yes."

The rest of the note read:

> . . . we have notify your already in what kind of bills. We warn you not to set any trapp in any way. If you or someone els will notify the Police ther will be a further delay After we have the mony in hand we will tell you where to find your boy You may have a air-plain redy it is about 150 mil awy. But befor telling you the odr. a delay of 8 houers will be between.

"Is that all?" Lindbergh asked. He sounded as though he had lost interest.

"That is all," Condon replied. Then, as a postscript Dr. Condon mentioned the odd symbol of two intersecting circles.

Lindbergh suddenly came to life. His voice was tense, "Circles? Intersecting?"

"I would call them sectant circles," Condon said.

"Yes, yes, I understand," Lindbergh replied. He sounded excited about the kidnapper's symbol.

Condon went on, "There are three dots or holes across the horizontal diameter of the three circles. The circles are tinted—one red, one blue. This symbol might have something to do with the Mafia."

Lindbergh said that the letter in Condon's possession was very important. He wanted to know where he could find Condon, he wanted to meet him tonight. Condon said he was in the Bronx but could arrange immediate transportation to Hopewell if the Colonel so desired. Lindbergh said that he would be waiting.[3]

It was a little after midnight when Condon, Rosenhain, and Gaglio, in Gaglio's car, set out for Hopewell. Two hours later Condon and his friends were standing in the Lindbergh kitchen. They were greeted by Col. Henry Breckinridge, who took Condon to an upstairs bedroom. A few minutes later Colonel Lindbergh entered the room. He shook hands with Condon, then took possession of the notes and envelopes. After examining the documents carefully, Lindbergh proclaimed them authentic.

The symbol on Dr. Condon's letter was identical to the ones on the nursery note and the two ransom letters already received. The description of the symbol was not known to the public, so the person who had written to Condon must have been one of the kidnappers. There were other similarities. Dr. Condon's documents and the other letters were written in ink of the same color, were on the same sized and textured paper, and contained the same misspellings and Germanic construction. The dollar signs in Doctor Condon's letter were on the wrong side of the money figures—just like the others.

Colonel Lindbergh was interested in the note writer's drawing of the box—the ransom money container that was to be made in accordance with the kidnapper's specifications. The three-dimensional drawing was like something a carpenter might sketch.

Lindbergh and Breckinridge said they were sure that Dr. Condon was in touch with the kidnappers. At last they had found their intermediary.

It was late, so Colonel Lindbergh asked Dr. Condon to spend the night at the estate. But there was no room for his friends Max Rosenhain and Milton Gaglio. Before the two New Yorkers left for the Bronx, they promised not to breathe a word of what had happened to anyone.

That night, Dr. Condon slept on the floor of the only vacant room in the house—the nursery. Early the next morning, before breakfast, Condon studied the room. In the crib he noticed the two large safety pins. They were still holding the baby's blanket to the mattress. Condon reached in and unhooked the pins, placing them in the small canvas pouch he carried with him. He then opened the chest beneath the large French window and removed three wooden toys—a hand-carved lion, a camel, and an elephant. He was fondling these playthings when Colonel Lindbergh appeared at the door. Condon asked if he could borrow the wooden animals. When he met the kidnappers and saw the baby he would show him the toys to get his reaction. It was a way to identify the baby. The Colonel nodded, it sounded like a good idea.

How did the baby pronounce the animals? Condon asked. Lindbergh said that his son didn't have any difficulty saying *lion* or *camel,* but he mispronounced *elephant* as "el-e-pent."

Finally, Condon asked permission to keep the two safety pins. "I am taking these so that when I meet the man who wrote to me I can ask him where he saw them. If he can tell me exactly where they were fastened then we will know we are dealing with the man who actually entered this nursery and took your son."

"They are yours," Lindbergh replied.

After breakfast Dr. Condon, Colonel Lindbergh, and Henry Breckinridge conferred in an upstairs bedroom. Colonel Lindbergh handed Condon a note dated March 10, 1932. It read: "We hereby authorize Dr. John F. Condon to act as go-between for us." The note was signed by Charles A. Lindbergh and Anne Lindbergh.

Colonel Breckinridge said he would place the message, "Money is ready," in the *New York American.* This was in compliance with the kidnapper's instructions. He would do it this afternoon. But there was a problem—the message had to be signed. But if Condon put his name to the ad, the press would know he was the intermediary. If this happened, reporters would converge on him. The negotiations would never get off the ground. A code name was needed.

Condon had an idea. "By putting my initials together—J.F.C.—I get 'Jafsie,'" he said.

"Jafsie," Lindbergh replied. "That will be the code name we will use."

Condon spent the next hour or so studying photographs of the baby. When he was satisfied that he could recognize the child on sight, Colonel Breckinridge drove him back to the Bronx. He arrived there just in time to give a lecture at Fordham. From now on, Colonel Breckinridge would spend his evenings at Condon's house. They would wait there to hear from the kidnappers.

That afternoon Colonel Breckinridge placed the "Money is ready" ad in the *New York American.* As he did this, another distinguished gentleman, a resident of Norfolk, Virginia, was telling the rector of Norfolk's largest church a remarkable story.

The teller of this tale was John Hughes Curtis, the owner of one of the largest shipbuilding companies in the South. He was speaking to the Reverend H. Dobson-Peacock. Mr. Curtis said that at ten the previous evening, as he was leaving the Norfolk Country Club, he was approached by a man he hadn't seen for several years, a man he knew only as Sam. Sam was a big, lumbering fellow with a foreign accent who had worked on a fishing boat that had undergone repairs at Curtis's dock. According to Sam, he had come to Norfolk to seek Curtis's help in getting in touch with Colonel Lindbergh. Sam said that he represented the gang that had stolen the Lindbergh baby!

"My God!" the Reverend Mr. Dobson-Peacock exclaimed. "This has to do with the Lindbergh case!"

John Curtis continued his story: The kidnap gang had designated Sam to ask Curtis to form a committee of a few prominent Norfolk citizens who would act as intermediaries between the kidnappers and Colonel Lindbergh. The gang had come to Virginia because the Mafia in New Jersey and in New York City would demand a split if the deal was made on their turf. The people who had the Lindbergh baby had no intention of dealing with Spitale or Bitz.

Curtis said that he had told Sam that under no circumstances would he ask Colonel Lindbergh for any money. Sam said that he understood this. Here was the deal—the ransom would be deposited in a Norfolk bank, then paid to the kidnappers *after* the baby had been delivered safe and sound.

Curtis spent the night thinking over Sam's proposal. In the morning he called Sam and agreed to get in touch with a few prominent Norfolk citizens. He really didn't want to get involved, but he was compelled to do so out of a sense of duty to the Lindberghs.

Dobson-Peacock, the dean of the Christ Episcopal Church, had become acquainted with the Morrow family when he was in charge of a church in Mexico City. If anyone else had told him this story, the fifty-two-year-old churchman would have been skeptical. But John Hughes Curtis was a pillar of the community. In addition to being a successful businessman, the round-faced, gray-haired, forty-three-year-old belonged to Norfolk's exclusive social organizations. He was the former president of the Norfolk Country Club and commodore of the local Yacht Club. If the six foot two inch, two-hundred-pound shipbuilder believed that Sam was on the level, then Dobson-Peacock had to assume this as well.

Since time was of the essence, Dobson-Peacock decided to move quickly. He would telephone Colonel Lindbergh and inform him of the developing situation in Norfolk. The Colonel would have questions as well as instructions.

When Dobson-Peacock called Hopewell he talked to a man who said that neither Colonel Lindbergh nor Mrs. Morrow were available to speak to him. Dobson-Peacock impatiently asked who *was* available. He was told that Colonel Lindbergh's personal secretary, Morris Rosner, would talk to him.

Rosner came on the line and the Reverend identified himself and explained how he had known the Morrow family in Mexico City. He introduced John Curtis and put him on the phone. Curtis told Rosner about Sam, the kidnap gang, and their proposal to deliver the Lindbergh baby. When he had finished there was a long silence. Curtis finally asked Rosner if he had any questions. Rosner replied that he did not. This was followed by another pause in the conversation. Frustrated by Rosner's obvious disinterest, Curtis hung up.

Dobson-Peacock was also upset—Lindbergh's personal secretary had sounded like a hood! What was going on at the Lindbergh estate?

While the Reverend Mr. Dobson-Peacock and John Curtis pondered their next move, Colonel Lindbergh and John Condon waited anxiously for a response to their ad in the *New York American*. Meanwhile, the police were pursuing their own leads. Lieutenant Keaten and his men were questioning the twenty-nine servants in the Morrow household.

These routine servant interviews were conducted at the Lindbergh house. Each interviewee would be picked up at the Morrow mansion and driven to Hopewell. While the servant was away from the Morrow house, a pair of detectives would search his or her room.

On March 10, a pair of detectives from the Newark Police Department were scheduled to question a twenty-eight-year-old Morrow maid named Violet Sharpe. Like the other interviews, it was strictly routine.

Of the twenty-nine domestics, Violet Sharpe was the most popular. In 1929 she had come to America via Canada from the little village of Tult's Clump in Bradfield, England. She had worked for nine months in Toronto before moving to New York City, where she registered with the Hutchinson's Employment Agency on Madison Avenue. Ten days later she was interviewed by Mrs. Cecil Graeme of the Morrow staff, who recommended her for employment. The woman Violet had worked for in Toronto described her as "sober, industrious, willing and loyal."

Violet's sister Emily worked as a maid for Miss Constance Chilton. Miss Chilton and Elisabeth Morrow, Anne Lindbergh's sister, were co-owners of a private school for children.

Violet had short, dark hair and sparkling brown eyes. Her protruding front teeth and round, rosy working-girl's face gave her the look of a chipmunk. Overall, she was plump and somewhat bottom-heavy.

Everyone in the Morrow house knew that someday Violet would marry Septimus Banks, the middle-aged English butler who had served Ambassador Morrow before his death. Banks was the head of the domestic staff. Although he was the head domestic, Septimus, whose former employers included Lord Islington and Andrew Carnegie, was an alcoholic who was having a hard time staying sober. He had been fired several times for being drunk on duty, but in each instance Septimus had been reinstated by Mrs. Morrow.

Other men had taken Violet dancing and to the movies. On occasion she would even sneak an illicit beer at one of the local speakeasies. Violet had to be very discreet, however. Mrs. Morrow was old-fashioned and straightlaced, and Violet couldn't afford to lose her job. Without Mrs. Morrow's endorsement she wouldn't be able to find work in the midst of the Depression. And things were even worse in England.

On March 10, Detective Sergeant McGrath and Det. James F. Schiable of the Newark Police Department came to the Morrow house and asked Violet to accompany them to Hopewell for a routine questioning. The officers had expected Violet to go along willingly like the others. But she was not as docile as the other domestics—in fact, she was rather sharp-tongued. She made it clear that she resented being questioned and that she was cooperating because she had no choice. She was also very nervous. Assuming that Violet was the temperamental type, the detectives gave little thought to her abrasiveness. But once the questioning began, they realized that Violet was also being evasive.

The officers tried to calm her. They explained to her that they were asking everyone the same questions. They just wanted to her to recall, as best she could, her movements on the days preceding the kidnapping and her activities on the night of the crime. All of the other servants, they said, had been cooperative and straightforward. Why was she so different?

Violet had a few questions of her own. Why were the police so interested in her personal life? Why didn't they mind their own business and get on with the job of catching the kidnappers?

Detectives McGrath and Schiable were patient but persistent. Look, they said, we're just doing our job. Surely you don't have anything to hide? All of the others have been so cooperative. Don't you want to help Mr. and Mrs. Lindbergh get their baby back?

Violet opened up a bit—but reluctantly. She said that on the afternoon of Sunday, February 28, she and her sister Emily were walking along Lydecker Street in Englewood when a man drove by and waved at them. Believing she knew him, Violet waved back. The driver stopped and offered them a ride home. As it turned out, they didn't know the man, but he seemed nice enough, so they climbed into his car. On the way home Violet agreed to go out with the man. He said he'd call and let her know when.

At 11:30 A.M. on the day of the kidnapping, Violet answered the telephone at the Morrow house. It was Mrs. Lindbergh calling from Hopewell. She wanted to speak with Betty Gow, the baby's nursemaid. Violet called Betty to the telephone. Later in the day Betty told Violet that the baby was suffering from a cold and she was going to Hopewell to look after him.

The detectives listened intently. As Violet spoke they nodded their heads as though they approved of what she was saying. Whenever she paused they gently prodded her on. She was still fidgety and her voice was tense: At eight o'clock the man she had met on Lydecker Street called. He wanted to take her to the movies. About an half hour later her date was at the Morrow estate to pick her up.

When Violet got to the car she looked into the back seat and saw another man and his date. Violet was introduced to this couple and the four of them went to a movie. After the show the man drove Violet home and walked her to the servant's entrance. It was eleven o'clock. They said good night and that was it.

Violet said that she had made a second date with this man for March 6 but had broken the engagement. Since then she hadn't talked to or seen him.

The detectives were pleased—this was a good start. If she'd just fill in a few blanks the interview would be over. The detectives noticed, for example, that Violet had not mentioned her date's name. So they asked—who was this man?

Violet said she didn't know his name. That is, she couldn't remember.

"Look," Detective McGrath said, "we know you are nervous. Relax and the name will come to you."

"I am not nervous," Violet snapped, "and I can't remember his name!"

"What about the other couple? Can you remember who they were?"

"No. I can't recall their names either," Violet replied defiantly.

Detective McGrath was losing his patience. "You were out with these people a little over a week ago. How could you have forgotten their names?"

Violet folded her arms across her chest and looked away. She was trembling.

The other detective, Officer Schiable, wanted to calm things down. Violet was, after all, one of Mrs. Morrow's favorite maids. If they pushed her too hard they might get in trouble with the Morrows—and even worse—Colonel Lindbergh. "All right, Violet," he said. "Tell us about the movie you saw."

"You have no business prying into my private life!" Violet shouted.

"Just tell us what the movie was *about,*" Detective Schiable pleaded. "Tell us *something* about the film."

Violet didn't respond.

"What was the name of the theater?"

"It was in Englewood," Violet muttered. "That's all I know."

"And the movie?"

"I can't remember."

The detectives gave up. They could tell they had gotten all they could out of Violet. She was put into the car bound for Englewood and rode all the way back in silence.

In the meantime, the officers who had searched Violet's room had found nothing suspicious. There were, however, a couple of items that had caught their attention. They were interested in Violet's savings book from a New York City bank. Her account showed a balance of sixteen hundred dollars. Considering that Violet only earned a hundred dollars a month and had been working for the Morrows less than two years, this was a rather substantial amount. She had also been sending money regularly to her parents in England. The officers concluded that since Violet's room and board came with her job, she only had few expenses. Maybe that was how she had been able to save so much money.

The police had also found a small leather notebook that contained ribald handwritten stories. There was also a slip of paper with the hand-written notation: "Banks promises to try to be straight for 12 months." Septimus had apparently been spending too much time at the local speakeasy.

The search had also produced a silk-covered notebook containing twenty-six names and addresses. Although none of the entries in Violet's book was particularly revealing or suspicious, each was taken down for future reference.

Violet Sharpe's curious loss of memory, her evasiveness, and general uncooperativeness meant that the book couldn't be closed on her. The detectives couldn't overlook the fact that she had known, hours before the kidnapping, of the Lindberghs' plans to remain in Hopewell that night. The police were now interested in the man who had taken Violet to the movies. They were also interested in his friends.

Violet had brought upon herself exactly what she had hoped to avoid—police attention. But for the time being, she would be left alone—right now the police had bigger fish to fry.

It was Friday, March 11, the day following Violet Sharpe's interview and the day Dr. Condon's ad—"MONEY IS READY. Jafsie"—appeared in the classified section of the *New York American.*

50   In the Bronx, at noon, the telephone rang at the Condon house. Condon was giving a lecture at Fordham, and Colonel Breckinridge was working in Manhattan. Mrs. Condon answered the phone. The caller was a man with a heavy German accent. He said he wanted to speak with Dr. Condon. When advised that Dr. Condon was not at home, the man said he would call that evening. He didn't leave his name. "Tell the doctor to stay at home," he instructed.

At six o'clock, Dr. Condon returned home. Shortly thereafter Colonel Breckinridge showed up. Condon's friend, Al Reich also stopped by the house in case he was needed.

Since his March 9 letter to the *Bronx Home News*, Condon had been getting a lot of mail. He was sorting through the day's letters when his wife told him about the telephone call.

Condon and Breckinridge believed the caller was the kidnapper. He had probably seen the ad in the *New York American*. In his March 9 letter, the kidnapper had written: "Be at home every night between 6–12 by this time you will hear from us."

Condon and Breckinridge could do nothing but wait and hope that the man would call again. An hour later the telephone rang—it was the man with the German accent. Dr. Condon took the call.

"Did you *gottit* my letter with the *sing-nature?*" he asked. Condon noticed that the man had pronounced *signature* as "sing-nature," the way it was misspelled in one of the ransom letters.

Condon replied that he had received the letter.

"I saw your ad," the caller said, "in the *New York American.*"

"Where are you calling from?" Condon asked.

"Westchester," the caller replied. There was a pause than the man asked, "Doctor Condon, do you write sometimes pieces for the papers?"

Condon said that he did. He then heard the caller speaking to someone else—"He says sometimes he writes pieces for the papers," the caller said in a muffled voice. Now speaking directly into the phone, the caller instructed Condon to be at home every night for the next week. "Stay at home from six to twelve. You will receive a note with instructions. Act accordingly or all will be off."

Condon promised to stay at home. As he said this he heard a voice that wasn't the caller's. *"Statti citto!"* the voice said. Condon understood this as Italian for shut up! "All right, " the caller said, "you will hear from us." He then hung up.[4]

Breckinridge and Condon talked about the call until the early hours of the morning. They concluded that the caller was the writer of the ransom note.

Condon was intrigued by the *"Statti citto"* he had heard in the background. Was this another kidnapper—or was it the voice of someone who happened to be near the telephone? The kidnapper might have called from a restaurant or some other public place.

But what about the caller's statement: "He says sometimes he writes for the papers"? Was the kidnapper speaking to a conspirator, or was he just play-acting to make it appear as though several people were involved?

No arrangements had been made to trace the calls to Condon's house. Colonel

Schwarzkopf had strongly recommended this but had been overruled by Breckinridge. Tracing the kidnapper's telephone calls conflicted with Colonel Lindbergh's policy of keeping the police from getting in touch with the kidnappers.

Back in Norfolk, John Curtis's wife had figured a way for Curtis to get in touch with Colonel Lindbergh. Dobson-Peacock hadn't got beyond Morris Rosner. Mrs. Curtis realized that there was another man in Norfolk who was much closer to Colonel Lindbergh than Dobson-Peacock was. He was sixty-seven-year-old retired Adm. Guy Hamilton Burrage, who had been in command of the cruiser *Memphis,* which had brought Lindbergh back to America after his transatlantic flight.

Mrs. Curtis suggested to her husband that he tell Admiral Burrage about Sam and the kidnappers' efforts to find a group of prominent citizens to handle the ransom payment and the return of the baby.

Mrs. Curtis had come up with a marvelous idea. But before going to Admiral Burrage, John Curtis wanted to touch base with Dobson-Peacock. The Reverend liked the plan. Admiral Burrage should be contacted as soon as possible he said.

After hearing Curtis's story, Admiral Burrage offered to do whatever he could to help. Yes, he would be more than willing to call Colonel Lindbergh.

So, on Friday, March 11, the day John Condon's ad appeared in the *New York American,* Admiral Burrage telephoned Hopewell. He identified himself to several people before getting through to Colonel Lindbergh. At first, Lindbergh wasn't sure Burrage was who he said he was. But when the admiral related some of the private incidents that had taken place on the *Memphis,* the Colonel knew the call was legitimate.[5]

Burrage put John Curtis on the phone and the shipbuilder told Lindbergh of his conversation with Sam. When he finished, Curtis handed the telephone back to Admiral Burrage. The admiral asked Lindbergh if and when they should begin negotiating with the kidnappers.

Colonel Lindbergh was certain that John Condon was in touch with the kidnappers; his response was therefore less than enthusiastic. But in order to keep all of his options open, Lindbergh was careful not to pour cold water on the project. For that reason he didn't tell Burrage he already had a go-between who was in touch with the kidnappers. At this stage Lindbergh felt he had to keep all avenues open.

Admiral Burrage hung up a bit confused. The best course to take, he said, was to write Colonel Lindbergh a personal letter asking for a private meeting in Hopewell. Dobson-Peacock and Curtis agreed.

On this same day, Colonel Schwarzkopf and Capt. John J. Lamb were in Newark helping Insp. Harry Walsh of the Jersey City Police Department interrogate Henry ("Red") Johnson—Betty Gow's boyfriend.

Johnson, the Norwegian deckhand employed on Thomas W. Lamont's yacht, *Reynard,* had been a suspect from the very beginning. He and Betty had spent their time together visiting Palisades Amusement Park, boating, and going to dances. They also went to the movies regularly. When the Lindbergh baby was kidnapped, Johnson was living in a rented room in Englewood.

During the days immediately following the crime, Betty Gow, as the baby's nursemaid, had also been a suspect. She had been questioned several times and her background had been thoroughly checked. During the early days of the investigation the Detroit police announced that they were looking for one "Scotty Gow," a hoodlum who was mixed up in the Detroit mob and active in the "snatch racket." Betty had worked in Detroit—was there a connection? The police checked into this but found nothing.

Three days after the kidnapping, the New Jersey State Police asked the Hartford, Connecticut, police to pick up Johnson for questioning. He was arrested at his brother's house in that city and taken to the courthouse, where he was questioned by District Attorney Hugh M. Alcorn and his chief investigator, Edward J. Hickey. Alcorn and Hickey tired themselves out grilling Johnson, so they called in Capt. George J. Sullivan and Chief Joseph Grogan of the Hartford Police Department.

Throughout the interrogation Johnson denied any connection to the kidnapping. His answers were straightforward, matter-of-fact, and plausible. He didn't seem anxious, nor did he act indignant.

While Johnson was being questioned, his green Chrysler coupe was searched. The police were interested in his car because a green vehicle had been seen by a local resident near the Lindbergh home on the night of the kidnapping. But owning a green car didn't make Johnson a prime suspect. The police had already checked the registration of 374 such vehicles. In Johnson's car, however, the police had found an empty milk bottle. It was lying on the rumble seat. The quart container was stamped "Wednesday" and had been issued by a Newark dairy.

Johnson's interrogators wanted to know what a grown man was doing with an empty milk bottle in his car. Was it for the Lindbergh baby? Why didn't Johnson make it easy on himself and confess? Where was the baby?

Showing little emotion, Johnson said that he couldn't confess to something he didn't do. He had no idea where the Lindbergh baby was and he could explain the milk bottle.

Johnson said that he drank a lot of milk. In fact, he often drained a bottle as he drove. When finished he'd toss the empty into the back seat of his car. Later, he'd return the bottles for the two-cent deposit. He drank so much milk that he frequently told people that he was on a milk diet.[6]

Colonel Schwarzkopf had asked Capt. Henry Gautier of Jersey City to go to Hartford to see if he could get a confession from Johnson. Although Johnson was exhausted and had lost some of his composure, Captain Gautier couldn't shake his story. In the meantime, Johnson's fingerprints were en route to the FBI's Fingerprint Bureau in Washington, D.C., and photographs of his car had been distributed all over New Jersey.

On March 6, Captain Gautier drove Johnson to Newark, where he was held, without charge or bail, for further investigation.

On Friday, March 11, when Colonel Schwarzkopf, Captain Lamb, and Inspector Walsh went to Newark to question Johnson, the prisoner had been in custody for a week. He still hadn't been charged with a crime, and he hadn't confessed.

In the Bronx shipyard where Mr. Lamont's yacht was in drydock, the police checked to see if a homemade wooden ladder was missing. The investigators came up empty-handed.

Henry Johnson's brother had hired a lawyer to get him out of jail. But the lawyer ran into a brick wall—the FBI had discovered that five years ago Red had entered the country illegally. The police could now hold him indefinitely as an illegal alien. The suspect was told that if he didn't cooperate, he would be turned over to the immigration authorities and deported to Norway. Johnson said that he loved America. He pleaded with Colonel Schwarzkopf not to have him deported. He also said that he was innocent of the Lindbergh crime. He next gave Schwarzkopf, Walsh, and Keaten an account of his activities before, during, and after the kidnapping, a story that was no different than the one he had given the district attorney on the day of his arrest, and so far everything had checked out. Schwarzkopf was disappointed. Johnson was looking less and less like a suspect. Johnson would remain in custody, however, until the investigation on him was completed. If nothing turned up to change Schwarzkopf's mind, he would hand Johnson over to the immigration authorities.

Schwarzkopf and Captain Lamb left Johnson in Newark and returned to their headquarters in West Trenton, where Schwarzkopf supervised the distribution of the Lindbergh baby's wanted poster. The circular was being sent to fourteen hundred law enforcement agencies. Designed like the wanted posters of the old west, it carried two photographs and the following description of the baby:

Age, 20 months	Hair, blond, curly
Weight, 27 to 30 LBS	Eyes, dark blue
Height, 29 inches	Complexion, light

Deep dimple in center of chin
Dressed in one-piece coverall night suit

On March 12, Morris Rosner, Colonel Lindbergh's "personal secretary," granted reporters an interview. Speaking in a firm, confident voice, Rosner said that the baby was alive and well. He assured his audience that the baby was about to be returned to his parents. He set the crowd of journalists buzzing when he said, "This statement does not represent my opinion but is based on what I actually know." [7]

On the same day, Police Commissioner Mulrooney in New York City disclosed that Colonel Lindbergh's "personal secretary" had just been indicted on three counts of land fraud. The announcement infuriated Lindbergh and Breckinridge. Not only was it embarrassing, it could endanger the ransom negotiations. Breckinridge felt that Mulrooney's disclosure was nothing short of malicious.

Rosner's press conference was held amid speculation that he was holding secret talks with a top underworld figure who was in prison. Rumor had it that Rosner and this gangster were about to negotiate the return of the baby. As a result, there was a feeling among reporters that the case was about to break.

Dr. Condon, on this Saturday, was in the Bronx seeing to the construction of the box

54   he would use when it came time to deliver the ransom money. The kidnappers' last letter had been very specific about the shape and measurements of the money box. Although Condon was following the kidnappers' instructions, he was adding his own touch. The box under construction was a duplicate of a ballot box Condon kept in his study. The antique in his office had belonged to the lieutenant-governor of New York in 1820. It was fitted with two ornamental brass hinges and a casement lock. The ballot box had been a gift from an old friend.

Duplicating the ballot box had been Condon's idea. He wanted to hand over a container that could be easily and positively identified if recovered in someone's possession. The ballot box under construction would have a five-ply veneer of maple, pine, tulip, and two other species of wood.

The box was being fashioned by a cabinetmaker in the Bronx at the cost of three dollars. The job would be completed in four days.

At six o'clock Saturday night, Condon, Colonel Breckinridge, and Al Reich were seated in Condon's living room waiting for the kidnappers' next move. At 7:30 the doorbell rang—it was Milton Gaglio and Max Rosenhain, the men who had taken Condon to Hopewell three nights ago. They had stopped by to lend a hand. Colonel Breckinridge was alarmed by their impromptu visit. They couldn't have picked a worse time to pop in. Breckinridge hoped the kidnappers weren't watching the house. If they were, they might be frightened off by the activity.

Condon and his guests waited. Breckinridge looked nervously at his watch—it was now 8:30. Condon reminded him that the ransom note had said the call would come between six and twelve. A few minutes later the doorbell rang. Condon hurried to the door. The man standing in the doorway asked if he were Dr. Condon.

The stranger handed Condon an envelope that was addressed: "Dr. John F. Condon, 2974 Decature Ave." The letters and numerals were large and hand-printed. Condon recognized the childlike printing at once. He had seen it on the envelope he had received from the kidnapper.

Condon asked the man to step inside. A taxicab was parked along the curb in front of the house. In the presence of Colonel Breckinridge and the others, Condon opened the envelope. It read:

> Mr. Condon
>
> We trust you, but we will note come in your haus it is to danger. even you can note know if Police or secret servise is watching you
>   follow this instruction.
> Take a car and drive to the last supway station from jerome Ave here. 100 feet from this last station on the left seide is a empty frankfurther stand with a big open Porch around, you will find a notise in senter of the porch underneath a stone.
>   this notise will tell
>   you were to find us.
>   act accordingly.
> After 3/4 of a houer be on the place. bring the mony with you.

The message was written, in ink, on one side of the note. It bore the symbol of interlocking circles.

Breckinridge read one sentence out loud—"Bring money with you." He turned to Condon and said, "But we don't have the money! It'll be several days before we can get the ransom together. The box to carry it in hasn't even been made yet."

"I know," Condon replied. "But the important thing is for me to get to that hot dog stand in forty-five minutes!"

"But we don't have the money!" Breckinridge protested.

"I'll explain that to the kidnappers when I get there," Condon said.

"Yes," Breckinridge said. "You'll have to tell them that we need more time."

Al Reich said that he would drive Condon to the spot in his Ford coupe. Condon put on his coat and walked to the door, where the cab driver was still waiting. The man's name was Joseph Perrone. Milton Gaglio had asked to see his driver's badge. Gaglio had checked the badge number against the identification card inside the cab.

Perrone said that a man had hailed him on Gun Hill Road at Knox Place and had asked if he could find 2974 Decatur Avenue. Perrone said that he could. This man wore a brown topcoat and a brown felt hat. He pulled a white envelope out of his overcoat pocket then reached into the same pocket and brought out a dollar bill. He handed the envelope and the bill to Perrone. The man told Perrone to deliver the letter to Doctor Condon at the Decatur Avenue address. He then walked around to the rear of the car and jotted down Perrone's license number. The man spoke with a heavy German accent.

As Condon climbed into Al Reich's Ford, Breckinridge told him to be careful. He reminded Condon that he would be dealing with gangsters. Breckinridge said that he would be waiting anxiously for their return.

A blast of March wind chilled Breckinridge as he watched the old schoolteacher and the ex-prizefighter drive off to the rendezvous with the people who had Colonel Lindbergh's son.

What if the baby is dead. Would I burn if the baby is dead?
—THE   MAN   IN   THE   CEMETERY

5 JAFSIE AND THE RANSOM NEGOTIATIONS

FROM CONDON'S HOUSE, Al Reich drove his car eight blocks west before turning north on Jerome Avenue. The little Ford then made its way up the deserted thoroughfare beneath the hazy glow of the streetlights.

They were now approaching the last subway station on Jerome Avenue, just south of the sprawling Woodlawn Cemetery and Van Cortlandt Park. As they drove by the subway station Condon spotted the frankfurter place. It was on the left side of the street. Strictly a summertime operation, the refreshment stand was deserted and deteriorating. Its sagging front porch and abandoned appearance were forbidding and melancholy. Al made a U-turn and stopped along the curb in front of the stand.

Condon stepped out of the car and walked to the creaky porch, where he found an envelope under a rock. As he hurried back to the car he tore it open. Standing under the streetlight, Condon read the note out loud so that Al Reich could hear him. The note said:

> Cross the street and follow the fence from the cemetery direction to 233rd Street. I will meet you.

The note was referring to the fence enclosing Woodlawn Cemetery to the north. The western boundary of the graveyard bordered Jerome Avenue. Two hundred thirty-third Street was an east-west street that intersected Jerome Avenue about a mile north of the frankfurter stand. It formed the northern boundary of the cemetery.

The car was facing south, so Al Reich made another U-turn then headed north on Jerome to 233rd Street. As they drove, Condon watched the big iron fence pass by on his right. Beyond the nine-foot fence was the cemetery—and possibly the kidnappers. Al Reich looked over at Condon and said, "When they shoot you they won't have to carry you far to bury you."

Reich brought the car to a stop fifty feet south of 233rd Street. Ahead at the intersection, Condon saw the large gates at the main entrance to the cemetery. He got out of the car.

"I'll go with you," Al said. Condon shook his head. "I should go alone. He's expecting one person. You stay in the car."

"I don't like it. He may try something. We could at least nab him."

"My job is to get the baby back. I wasn't sent here to arrest the kidnappers."

"I still don't like it," Reich mumbled. "I'm here if you need me." [1]

Condon walked slowly toward the main gate. On his left was Jerome Avenue, on his right the iron fence and Woodlawn Cemetery. He got to the big gates and stopped. There was no sign of the kidnapper. Condon reread the note to make sure he was at the right place. He stuffed it back into his pocket and started pacing beside the fence. He was waiting for a hand to come out through the fence and grab him by the neck. Condon walked back and forth along the fence for another ten minutes, then started back to the car. It was cold, but he was perspiring heavily.

Al Reich saw Condon coming and opened the driver's side door. "Well?" he asked. He looked worried.

"Something's wrong. There's no one out there! We're on time. Did we do something wrong?"

Al Reich shrugged his shoulders. "I don't know," he said. He looked at his watch, "It's nine fifteen. Maybe we're early."

Just then they saw a man walking toward them along Jerome Avenue. Condon approached the figure, but when they met, the man kept walking. Condon watched him until he was out of sight, then returned to the car.

Not sure what he was supposed to do, Condon walked back to the big gates. He waited. Fifteen minutes passed. He was thinking about returning to the car when he saw something white. Someone was waving a handkerchief through the bars of the main gate. There was someone in the cemetery signaling him.

As Condon walked toward the gate he saw a shadowy figure moving among the tombstones. He was wearing a dark overcoat and a felt hat with the brim pulled down. Condon and the man approached the gate. The man in the cemetery held the handkerchief over his nose and mouth. Condon was now face to face with him. They were separated by the fence.

"Did you *gottit* my note?" the man asked.

Condon recognized the accent and the voice. It was what he had heard on the telephone the other night.

"Have you *gottit* the money with you?"

"No," Condon replied. "I can't bring the money until I see the baby."

Both men heard footsteps. Someone from inside the cemetery was approaching. The man turned abruptly to see who it was. He turned back to Condon, "A cop! He's with you!"

"No!" Condon said. "I wouldn't do that!"

The man shoved his handkerchief into his coat pocket and seized the bars of the gate with both hands. He then pulled himself up and over the fence. He landed on his feet next to Condon. For a split second the two men stood face to face outside the cemetery. Before Condon could speak, the man said, "It's too dangerous!" He then turned and ran north on Jerome Avenue.

The footsteps they had heard belonged to a cemetery guard. "Hey," the security man shouted, "what's going on?"

"He's all right," Condon said, "he's with me."

The man with the handkerchief turned west off Jerome Avenue and headed into Van Cortlandt Park. Condon lumbered after him. He thought the man might have injured himself when he jumped over the fence. The old teacher did the best he could to keep his prey in sight as the man he was chasing ran southwest through the park.

"Come back!" Condon shouted.

About half a mile from the cemetery's main gate, the man ran into a clump of trees at the southwestern tip of Van Cortlandt Lake. It was here the chase ended. The man simply stopped running. Condon caught up to him and grabbed him by the arm. When he caught his breath, he said, "You should be ashamed of yourself. No one will hurt you."

The man pulled up his coat lapels to cover the lower portion of his face. "It was too much risk," he said. "It would mean thirty years."

Condon led the man to a bench near a shack used by tennis players to change their clothes. They took a seat. It was nine-thirty. About a mile to the northwest Al Reich waited anxiously in his car.

The man spoke uneasily: "The risk was too much. I would get thirty years if I am caught. And I am only go-between. I might even burn."

Condon was alarmed by the word *burn*. "What was that you said—about burning?"

"What if the baby is dead?" he asked sullenly. "Would I burn if the baby is dead?"

Blood rushed to Condon's face. What was this man telling him? He looked into the eyes peering from the shadow of the felt hat. "What is the use of this? What is the meaning? Why should we be here, carrying on negotiations if the baby is dead?"

"The baby is not dead," the man said matter-of-factly. "The baby is better than it was. We give more to him to eat than we heard in the paper from Mrs. Lindbergh. Tell her not to worry. Tell the Colonel not to worry. The baby is all right."

Condon was relieved. He believed the man. Assured that the child was not in danger, Condon turned to other business. "Tell me, how do I know I'm talking to the right person?"

"You *gottit* my letter with the *sing-nature*," he replied. "It is the same like the letter with the *sing-nature* which was left in the baby's crib."

Crib? Condon thought. It was his understanding that the note had been left on the window sill.

Still seeking proof that he was dealing with the right man, Condon pulled his little canvas bag from his pocket. It contained the four-inch safety pins that had held the baby's blanket to the mattress. Dangling the pins in the air, Condon asked, "Have you ever seen these before?"

"Yes," the man replied. "Those pins fastened the blankets to the mattress in the baby's crib. Near the top. Near the pillow."

"What is your name?" Condon asked.

"John."

"My name is John, too. Where are you from, John?"

"Boston," he replied.

"What do you do?"

"I am a sailor."

"Are you German?" Condon asked.

"No, I am Scandinavian."

"You don't look like the kind of man who would be involved in a kidnapping. Is your mother alive, John?"

"Yes."

"What would she say if she knew you were mixed up in a thing like this?"

"She wouldn't like it. She would cry," he answered.

As they talked, Condon made a mental note of the man's appearance. Despite the fact it was dark, and the man's face was partially hidden beneath his hat and coat collar, Condon could see that he had a triangular face, deep-set eyes, and a small mouth. Condon figured him to be thirty-five. The man was about five foot ten and weighed approximately 160 pounds.

"Where is the baby?" Condon asked.

"Tell Colonel Lindbergh the baby is on a boat." (pronounced "boad" by the man.) The boad, he said, was six hours away. The child was being cared for by two women.

Condon asked John about the other kidnappers. John replied that the gang consisted of six people, the leader being a high-level government employee. He said that the second-in-charge knew Condon. The number two man had assured the others that Dr. Condon could be trusted.

"Then why doesn't Number Two come to see me?" Condon asked.

"He's afraid. He might be caught from you."

"What are *you* getting out of this, John?"

John explained that the top man would get twenty thousand dollars while John and the other two men would receive ten thousand dollars each. The two nurses would split the remaining twenty thousand dollars.

Condon asked the man why the ransom had been raised to seventy thousand dollars.

John said that Colonel Lindbergh had made things more difficult when he brought in the police. Because of this the negotiations would take a lot longer. One of the nurses was already getting impatient. The extra money would be used, John said, to pay for lawyers if something went wrong.

So far, Condon thought, John had shown two emotions—fear and greed.

"It seems to me, John, that you are doing the most dangerous work in this case."

"I know it," he answered.

"You are getting only ten thousand dollars. I don't think you're getting what you deserve," Condon said.

"You could be right," John said.

"Turn yourself in," Condon said. "Help the Lindberghs get their baby back."

"I can't do that."

"Then take me to the baby," Condon said. "Take me there now. I will be your hostage until every cent of the ransom money is paid."

"What do you mean hostage?"

"I'll stay with the baby until the money is in your hands."

"No, they would smack me out. They would drill me," John said.

"Leave them. Don't you see that sooner or later you will be caught?"

"Oh no," he replied. "We have planned this case for a year already."

"Come, now, John. You can't expect us to pay the ransom without seeing the baby. We must know that he is alive. I have some of his toys. And I know some of the words he can speak. I will be able to tell if he's the right one. I'll stay with the baby until the money is paid. You must take me to the baby—let me see him."

"No, the leader would drill the both of us. He would be mad if he knows I said so much and stayed so long."

"Don't go," Condon pleaded. "We have to make arrangements. Give the baby to a priest—he will keep your name a secret. He will see to it that the baby is safely returned to his parents."

The man stood up. "I go now. I have stayed too long already. Number One will be mad. I should have *gottit* the money."

"All right," Condon replied. "Get your men together and work something out on a cash-and-delivery basis. Are you sure the baby is all right?"

"The baby is better than it was. It is happy and well. Number One told me I should tell you the baby is well. So you put an ad in the *Home News,* Sunday, to show Number One that I gave you the message. You say—'Baby is alive and well' and you put this in, too: 'Money is ready,' to show my friends I saw you and you will pay the money."

"I'll do that," Condon said. "But before you go, tell me about Henry Johnson."

"Red Johnson?"

"Yes."

"Red Johnson is innocent. Betty Gow—she is innocent too. Red Johnson must be freed. The girl too. Red Johnson had nothing to do with it. It was worth my life to come here and now it seems you don't trust me. Don't you believe that we are the ones who *gottit* the baby, that we are the ones who should *gottit* the money?"

Again, the same two emotions, Condon thought. Greed and fear.

"Now, I go," John said. "I will send by ten o'clock Monday morning, a token."

"What token?" Condon asked.

"The sleeping suit from the baby."

"I will put the ad in the *Home News* tomorrow," Condon said.[2]

The two men shook hands, not as friends, but as negotiators who had come to a preliminary agreement.

"I must go. Goodnight," John said.

Condon watched the man walk north and disappear into the woods. Condon then hurried back to Al Reich and the car. He looked at his watch, it was 10:45. He had been on the bench with John an hour and fifteen minutes. He felt drained.

Al Reich drove Condon back to the house, where he was greeted eagerly by Breckinridge, who asked Condon to relate every last detail about the meeting. After describing John, Condon went over their conversation word by word.

Breckinridge was particularly interested in John's comment that "We have planned this case for a year already." In the kidnapper's third letter he had written that the crime had been a year in the planning. Condon had not seen that letter and had no knowledge of its contents. Breckinridge considered this further proof that Condon was in touch with the kidnappers.

Thoroughly debriefed, Condon helped Breckinridge compose the message for the *Bronx Home News*. It read:

> Money is ready. No cops. No Secret Service. No press. I come alone, like last time. Jafsie.

Breckinridge telephoned Lindbergh and filled him in. Lindbergh had been waiting for the call—Breckinridge had telephoned him the minute Condon and Al Reich had driven off to meet the kidnappers. Like Breckinridge, Colonel Lindbergh was certain that Condon was dealing with the people who had his baby.

Anticipating the upcoming ransom payment, Lindbergh called the head of the U.S. Treasury Department and asked for the assistance of Elmer Irey. Lindbergh had been impressed by the way Irey had advised him on the Al Capone matter. As a result, he wanted Irey on hand when it came time to gather and package the ransom money. The head of the Treasury Department said that Irey would be sent to Hopewell immediately.

On Sunday, March 13, Dr. Erastus Mead Hudson, a New York City physician and fingerprint expert arrived at the Lindbergh estate. The curly-headed, bespectacled thirty-five year old had come to do what Corporal Kelly of the New Jersey State Police had failed to do—get fingerprints off the kidnap ladder. Although Dr. Hudson had volunteered his services shortly after the kidnapping, Maj. Charles Schoeffel hadn't responded back to him until a few days ago.

Dr. Hudson had been working with fingerprints since his medical school days in 1917. As a young medical officer in the navy, Doctor Hudson had fingerprinted navy personnel. While serving in England he had studied fingerprinting under the great masters at Scotland Yard where, in 1901, the world's first fingerprint bureau was established. Dr. Hudson had returned to New York City after World War I and had worked with Frederick Kuhn, who was in charge of the police department's fingerprint bureau.[3]

Dr. Hudson began experimenting in 1920 with a method of making visible invisible fingerprints, called latents, through the use of a silver nitrate solution. The process was invented in 1892 by a Frenchman, Dr. René Forgeot. Forgeot was a colleague of Alphonse Bertillon, the first man to develop a scientific way of individualizing and therefore identifying people. Bertillon's system, called anthropometry, involved measuring certain parts of a person's body—length of arm, sitting height, head circumference, and so forth. Bertillon is recognized as one of the fathers of scientific crime detection.[4]

In 1932, only a handful of American fingerprint experts knew of the silver nitrate method. The only other American who had worked with silver nitrate as early as 1920 was a private criminalist in Seattle, Washington, named Luke S. May. Silver nitrate was not being used in 1932 by the New Jersey State Police or any other major law enforcement agency in America.

Dr. Hudson's process involved spraying a fine mist of the silver nitrate solution over the object to be examined. The solution would mix with traces of salt in the latent fingerprint, causing the silver nitrate to turn to silver chloride. Since silver chloride is sensitive to sunlight, the places that have been touched come out reddish-brown when the object is exposed to the sun. If the object has been handled right, the reddish-brown stain will come out in the form of a latent fingerprint.

Dr. Hudson explained his method to Major Schoeffel. He pointed out that its principal advantage was that it worked better than fingerprint powder on wood and other porous surfaces. The silver nitrate would therefore be ideal for the kidnap ladder.

On Sunday morning, with Cpl. Frank Kelly at his side, Dr. Hudson applied his solution to the baby's toys. Since the child had been born at home and had never been fingerprinted, Doctor Hudson wanted to get a set of the baby's latent prints from the objects he had touched. Colonel Schwarzkopf thought that someday these prints might be useful in identifying young Charles Lindbergh.

Using a small glass atomizer to produce the mist, Doctor Hudson sprayed the child's building blocks, wooden animals, and books. Hundreds of the reddish-brown stains appeared when Dr. Hudson exposed the toys to the sun. From these the doctor found thirteen identifiable latents. Corporal Kelly, using a special fingerprint camera, photographed the stains before they faded.

In the afternoon, Dr. Hudson and Corporal Kelly began working on the ladder. It had gotten cloudy so Doctor Hudson sprayed just a part of the wood. Corporal Kelly helped him apply the silver nitrate. After they had covered an area with the substance, Dr. Hudson exposed the ladder to an ultraviolet light. Although this light was not as effective as the sun, dozens of fingerprint stains came out.

The following day, Doctor Hudson was back at the estate spraying the rest of the ladder. He was being assisted by another New Jersey State Police fingerprint man, Sgt. Louis Kubler. The three ladder sections, soaked in silver nitrate, were taken outside and laid in the sun. In moments hundreds of marks appeared. Hudson and Kubler scrutinized these stains for hours, classifying them as complete prints, partials, and useless smudges.

The fingerprint man found a total of 500 stains. But only 206 of them represented complete latents—the rest were merely fragments, too incomplete to identify. Of the 206, only 8 were clear enough to be useful. The rest were worthless smudges.[5] Seven of the eight latents were never identified. The eighth belonged to Lt. Lewis J. Bornmann of the New Jersey State Police.[6]

Dr. Hudson was not surprised that the ladder contained so many prints. It had been handled by hundreds of people. But there was always the chance that among all of those prints, there was one that had been left by someone connected to the kidnapping.

Under ideal circumstances, fingerprints a year old could be brought out by silver nitrate. So even if the ladder had been built a year earlier, the prints of the person who had constructed it could still be there. But Doctor Hudson realistically assumed that if the ladder contained the builder's and/or kidnappers' prints, they were buried under those left by policemen and others who had handled it. Moreover, the person who had climbed up and down the ladder might have worn gloves. The fingerprint angle was therefore a long shot.

The next day, on a nationwide radio broadcast, Colonel Schwarzkopf appealed for help. The kidnapping had been committed twelve days ago. Although still active, the police were running out of solid leads. The investigation had become less frantic. Most of the servants had been checked, and there were fewer cranks and wild goose chases. So far, all of the so-called underworld contacts had proved useless. Schwarzkopf was starting to question the notion that the kidnappers were professional criminals.

On Monday, the ad written Friday night by Colonel Breckinridge and John Condon—"Money is ready. No cops. No Secret Service. No press. I come alone, like last time. Jafsie"—appeared in the *Bronx Home News*.

When Doctor Condon checked his mail Monday morning he found nothing from the man he was now calling John. About an hour later, when Condon was starting to wonder if John had broken his word, the telephone rang. It was John: "Doctor Condon?"

"Yes. What is wrong? I have been waiting . . ."

"There has been a delay sending the sleeping suit. It will come. You will have it soon."

Before Condon could respond the caller hung up.

From outside the case, it looked as though the investigation had come to a stop. The newspapers were running out of stories to print and the public was getting restless. People were demanding results.

Schwarzkopf was being accused of withholding information from the press. The controversy had started at a press conference held by Governor Moore. Although there were persistent rumors that the kidnappers had made a ransom demand in the form of a note left in the nursery, Schwarzkopf and Lindbergh had flatly denied its existence. Colonel Breckinridge told a reporter that there was such a note. When a newsman at the press conference confronted the governor with this contradiction, the politician replied that whatever Colonel Breckinridge had said was probably correct. Later that day, Capt. John J. Lamb kept the debate alive when he denied that a ransom demand had been made. He said the Lindberghs' public offer of fifty thousand dollars to the baby's kidnappers had been made on their own initiative.[7]

The press was also being kept in the dark about John Condon and his dealings with the man in the cemetery.

Having nothing factual to report, the New York tabloids, principally the *Daily Mirror* and the *Daily News,* were speculating about an inside job. There were numerous stories suggesting that Betty Gow and the Whateleys were somehow behind the kidnapping.

The papers were also reporting that Governor Moore, at Colonel Lindbergh's request, was about to take the state police off the case. Stories of friction between Colonel Lindbergh and Colonel Schwarzkopf were popping up in the papers. Schwarzkopf was also being criticized for not cooperating with the New York City police. Meanwhile, as the ransom negotiations dragged on in secret, Schwarzkopf hoped for a break that would divert the press and the public.

On March 14, amid the criticism and public unrest, Colonel Schwarzkopf issued a statement claiming that his men were cooperating with all agencies and that he did not have the authority to grant prosecutorial immunity.

On this date, a Monday, Morris Rosner made his own statement to the press, announcing that he knew for sure that the baby was safe and alive. Colonel Schwarzkopf, as soon as he got wind of Rosner's statement, told reporters that Rosner's comments were strictly unofficial and that the New Jersey State Police could not verify his statement.

Rosner's associates, Salvatore Spitale and Irving Bitz, were more candid; they were not getting any results. Despite the fact they hadn't made contact with the kidnappers, they still believed the crime had been committed by an underworld gang. Bitz told reporters, "I can't believe any boob stumbled through a job of this kind and was lucky all the way. But where that boy is or who's got him is certainly beyond me. This is a mystery."[8]

The tabloids continued to print every scrap of Lindbergh information they could find. For example, the *New York Daily News* reported that the police in Pittsburgh were looking for two men who had worked as gardeners on the Lindbergh estate. Similar investigations were being carried out in Detroit, Nashville, and a dozen other cities.

Monday was a beautiful spring day, and this brought to the Lindbergh estate a large number of sightseers. State troopers and local police were kept busy directing traffic away from the Lindbergh grounds. Sightseeing airplanes, charging $2.50 a ticket were flying over the house all day. These sightseeing planes were operating from an emergency airfield three miles from Hopewell.

On Tuesday, two weeks after the kidnapping, Colonel Schwarzkopf made a statement to the press in which he stated that Henry Johnson had been cleared of any wrongdoing in the Lindbergh case. Johnson was now in federal custody on charges of entering the country illegally. Schwarzkopf said that Betty Gow was no longer under investigation.

Dr. Condon didn't hear from John on Tuesday. He was still waiting for John to send the baby's sleeping suit.

The next day, when Condon checked his mail, he found a soft oblong package wrapped in brown paper. He recognized the hand-printed address on the bundle as John's handwriting. Certain that the package contained the baby's sleeping garment, he telephoned Colonel Breckinridge's office in Manhattan. It was ten-thirty in the morning.

Forty-five minutes later, Breckinridge was in Condon's living room. He had called Colonel Lindbergh, who said that he'd be on his way to the Bronx as soon as he could figure a way to slip by the reporters posted on the roads surrounding his house.

Condon had not opened the package—he was leaving that for Colonel Lindbergh, but Breckinridge insisted that they open it to make sure it contained a sleeping suit. Breckinridge didn't want Colonel Lindbergh driving to the Bronx for nothing.

Colonel Breckinridge carefully unwrapped the package. Inside he found a folded garment of gray wool. It was a one-piece sleeping suit with closed feet and buttons in the back. Breckinridge thought it looked like the one the baby was wearing the night he was kidnapped. But he couldn't be sure. Colonel Lindbergh would know.

Attached to the sleeping suit was a one-page note bearing the familiar symbol of interlocking circles. The note contained writing on both sides and read:

> Dear Sir: Ouer man faill to collect the mony. There are no more confidential conference after we meeting from March 12. Those arrangemts to hazardous for us. We will note allow ouer man to confer in a way like befor. circumstance will note allow us to make transfare like you wish. It is impossibly for us. wy shuld we move the baby and face danger. to take another person to the place is entirely out of question. It seems you are afraid if we are the rigth party and if the boy is allright. Well you have ouer singnature. It is always the same as the first one specialy them 3 holes.

On the reverse side, John had written:

> Now we will send you the sleepingsuit from the baby besides it means 3 $ extra expenses because we have to pay another one. please tell Mrs. Lindbergh note to worry the baby is well. we only have to give him more food as the diet says.
>
> You are willing to pay the 70000 note 50000 $ without seeing the baby first or note. let us know about that in the New York-American. We can't do it other ways because we don't like to give up ouer safty plase or to move the baby. If you are willing to accept this deal put these in paper.
>
> *I accept mony is redy*
> ouer program is:
>
> After 8 houers we have the mony received we will notify you where to find the baby. If there is any trapp, you will be
> responsible what
> will follows.

Dr. Condon placed the brown wrapping paper on the piano in his living room and carefully, almost reverently, laid the woolen garment on it. There was nothing to do now but wait for Colonel Lindbergh.

Colonel Breckinridge was studying the note. There was one sentence that puzzled him: "Circumstance will note allow us to make a transfer like you wish." What did that mean?

Condon explained that he had told John that he could, if he wanted, hand the baby over to a Catholic priest—or if he preferred, the baby could be moved to a different hiding place where he (Condon) would be able to see him to make certain they had the right baby.

It was now midnight, and they were still waiting for Colonel Lindbergh. Finally, at 1:30, they heard a car door slam. A few moments later there were footsteps on the front porch. Dr. Condon opened the door and saw a tall man wearing a hunter's cap and oversized sunglasses. When the man spoke Condon knew it was Colonel Lindbergh. He had used this disguise to slip by the reporters.

Lindbergh followed Condon into the living room. He picked up the sleeping suit, examined it front and back, then spread it out on top of the piano. He studied it some more, then picked it up again and looked at the red manufacturer's tag in the neckband. It was a Dr. Denton brand—number 2. Lindbergh turned the suit around and inspected the buttons up the back and on the flap.[9] He laid the woolen garment down and turned to Breckinridge. "This is my son's sleeping suit," he said. "Why did they clean it?"[10]

"What?" Breckinridge asked.

"The sleeping suit, it has just been cleaned. I wonder why?"[11]

Breckinridge didn't know why, and neither did Condon.

"We must pay the ransom as soon as possible," Lindbergh said. "There should be no delays. After all, this man has kept his word with us throughout. And he knows that we've kept our word. I will not permit any schemes to trap him. He wants the money. And, if he gets it, I see no reason why he won't keep his end of the bargain and return my boy."[12]

At the risk of throwing cold water on Lindbergh's optimism, Condon said, "Don't you think, Colonel, that one of us should see and identify the baby before any money is paid over?"

"Yes, of course, if it can be arranged that way. But we can't let the negotiations go on too long. If the kidnappers lose patience, if word leaks out to the newspapers, if any one of a dozen things happen, my son's life could be in danger. The kidnappers are in a position to dictate their own terms."[13]

"I understand, sir," Condon said. "But I think it's important for someone to see the baby before the money is paid. I think we ought to word our ad as follows:

> I accept. Money is ready. You know they won't let me deliver without getting the package. Let's make it some sort of C.O.D. transaction. You know you can trust Jafsie.

"No," Lindbergh said. "I don't like that. We're going to play by their rules. Run the ad they want."[14]

Breckinridge and Condon followed Lindbergh's instructions and composed the following ad: "I accept. Money is ready." To that, they added: "John your package is delivered and is O.K. Direct me. Jafsie."

It was three in the morning. Mrs. Condon came into the living room and announced that she had prepared a light meal. After downing three sandwiches and two cups of coffee, Colonel Lindbergh said he had to leave. He gathered up the sleeping suit, thanked the Condons, and climbed into his car for the trip back to New Jersey.

Shortly after dawn, Lindbergh was pulling the car into his driveway. Anne Lindbergh heard the tires on the gravel and went to greet him at the kitchen door. She wanted to see the sleeping suit. Numb from over two weeks of constant worry and grief, she looked at the garment then at her husband. "Yes," she said, "it is his."

Colonel Lindbergh tried to comfort his wife by assuring her that this was a good sign. It meant that the kidnappers could be trusted and that the negotiations were finally getting underway.

On Thursday afternoon, armed guards from the J. P. Morgan and Company Bank delivered fifty thousand dollars to the Fordham branch of the Corn Exchange Bank. The money was placed into a special vault to which Dr. Condon had round-the-clock access.

Dr. Condon had urged Breckinridge to have a list made of the bills' serial numbers. But Colonel Lindbergh, in his desire to play fair with the kidnappers, wouldn't allow it.

Raising seventy thousand dollars in cash in the midst of the Depression wasn't easy, even for Colonel Lindbergh. He could have let Mrs. Morrow pay the ransom, and several wealthy friends had offered to give him money as well, but Lindbergh insisted on doing it himself. So far, he had sold off most of his holdings in the stock market. He had unloaded his shares at rock-bottom prices—compounding his economic loss. He still had twenty thousand to raise.

In a front-page story, the *New York Daily Mirror,* on March 17, declared that the J. P. Morgan Bank had given Colonel Lindbergh $250,000—money that was to be used to pay the kidnappers. Lindbergh and Breckinridge were enraged and alarmed. If the kidnappers read the story they'd think that Colonel Lindbergh was holding back. If the kidnappers upped the ransom, it would extend the negotiations and take Lindbergh longer to raise the money. This would cause further delay—something Lindbergh wanted to avoid.

Another story in the *Daily Mirror* told of Lindbergh's negotiations with a gang in Chicago. According to the newspaper, the gang was ready to return the baby as soon as they got the ransom money. The story terrified Lindbergh—there was no telling what effect it might have on Condon's man in the cemetery. If John saw the story he might think that Colonel Lindbergh was about to hand the money over to the wrong people.

On March 17, the *Home News* and the *New York American* carried Lindbergh's latest message to John:

I accept. Money is ready. John, your package is delivered and is O.K. Direct me. Jafsie.

These "Jafsie ads" had attracted some attention. The March 13 ad which read—"Baby alive and well. Money is ready. Call and see us. Jafsie."—was particularly revealing. Many suspected that this message was related to the Lindbergh case.

People had been calling and writing to the *Bronx Home News* about these ads. The editors of the paper knew that Condon was Jafsie and that he was communicating with the kidnappers. Concerned that Condon was about to be exposed, the editors published a statement denying that the "Jafsie ads" had anything to do with the Lindbergh investigation.

For the time being then, Jafsie's identity remained a well-kept secret. Lindbergh and Breckinridge realized, however, that a leak could occur at any time, and once Dr. Condon was exposed, a frenzied press would make further negotiations with the kidnappers impossible.

An inquisitive reporter had given Condon a scare Thursday evening, the night he and Colonel Breckinridge were waiting for Colonel Lindbergh to identify the sleeping suit. The reporter, from one of the morning newspapers, came to the house and spoke to Mrs.

68   Condon. When told that Dr. Condon was not at home, the reporter said he had wanted to ask Dr. Condon if he had received a response to his letter in the *Home News* offering himself as intermediary. Mrs. Condon said that except for a few crank letters, nothing came of her husband's offer. If the reporter had hung around and watched the house, he would have seen Colonel Lindbergh arrive. He would have had the biggest scoop of his life, and Lindbergh's ransom negotiations would have been left in shambles. It had been a close call. But it wasn't over.

On Friday, March 18, Dr. Condon woke up to find a group of reporters camped on the sidewalk in front of his house. Among them was the reporter who had come to his door the night before. Dr. Condon had a problem. He had to leave the house to give a lecture that morning at the College of New Rochelle. Al Reich was out front waiting for Condon in his car. Reich was wondering how Condon would get by the reporters when a strange-looking figure in a woman's ankle-length coat stepped out of the house. The creature approaching the car had on Mrs. Condon's favorite hat—a massive affair accentuated by a foot-long turkey feather.

Condon's disguise had worked. None of the reporters noticed that the big woman had a mustache. When Condon returned to the house later in the day, the reporters were gone. They had more important stories to chase than some nut who wanted to become a Lindbergh intermediary.

There was no word from John this day or the next. Breckinridge was worried. It had been two days since they had heard from John. Breckinridge wanted the kidnappers to know that Colonel Lindbergh was raising the money. He wanted to tell them that the Colonel was ready to deal. In an effort to get things rolling again, Breckinridge composed the following ad for the *Bronx Home News:*

> Inform me how I can get important letter to you. Urgent. Jafsie.

On the day the ad appeared, Henry Johnson was handed over to the immigration department. Despite the fact he had been treated roughly by the police, the young Norwegian wasn't bitter. He told reporters that he loved America. He said that someday he hoped to return to the United States—legally of course—and become an American citizen. He also said that he would miss his girlfriend, Betty Gow.

On Monday, March 21, when Doctor Condon checked his mail, he found the letter he had been waiting for. The envelope was postmarked March 19, 7:30 P.M. from Station N. It bore two one-cent stamps. The message inside was handwritten in ink on a single piece of paper stamped by the familiar symbol of interlocking circles. It read:

> Dear Sir: You and Mr. Lindbergh know ouer Program. If you don't accept den we will wait until you agree with ouer deal. we know you have to come to us anyway But why should Mrs. and Mr. Lindbergh suffer longer as necessary we will note communicate with you or Mr. Lindbergh until you write so in the paper.
>
> we will tell you again; this kidnapping cace whas prepared for a year already so the Police won't have any luck to find us or the child. You only puch everything farther out did you send that

little package to
Mr. Lindbergh? it contains
the sleepingsuit for the baby.
the baby is well.

On the reverse side of the page the message ended with the following line:

Mr. Linbergh only wasting time with his search.

Dr. Condon immediately telephoned Colonel Breckinridge, who hurried to the Bronx to read the letter.

Breckinridge and Condon didn't like the tone of John's letter. They were bothered by two sentences: "If you don't except den we will wait until you agree with ouer deal. We know you will have to come to us anyway." These lines reflected a certain hardness that worried them.

But even worse, it appeared that John hadn't seen the ads in the *Home News.* On March 18 and 19 the paper had carried the "I accept. Money is ready" messages.

Did John think that Colonel Lindbergh was stalling? In his letter John sounded jittery and impatient. If the kidnappers thought it was getting too risky to deal with Lindbergh, the baby's life would be in jeopardy.

Something would have to be done to get the negotiations back on track. Breckinridge would write another ad and run it for four days. "We'll tell the kidnapper," he said, "that we've received the sleeping suit—the package—and that we accept his terms and we'll pay the money *at once!"*

"Should we add that we expect to see the baby first?" Condon asked.

"No!" Breckinridge replied angrily. "What is the use insisting upon something the kidnapper won't agree to? He told you in the cemetery that you couldn't see the baby. He's persistently ignored our pleas for a C.O.D. arrangement."

Condon bowed his head. Breckinridge was probably right. The kidnappers didn't seem willing to go along with their demands to see the baby first.

Breckinridge said they had to look at things through Colonel Lindbergh's eyes. He wanted his son back, and the quickest way to do that was to go along with the kidnappers. Breckinridge reminded Condon that it had been almost three weeks since the baby had been taken. The Lindberghs were getting desperate.

Dr. Condon understood—he had great sympathy for the Lindberghs. He too was a parent. But still—what harm would be done by asking the kidnappers to show the baby? Wasn't that reasonable?

Breckinridge finally agreed that such a request was reasonable. "All right," he said, "it won't hurt to ask." [15]

Their new ad read:

Thanks. That little package you sent me was immediately delivered and accepted as real article. See my position. Over fifty years in business and can I pay without seeing the goods? Common sense makes me trust you. Please understand my position. Jafsie.

The ad appeared in the *Home News* on Tuesday, March 22. Condon didn't hear from John that day, but he did receive several calls from reporters, who were starting to connect Condon with the Jafsie ads.

Condon was on the verge of being identified as Jafsie. It was just a matter of time. Once this became known, the negotiations with John would stop. And once that happened, the baby's life was in danger.

We'll keep our end of the bargain.

—C H A R L E S   L I N D B E R G H
to John Condon

6 THE PAYOFF

ON TUESDAY, THE AFTERNOON OF MARCH 22, John Hughes Curtis, the Reverend Mr. Dobson-Peacock, and Admiral Guy Burrage arrived at the Lindbergh estate from Norfolk. They were taken into the study, where they waited for Colonel Lindbergh.

Twelve days earlier, the admiral had spoken to Lindbergh on the telephone. Dissatisfied with the results of that conversation, Admiral Burrage had written Colonel Lindbergh a letter in which he discussed the kidnappers' attempts through Sam to have John Curtis assemble a committee of prominent Norfolk citizens to act as negotiators. Admiral Burrage had also requested a meeting with Lindbergh so John Curtis could tell his story in person.

A week later, Burrage received a letter from Colonel Lindbergh inviting him and his friends to Hopewell.

In the meantime, John Curtis had been contacted again by Sam, who told him that the kidnappers were getting restless. Sam had hastened to add, however, that the baby was all right. The gang had hired a special nurse who was following the diet Mrs. Lindbergh had published in the newspapers. The woman had also purchased a new outfit for the little boy.

Curtis said he had learned from Sam that the baby was being kept on a boat. He figured the ship was either hidden in one of the many coves and inlets along the Chesapeake Bay or was out to sea beyond the international limit.

Four days earlier, Sam got in touch with Curtis again. This time Sam had a very specific proposal. Colonel Lindbergh was to deposit twenty-five thousand dollars in a Norfolk bank under the names of Curtis, Dobson-Peacock, and Burrage. This would be a sign of good faith.

Curtis said that he had made it clear to Sam that Colonel Lindbergh would not release any money until after he had received the baby.

Colonel Lindbergh greeted his visitors in the study, apologizing for not responding to

Admiral Burrage's letter sooner. He said he was getting so much mail a letter from the White House had been misplaced and had gone unanswered for ten days.

Following a bit of small talk, John Curtis told Lindbergh of his meetings with Sam. It took him quite a while to do this because Lindbergh kept being called out of the room. When Curtis had finally finished his story, Lindbergh wasn't quite sure how to respond. An awkward silence followed. When it became obvious that Colonel Lindbergh didn't have anything to say, Curtis asked him how much ransom money he was planning to pay. Curtis didn't know of the nursery note.

"I have been advised," Lindbergh said, "that the amount should be named by the kidnappers."

Admiral Burrage spoke up: "The sum I presume they have in mind is the amount mentioned in the newspapers—fifty-thousand dollars."

"I cannot agree on any sum," Lindbergh replied, "until I have positive proof that I am dealing with the right people. They must show me that they are not imposters. If they really have my child, they can easily prove it by describing certain characteristics which have not been made public." Lindbergh suggested that the kidnappers send a photograph of the baby or a written message that contained a certain symbol. "I must insist on this identification before any negotiations," he said.

"Of course," Admiral Burrage replied.

"I want you to know how much I appreciate your willingness to help me get back our boy. But I have to tell you that I think this Sam is deceiving you. I don't know what his game is, but I think he's a phony. I can't tell you how I know this, but I'm certain it's true."[1]

Burrage and Dobson-Peacock were disillusioned. They had made the trip north for nothing. To soften their disappointment, Lindbergh assured them that he was keeping all his options open—if Sam could bring them proof that he was representing the people who actually had the baby negotiations would start immediately. Lindbergh then asked the three southerners to stay for dinner.

On Thursday, March 24, word leaked out in Norfolk that John Curtis was negotiating with the kidnappers for the return of the Lindbergh baby. Rumor had it that Curtis was about to pay the kidnappers fifty-thousand dollars. Curtis, Burrage, and Dobson-Peacock were suddenly hounded by reporters from all over the country who sensed that the Lindbergh case was about to break.

On Thursday afternoon, Dobson-Peacock agreed to be interviewed by a reporter. The Reverend said that it was true that he, Curtis, and Admiral Burrage had just come from Hopewell where they had met personally with Colonel Lindbergh. And yes, they were definitely in touch with the kidnappers, who had agreed to deliver the baby *before* demanding the ransom money.

That evening the story hit the Norfolk papers. The next day it was in every newspaper in the country. The Friday, March 25, edition of the *New York Daily News* carried the headlines: "LINDY AGENTS READY TO PAY $50,000 FOR BABY—'ON BOAT'"[2] The lead story quoted Dobson-Peacock as saying that the baby was on a boat in the Chesapeake Bay. "We are convinced he [the kidnapper] has the baby and is acting in good faith," the minister was reported as saying. "We expect to have the child within two or three days if everything goes well. The baby, as soon as the money is paid, will be delivered to me."

The Norfolk story broke at a time when Breckinridge and Condon were waiting anxiously to hear from John. The last Jafsie ad, the one thanking John for sending the baby's sleeping suit, had been in the papers three days. The most recent letter from the kidnappers, the one dated March 21, had caused Breckinridge to wonder if communications had broken down. Dobson-Peacock couldn't have picked a worse time to talk to the press about the so-called Curtis negotiations.

Colonel Lindbergh was beside himself. When the Norfolk story came out he immediately authorized Schwarzkopf to make the following statement: "The three citizens of Norfolk who visited Colonel Lindbergh gave him information which, on being investigated, was found to have no special significance."[3]

In Norfolk, John Curtis took exception to Schwarzkopf's statement. His pride wounded, Curtis told reporters that he regretted all of the publicity, but he wanted Colonel Schwarzkopf to know that after he had returned from Hopewell, Sam had called him from Philadelphia promising to give him proof that the people he represented had the Lindbergh baby.

On Saturday, March 26, the papers were full of stories about the kidnap negotiations in Norfolk. According to the press, Dobson-Peacock still insisted that Colonel Lindbergh had given him and his two partners "full authority" to negotiate the return of the baby. When asked about Colonel Schwarzkopf's statement, the clergyman was quoted as saying, "That's exactly what he [Lindbergh] would tell him [Schwarzkopf]. That man Shootskoff, or what ever his name is, has tried to hinder us from the outset."[4]

The news story about the Norfolk men and the mysterious Sam was making John Condon very uneasy. He found it hard to believe that Colonel Lindbergh was dealing with two sets of kidnappers. Could things be that confused at the Lindbergh estate?

Condon telephoned Colonel Breckinridge and asked for an explanation. Breckinridge assured him that although Colonel Lindbergh had met with the three men from Norfolk, Lindbergh didn't believe for one second that they were in touch with the real kidnappers. Breckinridge said that both he and Lindbergh were certain that John was the real article.

Meanwhile, Colonel Schwarzkopf was having problems of his own. The state police were running out of money. On March 24, he had appeared before the State Finance Committee and had asked the legislators to replenish the State Police Emergency Fund. The Lindbergh case had exhausted the kitty's five thousand dollars. So far the investigation had cost New Jersey over fifty thousand dollars. Schwarzkopf told the committee that the food supplied to his troops at the Lindbergh estate was being cooked at the Lambertville Barracks and transported by car every day to Hopewell. The Colonel said that he had reduced the number of men stationed at the Lindbergh estate and had removed several telephone lines. He was, he said, "curtailing all unnecessary expenses."[5]

On March 25 and 26, there was no word from John. On March 26, a Saturday, Breckinridge and Condon drew up another Jafsie ad that was to appear in Sunday's *Home News:*

Money is ready. Furnish simple code for us to use in paper. Jafsie.

On Saturday, John Curtis told Dobson-Peacock and Burrage that Sam had called and requested a meeting at one o'clock the next day in New York City. Curtis and Sam were going to meet at a Manhattan cafeteria on Seventh Avenue near Forty-first Street. Curtis said that he would keep them advised of any important development.

On Monday, March 28, there was no word from John, but the next day Condon found a letter in his mail box. The one-page note bore the familar handwriting, the misspellings, and the symbol of intersecting circles. It read:

> dear Sir: It is note necessary to furnish any code. You and Mr. Lindbergh know ouer Program very well. We will keep the child in ouer same plase until we have the money in hand, but if the deal is note closéd until the 8 of April we will ask for 30000 more. also note 70000−100000.
>
> How can Mr. Lindbergh follow so many false clues he knows we are the right party ouer singnature is still the same as in the ransom note. But if Mr. Lindbergh likes to fool around for another month, we can help it.
>
> Once he has come to us anyway but if he keeps on waiting we will double ouer amount. There is absolute no fear aboud the child it is well.

The kidnapper was irked by the Norfolk business. He was blaming Lindbergh for the delays in the negotiations. The kidnapper was also showing a little muscle—threatening to double the original ransom if the deal didn't go through within ten days. Even though the kidnapper held all the cards, he didn't threaten to harm the baby if things didn't move. Most kidnappers got their way by threatening to kill the victim.

Breckinridge was with Condon when John's letter came. He telephoned Lindbergh. There would be no more delays, Lindbergh said. It was time to act.

Lindbergh arrived at midnight. He was coatless and disguised in the hunting cap and sunglasses. He read John's letter. When he put it down he declared that the ransom money was ready. (Lindbergh had sold over $350,000 worth of stock to raise the $70,000 ransom.) "I want you to place an ad accepting John's terms," he said to Breckinridge. "We must pay the money as soon as possible. The end is finally in sight."

Sensing that the Colonel was in a good mood, Condon ventured, "Why can't the kidnappers take me to the baby? I'm willing to be their hostage. Let's confirm everything—then pay."

Breckinridge spoke: "The best answer to that, Doctor, is that John has repeatedly refused—and still refuses—to take you to the child."

"And," Colonel Lindbergh added, "if the ransom is raised again, I'm afraid . . ."

"I don't think there's any danger of that," Condon replied. "The kidnapper originally asked for fifty and he'll still take that amount. Let's make it clear that one sight of the baby will guarantee payment."

"But he's refused to do that from the beginning," Lindbergh said. "He's proven to us that he has the baby. We have no choice but to follow his demands."

"But how do we know he'll keep his promise? Once the money is paid, we've lost our leverage." Condon was afraid he had gone too far.

Breckinridge looked at Lindbergh then turned to Condon. "I'm sorry, you're overruled."

"All right," Condon said. "You're the boss. What should we do?"

"We'll prepare the ad," Breckinridge said. Following a brief discussion, Lindbergh and Breckinridge agreed upon the following language:

"I accept. Money is ready. Jafsie." [6]

The conference broke up at 3:30 in the morning. Lindbergh thanked Condon and assured him that the ordeal would soon be over. He then climbed into his car and drove back to Hopewell.

The Jafsie ad appeared in the *Home News* and the *Journal* on Tuesday, March 31. On the morning of the following day, Condon received a letter from John which read:

> Dear Sir. please handel inclosed letter to Col. Lindbergh. It is in Mr. Lindbergh interest not to notify police.

The envelope bore a Fordham Station postmark and contained a separate enclosure addressed to Colonel Lindbergh. It read:

> Dear Sir: have the money ready by Saturday evening. we will inform you where and how to deliver it. have the money in one bundle we want you to put it in a sertain place. Ther is no fear that somebody els will take it, we watch everything closely. Blease tell us know if you are agree and ready for action by Saturday evening—if yes put in paper
> "Yes everything O.K."
> It is a very simple delivery but we find out very sun (soon) if there is any trapp. After 8 houers you gett the Adr: from the boy. on the place
> you finde two
> ladies. the are
> innocence.

On the reverse side of the note John had written:

> "If it is too late we put it in the New York American for Saturday morning. Put it in New York Journal."

Condon called Breckinridge, who in turned telephoned Lindbergh. Two hours later, around noon, both men were in Condon's study. It was the first of April, a Friday.

Colonel Lindbergh read John's notes. He was particularly interested in the line— "After 8 houers you gett the Adr *from* the boy." The kidnapper had meant—*of* the boy.

76   This was disturbing. John was saying that Colonel Lindbergh would not get the baby immediately upon payment. Why the delay? Again Condon was skeptical. He wanted to make payment contingent upon seeing the baby. Colonel Lindbergh wouldn't hear of it. There was no time to complicate things with a counter-demand.

Lindbergh told Breckinridge to place the following ad:

> Yes. Everything O.K. Jafsie.

The ad would run in the *New York American* and the *New York Journal* on Saturday, April 2.

Colonel Lindbergh sat down at Condon's desk and wrote out a new authorization for Condon to deliver the seventy thousand dollars "to whomsoever in his judgment he believed to be the kidnappers of Charles Augustus Lindbergh, Jr."

Before coming to the Bronx, Lindbergh had informed Colonel Schwarzkopf of the impending ransom payoff. Schwarzkopf suggested that Condon be put under surveillance and followed to the rendezvous site. After the payment had been made, Schwarzkopf's men could follow John. Once the baby was in safe hands the kidnapper and his gang would be arrested.

Lindbergh emphatically rejected Schwarzkopf's idea. He said he didn't want the police anywhere near the payoff area. No one was to be followed. Schwarzkopf was to give his word on this.

Schwarzkopf could see there was no way to change Lindbergh's mind, so he agreed to stay out of the ransom picture. He gave his word.

Although everything was finally falling into place, Lindbergh was worried that the press would somehow get wind of the deal and destroy everthing. He was also worried that John would back out at the last moment.

With the final arrangements in place, Lindbergh drove back to Hopewell. He said he would return to the Bronx the next day. He was determined to make the deal before the weekend was out and to drive Condon to the rendezvous site himself.

While Lindbergh and Condon were awaiting their final instructions from John, the tabloids were full of stories about Curtis and Dobson-Peacock. The latter had apparently acquired a taste for publicity and was thoroughly enjoying his new status as a celebrity. On April 2, the *New York Daily News* reported that Curtis's wife had disappeared on a secret kidnap mission while her husband was at a designated spot waiting to be contacted by Sam. The lead-in to the article read: "Although members of the Lindbergh family have abandoned hope in their Norfolk emissaries, the three citizens of the Southern city declared yesterday that definite developments in their attempt to gain return of the kidnapped baby had occurred in the last twenty-four hours."[7]

Colonel Lindbergh hoped that the press would continue to look the wrong way while he, Condon, and John pulled off the deal.

A few days earlier, Elmer Irey of the IRS had come to Hopewell with three of his top investigators, Frank J. Wilson, Pat O'Rourke, and Arthur P. Madden. Lindbergh wanted Irey present when the final ransom arrangements were being made.

Irey didn't approve of the way the Lindbergh case was being handled. He agreed with Condon that unless Lindbergh got proof that the baby was alive, no ransom should be paid. Moreover, he liked Schwarzkopf's idea about following Condon to the ransom spot and arresting the kidnapper when the time was right. Irey believed the baby was probably dead. If that were true, all of Lindbergh's restraints on the police were unnecessary. Irey was worried that Lindbergh was giving the kidnappers a chance to get away.

As for the ransom money, Irey had a suggestion. In a year or so, the country was going off the gold standard. This meant that gold coins and gold certificate paper currency would be called in. The seventy thousand dollars that Lindbergh was about to release didn't contain a single gold certificate. These gold notes bore a round yellow seal that set them apart from ordinary bills. Once they became illegal, they would call attention to anyone who spent them. As ransom money, the gold notes would be easy to spot.

Irey found it hard to believe that no one had bothered to record the serial number to each ransom bill. Without such a list, the bills could not be identified as part of the ransom payment. The kidnappers could spend the unrecorded money without risk of detection. Lindbergh had chosen not to record the serial numbers because the kidnapper had warned him not to.

Irey put his foot down. Fair play was one thing—but this was absurd. He insisted that the ransom package be reassembled. The new bundle of money would contain gold notes and every serial number would be recorded.

Colonel Lindbergh objected to Irey's plan. He was convinced that the kidnappers would keep their word, and he was determined to keep his promises.

Irey held his ground. The Colonel was dealing with criminals. Besides, spiking the ransom package with gold notes and recording the serial numbers did not endanger the baby. The police had a right to go this far—and a duty to catch the criminals. Lindbergh must not be naive about this.

After thinking it over, Colonel Lindbergh reluctantly accepted Irey's plan for the ransom money. But he continued to insist on no police interference, and Dr. Condon was not to demand to see the baby before paying the money.[8]

The original ransom package was taken out of the special vault at the Fordham bank and returned to the J. P. Morgan company where IRS agents, with the help of fourteen bank clerks, assembled two new ransom packages in accordance with Irey's specifications.

It took eight hours to gather, package, and record the ransom money. The bills were divided into two bundles. The first package contained fifty thousand. All but fourteen thousand of it was in gold notes. The second, smaller package contained 400 fifty-dollar gold notes, which Irey thought would be the easiest to spot when spent. Together, the packages contained 5,150 bills. No two of the serial numbers were in sequence.

The ransom packages contained the denominations John had ordered—twenty-five thousand in twenties, fifteen thousand in tens, and ten thousand in fives. Bundles of the money were bound together by string. These stacks were made up of smaller packets held together by paper bands from the Morgan bank.

Samples of the string and the paper bands were placed into a J. P. Morgan bank vault. The samples might later be useful in identifying similar material found in the possession of a suspect.

The two ransom packages were placed in Al Reich's Ford and driven to Condon's house by Colonel Lindbergh himself. Colonel Breckinridge followed in his car.

Lindbergh and Breckinridge carried the bills into Dr. Condon's study where Condon was ready with the ballot box made to hold the money. When the bundles containing the fifty thousand dollars were packed into the box, there was no room for the remaining twenty thousand dollars. Colonel Lindbergh tried to stuff the second packet of bills into the box with his knee, but they wouldn't go. In the process he split one side of the box. He finally gave up and removed the twenty thousand dollars, which he wrapped into a separate package.

Since John might ask to see the money, Condon didn't lock the ballot box. He would save the key, however. It might later prove useful in identifying the box as the ransom carrier.

On Friday afternoon, the day the ransom money was being packaged in New York City, Betty Gow and Elsie Whateley had been strolling on the Lindbergh grounds. They were talking with the state policeman at the entrance gate. As they walked back to the house along the gravel driveway, something shiny caught their eye. Betty Gow bent over for a closer look. It was one of the baby's missing thumbguards. It was still attached to the string that had tied it to the baby's wrist. The servants ran into the house to show Mrs. Lindbergh.

Betty Gow and Elsie Whateley had walked up and down that driveway everyday since the kidnapping, but this was the first time either one of them had noticed the thumbguard. The discovery, coming on the day the final preparations were being made for the return of the baby, was interpreted as a good omen.

In Washington, D.C., Mrs. Evalyn Walsh McLean, the wealthy socialite and estranged wife of the owner of the *Washington Post,* was expecting to be holding the Lindbergh baby in her arms within the next few days. Her optimism had nothing to do with Dr. Condon and his progress with John. She knew nothing of that. Mrs. McLean was relying upon the word of Gaston B. Means, the man who had been entrusted with her hundred thousand dollars—money he would use to buy back the Lindbergh child.

On this day, Means had assured Mrs. McLean that within the week she would be delivering the baby to the Lindberghs. The gangsters had been very cautious, but thanks to Gaston's skillful negotiations, the deal was about to go through. Consumed by anticipation, Mrs. McLean sat by her telephone and waited.

On Saturday, John Hughes Curtis telephoned the Lindbergh estate with urgent news. Colonel Lindbergh wasn't home, so Curtis talked with Morris Rosner. Curtis said he had a person with him who had been sent by the kidnappers. This man possessed a letter that he would only give to Colonel Lindbergh.

Since his March 22 visit with Lindbergh, Curtis had been busy. On March 26, 27, and 28, he had met with Sam at the cafeteria in Manhattan. Sam had said that the Lindbergh child was being cared for by a German nurse. He had agreed, at some later date, to take Curtis to meet the other members of the kidnap gang.

A few days earlier, Curtis had telephoned Dobson-Peacock with the latest news. The kidnappers had lowered their ransom demand to twenty-five thousand. Excited about these developments, the Reverend had driven to Hopewell, where he had met with Lindbergh, who told him that he would not deal with the kidnappers until they proved they had the baby. The churchman returned to Norfolk feeling a bit deflated.[9]

John Curtis was talking to Morris Rosner on this very day that Lindbergh was in the Bronx awaiting final word from John. Curtis told Rosner that he had an urgent message. Several hours later, Lindbergh managed to get back to Curtis. The Colonel said the messenger would have to wait. He could deliver his letter later. Lindbergh said he was sorry, but he had urgent business. He then hung up.

On Saturday morning, April 2, the ad—"Yes. Everything O.K. Jafsie."—had appeared in the two newspapers.

Later that afternoon, Breckinridge, Reich, Condon, and Lindbergh were gathered in Condon's living room. They were waiting to hear from John. Colonel Lindbergh was in a good mood—but he was nervous—afraid that at the last minute something would go wrong. Condon's wife and daughter were worried about the old man. He was, after all, the only one who could identify John. Once the kidnapper had the money, Jafsie could be shot. Lindbergh, aware of the danger, had tucked a small handgun into his belt.

Everything was ready. John had said—"have the money ready by Saturday evening. we will inform you where and how to deliver it." The money was ready and Lindbergh and Condon were poised to deliver it. They would use Al Reich's Ford. Lindbergh looked at Condon and said, "We would all understand if you chose at this point to withdraw from the case. As intermediary you are not expected to deliver the money and risk your life. It is *my* son and I'm willing to take the money to them."

"Nonsense, Colonel. I *want* to do it. I want to see those little arms around his mother's neck. I'm not afraid." Condon said.[10]

They waited. It was starting to get dark. Since they hadn't received a letter that day they were waiting for a messenger or a phone call.

At 7:45 the doorbell rang. Doctor Condon rushed to the door. He opened it and saw a man wearing a taxi driver's cap walking down the front steps. The cab driver had left an envelope. Condon tore it open. With Lindbergh and Breckinridge at his side, Condon read the note out loud:

> Dear Sir: take a car and follow east tremont Ave to the east until you reach the number 3225 east tremont ave.
> It is a nursery.
> Bergen
> Greenhauses florist

ther is a table standing outside right on the door, you find a letter undernead the table covert with a stone, read and follow instruction.

On the reverse side of the note there were further instructions and warnings:

don't speak to anyone on the way. If there is a ratio alarm for policecar, we warn you, we have the same eqipnent. have the money in one bundle.
We give you ¾ of a houer to reach the place.

Lindbergh and Condon hurried to the car. Lindbergh slid behind the wheel and Condon climbed in next to him. He held the ballot-box and the twenty-thousand-dollar ransom packet on his lap.

The little Ford sputtered east on Gun Hill Road. After traveling a mile and a half, Lindbergh swung south onto Westchester Avenue. When they reached Tremont, Lindbergh wheeled east again. At this point they were less than a mile from the J. A. Bergen Greenhouses.

As they drove, Condon couldn't help thinking about Lindbergh's gun. He didn't dare let on that he knew about it, but if Lindbergh decided at the last minute to deliver the money himself, or to come along to witness the exchange, things could get out of hand. Condon was worried. There was no telling what Lindbergh might do if he came face to face with the kidnapper. Condon realized that he might have to persuade Colonel Lindbergh to stay in the car.

As the car approached Whittemore Avenue and the Bergen Greenhouses, Condon knew that John had brought them to another graveyard. This time it was St. Raymond's, an East Bronx cemetery bordered on the north by Tremont Avenue.

Whittemore Avenue cut through St. Raymond's and came to an end at Tremont. The Bergen Greenhouses and flower shop were on the north side of Tremont facing Whittemore and the cemetery.

Condon spotted the table. It was to the right of the flower shop's entrance. Lindbergh drove past the shop then made a U-turn and pulled up in front of it. Condon hurried to the table. He saw the note, held down by a rock. He carried it back to the car. Lindbergh unfolded the paper, and using the light from the dash, read:

Cross the street and walk to the next corner and follow whittemore Ave to the soud [south] Take the money with you. Come alone
and walk
I will meet you

Lindbergh switched off the engine. "I'm coming with you," he said.

"The note says to come alone," Condon blurted as he scrambled out of the car.

"All right," Lindbergh replied. He handed Condon the ballot box and the other package.

"I don't need the money yet," Condon said, "I'll come back for it." [11]

Condon walked east. He stopped under the streetlight on the corner of Whittemore and Tremont and looked down the dark and deserted road leading into the cemetery. Along the eastern side of the lane were bushes, and beyond the shrubbery stood the tombstones, statues, and crosses. Condon realized the gang could be hiding behind the bushes or among the gravestones. He was an easy target for an ambush.

Instead of following John's instructions to walk south on Whittemore into the cemetery, Condon proceeded east along Tremont, which was better lit. By taking this route, he could see behind the shrubbery and the tombstones.

Condon walked about a hundred yards along Tremont, keeping his eyes on the bushes and the tombstones. He then turned around abruptly and headed back to the street lamp on the corner. Condon crossed the street to Colonel Lindbergh and the car. "There doesn't seem to be anybody here," he said. Condon hoped his fear didn't show. He tried to be calm.

Before Lindbergh could speak, Condon heard a voice. It came from the tombstones: "Hey, Doctor!"

"All right," Condon answered back. Beads of sweat were on his forehead. His heart pounded wildly. The voice was John's. Colonel Lindbergh had also heard it.

John called out again, "Here, Doctor. Over here! Over here!"

Leaving Lindbergh, Condon walked briskly down Whittemore Avenue into the cemetery. When he got inside the graveyard he saw a figure moving through the tombstones in the direction he was walking. As Condon headed down the hill into the cemetery, the figure moving with him edged closer to the road. Wary of an ambush, Condon kept to the middle of the lane.

About a hundred feet south of Tremont, the man in the cemetery came to an access road that shot east off Whittemore. A five-foot cement wall ran along this road, cutting across the path of the man who was keeping up with Condon. Condon watched the figure climb the wall, cross the access road, then scale a low fence that ran along the south side of the little road. After jumping to the ground on the other side of that fence, the man crouched behind a shrub directly to Condon's left.

"Hello," he said from behind the bush.

Condon walked slowly to the spot where the man was hiding. "How are you?" Condon said. "What are you doing crouched down there?"

The man stood up. Condon recognized him as John. The two men were standing three feet from each other. John made no effort to hide his face. He was wearing the same fedora hat, and a black suit. "Did you ever see me before?" Condon asked.

"Yes. Don't you remember? Saturday night in the cemetery at Woodlawn. Have you gotitt the money?"

"No, it's in the car."

"Who is up there?"

"Colonel Lindbergh."

"Is he armed?"

"No," Condon lied. "Where is the baby?"

"You could not get the baby for about six, eight hours."

"You must take me to the baby."

"I have told you before that is impossible. It cannot be done. My father won't let me."

"Is your father in this too?" Condon asked.

"Yes. Give me the money."

Condon shook his head. "Not until you give me a receipt, a note showing where the baby is."

"I haven't got it with me."

"Then get it," Condon said.

"All right. You will wait."

"Yes. And John—these are hard times. Colonel Lindbergh is not so rich. He had a hard time raising the fifty thousand dollars. I can go to the car and get that much."

John shrugged his shoulders. "Since it is so hard it will be all right, I guess. I suppose if we can't get seventy we'll take fifty."

"Now where is the receipt—the note showing where the baby is?"

"I'll be back with the note in ten minutes," John replied. He turned and disappeared behind the tombstones.

Condon headed back to the car. It was 9:16.

Lindbergh watched anxiously as Condon crossed Tremont Avenue. As soon as the old man was in earshot, Lindbergh asked, "Well?"

"I've met him. He wants the money."

Lindbergh reached into the car for the ballot box and the package containing the twenty thousand.

"Just the box," Condon said. "I talked him out of the other twenty."

Lindbergh was grateful but his mind was on the child. "What about the baby?"

"John is giving us a receipt—a note that will direct us to the child. I must hurry back."

Carrying the ballot box under his arm, Condon retraced his steps across Tremont Avenue.

Nervous and full of anticipation, Lindbergh watched the black overcoat and derby hat pass beneath the street light and disappear in to the darkness.

Condon had reached the access road and the low fence running beside it. He stopped there and waited. A few minutes later he heard footsteps coming from within the cemetery. It was 9:29. John had been gone thirteen minutes.

The moment John reached the bushes along Whittemore Avenue, he asked. "Have you *gottit* the money?"

"Yes. Have you got the note?"

"Yes."

Condon handed the ballot box as John tendered the note. Condon stuffed the envelope into his coat pocket. John was on his knees inspecting the money. "Wait until I see if it is all right," he said.

"The box contains fifty thousand dollars in fives, tens, and twenties—just as you instructed. And the bills are not marked," Condon said.

"I guess it is all right," John replied. He put a packet of the bills into his left-hand coat pocket, then stood up. He held the box in front of him. "Don't open the envelope for six hours," he demanded.

Condon shook his head affirmatively. "I will not open it. You can trust me."

"We trust you," John said. "Everybody says your work has been perfect."

The two men shook hands. As they did Condon made a last-minute plea to see the baby. "You have the money. Take me to the child. Please."

"That is impossible."

"If you double-cross me—"

"The baby is all right," John said. "You'll find him on the boad *Nelly,* like the note says."

John turned and disappeared into the cemetery with fifty thousand dollars of Colonel Lindbergh's money. Condon hurried back to the car.

"The baby—where is the baby?" Lindbergh asked.

"He's on a boat. The details are in this note." Condon handed Lindbergh the envelope. "John said that we are not to open it for six hours. He said the baby is all right. They need six hours to escape. The boat is called *Nelly.*"

Lindbergh slipped the envelope into his pocket and started the car. "We'll keep our end of the bargain," he muttered as they pulled away from the curb.

Condon was sorry he had mentioned his promise not to open the envelope. It was not a pledge he had intended to keep. Condon should have known that the Colonel, with his sense of fair play, would keep his word. Lindbergh would even keep a promise to the people who had stolen his son.

They were now driving west on Tremont Avenue approaching Westchester Square. Condon pointed to a house he owned and asked Lindbergh to stop in front of it. The house was located about a mile west of the cemetery. Colonel Lindbergh pulled up and stopped in front of the house. Both men got out of the car and climbed the steps to the front porch. "This is a good place to open the note," Condon said. Lindbergh was hesitant. He had made a promise, and so far John had kept his word. The men were sitting on the porch with their feet resting on the top step.

Condon gave Lindbergh an excuse to open the envelope: "You didn't promise the kidnapper anything," he said. "*I* made the promise. Besides we should make sure the note contains good enough instructions. And a delay could endanger the baby's life."

Lindbergh slapped the palm of his hand with the envelope. He looked at Condon, then tore it open. Scrawled on the little piece of paper were the following instructions:

> The boy is on the Boad Nelly. It is a small boad 28 feet long. Two persons are on the boad. The are innosent. you will find the Boad between Horseneck Beach and gay Head near Elizabeth Island.

Colonel Lindbergh could barely contain his joy. It had been a month and a day since the kidnapping and now he was about to get his baby back. His hands were trembling as he reread the note. When he finished he put the note back into his pocket. He grabbed Condon's arm and said, "Let's go back to the house, Doctor."

> We've been double-crossed.
>
> —CHARLES LINDBERGH

7 THE "BOAD" *NELLY*

COLONEL LINDBERGH and his seventy-two-year-old intermediary returned to Condon's house with good news—thanks to Dr. Condon's courage, the kidnapper had been contacted and the ransom money paid. In exchange, Condon had learned that the baby was on a twenty-eight-foot boat called *Nelly* at sea somewhere near the Elizabeth Islands off the coast of Massachusetts. Amid the jubilant handshakes and pats on the back, Colonels Lindbergh and Breckinridge slipped out of the living room to confer privately and to make a few telephone calls. A short time later Lindbergh and his advisor came back into the room and announced that they were leaving. Lindbergh asked Condon and Reich if they could come along. Condon and his friend said yes.

Lindbergh and his three passengers drove to a house in mid-Manhattan owned by his mother-in-law. Elmer Irey, Frank Wilson, and several other IRS men were waiting for them in the expensively furnished library.

While Lindbergh and Breckinridge conferred in another room, Elmer Irey questioned Condon about his two meetings with John. Condon described John as being five feet ten and weighing 160 pounds. The kidnapper had a triangular face with high cheekbones, almond-shaped eyes, large ears, and a straight nose. John's eyebrows were straight and thick and his shoulders were slightly stooped.

An IRS agent made a sketch of John based on this description. Condon viewed the drawing and was amazed at how closely it resembled the kidnapper.

The old man was proud of himself. He had performed a successful mission for the world's most beloved hero—a man he personally idolized. His efforts as intermediary would bring him the gratitude of the Lindberghs, the Morrows and the American people. He would, in effect, become a member of the Lindbergh family.

Trying hard to conceal his self-satisfaction, Condon told Irey how he had saved the Lindberghs twenty thousand dollars. Irey leaned forward in his chair.

"Wait a minute," he said. "What did you do?" The government agent looked concerned.

Condon was confused. He explained that he had withheld the small package containing the twenty thousand dollars. Did he do something wrong?

He had done something terribly wrong. That little package was full of fifty-dollar gold certificates—four hundred of them. These were the big bills, the ones that would be the easiest to spot—and to trace. That was the idea behind that package. The largest bills in the big package—the twenties—were much less conspicuous.

Condon could see what he had done. He had great respect for Irey and he realized that he had let his government down.[1]

Irey saw that Condon was devastated. A moment earlier he had been patting himself on the back, now he was sullen. Suddenly Irey felt that he had been too hard on the old man. He put his hand on Condon's shoulder and said that it wasn't his fault. No one had taken the time to tell him about the fifty-dollar gold notes and what they were all about. Condon had just been looking out for Colonel Lindbergh's financial interests. Unlike Rosner and his sleazy assistants, Condon was doing this for free. He was even paying his own expenses.[2]

"Don't worry about it, Dr. Condon," Irey said. "It would have been months before they got around to those bills."

Irey laid a map of the Bronx on top of the large mahogany library table. Condon pointed out the places in the two cemeteries and Van Cortlandt Park where he had encountered John. Condon said that John had jumped over the fence along the southern border of the access road leading into St. Raymond's Cemetery. When he did, his left foot sank into the mud of a freshly covered grave. Irey asked Condon if he could find that spot. Condon replied that he could. Irey said that there was a good chance that John had left a shoe print.

Colonel Lindbergh, Breckinridge, and two men Condon didn't know entered the library. They all took seats around the big table. Lindbergh said that he had just called Washington, D.C., and that navy airplanes were being readied to assist in the search for the boat *Nelly*. Lindbergh had also arranged to have a large amphibious aircraft, a giant Sikorsky, waiting for him at an airport outside Bridgeport, Connecticut.

At two in the morning, Breckinridge, Condon, Reich, and Irey climbed into Lindbergh's car and headed for the airstrip. When they arrived there two hours later, it was still dark. Condon and Reich waited in the car while Lindbergh and the others conferred with officers of the airport.

At dawn, the huge Sikorsky landed at the airstrip. Lindbergh inspected the ship, talked with the pilot, then took off with his four passengers. Al Reich stayed behind—he had agreed to drive Lindbergh's car to the Aviation Country Club near Hempstead, Long Island, where Lindbergh would be landing with the baby.

Lindbergh circled the field and flew east to the Connecticut shore. He then headed north. Before long Lindbergh and his crew were over the northern end of Long Island Sound heading toward Martha's Vineyard off the coast of Massachusetts, near which the Elizabeth Islands were clustered.

Breckinridge was sitting in the front seat next to Lindbergh. Irey and Condon were directly behind them. Although everyone was excited and in high spirits, Condon was the only one talking. Above the roar of the engines he was reciting *Hamlet* and biblical quotes. Irey found himself wondering about this strange old man and his unusual connection to the Lindberghs.

As they approached Cuttyhunk Island, one of the Islands in the Elizabeth group, six Coast Guard cutters came into sight. Lindbergh also saw a navy man-of-war steaming toward the islands. Lindbergh was flying low so his passengers could scan the waters for a craft answering the description of the *Nelly*. For the next six hours, the aircraft roared over dozens of boats. None matched John's description of *Nelly*, so Lindbergh widened his search. As the morning wore on, the hunt became less systematic. Eventually Lindbergh was flying randomly, buzzing over everything afloat. No one had spoken for several hours—even Condon was quiet. Colonel Lindbergh's face was pale and drawn and he looked tired and beaten.

At noon, Lindbergh landed in the waters off Buzzard's Bay and taxied to Cuttyhunk Island. He wasn't hungry, but he thought his passengers were ready for lunch. As the men walked to the only place to eat on the island, an old hotel, Lindbergh was accosted by a group of reporters. The newsmen didn't know about the ransom payment, but they knew Lindbergh had been flying in the area. Mistaking Dr. Condon for John Curtis, they concluded that Lindbergh was searching for his son.

Lindbergh strode past the reporters while Breckinridge pleaded with them to stop asking questions.

Lindbergh ordered lunch but didn't eat. He only spoke when spoken to, and his responses were brief and sullen.

After lunch Lindbergh and his party searched the waters off southern Massachusetts. They saw nothing resembling the boat *Nelly*.

Just before dark Lindbergh landed the plane on Long Island where Al Reich waited with the car. The five men squeezed into the car and Lindbergh drove back to New York City. No one spoke.

In mid-Manhattan Lindbergh broke the awful silence. To Condon he said, "I'll drive you and Al home."

"Please don't, Colonel. We can get home on the El."

"I'll take you home," Lindbergh said.

"It isn't necessary," Condon replied.

Lindbergh stopped the car near the stairs to an uptown subway station. He stepped out of the car with Condon and Reich. "We've been double-crossed," he said matter-of-factly.

Condon was speechless—he looked blankly into Lindbergh's face.

"Well, Doctor," Lindbergh said in a dull voice, "what's the bill for your services?"

Condon blanched. The Colonel had insulted him. But that was all right—Lindbergh wasn't himself. He was anguished and bitter. It suddenly dawned on Condon that Lindbergh hadn't been prepared for this. He had actually trusted the kidnappers. The Colonel still wasn't sure what all of this meant, and he didn't know what to do. Condon marveled at the Colonel's naiveté. He should never have counted on the goodwill of those people. They were, after all, criminals who had stolen his son.

"I have no bill," Condon replied.

Lindbergh's face expressed a silent apology. "But I would feel better about it if you'd let me—"

"No," Condon said. "My family and I don't need the money. Besides, I never accept money from a man poorer than myself." The old teacher smiled.

Lindbergh climbed back into the car. "I'm grateful," he said. The vehicle lurched forward. Standing there, Condon and Reich watched the car until it drove out of sight. When it was gone the two men turned and climbed the stairs to the uptown subway.[3]

Lindbergh dropped Irey and Breckinridge off in Manhattan, then headed back to Hopewell. He hadn't been alone much since the kidnapping. Now, by himself for the first time in several days, he could think. He thought of his wife waiting at home for the baby. How would she react when she realized he had come back empty-handed? He would have to make her understand that this was only a delay. She was not to lose hope. Tomorrow he would continue looking for the boat. Maybe it had been premature to conclude that they had been double-crossed. There were dozens of reasons why the boat *Nelly* was not where John had said it was. The kidnappers might have been frightened off by all of the naval activity. Maybe they had hidden the boat or disguised it.

Lindbergh turned off Amwell Road onto the dirt lane that led to the estate. The brightly lit house came into view. Lindbergh noticed that the lights were on in the nursery. They hadn't been on since the abduction.

Mrs. Lindbergh heard the car on the gravel and rushed to the door to accept her baby. Although she had prepared herself for the worst, the sight of her husband without the child terrified her. Before she could speak, Lindbergh, pale and exhausted, assured her that it was only a delay. The search would continue, he said, and if necessary they would recontact the kidnappers. Everything would be all right. They would just have to be patient.

As long as her husband was optimistic, Mrs. Lindbergh was too. She had confidence in his abilities and judgment.

On Monday, April 4, the earlier message to John appeared in the *Home News* for the second time. The ad was now a cruel mockery: "Yes. Everything O.K. Jafsie."

Meanwhile, Lindbergh reporters, aware that something was afoot, were speculating wildly. On April 4, the *New York Daily News* reported that Lindbergh had "slipped through the cordon of watchers about his Sourland home and is absent on a mysterious mission."[4]

Dr. Condon returned to St. Raymond's Cemetery on Monday morning with his son-in-law, Ralph Hacker, and a FBI agent named Thomas Sisk. Condon led the men to the freshly covered grave John had landed on when he scaled the fence bordering the access road into the cemetery. As Condon had expected, there was a shoe impression in the dirt mound. Agent Sisk and Ralph Hacker made a plaster-of-paris cast of the foot print.

At daybreak Colonel Lindbergh was back in the air searching the Atlantic coastal waters. He was flying a Lockheed-Vega monoplane from the Teterboro Airport in New Jersey. Today he searched alone.

Lindbergh flew over the Elizabeth Islands, Martha's Vineyard, and the Coast Guard cutters that were still patrolling these seas. By noon his hopes were fading—he had spotted nothing that looked like the *Nelly*. That afternoon he searched as far south as Virginia.

At 6:30 Lindbergh landed at the Teterboro Airport. When he got off the plane he was carrying a small suitcase and the baby's favorite blanket.

It was dark when he got back to Hopewell. The windows of the big house were still ablaze in anticipation of the baby. He dreaded the idea of facing his wife at the door. When she came to him this time he couldn't mask his depression. He was too distraught and exhausted. They embraced.

"I'm sorry," he said.

This time she was the one who comforted. Everything would be all right, she said. They would just have to be patient.

Breckinridge spent Monday evening in the Bronx at Dr. Condon's house. He telephoned Hopewell and learned that Colonel Lindbergh had again returned without the baby. Breckinridge said that it was too early to concede that they had been double-crossed. He still believed the baby was alive. He was sure that John would get back in touch with them. He told Condon that no one in his right mind would murder the child of Charles A. Lindbergh. That would be suicide.

Dr. Condon was less optimistic. Even so, he felt there was a fairly good chance that the kidnappers would make good their promises to deliver the baby. Condon suggested they run the following ad in the *Bronx Home News* for fifteen days:

What is wrong? Have you crossed me? Please, better directions. Jafsie.

Breckinridge authorized the ad and Condon called it in to the paper that night. The next day, Tuesday, April 5, it appeared in the *Home News*.

Amid conflicting press reports, Schwarzkopf announced, "No definite nor authentic information concerning the restoration of the baby has been received by the police."[5] While Schwarzkopf was telling reporters that Colonel Lindbergh had not left his estate, several newsmen saw Lindbergh at various places wearing goggles, a pilot's jacket, and a flying hat. Other reporters had seen him in his 180-mile-per-hour Lockheed Vega monoplane with its familiar number—NC-49-M.

Condon stuck close to home all day Tuesday. He wanted to be available in the event John tried to get in touch with him. The day's mail carried no message from John. That night Colonel Breckinridge went to the Bronx to wait with him. The intermediary and the lawyer waited patiently in Condon's living room for the phone to ring or for a messenger to knock on the door. They waited in vain.

The following day, April 6, the treasurer of the United States, W. O. Wood, authorized the distribution of a fifty-seven page pamphlet listing the serial numbers of the 4,750 bills that had been given to John. The booklet was sent to financial institutions through-out the world. (Later the serial numbers were printed on a single sheet measuring seventeen by twenty-eight inches.) Bank tellers, without being told why, were asked to get in touch with the Treasury Department if they came across one of these bills. Since bank employees didn't make a habit of noting the serial numbers of the bills they handled, no one seriously expected that the pamphlet would lead to the capture of the kidnappers. There was always a chance, however, that a teller's suspicion would be aroused by some-one making a large cash deposit. But even this was unlikely, since the pamphlet made no mention of the Lindbergh case.

On Wednesday, the day the books were being sent out of Washington, D.C., a brush fire swept through two hundred acres of the Lindbergh's property. Colonel Lindbergh, Oliver Whateley, and a dozen or so state troopers used brooms and shovels to beat it out before the flames reached the house.

Back in the Bronx, Condon and Breckinridge were still waiting to hear from the kidnappers. The days passed—the sixth, the seventh, and the eighth. There was no word. The case had suddenly come to a standstill. In a letter to her mother-in-law on April 8, Mrs. Lindbergh complained about the press:

> The *Herald Tribune* of Wednesday 6 had a short good editorial by Walter Lippmann, called 'Let Lindbergh Alone,' quoting C.'s statement about feeling he did not have to report every action of his and that he should be left free to carry on his actions privately. The *Herald Tribune* and the *Times* and others have been very good, but the tabloids I believe have cost us this terrible delay and waiting and we don't know what in the future. I think such papers are really criminal outside of their inaccuracies.[6]

The *New York Daily News* was responsible for some of the most inaccurate and sensational reporting. On April 6 it carried the headline: "ANNE WAITS IN HIGH HOPES, EXPECTING BABY'S RETURN"; on April 7: "'MET GANG, SAW LINDY,' SAYS CURTIS AFTER TRIP"; on April 8: "LINDY SPURS AGENTS ON; THEY WAIT KIDNAP CALL"; and on April 9: "BABY'S CLOTHES SIGHTED ON RUM SHIP, LINDY TOLD."

On April 8, a teller in a Newark bank figured out that the bills in the fifty-seven page booklet pertained to the Lindbergh case. From this he deduced that the Lindberghs had paid the money but had not gotten their baby. The teller tested his theory on a reporter for the *Newark News,* who was so sure it was correct he published it. The wire services picked up the story and within hours it was being reported in every newspaper in the country.

Colonel Lindbergh's worst fear had become reality. His dealings with the kidnappers were no longer secret. The revelation had come at a most sensitive time—just when he was trying to reestablish communications with John. Now the kidnappers knew that the serial numbers had been recorded and sent to every bank in the world. Lindbergh was terrified that the gang would consider this a betrayal. What would this do to the baby? Did this mean more delays in the negotiations?

On April 9, Colonel Lindbergh authorized Colonel Schwarzkopf to release a statement confirming that fifty thousand dollars had been paid to the kidnappers, who had not kept their end of the bargain.[7]

The *New York Daily News* responded to this revelation by offering a fifty thousand dollar reward for the safe return of the baby.

In a letter to her mother-in-law on April 10, Anne Lindbergh said that it was true that they had paid $50,000 to one of the kidnappers. Mrs. Lindbergh then raised the subject of the baby's well-being:

> C. does not think (nor do others)—though of course there is always that possibility—that the baby has been killed. They say it is harder to dispose of a dead baby than a live one. There is the chance that he died, but he was over his cold and was a strong baby. C. doesn't think there is much chance of that. He tells me not to be discouraged.[8]

On Monday, April 11, nine days after Condon handed the ballot box to John in St. Raymond's Cemetery, the *New York Times* broke the story that Condon was Jafsie. Several months before the kidnapping, Dr. Condon had showed a young man some poems he had written. They had been signed J.F.C. When the young fellow saw the ads in the *Home News* he made the connection. A few days later the young man, an aspiring journalist, told a reporter for the *New York Times* that Jafsie was John Condon. The secret was out.[9]

Now, Condon's home on Decatur Avenue became a journalistic hot spot. Reporters rang his doorbell, tapped on his windows, trampled his flower beds, and gathered in his yard, sidewalk and front porch. Condon had no choice but to agree to a press conference in his living room. Reporters poured into the house until there wasn't room for another person. When things quieted down, Condon said there was much he couldn't tell. He was sure, however, that the kidnappers would keep their word and return the baby. The kidnap gang had feared a trap, he said. There had been too much naval activity around the area where the baby was to be picked up. So new arrangements would have to be made. Condon wanted to assure everyone that Colonel Lindbergh had not been duped.

Condon had nothing more to say. The reporters and photographers were ushered out of the house. But they didn't go away—the Lindbergh case was too big a story, and Condon was too hot to ignore. He was dealing directly with the people who had stolen Lindbergh's son. So, instead of leaving, the reporters camped on the sidewalk of Condon's house. The bolder ones took up positions in his yard and on his porch.

Several times during the day Condon appeared at the door to plead with the reporters to leave—he explained that he still had important business with the kidnappers. How could he arrange for the return of the baby with an army of reporters on his tail? The baby's life was at stake.

The situation at Condon's house worried Colonel Lindbergh. As long as the press camped at Condon's door, he was useless as an intermediary. Without Condon, it would be extremely difficult to establish contact with the kidnappers. Without Condon, how was he to get the baby back?

Lindbergh met with Colonel Schwarzkopf and representatives of the New York City Police Department and asked them to see if they could get the newspapers to call off their reporters. The next day, Schwarzkopf reported that the editors and publishers of the various news organizations in the city were sympathetic and pledged their support. For a day or so things at the Condon house were back to normal. But it didn't last. The *New York Daily News* decided not to cooperate, and when its competitors got word of this, they sent their newsmen back to the neighborhood. Once again Condon was under siege. Everywhere he went he was surrounded by reporters. The old man nearly caused a riot when he went to Long Island Sound to enjoy a few hours of leisure boating. As he rowed his canoe an unruly mob of reporters and curious onlookers ran along the shore. Word had gotten out that Jafsie was about to find the body of the Lindbergh baby.

Condon had become a celebrity. Although the publicity had stripped him of his role as intermediary, he still had a vital role to play in the investigation. He was the only person in the world who had seen John.

As the only eyewitness, much of Condon's time was taken up by the police. They showed him hundreds of mug shots and took him to jails in New Jersey and New York City to view prisoners. He was virtually police property.

Condon had also become public property. All of a sudden total strangers were telephoning him at all hours of the day and night. It got so disruptive he had to get an unlisted phone number.

On the days following his unmasking, Condon received over two thousand letters, many from people who thanked him for his services to the Lindberghs. But there was also crank mail, letters from spiritualists and the like who told him of their dreams, visions, and contacts with the dead. Most disturbing was the hate mail. Many of those who wrote Condon accused him of stealing Colonel Lindbergh's fifty thousand dollars. One letter simply said: "Enclosed you will find a picture of 'John,' the kidnapper." The enclosure was a mirror.

Condon was shocked and humiliated by this. It was bad enough that he had been unable to get the baby back; now he would have to live with the knowledge that many people believed that he had something to do with the kidnapping.

At noon on April 13, two days after the *New York Times* broke the story about John Condon being Jafsie, Insp. Harry Walsh of the Jersey City Police Department went to the Morrow estate in Englewood to question the maid, Violet Sharpe. The plump twenty-eight-year-old had been questioned on March 10 at the Lindbergh estate by Det. Edward McGrath and John F. Schiable of the Newark Police Department. The initial interview had been part of a routine questioning of all the domestic employees.

In her first interview, Violet had been unfriendly and very nervous. Not only that, her answers had been evasive and vague. The dark-haired, high-strung Englishwoman had told the Newark officers that on the evening of the kidnapping a man she knew had called her and asked her out to a movie. She had accepted, and at 8:30 he and another couple came to the Morrow estate to pick her up. After the movie this man drove her directly back to the Morrow house. She got home slightly before eleven o'clock.

92   As the detectives pressed Violet for details, she became evasive and coy. For example, she couldn't remember her date's name or the names of the other couple. As for the movie, she didn't remember its title or what it was about.

As a rule, detectives become suspicious when the person they are questioning is uncooperative or evasive. They often interpret this as a sign of guilt. And once their suspicions are aroused, they are reluctant to let go until they have resolved the issue. This is why, over a month later, Violet Sharpe was being questioned again by Schwarzkopf's friend and colleague, Inspector Harry Walsh.

Walsh had decided to talk to Violet at the Morrow estate in the hope that the familiar surroundings would reduce the tension and allow a more cordial interview.

Walsh asked Violet about her former employment, residence, and social habits. His tone was conversational and his manner friendly. The maid seemed to be in a cooperative mood. She had been born, she said, in 1904 in Berkshire, England. She left England for Canada in 1929, and nine months later entered the United States. She took up residence at the YWCA on Thirty-eighth Street in New York City. She lived there for two or three weeks. She signed up with a Madison Avenue employment agency and through that company was found employment as a waitress in the home of Mrs. Morrow in Englewood.

Violet said she had a sister named Emily who had worked in the home of Miss Constance Chilton, a friend of the Morrows. Emily was currently back in England.

Walsh carefully brought the questioning around to the night of the kidnapping—the night she and her date and the other couple went to the movies. Walsh wanted to know if she had since been able to recall anything about that picture.

Violet said that she hadn't gone to the theater that night. She had been mistaken about that. Instead, she, her escort, and the other couple drove to a roadhouse called the Peanut Grill. She couldn't say where the bar was exactly, except that it was an hour's drive from Englewood. It was in one of the "Oranges." (Orange, New Jersey, or Orangeburg, New York).

A few days later, when Violet's date telephoned her at the Morrow estate, she learned that his name was Ernie. She didn't know his last name and still couldn't provide the names of the couple.

Walsh was puzzled. A roadhouse was an unlikely place for a respectable girl like Violet—particularly when she was there with people she hardly knew.

Upset over the implication that she wasn't respectable, Violet became defensive. She explained how she had come to meet this Ernie man. Her account of their meeting was the same as the one she had given the Newark officers a month earlier. She and her sister had met a man in a car along Lydecker Street. They were on foot and he gave them a lift home. At eight o'clock on the night of March 1, this man called and set up the date.[11]

When she got home that night Violet answered the Morrow telephone and learned of the kidnapping.

On March 6, Ernie called and asked her to go to the movies. She said she was too busy. He never called again.[12]

Harry Walsh asked Violet to describe Ernie and the other man and woman. Violet said that Ernie was tall and thin and that he had fair hair and a light complexion. He was dressed in a dark-gray overcoat, a light-gray hat, and a navy blue suit. He was about twenty-four years old. The other man was short, had blond hair, and was of medium build. He was wearing a soft felt hat and a dark-gray overcoat. He was Ernie's age. The woman was dark-skinned, good-looking, and of average height and build. She was dressed in a navy blue suit, a little black hat, and black shoes. Walsh realized that he would be leaving the Morrow estate with more questions than answers. Was there any conversation that night, he asked, about the Lindberghs or the baby?

"Yes," Violet replied. "The girl asked me 'How is Lindy's baby?' I responded by saying that he was a very cute little fellow."

Following the interview, Walsh drove to Hopewell to discuss Violet Sharpe with Captain Lamb. Walsh told the Captain that Violet's statement didn't ring true. She had been dating Septimus Banks; in fact, there had been talk that they were getting married. According to the other servants, Violet never socialized with anyone outside the household staff. So why did she go to a speakeasy with a strange couple and a man who had picked her up on the street? The fact that she and her sister had gotten into a strange car was in itself hard to believe.

Captain Lamb said that Lieutenant Keaten's investigators had turned up something disturbing about Violet's sister Emily. On the day of the kidnapping, she had applied for a visa to return to England, and on April 6, just four days after the ransom payment, she had set sail for home. She had done this without notifying the police.

Inspector Walsh and Captain Lamb knew that Mrs. Morrow stood squarely behind all of her employees, including Violet. But how could a person of Mrs. Morrow's background judge such things? In matters like this a detective had to rely on his own instincts.

Schwarzkopf and his men were frustrated—after six weeks of hard work in the United States and in Europe, the investigation was floundering and running out of steam. It had produced more questions than answers. The kidnappers had taken the baby, had gotten the ransom money, and had double-crossed the Lindberghs. The police had been left holding the bag. They didn't have much to go on—a homemade ladder, a chisel, fifteen ransom notes, and an eccentric old eyewitness.

Now that everything about the case was public, Schwarzkopf found himself under tremendous pressure to get the baby back and catch the kidnappers.

Schwarzkopf's task was complicated by the possibility that the Lindbergh baby was still alive and at the mercy of the kidnappers. Although he secretly believed that the child was dead, he had to operate on the assumption that the baby was alive.

It was a bad time for everyone in the case. Anne Lindbergh, in a letter to her mother-in-law, summed things up this way:

> . . . we are at a standstill of course until the publicity dies down. It is still front-page headlines here.

In the meantime all tips from telephone calls, letters, etc. are followed up daily. They never seem to come to anything, but there's always the chance one may. You know the kind of thing: Child seen in a boat somewhere and evidently did not resemble people caring for it or child seen in a hotel window of a room whose blinds were usually pulled down, etc., etc. They investigate all of these.[13]

In Washington, D.C., Evalyn McLean was also frustrated. When she read that the Lindberghs had paid fifty thousand dollars to a man in a Bronx cemetery she summoned Gaston Means to her house for an explanation.

The meeting took place on April 14 in Mrs. McLean's luxurious living room. It had been her understanding that Means was in touch with the kidnappers. She had given him the money and now she had doubts. It seemed the real go-between was a school-teacher from the Bronx named John Condon—the man they called Jafsie.

Mrs. McLean also wanted to know about the people in Norfolk who were supposedly negotiating with the kidnappers. They seemed legitimate, too. If they weren't, a man like Admiral Guy Burrage wouldn't have anything to do with them. What was going on here? How many kidnap gangs were there and which group had the baby?

Gaston smiled. He assured Mrs. McLean that he could explain everything. Jafsie's kidnappers, Curtis's, and the Fox's were the same people. There *was* only one gang.

Means explained that Jafsie had been unable to get the baby because the kidnappers found out the ransom bills had been recorded. Moreover, the gang had been frightened off by the Coast Guard around the Elizabeth Islands. Like Jafsie, Curtis and his people were having difficulty negotiating with the kidnappers. They weren't having any luck because the kidnappers had decided that the only man they could trust was Gaston Means.

Having convinced Mrs. McLean that all was well, Means announced that he had some very exciting news: *He had seen the Lindbergh baby!* Yes! He had actually held the little boy in his arms!

The Lindbergh baby was alive and well, Means said. The child was being held in Aiken, South Carolina, where Mrs. McLean owned a summer home. It was there they would make the exchange. The Fox was in Aiken, too, waiting to meet with Mrs. McLean. She was to go there as soon as possible. Oh, yes—not a word of this to anyone!

The next day, Mrs. McLean waited eagerly in her summer home while Gaston set out to contact the Fox. About an hour later he returned with a chubby, middle-aged man with horn-rimmed glasses and a pencil-thin mustache. He had found the Fox.

Gaston said that the Fox was worried about a trap. So, before getting down to business, the gangster would have to search the house for hidden microphones. Mrs. McLean said that she understood.

Mrs. McLean didn't know it but the Fox was Norman Whitaker, a disbarred lawyer with degrees from Georgetown University and the University of Pennsylvania. A former chess champion, Whitaker had served time for automobile theft and had recently been arrested in Pleasantvale, New Jersey, for feeding slugs into a pay telephone.[14]

The Fox had completed his search. The house was clean. But he was still nervous. Casting his beady eyes about the room, the Fox told Mrs. McLean that he would confer with his underworld colleagues then get back to her. In the meantime, if she mentioned this to anybody, a member of the gang would rub her out with a machine gun. Did she get the picture? Literally trembling with fear, Mrs. McLean said that her lips were sealed.

The next day the Fox returned to the McLean house with bad news. The other members of the gang, fearing a police trap, had left Aiken. They were now in Juarez, Mexico, just across the border from El Paso. If she really wanted the baby, she and Means would have to go to Texas. Because of the child's condition, the Fox suggested that Mrs. McLean bring along a nurse.

A few hours later, Mrs. McLean, Gaston, and a professional nurse named Elizabeth Nelson were on their way to El Paso. When they got there, Mrs. McLean and the nurse waited in a hotel room while Means crossed the border into Juarez. A short time later he returned to the hotel with bad news. The kidnappers knew that the serial numbers to the ransom bills had been recorded, and as a result they couldn't spend the money. They needed an additional thirty-five hundred dollars in unmarked and unlisted bills. Once they got this money, Mrs. McLean would get the baby and the unspent ransom.

Mrs. McLean agreed to the kidnappers' terms but she said she needed some time to raise the extra money. Gaston understood, but reminded her that she must do it as quickly as possible. Mrs. McLean left immediately for Washington to get the cash while Means and the nurse stood by in El Paso.

Mrs. McLean couldn't go to the bank without arousing the suspicions of her bankers, so she asked a friend who worked at the *Washington Post* to help her. When Mrs. McLean gave this friend, Elizabeth Poe, several diamond bracelets and a diamond necklace to pawn, Miss Poe became suspicious and called Mrs. McLean's attorney. The lawyer stepped in and advised his client that she was being swindled.

On April 17, when Means called Mrs. McLean from a hotel in Chicago, she told him she knew he was a fake. She demanded her money back. Means exclaimed that he was insulted, and if necessary, he would kidnap the baby from the kidnappers to prove he was legitimate. He also promised to return the hundred thousand dollars he said was buried near his brother's home in Concord, North Carolina.

A few days later Gaston showed up at Mrs. McLean's house. When she demanded her money, he said he didn't have it. On his way to Washington he had met a man who was waving a lantern at a bridge. The man stopped him and whispered "Number eleven," the code name for one of the kidnappers. With that, Means handed him the money.

After ordering Means out of her house, Mrs. McLean telephoned her lawyer, who called J. Edgar Hoover.

Back at Hopewell, the investigation sputtered along. There was nothing the Lindberghs could do but wait for the kidnappers to resurface with word of the baby. On Monday, April 18, in a letter to her mother-in-law, Anne Lindbergh wrote:

> . . . there have been terrible rumors here. I don't know what comes out in Detroit. There are probably entirely different rumors there. So I feel it is useless to call you on them—for instance, last night C. had shot himself. That made him and me very angry.
> . . . no news yet, but they are not discouraged here. We follow everything, never

knowing what calls, or what strange-appearing person, may be from the kidnappers, to test us out. Only of course when a person starts by asking for money we are suspicious. We demand absolute identification before we will hand over the money.[15]

Over two weeks had passed since the ransom money had been paid, and there was no sign of the baby or the kidnappers. The police were probing in the dark, Mrs. McLean had been swindled out of $104,000, and the Lindberghs had been double-crossed. The baby had been missing six weeks and the Lindberghs were doing their best to keep their hopes up. As time passed this was becoming more and more difficult. The parents were hungry for any sign that the kidnappers, although hardened criminals, were reasonable men who would eventually keep their end of the bargain.

> If this gang of saps had any nerve, I'd sell the brat to the highest bidder.
>
> —J O H N   H U G H E S   C U R T I S
> *quoting a member of the kidnap gang*

8   LINDBERGH GOES TO SEA

ON APRIL 18, John Hughes Curtis came to Hopewell with an astonishing tale. He arrived at the Lindbergh estate with his longtime friend E. B. Bruce, a successful businessman from Elmira, New York.

Curtis and Bruce were escorted into Colonel Lindbergh's den. There Curtis, in the presence of Lindbergh, Schwarzkopf, Captain Lamb, and Lieutenant Keaten, told of his dealings over the past two weeks with the gang that had the baby. Following his April 3 meeting with Sam in the cafeteria, he and Sam, in Curtis's car, drove to the Hudson-Manhattan Railroad station in Newark, New Jersey, where Curtis came face to face with the four men who had masterminded the kidnapping.

The leader of the gang was a thirty-five-year-old Scandinavian named John. John was good-looking and had a splendid physique. He was five foot nine and weighed 160 pounds, with an air of importance about him.

The second man was George Olaf Larsen, another Scandinavian who was in his early forties. Larsen was of medium height and build and had straight, sandy-colored hair combed straight back. Nicknamed "Dynamite," Larsen had the ruddy complexion of a seafaring man. Curtis was told that Larsen was the captain of the schooner where the baby was being held.

The third person at the railroad station was a thirty-two-year-old Scandinavian named Nils. Five foot nine and 140 pounds, he had blond hair and a florid complexion.

The group was rounded out by Eric, described by Curtis as colorless and nondescript. Eric was Norwegian or Dutch and was in his thirties. He was a small man with a round face. Except for Sam, who was stylish in his gray topcoat and lighter-gray fedora, the kidnappers were drably clad in baggy suits and brown overcoats.[1]

The five gangsters squeezed into Curtis's car and rode to Larsen's house in Cape May, at the southern tip of New Jersey. As Curtis drove, John told how he and the gang had kidnapped the baby. Imitating John's Scandinavian accent, Curtis repeated John's story: "One night, about one month before the kidnapping, I go to some party with a girlfriend of mine, a German trained nurse, at a roadhouse outside Trenton. There I meet a member of the Lindbergh and Morrow household—which one I don't say. For some time I think I do this job, and put the child with my girlfriend, the nurse. I know I need inside help, so I get this person to help me. I promise plenty good money for the trouble . . ."[2]

Before John could finish his story, the group arrived at Larsen's cottage, where they met his wife, Hilda. According to Curtis, she operated a two-way radio out of a Ford sedan, relaying messages to and from the kidnappers when they were at sea.

Curtis and the gang sat around and listened as John finished his story about how he and the others had stolen the baby. Curtis, in the role of John, repeated the tale in Colonel Lindbergh's den: "On this night, March 1, Nils, Eric, the German nurse, and myself, we drive in a green Hudson sedan to the lane leading up to the Lindberghs. We park some 300 feet away. Sam follows us in his car. He parks still further away, on a high spot by the main road, so he can signal me with his lights if some other car comes into the lane.

"Nils and me, we walk to the nursery window and put up the ladder which we have with us. It is in three parts so as to fit in the car. When we climb through the window, we have a blanket, a rag, and some chloroform, just enough. We do not leave by the way of the window because the ladder is so unsteady. We come down the stairs and out the front door."[3]

Curtis paused to give emphasis to his last sentence. If Schwarzkopf and his two detectives were taken aback about the front door business, they weren't showing it. Colonel Lindbergh was keeping his thoughts under wraps as well.

Curtis said that John then showed him a twenty-four-by thirty-inch floor plan of the first and second floors of the Lindbergh house.

"You see this here," John said, pointing to a small passageway near the front door. "That's a pantry and it's a hallway between the kitchen and the front hall. We had this locked on the hall side, so if they got wise in the kitchen or servants' quarters they'd have to go all the way around through the dining room and living room to get to the front hall. You'll find that key on the hall side even now."

Lindbergh jumped up and strode from the den. He returned a few minutes later. He had checked to see if the key was still in the lock—it was.

Curtis said he was told that Larsen's wife had written the nursery note and the other ransom letters.

According to John, the baby was driven to Cape May where Inez took him out to the schooner.

When John finished his account, he took Curtis to the garage and showed him a green Hudson. Curtis looked inside the car and saw a pine box about two feet wide and three feet long. The bottom of the box was padded with blankets. John said that the baby had been transported in this custom-made container.

At seven the next morning, Curtis and George Olaf Larsen were in Trenton, New Jersey. Larsen had agreed to meet with Colonel Lindbergh. The kidnapper waited in the car while Curtis called the estate from a pay phone. Colonel Lindbergh interrupted Curtis to say that he remembered the call. At the time he had been tied up with Condon and the other John. He had asked Curtis to call back at eight o'clock that evening.

Because Lindbergh had put him off, Curtis had eleven hours to kill with a nervous kidnapper who thought he was being trapped. Larsen was holding a note for Lindbergh, a note that contained a description of the baby so detailed there would be no doubt in the Colonel's mind that Larsen and his people had the child.

Curtis and Larsen drove to Plainfield, New Jersey, where Curtis visited some relatives and Larsen went to a movie. At six that evening Curtis picked up Larsen in front of the theater and drove him to the Reading Railroad Station in Trenton; from there he called Hopewell again. Colonel Lindbergh had not returned to the estate. By now a bundle of nerves and energy, Larsen demanded to be driven back to Cape May.

Later that night Curtis realized that he had let Larsen walk off with the letter containing the baby's description.

That same evening, a reporter from the *New York Times* called Curtis and advised him that Colonel Lindbergh had paid a fifty thousand dollar ransom through an intermediary named John Condon.

The next day, while driving to Newark for a second meeting with the kidnappers, Curtis realized that the John who had taken the fifty thousand dollars from Dr. Condon was the John he had met at Larsen's cottage in Cape May. His John was the only member of the group whose age, height, and weight tallied with Condon's man in the cemetery.

When Curtis arrived at the railroad station in Newark he found all of the kidnappers but Larsen in Sam's car. Curtis got into the vehicle and was driven to a three-story brick house. In a shabby bedroom in the rear of the dwelling, Curtis asked John about Condon and the ransom.

"Yes, I did work with Condon," John said. "That was the idea all along—to chisel Lindbergh through Condon, then turn the boy over to you. That's why we are willing to let the kid go cheap."

"Do you call twenty-five thousand dollars cheap?" Curtis asked in disbelief.

"Yes!" John exclaimed. "Lindbergh is rolling in money. If this gang of saps had any nerve, I'd sell the brat to the highest bidder."

"Where's the letter describing the baby?" Curtis asked.

John smiled. "Torn up, of course. Do you think Larsen is fool enough to keep something that hot?"

"Is the baby better now?"

"Not so good," John replied, "but we got a doctor looking after him, and my girlfriend, the nurse."

"How did you find a doctor who wouldn't turn you in?" Curtis inquired.

A smirk crossed John's face. "You can get anything you're willing to pay for."

"I've got to have hard proof that you're the kidnappers," Curtis said.

"How would you like to see some of the ransom bills?" As John spoke, Eric and Nils pulled out fifteen hundred dollars in fives, tens, and twenties. John handed Curtis a newspaper clipping containing a list of the serial numbers. Curtis checked a few of the bills against the list—these were the men who had Colonel Lindbergh's money.[4]

Schwarzkopf didn't have to confer with his two detectives to know what they were thinking. The officers had already exchanged glances and the message was clear—Curtis was making it all up, Schwarzkopf was trying to understand why a wealthy and prominent businessman was spinning such a tale. Why would he do this to Colonel Lindbergh?

Schwarzkopf sympathized with the Colonel. Lindbergh had no choice but to go along. He could hardly ignore such a detailed, bold-faced story from a prominent country gentleman who had the backing of a well-respected churchman and a retired admiral known personally to Lindbergh.

It was bizzare. Curtis sounded so sincere—and there was no apparent reason for him to play such a cruel hoax on the Lindberghs.

A hopeful but very skeptical Lindbergh suggested that the next time Curtis met with the kidnappers, he, Lindbergh, should be close by. This would help avoid further delays. Curtis liked that idea—this was what he had wanted all along.

Curtis said that he'd get Lindbergh a hotel room in the village of Cape May Court House. Curtis would stay at a nearby hotel.

The meeting broke up and Schwarzkopf and his officers returned to West Trenton. They had Lindbergh's instructions to stay away from Curtis and the people he was dealing with. It was just like before, when Lindbergh, Breckinridge, and Condon were negotiating with "Cemetery John." Only this time Schwarzkopf didn't feel he was being shut out of the case. Although he would help Colonel Lindbergh in any way he could, Schwarzkopf considered the Curtis thing a farce and a waste of time. Right now he was more interested in Curtis and his motives than his phantom kidnappers. There was a chance, he guessed, that Curtis himself was being duped by a bunch of con artists.

Schwarzkopf found it interesting that Colonel Breckinridge wasn't at the meeting. He wondered if this was a sign that Lindbergh and his advisor didn't see eye to eye on the Curtis matter. Schwarzkopf knew that Breckinridge was committed to Condon and believed that Condon's "man in the cemetery" was the real kidnapper. Schwarzkopf also realized, however, that nobody had all the answers in this case. He recalled that in the very beginning Breckinridge had been convinced that the baby had been taken by the Mafia.

The next night, April 19, Lindbergh, Lt. George L. Richard (the commandant of the Norfolk Naval Air Station assigned to assist Curtis and his people), and E. B. Bruce drove to Lindbergh's hotel in Cape May Court to await word from Curtis.

Around midnight, Curtis came to Lindbergh's room with exciting news—the gang had agreed to take him on board Larsen's schooner. But there were two conditions: There was to be no Coast Guard surveillance of the area and there was to be no recording of the ransom bill serial numbers. Lindbergh agreed to both terms. Curtis left to meet with the kidnappers.

At dawn, Curtis returned to the hotel with quite a story. Under cover of night, he and the five kidnappers had driven to Schellinger's Fish Dock, where they had boarded a twenty-eight-foot sea-going skiff. Fourteen miles out to sea the skiff came to a larger vessel riding at anchor. The larger ship was named the *Theresa Salvatora*. Curtis suspected this name was an alias: it was painted on three boards screwed on to the hull, probably covering the ship's real name.

Curtis said the *Theresa Salvatora* was about eighty feet long and twenty feet wide. The ship contained a trolling outfit and was powered by a new 270-horsepower Fairbanks-Morse engine. The vessel had been freshly painted dark green. The mainmast was a little taller than the foremast, and between the two there was a radio antenna. The ship had a small cabin, a large gas tank, and a hatch into the forecastle.

The sea was running high, so Curtis and the kidnappers crowded inside the cabin to discuss how the baby would be returned. The kidnappers were leaving to rendezvous with a small boat from Falmouth, Massachusetts. Curtis said he was told to meet them in two days—on Thursday, April 21—off Block Island. One of the gang members would call Curtis at the Prince George Hotel in New York City and give him the exact meeting point. If for some reason Curtis missed the gang off Block Island, he could get back in touch with them through Hilda.

The moment Curtis finished his story Lindbergh asked if he had heard anything about the baby. Curtis said the baby was receiving excellent care.

Lindbergh and his party returned to Hopewell while Curtis drove to the Prince George Hotel. Lindbergh had said that he would arrange for the use of a boat.

The next day, Curtis called Lindbergh and advised that the rendezvous point was a spot near East Quarter Light just off the high cliffs of Block Island.

At dawn on Thursday, Lindbergh, Curtis, Lieutenant Richard, and E. B. Bruce were at sea in a small boat Lindbergh had rented. They were anchored off the coast of Block Island, where they were to meet the dark green, two-masted *Theresa Salvatora*.

The eighty-foot vessel didn't appear. There were several fishing boats in the area, and perhaps the kidnappers had feared a trap. Lindbergh and his party returned to the Prince George Hotel to wait for further word.

That night, while Lindbergh and the others slept, Curtis received a call from Hilda, who said they had feared a trap. The gang would like to make contact the next day off the Virginia Capes near the Chesapeake Lightship. She told Curtis to go out to the Chesapeake Lighthouse then sail twenty miles due east.

Curtis woke up Captain Whiting, a naval officer from the Norfolk Naval Base assigned to help the Lindbergh party. Curtis and Whiting studied several maps, so that when it came time to rendezvous they would be at the right spot.

At six o'clock Friday evening, Lindbergh and his party were in Norfolk, boarding the yacht *Marcon*. The ship was owned by Curtis's friend Colonel Consolvos, the owner of the Monticello Hotel in Norfolk. Colonel Consolvos said that Lindbergh could use the yacht and its captain, Frank Lackmann, as long as he needed them.

Two hours after the *Marcon* cast off, Curtis entered the pilothouse and told Captain Lackmann and the others that they would be looking for the *Mary B. Moss,* a Gloucester fisherman with a black hull.

The sea was so rough that Captain Lackmann had a hard time staying on course. It was also going to be difficult to stay at one spot for any length of time. To make things worse, a dense fog had moved in, dropping visibility to near zero. The *Marcon* pushed on anyway, reaching the rendezvous area in the early morning of Saturday.

The *Mary B. Moss* wasn't in sight. The fog had lifted, and Captain Whiting was searching the area in a seaplane. Captain Lackmann and Curtis decided to turn back because of the rough seas. They made this decision without consulting Lindbergh, who was napping below deck. As Lackmann was about to change course, a huge wave slammed into the yacht. Lindbergh was pitched out of his bunk, Curtis was thrown across the pilothouse, and the pilotwheel was wrenched from Captain Lackmann's hands.

When Lindbergh came on deck he was surprised and angry that the *Marcon* had turned back. Had he been consulted he would have insisted that they stay at sea a little longer. But by the time they reached calmer waters, Lindbergh admitted he had been wrong. He said he was feeling a bit seasick. He was a man of the air, he said, not of the sea.

On Saturday afternoon the *Marcon* sailed into port at Norfolk. Later that night Curtis reported that he had received a call from Hilda. She said that Larsen's ship had broken down in the storm and had limped back to port for repairs.

At two in the morning on Sunday, Lindbergh and his party were on the *Marcon,* passing through the Virginia Capes on their way back to the rendezvous spot east of the Chesapeake Lightship. But once again the *Marcon* and the kidnappers failed to make contact.

Lindbergh and his colleagues spent all day Monday aboard the *Marcon.* Because of bad weather they couldn't leave port. On Tuesday the skies cleared and the yacht cast off for the rendezvous point. Captain Whiting had radioed from his seaplane that he had spotted a craft that resembled Larsen's boat. It looked as though they'd finally make contact with the kidnappers! But it was a false alarm. The ship in question was not the *Mary B. Moss.*

On Wednesday, April 27, more bad weather kept the *Marcon* in port. Lindbergh and the others remained on board while Curtis flew to New York City. Although Curtis said he was going to New York to see Hilda, he was going there to meet someone else. He was meeting William E. Haskell, Jr., the assistant to the president of the *New York Herald Tribune.* The purpose of the meeting was to discuss the sale of an exclusive story about Curtis's dealings with the kidnappers. The *New York Daily News* had already put in a bid for the story. The *News* said they would pay Curtis an unspecified amount provided he make the baby exclusively available to their photographers.

Curtis was thought to be well-to-do, but in fact his ship-building business was doing poorly and his wife Constance was ill. He had also spent a lot on the Lindbergh case and hoped to get some of it back.

Curtis told Haskell he wanted twenty-five thousand dollars in advance. In return, he promised to give the *Tribune* the exclusive rights to his Lindbergh story. Haskell replied that his paper would pay this advance when the baby was recovered and after Lindbergh approved of the story and consented to its publication. Curtis accepted.

On Thursday, more bad weather kept Lindbergh in port. Admiral Burrage visited him and brought along a newspaper that carried a story about Salvatore Spitale and Irving Bitz. Apparently Rosner's assistant had decided to call it quits. According to the newspaper, they were withdrawing from the case because Lindbergh had ignored their advice. Both men criticized Condon for paying the ransom money without first seeing the baby.

Lindbergh was getting daily cable reports from Schwarzkopf, but unfortunately there was nothing to report except the fruitless results of Schwarzkopf's investigation.

On Friday the weather was better and John Curtis was back from his trip. By midafternoon the *Marcon* was heading toward Cape Henry off the Virginia coast.

Lindbergh hadn't been home for several days. While he was in and out of port in search of the *Mary B. Moss*, Anne Lindbergh could do nothing but wait and hope. On April 29, she wrote to Colonel Lindbergh's mother:

> . . . I know I am counting too much just now on Reuben's [Lindbergh's code name] lead, and by the time you get this it will probably have fallen through. It has less to recommend it than the majority we follow, and everyone I respect (except Reuben who is slightly more hopeful) thinks it is a lot of "hooey," an absolute waste of time, and the sooner they get Reuben clear of it and started on something else, the better."[5]

On Saturday, April 30, the *Marcon* was patrolling the waters twelve miles east of the Chesapeake Lightship. There was no sign of the *Mary B. Moss*.

Stormy weather kept the *Marcon* at port on May 1. The next day Lindbergh went to sea but returned several hours later empty-handed.

Lindbergh was starting to show the effects of the tedium and the repeated disappointments. He was getting plenty of sleep but was still exhausted. He was also irritable, and he lashed out bitterly against the news media. He said he would never forgive the press for reporting the ransom payment. He had pleaded with them not to do it, but they had published it anyway—even though they knew it would endanger his child.[6]

Lindbergh didn't stay discouraged for long. Just when it looked as if he'd never make contact with the gang, Curtis would come back from one of the excursions with hopeful news.

On Tuesday, May 3, Curtis returned to the yacht with word that the kidnappers wanted to make the rendezvous point farther north. Ever since the press had found out that Lindbergh was on the *Marcon,* the rendezvous waters had been teeming with ships. A new place would improve the chances of a successful exchange.

Because the seas were rougher up north, a more rugged boat was needed. Curtis said he would contact a friend, A. L. Foster of Atlantic City. Foster would lend them his eighty-five-foot ketch, the *Cachalot.* The *Cachalot* was a larger, sturdier ship. The men could change boats in a couple of days, when Curtis learned of the new rendezvous location.

On Wednesday and Thursday, May 4 and 5, the *Marcon* sailed the familiar waters off

Norfolk in search of the kidnappers. It was the same old story—no sign of the *Mary B. Moss*. Although Lindbergh was disappointed, he was hopeful they'd have better luck north in the *Cachalot*.

On May 5, as Lindbergh and his crew searched for the kidnappers off the coast of Virginia, Gaston B. Means climbed into a chauffeur-driven limousine waiting for him outside his home in Chevy Chase, Maryland.

The FBI had been investigating Evalyn McLean's allegation that Means had swindled her. Since the crime had been committed in the District of Columbia, the FBI had jurisdiction. A warrant had been issued for Gaston's arrest, but it couldn't be served outside the District.

The moment the limousine entered Washington, a pair of FBI agents pulled it over, yanked Means out, and placed him under arrest.

Means was taken to the Department of Justice building, where he was questioned by Hoover himself. Gaston told Hoover that he was shocked that Mrs. McLean's money hadn't been returned to her. He said that he had given the money to a man on a bridge who identified himself as one of the kidnappers. The chubby ex-agent smiled at Hoover and assured him that he wouldn't sue the FBI for false arrest. Not known for his sense of humor, Hoover immediately had Means arraigned and thrown into a cell with a prisoner who had just murdered a hit man. Means couldn't make his hundred-thousand-dollar bail, but he had made a new friend out of the Mafia killer.

The news of Means's arrest reached Lindbergh by cable. It was Friday, May 6, and high winds and a rough sea had kept the *Marcon* at port.

The next day, Anne Lindbergh wrote her mother-in-law a letter:

> . . . about the Englewood rumor, Col. Schwarzkopf had been moving more and more men away from here as the base of operations has been New York and environment. Trenton is the usual headquarters so there are always men there. Everything that can be done around here has, as far as possible, been done. He [Schwarzkopf] tells me that C. is seriously considering moving to Englewood to be nearer the base of operations. However, C. has not told me anything about it yet. I can see how it might be a good idea but I rather dread doing it. There is more to do here in my own house and woods, even though just futile routine.[7]

Early Saturday morning the sea was calm and Captain Lackmann was ready to sail—but when he went to wake up Lindbergh and the others they were gone. Curtis had left him a note: "Frank—You will hear from me. Please stay here at least two days before you move. Then stand by. Thanks. J.C."

Lindbergh and his crew would soon be moving into the *Cachalot*. But before they did, they drove to New York City. Curtis dropped Lindbergh off at the Morrow house on Fifth Avenue, where Anne Lindbergh was waiting to greet him. Curtis, Bruce, and Lieutenant Richard drove to the Prince George Hotel to sleep.

Sunday morning, William E. Haskell of the *New York Herald Tribune* came to the hotel to see how Curtis was progressing with his article. Haskell brought a secretary to take shorthand. Curtis dictated for a couple of hours, then said he had to leave on urgent business. He said he'd finish the piece later.

On Sunday night Curtis was off to meet Hilda. He returned to the hotel several hours later and said that Hilda had taken him to a house in Freeport, Long Island. From there they drove to southern New Jersey, where Hilda made radio contact with the kidnappers. Curtis said he would call Hilda as soon as they got to Atlantic City, and Hilda would tell then when and where to meet the gang.

When Lindbergh and the others reached Atlantic City, they drove to the house of A. L. Foster, the owner of the *Cachalot.* Foster took the men to the ship and helped them settle in while Curtis made the all-important call to Hilda. When Curtis returned, he happily reported that Hilda had given him the new rendezvous spot. The gang would be waiting in the waters off Cape May, near Five Fathoms Banks.

Lindbergh was elated. He was so sure he was getting his baby he established a radio code that would be sent to his friends on shore when young Charles was safely aboard the *Cachalot.*

At seven o'clock Monday night, May 9, the *Cachalot* cast off for the rendezvous spot. Five hours later the ship was in the waters off Cape May. During the next six and a half hours the *Cachalot* sailed aimlessly about these waters in search of the *Mary B. Moss.* By dawn, a distraught Lindbergh realized that another chance to meet the kidnappers had been lost.

When the *Cachalot* returned to port at ten o'clock Tuesday morning, Lindbergh remained on board to avoid being seen by reporters. Curtis went ashore to get things straight with the kidnappers. The weather had turned nasty, so Bruce and Richard left for New York City to wait until the skies cleared.

When Curtis returned to the *Cachalot* he reported that he had met with Hilda in the Freeport bungalow. Hilda said the gang members had been fighting among themselves. They had almost split into two factions—one headed by John and the other by her husband. According to Hilda, her husband had threatened to sell the baby to the highest bidder. It was only through Sam's efforts that the gang had agreed, at least for the time being, to hang together. As for the rendezvous, Larsen said he was going to wait until the seas had calmed. When the time was right, he'd get back to Curtis through Hilda.

On Wednesday, May 11, Lindbergh spent most of the day alone aboard the rolling, swaying ship. Curtis was busy shuttling back and forth between the ship and shore sending and receiving coded cables between Lindbergh and Schwarzkopf.

At Cape May, on the morning of May 12, it was blowing hard and raining harder. John Curtis had spent the previous night with friends in New York City. By one in the afternoon it was still raining, but the sea had quieted. Curtis was aboard the *Cachalot* having lunch with Lindbergh. Since the weather was beginning to clear, plans were made for Curtis to go to Atlantic City to see Hilda about arranging for another rendezvous. Curtis would be returning to the ship at eleven that night. Colonel Lindbergh said that he would wait up for him.

It was a quarter to five when Curtis walked into the Hotel President in Atlantic City

106   to cable Lindbergh's coded message to Schwarzkopf. Fifteen minutes later Colonel Schwarzkopf's return message, also in code, came through. Curtis didn't know what it said, but it was classified as urgent. Since he was not returning to the *Cachalot* until later that night, he called E. B. Bruce in New York and read him the message. Bruce said he and Lieutenant Richard were about to leave for Cape May to join Lindbergh on the boat. Bruce said that he would deliver the message personally.

9 THE BABY IN THE WOODS

LESS THAN A HALF MILE NORTH of the tiny village of Mount Rose, New Jersey, William Allen pulled his truck to the side of the narrow muddy back road that led to Hopewell. The thin, forty-six-year-old truck driver put on the hand brake, then climbed out of the cab onto the rutted road. Orville Wilson waited inside as his partner stepped into the woods to relieve himself. It was 3:15 on the afternoon of Thursday, May 12, and the two men were en route to Hopewell with a load of timber. Because of the light rain, the underbrush Allen was walking through was wet and chilly.

When Allen was about seventy-five feet into the woods, he ducked to pass under a low-hanging branch. As he ducked under the branch he looked down. There in the dirt he saw a baby's head. It looked more like a skull covered with patches of hair. He also saw a foot protruding from the ground. The startled truck driver bent over to take a closer look. Sure enough, he had found, half-buried in the leaves and dirt, the badly decomposed body of an infant.

Forgetting why he had entered the woods, Allen stumbled back to the road calling for Wilson. Wilson scrambled out of the truck and followed Allen back through the underbrush.

"I think it's a baby," Allen said as the two men examined the remains. The child's hair was blond and fragments of clothing still clung to the body.

"What are we going to do?" Wilson asked in a trembling voice.

Allen said they'd drive down the hill into Hopewell and find Officer Charles Williamson and report the matter to him.

Allen and Wilson found Officer Williamson in the local barbershop. The policeman was in the chair when the two truckers approached him.

It was Allen, a black man, who spoke: "Could you talk to me for a few minutes?"

"Sure," Williamson replied with a smile, "you can talk to me for five minutes."

"There's a baby in the woods." Allen blurted out.

"Jesus!" Williamson cried as he threw off the barber's sheet and scrambled out of the chair.

107

108   Moments later Williamson, with Allen and Wilson on his heels, burst into the police station. Chief Harry Wolfe was seated at his desk.

"These men found a body off the road on Mount Rose Hill—it could be the Lindbergh baby!"

Chief Wolfe grabbed the telephone and called Schwarzkopf, who said he was dispatching several detectives to the scene.

A few minutes later, Det. James Fitzgerald of the Jersey City Police Department and Sgt. Andrew Zapolsky of the New Jersey State Police arrived at the police station. Allen and Wilson were told to get back into their truck and drive to the spot where they had found the baby. Fitzgerald and Zapolsky and the two officers from Hopewell followed in two cars. In a matter of minutes the vehicles arrived at the place along the Princeton-Hopewell road. From this spot on the hill the Lindbergh house was visible across the valley.

Sergeant Zapolsky and Detective Fitzgerald found a burlap bag lying in the weeds just off the road. Picking it up, they walked seventy-five feet into the woods, where they came upon the remains. The officers asked William Allen and Orville Wilson to leave the scene. They were told they would be questioned later. The truck drivers eagerly departed.

Taking care not to disturb the body or the area immediately around it, the four officers knelt down to take a closer look. Although none of the men had seen the Lindbergh baby in person, they had seen photographs of him. The size and apparent age of the corpse, its golden curly hair, the general shape of the head, and the type of clothing on the body told them they were looking at the Lindbergh baby.

After making their tentative identification, Zapolsky and Fitzgerald walked out of the woods and drove to a store in Hopewell. From there they called Capt. John Lamb and informed him of the situation. Captain Lamb said that Lieutenant Keaten, Insp. Harry Walsh and Det. Robert Coar were on their way to the scene.

Inspector Walsh and Detective Coar were officers from the Jersey City Police Department. Walsh was the officer who had most recently questioned Violet Sharpe, the maid in the Morrow household whose statements and actions had been more than a little suspicious.

After calling Lamb, Zapolsky and Fitzgerald flagged down Keaten and Walsh, who were en route to the gravesite. Keaten and his partner then followed the detectives, who led them to the spot on Mount Rose Heights. The four officers arrived at the scene at about 3:45 P.M.[1]

Frank Kelly, the New Jersey State Police fingerprint man and crime scene photographer, arrived at the gravesite a few minutes after Lieutenant Keaten and the others. Corporal Kelly photographed the body in its half-buried, face-down position.[2] After Kelly had photographed the undisturbed remains Sergeant Zapolsky gingerly lifted the corpse out of its shallow grave and laid it face up. Zapolsky then took out a photograph of the Lindbergh child and compared the facial characteristics.

Although the corpse was in a state of advanced decomposition, the face was in relatively good shape. The forehead was well formed, as were the baby's eyes, nose, and chin.

The face lying on the ground matched the face in the Lindbergh photograph. Keaten, Walsh, and the others agreed.

The hunt for the Lindbergh baby was over. The little boy was dead, and it looked as if he had been dead all along. Apparently he had been killed shortly after the kidnapping. The officers at the scene took note of two other points of identity. There was the golden, curly hair and the deep-set dimple or recession beneath the baby's lower lip. This dimple had given the Lindbergh baby that endearing pouting expression. This recession was clearly visible on the face of the corpse.

As the officers stood over the body, Mrs. Lindbergh was waiting to hear from her husband, who was hoping for a break in the weather so he could rendezvous with John Curtis's "kidnappers." Lieutenant Keaten was thinking of the Lindberghs as he gazed at the body of their son. What he saw was not a pleasant sight. The child's skin, wet and shiny from the rain, was leatherish and almost black. The left leg was missing from the knee down—probably devoured by wild animals. Both hands were gone. That meant the corpse could not be identified by fingerprints. Keaten suddenly realized that the latent fingerprints taken off the baby's toys by Dr. Hudson would be useless.

Inspector Walsh had an idea. Before notifying the Lindberghs, they should make a more positive scientific identification. Lieutenant Keaten agreed. But what did Walsh have in mind? Walsh said that he and Newark Detective Warren Moffat, who had just arrived at the scene, would go to the Lindbergh estate, and without letting on about the corpse, get a more detailed description of what the boy had been wearing on the night of the kidnapping. They would talk to Betty Gow, the child's nurse.[3]

Inspector Walsh and Detective Moffat headed for the Lindbergh estate. Keaten and Zapolsky stayed behind to guard the corpse. The other officers, Fitzgerald and Coar, and the two policeman from Hopewell, began searching the area for evidence.

Betty Gow said that she remembered exactly what the child had been wearing on the night of the kidnapping. Just before he was put to bed she had made him a nightshirt to wear next to his skin. This shirt had been cut from a piece of flannel that was in the baby's room. She stitched the improvised garment with some blue Silco thread she had borrowed that night from the maid, Elsie Whateley. Betty told the detectives that she had also fashioned diapers from the same flannel remnant. Inspector Walsh asked Betty if she still had the leftover cloth from the nightshirt. The nurse said that she did and went off to fetch it. She returned a few minutes later with the flannel remnant and the spool of blue thread.

The nursemaid told the officers that the child was wearing a woolen T-shirt over the homemade garment. The T-shirt came from a batch of ten that had been purchased at the same time. All of the T-shirts had the "B. Altman & Co., N.Y." label sewn into the inside shirttail. The baby had also been wearing a diaper, a rubber diaper cover, and the one-piece Dr. Denton sleeping suit the kidnappers had mailed back to Dr. Condon eleven days after the crime.

Inspector Walsh was about to leave when Betty Gow reminded him that a Baby Alice Thumbguard had been tied to each sleeve of the child's sleeping suit.

110   Betty Gow had gotten used to having the police around, and she was accustomed to being questioned. As a result, Inspector Walsh's sudden interest in what the baby had been wearing didn't arouse her suspicions.

Inspector Walsh and Detective Moffat checked in with Colonel Schwarzkopf after questioning Betty Gow. Schwarzkopf, fearing the worst, accompanied them back to the woods.

At the gravesite, with Schwarzkopf and the others looking on, Inspector Walsh began the unpleasant task of removing the clothes from the corpse. Walsh noticed that the body was clad in a pair of undershirts like the ones described by Betty Gow.

Walsh was using a stick to manipulate the body while he cut off the shirts. As he did this he accidentally poked the stick through the baby's decomposing skull, just below the right earlobe. The accident left a hole about the diameter of a pencil.

After the garments had been removed, Walsh laid them on the ground so the officers could compare them to the samples he had obtained from Betty Gow. Walsh placed the flannel nightshirt found on the body next to the cloth remnant. The finely scalloped, embroidered edges of the flannel remnant and the nightshirt fit together like two pieces of a puzzle.[4]

There was no longer any doubt—the corpse found a little over two miles from the Lindbergh house was wearing the nightshirt Betty Gow had made on the night of the kidnapping.

Inspector Walsh also checked the label on the corpse's store-bought T-shirt and found that it matched the labels on the nine remaining shirts that had been purchased in a batch of ten.[5]

Walsh made his final textile identification by comparing the thread on Elsie Whateley's spool with the thread in the tattered and soiled nightshirt. The two sets of threads matched perfectly.

The burlap bag Detectives Fitzgerald and Zapolsky had found contained strands of blond hair. Some of this hair, in five-inch lengths, was also found in the hole. Apparently it had separated from the baby's skull. The officers noted that the hair on the corpse, in the grave, and inside the burlap bag matched the Lindbergh baby's. (The gravesite hair was later sent to a private laboratory in Newark and compared with samples that had been cut from the baby's head a couple of weeks before his abduction. The two sets of hair were found to be microscopically identical.[6]

The burlap bag, the hair, the gravesite clothing and the two safety pins that had been attached to the homemade undershirt were taken into custody by Colonel Schwarzkopf.[7]

Colonel Schwarzkopf, Inspector Walsh, and Lieutenant Keaten drove back to the Lindbergh estate carrying the gravesite garments in the burlap bag. They had left the baby's corpse in the woods. Sergeant Zapolsky, Detective Fitzgerald, and Chief Wolfe also departed. The remaining officers would wait for the detail of uniformed state troopers dispatched to protect the scene. Zapolsky and his group had been instructed to round up and question William Allen and Orville Wilson.

As soon as Schwarzkopf and his party arrived at the Lindbergh house they telephoned Walter H. Swayze, the Mercer County coroner.

It was now time to talk to Betty Gow. About 4:30 in the afternoon, Keaten and Walsh brought her into Schwarzkopf's office. The colonel handed her the two undershirts, still wet from the rain, and asked if she could identify them. The nurse recognized the shirts immediately. As she examined the garments the skin on her face lost its color and her lips started to quiver. She asked Schwarzkopf where he had found these things.

Schwarzkopf told Betty that the Lindbergh baby was dead. He said that the baby's remains were lying in the woods across the valley on Mount Rose Heights. Betty said she didn't believe it. Colonel Lindbergh and his associates were about to meet the kidnappers at sea off Cape May. The baby was going to be returned. He had been on the kidnappers' boat all along. Hadn't he?

Colonel Schwarzkopf shook his head. The baby's remains were in the woods, he said. Efforts were being made to contact Colonel Lindbergh. Schwarzkopf said that in a few minutes he would be breaking the news to Mrs. Lindbergh.

There was nothing more to say. The shaken nurse was escorted from the room and asked not to say anything until Mrs. Lindbergh had been notified.

The cabled message Colonel Lindbergh had sent from the *Cachalot* through John Curtis had just come in. Colonel Schwarzkopf prepared his return message. He advised Lindbergh that the baby's remains had been found and that Lindbergh was to return home at once. Schwarzkopf's message was put into code and sent to Curtis. Schwarzkopf realized that it would be several hours before Lindbergh got the message, and because of his isolation aboard the *Cachalot,* the entire world would know of his tragedy before he did.

The time had come to tell Mrs. Lindbergh, and the painful task fell upon Colonel Schwarzkopf. Since Schwarzkopf had virtually become a member of the Lindbergh family, it was appropriate that he break the news.

Anne Lindbergh and her mother, Mrs. Dwight Morrow, were in the master bedroom. When he entered the room, the Colonel was struck by Mrs. Lindbergh's frail beauty. He found it hard to believe that she was an accomplished pilot, navigator, radio operator, and world traveler.

"Mrs. Lindbergh, I have bad news," Schwarzkopf began. He paused but neither women spoke. Mrs. Morrow got up from her chair and walked to the desk where Anne Lindbergh was sitting. The mother put her arms around her daughter's shoulders.

Schwarzkopf continued, "The baby is dead. His body was found this afternoon about two miles from here. Betty Gow has identified both of his undershirts. There is also the hair. We're certain it's him. The kidnappers must have killed him shortly after taking him from the house. So there was no pain—no suffering. There's no reason to identify the remains. We can spare you that. We have gotten in touch with John Curtis in Atlantic City who will pass the message on to people who will notify the Colonel. They'll see him later tonight on the *Cachalot*. We are all very sorry."

112   There were no tears or screams of anguish—no fainting—just silence. Schwarzkopf felt that Mrs. Lindbergh had prepared herself for such a message. The tiny woman with the melancholy face and shy ways bowed her head. The realization that her "Fat Lamb," as she called him, was dead was a numbing jolt. There was no way to totally prepare for such a thing.

Without raising her head Mrs. Lindbergh asked, "How was he killed?"

"We don't know for sure. There hasn't been an autopsy. But it looks like he was killed by a blow to the head." [8]

Mrs. Lindbergh and her mother had no further questions, so Schwarzkopf slipped quietly out of the room, closing the door on the two bereaved women.

Schwarzkopf returned to his office. It was time to notify the public. He called the press room at the State House in Trenton and left word that in an hour he would be making an important announcement. He then called Paul Gebhart's general store in Hopewell, the local hangout for newspapermen and radio reporters. The newsmen were summoned to the New Jersey State Police Headquarters in the Lindbergh garage. It was five o'clock.

Walter H. Swazye, the Mercer County coroner, had arrived at the gravesite. Like most coroners, Swayze was a mortician. His funeral parlor, located at 415 Greenwood Avenue in Trenton, doubled as the Mercer County morgue.

Swayze, in his mid-fifties, was as bald as a billiard ball. A tall, big-framed outdoorsman type, he spent a lot of his time hunting and fishing.

Swayze made a cursory, on-the-scene examination of the body. Its size, apparent age, blond hair, and facial features led him to believe the remains were those of the Lindbergh child. Swayze looked over the spot where the body had been lying face down in the mud. It wasn't really a grave, it was more like a depression someone had shallowed-out by kicking the ground with his foot.

The sky was overcast, and it was still drizzling when Swayze gathered up the corpse and put it into a small body bag. The remains would be taken to his funeral parlor in Trenton, where the county physician, Dr. Charles H. Mitchell, would perform the autopsy.

After Swayze had removed the corpse, several police officers raked the area for evidence, collecting ten barrels of leaves, sticks, and dirt. When the officers sifted this debris, they found tufts of blond hair, fragments of the baby's clothing, a toe nail, and twelve small bones, six of which were human.

Four of the human bones were metatarsals from the baby's foot. The fifth was a human heel bone (calcaneous bone), and the sixth was not specifically identified. Several months later these skeletal remains were sent to the Edel Laboratories in Newark, where scientists determined that the bones could have come from the body of a twenty-month-old child. [9]

Colonel Schwarzkopf, after he had summoned the reporters to the Lindbergh estate, called Gov. A. Harry Moore and advised him of the discovery. A young reporter named Francis Jamieson, who covered the State House for the Associated Press, just happened to wander into Governor Moore's office a few minutes after Schwarzkopf's call. Moore **113** passed the information on to Jamieson, who ran down the marble hall to the nearest telephone where he called in his scoop. (For that piece of reporting, Jamieson received the Pulitzer Prize in journalism for 1932.) A short time later, Governor Moore made a formal announcement. He concluded with the following statement: "Now, of course, we will do everything in our power to get the murderers. It is a perfectly horrible crime and we shall do everything in our power to find those responsible. This is a great shock to the whole country."

Governor Moore's announcement hit the wires and was carried to every radio station in America. The first radio bulletin was broadcast at 6:12 P.M. in New York City over station WOR. Three minutes later the story was flashing across the *New York Times'* electric bulletin at Times Square. By 6:30 NBC and CBS were broadcasting the story nationwide.

Less than an hour after learning of her baby's death, Mrs. Lindbergh telephoned Detroit to break the news to the Colonel's mother, Mrs. Evangeline Lindbergh. Anne wanted to inform her mother-in-law of the tragedy before she heard the news over the radio. When she hung up, the distraught mother went to her desk and wrote:

> Everything is telescoped now into one moment, one of those eternal moments—the moment that I realized the baby had been taken and I saw the baby dead, killed violently, in the first flash of horror. Everything since then has been unreal, it has all vanished like smoke. Only that eternal moment remains. . . .
>
> I look at it now as a police case, a murder case, and I am interested in it as such and can and *have* to ask and talk about it. Soon it will be personal, but I do not face it yet.
>
> I feel strangely a sense of peace—not peace, but an end to restlessness, a finality, as though I were sleeping in a grave. . . .[10]

It was 6:30, and most of the reporters who were coming to the Lindbergh estate were already there. The ones who had arrived earlier and had been waiting the longest were getting impatient. This was the first time reporters had been on the Lindbergh grounds since the press had been barred from the estate a few days after the kidnapping. The reporters were seated around a long wooden mess table and speculating on the nature of Schwarzkopf's forthcoming announcement. None of the newsmen had heard the radio bulletin that had been broadcast while they were in the garage.

Schwarzkopf finally walked into the room. He was accompanied by Captain Lamb, Inspector Walsh, and Lieutenant Keaten. Looking very much the military man, the colonel stepped to a small stand that functioned as a stage, and with his subordinates standing at his side, cleared his throat. The only sound was the rain pelting the roof. Schwarzkopf withdrew a sheet of paper from his pocket and in the gravest voice possible read his statement:

"We have to announce that apparently the body of the Lindbergh baby was found at 3:15 P.M. today by William Allen, Negro, of Trenton, who was riding on the Mount Rose Road toward Hopewell."

Schwarzkopf paused. For a moment the twenty-four reporters in the room sat in silence, gazing blankly at Schwarzkopf. They were frozen—stunned. Then all of a sudden their pencils began moving. Schwarzkopf continued:

"He was riding with Orville Wilson on a truck load of timber. They stopped the truck so he could answer a call of nature. He went into the woods for this purpose on the Mount Rose Hill, in Mount Rose, New Jersey. . . ."

Schwarzkopf went on with his statement, telling the reporters that detectives had positively identified the flannel undershirt on the corpse as the Lindbergh baby's. When Schwarzkopf finished describing the condition of the corpse and how it was positioned in the shallow grave, several reporters jumped up and scrambled for the door. They were so eager to call in their story, they couldn't wait for him to finish.

"No!" Schwarzkopf shouted. "No one is to leave this room until I have finished my statement!" When order was restored, Schwarzkopf concluded his announcement:

"Mercer County physician, Dr. Charles H. Mitchell, and the County Coroner, Walter Swayze, were immediately called in."[11]

Having finished his announcement, Schwarzkopf said that he had no additional comments and would not answer questions. With that, he dismissed the excited reporters, who raced out of the garage to call in their offices.

By 7:00 P.M., the news of the baby's death was spreading throughout America and the world. Americans would soon be talking of little else. May 12 was a day people would remember the rest of their lives. From now on they would recall exactly what they had been doing when they heard the news. Ironically, one of the persons who still hadn't heard the news was the child's father.

At 7:00 P.M., Lowell Thomas, the nationally known journalist and commentator, mentioned the Lindbergh baby on his regular news broadcast over NBC radio. At the same time, New York City Mayor Jimmy Walker referred to the matter during an address over another station. Walker digressed from his previously scheduled topic to announce that the New York City Police, eighteen thousand strong, would make every effort to capture the baby's murderers, whom he called "the most miserable criminals and scoundrels in the annals of criminology."

About this time the first newspapers carrying the story hit the streets. The papers, proclaiming the baby's death in huge, front-page headlines, were immediately snatched up from newsstands and newspaper boys.

The death of the Lindbergh baby had so ignited the country that the news media were unable to satisfy the public's appetite for Lindbergh information. The switchboards at *The New York Times* were jammed. During the three hours following the first news of the baby's death, the *Times* received over three thousand telephone calls from people demanding more information.

The baby's corpse was deposited at the Swayze Funeral Parlor around six o'clock. Shortly thereafter, Det. Robert Coar of the Jersey City Police Department and Det. Samuel Leon of the state police arrived at the Mercer County morgue with Betty Gow. The baby's nursemaid had agreed to view the remains to make sure there had been no mistake in his identification.

Betty was led into the sterile embalming room. The body was on a stainless steel autopsy table covered by a white sheet. The two detectives stood at Betty's side as Coroner Swazye pulled back the cover. The nursemaid groaned, brought her hand quickly to her mouth, then turned away. She hadn't been prepared for such a gruesome sight. No one had told her the baby would look like that. Having to force herself, she looked again at the black object on the table. She inspected its right foot and noted that the little toe was curled under the one next to it. She examined the mouth and recognized the four eye-teeth that were barely showing through the gums. And the face—there was still enough of it to recognize—particularly the nose, chin, and forehead.

Betty Gow turned from the table and walked out of the room. The examination had taken three minutes. She said there was no doubt. That horrible object on the table was Baby Lindbergh.[12]

Henry Breckinridge and Dr. Philip Van Ingen had come to the morgue. Dr. Van Ingen was the prominent New York City pediatrician who had attended the Lindbergh baby. He had given the baby a routine checkup ten days prior to the kidnapping. The physician had brought the child's medical records, which showed him to be twenty-nine inches long and to weigh twenty-seven pounds.

Dr. Van Ingen examined the body on the table. He counted the teeth—there were sixteen of them—eight on top and eight on the bottom. He also noted the absence of dental work. Van Ingen measured the circumference of the baby's skull, then studied the overlapping toes on the right foot. When he was finished, the doctor said to Coroner Swazye that he believed the corpse was the Lindbergh baby.[13]

As county coroner, Walter Swazye signed death certificates and proclaimed people dead. But in cases of sudden, unexplained, or violent death, the county physician was called in to perform the autopsy to determine, among other things, the cause, manner, and time of death. In Mercer County in 1932 this man was Dr. Charles H. Mitchell.

Dr. Mitchell came to the Swazye Funeral Parlor at 6:45 that evening. A University of Pennsylvania graduate and former assistant surgeon at St. Francis Hospital in Trenton, Dr. Mitchell had been the Mercer County physician for eleven years. During this time, the sixty-year-old physician had performed over a thousand autopsies, including a hundred or so on children.

The doctor was a big, blustering man who had a large, hawkish nose that supported a pair of steel-rimmed, hexagon-shaped glasses that were much too small for his face. The physician's snow-white pompadour stood out against his dark gray hair, and his jellylike neck, swollen like a water balloon, made him unusual looking. In cases like this, it was Dr. Mitchell's job to find out what had caused the baby's death. He would attempt to find out if the baby had died from, among other things, asphyxia, exposure, or injury to a vital organ. Concerning the manner of death, the baby might have been killed by strangulation, suffocation, a blunt instrument, or a gunshot.

As for time of death, this was often the most difficult thing to fix. To estimate how long a body had been dead, the county physician took note of certain biological and chemical changes that normally occur after death. These postmortem conditions included body temperature, the presence of rigor mortis (stiffening of the body), and the state of decomposition.

Since the rate and degree of these postmortem changes varied according to such things as the climate and the age of the deceased, fixing time of death was an imperfect science. Dr. Mitchell also knew that the longer a corpse had been dead, the more imprecise the time of death estimate. He realized, for example, that once a person had been dead long enough to be reduced to a skeletal state, it was impossible to pinpoint when death had occurred.

Although Dr. Mitchell had performed over a thousand autopsies, he was not, by profession, a forensic pathologist. Although there were two prominent forensic pathologists and one toxicologist working within sixty miles of Trenton, no outside help was summoned.[14] Since Dr. Mitchell had never in the past called upon an expert to help him with a death, the thought of doing it now never crossed his mind.[15]

Upon his arrival at the morgue, Dr. Mitchell conferred briefly with Walter Swazye and Dr. Van Ingen. He then walked into the autopsy room to look at the remains.

Dr. Mitchell could tell that the baby had been dead for a while. The body was in a state of advanced decomposition. Lying before him was a corpse that had been exposed to the elements for several weeks. He noted that it had been seventy-two days since the kidnapping.

The baby's left leg was missing from the knee down. Also gone were the left hand and right arm below the elbow. The lower portion of the torso had been eaten away by animals—probably skunks, foxes, and rats.

Flanked by the Coroner and Dr. Van Ingen, Dr. Mitchell examined the baby's right foot. One toe overlapped the little one next to it. Dr. Mitchell then found a section of skin on the right foot that was not discolored. This patch indicated that the corpse was white.

A close examination of the baby's face showed that it was in much better condition than the rest of the body. Although the skin of the baby's head had turned a dark brown, the facial muscles had not deteriorated as much as the other muscle tissue. Dr. Mitchell attributed this to the fact that the baby had been face down in the mud, where it had been protected from the elements. Both eyeballs, for example, were soft but still intact. Had the body been in a face-up position, the eyeballs would have liquefied and drained out of their sockets. Looking at the face, the doctor recognized the high, prominent forehead—one of the Lindbergh baby's most identifiable features.

The baby's lips were swollen and pulled back over his teeth—which Dr. Mitchell counted. There were eight on top and eight on the bottom—the number normally found in the mouth of a twenty-month-old child.

Having completed his visual examination, Dr. Mitchell laid a tape measure along the corpse. The body measured 33½ inches long—4½ inches longer than the height recorded by Dr. Van Ingen ten days before the kidnapping.

Dr. Mitchell didn't consider the height differential particularly significant. He knew that discrepancies like this were normal. There was no guarantee that Dr. Van Ingen had precisely measured the baby. The quick, routine measuring of a squirming infant on a baby scale was not a scientific procedure.[16] And there were other reasons why the height discrepancy didn't cause Dr. Mitchell any concern. He had learned from experience that when comparing the measurements of a body before and after death—particularly when the corpse had been exposed to the elements for several weeks, then jostled about by the police—discrepancies were bound to crop up. Dr. Mitchell didn't give the matter much thought—he wasn't trying to identify the corpse—the police had already done that. He was there to find out what had caused the baby's death.

Upon completion of his superficial examination, Dr. Mitchell said it was time to start the autopsy. Walter Swazye immediately put on a pair of surgical gloves. Dr. Van Ingen was puzzled. Why was the coroner preparing for the operation? Dr. Mitchell was the one who should have been putting on the gloves. Instead, he was telling the mortician to rule out choking as the cause of death. Dr. Van Ingen spoke up: "Who's performing the autopsy?"

Dr. Mitchell's face reddened slightly. "I can't," he said. The county physician looked at his hands, then held them up for Dr. Van Ingen to inspect. "Arthritis," he said. "The gloves cut off the circulation—I can't do much with my hands."

The pediatrician looked dumbstruck. Lying on the autopsy table was the Lindbergh boy. Outside, tens of millions of people were learning of the child's death. Dr. Van Ingen was about to watch a laymen perform one of the most important autopsies in history.

The expression on Dr. Van Ingen's face gave him away. Swayze broke the silence: "We're not doing anything wrong here. I'm gonna be the doctor's hands—that's all."

"I tell him what to do," Dr. Mitchell cut in, "we work as a team. He handles the instruments but I perform the autopsy. If I could do it myself, I would—but I can't. It's the arthritis."[17]

As a physician, Dr. Van Ingen must have understood the severity of Dr. Mitchell's position. He was a doctor who couldn't use his hands anymore. Dr. Mitchell's career as a surgeon was over—but as long as he had this arrangement with Coroner Swayze, he could hold on to his job as county physician.

"Does Schwarzkopf know of this?" Dr. Van Ingen said.

"Of course not," Dr. Mitchell snapped. "Why should he?"

"And Colonel Lindbergh—does he know?"

"Know what?" Dr. Mitchell asked. "What is there to know? I'm the county physician and Walter is the coroner. We work as a team. What's wrong with that? If you want to stay, Doctor—and help—you're welcome. But if you'd rather leave—that's okay."

"I'll stay," Dr. Van Ingen replied.

"Let's get on with it then," Swayze said.[18]

Dr. Mitchell wanted to rule out choking as the cause of death, so he had Swazye pry open the child's mouth and insert his finger past the swollen tongue into the baby's throat. He wanted to see if anything was obstructing the windpipe.[19] The coroner withdrew his finger and reported, "He didn't choke on anything."

Dr. Mitchell said it was time to dissect and examine the brain. He told Swayze to make an ear-to-ear incision across the back of the baby's head. Swayze made the cut, then peeled the flap of skin forward over the baby's face, exposing the top of the skull. He picked up a small hand tool and began sawing off the top of the head. But he ran into trouble when the soft, pliable bone started coming apart on its own. The mortician tried his best to hold the skull together, but he couldn't; the bone was too soft. It could be peeled off like the skin of an orange.

The baby's brain had decomposed into a thick souplike substance, and as the skull came apart in Swayze's hands, it spilled out onto the table. There was nothing Swayze could do to stop it. Suddenly the room was filled with a horrible and sickening odor. The men had to step back from the table.

Swayze forced himself back to the body. He swirled a finger through the green, soupy substance. As far as he could-tell, the brain didn't contain anything foreign. He was specifically looking for a bullet.

Inside the baby's skull, below and to the right of the left ear, Dr. Mitchell discovered four fracture lines radiating from a point of impact. At this spot he found a decomposed blood clot, evidence of a hemorrhage. This meant that the baby was alive when the wound was inflicted. The skull fracture and the blood clot led Dr. Mitchell to the conclusion that the baby had been killed by a blow to the head. But he didn't know how the injury had been delivered.

Upon examining the skull, Dr. Mitchell found a one-quarter-inch hole opposite the fracture. This opening was located below the right ear. This "perforated fracture," as the doctor called it, was the hole Insp. Harry Walsh had made when he accidentally poked the body with a stick.[20] The county physician concluded that this wound had been inflicted after death. The doctor was satisfied, he said, that the Lindbergh baby had died from a "fractured skull due to external violence." In Dr. Mitchell's mind, this finding was consistent with the fact that there were no bloodstains in the nursery, on the kidnap ladder, on the chisel, or on the baby's sleeping suit.[21]

Dr. Mitchell explained to Swayze and Dr. Van Ingen that skull fractures seldom cause external bleeding, especially in infants whose heads are gristly and soft. A baby's head, because it is soft and pliable, does not crack like an egg when bludgeoned. Just because there were no bloodstains in the nursery did not mean that the baby couldn't have been murdered in his room. Moreover, simply because an object, like the chisel, didn't have blood on it, didn't rule it out as the murder weapon.[22] This also explained why there were no bloodstains on the baby's clothes.[23]

Dr. Mitchell next inspected the "soft spot" on top of the baby's skull. This area of the head, called the fontanelle, is open until the child matures. When sufficient bone is formed, the hole closes. Dr. Mitchell measured this opening on the corpse and found it to be one inch in diameter.[24]

Having concluded his examination of the baby's head, Dr. Mitchell asked Swayze to open up the chest in order to inspect the internal organs.

There wasn't much left of the baby's heart, and his liver, stomach, lungs, bladder, and intestines were gone. Because of this, Dr. Mitchell's internal examination yielded little information. There was nothing else the doctor could do. The autopsy was over.

Coroner Swayze and the two physicians had been in the autopsy room ninety minutes. No one had photographed the body, the internal organs, or the blood clot.

After the autopsy, the three men walked into the coroner's office, where Dr. Mitchell dictated his report to Swayze, who typed it. Swayze finished the one-page report, pulled it from his typewriter, and handed it to Mitchell. The county physician read it over carefully and signed it.

By now the world had learned of the baby's death. Sightseers, souvenir hunters, cameramen, and reporters were rushing to the gravesite on Mount Rose Heights. Although the area immediately around the shallow grave was being protected by the New Jersey State Police, the Princeton-Hopewell road was already bumper to bumper with cars. A growing number of people were milling about the spot where William Allen had entered the woods. Peddlers were in the area selling peanuts, popcorn, and postcards of the Lindbergh house. A merchant from Trenton had set up a hot dog stand.

The aroma of hot dogs, peanuts, and popcorn filled the night air as people chatted excitedly among the cars, headlight beams, and movie cameras. On this damp, chilly Thursday night in May, the crowd on Mount Rose Heights was in a festive mood. It was a night that would stick in their minds for years to come. Ten weeks and two days after the kidnapping, and six weeks after John Condon had paid fifty thousand dollars to the man in the cemetery, the Lindberghs got their baby back.

If William Allen had not picked that particular spot along the Princeton-Hopewell road to relieve himself, the body of the Lindbergh baby might never have been found. It is hard to say what course the case would have taken had this not happened. But the baby in the woods *was* found, and this changed everything. Colonel Schwarzkopf and his men were no longer restrained—from now on they wouldn't have to worry about jeopardizing the child. The investigation had entered a new phase.

I am perfectly satisfied that it is my child.

—CHARLES LINDBERGH

10 A NEW BALLGAME

BY THE TIME E. B. BRUCE and Lt. George Richard got to Cape May Harbor with Colonel Schwarzkopf's coded message, news of the baby's death was being broadcast on the radio and was the big story in the evening papers. The two men boarded the *Cachalot,* knowing that Colonel Lindbergh hadn't heard the bulletins or seen the headlines.

Lindbergh greeted the men and knew at once something was wrong. "What is it?" he asked.

"We have bad news, sir," Lieutenant Richard said. He looked at Bruce, and both men lowered their eyes.

Lindbergh suddenly knew what was coming. He turned away so they couldn't see his face.

Speaking to the Colonel's back, the lieutenant said, "Colonel, I have a message for you. They have found the baby."

Lindbergh whirled around, "They have *found?*"

"He is dead," both men blurted.

The Colonel's face flushed. "Does Mrs. Lindbergh know?"

"Yes," Bruce replied.

"Is she all right?"

"Yes sir, as far as we know."

"Do you have the details?"

"Yes sir—they found him this afternoon."

"Who found him?"

"A truck driver came upon the remains when he went into the woods."

"The woods?"

"Near Mount Rose—along the Princeton-Hopewell road. About two miles from your house, sir."

Lindbergh massaged his forehead as though he had a headache. His eyes were bloodshot and he looked a little unsteady. "Do they know how he died?" he asked.

120

"We don't know that," Bruce replied. "We're very sorry, sir."

Lindbergh placed a hand on Bruce's shoulder. "I want to thank you fellows for everything."

"We are honored sir," Lieutenant Richard said, fighting back the tears.

Lindbergh cast his eyes about the cabin and said, "I'm going home."[1]

John Curtis was in Atlantic City when he heard the news. He ran to a pay phone and called Schwarzkopf. Schwarzkopf confirmed the story and advised that arrangements had been made to notify Colonel Lindbergh. He said a police car was on its way to Atlantic City to bring Curtis back to Hopewell.

When Curtis got to the Lindbergh estate he was ushered into Colonel Schwarzkopf's office. There were several men in the room—Captain Lamb, Lieutenant Keaten, Inspector Walsh, Detective Sergeant Moffatt, and Frank Wilson of the IRS. Anthony M. Hauck, the Hunterdon County Prosecutor was also there.

Schwarzkopf had been eager to get at Curtis. From the very beginning he and his men had been convinced that Curtis, like the gangster Morris Rosner, was pulling some kind of hoax.

Up until now, Schwarzkopf could only speculate on what Curtis had up his sleeve. As long as there had been a chance that the baby was alive, Colonel Lindbergh had called the shots. The police had kept at arm's length. People like Rosner, Bitz, Spitale, Condon, and Curtis had operated under Lindbergh's protection. With the baby dead, these men were of no further use and were fair game for the police.

Before Curtis could take off his overcoat, Schwarzkopf said, "You can speak with us frankly. Colonel Lindbergh has kept us informed of your activities."

"Would it not be better for us to wait until Colonel Lindbergh arrives?" Curtis asked. "I would prefer he be here when I tell what I know."

Ignoring Curtis's request, Schwarzkopf asked him to describe Sam, Nels, Eric, John, Hilda, and the others. Schwarzkopf also wanted descriptions of all the boats Curtis had been aboard in his negotiations.

The officers didn't bother to conceal their skepticism. As soon as the questioning began Curtis knew that they doubted his story. The questions were pointed, accusatory. Schwarzkopf wanted to know about automobile license plate numbers and boat registrations. Curtis said that he couldn't answer these questions without consulting his records and notes, documents that were still on the *Cachalot* and in his room at the Prince George Hotel.

The officers questioned Curtis for two hours. It was getting late and Colonel Lindbergh would be arriving soon. Although it was obvious that the detectives didn't believe Curtis, no one specifically accused him of lying.

After the interview, Curtis followed the policeman into the Lindbergh kitchen for a bite to eat. Curtis and the officers were seated at the kitchen table when Colonel Lindbergh walked through the door.

Curtis seemed relieved to see a friendly face. After huddling with Schwarzkopf, Lamb, and Keaten, Lindbergh approached Curtis with his hand extended. Curtis virtually jumped out of his chair, clutching Lindbergh's hand with both of his. The Colonel seemed glad to see his old sea mate.

"You and Mrs. Lindbergh have my deepest sympathy," Curtis said. "I can't tell you how shocked I am that we have been deceived. The gang had me totally convinced that the baby was alive."

Lindbergh and Curtis walked into the den and sat down on the sofa. They were alone.

"John," Lindbergh said, "what do you make of this?"

"I can't fathom it," Curtis replied. "But I'll do everything in my power to help you. If we move fast, we ought to be able to get Hilda and Sam right away—neither one of them is on the *Mary B. Moss.*

Before Lindbergh could respond, a state trooper stuck his head in the door. The Colonel was wanted, he said, for a conference. Lindbergh hurried from the room.[2]

The trooper took Curtis back to Schwarzkopf's office, where he was questioned by Captain Lamb. Curtis described the *Mary B. Moss,* and this information was immediately passed on to the Coast Guard.

At daybreak, Curtis and two state troopers, Mullins and Holt, left Hopewell for Cape May. Curtis was to take the troopers to the various places he had met with the kidnappers. Curtis was exhausted and uneasy in the company of the police. He missed the good-old-boy camaraderie he had in the company of Colonel Lindbergh, E. B. Bruce, and Lieutenant Richard.

In Trenton, a crowd of reporters, cameramen, and sightseers had gathered outside Walter Swayze's funeral parlor. Many of these people had been standing in the rain all night. One of them was Dr. Condon, haunted by the notion that he had in some way failed the Lindberghs.

Early Thursday night, shortly after the baby had been identified, Colonel Schwarzkopf had summoned Condon to the Lindbergh estate. Condon spent an hour in Schwarzkopf's office. After the interview Schwarzkopf told Condon to be available for further questioning the following day. Before leaving, Condon asked to speak to Mrs. Lindbergh. Schwarzkopf said no, Mrs. Lindbergh was only seeing relatives and close friends.

Sometime Thursday night, amid the excitement and confusion around the funeral home, a reporter and a cameraman slipped into the morgue and photographed the baby. How the unidentified intruders got into the building remains a mystery. On Friday, photographs of the corpse were being sold on the street at five dollars apiece.[3]

That night, Schwarzkopf and Lindbergh had a long discussion in Lindbergh's den. Schwarzkopf said that he considered Curtis, Condon and Rosner suspects. He understood that during the past two months Colonel Lindbergh had developed a personal relationship with these men, but it would be better for the investigation if he cut his ties with them.

Lindbergh asked if there was any doubt that the corpse was his son. Schwarzkopf said that there wasn't and explained in great detail why he was so sure of the identification. Schwarzkopf didn't think it was necessary for Colonel or Mrs. Lindbergh to view the remains.

The meeting broke up at dawn. Lindbergh, exhausted and emotionally drained, climbed the stairs to his bedroom. At this moment he was more concerned about his wife than Colonel Schwarzkopf's investigation.

With the discovery of the body, the newspapers were once again full of the case. Hundreds of reporters and cameramen had moved back into Hopewell, where squads of telegraph operators were dispatching, around the clock, thousands of words a day.

President Hoover announced that he had directed the federal law enforcement establishment to aid Colonel Schwarzkopf and the New Jersey State Police in the hunt for the kidnappers. Acting on the advice of his attorney general, Homer S. Cummings, President Hoover asked J. Edgar Hoover to coordinate this effort.

Elmer Irey considered the President's selection of J. Edgar Hoover a slap in the face. Although humiliated by the President's decision, Irey, a good soldier, was willing to cooperate. But J. Edgar Hoover poured water on Irey's spirit of cooperation when he ordered the Secret Service and the IRS off the case. Hoover said that he wanted the FBI to have control over the federal operation.

Irey called Hopewell and talked to Lindbergh. The Colonel couldn't believe his ears. Why was an outstanding law enforcement man like Irey being taken off the case? Lindbergh telephoned the secretary of the treasury and complained bitterly about Irey's removal. Several calls and a couple of high-level conferences later, Irey and his agents were back on the case. J. Edgar Hoover was still in charge, however.

J. Edgar Hoover's attempt to grab everything for himself didn't sit well with Lindbergh or Schwarzkopf. Since kidnapping hadn't been a federal offense when the baby was taken, the FBI didn't have jurisdiction. Hoover would have to settle for a support role in the case, a position he didn't like.

Schwarzkopf hadn't been inclined to cooperate with the New York City Police or the FBI. He hadn't given either agency access to the Lindbergh estate or to the physical evidence. The New York police and the FBI had been forced to rely on newspaper accounts of the crime. Both agencies had been busy, however, running down countless tips and leads. Meanwhile, Schwarzkopf and his men were content to work with the IRS and the Newark and Jersey City police departments.

At this point in the investigation, Schwarzkopf was operating on the assumption that the kidnappers had killed the baby on the night of the kidnapping and had dumped him in the woods before leaving the area. In all probability the baby had been taken from the nursery to the kidnappers' car, then transported to the place where it was found along Princeton-Hopewell road. The baby had probably been carried from the house in the burlap bag the officers had found along the road. The sack had contained strands of the baby's hair.

In Norfolk, Virginia, Adm. Guy Burrage refused to comment on John Curtis. Burrage's colleague, Dobson-Peacock, was not so closemouthed. He told reporters that he was puzzled by the whole affair. He couldn't understand why Sam and the gang had gone to all of that trouble when they knew that the baby was dead and that Colonel Lindbergh wouldn't pay until he got the baby.

124   On Friday morning, Morris Rosner arrived at the Lindbergh home to be questioned by Captain Lamb, Lieutenant Keaten, and Inspector Walsh. Colonel Schwarzkopf was in Trenton conferring with Governor Moore and members of the state attorney general's office.

Captain Lamb asked Rosner how many people he had shown his copy of the nursery note to. Much to the captain's dismay, Rosner said he had shown his copy of the note to hundreds of people, including thieves, racketeers, gamblers, and con men. This meant there was an outside chance that the man Condon had dealt with was merely an extortionist who had gotten a look at the secret symbol on Rosner's copy of the nursery note.

As Captain Lamb and the others questioned Rosner and Condon, John Curtis was in Cape May taking the state troopers to the various places where he had met with the kidnappers. Curtis and the troopers returned to Hopewell late Friday night. Troopers Holt and Mullins reported that the trip had been a waste of time.

Schwarzkopf told Trooper Mullins to drive Curtis to the Hildebrecht Hotel in Trenton, where he was to be kept under wraps. Schwarzkopf didn't want the press to get their hands on Curtis until he was finished with him.

On Friday afternoon, shortly after Schwarzkopf had returned from his conference with Governor Moore, he met with Colonel Lindbergh, who said the baby would be cremated. Burying the body in a cemetery would create problems: the gravesite would have to be guarded around the clock against souvenir hunters and grave robbers. The place would have to be protected for years, maybe decades. The body would be disposed of that afternoon at the Rosehill Crematory in Linden, New Jersey.

Lindbergh looked tired and on edge. "I've been thinking about the body," he said. "Maybe I ought to see it for myself."

"There's no need for that," Schwarzkopf said. "The body had been identified. There is no doubt."

"I know, but I think I should see for myself. I won't get a second chance."

"Are you sure you want to do this?" Schwarzkopf asked. "It's not necessary."

"I'll know the teeth," Lindbergh replied, "and the toes."

In Trenton, Walter Swayze was preparing the baby's death certificate. In the blank calling for the principal cause of death, Swayze typed, "Fractured Skull due to External Violence." In the space relating to the manner of injury, Swayze put "Fractured Skull Due to Homicide." The coroner then signed the document.

At four in the afternoon, Schwarzkopf pulled the car containing Colonels Lindbergh and Breckinridge into the alley behind the funeral parlor. The three men slipped into the building through a back door to avoid the crowd of onlookers gathered out front.

Inside, they were greeted by the Mercer County Prosecutor, Erwin E. Marshall, and James S. Kirkham, Chief Mercer County Detective. Lindbergh followed Walter Swayze into the room that had the baby. The corpse was on a table and covered by a sheet. Lindbergh stepped up to it and said, "Take that off."

Swayze pulled back the sheet, exposing the black, leathery remains. The stench was almost overwhelming. Lindbergh stood stiffly over the body—he didn't move or speak—

he just stood there, marble-faced. A few seconds later he stepped closer to the table and bent at the waist to get a better look at the teeth, which he counted. He then examined the foot with the overlapping toes. Lindbergh straightened up and without a word strode out of the room. He had been in there three minutes.

Lindbergh was met in the adjoining room by Erwin Marshall. "Are you satisfied that this is the body of your baby?" Marshall asked.

Lindbergh cleared his throat. "I am perfectly satisfied that it is my child."

Swayze wrapped the body in a shroud and placed it into a small oak coffin.

At four-thirty a gray hearse carried the little coffin from the funeral home. The hearse was followed by a police vehicle and several cars of reporters and cameramen.

When the sightseers on Greenwood Avenue saw the hearse, about half of them ran after it trying desperately to catch a glimpse of the coffin. Most of the others contented themselves by touching the hearse as it drove by and looking into the cars for Colonel Lindbergh.

Lindbergh and Breckinridge stayed behind at the morgue. Ten minutes later, when the crowd was gone, they left.

The thirty-mile trip to Linden took an hour. Lindbergh and Breckinridge waited in the home of the man who ran the crematorium while Schwarzkopf and the reporters proceeded to the Rosehill Cemetery and Crematory.

Schwarzkopf waited in an adjoining room as the body was put into the furnace. At 6:15 it was over. Lindbergh had said he would scatter the ashes into the Atlantic Ocean, but for now they would be kept in an urn at the crematory.

That afternoon Dr. and Mrs. John Hibben came to Hopewell to console Mrs. Lindbergh. Hibben, the president of Princeton University, spoke to reporters later that evening. "Since the child was dead, it was fortunate that it was found for it saved the parents years of anxiety and doubt," he said. "However, one would have thought the authorities would have made a thorough search of a ten-mile radius around the house, but perhaps they had a reason for not doing so."[4]

Doctor Hibben's last comment foreshadowed a difficult time for Schwarzkopf and his men.

They searched all places except those under their feet.
I'm inclined to believe that the Lindbergh garage was too
comfortable, a loafing place for the boys.

— V A L   O ' F A R R E L
a former detective and columnist for the New York Daily News

11 CRITICISM

ON SATURDAY MORNING, MAY 14, John Curtis was picked up by Trooper Agnew at the
Hildebrecht Hotel in Trenton and driven to Hopewell. From there Detective Cobb and
Sergeant Hastings of Newark would be taking him to Newark to find the house where he
had conferred with the kidnap gang.

Curtis couldn't find the house, the best he could do was take the officers to the
neighborhood where it was located.

After lunch, the officers drove Curtis to Newark's main police station, where he leafed
through several large photograph albums. In one of these he came upon a mug shot that
resembled Nils. An officer looked up the man's record and found that he had been in an
insane asylum when the baby was kidnapped.

That night, Curtis and the detectives were back driving around the neighborhood.
Curtis couldn't find the kidnappers' house, so at two-thirty in the morning, they
checked into a hotel. Since Curtis had been wearing the same clothes for three days,
he said he would like to run over to the Prince George Hotel and pick up his laundry.
He could also gather up his paperwork on the case. The detectives were sorry, but they
had orders not to let him out of their sight. He wasn't under arrest, they said, Colonel
Schwarzkopf just didn't want him talking to the press.

Schwarzkopf, Lamb, Keaten, and Walsh were mulling over Curtis's story, and it still
didn't ring true. Why would John, Eric, Nils, and the others go through all of that
rendezvous-at-sea business when they didn't have the baby? They had been told there
could be no ransom payment until *after* Colonel Lindbergh had gotten his son.

The sympathy and concern for the Lindberghs was reaching its peak. The public,
whipped up by grandstanding politicians and sensational journalism, was getting restless—and angry. The public demanded that the murderers be caught and punished.
With the baby dead and Schwarzkopf and his men unfettered, the public expected results—and wanted blood.

But there was a problem. By the time Schwarzkopf got a free hand, the trail was cold.

The time to catch kidnappers is when the ransom is exchanged. When Colonel Lindbergh denied Colonel Schwarzkopf this opportunity he gave the kidnappers a head start. And now, with politicians, mental cases, and reporters on his back, and a cold trail to follow, Schwarzkopf had to catch up.

At this point, the future didn't look bright for Schwarzkopf. He had a lot of evidence, plenty of advice, a number of political rivals, and more than a few discontented, bitter, and jealous colleagues who enjoyed heckling him from the sidelines. He was dangerously close to becoming a scapegoat.

Schwarzkopf's critics faulted him for not finding the baby's body. The fact that the corpse was discovered so close to home made the criticism even sharper. Many wondered out loud why the State Police hadn't used bloodhounds. Local dog owners told reporters that a hundred hounds could have been assembled in two hours. Schwarzkopf had said earlier that bloodhounds weren't available. Now people were saying otherwise. In private, Schwarzkopf explained that he didn't use dogs because of the rain and all of the people in the area. He said he had been told that these factors would have rendered them useless.[1]

Others couldn't understand why the area around the estate hadn't been searched by volunteers. Dr. Hibben of Princeton University had offered student help. Several local Boy Scout troops had made similar offers.[2] Fearing that evidence would be trampled, Schwarzkopf had kept volunteer groups out of the area. He realized that regardless of the number of searchers, finding the remains of a tiny corpse within a two-mile radius of the Lindbergh estate was like finding a needle in a hay stack. Telephone workers had laid cable along the Princeton-Hopewell road only a few yards from the gravesite, but no one had seen the body.

Schwarzkopf was also accused of not cooperating with the FBI and the New York City Police. Representatives of both agencies complained that he wasn't sharing information. They said their investigators hadn't seen the physical evidence, crime scene photographs, copies of the ransom notes, or key investigative reports.

The most severe and vocal complaints came from the New Jersey County Detectives Association, a statewide law enforcement organization made up of county investigators. Frank J. Harrold, a detective from Atlantic County, told reporters that several members of the organization were demanding Schwarzkopf's resignation.[3]

Ellis Parker, Sr., the veteran detective from Burlington County, was one of Schwarzkopf's most outspoken critics. Parker had been a county detective for forty years and had built a reputation as a real-life Sherlock Holmes. A law enforcement celebrity, Parker was called the small-town detective with the worldwide reputation.

Parker claimed to have investigated three hundred homicides, including several "baffling murders." According to his own account, all but twelve of these cases had resulted in convictions. As a result, Detective Parker had acquired a taste for publicity and was accustomed to the lion's share of the limelight. When the Lindbergh crime was committed one county away, Parker saw the chance to make himself one of the most famous detectives in the world. But things hadn't worked out that way—Colonel Schwarzkopf had been put in charge of the investigation. It was Schwarzkopf's name in the papers, his voice over the radio, and his presence that brought the reporters, photographers, and newsreel people running.

Parker might have been able to work his way into some of the limelight, but he was on the outs with Governor Moore. Although he had made several overtures to Schwarzkopf, he had been rebuffed.

Bitter and almost insane with jealousy, Parker could only hope that Schwarzkopf would stub his toe. He had been critical of everything Schwarzkopf had done, and now, two days after the baby had been found, he was telling *The New York Times* that Schwarzkopf's "failure to make a thorough search of the entire community within a wide radius of the Lindbergh house after the kidnapping is inexcusable and shameful."[4]

Colonel Lindbergh was disgusted by all the cheap shots, second-guessing, and theorizing. He was squarely behind Schwarzkopf and knew that if he made a public statement praising him it would take off much of the pressure. But Lindbergh chose to remain silent. He hated the press and felt that Schwarzkopf could take care of himself.

Schwarzkopf did get public support from Governor Moore, who announced that Schwarzkopf would continue running the investigation. The governor claimed that the state police had cooperated with other agencies and would continue to do so. Moore said that the proposals calling for Schwarzkopf's ouster were "silly and ridiculous." The governor concluded his remarks with the following statement: "This [the Lindbergh case] is a brilliant opportunity for every policeman. The cop who arrests the murderer of the Lindbergh child is made for life. Why, he could get fifty-two weeks' booking at $10,000 a week."[5]

So Schwarzkopf had the governor's support—for whatever it was worth. He also got some help from an unexpected source—Hans Schulz, the police commissioner of Berlin. In a widely published statement, the commissioner said that the American police should not be criticized for failing to find the baby's body. He noted that he had worked on many murder cases where the body had not been found until several months after the crime.

On Saturday, May 14, two prominent criminalists traveled to Hopewell to meet with Colonel Schwarzkopf. They were Dr. Calvin Goddard, director of the Scientific Crime Detection Laboratory at Northwestern University Law School, and Leonarde Keeler, a nationally known polygraph expert on Goddard's staff. The two experts had come to Hopewell to offer Keeler's lie-detection services. John Wigmore, the dean of Northwestern's Law School and noted author of *Treatise on Evidence,* had written to Colonel Lindbergh urging him to take advantage of Keeler's expertise.[6] Colonel Lindbergh had turned Dean Wigmore's letter over to Breckinridge, who had referred the matter to Schwarzkopf.

Schwarzkopf told Keeler and Goddard that although he had heard of the polygraph, he didn't know much about it. Keeler explained how the lie detector worked, and outlined its eleven-year history. He said the machine was over 90 percent accurate.

Schwarzkopf thought that Keeler made sense. He thanked Keeler and Goddard for their time and willingness to contribute their services. He told them that Colonel Lindbergh was also grateful.

Before the experts departed, Schwarzkopf promised to give the polygraph some thought. He said he would discuss the matter with Colonel Lindbergh.

Schwarzkopf hoped that the polygraph idea would appeal to Lindbergh. Since the Colonel was fascinated with science, technology, and all manner of gadgetry, Schwarzkopf figured that he might be interested in the polygraph. But when Schwarzkopf brought the subject up, Lindbergh showed little interest. He didn't like the idea of subjecting the servants to a lie-detection test. Why humiliate and insult innocent people?

Schwarzkopf didn't get back to Goddard or Keeler. Without Colonel Lindbergh's support, there could be no polygraph. The subject was dropped—for the time being.

A few of those who believed that the kidnapping had been an inside job were critical of Schwarzkopf for not subjecting the servants to the lie detector. One of these critics was Al Dunlap, the editor of a popular police and crime magazine called *The Detective.* In an article entitled, "Why No Lie Detector for the Lindbergh Case?" Dunlap called the Lindbergh investigation a "monumental fizzle," stating that it had been "miserably bungled from every angle."[7]

Since the discovery of the baby, more and more information about the investigation was leaking out. Many were wondering how the kidnappers had managed to get the money without proving that the child was alive.

In the midst of all this criticism, Ellis Parker, Sr., got his hands on one of the pirated photographs of the baby's corpse—one of those taken by the photographer who had gotten into the morgue. Parker had studied the photograph of the decomposed corpse and from its condition suspected that the baby had been dead for more than seventy-two days. Parker checked the weather records for the months of March, April, and the first part of May and found that temperatures during this period had been cooler than usual. Parker knew that bodies decompose more slowly in cool temperatures, and from this concluded that the corpse in the photograph, by virtue of its condition, had been dead long before the Lindbergh baby was kidnapped.

Parker showed his photograph and weather data to a "medical man" who agreed that the baby whose body this was had been dead at the time of the kidnapping. Parker was now asserting that the corpse found on Mount Rose Heights was not young Lindbergh.

Parker compared Dr. Mitchell's autopsy report with Dr. Van Ingen's medical records and found the four-and-one-half-inch discrepancy in the baby's height. Parker was now doubly sure that Colonel Lindbergh had cremated somebody else's baby. As far as he was concerned the Lindbergh child was still alive.

Although he was still an outsider, Detective Parker had found a role to play in the Lindbergh case. He was a missionary with a cause, preaching his theory to anyone who would listen. But he soon became frustrated because nobody took him seriously. Even the tabloids, always eager to publish outrageous material, ignored him—his theory was too bizarre. The Lindbergh baby had been positively identified through its hair, clothing, teeth, and toes.

130   Although Parker didn't know whose ashes were in Colonel Lindbergh's urn, he had a pretty good idea how that body had ended up on Mount Rose Heights. His theory was this: The Princeton-Hopewell road was a major bootlegging artery that had been shut off when the police started stopping cars in search of the baby. The bootleggers figured that until the baby was found, things would not get back to normal. To remedy the problem, they had dug up a twenty-month-old baby that had been dead for several months and planted it in the woods so the police could find it.

Parker had few converts to his theory. But the world hadn't heard the last of Detective Ellis Parker. There was nothing he wouldn't do to get into the Lindbergh limelight.

I cannot understand how he could have done such a thing. It just seems impossible.

— THE REVEREND H. DOBSON-PEACOCK
referring to John Hughes Curtis

12 THE HOAX

ON SUNDAY, MAY 15, John Curtis was in Newark with Detectives Cobb and Hastings. The men had spent the previous day looking for the house where Curtis had negotiated with the kidnappers. Detective Cobb had stayed in the car while Hastings and Curtis walked up to several houses to look in their windows. Curtis had said that a couple of the houses looked familiar but he couldn't be sure.

That evening, at the Lindbergh estate, Curtis was questioned twice, each time by a different set of detectives. Both times he went over his entire story, complaining to his interviewers that without his notes and other documents he couldn't be as detailed and accurate as he'd like. Curtis was questioned until 2:30 in the morning, then driven back to the Hildebrecht Hotel. He was told not to use the telephone or try to get in touch with the press. A trooper would come back for him at seven o'clock.

The next morning, as Curtis wandered about the Lindbergh grounds, none of the troopers stopped to talk to him. They were giving him the silent treatment. Curtis stopped a passing detective and said that he had an important message for Colonel Lindbergh. The detective said that he'd pass that information on to the Colonel.

At one in the afternoon Curtis was still in exile. He hadn't eaten, and instead of having lunch, he was sitting on the running board of Colonel Lindbergh's car. Anne Lindbergh noticed Curtis as she and her mother started on their daily walk. The two women stopped and chatted with him for a few minutes. In her diary, Mrs. Lindbergh wrote: "Curtis sitting dejected, broken, on the running board of C.'s car all day, being questioned."[1]

Tired, nervous, and on the verge of panic, Curtis approached one of the troopers and demanded to see Colonel Lindbergh. The officer said he would see what he could do and walked into the house. A few minutes later Colonel Lindbergh strode out the door. Curtis got off the running board and the two men shook hands.

"Colonel, what is this all about? Why am I being treated like this?" Curtis asked with a nervous smile.

"I don't know anything about it," Lindbergh replied. His voice lacked warmth or concern. "I'll go in and check on it."

"I'd appreciate that, sir," Curtis said with a tinge of relief.

"I do know that some of the information you gave us didn't check up," Lindbergh said. He looked Curtis square in the face.

"But Colonel," Curtis whined, "they should have given me a chance to consult my notes! I could have been mistaken about some of the phone numbers and so forth."

"I believe you were," Lindbergh said, shifting his weight. Suddenly he looked uncomfortable. "I'll look into it." He turned and walked back into the house.[2]

At two o'clock Curtis was still outside—waiting. Tired, worried, and now very hungry, he walked uninvited into the mess hall and helped himself to lunch.

Several troopers spoke to Curtis, but no one sat down to chat. Later in the afternoon, he was told that he would be spending the night in the den on Lindbergh's couch. At dinner time Curtis called home and spoke to his wife Constance and their two children. Constance didn't understand why he was being detained; she was ill and needed him at home.

Curtis spent the evening in Lindbergh's den listening to the radio. He heard several news broadcasts about the Lindbergh case, including the story about the Coast Guard searching the Atlantic Ocean for the *Mary B. Moss.*

Just before midnight, Inspector Walsh stuck his head into the room to say hello and to see if there was anything Curtis needed. It was the first kind word Curtis had heard all day. Curtis asked Walsh if he had time for a game of checkers. Walsh said sure, and the two men sat on the sofa with the checkerboard between them.

As the game progressed, Walsh asked Curtis about his wife and children. Curtis said he had talked with Constance several hours ago and she was puzzled why he couldn't come home. Inspector Walsh laid the checkerboard aside and suggested that they get a breath of fresh air.

Outside, Curtis said that things hadn't been going well for him. His wife was sick and his ship-building company had gone bankrupt. If it hadn't been for his wife's personal fortune, he wouldn't have been able to pay off his debts. His business problems had almost driven him crazy. To be honest about it, he had suffered a nervous breakdown.

As the two men strolled, Curtis talked and Walsh listened. Walsh said he understood why Curtis was under so much stress. Why didn't Curtis relieve some of this pressure by telling the truth about Sam and the kidnap gang. This would also help Colonel Lindbergh.

"But I have told the truth," Curtis said.

Walsh thought he detected a lack of conviction in Curtis' voice. "Please, John," Walsh replied, "tell Colonel Lindbergh the truth."

The two men continued walking: Curtis was deep in thought. "The only thing that I told Colonel Lindbergh that wasn't true is that I saw the ransom money," Curtis blurted.

"Let's go in and tell that to Colonel Lindbergh right now," Walsh said. "That's the thing that convinced him that you were in touch with the kidnappers. It's a good start, John. I'm proud of you," Walsh said putting a hand on Curtis's shoulder.

Curtis shook his head, "Why not," he sighed. "I hate to do it—I hate to face the Colonel." He looked at Walsh, "I did it because I was afraid he wouldn't believe me when I said that I was in contact with them. I did it for his own good—I hope he'll understand. I am not a liar. You can ask my friends and business associates—they will say I'm an honest man. My word is good."

The two men entered the house and Walsh sent a trooper for Colonel Lindbergh. In a matter of minutes the Colonel walked into the dining room.

Curtis's eyes were watery and his voice strained as he told Lindbergh that he hadn't seen any of the ransom money. He had lied. As Curtis explained why he had lied, Lindbergh made a gesture of disgust, then walked out of the room. Curtis stopped talking and slumped into a chair. He sat there with his face in his hands while Inspector Walsh went to get Lieutenant Keaten, Frank J. Wilson, and a police stenographer.

With the stenographer looking on, Walsh asked Curtis to tell Lieutenant Keaten and Wilson how he had lied to Colonel Lindbergh. Curtis repeated the story. When that was done, Walsh, speaking very softly, suggested that Curtis clear the air with the whole truth. It was time, he said, for Curtis to admit once and for all that the entire episode was a hoax. People would understand, he said. Everybody knew how much stress he had been under.

Curtis insisted that he had not lied about the kidnappers, all of that was true.

The police stenographer was dismissed and the three detectives took Curtis to the den to question him further. It was two in the morning. Frank Wilson took charge of the interrogation. The IRS agent was a poker-faced, ex-real estate salesman from Buffalo, New York. He chain smoked nickel cigars and was as hard-nosed as Schwarzkopf and Keaten. He disliked big, blustering backslapping types like Curtis. After a loud, profane, two-hour grilling, Curtis was getting confused and starting to babble. Just when Curtis was on the verge of breaking, Walsh, the nice guy, took over.

In a soothing, sympathetic voice, Walsh said he understood Curtis's reluctance to confess. Such an admission would surely bring him immediate disgrace. But the Inspector had an idea: If Curtis admitted his hoax and signed a written confession, Walsh would get Colonel Lindbergh and Colonel Schwarzkopf to agree not to make the confession public. And that meant there would be no criminal charges. As soon as Curtis signed his confession, he'd be free to go home to his wife and children. But if he didn't confess, Curtis would be ruined—because he would be sent to jail.[3]

Curtis was about to collapse physically. The detectives were exhausted too. No one spoke for several minutes. Then Inspector Walsh said, "I've had it. I'm going to bed."

The detectives were at the door when Curtis leaped out of his chair, causing it to bang against the wall. "All right, I'll make a statement!" he cried. "Get me a typewriter. I'll make a statement and sign it."

Lieutenant Keaten fetched a typewriter and several sheets of paper. Curtis pulled a chair up to Lindbergh's desk and began to peck. A half hour later, he pulled a statement from the carriage which in part read:

> At the present time I am sane but I honestly believe that for the last seven or eight months I have not been myself, due to financial troubles. I became insane on the subject

of the Lindbergh matter which caused me to create the story in its entirety which was untrue in every respect.

I never knew such people that I named to Colonel Lindbergh and they were creatures of a distorted mind.

I exceedingly regret that I caused Colonel Lindbergh and others any inconvenience and wish it were in my power to correct my wrong.[4]

Curtis signed the paper and handed it to Walsh and Keaten who also signed it as witnesses. Walsh wrote down the time—4:35 A.M.—and the date—May 17, 1932—on the bottom left-hand corner of the page.

Walsh felt sorry for Curtis, but he had to tell him that he considered the hoax unbelievably cruel—and one other thing—Curtis would be prosecuted, and he would probably go to prison for a long time.

Curtis sank into the sofa and cried. He was ashamed of himself and he hoped that Colonel Lindbergh would forgive him. Regaining his composure somewhat, Curtis asked when he could return to Norfolk. This was out of the question, Walsh said. Curtis would be spending the night on Colonel Lindbergh's couch.

Early the next morning Curtis was walking about the Lindbergh estate in the company of a guard. He hadn't shaved or bathed for several days and his clothes were rumpled.

Later in the morning Curtis was visited by Schwarzkopf and Keaten. They wanted to know if he had anything to add to his statement. Curtis said that he was concerned about the effect his confession would have on his reputation. He was also worried about prison and wanted to know what he'd be charged with. Schwarzkopf said he didn't know. Curtis asked to speak to Colonel Lindbergh; he said he wanted to apologize to him personally.[5] Schwarzkopf promised to tell Lindbergh that Curtis had asked to see him.

Schwarzkopf brought the conversation around to Admiral Guy Burrage and the Reverend Mr. H. Dobson-Peacock, the other members of the so-called Norfolk Negotiating Committee. Schwarzkopf wanted to know if either of them had been a party to the hoax. Curtis said that neither man had any idea he was making it all up. However, when he had tried to drop the matter, before meeting with Colonel Lindbergh, Dobson-Peacock talked him out of it. Curtis said the cleric had urged him on out of his own desire for publicity. According to Curtis, Dobson-Peacock had become a full-fledged publicity hound, continuously pressing him for news. In fact, as the negotiating committee's spokesman, the cleric started fabricating some of his own stories.[6] His penchant for the limelight became such a problem that Admiral Burrage had to take over as spokesman.

Curtis and the two officers walked to the guardhouse at the entrance to the estate. Inside the shanty, Curtis wrote out his comments about Dobson-Peacock. When he finished, Schwarzkopf and Keaten carried the statement back into the house to get it typed.

Curtis was ignored the rest of the morning. His guard didn't even take him into the mess hall for lunch.

At 3:30 that afternoon Schwarzkopf held a press conference in Lindbergh's garage.

With Curtis at his side, Schwarzkopf read the confession to a hundred or so reporters. When he finished, he read Curtis's statement about Dobson-Peacock and how he had pushed him into the hoax.

Schwarzkopf announced that he had asked Dobson-Peacock to come to Hopewell to be questioned about any false statements he might have made. Schwarzkopf said that he had sent the churchman two telegrams and had talked to him on the telephone. Dobson-Peacock had made it clear that he was not coming to Hopewell. Since he was not a resident of New Jersey, Schwarzkopf couldn't force him to.

The news that Curtis had concocted the entire kidnapper business had devastated Dobson-Peacock. When he learned that Curtis was telling the police that it was *his* fault and that *he* had lied to the press, he was furious. He had torn up Schwarzkopf's two telegrams, and when the colonel called him, he angrily denied any responsibility for the hoax. He also denied being a publicity-seeker and a liar. He couldn't see why he should travel to Hopewell at his own expense to be humiliated by police interrogators. Dobson-Peacock reminded Schwarzkopf that the only reason he had gotten into the case was to help free the Lindbergh baby. Curtis had come to him with the story and had asked for his help. Now he was being subjected to this! He said he was as much a victim of the hoax as the Lindberghs.

That evening, as Curtis floated aimlessly about the grounds, he saw, through the dining room windows, Lindbergh, Schwarzkopf, Anthony Hauck, and others conferring about his future. When darkness came, a second guard was added to the Curtis detail.

The news that Curtis had been driven insane by the Lindbergh case triggered a series of false confessions. Lunatics everywhere were turning themselves in as Lindbergh kidnappers.

Amid all of this madness, Mrs. Lindbergh was living in seclusion, trying to distance herself from the case. She was puzzled and a little frustrated by her husband's continued interest in the day-to-day investigation. The baby was dead, and catching the murderers was a job for the police. Her main concern was her second child, due in three months. Once the baby was born, Anne Lindbergh could start a new life.

On Tuesday, just before midnight, Schwarzkopf arrived in Trenton to attend a conference in the state attorney general's office. William Stevens had summoned Schwarzkopf and the prosecutors from Mercer and Hunterdon counties. The purpose of the meeting was to determine what to do with Curtis. Following a lengthy discussion, it was decided that Curtis would be prosecuted in Hunterdon County for the relatively minor but broad offense of obstructing justice and giving false information. Charges would not be brought against Dobson-Peacock.

The next morning, John Condon was blaming Curtis for killing his deal with "Cemetery John." "I knew all along that this Curtis was a faker," Condon said. "He was not only guilty of a cruel hoax, he ruined my chances of maintaining contact with the kidnappers."[7]

About the time Schwarzkopf got back to Hopewell from his meeting in Trenton, Trooper Agnew, one of the officers who had accompanied Curtis to Newark a couple of days earlier, started to question the hoaxer. For the next four hours, Curtis was put through another intensive grilling. Helping Agnew were Sgt. Warren Moffatt and Det. Robert Coar of the Newark Police Department.

Seated at the Lindbergh dining room table, Curtis pleaded exhaustion and stated that he didn't understand why he was still being interrogated. He had already confessed—what else did they want? When Agnew accused him of holding back, Curtis said that he had confessed fully. Surely the police didn't believe that he had something to do with the kidnapping itself. Ignoring Curtis's denials, the detectives grilled him until dawn. In a fit of frustration, Agnew tossed a copy of the *New York Daily News* on the table. On the front page, under the headline: "FAKE BABY HUNT, CURTIS CONFESSES," there was a story of the hoax and a picture of Curtis, his wife, and two children.

"Now, goddammit," Agnew shouted, "you're ruined for life!" With that, the interrogation was over. At a quarter after five, Agnew took the suspect to the laundry room in the basement. Curtis was told that he would be held there until his arraignment later in the day. The laundry room door was locked and a guard posted outside.[8]

In Norfolk, Curtis's wife and many of his friends refused to believe that Curtis had perpetrated a hoax. They believed that Sam and the other gangsters had forced Curtis to participate in a scheme to swindle Colonel Lindbergh. They thought that Curtis had gone along after they had threatened his family.

Late Wednesday afternoon, a local magistrate named George Webster arrived at the Lindbergh estate to preside over John Curtis's arraignment. Curtis was taken to the garage, where Lieutenant Keaten formally placed him under arrest. Keaten advised Curtis that he was being charged with giving false information for the purpose of hindering the investigation of the Lindbergh case. The offense, contained in Section 13b of the New Jersey Crime Laws of 1898, carried a fine of a thousand dollars and/or a maximum prison sentence of three years.

Curtis was escorted into Colonel Lindbergh's den, where the arraignment was to be held. The magistrate and the complainant, Hunterdon County Prosecutor Anthony M. Hauck, were present along with Colonel Lindbergh, Henry Breckenridge, Colonel Schwarzkopf, and several detectives, including Inspector Walsh, Frank Wilson, Sergeant Moffatt, Detective Coar, and Trooper Agnew.

After Huack read Curtis the charge, the prisoner waived a preliminary hearing. The magistrate then fixed his bond at ten thousand dollars. Curtis said that he couldn't make the bail, so he was placed into a car and driven to Flemington, the site of the Hunterdon County jail.

The impatience of the public for quick results has resulted in much criticism of the police management of the case, most of it probably unwarranted, all of it premature.

— D R .   G E O R G E   W.   K I R C H W E Y
former dean of Columbia Law School.

13 THE EXPERTS

ON MAY 17, the day following Curtis's confession, District Attorney Charles B. McLaughlin of the Bronx initiated his own investigation into the case by convening a grand jury. McLaughlin's inquiry focused on the extortion aspect of the case.

McLaughlin's first witness was Henry Breckinridge, who chronicled Colonel Lindbergh's prolonged ransom negotiations with Condon's "Cemetery John." Breckinridge was followed to the stand by Jafsie's friend Al Reich and the two other men who had accompanied Condon to Hopewell the night Colonel Lindbergh made Condon a go-between.

The grand jury adjourned at two o'clock without hearing from Dr. Condon—he was told that his testimony would be taken on Friday, May 20. When Condon walked out of the Bronx Supreme Court Building, he was surrounded by a crowd of reporters. Showing signs of exhaustion and strain but insisting that he was not afraid of the kidnappers, Condon declared, "I will readily identify them. They broke contact with me, thus placing me in a position of discredit in the eyes of the world, but I am not afraid of them."[1] Condon then launched an attack on Curtis, calling his hoax stupid and cruel.

While Breckenridge and the others were testifying in the Bronx, Schwarzkopf got in touch with Commissioner Edward Mulrooney of the New York police and arranged for Condon to make daily visits to numerous station houses in the city where he would view lineups of recently arrested men. It had occurred to Schwarzkopf that if things got too hot for Condon's John, he might get himself arrested and take refuge in jail.[2]

The next day Condon was scheduled to examine two thousand mug shots at the Mount Vernon (N.Y.) Police Department in Westchester County. Condon was summoned whenever a person meeting John's description was taken into custody in New York, New Jersey, eastern Pennsylvania, or Delaware.

Colonel Schwarzkopf was still being criticized. On the day the Bronx grand jury convened, New Jersey State Senator Emerson L. Richards told reporters that Schwarzkopf was bungling the Lindbergh case the way he had mishandled another celebrated case (the Hall-Mills murder case) six years ago. "This probably will be just another Hall-Mills case and for the same reason," Richards said. The senator added that the state police were "fine for catching speeders" but were not equipped for detective work. "I think the Colonel is doing a job that's all right for the kind of job he is equipped to handle. We won't gain anything by throwing Schwarzkopf out and putting someone else in. It is just a matter of having the case handled by the proper authorities."[3]

In response to Richards's criticism, Colonel Lindbergh wrote a letter to Governor Moore, who read part of it at a press conference: "The untiring energy, efficiency and cooperation with which Colonel Schwarzkopf has conducted his investigation has been of the most help and satisfaction. I feel that I cannot speak too highly of the New Jersey Police and the officers detailed from other organizations."[4]

In Flemington, at the Hunterdon County Jail, John Curtis awoke Thursday morning feeling well rested and in high spirits. He hadn't felt this good in weeks.[5] Curtis spent the day reading, doing light exercise, and conversing with the guard stationed outside his cell. Prosecutor Hauck looked in on him late in the afternoon, advising Curtis that so far no date had been set for his indictment. Curtis had not retained an attorney and had made no effort to raise the money to post his bail. One of the reasons Curtis was in such high spirits had to do with the bulletin Schwarzkopf had issued earlier in the day exonerating him from any involvement in the kidnapping.

In Norfolk, Dobson-Peacock told the press that he would submit to a New Jersey State Police interview if Schwarzkopf sent an officer to Virginia to conduct it. Schwarzkopf declined, saying he wanted Dobson-Peacock in New Jersey where he could be confronted by John Curtis.

Thursday morning, Dr. Condon's daughter Myra telephoned Colonel Schwarzkopf to tell him that her father had been ordered by his physician to take the day off. Condon would not be able to examine the mug shots at the Mount Vernon Police Department. Earlier in the week Condon had looked at thousands of rogues' gallery photographs at the White Plains and Yonkers city jails. He had also visited the county lockup in East View, New Jersey, and was scheduled to view mug shots at Sing Sing Penitentiary in Ossining, New York.

On his day off, Dr. Condon drove to West Point to visit a friend who was an instructor there. Condon's automobile was followed by a caravan of New York City detectives, New Jersey State Police officers, newsreel people, cameramen, and newspaper reporters.

The same day, Colonel Lindbergh called the principal investigators in the case to a meeting in his office. The purpose of the conference was to reenact the kidnapping and to trace the trail of the kidnappers from the nursery to Featherbed Lane where their car had probably been parked. Lindbergh hoped the reenactment would uncover clues that had been overlooked.

Looking haggard and wearing a baggy gray suit, Lindbergh looked on as a detective positioned the bottom two sections of a duplicate kidnap ladder against the house where the real one had been placed. Colonel Schwarzkopf then climbed up the ladder and into the nursery. When he came down, the 165-pound Schwarzkopf was carrying a bag of sand that weighed the same as the baby. When Schwarzkopf put his weight on the top rung of the bottom section of the ladder, the fourth one from the ground, the side rails split. The break occurred at the place where the dowel pin traversed the two ladder sections.

When the ladder split, Schwarzkopf dropped the sandbag and fell to the ground. On the way down, the bag struck the cement windowsill to Colonel Lindbergh's den.

The reenactment suggested two things: The intruder weighed about 160 pounds and the Lindbergh baby might have been killed when the ladder broke. The baby's skull could have been fractured by Colonel Lindbergh's windowsill.

The break in the duplicate ladder, constructed the same way and with the same kind of wood as the original, occurred in the place the real ladder had broken. Both ladders had held the weight of the kidnapper but had broken under the additional burden of the baby.

At 10:15 Friday morning, Dr. Condon appeared before the Bronx grand jury. He testified for two hours. After lunch, several New York City detectives took the stand. Outside the courthouse, the crowd of fifteen hundred people looked on as Condon strode from the building to a waiting car driven by Condon's son-in-law, Ralph Hacker. Hacker drove Condon directly to the New Rochelle Police Department, where Condon looked at several hundred photographs. While he was there, he and the police chief got into a heated argument over Condon's refusal to describe "Cemetery John" to him.

Back in Hopewell, Lieutenant Keaten and his men were investigating a gangster in Maryland who had said in a statement that he had inside information about the kidnapping. New York City detectives were questioning Joseph Perrone, the cab driver who had delivered the ransom note to Condon's home on March 12.

Dobson-Peacock, speaking to reporters outside the Christ Episcopal Church in Norfolk, announced that his legal advisors had instructed him not to go to New Jersey to be questioned by the police. Meanwhile, a letter he had written to his mother in England had been published in the *London Daily Express* and *The New York Times*. Undated, it had been written from a New York City hotel shortly before the baby was discovered. The letter embarrassed Peacock because it showed that he was prone to a little hoaxing himself.[6]

On May 21, the *New York Times* quoted Dr. George W. Kirchwey, the former dean of Columbia Law School and one-time warden of Sing Sing: "The impatience of the public for quick results has resulted in much criticism of the police management of the case, most of it probably unwarranted, all of it premature."

Kirchwey conceded that the police had talked too much and had thus inflamed public expectations. He said that even though the baby had been found in an area where it might have been discovered had a more thorough search been conducted, this was not grounds for major criticism of the police. Kirchwey said "The search for clues and the follow-up work may have been as well done as was humanly possible under the circumstances. There is no science of detection. It is a matter of following hunches, a process of trial and error."[7]

140   On May 23, the New Jersey State Legislature authorized Governor Moore to offer a twenty-five-thousand dollar reward for information leading to the arrest and conviction of the kidnappers. Because the baby's safety was no longer a factor, Colonel Lindbergh had no objections.

On the day Governor Moore authorized the reward, Schwarzkopf mailed a circular to hundreds of prisons and police agencies across the country. The flier contained photographs of two of the ransom letters. Prison wardens, jail keepers, and law enforcement heads were asked to compare the handwriting of criminals in their custody against the notes.

Schwarzkopf's handwriting investigation was two-pronged—it involved a random search for handwriting that matched the ransom notes, and it consisted of comparing the writing of particular people to confirm or eliminate them as suspects.

Back in April, Schwarzkopf had sent all of the handwriting evidence, including the ransom-note envelopes and the sleeping-suit package mailed to John Condon, to Dr. Wilmer T. Souder, chief of the National Bureau of Standards in Washington, D.C. Dr. Souder was one of two handwriting experts, called questioned documents examiners, working for the federal government. The other was Bert Farrar of the United States Treasury Department. After studying the evidence, Souder reported that all of the writing had been penned by the same person—there was only one ransom-note writer.

In May, Schwarzkopf sent the handwriting evidence to Albert Sherman Osborn, a private questioned documents examiner in New York City. Osborn was the most prominent and successful questioned documents examiner in the world. A portly, white-haired seventy-four-year old, he had been in the business since 1887. By 1932, he had testified in thirty-seven states and in most of the provinces of Canada. He had also taken the stand in London, Puerto Rico, and New Zealand. He had been a friend and colleague of scientific crime detection advocates John W. Wigmore, the dean of Northwestern Law School, and August Vollmer, the progressive chief of the Berkeley, California police. In 1910, Osborn had written a massive textbook, called *Questioned Documents,* that was now the standard in the field.[8] At the peak of his career, Osborn was considered the dean of the world's questioned documents examiners.[9]

Osborn had been following the Lindbergh investigation closely and was delighted when Colonel Schwarzkopf sent him all of the handwriting evidence. Like Dr. Souder, Osborn concluded that one person had written all the ransom writings. He found that the same words had been misspelled throughout—words like *boad* for "boat," *singnature* for "signature," *mony* for "money," and *ingnore* for "ignore." The kidnapper also transposed his *g*'s and *h*'s such as in *lihgt* for "light" and *rihgt* for "right." Moreover, he had neglected to cross his *t*'s and dot his *i*'s and *j*'s. According to Osborn, the contents of the letters supported the one-writer theory. The notes were full of references to earlier statements regarding the amount of the ransom, warnings not to notify the police, and assurances that the child was safe, well, and in good hands. There were also two remarks in separate notes that the crime had been a year in the planning. Osborn concluded further that the holes in the ransom note symbols had been punched by the same instrument.

The presence of the same symbol on eleven of the fifteen ransom notes and the fact that all of the letters had been written on the same kind of paper with the same ink was further indication of a single ransom writer.

In addition to the misspellings, Osborn was struck by the letters' construction and phraseology. He concluded that the writer's nationality was German. For example, the word *New York* usually appeared as "New-York," a European form, and the word *good* had been written as "gut." Osborn guessed that the writer, in composing the notes, had used a German-English dictionary.

Osborn noted that entire sentences were completely jumbled, but when translated literally into German, made sense. The word *sleeping suit*, for example, mentioned in the March 20 letter, was written as one word—in German that word would be *schlaf-anzug* or *schlafrock*. The writer had addressed Dr. Condon as "Mr. Doctor John F. Condon," a proper Germanic salutation, and there was the writer's custom of placing the dollar sign after the money figure. Other typically Germanic words were *dank* for "thank," *ouer* for "our," and *aus* for "out." Finally, the words *private mail* contained in the March 20 note were run together and the letter *e* omitted, characteristic of such words in German, which are often formed by the placing together of an adjective and a noun.

Realizing that policemen all over the country would be taking handwriting samples from hundreds of people in their custody, Osborn composed a paragraph the police were to dictate to them when obtaining samples of their handwriting. This paragraph contained the words *our, were, place, money, later, not, anything*, and *something*, the words most frequently misspelled by the kidnapper. Osborn's paragraph was disguised so that the subject of the test would not be aware of its relationship to the Lindbergh case.[10]

Osborn completed his study and mailed his report and the paragraph to Schwarz-kopf. In his cover letter he stressed the importance of having the paragraph *dictated* to suspects. If the suspects were allowed to copy the test, the ransom writer's misspellings would not be revealed.

While Albert Osborn was studying the handwriting evidence, Schwarzkopf sent pieces of the kidnap ladder to Carlile T. Winslow, the director of the Department of Agriculture's Forest Service Laboratory in Madison, Wisconsin. Winslow turned the specimens over to his chief wood technologist, Arthur Koehler.

Koehler, a quiet, unassuming government technocrat had testified as an expert in several criminal trials, the most celebrated being the Magnuson bombing case in Madison, Wisconsin. He had been born in 1885 in Mishicot, Wisconsin, and grew up on a farm. His father was a carpenter, and this led to young Koehler's interest in wood and fine tools. In 1911 Koehler earned a B.S. degree in forestry from the University of Michigan. As a senior, he lectured on wood identification, and a year later he joined the U.S. Forest Service. In 1914 he began work at the Forest Products Laboratory in Madison.

142 Koehler earned his M.S. degree in wood anatomy from the University of Wisconsin in 1928. By 1932, as chief of the division of Silvicultural Relations at the U.S. Forest Products Laboratory, he was the most prominent wood expert in the world. He had written fifty-two government booklets and bulletins dealing with wood and its identification. He had also published a book on the subject, *The Uses and Properties of Wood.*

In March, a few days after the kidnapping, Koehler had written to Colonel Lindbergh to volunteer his services. His letter, one of thousands received at the Lindbergh estate during that period, had been ignored. Now Koehler was being invited into the case.

From the slivers of wood Schwarzkopf had sent, Koehler determined that the ladder was made of at least four kinds of wood. There was pine from North Carolina, Douglas fir from the West, birch, and Ponderosa pine.

Late in May, Koehler mailed his report. In his cover letter he said that he was willing to come to New Jersey to study the ladder itself. If he could get a look at the whole ladder, he might be able to determine something about the person who had built it.

Several months later Schwarzkopf would ask Koehler to come to New Jersey. Schwarzkopf believed that if the Lindbergh case was ever to be solved, experts such as Osborn and Koehler would become extremely important.

> Gee, life is getting so sad. I really don't think there is much
> to live for any more.
>
> — V I O L E T   S H A R P E
> *in a letter to a friend three days before she committed suicide*

14 VIOLET SHARPE

NOW THAT THE JOHN CURTIS BUSINESS was resolved, Colonel Schwarzkopf was in a position to tie up a few loose ends. The most pressing business at hand had to do with Violet Sharpe, the twenty-eight-year-old maid who lived at the Morrow estate in Englewood.

Violet was first questioned about her date on the night of the crime by two detectives from the Newark Police Department. She told the officers that she couldn't remember her date's name or the names of the other couple. She wasn't able to recall the title of the movie and couldn't remember what it was about. Because she had been uncooperative and at times hostile with the detectives, Schwarzkopf had decided that Violet should be interviewed again.

On April 6, four days after the ransom money was delivered to the man in St. Raymond's Cemetery, Violet's sister, Emily, sailed for England. She had left the country without telling the police.

One week later, on April 13, Violet was questioned at the Morrow home by Insp. Harry Walsh of the Jersey City Police Department. Although still elusive and sometimes openly hostile, Violet was a little more forthcoming. She told Inspector Walsh that she had not gone to the movies on the night of March 1. Instead, she and her date, a man named Ernie, had spent the evening at the Peanut Grill, a roadhouse in Orangeburg, New York. They were accompanied by Ernie's friend and his date.

Inspector Walsh had reported the results of the second interview to Schwarzkopf who was still not convinced that Violet was telling everything about her activities on the night of the kidnapping. For example, why would a woman who had supposedly never dated an outsider, a woman who knew that the Morrows' head butler, Septimus Banks, was about to ask her to marry him, go to a speakeasy with three strangers? Why would she accept a date with a man she had met for the first time two days earlier? And why couldn't she remember this man's last name? She had described him as a tall, thin, twenty-three-year-old. She said he was a native American who had fair hair and a light complexion.

143

Schwarzkopf became even more suspicious when Violet's sister sailed for England without notice. So, he decided that Violet would be questioned for the third time.

On May 9, three days before William Allen stumbled upon the baby's corpse, Violet was admitted to the Englewood Hospital with infected tonsils. The next day her tonsils and adenoids were taken out. She had spent an uncomfortable night following the operation, so her surgeon urged her to remain in the hospital a little longer than usual. Violet was recouperating from her operation when the Lindbergh baby was found. After learning of the baby's murder, she became very despondent. On May 14, against the wishes and advice of her personal physician and the surgeon, Violet checked herself out of the hospital.[1]

On Saturday, May 21, Colonel Schwarzkopf sent Dr. D. Leo Haggerty, the state police surgeon, to the Morrow estate to examine Violet. Anxious to put the Sharpe business behind him, Schwarzkopf was in a hurry to have the maid interviewed. But before he approved a third session, Schwarzkopf wanted to make certain that Violet had recovered from her illness.

Dr. Haggerty and a local physician, Dr. Harry D. Williams, examined Violet that Saturday. In a letter to Colonel Schwarzkopf dated May 21 and signed by both physicians, Dr. Haggerty wrote: "We have examined Violet Sharpe and find that she is running a temperature of 99.3 and a pulse rate of 120 and is in a slightly weakened condition due to the removal of her tonsils eleven days ago and *would not advise further questioning at this time.*"[2]

Ignoring the physicians' advice, Inspector Walsh arranged an interview for Thursday, May 23, in the study of the Morrow mansion. At 7:15 P.M. Inspector Walsh led Violet into the study, where she was greeted by Colonel Schwarzkopf, Lieutenant Keaten, and Colonel Lindbergh himself. Violet had lost weight since her illness and looked pale and tired. She was nervous and obviously flustered in the presence of Colonel Lindbergh.[3]

Inspector Walsh began the interview by asking Violet to describe her background. Violet complied, speaking with her head bowed, occasionally stealing a glance at Colonel Lindbergh. Lindbergh's presence, or possibly Violet's illness, made her quite docile. This was in sharp contrast to her first two interviews. She was almost polite—but very nervous. Inspector Walsh asked Violet to repeat how she had met Ernie on Lydecker Street on the day of the kidnapping. After doing this, Violet said that she and the others had gone to the Peanut Grill in "one of the Oranges." Her date had brought her home around eleven o'clock that night. When questioned previously, Violet had said that on the night of the kidnapping Ernie had called her at eight o'clock, thirty minutes before he had picked her up for the date. When Walsh asked her about this again, he was surprised by her answer. She said that Ernie had called her at one in the afternoon. Walsh repeated the question and Violet gave him the same answer. This was new, and it was important. It meant that on the day of the kidnapping, Ernie had called Violet an hour and a half after Violet had learned that the Lindbergh baby would remain at the Hopewell estate that night. The implication was clear—Violet could have informed Ernie of this and he would have had time to tell others—possibly the kidnappers.

Inspector Walsh pressed Violet about the other contradictory statements she had made to the police. "You told me that you were to a moving picture show when I first questioned you?"

"Yes," Violet answered.

"You also told the Newark police that?"

"Yes."

"Will you explain why you told a lie about that?"

"I could not explain why, I don't know." Violet shot a glance at Colonel Lindbergh.

"You did not have any conception that you were going to the roadhouse when you made this telephone appointment to go to the movies?"

"No."

"Why didn't you object when you found out you were not going to the moving pictures?"

"I did not know anything about it then."

"Are you in the habit of going out with people you don't know, and going and having a drink with them?"

"No, I don't know why I did it."

"Are you in the habit of picking up strange men on the street?"

"No, I don't know why I did it, I just did it and that is all."

Inspector Walsh asked about the Peanut Grill. "How do you know it was the Peanut Grill that you were to?"

"Because I saw the name on a sign."

Violet went on to say that she had a cocktail and a cup of coffee. The other woman had a beer and the men had cocktails. Violet then told Inspector Walsh and the others how she had learned of the kidnapping. "When I got into the house I answered the telephone and found out."

"Who telephoned it?"

"It was Mr. Weidner of *The New York Times*. He asked me if I could tell him anything further about the baby being kidnapped and I told him that it was a lot of bull and I did not think there was anything to it. A minute after the police called up and asked me to give a description of the baby and I went up to Mrs. Morrow and asked her if it was true."

Back in March, when Violet was taken to the Lindbergh estate and questioned, the police had searched her room. Among the items they had inventoried was a slip of paper upon which she had written: "Banks promises to try and be straight for 12 months." Inspector Walsh now asked Violet to explain what that meant. "You have a slip among your personal belongings that we would like to have an explanation of. It said, 'Banks promises to try and be straight for 12 months.' What does this mean?"

"It is a private thing, something I don't wish to answer."

Walsh's question had made Violet uneasy. She shot another glance at Colonel Lindbergh then lowered her eyes. Inspector Walsh pressed on, "Was it something you don't wish to answer?"

"Yes."

"Are you acquainted with him [Septimus Banks]?"

"Well, I work with him."

"I mean are you intimately acquainted with him?"

"I don't know what you mean."

"Well, what do you mean by saying, 'Go straight for twelve months'?"

"That is a thing that I don't want to answer." Violet's face reddened a bit.

"We know that he drinks."

"Well that is the thing I meant."

"Where does Banks get his liquor?"

"I don't know. It is not so much for Banks I mind, it is because I want Mrs. Morrow to have a fair deal."

Walsh asked Violet about a $500 deposit she had made in October, 1931. She explained that she had not made a deposit for several months and that her cash had accumulated. She had also deposited $240 in the bank in January and Walsh wanted to know where she had obtained that money. Violet explained that Mrs. Morrow had given her a Christmas present of $100. She had also been given Christmas money by the Lindberghs. Walsh then brought the questioning back around to Ernie: "What was this man Ernie's business?"

"I don't know."

"Have you ever seen any of these three people after that?"

"No."

"Did you ask what their occupation was or something about them?"

"No, I did not."

"Can you give us a description of Ernie?"

"He is fairly tall and thin, wore a navy blue suit and had a sort of dark gray overcoat on and as far as I know a soft felt hat, more dark than fair."

Keeping on the subject of Ernie, Walsh got a little personal, "The fellow that you were out with, did he make any attempt to love you?"

"No."

"Not even attempted to kiss you?"

"He tried to kiss me when he left me."

Walsh had Violet describe the other woman in the foursome. She then answered several questions about Septimus Banks and his drinking habits. Walsh wanted to know where Banks normally obtained his liquor and so forth. When Violet finished answering these questions, Walsh declared that he had nothing further to ask. Colonels Lindbergh and Schwarzkopf said that they had no questions. The interrogation was over.[4]

Violet said goodbye to Colonel Lindbergh then walked out of the room. In the wake of Violet's exit there was an awkward silence. Inspector Walsh spoke up, "Well, what do you make of it?" He looked at Colonel Schwarzkopf.

Knowing how Colonel Lindbergh felt about the servants, Schwarzkopf picked his words carefully, "We need to find this man Ernie to see if he knew about the plans to stay in Hopewell."

"But what about Violet?" Walsh asked. "Do you think she was in on it?"

"I don't know," Schwarzkopf answered. He shot a look at Colonel Lindbergh, who looked lost in his thoughts.

Walsh continued, "I'm still not satisfied. She's lied before. I think she's hiding something."

"She's scared," Colonel Lindbergh said, "and she's upset about the baby. She's also been ill."

"That's true, sir," Inspector Walsh said, "But she wasn't sick when we talked to her back in March and in April. I'm sorry, sir, but I still have my doubts. I'm sorry."

Colonel Lindbergh stood up. "She lied about going to the movies because she didn't want Mrs. Morrow to know that she'd been to a roadhouse. If she did pass information on to the kidnappers, she wasn't aware of it. Violet Sharpe had nothing to do with the kidnapping," he said as he walked from the room.[5]

On Monday, May 23, the day Violet Sharpe was interviewed, the Lindberghs were back at the Morrow home in Englewood. They had abandoned their home in Hopewell and were now living permanently at the fifty-two-acre Morrow estate. Ten days earlier Colonel Lindbergh had resumed his work at the Rockefeller Institute for Medical Research in New York City.

On Monday, June 6, Colonel Lindbergh resumed another facet of his work. He drove to his office at Transcontinental and Western Airways in New York City. He hadn't been there since March 1. The resumption of his regular work schedule was big news. A gang of reporters chased after the secretaries and clerks at the company, asking them to describe how the Colonel looked, what he had done, and so forth. All of the employees said the same thing—Colonel Lindbergh looked older, and thinner.

June 6 was also a big day for William Allen, the truck driver who had found the Lindbergh baby. Allen was making his debut as a Coney Island sideshow star. He spent his opening day posing with a troupe of wax figures amidst a re-creation of the Mount Rose gravesite. Word of the Allen display got back to Governor Moore of New Jersey, who called the New York City Police Department to see if they could shut it down. Inspector James Fitzpatrick of the Coney Island precinct said that he would revoke Allen's exhibition permit.

The next day William Allen's career as a sideshow attraction came to an end. The unemployed truck driver found himself looking for another way to support his wife and four children.

On Tuesday, June 7, Violet Sharpe, despondent and physically weak, penned a letter to her girlfriend back in England. She wrote:

Dearest Fan,

Just a hurried line. At last so glad to get your letter this morning. I hope you will forgive me for not writing before but really we have had so much trouble here over the Lindbergh baby. We have all been questioned by the Police and I have been in hospital a week with a Poisoned throat—had my tonsils out and I only weigh seven stones [98 pounds] the least I have ever been in my life and I just feel as weak as a rat. I want to come home so much but I can't leave the country or they would think I knew something about the baby. You have no idea what we have been through when the Police had me for questioning. I fainted 2 in 2 hours so you can guess how weak I was. I was so sorry to hear about that little girl, Fan, Gee, life is getting so sad I really don't think there is much to live for any more."[6]

On June 3, the trial of Gaston B. Means, the man who had swindled Mrs. Evalyn McLean out of $104,000, got under way in a federal court in Washington, D.C. A month earlier Means had spent a week in jail before posting his $100,000 bond. Means had been out on bail one day when he hit a *Washington Times* reporter in a drugstore. Charged with disorderly conduct, Means was put back in jail until he sobered up.

The FBI, the agency investigating Means, had been looking for the $100,000 that Mrs. McLean had given Means to ransom the Lindbergh baby. Means said that he had spent the expense money but claimed that he had given Mrs. McLean's $100,000 to a shadowy figure Means thought was collecting the money for Mrs. McLean. The FBI had rejected this story as absurd and was frantically looking for the money. They had searched several safety deposit boxes, questioned Gaston's wife, and ransacked his house. So far there was no trace of the money, and the FBI didn't know where to look next.

As he climbed the courthouse steps in the company of his lawyer, Means was all smiles. Having acquired a taste for publicity, he eagerly confronted the photographers and reporters outside the courtroom. "Mrs. McLean don't have a leg to stand on," he declared.

J. Edgar Hoover, the man who had fired Agent Means shortly after becoming FBI director in 1924, countered the defendant's remark by announcing that Means was "the greatest faker of all time." Hoover added that he was confident United States Attorney Leo A. Rover would convict the swindler.

Rover's star witness was Mrs. McLean herself. The victim testified that she had withdrawn the cash from her bank and had given it to Means in two thousand fifty-dollar bills. She had also given him an additional four thousand dollars for expense money. "I told Means," she said, "that I had great sympathy for the Lindbergh family. I told him that for five or six years my first son was the subject of kidnapping threats and I had to keep guards around him, and it made me a nervous wreck."

During Mrs. McLean's testimony, Means sat at the defendant's table with a smirk on his face. Every so often he would wink at the courtroom reporters as if to say there was much more to the story than Mrs. McLean was letting on—revelations that would be forthcoming when he took the stand.

Following a weak and ineffectual cross-examination by Means's lawyer, Mrs. McLean stepped from the witness box. Instead of weakening her story, the defense attorney had made the jury feel sorry for her. Several of the jurors were scowling at Means. Mrs. McLean was followed to the stand by several prosecution witnesses who corroborated her testimony.

On Thursday, June 9, the second day of the trial, Inspector Harry Walsh of the Jersey

City Police Department was driving to the Morrow estate in Englewood to show Violet Sharpe a mug shot of a petty thief named Ernest Brinkert. Brinkert had operated the Post Road Taxi Company in White Plains, New York, a firm that had been bankrupt for over a year. Back in March, the police had found six of Brinkert's business cards in Violet's room. Brinkert had an arrest record, and Walsh wanted to know if he was the man who had taken Violet and the other couple to the Peanut Grill on the night of the kidnapping.

Walsh arrived at the Morrow estate at eleven in the morning and was escorted into the study, where he and Laura Hughes, a secretary in the Morrow house, waited for Violet to come down. Miss Hughes was there to make a record of the interview. Violet walked in to the study a few minutes later. Walsh hadn't seen the maid in two weeks and was shocked at her appearance. Violet looked old beyond her years and almost wasted. Fifty pounds lighter than she had been when she and Walsh had first met, Violet looked like the mother of the perky girl the police had first questioned.

The Inspector began by asking Violet to account for her activities on the night of the kidnapping. Trembling, and on the verge of tears, Violet went over the familiar story. Whenever her answers sounded tentative, or when she hesitated, Walsh tested her resolve by asking probing, accusatorial questions. Although she was shaky, Violet managed to hold herself together. Walsh then showed her a mug shot of Brinkert. Instead of asking Violet if she had ever seen this man before, the Inspector asked a more leading question: "Is this one of the men you were with at the Peanut Grill?"

"Yes," she answered.

"Is this the Ernie you were with that night?"

"Yes," she replied. "Yes, that's the man."

Walsh looked at the Morrow secretary to make sure she was getting all of this down. Satisfied that she was, he put Brinkert's photograph back into his pocket.

"Why didn't you tell us before that you were out with Ernie Brinkert?"

"Because I didn't know who he was," she replied.

"Yes, you did, you had his business cards in your room. How do you explain that?"

"I did not," Violet protested.

Walsh shook his head in disgust. "All right, I'm not going to argue with you, all I want to know is this—is he or is he not the man you were with that night?"

"Yes, it is—it looks like him."

"Are you sure?"

"Yes, it is!" Violet screamed. She brought her hands to her face and burst into tears. A moment later she was sobbing uncontrollably. The secretary, Laura Hughes, became alarmed. She ran to the telephone and dialed the number of the Morrow family physician. She hung up a few minutes later and announced that the doctor would be right over.

Inspector Walsh and the two women waited for the doctor. Laura Hughes was seated on the sofa with her arms around Violet, trying to calm her down. Walsh was skeptical. As a hard-nosed cop, he had seen it all. He thought the secretary had been a little rash in calling the doctor. It was not unusual for a person to break down under questioning—particularly if he or she had something to hide.

Ten minutes later the doctor strolled into the study. He gave Walsh a quick, cold look and turned his attention to Violet who was now whimpering.

After a cursory examination, the doctor said that Violet was on the verge of hysteria. Because of this and the fact that her blood pressure was very high, he told Walsh that he would have to terminate the questioning. The doctor's order angered Walsh. He was certain that Violet was faking—she was using the doctor to keep the police away. "We'll call it quits for today," Walsh said. "But tomorrow we'll have you brought to our offices in Alpine for more questioning." Anticipating an argument, he looked the doctor square in the face. When the physician didn't protest, Walsh shook his head in approval as though he approved of his own decision. Like all good cops, he liked to be in charge.

Violet got to her feet and walked unaided out of the room. Laura Hughes was seated at the desk working on her notes. She looked up sympathetically as Violet passed by. To the secretary's utter amazement, Violet flashed a sly smile, then winked. Walsh didn't see this, and neither did the doctor. The secretary decided not to tell them—Violet had enough trouble.[7]

They'll never take me from this house again!

— V I O L E T   S H A R P E
on the eve of her death

15   THE SUICIDE AND ITS AFTERMATH

FOLLOWING HIS SESSION WITH VIOLET SHARPE, Inspector Walsh drove to Trenton, where he reported to Schwarzkopf that it was Ernest Brinkert who had called the Morrow house at one in the afternoon on the day of the kidnapping. Brinkert had also taken Violet to the Peanut Grill on the night of the kidnapping. Schwarzkopf was excited. This was a major breakthrough. Brinkert would be brought in for questioning. His whereabouts were unknown, so Schwarzkopf put out an all-points bulletin describing the five foot four inch Brinkert and his car, a green 1926 Nash. He was to be arrested on sight.

That night, at the Morrow estate, Violet Sharpe was telling Betty Gow and another servant about her ordeal with Walsh. Violet had whipped herself into a state of near hysteria. Referring to the Lindbergh investigators, she ranted, "They'll never take me from this house again. I'm not going to Hopewell and I'm not going to that place in Alpine! They're not going to question me again! Never!" Violet then collapsed onto the floor of the servant's hall.

The next day, at ten o'clock in the morning, Inspector Walsh telephoned the Morrow house and asked Arthur Springer, Mrs. Morrow's personal secretary, to tell Violet that Lieutenant Keaten from the New Jersey State Police would be by the house in an hour to take Violet to Alpine for further questioning. Springer picked up the house phone and relayed the message to Violet, who, in a state of panic, slammed down the phone and ran to Septimus Banks.

"Walsh wants to question me again," she cried. "I won't go! I won't! I won't!"

Septimus tried to calm her. She ran to the pantry, where she pulled a large measuring glass off the shelf.[1] She hurried up the stairs to her room, and from the top shelf of her wardrobe closet, she took down a can that was about six inches tall. The container was wrapped in yellow paper. The warning, "Poison. Do Not Unpack," was penciled on it. As she tore off the wrapping she spilled some of its contents, a fine white powder, onto

151

herself and the closet floor. She then ran into the bathroom and poured some of the crystals into the measuring cup she had brought from the downstairs pantry. Her hands were trembling so much she spilled some of the crystals into the bathroom sink. She filled the measuring cup with water, then walked back into her room, where she gulped down the milky white liquid. She wiped her lips with the back of her hand, then walked out of her room to the head of the stairs. Slowly, she started down the stairs with the measuring cup dangling from her right hand. Except for the filigree of undissolved crystals on the bottom of the glass, it was empty.

Once Violet had reached the bottom of the stairs, she shuffled to the pantry, where she met Emily Kempairien, another maid. Swaying back and forth, Violet tried to speak, but all she could manage was a gurgling sound. She then collapsed to the floor at the feet of the terrified maid.[2]

Septimus Banks and another servant heard Miss Kempairien cry out. They both ran to the pantry. Dwight Morrow, Jr., home from college, joined the group a few seconds later. Mrs. Morrow wasn't home, and neither were the Lindberghs. Young Morrow and Septimus Banks were unable to revive Violet, so they carried her upstairs to her room and laid her on the bed. Arthur Springer called the doctor, the Englewood Police, and the New Jersey State Police.

The physician arrived in a matter of minutes, but he was too late. Violet was dead.

Chief Peterson of the Englewood Police and Lieutenant Keaten had also arrived. Keaten had come to drive Violet to Alpine. A few minutes later, Detective Nathan Allyn of the county prosecutor's office pulled up to the house.

Shortly before noon, the County Coroner examined Violet and pronounced her dead. Her body was taken to Greenleaf's Morgue in Englewood, where the county physician, Dr. Ralph W. Gillady, was standing by to perform the autopsy.

Some of the evidence of Violet's suicide was in her bedroom. The can containing the white crystals was still on the table next to her bed. The printed label on the container read: Cyanide chloride, 73–76 percent. *Not to be used as an insecticide or fungicide.* This substance was commonly used to clean silver. (The police determined later that the cyanide had been bought from a wholesale drug house in New York City. Violet had brought the can with her to the Morrow house two years earlier.)[3]

Walsh and Keaten examined the moist measuring glass Violet had carried to the pantry and noticed that it contained a thin layer of undissolved crystals. They found traces of poison on her clothes, on her closet floor, and in the bathroom wash basin.

Lieutenant Keaten telephoned Schwarzkopf from the Morrow house to tell him the news. Schwarzkopf was dismayed at losing his best lead so far in the kidnapping case, and worried about the effect of the suicide on the Lindberghs and the public.

Later that afternoon, Schwarzkopf called reporters to his office in West Trenton and issued the following statement:

> Violet Sharpe has been under constant suspicion in this investigation since she was first interviewed at Englewood, N.J., in the early days of the kidnapping, because she gave conflicting statements as to her whereabouts on the night of the kidnapping, and

because she refused to reveal the identity of the man with whom she went out that night. She also refused to reveal the places visited on their trip that night. It has since been found that she had been in communication with this man [Brinkert] at one o'clock on the afternoon of March 1st. She knew that the Lindbergh family expected to remain in Hopewell.

Schwarzkopf also announced that the New Jersey State Police would be closing their headquarters at the Lindbergh estate. From now on the case would be run out of Schwarzkopf's office in West Trenton.

At the conclusion of his prepared statement, reporters bombarded Schwarzkopf with questions. They wanted to know exactly how Violet had killed herself, why she had done it, and what connection it had to the investigation. Did it mean that she had had something to do with the kidnapping? Since Mrs. Morrow and Colonel Lindbergh had refused to comment on the suicide, the reporters were counting on Schwarzkopf for answers. Careful not to disclose his own opinion that Violet's suicide was directly connected to the crime, Schwarzkopf told them that Violet had not left a suicide note. The reason for her suicide was still a mystery, Schwarzkopf said. Schwarzkopf downplayed the fact that Violet had been ill, had broken under Walsh the day before, and had hysterically declared that she would not be taken from the Morrow house.

At the close of the press conference, Schwarzkopf believed that he had headed off any forthcoming criticism.

At nine o'clock that night, Dr. Condon entered the police station at White Plains, New York. As usual, the doctor was accompanied by an entourage of uniformed policemen, detectives and his old friend Al Reich. Condon was no stranger to the White Plains police; he had been to the station house several times to look at lineups and mug shots. This night hopes ran high that Condon would identify Brinkert's photograph as "Cemetery John." This would tie the case up quite nicely and explain why Violet Sharpe had killed herself.

As usual, Condon's presence created a stir. The famous "Jafsie," basking in all of the attention, was escorted, like a distinguished visitor, into the police chief's office. Inside, Lieutenants Keaten and Walsh and several other officers looked on as Condon examined Brinkert's photograph. No one spoke as Condon studied the picture. All eyes were on him as he focused upon the mug shot. Several minutes passed. The chief shifted impatiently in his chair. Finally, Lieutenant Keaten couldn't stand it any longer. "Well, Doctor," he said, "what do you say?"

The old schoolteacher in the familiar black overcoat and derby hat didn't reply. He had heard Keaten but he didn't like being rushed in such matters. Finally, Condon spoke, "It looks something like the man who got the money, but this picture is too light to tell. I can't be sure."

"Then it could be the man?" Keaten asked.

"It could be. But I can't be sure. Do you gentlemen have anything else for me to examine?"

"That's it," Keaten said. He had hoped for something more positive.

"If there's nothing else, I'll be on my way," Condon said. "I have a busy day tomorrow."

Condon and his entourage left the building, leaving Walsh, Keaten, and the others no wiser. What they needed was Ernest Brinkert.

Later that night, at 10:45, Brinkert telephoned a friend of his named Thomas Fay. This was the break the police had been waiting for. When Brinkert had operated his cab company, Thomas Fay had handled Brinkert's business calls at his house. The White Plains police had stationed Det. Roy Turner at Fay's house in the hope that Brinkert would get in touch with his old friend. Detective Turner was there when Brinkert called. Fay spoke briefly to Brinkert, then handed the telephone to Detective Turner. The officer identified himself and asked Brinkert where he was hiding. Brinkert said that he had heard that he was wanted in connection with the Lindbergh case. He swore that he didn't know Violet Sharpe and that he had nothing to do with the kidnapping. He said that he couldn't understand how he had gotten named in the Lindbergh case. Detective Turner didn't want to talk about that right now, he just wanted Brinkert to tell where he was. Brinkert didn't say, and after protesting his innocence, hung up.

Detective Turner traced the call—it came from a store in New Rochelle, New York. Turner notified the New Rochelle police, who dispatched several patrol cars to the store. At eleven o'clock that night, Brinkert was arrested while sitting outside the place in his 1926 Nash. The police hauled him to the station house in New Rochelle where detectives interrogated him about his date with Violet Sharpe.

Brinkert insisted that he didn't know Violet Sharpe. He said that on March 1 he was visiting a friend in Bridgeport, Connecticut. This friend was a black man named Frank Page. Brinkert said that he and Page had spent the evening playing cards.

The detectives weren't satisfied with Brinkert's story. They asked him to explain how six of his business cards had gotten into Violet Sharpe's room. Brinkert said that he couldn't explain that. He seemed genuinely dumbfounded.

A few minutes after midnight, Keaten and Walsh arrived at the New Rochelle Police Department to take over Brinkert's interrogation. The two investigators had to push their way through a crowd of five hundred people. Word had already gotten out that the police had a hot suspect in the Lindbergh case. The crowd was getting unruly so the police chief, to maintain order, dispatched a squad of uniformed officers to control the crowd. At one point the police were getting worried about Brinkert's safety.

Keaten and Walsh talked to Brinkert for an hour. The suspect stuck to his story, maintaining that he didn't know Violet Sharpe and that on the night of the kidnapping he was in Bridgeport, Connecticut.

Dr. Condon had arrived at the police station. He was there to find out if Brinkert was "Cemetery John." The moment Condon laid eyes on the suspect he shook his head and said, "This man is too short!" Without another word, Condon turned and walked out of the building.

Keaten and Walsh shrugged their shoulders and resumed their interrogation. Apparently Brinkert wasn't the man in St. Raymond's Cemetery. That didn't mean, however, that he had nothing to do with the kidnapping.

The two police officers questioned Brinkert until three in the morning. The suspect still hadn't budged from his story. At dawn, the police put Brinkert into a car and drove him to Alpine, New Jersey where the interrogation would continue.

When Brinkert was told that he was being released to the custody of the New Jersey State Police, he asked to be examined by a physician. "I'm wise enough to know about Jersey police methods," he said. "And I'm not going to take any chances on being beaten up."[4]

At Alpine, Lieutenant Keaten took samples of Brinkert's handwriting. Brinkert wrote as Keaten read to him the special paragraph composed by Albert S. Osborn, the questioned documents expert. When Keaten was finished, the handwriting samples were taken to Osborn's office to be compared with the ransom notes.

Detectives from the White Plains Police Department questioned Brinkert's wife, who said that she and her husband had been together on the night of March 1. Ernest Brinkert now had two different alibis for the night in question.

On Saturday morning, June 11, Dr. Ralph Gillady, the physician who had performed Violet's autopsy, reported that the poison had killed her a few minutes after she had taken it. He said that she hadn't been suffering from any disease and that she wasn't pregnant.

This Saturday, the case took a bizarre turn when a man named Ernest Miller from Closter, New Jersey, walked into a police station and announced that *he* was the one who had been out with Violet Sharpe on the night of the kidnapping. The Closter police called Lieutenant Keaten, who immediately dispatched Detectives Moffatt and Coar to Closter. At noon the detectives returned to Alpine with Miller. Keaten and Walsh were still questioning Brinkert, but when Miller arrived, they gave Brinkert a break and began grilling the new Ernie.

Initially, the officers treated Miller as just another Lindbergh nut. But as the questioning proceeded the detectives began to have second thoughts.

Miller said that he had met Violet and her sister on the Sunday preceding the kidnapping. The girls were walking along Lydecker Street that afternoon when he drove by. Because they waved to him he stopped. The twenty-three-year-old bus driver gave the girls a lift to the Morrow house, and on the following Tuesday, he called Violet and asked her out that night. He said he called the Morrow house at one o'clock in the afternoon. Around eight that night he and another couple, Elmer Johnson and Katherine Minners, picked Violet up at the Morrow estate. Miller drove the group to Orangeburg, New York, near Tappan, where they danced and had a few drinks at a place called the Peanut Grill. Around midnight he took Violet home.

Miller's story matched Violet's. He had never been in trouble with the law, he said. And he had nothing to do with the Lindbergh crime.

Walsh and Keaten found it hard not to believe Miller. But they were confused. Why hadn't Violet remembered his name, and what had possessed her to identify Brinkert's photograph? They put these questions to Miller, who could only say that it was a mystery to him, too. "Violet knew my name," he said. "I told her my name that afternoon when we met on Lydecker Street."

"Why did Violet identify Brinkert?" Keaten asked. "He doesn't even look like you."

Miller shrugged his shoulders, "You're asking the wrong guy," he said.

Keaten informed Miller that he would be held until Elmer Johnson and Katherine Minners were questioned. Miller said that he didn't mind. Until everything got sorted out, they'd have to keep Brinkert in custody as well.

Katherine Minners, a good-looking brunette from Palisades Park, New Jersey, was rounded up and brought to Alpine for questioning. The twenty-one-year-old stenographer from New York City told the officers that on March 1 she was on a double date with Elmer Johnson and another couple. The other two people were Ernest Miller and Violet Sharpe. She said she hadn't come forward on her own with this information because she was afraid of being sucked into the Lindbergh investigation. She told Keaten and Walsh that she had known Ernest Miller for several years but had first met Violet Sharpe on the date. That Tuesday evening she and the men had picked Violet up at a quarter to eight. They drove to the Peanut Grill where they "sat around for a while" before returning to Englewood. They dropped Violet off around midnight.

Walsh and Keaten also questioned Elmer Johnson that afternoon. His account of that night matched the others'. There was little doubt that Miller was the real "Ernie."

While Keaten and Walsh questioned Miller and his friends, detectives were talking to Thomas Fay, Brinkert's former business associate. Fay said that on March 1 he and Brinkert were in Bridgeport, Connecticut, playing cards.

Having questioned all of the principals, Keaten called Albert S. Osborn to find out if Brinkert had written any of the ransom notes. The questioned documents examiner reported that Brinkert had not written any of the ransom documents. Lieutenant Keaten was not surprised.

Inspector Walsh telephoned Colonel Schwarzkopf and advised him that Violet Sharpe had put them on to the wrong Ernie. Schwarzkopf was furious. He was also worried. His law enforcement and political rivals would rejoice over his misfortune. They would take this opportunity to embarrass and humiliate him. He shuddered to think about the press. They were going to have a field day. He and his men would be back on the defensive. Over night, the Violet connection had turned from a promising lead to a serious liability.[5]

"What about the press?" Schwarzkopf asked. "Have they gotten on to this?"

"Not yet," Walsh replied. "We just got done talking to Miller and his friends."

"All right. I want you to call a press conference in Alpine and make the announcement. If it comes from us it'll be a lot better than if they pick up the story themselves. And be sure to emphasize that Violet identified Brinkert's mug shot and that his business cards were found in her room."

An hour later Walsh was speaking to a group of reporters. "This is a peculiar turn of events," he said. "It is no fault of ours. I can't understand why Violet Sharpe, if she had nothing to do with the kidnapping, preferred death to revealing Miller's name. I can not understand it at all."

Walsh said that there were still many unanswered questions about the Brinkert-Sharpe connection. Why, he asked, did Violet have Brinkert's business cards in her room? Walsh said that despite the fact that Miller had backed up Violet's story, he was certain her suicide was related to the crime.[6]

While Walsh was talking to the reporters in Alpine, Schwarzkopf was making his own move to head off criticism. He released to *The New York Times,* Violet's Sharpe's three statements to the police. These documents included the statement she had given to the Newark detectives on March 10 and the two statements given to Inspector Walsh on April 23 and May 23. Schwarzkopf also released, for publication, a New Jersey State Police report highlighting all of Violet's discrepancies, inconsistencies, and lapses of memory. It was an unprecedented act.

Schwarzkopf hoped the public would understand why Violet was considered a prime suspect. Her responses would show why the police had kept pressing her for more information. He hoped her statements would show that she had killed herself out of guilt and fear, not because of police harassment.

The previous afternoon, Schwarzkopf had called Scotland Yard to have Violet's sister Emily questioned. Emily had left the country four days after John Condon had handed over the ransom. Schwarzkopf didn't consider this a coincidence. He was certain that Emily was somehow tied into the crime.

Shortly after receiving Schwarzkopf's cablegram, Scotland Yard's Chief Inspector John Horwell telephoned Stourbridge, in Worcester, where Emily's brother-in-law was employed on an estate as a servant. Emily was at the estate visiting her sister. At seven o'clock that evening, Emily returned to her parents' cottage in Beenham at the request of Inspector Horwell and Inspector Braby of the Berkshire County Police.

The English police officers questioned Emily for three hours. Inspector Horwell then sent Schwarzkopf the following cable:

> I am satisfied that Emily Sharpe knows nothing about the Lindbergh business. She appears to be a girl of excellent character and has been in the best of situations.

This was not what Schwarzkopf wanted to hear. So far nothing connected to Violet Sharpe made any sense. The pieces of the puzzle weren't falling into place. The investigative gods were not smiling upon Schwarzkopf and his men. They were·conspiring to make him and the New Jersey State Police look like fools.[7]

Inspector Horwell had picked up an interesting tidbit about Violet Sharpe that he passed along to Schwarzkopf. According to Emily, Violet had married a man named George Payne just before she sailed for Canada two and a half years ago. Emily said that her sister had married this man in London. Emily had never met the man and didn't know where he was. The fact that Violet had been married was news to her parents. Violet had also withheld this information from Mrs. Morrow. Because Schwarzkopf didn't see any connection between Violet's marriage and the Lindbergh case, he gave it little thought.

The next day was June 12, a Sunday, and the newspapers were full of the Lindbergh case. Inspector Walsh's comments were in the news and the *New York Times* ran Violet's

158 three statements. And there were several articles about the two Ernies. But the news that rang the most bells dealt with Emily Sharpe. After being questioned by Inspector Horwell she had addressed a group of British reporters. Her comments, appearing in every Sunday newspaper in America, opened the flood gates to a tidal wave of criticism against Schwarzkopf and the Lindbergh investigators. Her statement:

> Ever since the baby disappeared, Violet was badgered and was questioned until she did not know what she was saying or doing. She was driven nearly mad. After the baby was stolen Violet wrote me and I went to Englewood to see her. She was terribly distressed and said the police had been questioning her for hours. She asserted that she knew nothing about the child's disappearance, but she said the police would not believe her. It was all so cruel. Violet would never had done anything to the child or to anyone who wanted to find it."[8]

When Inspector Walsh read his Sunday newspaper, he felt that Emily Sharpe was accusing him personally of driving her sister to suicide. Later in the day he told reporters that there was no basis for Emily's accusations. "She [Violet] was always treated gently, never roughly," he said. "We pleaded with her to help us." Walsh then reiterated why Violet was treated like a suspect in the first place.

Mrs. Morrow had not spoken to the press, but a friend of the family told reporters that Mrs. Morrow believed that Violet was innocent. "If Violet had given any information that might have reached the kidnappers, she must have done it unwittingly," the spokesperson said.

All of a sudden, the public was in no mood for Walsh's explanations or Violet's published statements to the police. The pathetic remarks of Emily Sharpe and her mother had struck a sympathetic chord. On Monday, June 13, newspapers all over the country carried editorials that were sharply critical of the Lindbergh investigation. Walter V. Hogan, the editor of Brinkert's hometown newspaper, the *White Plain's Daily Reporter,* criticised Schwarzkopf and the New Jersey State Police for arresting Brinkert on such flimsey evidence and dragging his name through the mud.

Hogan accused the police of causing Violet Sharpe's death. "Miss Sharpe had nothing to do with the kidnapping, and there is every reason to believe that she was so hounded by the New Jersey State Police for more than three months she would rather be dead than submit to more questioning. She drank cyanide of potassium."

The American tabloids, never on good terms with the police, published a series of wild headlines like: "PUNISH COPS WHO DROVE MORROW MAID TO DEATH!"[9]

Schwarzkopf and his men were getting bad press in England, too. In London, the *Daily Herald* accused the American police of "venting their chagrin at their failure in the Lindbergh case on a poor English servant girl." The *London Daily Telegraph,* under the headline "DISGRACE TO AMERICAN JUSTICE" accused the New Jersey State Police of torturing the girl. The editors of the *Manchester Guardian* were no less harsh: "They [the New Jersey State Police] stand, or should stand, condemned in the eyes of all decent persons in the United States."[10]

Concerned about protecting British citizens from the brutality of the American police, Labor Party members of Parliament demanded to know what steps His Majesty's Government was taking to protect British subjects. British officials assured Parliament that appropriate measures were being taken. For example, His Majesty's Acting Consul-General in New York City had been instructed to investigate Violet Sharpe's suicide.

From his cell in the Hunterdon County Jail, John Hughes Curtis couldn't resist joining the anti-Schwarzkopf chorus. Curtis was in jail because he hadn't been able to raise the ten-thousand-dollar bail on his obstruction of justice charge. His trial was coming up in two weeks. "Personally," he said, "I can deeply sympathize with Miss Sharpe's family and think it perfectly justified in the English in raising a howl. Beatings, as I noticed, evidently are a common practice with the New Jersey police in gaining their ends, but are not always necessary. Lying promises often work just as well."[11]

In response to charges that he had used the "third degree" on Violet, Inspector Walsh told reporters that "she was always questioned either at the Lindbergh home or the Morrow home in Englewood, never in the station house. She was always treated gently and kindly—never roughly. Colonel Lindbergh would not have permitted any rough treatment. We really pleaded with her to help us."[12]

In Trenton, reporters asked Schwarzkopf if, in view of Brinkert's alibi and Ernest Miller's statement, he would publicly exonerate Violet Sharpe. Schwarzkopf responded that Violet's guilt or innocence was a matter of opinion. "The fact remains," he said, "that conflicting statements were made, that a false identification was made, that the identity of Miller was concealed, and that truths were denied."[13]

Schwarzkopf was asked to give a detailed explanation of how Brinkert's business cards had gotten into Violet's room. Schwarzkopf responded by saying that "three investigators made a careful search of Violet Sharpe's room in Englewood during the time that she was in Hopewell being questioned. Among her effects were found a number of cards, probably four or five from The Post Road Taxi Company owned by Ernest Brinkert. The similarity of his first name with the nickname Ernie formed the basis for further investigation concerning Ernest Brinkert."[14]

One of the reporters asked Schwarzkopf point-blank if the police had planted Brinkert's business cards in Violet's room. Schwarzkopf simply ignored the question.

There *were* rumors floating about that the police had planted Ernest Brinkert's business cards. The theory went something like this: Initially Walsh had no reason to connect Brinkert to Violet other than the fact that his first name was Ernest and that he had an arrest record. Taking Brinkert's photograph to Violet had been a longshot. Therefore, no one was more surprised than Walsh when Violet identified Brinkert as the man she had been out with on the night of the kidnapping. At that point, as the theory goes, Brinkert's old business cards were planted in Violet's room. The idea was to cement the

160   connection between Brinkert and Sharpe so that the suspect would be less likely to deny that he had been Violet's date that night. But when it turned out that he hadn't been Violet's date, the whole thing backfired. When the real Ernie came forward, Brinkert's business cards suddenly became a mystery and an embarrassment. If Ernest Brinkert hadn't known Violet Sharpe, what *were* his business cards doing in her room? One explanation was that the police had planted them there.

Schwarzkopf and his men were being accused of things much more serious than planting a little evidence, so the matter of Brinkert's business cards never caught the public's attention. As a result the controversy was soon forgotten. (It should be noted that a six-page inventory listing the personal effects found in Violet's room, seventy-three items in all, did not include Brinkert's business cards. This document was prepared by the New Jersey State Police on June 15, 1932.)[15]

The Violet Sharpe controversy put Colonel Lindbergh in an awkward position. He wanted to defend Schwarzkopf against the charges of incompetence and brutality, but couldn't. If he allowed himself to be drawn into the debate, he would have to publicize his opinion that Violet Sharpe was innocent. Knowing that Schwarzkopf believed otherwise, and that such a statement would weaken Schwarzkopf's position, Lindbergh kept his silence.

Violet's suicide had a profound effect upon Anne Lindbergh. Reflecting on the tragedy, She wrote, " . . . Terrible criticism of police, in papers: 'Bullied innocent girl to death.' Blaze of criticism in papers in England. Girl appears innocent. It is very sickening. What a crude, imperfect world—we understand nothing."[16]

On Monday, June 13, the jury in the Gaston Means trial heard the last of the prosecution witnesses. If the Means jury, comprising eleven men and one woman, had been looking forward to hearing his side of the story, they were disappointed. The defense rested its case without putting on a single witness.

Judge Proctor gave his instructions to the jury and sent them off to deliberate. Two hours later they were back in the courtroom with their verdict. The foreman stood up and announced that the jury had found the defendant guilty of larceny on two counts. The first count involved the hundred thousand dollars—the so-called ransom money—and the second had to do with the four thousand dollars given to Means for expenses.

Making no effort to hide his approval of the verdict, Judge Proctor declared that Means would be sentenced on Wednesday, June 15. As the defendant was led from the courtroom he grinned at the reporters. He smiled all the way back to his cell. A latecomer to the proceeding would have thought he had won.

The next day Violet was buried in Englewood at the Brookside Cemetery, not far from the tomb of Dwight Morrow. The British Acting Consul-General had sent red roses. Violet's fellow servants had sent several wreaths.

The next day, Judge Proctor sentenced Gaston Means. Referring to his crime as a "clever and adroit plan" the judge said, "The verdict of the jury in this case reveals that the defendant capitalized not only on the sweetest and tenderest emotions of the human heart, but also on the basest." The judge then slapped Means with a fifteen-year prison sentence.

Judge Proctor's sentence would have sent most men reeling, but not Means. The judge asked the prisoner if he had anything to say for himself. Means shook his head— no, he had nothing to offer. He just stood there and smiled. Means wasn't a stranger to prison, he'd been there twice before. But this time he had drawn a long stretch, and although he didn't know it, he'd never get out.[17]

On the day Means was sentenced, the New Jersey State Police released Ernest Brinkert.

On June 17, Inspector Thomas of Scotland Yard located George Payne, the man Emily Sharpe said Violet had married in London before sailing for Canada. The inspector had found out that Payne, a sixty-three-year-old warehouse worker for a London publishing house, had been married for thirty-six years to his present wife. Payne met Violet in 1926 when they were domestic servants in the same house. They had been friends for six months he said, but were never intimate. They were never married either.[18]

The furor over Violet's suicide quickly faded. Acting British Consul-General Shepherd had completed his investigation of the incident and had forwarded his report to Anthony Eden, the Under-Secretary of His Majesty's Foreign Office. Speaking in front of the House of Commons on June 29, Eden reported that Mr. Shepherd had interviewed all of the Morrow servants and was satisfied that "no physical violence whatever or so-called 'third degree' methods" were used by her interrogators. "Miss Sharpe," he said, "had not been questioned under conditions of severe physical strain by lack of sleep or want of food."[19] Eden concluded his speech by saying that he was convinced that Violet had not been maltreated by the American police. As far as the British were concerned, the matter was closed.

The results of the British investigation were published without fanfare on the back pages of the English press. The American papers didn't bother to report them at all.

For some time Colonel Schwarzkopf harbored the belief that Violet Sharpe had been involved in the kidnapping. Although he later changed his mind about this, Schwarzkopf theorized that Violet had been the kidnappers' inside contact.

Four years after Violet's death, the New Jersey State Police uncovered information that probably explains her suicide. Investigators disclosed that while Violet was employed at the Morrow estate, she went out with five men with whom she had been sexually intimate. One of these men, William O'Brien, was a sodajerk at Dr. Wilmer's Drug Store on the corner of Lexington Avenue and Thirty-ninth Street in Manhattan. O'Brien met Violet when she was living at the nearby YWCA.[20]

Violet probably had been afraid that the Lindbergh investigators would find out about her relationship with these men. If Mrs. Morrow had found out about this, she would have fired Violet. The thought of being jobless and having no one to recommend her in the midst of the Depression had terrified her. She would have no choice but to return in disgrace to her parents' crowded cottage in England.

162   Violet was probably also thinking about Septimus Banks. He had planned to marry her. Worried about her job and future in America, sick and weak from her recent hospitalization, and under relentless attack by investigators who believed that she had helped the kidnappers, Violet had ended her dilemma by taking her life.

Violet's death had left a gaping hole in Schwarzkopf's investigation. What had once been a promising lead was now nothing more than a troublesome loose end. Violet Sharpe had given the Lindbergh investigators something to focus upon. Now that she was gone, the police were on the defensive, and somewhat adrift.

... he would be very methodical and extremely cautious, with full confidence in himself but no real confidence in those close to him; and this caution would make it very difficult to apprehend him since, considering everybody an "enemy," he would be constantly on guard.

—*A psychiatric profile of the kidnapper by Dr. Dudley D. Shoenfeld*

16 A FLOUNDERING INVESTIGATION

NOW THAT VIOLET SHARPE WAS DEAD, the two Ernies freed, Betty Gow and her boyfriend cleared, and John Hughes Curtis reduced to a cruel joke, the embattled Lindbergh investigators had run out of promising leads. As a result, they began reaching for suspects, and one of the persons they reached for was Dr. Condon—the one and only Jafsie.

Inspector Walsh had suspected Condon all along. Back in May at a press conference, he told reporters that John Condon wasn't on the level.[1] Walsh, and those who agreed with him, had their reasons for suspecting Condon. For one thing, they questioned the kidnappers' prompt reply to Condon's letter to the *Bronx Home News*. How did Condon know that the kidnappers read this paper? Why didn't he publish his letter in *The New York Times* or some other city-wide newspaper?

Walsh suspected that Condon had used his role as go-between to ensure the ransom payment. He doubted that Condon's March 12 conversation with John on the park bench in Van Cortlandt Park ever took place. Walsh didn't believe that a seventy-two-year-old man could chase after and catch up to a fleeing kidnapper. He was sure Condon had fabricated that part of the story.

Walsh also believed that if Condon was a crook, so was his friend and sometime chauffeur, Al Reich, who had driven Condon to the Woodlawn Cemetery that night.

On June 16, a Saturday, the day Ernest Brinkert was released from custody, Detective Robert Coar from Jersey City and Detective Sam Leon of the New Jersey State Police called on Dr. Condon at home. They asked if he would accompany them to the police station in Paterson, New Jersey, to look at some photographs. Condon and the two detectives had visited dozens of police departments together. Condon had come to enjoy these outings. A camaraderie had developed between the old man and the good-natured young detectives. The three of them had traveled all over New Jersey, New York, and parts of New England. Lately they had been playing practical jokes on each other.

Although the detectives hadn't given Condon any notice, he said that he'd be willing to ride over to Paterson. It was, after all, for a good cause.

Along the way, Detective Leon stopped at a pay phone. He said he was checking in with headquarters. When he returned to the car he said, "I've got orders, Doc, to take you to Alpine."

"But I thought we were going to Paterson."

"I got orders," Leon replied.

"All right," Condon said. "Whatever you say."

All of a sudden the mood had changed. The three men rode to Alpine in silence.

At Alpine, Condon was taken into a large office with a big conference table in the middle of the room. Around it sat six or seven uniformed policemen Condon didn't know. None of them came forward to greet him—they just stared at him with expressionless faces.

Detective Coar leaned against the wall with a dejected look. Officer Leon offered Condon a chair. The old man said he would rather stand. The business about going to Paterson had been a pretext. Although he didn't know why he had been hauled to Alpine, Condon didn't like it. He didn't like the atmosphere and he wasn't fond of being tricked.

Condon stood and waited. No one at the table spoke or looked his way. Detectives Coar and Leon had nothing to say either. They looked embarrassed.

Fifteen minutes passed. Condon was about to protest when Walsh strode into the room. Condon recognized him from his pictures in the newspapers.

Walsh walked straight up to Condon, folded his arms in front of him, and snapped, "It's about time you confessed."

So much for small talk. Condon was momentarily stunned. Finally he said, "Confess what?"

"Come now, Professor—you know exactly what I'm talking about." Walsh gave Condon a menacing look. "We don't want to hear any more of your shit."

Condon fought the urge to step backward. He was more than a little frightened of this man. But he was also angry. He didn't like being spoken to like that—particularly in the presence of others. He had been a teacher and a scholar for fifty years. His record was spotless. Hundreds of professional men, political leaders, and successful businessmen had been his students. As a patriotic American he had risked his life to help the Lindberghs in their hour of need. And now, some clumsy, heavy-handed cop was treating him like a common criminal.

"Who do you think you're talking to?" Condon replied.

"I know who I'm talking to. Let me tell you who *I* am. I'm a cop—first, last, and always! And I'm not listening to any more of your bull!"

The two men exchanged insults, then began shouting at each other. The officers sitting at the big table looked on silently. Walsh had used the wrong approach on Condon, and he knew it. But it was too late to back down—he couldn't lose face in front of the other policemen. In an attempt to gain control, Walsh reached out and grabbed Condon by the arm. That was his second mistake. Although he was seventy-two, Condon was well built and in good condition. He pulled his arm free of Walsh's grip, causing Walsh to lose his balance and stumble backward against the window sill.

"Arrest me," Condon said, "or keep your hands to yourself!"

Several of the officers at the table squirmed uneasily. The much shorter policeman regained his balance and repositioned himself in front of Condon. He stuck a stubby finger into Condon's chest and said, "When it comes time for me to arrest you, Condon, you'll know it." He then reduced the tension by smiling, "Look, Condon, you don't expect us to believe that you helped Colonel Lindbergh out of the kindness of your heart? What was in it for *you?* What was your cut of the action?"

"I've been asked that before," Condon replied. "And I'll tell you what I told the others—I did it so I could see the baby's arms around his mother's neck. That's why I volunteered my services, spent my own money and put my life in jeopardy."

Walsh shook his head. "That's the kind of bullshit I didn't want. Look—Condon, the truth will out. Make it easy on yourself."

"I have nothing to confess."

Walsh had run into a brick wall. He fired his big gun. "*Colonel Lindbergh is not a friend of yours,*" he said.

The statement rocked Condon. He felt his face get hot. He idolized Lindbergh. He had laid his life at his hero's feet. Condon had wanted nothing in return but Lindbergh's friendship and gratitude. He thought he had earned these things and this knowledge was a constant source of comfort and pride. It meant everything to him.

Walsh knew that he had hit a nerve and hoped it would loosen the old man's tongue. Walsh pulled a chair away from the table and said, "Have a seat, Doctor Condon. Please—make yourself comfortable." All of a sudden Walsh was a nice guy—Condon's friend. This had worked on John Curtis.

Condon suddenly felt tired and heavy on his feet. He plopped onto the chair. "What do you mean? Who says Colonel Lindbergh isn't a friend of mine?" he asked.

"There are certain things I can't divulge," Walsh answered.

"Did Colonel Lindbergh tell you that?"

"I can't say," Walsh replied sympathetically.

"Well, you're wrong about that. I'm a friend of the Lindberghs. They know my motives—and my integrity."

Walsh pulled up a chair and sat down himself. He and Condon would have a heart-to-heart talk.

Four hours later, Walsh was no closer to a confession. But he wasn't giving up. Rising from his chair he said, "You're going to stay here until you confess. You'd better telephone your family."

"Don't worry about my family. They know I can take care of myself."

"You may be here for three months."

"Whatever you say." Condon said with a smile. He could play the same game.

166   It was late in the afternoon, so Walsh announced that it was time to eat. Everyone got up and left, leaving Condon in the room with a uniformed guard. Hungry and tired, he fell asleep in his chair.

An hour later, Walsh and the other policemen returned. "Well, I'll be a son of a bitch," the inspector said, "will you look at that. You'd think he was home in bed. Get your hat, Doctor, you and I are taking a walk."

Condon and Walsh strolled along a path that followed the edge of a cliff overlooking the Hudson River. Walsh was now talking in a fatherly tone. This was how he had coaxed a confession out of John Curtis. It had worked on the hoaxer, but not on Condon. Two hours later, Condon was released.[2]

In the wake of Violet Sharpe's suicide, Colonel Schwarzkopf had sent Corporal Frank Kelly, the New Jersey State Police fingerprint man, to Washington, D.C., with the kidnap ladder. In May, pieces of the ladder had been sent to Arthur Koehler at the Department of Agriculture's Forest Service Laboratories in Madison, Wisconsin. Schwarzkopf had sent the entire ladder to Dr. Wilmer T. Souder at the National Bureau of Standards. Dr. Souder had analyzed the ladder and had submitted his report. Although he wasn't a wood expert, he concluded that the ladder had been crudely but ingeniously fashioned by someone who possessed basic carpentry skills. The lightweight portability of the ladder suggested to Souder that it had been specifically designed for the kidnapping. When the three sections were compressed together, the ladder could fit nicely into the back seat of a car.

On June 22, Congress finally passed a kidnapping bill. Under the new statute, called the Lindbergh Law, if the victim was not returned within a week, it was presumed that the kidnappers had taken the person across a state line. This in turn would give jurisdiction in the case to the FBI. The crime carried a maximum penalty of life imprisonment. When the federal law was passed, kidnapping in New Jersey was classified as a high misdemeanor, carrying a sentence of five years to life. One year later, the federal statute was amended to make kidnapping a capital offense when the victim was harmed. Pursuant to this amendment, the death penalty could be imposed at the recommendation of the jury. The amendment also allowed the FBI to enter the case within twenty-four hours of the crime.

The obstruction-of-justice trial of John Hughes Curtis got underway on Monday, June 27, at the Hunterdon County Courthouse in Flemington. A large crowd of spectators had gathered in the town in the hope of seeing Colonel Lindbergh, the prosecution's star witness.

Curtis was represented by C. Lloyd Fisher, a well-respected Flemington attorney.[3] Constance Curtis, the defendant's eleven-year-old daughter, sat between Fisher and his client at the defense table. She was holding her father's hand. Pale and thin, she looked out of place and a little frightened.

Curtis was being prosecuted by Anthony Hauck, the Hunterdon County district attorney. Joseph Lanigan from the state attorney general's office was assisting him.[4] Colonel Lindbergh sat next to Lanigan.

When Lloyd Fisher saw the fourth man at the prosecution table, a local attorney **167** named Harry Stout, his heart sank. Curtis had consulted with Stout after his arraignment at the Lindbergh house. Although Curtis never retained Stout, the two men had discussed possible defenses. In fact, Curtis's defense that he *had* been in touch with the kidnappers, that his story was *not* a hoax, had been Stout's idea. Fisher was therefore more than a little shocked and disheartened to see Stout conferring with the enemy.

By noon, with Judge Adam O. Robbins presiding, the attorneys had selected the jury of seven men and five women.

Fisher was shocked again when Hauck, in his opening statement, declared, "We will prove beyond a reasonable doubt that Curtis *was* dealing with the kidnappers, that he knew *who* they were and *where* they were."

This was a complete turnaround. Instead of prosecuting Curtis for making up a story, the defendant was being charged with confessing to a hoax in order to protect the kidnappers.

In preparing Curtis's charge, the prosecution had run into a legal dilemma. In New Jersey, it was not a crime to report false information to the police. The closest thing to it was obstructing justice by willfully pointing the police in the wrong direction—to take them off the trail of the perpetrators. In order to have a case against Curtis under New Jersey law, the prosecution had to prove that Curtis's "kidnappers" did exist and that Curtis had confessed to a hoax in order to throw the police off the kidnappers' trail. In effect, the prosecution was saying that Curtis was not a hoaxer but an accomplice after the fact.

Although it was common knowledge that Sam, John, Eric, and the others did not exist, and that the charge was therefore absurd on its face, it robbed Fisher of his defense. Having made a case that Curtis's kidnappers did exist, he now had to argue that they didn't. Instead of defending against the hoax, he would have to argue for it. It was a strange case.

Two and a half days later, the jurors filed back into the jury box. The foreman stood up and declared that the jury had found the defendant guilty as charged. Speaking on behalf of his fellow jurors, the foreman asked Judge Robbins to be lenient with Curtis.

The judge sentenced Curtis to one year in prison and fined him one thousand dollars.

The jury had overlooked the gap in New Jersey's penal code. By letting the case go to the jury, Judge Robbins had done likewise.

The verdict shocked and infuriated Fisher. It was an outrage, he said. He would appeal. But Curtis was all smiles as he was taken back to his cell. He was relieved, he said.

A week later, Fisher made Curtis's bond, allowing the shipbuilder to return to his wife and children in Norfolk.

The Lindbergh case dropped out of the news after Curtis's trial; there was nothing left to report. It had been four months since the crime, and the police were still baffled. Many thought that Schwarzkopf had bungled the investigation and that the case would never be solved.

Because of the depression, Governor Moore was under pressure to cut expenses.

168 Hundreds of workers had already been cut from the state payroll. Moore had planned to reduce the size of the New Jersey State Police, but the Lindbergh crime had made this measure politically unwise.

In July of 1932, with the Lindbergh case out of the news and the investigation slowed to a crawl, Governor Moore laid off fifty New Jersey state troopers.

Out of leads and solid suspects, Schwarzkopf, desperate for a break in the case, turned again to John Condon. During July and August, his men and detectives from New York City searched Condon's house for his share of the ransom money. They intercepted his mail, tapped his telephone, stripped the paper off the walls of his study, and dug holes in his yard.[5]

In August 1932, Colonel Schwarzkopf sent Hugo Stockberger, a German-speaking trooper, to England to conduct further background investigations of Oliver and Elsie Whateley, Betty Gow, and Violet Sharpe's sister Emily.

Stockberger spent two months in England working with detectives from New Scotland Yard. He didn't find any evidence that connected the Lindbergh-Morrow servants to the kidnapping.

Stockberger reported that detectives at New Scotland Yard were interested in the ransom note symbol. They concluded that it had been designed by a man with the initials BRH (not necessarily in that order). The English detectives had interpreted the ransom symbol as follows: The two large circles outlined in *blue* represented the letter *B*, the solid *red* circle in the middle represented the letter *R*, and the three *holes*, the letter *H*.[6]

In June, the Lindberghs moved out of the house in Hopewell. The new baby was due in August and they wanted to avoid the publicity that had greeted the birth of Charles, Jr. The Lindberghs were living at the Morrow estate in Englewood.

The move to Englewood also provided better security. There had been repeated threats to kidnap the new baby, and the family could be better protected there. The estate was patrolled around the clock by a state trooper and three private guards, and the Lindberghs had purchased Pal, a large German police dog the Colonel had renamed Thor.

The move to the Morrow mansion didn't rid the Lindberghs of the press or the public's attention. Reporters camped outside the gates of the estate, and the roads around the Lindbergh house were clogged with cars full of sightseers. Next Day Hill, the Morrow estate in Englewood, had become a popular tourist attraction, and for the Lindberghs, a prison.

Mrs. Lindbergh went into labor at 4:00 A.M., on Tuesday, August 16. Shortly thereafter she was driven to her mother's apartment at 4 East Sixty-sixth Street in Manhattan. She was met there by her obstetrician, Dr. E. M. Hawks, and Dr. P. J. Flagg, the anesthetist. Three and a half hours later the baby was born. It was a seven pound fourteen ounce boy.

The next day, Colonel Lindbergh and Dr. Hawks spoke to a large group of reporters gathered outside Mrs. Morrow's apartment. Dr. Hawks described the baby, named Jon, and announced that mother and son were doing fine. Colonel Lindbergh then read the following statement:

Mrs. Lindbergh and I have made our home in New Jersey. It is naturally our wish to **169** continue to live there near our friends and interests. Obviously, however, it is impossible for us to subject the life of our second son to the publicity which we feel was in large measure responsible for the death of our first.

We feel that our children have a right to grow up normally with other children. Continued publicity will make this impossible. I am appealing to the press to permit our children to lead lives of normal Americans.

Colonel Lindbergh's appeal had no effect. The press continued to follow him, reporting everything he did, and hordes of people drove by the estate every day hoping for a glimpse. A few days after Jon's birth, the Lindberghs started getting letters threatening to kidnap and murder the new baby. Horrified and depressed by the continuing publicity and the threats, the Lindberghs were beginning to wonder if their lives would ever be normal.

In the fall of 1932, a New York City psychiatrist named Dr. Dudley D. Shoenfeld began studying photographs of the ransom notes that had been published in the newspapers. The balding, thirty-nine-year-old graduate of New York University and Bellevue Medical College was using the ransom notes to formulate a profile of the kidnapper. So far, he had concluded that the crime had been committed by one man—the ransom note writer—who was not a professional criminal.

In October, hoping that his theoretical deductions would be of some use to the police, Shoenfeld contacted Det. James Finn, the New York City officer assigned to the Lindbergh case.

James Finn was a slender, high-strung fifty-one-year-old who resided in Belle Harbor, Long Island, with his wife and two children. A New York City cop for twenty-seven years, he was bright and energetic. Finn had been promoted to detective shortly after joining the force in 1905. But eleven years later, he was demoted to patrolman and transferred to Staten Island. Five years after that, under a new police commissioner, Finn climbed back to the rank of second-grade detective. In 1927, Finn was one of the bodyguards at Lindbergh's New York City ticker-tape parade.

After the kidnapping, Colonel Lindbergh's former press secretary, Harry A. Bruno, remembered Detective Finn from those glory days. Bruno asked Police Commissioner Edward Mulrooney to assign Finn to the Lindbergh investigation. The next day Finn was dispatched to Hopewell.

Detective Finn put himself at the disposal of Colonel Schwarzkopf, but after a few days it was obvious that he was not going to be brought into the inner circles of the investigation. Rather than hang around the fringes and get in the way, Finn returned to his office in Manhattan.

During the next several months, Finn made several attempts to get Colonel Schwarzkopf to send him photocopies of the ransom notes. Schwarzkopf ignored his requests. In the meantime, Finn kept busy keeping track of the ransom bills that were occasionally turning up in the city. So far, he hadn't found anyone who remembered how they had come into possession of a Lindbergh bill. Finn kept a city map that was dotted with pins representing places the gold notes had turned up.

170   Although skeptical of what a psychiatrist would have to say about the case, Finn gave Shoenfeld a hearing. When the doctor was finished, Finn was impressed. He was so impressed he wrote another letter to Schwarzkopf requesting copies of the ransom notes. Finn carefully explained that he was not asking for the documents himself—they were for Dr. Shoenfeld whose psychiatric insights might prove useful.

Instead of sending Finn the photocopies, Schwarzkopf arranged to have Dr. Shoenfeld come to the Morrow estate to discuss his work with Colonel Lindbergh.

Early in November, Shoenfeld was in the Morrow library presenting his preliminary findings to Lindbergh, Breckinridge, Schwarzkopf, Keaten, Walsh, and several federal officers. Everyone was there except Detective Finn.

When the meeting broke up, Shoenfeld was driven back to New York City. He carried with him the photocopies Detective Finn had been trying to get for seven months. Shoenfeld had been given the documents over the objections of Schwarzkopf and Keaten. The psychiatrist had convinced Lindbergh and Breckinridge that he would be able to profile the kidnapper more fully once he had studied all of the letters.

Dr. Shoenfeld spent a week poring over the ransom material. On November 10, he submitted a lengthy report, in the form of a memorandum, to Colonel Schwarzkopf. He sent a copy to Detective Finn.[7]

Shoenfeld wrote that in his opinion the kidnapper had a mental disease called dementia paralytica (today called schizophrenia). Although the kidnapper felt omnipotent or all-powerful, he was, in reality, a powerless man who occupied a low station in life. Angered and frustrated by his status, he blamed others for his inadequacies, laboring under the illusion that certain forces in society were preventing him from realizing his grandiose goals in life.

Colonel Lindbergh was everything this man wasn't and wanted to be—powerful, wealthy, and universally revered. The kidnapper saw him as a rival, someone to defeat, outsmart, and humiliate. This was the unconscious motive for the crime. Shoenfeld said that such a man would work alone and take great personal risks.

In the ransom writings, the psychiatrist noticed that the kidnapper had overdecorated many of his letters—a trait common among sufferers of dementia paralytica. In the last note he had written that the baby was on the "Boad between Horseneck Beach and Gay Head near Elizabeth Island." Shoenfeld said that the word *Gay* had been initially written as Gun. The writer had changed the *u* to an *a*. Shoenfeld noted that the kidnapper may have been thinking of Gun Hill Road, a major street in the Bronx.

Shoenfeld concluded that the kidnapper was a forty-year-old German who had served time in prison. He had homosexual tendencies, was mechanically inclined, secretive, and not prone to confess. The psychiatrist speculated that the kidnapper was physically similar to Lindbergh, and if married, would be tyrannical. He would have female friends but his life would revolve around men. Because he was secretive, cautious, and untrusting, the kidnapper would be very difficult to catch.

Although Shoenfeld's profile fit thousands, it would be useful in evaluating and eliminating suspects. Schwarzkopf and Finn were very impressed.

During September and October, Dr. Condon widened his search for John. He looked at hundreds of lineups and rogues' gallerys between Montreal and Miami. According to his own estimate, he looked at thirty-seven thousand mug shots and spent twelve thousand dollars of his own money.

On November 6, John Curtis appeared before Judge Robbins to be resentenced. Pursuant to Fisher's agreement to drop his appeal, Curtis only received a thousand dollar fine. Curtis handed the money over, then shook everybody's hand—including the judge's. He had no hard feelings, he said. The next day in Norfolk he told reporters that he had been vindicated. He said he had dropped his appeal to avoid what he called the "uncertainties of Jersey justice." After giving the police and the press a run for their money, John Hughes Curtis dropped out of the case for good.

During the next eighteen months the Lindbergh case slipped out of sight. People weren't tired of it—there just wasn't much to report. The investigation had slowed to a crawl, and the great sideshow attractions—Rosner, Means, Sharpe, and Curtis—had closed.

Two days after Curtis was resentenced, Franklin Delano Roosevelt won a landslide victory over President Hoover. Roosevelt and his New Deal politics would dominate the domestic news.

> I still consider Colonel Lindbergh the most wonderful
> man whom it has been my pleasure to know.
> —DR. JOHN F. CONDON
>   *in* Jafsie Tells All!

17   TRACKING THE LADDER

ON JANUARY 1, 1933, Detective Finn was assigned full time to the Lindbergh investigation. His new assignment was accompanied by a promotion to the rank of lieutenant. He was working under the supervision of Deputy Insp. J. Sullivan, the city-wide head of the detective bureau.[1]

Because Schwarzkopf wasn't cooperating with the New York police, Finn's investigation consisted of keeping track of the ransom bills that were popping up in the city. So far, only a handful of the gold notes had been identified as ransom money.

In February, Schwarzkopf asked Arthur Koehler to come to New Jersey to examine the kidnap ladder. Koehler had previously only studied pieces of the ladder. Two days after receiving Schwarzkopf's invitation, he was on a train for Trenton.

Seeing the ladder for the first time, Koehler was impressed by its ingenious design and fascinated by how crudely it had been made. It was both crude and clever, an unusual combination.

On Koehler's fourth and final day in New Jersey, he went over his findings with Colonel Schwarzkopf. The next morning, he was on the train back to Wisconsin. Lying in the aisle next to his feet was the kidnap ladder.

In his own laboratory, Koehler labeled and numbered the eleven rungs and the six side rails. The rungs were numbered one through eleven and the side rails twelve through seventeen. The two rails on the bottom of the ladder were twelve and thirteen, the two in the middle fourteen and fifteen, and the ones on top sixteen and seventeen.

Rail number sixteen, the left-hand side board to the top section, had four nail holes in it. These holes had nothing to do with the ladder—they had been in the board before the ladder had been made. This meant that rail sixteen had been used for something else. From the shape of the holes, Koehler could tell that it had been fastened by old-fashioned square nails. Koehler figured that the ladder's builder had used rail sixteen when he ran out of wood. Maybe the kidnapper had taken something apart to get it.

Koehler found that eight of the Ponderosa pine rungs had been cut from a single board that had been five and five-eighths inches wide and at least four feet eleven and one half inches long. The edges of these rungs had been planed by a dull hand-plane, which had left distinctive marks on the wood.

In cutting the places in the side rails for the rungs, the builder had used a three-quarter-inch wood chisel. After making test cuts with the crime scene chisel, Koehler couldn't say for sure that it was the tool that had been used on the ladder.

Koehler believed that most of the ladder's rails had been planed at the same lumber mill. The mill's planer had a cutting irregularity that had left a unique and clearly identifiable mark on the wood. Koehler concluded that these boards had been fed through a planer at the speed of 230 feet per minute. This was a rate used by mills in the South.[2]

On March 8, one year and one week from the day of the crime, Koehler submitted his report to Schwarzkopf.

About the only aspect of the Lindbergh case getting into the newspapers was Condon's unrelenting hunt for John. A month earlier he had gone to Newark to see if a jewel thief named Arthur Barry was his man. Barry wasn't John, but before Jafsie left the police station, he and the prisoner fell to their knees and recited the Lord's Prayer in Latin. The following day a New York City tabloid carried the headline: "JAFSIE VINDI-CATES BARRY AND BOTH HAVE A GOOD CRY."[3]

Schwarzkopf was desperate for a way to resolve his doubts about Condon. He asked Colonel Lindbergh to invite Condon to Englewood for dinner. Maybe this would throw the old schoolteacher off guard. Lindbergh could watch and listen to him closely for hints of guilty knowledge.

Lindbergh said that he didn't have a fix on Condon either—but he was sure that Jafsie was on the up and up. But he'd go along with Schwarzkopf's plan. Having Condon over for dinner was the least he could do to show his gratitude. It had been almost a year since he had seen the old man.[4]

During the past year, the Lindberghs had been in Condon's thoughts. He had rejoiced over the birth of the Colonel's second son, railed at the press for its harassment of the Lindberghs, and prayed that all was going well in Englewood. Condon was sure that Lindbergh didn't know he was being treated so badly by the police. The Colonel probably didn't know about Walsh's interrogation, the search of his house, the wiretapping, and the interception of his mail. If the Colonel had known about these things, he would have put a stop to them. Just like the time he wrote that nice letter when he learned that Condon was getting hate mail.

Condon's dinner invitation came late in March. He showed the invitation to anyone who would stop and look at it.

Late in the afternoon of the big day, a chauffeured limousine pulled up at the Condon house. Twenty minutes later Condon was being greeted at the Morrow estate by Charles and Anne Lindbergh. The Colonel was surprised that Condon had come alone. Why didn't the doctor bring his family? Condon might have answered that they hadn't been invited. Instead, he said that he didn't want to impose. But since the Colonel had asked, his daughter Myra was living in nearby West Englewood. When Lindbergh heard that, he insisted on driving over to Myra's house and bringing her back to the estate. A few minutes later, Myra got the shock of her life: Standing in her doorway was Colonel Charles Lindbergh.

No one mentioned the kidnapping. Condon had decided not to bring the subject up. Lindbergh was in the kitchen showing Condon his dogs while Anne Lindbergh and Myra were in the living room discussing the book Mrs. Lindbergh was working on.[5]

After dinner, Condon asked if he and Myra could see the baby. Mrs. Lindbergh went upstairs and brought him down for Condon to fuss over. The baby was eight months old and as beautiful as their first. The excitement got to be too much for Jon and he began to cry, so Mrs. Lindbergh carried him back to his crib. The Colonel led Condon back into the kitchen. As he stroked his police dog, Lindbergh said, "I've been reading about your visits to the police stations, Colonel Schwarzkopf tells me you haven't seen the man."

"Not yet, no. But I won't stop looking until I do."

"It must be exhausting—and very expensive. Are you spending your own money?"

"Yes. I feel that it's my duty—as an American. And I don't like being double-crossed."

"I'd like to reimburse you for your expenses. You shouldn't have to spend your own money."

Condon stiffened. "You don't owe me a penny, sir. I'm doing it for myself. If you want to give me something, let me keep the wooden animals and the safety pins."

"You may have them," Lindbergh replied. "Anne and I are very grateful." The two men shook hands.

It was late in the evening when Colonel Lindbergh drove Condon and Myra to West Englewood where Condon would spend the night at his daughter's house. His evening with the Lindberghs had made everything worthwhile.[6]

A week later, Colonel Schwarzkopf called a conference at the Morrow estate to discuss the status of the case. Among the topics to be discussed was John Condon. The meeting was attended by Lindbergh, Breckinridge, Lamb, Keaten, Walsh, and several IRS and FBI agents. Lindbergh said if Condon were a younger man, he might be suspicious, but in the absence of evidence to the contrary, he didn't consider Jafsie a suspect.[7]

Inspector Walsh spoke up and said that in his mind Condon was a suspect—and a prime one at that. He believed there was a connection between Condon and Violet Sharpe. In fact, he wouldn't be surprised if Condon had masterminded the crime by using inside information the maid had given him.

Inspector Walsh's relationship with Schwarzkopf had become strained after Walsh had written an eight-part magazine article about the case. The piece, called "Hunt for the Kidnappers: Inside Story Of The Lindbergh Case," had been published in the *Jersey Journal*.[8] In the article, Walsh had accused the Lindbergh investigators of not following what he called, "usual police procedures."[9] He faulted Colonel Schwarzkopf for not arresting Violet Sharpe and John Condon and holding them until they confessed or were cleared.[10] Walsh was now suggesting that they arrest Condon and hold him as a material witness.

Walsh said, "Curtis didn't confess until he was in custody. He knew he wasn't going anywhere until he did."

"What if you arrest Condon and he doesn't confess?" Lindbergh asked.

"He will."

"He didn't at Alpine," Schwarzkopf said.

"It takes time."

"No," Schwarzkopf replied, "we don't have the evidence. He'd eventually get a lawyer and get out."

The meeting broke up with the general consensus that Condon was eccentric but clean. The lone dissenter was Inspector Walsh. A few weeks later, Walsh returned to regular duty at the Jersey City Police Department. Schwarzkopf wrote the mayor of that city a nice letter thanking him for the services of this fine detective.[11]

About the time the Lindbergh investigators were conferring at the Morrow estate, a newspaperman named Leigh Matteson presented an idea to Lieutenant Finn. Matteson suggested that Finn and his men check all of the motor vehicle registration cards in the Bronx that bore German names, then compare the writing on the cards with the handwriting in the ransom letters.

Finn was intrigued by the plan. The more he thought about it the better he liked it. It was logical, practical, and simple. And it came at a time when the Lindbergh investigation, on both sides of the Hudson, was running out of steam. Before taking any action on the lead, Finn called Albert S. Osborn, the chief documents examiner in the case. Osborn wasn't impressed with Matteson's idea. It would be a waste of manpower, he said. Motor vehicle registration cards didn't contain enough handwriting to make them useful as exemplars. The kidnapper's signature on one of these cards wouldn't necessarily match the ransom writings. Osborn said that document examiners needed more than signatures to make their comparisons. Moreover, much of the material on the registration cards would be hand-printed.

After talking to Osborn, Lieutenant Finn decided not to use Matteson's idea. The Lindbergh investigation didn't need another wild goose chase.[12]

Finn wasn't totally averse to long-shot leads, however. Working off the fact that the kidnappers had responded to Condon's ad in the *Bronx Home News,* New York City detectives, posing as door-to-door salesmen, called at the homes of every German American who got the paper. Every person who came close to John Condon's description of John was thoroughly investigated.

In May, Oliver Whateley died in a Trenton hospital. The fifty-year-old butler had been ill for several months. The Lindberghs were deeply saddened by his death.

In the summer of 1933, Arthur Koehler returned to Madison, Wisconsin, after spending several fruitless weeks in New York, Massachusetts, and New Jersey searching for remnants of the wood that had been used in the construction of the kidnap ladder. Det. Lewis J. Bornmann of the New Jersey State Police had been with him.

Back in his laboratory, Koehler studied his enlarged photographs of the five side rails made of southern pine—rails eleven through fifteen. Koehler was particularly interested in the boards' planing marks. He believed that these marks would eventually lead him to the lumber mill that had produced the rails.

But where to start? Koehler knew that although southern pine grew all over the country, it was reasonable to assume the lumber that he was interested in had been grown and dressed in the Atlantic states. That meant he would have to check 1,598 lumber mills.

Koehler began his search by mailing a form letter to each mill. He said he was looking for a lumber planer that fed boards at a speed of 230 feet a minute, a planer that had six knives in its edge cutters and eight in its face cutters.

Twenty-five mill owners replied that they used such a planer. After ruling out two of them because they had never handled one-by-four-inch boards, Koehler asked the rest to send samples of the boards dressed by their planers.

A few weeks later, Koehler examined a sample one by four board sent to him by a mill in McCormick, South Carolina. It had cuts on it that were very similar to the marks on the kidnap ladder. But the marks were not identical. The planer that had dressed the ladder's rails had an irregular cutting blade that had left a unique pattern in the wood, a cutting blade that would have since been replaced.

Excited by his find, Koehler hurried to South Carolina, where he met the officials of the M. G. and J. J. Dorn Lumber Company. Koehler told the mill owners that he was looking for a board with cutting marks identical to the ones on the ladder. If he found such a board, he would know where the rails had been planed—a starting point in tracing the lumber to its place of sale, and eventually, to the kidnapper.

Koehler didn't find his board, but he did learn that the ladder's rails had been planed during a twenty-nine-month period after September 1929. During this time, the Dorn Lumber Mill had been using a planer that ran the boards through at the same speed the kidnap rails had been fed. Koehler searched through the company's records and learned that during this period the company had shipped forty-six carloads of pine to twenty-five firms. Eighteen of these carloads had gone to two companies within a twenty-five-mile radius of the Lindbergh home. Since both of these firms had sliced the boards into short lengths to make crates, they were eliminated. Koehler started running down the other twenty-eight carloads by searching lumber yards in Boston, Springfield, Stamford, and New Haven. After that, he checked out all of the Dorn shipments to New York City. He still hadn't found a board that had been planed by the blades that had fashioned the ladder's rails. In Ozone Park, Long Island, a lumber dealer told Koehler that he remembered using some of the Dorn Company one by fours to build a storage bin. Koehler looked at a sample of this wood and found marks that had been made by the defective cutter blade used on the ladder. But the overall cutting pattern was not identical. The Long Island board had gone through the same planer, but it had been fed through at a faster speed than the rails of the ladder.

Through a series of complicated deductions, Koehler figured that the boards he was looking for had been part of a carload of southern pine the Dorn mill had shipped either immediately before or just after the shipment to Ozone Park. The shipment after had gone to Youngstown, Ohio—but these one by fours had been dressed one-eighth of an inch narrower than the ladder's boards. The previous shipment had gone to the Halligan and McClelland Company in New York, which in turn had sold it to the National Lumber and Millwork Company in the Bronx. This shipment had been bought on December 11, 1931, exactly three months before the kidnapping. Koehler was confident that he was finally closing in on his target.

At the National Lumber and Millwork Company, on White Plains Avenue, Koehler learned that the wood from the Halligan and McClelland Company had been sold. But when Koehler checked the company's storage bins he found what he was looking for—the perfect match. The boards used to build the bin had been cut from the same cutting machine that had dressed five of the six ladder rails. Koehler's discovery came on November 19, 1933, eighteen months after his initial involvement in the case.

The excited wood expert and his partner, Detective Bornmann, asked to see the store's sales records. If the kidnapper had purchased his wood here his name would be in their files. The manager killed Koehler's euphoria and his hopes when he announced that the store didn't keep sales records—it was a cash-and-carry operation. With that, Koehler's quest had suddenly ended. Although he hadn't identified the kidnapper, he had discovered where he had purchased some of his wood. The trail had led him to the Bronx, the origin of the extortion notes and the site of the ransom payment.

The next day, Lieutenant Finn placed every employee of the National Lumber and Millwork Company under twenty-four-hour surveillance. It was an enormous undertaking. Albert S. Osborn obtained handwriting samples from each employee and checked them against the ransom notes.

With nothing left to do, a disappointed Koehler returned to Madison.

In Trenton, Schwarzkopf was a little uncomfortable. Koehler's investigation had turned up another connection to the Bronx. The center of the investigation was slowly moving across the Hudson, and Schwarzkopf was not on very good terms with the New York City police. He had good cause to be worried about losing his grip on the case.

What's the matter? It's good ain't it?
—*The passer of a five-dollar ransom bill at the Loew's Sheridan
Theater in Greenwich Village on November 26, 1933*

18 THE GOLD NOTE TRAIL

IN NEW YORK, LIEUTENANT FINN had been keeping a large map of the city in which he had stuck pins that showed where the Lindbergh bills had turned up. He had been doing this since April 1932, when the first gold notes had surfaced. At the FBI office on Lexington Avenue, Special Agent Thomas Sisk was doing the same thing.

The first ransom bill to surface was a twenty-dollar gold note that showed up at the East River Savings Bank in Upper Manhattan. It was discovered a few days after the ransom payment.[1] Several of the tellers at the bank were questioned, but none of them had any idea who had passed it. This would be the last twenty to pop up for some time. During the next several months all of the bills that were recovered were fives and tens.

By the fall of 1932, a quarter of a million copies of the fifty-seven-page ransom booklets had been distributed. But the list was awkward and the typed columns were small and hard to read. Bank personnel and merchants were also becoming lax in checking incoming currency. In an attempt to revitalize interest in the ransom pamphlet, Colonel Lindbergh offered a two dollar reward to every person who reported a ransom bill. Meanwhile, Lieutenant Finn and his detectives visited banks to keep tellers alert and on the lookout for Lindbergh money.

On April 5, 1933, President Roosevelt took steps to stop the hoarding of gold, a practice that had become much too popular as the Depression deepened. By executive order, he directed all persons possessing gold bullion, coins, or certificates valued at more than a hundred dollars to deposit it at a Federal Reserve Bank on or before May 1, 1933. Noncompliance could bring a ten thousand dollar fine and a stretch in prison.

Lieutenant Finn hoped that Roosevelt's order would make people more alert to the ransom money. Although it wasn't a crime to possess and pass a twenty-dollar gold note (it was only a crime to own a hundred dollars or more in gold notes), these bills would become increasingly rare, and therefore noticeable. In May of 1933, Lieutenant Finn and Agent Sisk visited the officials and cashiers of the Federal Reserve Bank of New York and

178

asked them to check the serial numbers of all incoming gold certificates against the ransom booklet.

A week before President Roosevelt's gold exchange deadline, fifty ten-dollar ransom bills turned up at the Chemical National Bank in New York City. A few days later, fifty more ransom bills of five and ten-dollar denominations were discovered at the Manufacturers Trust Company. None of the bank employees could recall who had exchanged the gold certificates.

On May 1, 1933, the last day of President Roosevelt's deadline, a person walked into the Federal Reserve Bank in New York City and exchanged $2,980 in gold notes for the equivalent amount in greenbacks. Every gold note in the pack was a ransom bill. The only clue to the man's identity was a deposit slip bearing the name J. J. Faulkner and the address 537 West 149th Street, New York. Finn's detectives checked out the address and found no such person living there. The follow-up investigation produced more questions than answers.[2] No one at the bank could provide a description of J. J. Faulkner.

By the fall of 1933, about a year and a half since Lieutenant Finn started sticking pins into his map, a pattern had emerged. Originally, the bill passer had made an effort not to spend the money in the same area. But as time went on he had become more careless. The increasing number of red (ten-dollar) and black (five-dollar) pins were now clustered in the same places. The pins were along Lexington and Third Avenues in upper Manhattan and also clustered in the German-speaking district of Yorkville.

Finn's detectives and secret service agents had worked as waiters in restaurants in this part of the Bronx. They had also assumed roles as bartenders in Yorkville's speakeasies known to be frequented by German-Americans.

Whenever someone reported a ransom bill, Finn or one of his detectives would immediately question the store clerk or bank employee in the hope of getting a description of the bill passer. Usually the money wasn't identified until two or three days after it had been spent, making it difficult to connect the bills with a particular person. On occasion, however, the man who had tendered the gold note was observed and remembered. And so far, all of the descriptions were consistent: a white male of average height with blue eyes, high cheekbones, flat cheeks, and a pointed chin. He spoke with a German accent and wore a soft felt hat pulled down over his forehead. This composite portrait tallied with Condon's description and the one given by Joseph Perrone, the cab driver who had delivered one of the ransom notes to Condon's house. The accent fit in with Albert S. Osborn's belief that the ransom note writer was German.

So far, most of the ransom bills that had been recovered were in the same condition. Each note had been folded in half along its full length, then doubled over twice along its length, so that when it was unfolded and laid flat it had creases dividing it into eight sections. Lieutenant Finn had also discerned a pattern in the way the bill passer tendered the money. He would take a small, folded bill from his watch or vest pocket and toss it onto the counter for the bank or store clerk to unfold.

Finn sent each ransom bill to Dr. Alexander Gettler, the director of New York City's

Toxicological Laboratories. Gettler worked for Dr. Charles Norris, the city's Chief Medical Examiner. Gettler and Norris were two of America's most renowned forensic scientists.

Dr. Gettler found particles of glycerine and emory on each bill. He concluded that the person who had passed the currency had used an emory wheel to grind tools. Moreover, many of the bills contained a fatty substance that was probably oil or grease. Gettler believed the bill-passer was a person who worked with metal and who used a lathe or drill-press.

Dr. Gettler also found, on many of the bills, lipstick and mascara as well as traces of blond, brunette, and red hair. The toxicologists reported that the bills had a musty odor, suggesting that they had been buried or secreted in an enclosed place. None of the notes contained any discernable fingerprints.

As the gold notes turned up in the Bronx, the focus of the investigation moved slowly but surely from New Jersey to New York City. If Schwarzkopf wanted to keep his grip on the investigation, he would have to start working with Finn. Schwarzkopf, therefore, decided to open his files to Finn and to cooperate fully with the FBI. He then got permission for his men to cross the Hudson and to join in the hunt for the kidnapper. From now on, the Lindbergh investigation would be a joint effort.

James T. Berryman, the well-known political cartoonist, had drawn a portrait of John based on the Condon-Perrone descriptions. Berryman's drawing was shown all over Manhattan and the Bronx.

Lieutenant Keaten headed the group of New Jersey officers working in New York City. His principal assistants were Detectives William F. Horn and John Wallace. During the next year, the Lindbergh investigation in New York City would be spearheaded by Finn, Keaten, and Thomas Sisk of the FBI.[3]

On November 27, 1933, eight days after Arthur Koehler had traced the five ladder rails to the National Lumber and Millwork Company, a teller at the Corn Exchange Bank and Trust Company in Greenwich Village came across a five-dollar gold certificate. The bank clerk consulted the ransom list and discovered that he had a Lindbergh bill. The five was part of a Loew's Sheridan Theater deposit that had been dropped in the night deposit box. The Loew's Sheridan was housed in a large, red building in the heart of Greenwich Village two blocks south of the bank.

Lieutenant Finn hurried to the Loew's to question Miss Cecile Barr, the cashier who had taken the gold note. When he got there, he handed Miss Barr the bill, creased into eight sections, and asked if she remembered who had given it to her. She said that a man wearing a black suit and a black slouch hat pulled over his forehead had purchased a ticket with the tightly folded bill. This occurred at 9:30 Sunday night, just as the main feature, *Broadway Through A Keyhole,* was about to begin. The movie, written by Walter Winchell and starring Paul Kelly and Constance Cummings, was about crime in the big city. The man in the slouch hat had tossed the five-dollar gold note through the opening in the ticket booth and had asked for a seat in the orchestra section. When Miss Barr unfolded the bill, she noticed the yellow seal that identified it as a gold note.

Miss Barr didn't remember what the man did after he got his change. She guessed **181** that he entered the theater. The man was average in size and had a prominent, but not a big nose. His mouth was small, his eyes gray-blue, and his chin pointed. Miss Barr figured that the man was in his mid-thirties.

Miss Barr's description coincided nicely with the Condon-Perrone portrait, and the tightly folded bill tied this incident to the other bill passing episodes.

Lieutenant Finn examined all of the consecutively numbered ticket stubs from that night and discovered that one of them was missing. There had been six tickets sold after the one with the missing stub. Finn questioned the ushers and none of them recalled seeing a man meeting the bill passer's description. Finn concluded that the suspect had not entered the theater, he had probably purchased the ticket to convert his gold note into less conspicuous currency.

At the police station, Miss Barr identified Berryman's portrait of John as the man who had purchased the ticket.[4]

Six weeks after Finn's investigation at the Loew's Sheridan, Schwarzkopf was having second thoughts about the polygraph. Although all of the Lindbergh-Morrow servants had been thoroughly investigated, he was still concerned about the possibility of an inside job.

In January 1934, Captain Russell A. Snook, the man in charge of the Fingerprint and Identification Bureau, wrote to Chief August Vollmer of the Berkeley, California, police department. A Berkeley police officer named John Larson, a Vollmer protégé, had invented the polygraph in 1921. Since that time Vollmer and his officers had used it in hundreds of cases.

Captain Snook and Colonel Schwarzkopf believed that the polygraph, if properly used, was a reliable and useful investigative tool. Schwarzkopf was convinced that the instrument could resolve his inside job question. Once he had put that matter to rest, he could concentrate on the investigation in New York City. So, in April, Schwarzkopf approached Colonel Lindbergh for the second time about arranging a series of polygraph tests. Lindbergh was still hesitant—he had no doubts about the domestic help. The polygraph was once again rejected.

In January, Lieutenant Finn noticed that the ransom money was turning up at the rate of forty dollars a week. Although the bill passer was spending more of it, he was still being cautious. Finn also noticed that there were no more five-dollar bills turning up. So far, four hundred of the fives had been pulled out of circulation. In all probability the kidnapper had spent them all and was now dipping into his tens. Lieutenant Finn figured that before long, the twenty-dollar bills would start surfacing. The twenties represented the largest part of the ransom package and would be the easiest to spot. Finn looked forward to the day when the kidnapper started laying a trail of these notes.

While the hunt was on for the bill passer, John Condon was still searching for John in lineups, jail cells, and mug shot albums. The FBI had been to his house over a hundred times to show him thousands of photographs.[5]

182   In March 1934, Arthur Koehler was still working on the kidnap ladder. He was back in the Bronx trying to find the origins of two of the pine ladder rungs. Koehler and Det. Lewis Bornmann were in a Bronx lumberyard looking through the company's sales records when a man entered the store and tried to buy a forty cent piece of plywood with a ten-dollar gold certificate. When the sales clerk expressed some concern over the bill, the man abruptly walked out of the store. Since none of the sales personnel were aware of Koehler and Bornmann, the man with the gold note escaped their attention.[6]

In March, the New York City police offered a five-dollar reward for every person who turned in a ransom bill. Finn had also sent a form letter to every gas station in the city requesting attendants to write down the license number of any person passing a gold note. Finn suggested that gas station employees jot down the number on the margin of the bills themselves. If the kidnapper owned a car, he'd eventually pay for his gas with Lindbergh money.

In the summer of 1934, the ransom bills suddenly stopped appearing. Several days passed without a note being reported. Finn was concerned. Did this mean the kidnapper had moved? Or had the bill passer been frightened by the publicity now surrounding each discovery of Lindbergh money? The press had been paying more and more attention to the ransom bill angle—reporting every incident involving a recovery.

Although he couldn't be certain, Finn figured that the press and radio coverage had made the kidnapper gun-shy. He was probably lying low for a while.

In an effort to get the ransom money flowing again, Finn and Agent Sisk visited and wrote to dozens of newspaper editors. The editors were asked not to print any more stories about the ransom money. All of the newspapers that were contacted agreed to withhold this information.[7] Lieutenant Finn hoped that once the dust had settled, the kidnapper would start spending his money.

In August, when the ransom bills were just trickling in and the investigation on both sides of the Hudson had slowed to a crawl, John Condon, while riding a bus in the Bronx, spotted John.

It was late in the afternoon and the bus was travelling south on Williamsbridge Road toward Pelham Parkway. Condon was gazing out the window when he saw his man. The kidnapper was wearing workman's clothes and walking north along the southbound lane of Williamsbridge Road. Condon jumped to his feet and shouted, "I am Jafsie! Stop the bus!" The driver proceeded across the Pelham Parkway then stopped at the southwest corner of the intersection. By the time Condon got off the bus, John had disappeared. Condon ran to a pay phone and reported his sighting to the New York City police and the FBI.[8] Within thirty minutes dozens of policemen and FBI agents were combing the area for Condon's John.

The next day, news of Condon's sighting was on the radio and in the press. This was the kind of thing Finn was hoping to avoid. He was afraid the notoriety would drive the kidnapper further underground—or even worse—force him to move out of town.

At this point, Schwarzkopf, Finn, and the rest of the Lindbergh investigators didn't know what to make of Condon. The old man had gone from star witness to suspect then

back again. At times he had behaved like a publicity-seeking buffoon—making it difficult to take him seriously. Here was a man who had recently sat in a Bronx store window with a disassembled replica of the kidnap ladder.[9] J. Edgar Hoover was also having
his doubts about Condon. Following the so-called bus sighting, Hoover wondered out
loud how it was that Jafsie had seen John when the kidnapper had managed to escape
the attention of thousands of police officers looking for him.

Lieutenant Finn's worries about the decreased flow of ransom bills was short-lived. In
September, three ten-dollar gold notes turned up. One of them had been passed in a
grocery store and the other two in a pair of vegetable markets. Three days later, on September 8, a twenty-dollar gold certificate was discovered at the Bronx branch of the
Chase National Bank at 301 Fordham Road. Finn, Keaten, and Sisk traced this twenty to
an East Fordham Road shoe store where the clerk recalled taking the bill the day before
from a man who had purchased a five-dollar pair of women's shoes. But none of the
salesmen remembered the man well enough to identify him.

Two days later, several more bills surfaced, and the next day, still more. The money
was being passed on the east side of Upper Manhattan, in Yorkville, and in the Bronx.
The bill passer was getting bold, using tens and twenties to make small purchases. With
the newspapers still silent, John was laundering his money at an increasing rate.

On Sunday night, September 18, Finn's worst fears were realized. While listening to
the radio, he heard Walter Winchell report that the Lindbergh money was flowing again
in the Bronx and Manhattan. Referring to the city's bank clerks, he said: "Boys, if you
weren't such a bunch of saps and yaps, you'd have already captured the Lindbergh
kidnappers."[10]

The years 1932 and 1933 had been filled with false leads and frustrations. But in 1934
the Lindbergh investigation began to focus in New York City, and this had forced Schwarzkopf, out of sheer necessity, to cooperate with the New York City police and the FBI.[11]

In September 1934 the case was two and a half years old, and after tens of thousands
of investigative man-hours, the kidnapper was still unknown and still at large. But it was
just a matter of time before the kidnapper made a mistake that would lead to his arrest.

Tell me! Tell me if you did anything wrong!
— A N N A H A U P T M A N N
to Bruno the moment she
saw him handcuffed to a policeman

19 THE ARREST

ON TUESDAY, SEPTEMBER 18, 1934, the head teller of the Corn Exchange Bank in the Bronx came across two ten-dollar gold certificates. He checked the ransom bill circular and found that one of them was listed.[1] The teller called the FBI, and Agent Sisk notified Finn and Keaten. Earlier that morning FBI agents had run down two other ransom bills that had been passed at a pair of stores in the Bronx.

At the bank, the investigators found "4U-13-14 N.Y." penciled on the margin of the bill. Although no one at the bank knew who had deposited this note, the investigators figured that a gas station attendant had written a customer's license number on the bill. One of the bank's three nearby service station accounts was the Warren-Quinlan service station on the corner of Lexington Avenue and 127th Street in upper Manhattan. The officers went to the station and spoke to the manager, Walter Lyle, and his assistant, John Lyons. Both men remembered the gold certificate, they said it came from a man driving a blue, 1930, four-door Dodge. The driver was white, of average height and weight, and spoke with a German accent.

Lyle said the man had pulled into the station the previous Saturday at ten in the morning and asked for five gallons of ethyl—ninety-eight cents' worth. He paid for the gasoline with a ten-dollar bill he took from a white envelope he had in his pocket.

"What's wrong?" the man asked when Lyle examined the note. "That's good money."

"You don't see many of these any more," Lyle said.

"No," the man replied. "I have only about one hundred left."

Lyle said that he placed the bill in the cash register, then returned with the customer's change. As the Dodge pulled away, Lyle took down its license number. He later wrote the number on the margin of the gold note. He did this, he said, because he was afraid that the bill was counterfeit.

Finn called the New York Motor Vehicle Bureau and learned that 4U-13-14 was registered to Richard Hauptmann, 1279 East 222nd Street, the Bronx. Hauptmann's automobile registration card indicated that he was almost thirty-five, German-born, and a carpenter by trade. His car was a 1930 Dodge sedan, dark blue in color.[2]

184

It was almost too good to be true. After thousands of investigative manhours, hun- **185**
dreds of wild-goose chases, and countless deadends, the case had been broken by a Manhattan pump jockey. Everything seemed to fit—a German carpenter from the Bronx
who matched the Condon-Perrone description had passed a ten-dollar ransom bill.

When Finn, Sisk, and Keaten checked the criminal files of their respective agencies,
they were disappointed because they found nothing on a Richard Hauptmann. If Hauptmann had been arrested anywhere in the United States the FBI would have had this in
their files.

Finn and his partners agreed that it would be best not to arrest Hauptmann in his
house; instead, they'd watch his home, follow him, then arrest him someplace else.
They needed time to get search warrants for his car and his house, and by arresting him
on the street, they might catch him carrying a ransom bill or two.

That evening, nine officers representing the New York City police, the FBI and the
New Jersey State Police divided evenly into three Ford sedans and discreetly took up
positions in Hauptmann's neighborhood.

The suspect lived in the Williamsbridge section of the Bronx, an area located between
Woodlawn Cemetery and Pelham Bay Park in the north-central portion of the borough.
His tan, two-story dwelling sat on a quiet, residential street just east of White Plains
Avenue, a major north-south thoroughfare; eleven blocks north was busy 233rd Street
and twelve blocks south, Gun Hill Road. The structure sat above the street on a terraced
lot that was becoming overgrown with goldenrod and mountain daisies. Along the east
side of the house was Needham Avenue, a one-block-long dirt road lined with old oak
and poplar trees. Just behind the house was a small but rather thick patch of woods
where the underbrush reached a height of four to five feet.

On Needham Avenue, about fifty feet from the house, sat Hauptmann's weather-
beaten, one-car garage, which had freshly painted double doors. The garage was secured
by a large, new-looking padlock.

Most of the ransom bills had been passed in the vicinity of the Warren-Quinlan gas
station, about ten miles from Hauptmann's house. A few of the ransom bills had been
passed in Brooklyn and some as far south as Wall Street, but the greatest number had
turned up in Upper Manhattan and the Bronx.

Hauptmann's tree-shaded home was ten blocks from the National Lumber and Millwork Company, where lumber similar to that of the kidnap ladder had been traced, and
one mile from the spot in Van Cortlandt Park where Dr. Condon and John had negotiated
their ransom business. Dr. Condon's house was a mile south of Hauptmann's, and both
men resided less than four miles from St. Raymond's Cemetery, where the ransom was
passed. According to Finn's map, the one containing the ransom pins, Hauptmann lived
in one of the areas designated as the likely location of the bill-passer's home.

The next morning, at three minutes to nine, Hauptmann came out of the house. A
half block away, Finn, Keaten, and Sisk trained their binoculars on him as he walked
along East 222nd Street, then turned the corner onto Needham Avenue. Hauptmann
strolled to the garage, unlocked the big padlock, pulled open the double doors, then
disappeared inside. A few seconds later he backed his car onto Needham Avenue.

186   Hauptmann stepped out of the car, shut and locked the garage doors, then climbed back into his car. At the corner of Needham and East 222nd he turned left in front of the three black police sedans. The four-car parade wove its way south beneath the roaring elevated trains, past the bustling sidewalks and busy shops.

The Dodge picked up speed as the traffic thinned, but as the cars approached Manhattan, heavier traffic slowed the pace. The caravan came up to Tremont Avenue, a busy east-west street. The detectives didn't want to get too close and risk detection, but if they hung back they'd lose Hauptmann in traffic.[3] When a city sprinkler truck was stopped in the southbound lane of Park Avenue, a half block north of East Tremont Avenue, Det. William Wallace pulled the lead police car alongside Hauptmann's car, which had slowed down. From the passenger's side, Trooper Dennis Duerr ordered the suspect to pull over. Before Hauptmann brought his car to a stop, Det. John Wallace jumped out of the police sedan and ran to the passenger's side of the Dodge. Wallace opened the door and slid in next to Hauptmann. The other two police cars pulled up behind, and before they came to a stop, doors flew open and five officers, with their guns drawn, scrambled to the Dodge.[4]

Hauptmann, with a gun in his ribs, was yanked out of his car, quickly frisked, then handcuffed to Detective Wallace.

Lieutenant Keaten lifted the billfold from Hauptmann's pocket. Inside, he found a five-dollar bill, four ones and a twenty-dollar gold note that had been folded into eight sections—like the one passed at the Loew's Sheridan Theater back in November of 1933.[5]

The twenty was checked against the ransom list and found to be a Lindbergh bill. The suspect's identification confirmed that he was Bruno Richard Hauptmann of 1279 East 222nd Street, the Bronx.

"What is this? What is this all about?" Hauptmann stammered in a heavy German accent. He was trembling.

"Where did you get this gold note?" Keaten asked.

"I brought it from my house," Hauptmann said.

"What do you mean?" Keaten asked.

"I have three hundred of them. I was afraid of inflation, like in Germany, so I saved them. Now I spend the money."

"Did you spend one last Saturday at the Warren-Quinlan station on Lexington?"

"Yes."

"You told the gas station man you had a hundred gold notes. How many do you have?"

"Three hundred."

"So you lied to him."

"Yes."

Hauptmann had light-brown hair, a triangular face, deep-set blue eyes, prominent cheekbones, a small mouth, and a pointed chin. The suspect's hands, large and strong-looking, were the hands of a man accustomed to physical labor. Of average height,

Hauptmann was thin but broad across the shoulders. He was well dressed in a gray double-breasted salt-and-pepper suit cut from expensive cloth. He wore a blue shirt and a matching blue tie with a design on it.

Bruno Richard Hauptmann was a dead-ringer for John Condon's man in the cemetery.

The six officers initialed the twenty-dollar gold note, then placed the suspect into a police car, where he was questioned while Lieutenant Finn telephoned his superior, Inspector John A. Lyons. Agent Sisk called J. Edgar Hoover, and Lieutenant Keaten reported the arrest to Colonel Schwarzkopf.

Inspector Lyons said he would meet the arresting party at the intersection of White Plains Avenue and Gun Hill Road. From there they would all proceed to Hauptmann's house.

While the officers waited for Inspector Lyons, they questioned Hauptmann about his background but were careful not to mention the Lindbergh case. Right away, the prisoner declared that he had come to America illegally. He told the following story:

In July of 1923, when he was twenty-three and living in Germany, Hauptmann stowed away in the hold of the North German liner *Hanover*. When the ship docked in America, he was discovered and turned over to Immigration. Under the name Karl Pellmeier, he was taken before a special tribunal and ordered back to Germany. A month later, he stowed away on the same ship but was discovered before the vessel left the pier. He escaped arrest by diving overboard. Two months later he made it to America as a stowaway on the S.S. *George Washington*. He stepped ashore on his twenty-fourth birthday with no passport and two cents in his pocket.

He was taken in by an immigrant he met on the street and within a few days he found work as a dishwasher. He later got a better job as a mechanic, then became a dyer's helper before finding work as a carpenter. On October 10, 1925, he married a German waitress named Anna Schoeffler, and eight years later a son was born. The boy's name was Mannfried, but they called him Bubi.

As Hauptmann spoke to his captors, his wife, Anna, was at home bathing Bubi. The Hauptmanns rented the second floor of the house on 222nd Street. Their five-room apartment wasn't fancy, but it was well furnished and clean as a whistle. The fifty-dollar rent went to Mrs. Pauline Rauch, a seventy-one-year-old widow who lived on the first floor with her son Mac.

Most of the Hauptmann furniture was new, and expensive. They had a walnut bedroom suite and an ivory crib for Bubi. Their prize possession was the huge floor-model radio housed in a fine wooden cabinet.

Anna was a plain, sturdy woman of medium height and weight. She had blue eyes and strawberry blond hair that was naturally curly and usually tangled. That morning she was wearing a flowered robe and was still in her bedroom slippers.

In June of 1929, when Bruno, or Richard as his wife called him, was working as a carpenter, Mrs. Hauptmann took a job as a countergirl and waitress at a combination bakery-lunchroom on Dyre Avenue. The place was owned by a Danish baker named Chistian Fredericksen. Anna worked at the store ten to thirteen hours a day. She quit

188 the thirty-three-dollar a week job in December 1932 to devote all her time to her home and family.

Earlier that morning Anna had prepared a breakfast for Richard and had seen him off to another day at his stockbroker's office. He hadn't worked as a carpenter for two and a half years. Although Richard was close-mouthed about his stock market speculations and financial dealings, Anna knew that he was doing very well. While their friends and relatives were barely surviving the Depression, the Hauptmanns had everything they needed.

Anna was quick to say that Richard wasn't a spendthrift, he had her on a very tight household budget. He gave her twenty dollars a week, and not a penny more. When Anna and Richard argued, it was usually over money. She wanted more, while he claimed she was already spending too much. But when it came to something he wanted, it was a different story. There was always plenty of money for that. Richard had recently paid $126 for a pair of German field glasses, $56 for a hunting rifle, and was spending $190 a year for a Wall Street newsletter.

By eleven o'clock, Bubi had been scrubbed and dried and was romping in the sunny backyard under his mother's watchful eye. At that time, Anna noticed a man in a suit watching her from Needham Avenue. As she kept an eye on this man, four cars pulled up and parked in front of the house.

The man on Needham Avenue walked toward Mrs. Hauptmann. As he approached, she gathered up her baby.

"What is your name?" the man asked.

"Mrs. Hauptmann."

"Where is your husband?"

"He went to work."

The man flashed a badge and said he was a detective. "Come upstairs," he said. "We want to ask you some questions."

Anna called out to her downstairs neighbor, Mrs. Louisa Schuessler, and asked her to keep Bubi. Confused, and on the verge of panic, Anna accompanied the detective to her apartment.[6]

When they got upstairs, Anna found the apartment swarming with policemen. Some were in suits and others in uniform. They were shoving furniture around, going through drawers, and rummaging through closets. Anna was taken into the master bedroom where she found Richard standing next to the bed. He was handcuffed to a policeman. Several other officers were crowded into the room.

Anna rushed to Richard and gasped, "What is this?" When he didn't answer, she put her arms around him, and in German asked, "Did you do anything wrong?"

"No, Anna," Bruno replied in German.

"Tell me! Tell me if you did anything wrong!" she cried. "What are they doing here?"

"They're here over a gambling problem I had the other night," Hauptmann said, unaware that a trooper in the room who understood German was listening.[7]

As Mrs. Hauptmann was taken from the house she passed the baby's room and was horrified to see two police officers searching Bubi's closet and pulling the bedclothes off his crib.

Meanwhile, Bruno looked on helplessly as several officers searched his bedroom. Outside, the police were questioning Anna about his background and recent activities. Anna told the police that Richard had attended eight years of public school in Germany. After that he spent two years studying at a trade school, where he learned carpentry. When he was fourteen Richard was drafted into the German army and sent to the front, where he was gassed. In 1917 he was discharged.

As the police continued their search they found twenty-six gold coins, a pair of womens' black shoes, several road maps of New Jersey, a New Jersey hunting license and the German field glasses.[8] Finn and his party were frustrated. So far they had found nothing incriminating.

Hauptmann was still standing next to the bed, and although the police were tearing apart his apartment, he maintained his composure. He insisted that when he had said that he had one hundred gold notes, he was referring to the twenty-six gold coins the police had found.

Sergeant Wallace removed Hauptmann's handcuffs and pushed him into a seated position on the bed. The questioning became heated and loud. There was no more beating about the bush—Finn wanted to know about Hauptmann's role in the kidnapping and murder. The officers wanted to know where he had hidden the ransom money.

Hauptmann shrugged his shoulders and said he didn't know anything about any ransom money. He didn't know anything about the Lindbergh case either. All he knew about the case was what he had read in the papers.

Finn ordered Hauptmann onto his feet, then stripped the sheets off the bed and ripped open the mattress. There was no sign of the ransom money.

On the first floor, the landlady gave the police two ten-dollar gold notes Bruno had given her a few days ago in partial payment of his rent. Both of them were ransom bills. Mrs. Rauch said that Richard had given her gold certificates in the past—as far back as nine months ago.[9]

The detectives questioned Mrs. Rauch's other tenants, Victor Schuessler, an unemployed upholsterer, and his wife Louisa. The Schuesslers described Bruno Hauptmann as a decent, law-abiding man.

The officers also spoke with Mrs. Laura Urant, the landlady's daughter. Mrs. Urant told the detectives about a neighborhood gas station where she claimed Hauptmann had spent at least forty-five five-dollar bills. "He would go down there," she said, "and if the men didn't have change he would leave the bill and go back for it several days later."[10]

Thomas Sisk and Corporal Horn looked for the ransom money in Hauptmann's bedroom closet. They turned out pants' pockets and ran their fingers through coat linings and trouser cuffs. Every so often Hauptmann would raise himself off the bed a little and sneak a glance out the window. Sisk asked him what he was looking at.

"Nothing," Hauptmann replied.

The FBI agent walked over to the window and looked out himself. Down below he saw the weather-beaten garage. Pointing to the structure, he asked, "Is that where you have the money?"

"No," Hauptmann answered. "I have no money."[11]

From other rooms in the apartment, the police had seized seventeen notebooks containing Hauptmann's handwriting. They had also gathered up a batch of lottery tickets, several gas station maps, including two of New Jersey, and a German-English dictionary.

After Finn, Sisk, and Keaten walked out to the garage on Needham Avenue, Finn noticed that two of the eight-inch by two-inch floorboards, located in the middle of the garage, were loose. When Finn pried up the planks with a crowbar, he uncovered some freshly disturbed soil. He took a shovel and dug down a foot, where he hit a crock. The heavy jar was empty except for some water.

Finn carried the crock to the apartment and showed it to Hauptmann, who acted as though he had never seen it before.

"What were you hiding in this jar?" Finn asked.

Hauptmann shook his head and said, "I know nothing of that."

"Sure you do. This is where you hid some of the ransom money. Isn't that right?"

"I have no ransom money. I don't know what you're talking about." Hauptmann looked at Finn with an expressionless face. "I have no ransom money. No, sir."

At a quarter past noon, when Hauptmann was taken from his house, Anna was standing in the front yard with Bubi in her arms. She turned to the policeman standing next to her. "Why are they taking him?"

"He's under arrest."

"For what? What did Richard do?" There were tears in her eyes.

The officer just walked away. As the car with Hauptmann pulled off, Anna turned and looked up at her apartment. Through the two front windows she could see the invaders ripping the place apart. Holding Bubi tightly in her arms, she began to cry.[12]

On the way to the police station, the officers stopped at the Central Savings Bank where Hauptmann kept a safe deposit box. The container was stuffed with papers—but there were no ransom bills.

> Oh, God, it's starting again.
>
> — A N N E   M O R R O W   L I N D B E R G H
> *when she learned of Hauptmann's arrest*

20 THE INTERROGATION

ON THE DAY HAUPTMANN WAS ARRESTED the Lindberghs were in Pasadena vacationing on Will Rogers' ranch. Just before noon Schwarzkopf called with the news. When he hung up Colonel Lindbergh said to his wife, "They've arrested a man from the Bronx named Hauptmann. They caught him with a ransom bill—they think he's the one. He's a German and he looks like Condon's man. I'm sorry but we'll have to go home."

The news stunned Mrs. Lindbergh who muttered, "Oh, God, it's starting again."

"Yes," Colonel Lindbergh replied, "but they got him at last."[1]

In New York City, the police took Hauptmann to the 2nd Precinct on the Lower West Side of Manhattan. The old station house on Greenwich Street was selected because it was off the beaten path and rarely frequented by reporters. Finn wanted to keep things quiet as long as possible.

Hauptmann was fingerprinted and his prints compared to the seven complete latents Dr. Hudson had taken off the kidnap ladder. None of these prints were Hauptmann's. His fingerprints were also checked against the latents the FBI had recently developed off 310 of the ransom bills and 4 of the ransom notes. There was still no match.

While Hauptmann was being booked, Finn had the 1930 Dodge towed to the station, where a team of crime scene technicians processed it for hair, blood, fibers, and other traces of the baby.[2] The car was clean.

When Finn looked over Hauptmann's automobile license applications for the past four years, he came across something very revealing. In filling out the application for 1931, Hauptmann had written the word "Bronx" the way the writer of the ransom note had written it. In both cases the x in "Bronx" looked like two e's. Finn found other similarities—Hauptmann had hyphenated New York, and in response to a question about past convictions, had written: "Passed red *lihgt* paid fine 5$." Hauptmann had transposed his *g*'s and *h*'s and had placed the dollar sign *after* the money figure—just like the ransom-note writer.

At three o'clock, Hauptmann was taken to a small interrogation room and shoved

191

onto a straight-back wooden chair. He was surrounded by a dozen officers from New Jersey, New York City, and the FBI. Schwarzkopf had come to the station and was in the room as Hauptmann's chief interrogator, Insp. John A. Lyons, began the questioning. In response to questions about his background, Hauptmann said that he was born thirty-five years ago in Kamenz, Germany. In 1923 he came to America as a stowaway. He survived the ten-day crossing on two loaves of bread and the ship's garbage. Hauptmann said that he was drafted into the German army when he was fourteen and had served twenty months with the 103rd Infantry.

Hauptmann described his early days in America and how he eventually found work as a carpenter. He was paid a dollar an hour, at that time an excellent wage. He said he had purchased some of his lumber at the National Lumber and Millwork Company on White Plains Avenue and at one time had worked there.

With the preliminaries out of the way, Inspector Lyons asked Hauptmann what he had been doing in the spring of 1932. Hauptmann said that he was working as a carpenter at the Majestic Hotel in Manhattan. "When did you leave that job?" Lyons asked.

"I guess in April."

"When did you start the job?"

"I only had it a couple of months."

"Was it January or February?"

"I guess I left the job in April or May."

"In 1932?"

"Yes."

"You are quite sure it was April or May?"

"I am not quite sure."

"But you were continuously working on that job in the Majestic Hotel over a period of two months, say from February to May?"

"Yes, maybe it was April."

"You were working every day there?"

"Yes."

"What time did you get off?"

"I guess five o'clock, or six o'clock."[3]

Hauptmann said that after quitting the Majestic he had a few jobs at the National Lumber and Millwork Company. But in the spring of 1932, he got out of the carpenter business.

"In 1932, were you working at the National Lumber and Millwork Company?"

"Very seldom, because in 1931 I went to play the stock market."

Inspector Lyons looked at Schwarzkopf to make sure he had heard Hauptman say that he had quit work the month and year the ransom was paid. Schwarzkopf nodded that he had picked that up.

"How much was the greatest amount you invested in stocks at any time?" the Inspector asked.

"Twenty thousand dollars or twenty-five thousand dollars," Hauptmann replied.
"What year was that?"
"I guess it was two years ago, or last year."
"And that was in 1932?"
"I guess it was last year."
"Where did you work in 1933?"
"I worked a little."
"For whom?"
"Mostly for myself."
"What jobs did you do, and where?"
"Doing jobs mostly for myself."
"You have not worked doing any carpentry since 1932?"
"No."

Hauptmann said he had no idea the gold note he gave the gas station man was a Lindbergh bill. He admitted using another gold note to buy his wife a pair of shoes at a store on East Fordham Road. That was a few days ago.

"How many other gold certificates have you passed?" Lyons asked.
"I had about three hundred dollars in gold certificates."
"Where did you get them?"
"When the inflation started to come up I was keeping all the certificates I could get, and even all the gold I could get. I kept it."
"Did you try to pass one at Eighty-ninth Street and Third Avenue?"
"Yes."
"You bought some vegetables?"
"Yes."
"Where did you get that bill?"
"That is from the three hundred dollars I saved in with the gold."
"Does it not strike you odd that it was a Lindbergh bill?"
"Yes, it does."
"What explanation can you make?"
"None."

Inspector Lyons showed Hauptmann several.papers and notebooks from his apartment and asked if they contained his handwriting. Hauptmann said they did. At Lyons request, Hauptmann initialed these documents.

Inspector Lyons took Hauptmann into another room and sat him at a table. "We would like you to do some writing for us. Will you do that?" Lyons asked.

"Yes, I will write," Hauptmann said.

Lyons handed Hauptmann a pen and a sheet of typing paper, then slowly recited the paragraph composed by Albert S. Osborn. Although Osborn's passage made no reference to the Lindbergh case, it contained many of the words and letter combinations found in the ransom letters.[4] Schwarzkopf and the other officers looked on as Inspector Lyons dictated to Hauptmann. When the Inspector came to the word money, he didn't spell it "mony," and he made sure he didn't pronounce any of the words as they had been misspelled by the ransom note writer.

Lyons had Hauptmann write out Osborn's paragraph twice then escorted him back into the interrogation room where the questioning continued.

Hauptmann said that he had a license to hunt in New Jersey, and in November of 1932 he and a friend had gone deer hunting in Maine. Lyons wanted to know how familiar Hauptmann was with New Jersey: "When was the last time you were in Jersey?" he asked.

"About two months ago."

"Prior to that?"

"I go pretty near every two months."

"Where do you go?"

"Into Freehold." (About fifteen miles from Hopewell.)

"Did you ever pass through Hopewell?"

"I do not remember."

"Do you remember reading about the Lindbergh case?"

"Yes."

"Did you talk to anybody about it?"

"Yes, everybody was talking about it."

"And you remember the night the baby was kidnapped? It was a very dismal night?"

"I do not remember."

Lyons asked Hauptmann if he knew anyone who worked at St. Raymond's or the Woodlawn Cemetery. Hauptmann said he didn't. Did he know John Condon or Condon's friend Al Reich? No, he did not.

The interrogation was in its fourth hour and Hauptmann still looked fresh. In his slightly high-pitched voice he answered Inspector Lyons' questions calmly and matter-of-factly. Being in a room full of detectives and high-ranking police officials accusing him of the Lindbergh kidnapping apparently didn't unnerve him. Hauptmann hadn't asked to see a lawyer or his wife—he hadn't even asked for a glass of water. There were no hysterical protests of innocence. Hauptmann just sat in the wooden chair and in a casual, conversational tone answered the questions. Inspector Lyons and his observers were getting the feeling they were dealing with an extraordinary man.

Hauptmann said he had purchased his Dodge for $725 in 1931. He had three active bank accounts, and the previous year he sent his mother fifty dollars. She was living alone in Germany, so he sent her a few dollars every Christmas and Easter.

In their spare time, Hauptmann and his wife went to the movies, walked in the park, and swam in the Atlantic Ocean. Occasionally they would go to Coney Island. Hauptmann said he liked to play cards, hunt, go boating, and play the mandolin. He and his family had been living on East 222nd Street for four years. He said he had only one relative living in America and that was his sister in California.

Inspector Lyons asked Hauptmann about Bubi, "How old is your little boy?"

"Ten and one-half months."

"You would not like anybody to kill your child would you?"

Hauptmann didn't answer.

"You would not want to see anybody kidnap your child?"

"No, sir."

Lyons got back to Hauptmann's gold notes and where he had spent them, then asked Hauptmann if he had ever been to the Loew's Sheridan in Greenwich Village. Hauptmann said he had never been to that theater.

At 2:30, Hauptman's wife was brought to the station and questioned by a second set of interrogators. The frightened and bewildered woman said that on the night of the kidnapping she was working at the bakery in the Bronx. She learned of the crime through a customer. "It made me sick," Anna said. "I have a baby of my own. I prayed it would be brought back to them."

Anna said that Richard was a loving husband and a devoted family man. He had worked hard and had invested his savings wisely in the stock market. They attended St. Paul's Lutheran Church on 156th Street. They didn't go every Sunday, but almost. Her husband could not have been mixed up in the Lindbergh crime, that was impossible. Not Richard—they had arrested the wrong man.

Mrs. Hauptmann was driven back to her apartment at five o'clock. Her interrogators couldn't decide if she was playing dumb or was as innocent as she seemed. When Anna got home she found that her apartment was still full of policemen.

One of the apartment searchers had come across an interesting item. In one of Hauptmann's small notebooks they found pencil sketches of a homemade ladder and two windows. The ladder in the drawing was made just like the one used in the kidnapping.

From Hauptmann's garage, the searchers seized Bruno's tool chest, assorted carpenter tools, a keg of nails, and a handful of loose nails found in a carpenter's apron. The officers noticed that Hauptmann's tool chest was missing a three-quarter-inch chisel.[5]

At 7:30, Joseph Perrone, the cab driver who had delivered one of the ransom letters, was brought to the police station to identify Hauptmann as the man who had given him the note. Before taking Perrone into the interrogation room, Inspector Lyons gave him a little pep talk: "Now, Joe, we've got the right man at last. There isn't a man in that room who isn't convinced he is the man who kidnapped the Lindbergh baby. He answers the description of the man that gave you the note perfectly and there is no doubt about him being the man. Now we're depending on you, Joe. Take a look at him, but don't say anything until I ask you if he is the man."[6]

When Perrone entered the interrogation room he saw three men standing before him. Lyons then asked him to point out the man who had handed him the note on March 12, 1932. The two men flanking Hauptmann were a pair of New York City cops in civilian clothes.

Perrone walked over to Hauptmann and placed his hand on the prisoner's shoulder. "This is the man," he said. "He asked me to bring a note to Dr. Condon—2974 Decatur Avenue, Bronx."[7]

196   At 9:15, Inspector Lyons resumed the interrogation. Hauptmann had been in custody twelve hours and he was starting to show signs of exhaustion. He had been seated in the wooden chair almost seven hours.

Inspector Lyons asked Hauptmann to name everyone he knew in New Jersey as well as all of his former business associates. Hauptmann said that the only person he knew in New Jersey was a man who owned a chicken farm near Freehold. Hauptmann and a friend had hunted on this man's property. One of his former business associates was a German fur trader named Isidor Fisch. He and Fisch had been speculating in furs and pelts since 1930.

Lyons wanted to know more about Hauptmann's business with Fisch, "How long were these transactions going on?"

"A year and a half."

"And you have some furs in your house now?"

"Yes."

"Was he married?"

"No."

"Did he visit your home frequently?"

"Yes."

Hauptmann said that Fisch had lived on 127th Street and had returned to Germany three weeks before last Christmas. Four months later he died of tuberculosis.

"You were speculating on furs with Fisch at that time before Christmas?" Lyons asked.

"Yes."

"What's the value of the furs you have in your possession now?"

"About five hundred dollars."

"How old was Fisch?"

"I guess twenty-six or twenty-nine."

"Describe him, was he Jewish?"

"Yes, Jewish, skinny, about five foot four inches."

"How much money did you put up?"

"It was quite a lot."

"What do you call a lot?"

"It was about five thousand dollars. We made this money in buying and selling furs. It was extra money we made in the fur business."

"Where did you buy the furs?"

"I don't know. He kept the account of the fur business and I kept track of the stock account. We split the profits and go half and half."

Inspector Lyons dropped the subject of Isidor Fisch and turned to something else: "Did you ever make any ladders?"

"No."

"Never made a ladder?"

"No."

"You can make a ladder?"

"Oh, I can make one."

"On some of your repair jobs you used a ladder didn't you?"

'Never did."

"You never used a ladder at all?"

"No, when I hook on storm windows on the second floor I always hang them from the inside."

"What papers do you read?"

"*The Times, The News,* and sometimes a German paper."

"Don't you ever read *The Bronx Home News?*"

"Never read it."

"Why don't you read it?"

"I don't like it."

"Anybody in the house get it?"

"Sometimes the paper lays on the steps of the house there. Sometimes I take it up but I never read it."

"Did you ever know anybody by the name of Violet Sharpe?"

"No."

"Betty Gow?"

"No."

"Does your wife know them?"

"No."

"Did you ever work with anybody who worked on the Lindbergh house in Hopewell?"

"No."

"Did you ever hear any carpenters talking about the job over there on the Lindbergh house in Hopewell?"

"No."

"Did you ever work in Englewood?"

"No."

"Did you ever see Colonel Lindbergh?"

"No, only in pictures."

Inspector Lyons turned to the field glasses found in Hauptmann's apartment: "What did you use those night glasses for?"

"I'm a friend of nature."

"And do you need night glasses to be a friend of nature?"

"They are not night glasses they are regular field glasses."

Lieutenant Finn had cabled Germany to see if Hauptmann had a criminal record and was waiting for the reply. Inspector Lyons decided to ask Hauptmann himself about this. "Have you ever been arrested?"

"No."

"Were you ever arrested in Germany?"

"No."

198   Lyons came back to the gold certificates. "Now, Hauptmann, what explanation do you make for having these Lindbergh gold certificates in your possession?"

"I don't know I have any Lindbergh money in my possession until just now. As soon as inflation come up I started to accumulate gold coins and gold certificates."

"Doesn't it impress you as a strange coincidence that four of these bills you had should be Lindbergh ransom money?'

"Yes, it does."

"And you can't explain where you got it?"

"No."

"Why did you leave Germany?"

"Well, you couldn't make any future over there."

At ten o'clock, Deputy Chief Inspector Vincent J. Sweeney took over the questioning. After going over Hauptmann's stock market dealings, Sweeney asked, "How much would you say you made in 1933?"

"I didn't make anything."

"How much this year?"

"Nothing."

"So that you lost every year except 1932?"

"Yes."

"And you haven't worked in two years and you still have a balance of four thousand dollars with the broker. How do you account for that?"

"I made money in the fur account. I lose some. Isidor Fisch took half of the loss, when I make good he got half of what I made."

"You've been living good, maintaining a car?"

"The car is cheap like a Ford car."

"You sent your wife to Europe?"

"Yes."

"How much did she take abroad with her?"

"I don't know."

"When she went to Europe you had already accumulated your gold didn't you?"

"Yes."

"When did she go to Europe?"

"1932."

"Have you ever been arrested abroad?"

"No."

At eleven o'clock Inspector Lyons took over, "What have you got to say regarding this identification by Perrone?"

"I can't say anything. I never saw this fellow in my life."

"The identification was positive, he said: 'I am positive this is the man,' you heard him say that didn't you?"

"I did hear that."

"Do you know of any reason why he should say that?"

"I never saw this fellow before. I never was riding in a taxicab since owning a car."

At midnight, Lyons asked Bruno what he was doing on the night of the kidnapping. Hauptmann replied that he had worked that day at the Majestic Hotel on Central Park West and Seventy-second Street. He finished up at five. Later that night he drove to Fredericksen's Bakery to pick up his wife who worked until nine o'clock on Tuesdays.

Hauptmann couldn't say what he was doing on the evening of March 12, 1932, the night John Condon talked with the man in Van Cortland Park. On April 2, the day Colonel Lindbergh and John Condon drove to St. Raymond's with the ransom money, Hauptmann said he was working at the Majestic Hotel. It was his last day on the job. He got home at six o'clock, and that night his friend, Hans Kloppenburg, came to the apartment to sing and play his guitar. The two men got together on the first Saturday of every month to sing. Kloppenburg played his guitar and Hauptmann the mandolin. (Hans Kloppenburg, a thirty-five-year-old German-American carpenter, was also being questioned at the Greenwich Station.) Hans didn't leave the apartment until after midnight.

Inspector Lyons asked Hauptmann what he was doing on the evening of November 26, 1933, the night the five-dollar ransom bill was passed at the Loew's Sheridan. That was easy, Hauptmann said, November 26 was his birthday and the previous year on that night he and his friends celebrated at his apartment.

It was past midnight and Hauptmann had been seated on the hard, wooden chair ten hours. He hadn't eaten since breakfast and he was tired. Inspector Lyons said that the questioning was over for now. He asked Hauptmann if he was willing to do some more writing—like before. These handwriting samples would be compared to the ransom notes, Lyon said. Hauptmann would be writing the same paragraph Lyons had read to him before.

"I would be glad to write because it would get me out of this thing," Hauptmann replied.

At one in the morning, Sgt. Thomas Ritchie of the New Jersey State Police handed Hauptmann a pen and a sheet of paper and instructed him to write down the words just as they were read to him.[8] When Hauptmann finished, he was given a clean sheet of paper. Sergeant Ritchie told Hauptmann that they would be doing this again—and again.

As Hauptmann produced page after page of handwriting, Schwarzkopf, Finn, and Keaten studied his writing closely. The officers noticed two things—at first Hauptmann's writing was stiff and unnatural—as though he were attempting to disguise his hand. But the similarities between his writing and that in the ransom notes were gradually surfacing—even to an untrained eye. Hauptmann had hyphenated New York, and had transposed his g's and h's, and was spelling the same words in the same way as the ransom note writer.

When the officers compared Hauptmann's samples with each other, it became obvious that he was trying to alter his writing style. He was changing the slant of his lines, the size of his writing, and even the way he formed his letters. He was making these changes in the same paragraph.

The officers asked themselves why an innocent man would try to disguise his handwriting.

Hauptmann wrote nonstop for four hours, then declared that he couldn't do it any more. He put his head on the table and fell asleep. Thirty minutes later he was awakened by a poke and told to keep writing.

Lieutenant Finn was now dictating parts of the various ransom notes and asking Hauptmann to hand print Dr. Condon's address. FBI Agent Leon Turrou was in the room, and he had Hauptmann copy passages from a newspaper.[9] Turrou's samples were taken to Charles Appel, Jr., at the FBI Crime Laboratory, while copies of the other samples were delivered to Albert S. Osborn and to Bert C. Farrar, a documents examiner for the Treasury Department.[10]

Hauptmann's handwriting ordeal lasted until eight o'clock that morning. Exhausted and virtually incoherent, Hauptmann collapsed over the writing table.

It had been a frantic twenty-four-hour period for Hauptmann and his captors. Although the prisoner hadn't confessed, the police were fairly confident they had at least one of the kidnappers. Hauptmann looked and sounded like Condon's John, and the cab driver had identified him. Hauptmann had been too quick with an alibi, had tried but failed to disguise his handwriting, had gone from a carpenter before the ransom payoff to a Wall Street financier after it, and had admitted possessing several of the Lindbergh bills.

For the Lindbergh investigators, things were looking up. But they needed a confession, and Hauptmann looked like a tough nut to crack.[11]

As I sat in the Greenwich Street Police Station, while they
questioned my husband in a separate room, I was utterly numb.

— A N N A   H A U P T M A N N

21 THE FISCH STORY

ANNA AND THE BABY spent Wednesday night with Mrs. Hauptmann's niece, Maria
Mueller. That night two New York City police officers stood guard at her apartment. At
nine the next morning, while Bruno slept at the writing table, Anna surveyed her ransacked home.

A few minutes after Anna had arrived at the apartment, she was joined by New York
City detectives Edward Murphy, Frank Dunn, and James Petrosino. They were followed a
little later by Sgt. John Wallace of the New Jersey State Police and Special Agent Leon
Turrou of the FBI.

Although a thorough search of the apartment had failed to uncover a cache of ransom money, the police had found other, less obvious evidence. In Hauptmann's desk they
came across several sheets of white, watermarked paper that looked very similar to the
paper used by the ransom note writer.

Today, the officers were going to focus on Hauptmann's fifteen-by-eleven-foot garage.
He had built it with lumber purchased by the landlady and had put it up about the time
he bought his car. Sometime in the spring of 1932, Hauptmann ran a wire from his
bedroom window across Needham Avenue to the garage. By flicking a switch near his
bed Bruno could light up the little building.[1] After rigging the light alarm, Hauptmann
bought a hefty padlock to secure the doors.

The police had never seen so much security afforded a garage containing what
Hauptmann himself referred to as a cheap car.

At 10:30, the five officers and Mrs. Hauptmann walked to the garage. Anna watched
as the men began to search in earnest for the ransom money. An hour later, New York
City detectives Maurice Tobin and James Cushman joined in the hunt. Mrs. Hauptmann
went back into the apartment to gather things she and the baby would need.

At 11:00, an officer shook Hauptmann awake at the writing table and escorted the
groggy prisoner back to his chair in the interrogation room. Inspector Lyons, in the
presence of Schwarzkopf, Lamb, Keaten, and Sisk, placed his hand on Hauptmann's
shoulder and said, "Now, Richard, I understand you want to help us in this case."[2]

"I will do everything you want."

"You are willing to go further aren't you and answer any questions willingly for the purpose of cleaning up this case?"

"Yes."

"And you are perfectly willing to volunteer any information you can give us for that purpose?"

"Yes, sir."

"You understand you are not under arrest, we are just holding you for investigation until this matter is cleared up?"

"I don't know, I was never in a position like this."

"You are not under arrest, you are just assisting us in this investigation. I am going to ask you some names, see if you know them."

Inspector Lyons named twenty construction people, all of whom had worked on the Lindbergh house. Hauptmann said he didn't know any of these people.

Lyons asked Hauptmann if he had been to a number of places where the gold notes had been passed—clothing stores, a cafeteria, a sports shop, a burlesque theater, restaurants, butcher, pastry and poultry shops, grocery stores and so forth. Hauptmann, in his flat, matter-of-fact tone, said he had never been to any of these places.

Back in the Bronx, the police were still searching the garage. It was 11:30, and the officers were getting discouraged. Detective Petrosino was checking the area around Hauptmann's workbench. He noticed that a board had been nailed across two wall joists above the bench. He pried the board off and uncovered a shelf that held two packages wrapped in newspaper.

Detective Petrosino took one of the bundles off the shelf and unwrapped it. What he found caused him to yelp in glee. He had just uncovered a stack of ten-dollar gold notes—one hundred of them! The officers in the garage gathered around as Petrosino unwrapped the other package. It contained more ten-dollar gold certificates, eighty-three in all. The serial numbers were checked, and yes, they were Lindbergh bills—every one. Petrosino had just found $1,830 of the ransom money in Hauptmann's garage!

Sergeant Wallace drove to the nearest pay phone and called Schwarzkopf. Schwarzkopf was elated. "Go back to the garage," he said, "and find the rest of it."

"Yes, sir," Wallace replied.

"And when you find it, put it back like it was and bring the wife to the garage."

"I don't understand," Wallace said.

"I want the money found in the wife's presence—to get her reaction," Schwarzkopf said.

"I get it," the Sergeant replied.

The stacks of ransom bills were rewrapped and returned to the shelf. The search continued. At 12:40 Detective Murphy came across another board between two joists. When the plank was removed the officer found a one-gallon shellac can sitting in the recess of the garage window. In the can, beneath a couple of rags, were twelve packages of gold notes. The bills had been wrapped in newspapers—the June 25 and September 6, 1934 editions of the *New York Daily News*. The shellac can contained, in ten- and twenty-dollar denominations, $11,930 of Colonel Lindbergh's money! There were 390 tens and 493 twenties. The officers were so excited they could barely keep from jumping up and down. After a round of handshakes and pats on the back, the men carefully replaced the loot.

Sergeant Wallace, Detective Petrosino, and Agent Turrou went to the apartment and asked Mrs. Hauptmann to put on her hat and coat and to come with them to the garage.

With Anna Hauptmann looking on, the officers went through the motions of searching the garage. Then suddenly, they made their discoveries. First the two bundles of tens, then the shellac can and the twelve bundles of tens and twenties. Anna Hauptmann stood in the center of the garage with her hand to her mouth. She was dumbstruck. One of the detectives sat her on the workbench stool.[3]

"Where did this money come from?" she gasped.

"It's Lindbergh money. Where do you think it came from?" Sergeant Wallace asked.

"I know nothing of this," Mrs. Hauptmann replied.

"Are you sure of that?" Wallace asked.

"I am certain. I know nothing."

"Well, your husband knows about it, that's for sure," Wallace replied.

"I'm sure Richard will be able to explain," Mrs. Hauptmann said. "Maybe he doesn't know about it either."

"Sure, sure," Wallace said sarcastically. "Richard won't know a thing—not our Richard!"

By four in the afternoon, the only policemen around Hauptmann's garage were a couple of uniformed officers guarding the place. News of Hauptmann's arrest and the ransom find was already on the radio. Schoolchildren and local housewives were gathering on Needham Avenue. By dinner time, the crowd had swollen and people were tramping about Hauptmann's backyard. Others were rummaging through the lumber the searchers had tossed aside.

The women stood in little groups on Needham Avenue and along East 222nd Street pointing up at the apartment and at Mrs. Hauptmann's wash still flapping on the line.

Reporters and photographers were at the scene, and overhead two newsreel planes were circling. By six o'clock a hot dog vender was doing a brisk business in front of the house.

Newsmen were interviewing Hauptmann's neighbors. An old man who lived down the street said that Hauptmann wasn't much of a talker. None of the neighbors knew the Hauptmanns, since they kept to themselves. Bruno was occasionally seen puttering in the yard wearing a lumber jacket.

The crowd had gotten large and difficult to contain, so additional police officers were dispatched to the scene to protect the apartment and the garage.

When Inspector Lyon and the other interrogators learned that Hauptmann had over 25 percent of Colonel Lindbergh's ransom money stashed in his garage, they figured the game was over. Hauptmann would surely confess.

If there had been any doubts in anyone's mind that Hauptmann was deeply involved in this crime, they had vanished. The fact that Hauptmann had spent twenty-five thousand dollars on the stock market, and had fourteen thousand dollars hidden in his garage, meant that since the kidnapping he had come into possession of at least forty thousand dollars—80 percent of the ransom payoff. This was certainly a lot of money for a mere accomplice. It seemed to the police that they had captured the big guy—or maybe the lone kidnapper.

Around noon, Lyons, Schwarzkopf, Keaten, and Sisk left Hauptmann to confer about the ransom money. An hour later, after the second cache had been found, the officers returned to the interrogation room. Hauptmann, red-eyed and disheveled, was still in the chair. He had not been told of the discovery.

"Richard," Lyons said, "I want you to think before you answer—have you told us everything?"

"Yes, I have told all I know."

"You don't have any gold notes hidden away, do you?"

"No, sir."

"Are you sure?"

"Yes."

"Well, you're a liar!" Lyons screamed. "You're a goddamned lying son-of-a-bitch— aren't you?"

"I am not," Hauptmann said.

"You are—you are—you're a lying son-of-a-bitch because we found the money—the Lindbergh money—in your garage! What do you say to that? And goddamn it—no more lies. We're not going to listen to any more of your lies—we want to know everything— and now! Do you hear me?" Lyons shouted.

"Yes, I hear you."

"Well, are you going to lie to us?"

"I am not going to lie. No."

"Okay," Lyons said, "Good. No more lies then. So let's have it, Bruno—tell us the truth."

"I can explain the money."

"You can explain the money?"

"Yes," Hauptmann said. "I can explain."

"Well, let's hear it then."

Hauptmann crossed his legs. His suit was rumpled and his tie loose around his neck. He had a day's beard, and his face was drawn. He cleared his throat and proceeded to tell how he happened to have almost fourteen thousand dollars worth of the ransom money in his garage.

In December 1933, Hauptmann's friend and partner in the fur trading business, Isidor Fisch, sailed to his parents' home in Leipzig, Germany. Isidor was in poor health and was returning home to stay with his family. On March 29, 1934, Isidor Fisch died of tuberculosis in a Leipzig hospital.

Before sailing for Germany, Fisch had left some of his belongings with Hauptmann for safekeeping. There was a trunk, some suitcases, and a shoebox tied up with a string. Hauptmann placed the shoebox on the top shelf of the broom closet in his kitchen. About a month earlier, water from a heavy rain had leaked through the kitchen ceiling and into the closet. When Hauptmann removed the wet items he came upon Fisch's forgotten shoebox. When he opened it, Hauptmann had the shock of his life—Isidor Fisch had left him forty thousand dollars in gold certificates!

The money was damp, so Bruno took it to his garage, where he divided the cache into several piles, then wrapped each stack in newspaper. Without telling Anna about his find, he stashed the bundles about the garage where nobody could find them. A few days later, sometime in August, Bruno started spending Fisch's money. He felt privileged to do this because Isidor Fisch owed him $7,000. He was only going to spend that amount. He had no idea the gold notes were Lindbergh ransom bills.

Hauptmann looked at Inspector Lyons and said, "I have told the truth now, I said nothing before because I was afraid no one would believe me."

Lyons was grim-faced. He didn't respond. In all his years as an investigator and police administrator he had never come across a man like Hauptmann. After a twenty-four hour grilling in which the prisoner was denied food, sleep, and the consolation of family and friends, Hauptmann had the presence of mind to unravel this story of how Colonel Lindbergh's money had ended up in his garage.

Earlier in the day, J. Edgar Hoover had arrived from Washington.[4] He had been listening to Hauptmann, and now, with Inspector Lyons' permission, he began questioning the suspect: "How often did you count the money?"

"Only one time."

"When did you first learn money was in that box?"

"About three weeks ago when the rain came in."

"Did you ever open it before then?"

"No."

"You didn't know what was in the box?"

"I didn't open it yet; if the rain didn't come through—"

"How much money did you take out of there?"

"About eight or nine bills, about fifty dollars."

"You know the money didn't belong to you, didn't you?"

"Yes."

"You were stealing it?"

"Not exactly stealing it."

"You knew this money didn't belong to you?"

"This man owed me money."

Deputy Inspector Sweeney, the most emotional interrogator and the one who rattled Hauptmann the most, took over: "Listen, you heard yesterday that was Lindbergh money, didn't you?"

"Yes."

"If you were an innocent man or an honest man, as soon as you heard it's Lindbergh money you would come out and tell the truth. Instead of that for twenty-four hours you have sat there and lied."

Hauptmann had no answer.

Inspector Lyons had stepped out of the room and now he was back. He took Sweeney aside and said something to him privately. Sweeney nodded his head and informed Hauptmann that Inspector Lyons wanted to ask him some very important questions. The inspector began:

"Richard, do you remember telling me last night that on March first you were working at the Majestic Hotel?"

"Yes, I was."

"You were lying when you told me that."

"I was telling the truth."

"We just sent a man to check that story and he tells my investigator that you didn't come to work until the twenty-first of March and you quit on April second, the night the ransom was passed, is that true?"

"I said I was working in March."

"You said you were working the first of March, the day of the Lindbergh kidnapping."

"Yes, if it wasn't a Sunday. I was working."

"You said you were working in the Majestic Hotel on March first?"

"Yes."

"You will stick to that?"

"Yes."

"You said you worked there two or three months?"

"Yes, two or three months."

"We sent a man up to verify that and he said that you only worked ten days. You went there on the twenty-first of March and quit the second of April and the night of the second of April was the night the money was passed."

"I can remember, I was going to White Plains Avenue because that's where I bought the *News*. There was big headlines about the kidnap story. This morning, like every morning, I go to work to White Plains Avenue, over there I take the subway and that's where I bought the *News* and that's where I heard from the kidnapping."

"What hours did you work there?"

"Before seven o'clock in the morning."

"What time did you quit at night?"

"I guess five or six o'clock."

Referring to Isidor Fisch, Sweeney asked, "Where do you suppose he got this money?"

"He said to me one time, 'Bruno, do you like to come into business with me?'"

"When was that?"

"Around 1932, but he was in business long before. I asked him how much money you have, Fisch? I said I have only one thousand dollars. He said, 'Listen, I have twenty-seven thousand.' I didn't ask him where he got it."

"How much did he take abroad with him?"

"When he left he said, 'Dick, how is it, you want me to sell some of them furs we bought?' I said, 'No, you only bought it a couple weeks ago, what use to sell it again, leave it until you come back.' He said, 'I need the money to go to Germany.' I said: 'All right, take it from my account.' I thought he was playing fair with me. I took two thousand dollars from my stock account."

"Although at that time he owed you five thousand dollars?"

"Yes, but extra money he made in furs."

"But you gave him two thousand dollars to go abroad? Did you take a note for that?

"No."

"And although he owed you five thousand dollars you gave him two thousand more to go abroad?"

"Yes."

"And he was sickly at that time and likely to die?"

"Yes."

"You were a real friend?"

"Yes."

"Now you are talking him up out of the grave and stealing his money?"

"No."

"Don't you think it is kind of funny that on his deathbed when he was dying he told his brother about the trunk but said nothing about the shoebox?"

"He was saying to his brother that he got so-and-so many furs laying over here. That's what he told his brother a short time before he died, that's what his brother told me."

"As a matter of fact he did leave furs here and the furs are up in your house?"

"There is only four hundred dollars in furs."

"That's all he told his brother he had, furs in your custody."

There was a break in the interrogation. Several of the officers, many of them shaking their heads, walked out of the room.

At three o'clock, Albert S. Osborn called the Greenwich Station to report that his preliminary findings indicated that Hauptmann had written all of the ransom notes, including the one that had been left in the baby's nursery. Osborn said that his son, Albert D., was also studying the evidence and would report his findings shortly. The senior Osborn said that in a couple of days he would submit his final report.

Thirty minutes later, the younger Osborn called and said that his findings tallied with his father's.

By now, the news of the discovery in Hauptmann's garage was on every radio station in America.

Twelve hours earlier, at four in the morning, just a few hours after copies of Hauptmann's writings had been taken to the Osborns, young Osborn had called Schwarzkopf and expressed some doubt that all of the ransom writings had been made by Hauptmann.[5] Some of the Lindbergh investigators were wondering if Albert D.'s change of mind had anything to do with the news of the ransom cache in Hauptmann's garage. Others believed that the older Osborn had straightened his son out.

Anna Hauptmann was back at the police station being questioned about her knowledge of Isidor Fisch and the shoebox her husband said the dead man had left behind. At 6:30, after the police had finished with her, she walked out of the stationhouse into a group of frenzied newsmen.

At the other end of Manhattan, the president of the Warren-Quinlan Oil Company was telling reporters that the company had given Walter Lyle a hundred-dollar reward for his role in the capture of Bruno Hauptmann. Both Lyle and John Lyons had been given the day off. The president said there were so many sightseers at the station he had to close the place anyway.

Although Hauptmann had been in the hands of the police for thirty-two hours, he hadn't seen a lawyer or a judge. He still hadn't eaten, and it didn't look as if he'd get to bed for quite a while. The investigation was white-hot—and the police were determined to get a confession.

Hauptmann looks like a midget who has wandered through a
Turkish bath for two sleepless days and nights.

— F B I   A G E N T   L E O N   T U R R O U

22   THE LINEUP

AT 4:30 IN THE AFTERNOON, thirteen New York City policemen in civilian clothes were assembled in the deputy commissioner's office on the fourth floor of the Greenwich Station. The police were arranging a lineup. John Condon and the six other witnesses were on their way to the station.

While the witnesses were being rounded up, Hauptmann, his hands handcuffed in front of him, was led into a room full of reporters. He was seated in a chair on a raised platform. Wearing his hat, he sat with his hands resting on his lap. He kept his eyes lowered and every once in a while a reporter would ask him to look up. Hauptmann would lift his head for a second and blink as the flashbulbs popped in his face. At the request of a reporter, Hauptmann raised his handcuffed hands to take off his hat.

At five o'clock, John Condon arrived at the police station. Trying to walk erect and dignified, he entered the building behind three policemen who had to plow a path through the huge crowd of sightseers and reporters on the steps and in the lobby of the stationhouse. Condon was taken to a small room next to the office where the lineup was to be held.

At 5:15, Hauptmann was brought into the lineup room, where Inspector Lyons was seated behind a desk. Pointing to the thirteen men standing against the wall at the other end of the room, he said, "Richard, take a position in that line, any position you care to. We are going to bring a man in here to see if he can identify you. You choose your position."[1]

Leon Turrou, one of the FBI agents in the room, noted that Hauptmann stood out like a sore thumb. The police officers were all over six feet tall, neatly pressed and freshly shaved. "Hauptmann looks like a midget who has wandered through a Turkish bath for two sleepless days and nights," he whispered to the man next to him.[2]

A few minutes later, Dr. Condon, wearing an unpressed blue suit, strode into the room. If Condon had any doubts regarding the importance of this moment, they were erased when he saw New York City Police Commissioner John F. O'Ryan, J. Edgar Hoover, and Colonel Schwarzkopf. Also present to witness the identification were the top twenty Lindbergh case investigators from the three agencies.

From his desk, Inspector Lyons addressed the famous Jafsie: "Dr. Condon, start at the head of the line, look at all those men, and if you can identify the man whom you passed the money on the night of April 2, 1932, you just go over and put your hand on his shoulder."

Condon nodded and asked, "May I ask a favor?"

"Yes," the Inspector replied.

"Could I speak to each man one minute on something nobody else has heard but me?"

"Yes, go ahead," Lyons answered.

Condon walked up and down the line of men three times, eying each one carefully. *Twelve or more men,* he thought, *and perhaps eleven of them are broad-shouldered, florid-faced, bull-necked cops who could not by any stretch of the imagination be confused with the man I have described, over and over, as John.*[3]

Condon stopped in front of Hauptmann, scrutinizing him closely. He then walked down the line to the thirteenth man. "May I eliminate several men from the line now and have them come forward?"

"You want to eliminate some men?" Lyons asked.

"Yes."

"Who do you want to eliminate?"

Condon stopped in front of four men, including Hauptmann, and asked them to step forward. "Can I speak to them? You don't mind, do you?" he asked.

"Surely," Inspector Lyons replied.

As he stood in front of Hauptmann, Condon addressed the four men: "When I saw you I gave you my promise that I would do all I possibly could for you if you gave me the baby. The only way in the world I think you can save yourself at all is to tell the truth. I gave you a promise heard that day. Follow that promise." Condon looked over at Inspector Lyons and asked, "Would you mind if they showed me their hands?"

The Inspector nodded and said, "Hold your palms up, hands up."

Condon stepped in front of the first man (Officer James Kissane) and looked at his hands, "Did you ever see me before?" Condon asked.

"No, sir," the man responded.

Condon repeated this procedure with Hauptmann and the other two police officers. They all responded with a "No, sir." He then walked back to Hauptmann. "What is your name?" he asked.

"Richard Hauptmann."

This looks like the man, Condon thought. *He has the voice, military bearing, inverted triangle face, slightly stooped shoulders and straight nose. In every detail this is John.*[4] Condon turned to Inspector Lyons, "Could I have a pencil and paper, sir?"

"I guess so," Lyons replied. A police officer came forward with the supplies. Using the inspector's desk, Condon jotted something down on a slip of paper. Lyons was getting a little annoyed—he hadn't expected such a Cecil B. de Mille production. Why didn't Condon just make his identification? Inspector Lyons and Lieutenant Finn exchanged glances. The unspoken message was this: Knowing Condon, they should have expected this.

Condon walked back to Hauptmann and handed him the slip of paper, "Read it out loud," he ordered.

Hauptmann complied: "I stayed already too long. The leader would smack me out. Your work is perfect."

"I could not quite hear those last two lines," Condon said.

Hauptmann repeated the last two lines.

"Did you see me before?" Condon asked.

"Never."

Condon handed Hauptmann another slip of paper. "Say that," he instructed.

"John."

"And you've never seen me before?"

"No."

Condon walked down the line and spoke to each of the three men. When he finished, he ordered them to return to their original places in the line. That left Hauptmann standing alone in the forward position. Condon said, "I gave the money and you promised to restore the baby. Do you remember that?"

"No."

"And I said I would help out?"

"No, I never talked to you."

"I never broke my word in my life. What is your name?"

"Richard Hauptmann."

"Where were you born?"

"Germany."[5]

Condon then spoke to Hauptmann in German. When the prisoner didn't respond, Condon recited a poem in German. The officers in the room were getting impatient. There were a few throat clearings and some shuffling feet. Schwarzkopf was disgusted. The old guy was such a goddamn ham. He couldn't do anything straight.

Inspector Lyons had taken about all he could of this.[6] Trying not to sound frustrated and angry, he asked, "Would you say he was the man?"

Condon's reply stunned everybody: "I would not say that he is the man."

There was silence followed by pandemonium. The reporters in the room were firing questions, and the detectives were talking excitedly to each other. Schwarzkopf looked at Lieutenant Keaten and grimly shook his head as if to say—"I knew it."

Inspector Lyons restored order then asked, in a voice reflecting his amazement and disbelief, "You're not positive?"

"I am not positive."

"Do you recognize the voice?" Lyons asked.

"The voice [in the cemetery] was husky," Condon replied. "I'd like to say this quick—when it is a man's life, gentlemen, I want to be careful."

Condon asked Hauptmann several more questions then turned to Inspector Lyons: "He is the one who would come nearer to answering the description than anybody I saw. You gave me no hint and I picked him out. He is a little heavier. I couldn't say he is not the man."

"So it looks like him?" Inspector Lyons asked.

"Yes."

"But you cannot identify him?"

"No, I have to be very careful. This man's life is in jeopardy."

"Is that it then?" Inspector Lyons asked, making no effort to disguise his disgust.

"I guess so," Condon replied.

"Then get him out of here," Lyons said, referring to Condon.[7]

The room was buzzing as Agent Turrou walked over to Condon, "Come with me," he snapped. Someone in the room yelled, "The old bastard is in with them!"

"Wait a minute!" Condon shouted. Raising his arms to quiet the crowd, he said, "I am holding my identification in abeyance for the present!"

"Either you can pick the man or you can't," someone yelled back. "Which one is John?" someone else hollered.

"I shall not declare an identification at this time," Condon said as he was escorted out of the room by Agent Turrou.[8]

The other witnesses had arrived. One by one they were taken into the room and asked to pick Hauptmann out of the lineup. The gas station attendants, Walter Lyle and John Lyons, were the first two witnesses. They both selected Hauptmann as the man who had passed the ten-dollar gold certificate at the Warren-Quinlan Station.

Next came the cab driver, Joseph Perrone. He had identified Hauptmann the day before as the man who had given him the note to deliver to Condon's house. His identification of Hauptmann today was, therefore, no surprise.

The fourth witness to put the finger on Hauptmann was Amandus Hochmuth, an eighty-six-year-old veteran of the Franco-Prussian War. The old man lived at the corner of Mercer County Route 158 and Amwell Road, the lane leading back to the Lindbergh estate. Two days after the kidnapping, Trooper W. O. Sawyer of the New Jersey State Police talked to Hochmuth as part of a general police canvass of the area. The old man said that just before noon on the day of the kidnapping, he watched a man almost drive a dirty green car into the ditch at the intersection in front of his house. Watching cars slide into that ditch was Hochmuth's favorite pastime. He had told the police that in this particular car he had seen a ladder lying crosswise in the back seat.

Inspector Lyons asked Hochmuth if the driver of that car was in the lineup. The witness placed a hand on Hauptmann's shoulder.

"Is that the man?" Lyons asked.

"This is him," Hochmuth replied.

Hauptmann looked blankly into space as Hochmuth was helped from the room.

The next witness was Ben Lupica, a Princeton preparatory school student who lived in Hopewell. Late in the afternoon of March 1, Lupica made his usual stop at his mailbox near the gatehouse to the Lindbergh estate. After picking up the mail, he drove a few yards then pulled over to read it. A few minutes later, a car passed him and stopped a few feet down the road. Lupica described this car as a dark blue or black 1929 Dodge. When the witness passed the car, he got a look at the driver, a man he described as thirty-five to forty years old, wearing a dark coat and a dark fedora hat. Lupica said the car had New Jersey license plates that included the letter L (the code for Mercer County). In the back seat of the car he saw two sections of an extension ladder. The next morning Ben Lupica reported all this to the New Jersey State Police.

Like the four witnesses before him, Lupica picked Hauptmann out of the lineup.

The last eyewitness was Mrs. Cecile Barr, the cashier at the Loew's Sheridan in Greenwich Village. Mrs. Barr had come to the station to identify Hauptmann as the man who ten months earlier had passed the five-dollar gold note at the theater. Mrs. Barr looked over the men in the line then walked over to Hauptmann. "This is the man," she said.

"Are you sure?" Inspector Lyons asked.

"Yes, I am sure," she replied.

Inspector Lyons thanked the witness and she was escorted out the door.

Although Mrs. Barr and the others had come through with flying colors, Lyons and his colleagues were concerned. They were worried about Condon. The old guy was so eccentric and full of himself he couldn't be trusted. Many of the officers in the room felt that Condon's reaction to Hauptmann suggested that they had been accomplices in the kidnapping.

Following Condon's disappointing performance, Agent Turrou had taken him into an adjoining room. Turrou had instructions to keep Condon there while the other witnesses were brought before the lineup to identify Hauptmann.

Turrou took a seat behind the desk while Condon, with a worried and agitated look on his face, dropped heavily onto a guest chair. "I have an excellent memory," he said.

"Is that so?" Turrou replied.

"Yes. I will never forget John's face and accent. Mr. Hauptmann pronounced the word 'perfect' just like John."

"I see."

"Yes. I have a remarkable memory. It's one I've developed over the years. I could never make an incorrect identification."

When Turrou didn't respond, Condon asked, "Has Hauptmann confessed?"

"I'm not at liberty to discuss that," Turrou replied.

"I see. Well, the papers say he had the ransom money. How much did he have?"

"I'm sorry, Dr. Condon, but I can't discuss that either."

"Well, they obviously think they have the right man," Condon said. "He had the ransom money. I'm curious to know what he said about the money when he was arrested. I wonder if he said how he got it."

"Please, Dr. Condon, I can't answer those questions."

Two hours later, long after all of the other witnesses had gone home, Condon was still in the room with Turrou. Condon was getting impatient. "Am I being detained?" he asked.

"I am under orders to keep you here."

"Well, how long?"

"I don't know."

"Am I under arrest?"

"No, sir."

"Well then, I could put on my hat and walk out of here. I could just walk out that door," Condon said. Turrou didn't respond. "Well, I won't do it. I have too much respect for your boss, Mr. Hoover. I wish I could say the same about Colonel Schwarzkopf."[9]

Another two hours slipped by—it was nine-thirty—and Turrou and Condon were still in the room. Condon had been pacing back and forth but was now slumped in the chair with his chin on his chest. "I guess you know that my life isn't worth two cents. Hauptmann's accomplices are going to kill me."

"Is that why you haven't identified Hauptmann? Are you afraid of his accomplices?"

"I am not a coward."

At ten o'clock, another FBI agent came by and called Turrou out of the room. A few minutes later Turrou returned and advised Condon that he was being taken to the district attorney's office.

At midnight, after being shouted and sworn at in the D.A.'s office, Condon was driven home. It had been a long and unpleasant day. He was exhausted, depressed, and more than a little apprehensive. He wasn't sure who he feared the most—the kidnappers or the police.

On Thursday afternoon, when the eyewitnesses were at the Greenwich Station confronting Hauptmann, some interesting information about the prisoner was coming in from Germany. It seemed that Hauptmann had lied when he told the police that he had no criminal record. In June of 1919, the twenty-four-year-old Hauptmann had been convicted of grand larceny, petty theft, receiving stolen property, and armed robbery. He had also served over three years in the Bentzin Prison in Seconsen, Germany.[10]

Hauptmann's grand-larceny conviction had to do with three burglaries. In one of these cases, Hauptmann had broken into the mayor's house in the village of Bernhruch, Germany. He had gotten into the dwelling through a second-story window. He had reached this window by climbing up a ladder.

Hauptman was convicted of armed robbery after he and another man stole groceries from two women at gunpoint. The women had food, not babies in the carriages.

Hauptmann was released from prison in March of 1923. Three months later, he was arrested for another series of burglaries. To avoid going to prison for these crimes, he fled to America.

The information from Germany also revealed that Hauptmann had a history of escaping police custody. On one occasion he jumped out of a police van and on another he broke out of jail.

Hauptmann's criminal record indicated that he was a bungler and an amateur. It also showed that he wasn't afraid to commit serious crimes. His second-story caper with the ladder reflected the kind of daring shown by the Lindbergh kidnapper.

The German authorities advised that in the summer of 1932, Mrs. Hauptmann had sailed to Europe to see if her husband was still wanted there. She was told that if he returned to Germany, he'd be thrown into jail. This ended his hope of returning home.

Thursday evening, Colonel Schwarzkopf was in Hopewell updating Colonel Lindbergh on the status of the investigation. Schwarzkopf said that everything pointed to Hauptmann. He had the money, he had written the ransom notes, he had been placed, by two witnesses, near the Lindbergh estate on the day of the kidnapping, and he was an ex-felon. There were still a few snags, however. John Condon wasn't cooperating, and Hauptmann hadn't confessed.

Tell me, Richard, what have they done to you?

— A N N A   H A U P T M A N N
to her husband at the Bronx County Courthouse,
September 22, 1934

23   THE THIRD DEGREE

AT SIX O'CLOCK THURSDAY EVENING, after the fingerprinting, interrogation, handwriting session, and lineup, Hauptmann was taken to the Bronx where, before Magistrate Richard McKinery he pled not guilty to the charge of extortion. The prisoner said he didn't have a lawyer and that he didn't want one. The judge ordered that Hauptmann be held without bail until his arraignment on Monday, September 24. That night, Hauptmann was placed into the Bronx County Jail, where he was allowed to sleep without interruption for the first time in three days.

The investigation of Hauptmann's background revealed that in the summer of 1933 he had run into a pedestrian with his car. The victim, a Mr. Alex Begg, had since died from other causes. After initially offering the victim's wife $250, Hauptmann had settled the claim by agreeing to pay $300. Six months after the accident, the man's wife wrote Hauptmann and asked for the $60 Hauptmann still owed on the claim. Hauptmann sent $20.

The detectives looking into Hauptmann's background learned a lot from his landlady, Mrs. Pauline Rauch. She said that the Hauptmanns had moved into their apartment in October 1931. She said that sometime after that Hauptmann started paying his rent with gold certificates. Up until the past winter, Hauptmann had paid his rent on time, then he stopped. This is when she and her tenant started fighting. Mrs. Rauch, an Austrian Jew, called him a Nazi and threatened to take him to court. Hauptmann still didn't pay, so Mrs. Rauch followed up on her threat. Two months later Hauptmann was ordered to pay his rent to the court or be evicted. Mrs. Rauch said she had never liked Hauptmann, but she needed his rent money to pay off her mortgage.

The police were getting a picture of a man, who, with fifty thousand dollars stashed in his garage, was still frugal, if not stingy.

Hauptmann's friends, however, painted a very different picture of him. A man who had worked with Hauptmann in 1927 described him as a hardworking, shy man who was an excellent carpenter.

Detectives checked with the Matthews Construction Company in Princeton, New **217** Jersey, the firm that had built the Lindbergh home, to see if Hauptmann had been on the payroll as a carpenter. He had not.

The police also questioned Mrs. Hauptmann's niece, Maria Mueller. Maria lived on Marion Avenue in the Bronx and was taking care of the Hauptmann baby.

Mrs. Mueller said that Bruno was "a very fine man" and that it was "wrong to speak of him as cruel." She said that Hauptmann was very polite and considerate with his family and friends.

The *New York Daily News* published a statement by Frank Talksdorf, a Bronx cabinetmaker:

> He was a brave soldier, an absolutely fearless man. He was a machine-gunner during the war. He was wounded in the leg. All the veins in that leg were ripped to pieces.
> He smuggled himself aboard the *George Washington* in 1923. He lay in bilge-water in the hold all the way over. They caught him, and locked him in the washroom, but he cut his way out with a knife. They caught him again and took him back."[1]

Hauptmann was born in Kamenz, Germany on November 20, 1899, to a respected family. His father had died in 1917 and two of his brothers were killed in World War I. Another brother was residing in Saxony and a sister, Mrs. Emma Gloechiner, was living in West Hollywood, California. In Germany, Hauptmann's sixty-nine-year-old mother, Pauline, lived on a small welfare pension and the few dollars she got from Bruno every Christmas and Easter.

Several of the local police officers in Kamenz, a town of eleven thousand, remembered Hauptmann. They knew him by his alias, Karl Pellmeier. They reported that Hauptmann had served a few months in an infantry regiment, during which time he saw action on the front. After the war, in the wake of Germany's defeat and economic collapse, Hauptmann had turned to crime. This had made him the black sheep of the Hauptmann family.

The police had found several of Hauptmann's notebooks and ledgers. The books contained detailed records of his earnings and financial dealings. These records documented every penny that Hauptmann and his wife had ever made and showed that Hauptmann was a very methodical and meticulous man. The notebooks also reflected a certain preoccupation, if not obsession, with money.

At the end of each year, Hauptmann had calculated his net worth. In June 1931, he started recording all of his stock market transactions. There were no references, in any of his notebooks, to any fur-trading transactions. The only entries under Isidor Fisch's name had to do with small sums of money Fisch had given Hauptmann to invest in the stock market. The only evidence that Hauptmann and Fisch had been fur-trading partners were the pelts Fisch had left in Hauptmann's apartment.

The investigation into Hauptmann's financial status revealed that he had no cash assets on April 1, 1932. But in May and June of that year, Hauptmann, still unemployed, was able to pay $526 for a console radio and $126 for a pair of German field glasses. That summer, Hauptmann had also taken a hunting trip to Maine. On a second hunting excursion in the summer of 1932, he had purchased a $56 rifle for his hunting companion. This was the summer he sent his wife, at a cost of $706, to Europe to clear the way for his return to Germany.

When Anna returned, she came back to a husband who was leading the life of a playboy. But most disturbing was a friendship Richard had struck up with a young and beautiful woman named Gerta Henkel.

No longer a working man, Hauptmann had time on his hands. He played cards with his friends, spent leisurely afternoons with Gerta Henkel, and filled in the gaps watching the board at his stockbroker's office. In the midst of the Great Depression, at a time when most of his friends were unemployed and standing in breadlines, Hauptmann was leading a life of leisure and comfort.

In the winter of 1933, Hauptmann and his wife drove to Florida. The following summer, they spent several long weekends at Hunter's Island, where Hauptmann kept a canoe that had a little sail.

Back in the late 1920s, just before the big crash on Wall Street, Hauptmann had enjoyed small-scale success in the stock market. He had invested his meager savings quite shrewdly. But because his investments were moderate, he hadn't been able to take full advantage of the rising market.

After the kidnapping, Hauptmann's investments were no longer moderate. In fact, there were times when Anna fussed over the magnitude of his financial adventures. On one occasion, she objected vigorously when he wanted to take twenty-five thousand dollars from their account to speculate on silver. They argued, and she finally gave in. But by the time Bruno got into the market, silver prices had already shot up. He had missed the boat. After that, whenever Anna wanted to stick her nose into Bruno's financial business, he would remind her of this.

Early Friday morning, Hauptmann was awakened in his cell and told that he was being taken to the office of Samuel J. Foley, the Bronx County District Attorney.

Foley's office was in the recently constructed Bronx County Building, a massive structure of granite surrounded by four sets of gradually rising steps. The four main entrances to the building were flanked by neoclassical statues—warriors, sages, and barebreasted maidens. Yankee Stadium was just down the street. It was Babe Ruth's last year as a New York Yankee.

Foley's office had mahogany walls and a thick, green carpet. Hauptmann, wearing the clothes he had been arrested in and handcuffed to a detective, was escorted into the big room. The D.A. had Hauptmann uncuffed and seated in the big, cushioned chair on the opposite side of the desk. Foley was fifty-three, and wore steel-rimmed glasses. Without the glasses that gave him a scholarly look, Foley looked tough and street-wise.

Foley didn't have any more luck getting a confession from Hauptmann than the police had. As the morning wore on, Hauptmann slumped deeper and deeper into his chair. Speaking in a weary monotone, Hauptmann stuck to his Fisch story. At noon the prisoner was offered food but refused to eat. He asked Foley when he could see his wife.

Foley said that he could see his wife as soon as he told the truth. "Think of your wife and baby," Foley kept saying.

"I do! I do!" Hauptmann would answer.

At four in the afternoon, Foley gave up. Hauptmann was taken to another office where his wife was waiting to see him. They were given a few minutes together, then Bruno was taken back to his cell and Anna was escorted into Foley's office.

Mrs. Hauptmann told the D.A. that the first she knew of the ransom money was when the policeman found it in the garage. As for Isidor Fisch, she only knew him as Richard's friend.

The next day, the Lindbergh investigators received the results of the background investigation on Fisch in Germany. The fur trader was so poor his parents had to send him money. He was also sick and virtually starving to death. The German police also spoke to Pinkus Fisch, Isidor's brother, and learned that before he died, Isidor made no mention of Hauptmann. Isidor's German acquaintances characterized him as a harmless fur trader. The police in Leipzeig, Fisch's hometown, offered to exhume his body.

In the Bronx, the police questioned Harry Uhlig, a man who knew Hauptmann and Fisch. Uhlig said that on December 9, 1933, Fisch set sail for Germany on the liner *Manhattan*. He paid for his ticket with $420 worth of gold certificates Hauptmann had lent him. He had also purchased, with Hauptmann's money, $600 worth of Reichmarks. Hauptmann saw his friend off at the pier. Uhlig said that Isidor Fisch was very poor.

In investigating Fisch's activities in America, the police came across an interesting if not disturbing piece of information—Isidor Fisch had applied for his passport on May 12, 1932, the day the Lindbergh baby was found dead.

Mrs. Laura Urant, the daughter of Hauptmann's landlady, told investigators that she had met Isidor Fisch at a party at Hauptmann's apartment. After that she frequently saw him in Hauptmann's company. "Fisch knew he was plagued by an illness that would take many years to cure," she said. "Knowing that, I do not believe that if he had a great sum of money he would have delayed obtaining the medical attention he so greatly needed."[2]

Digging into Fisch's financial dealings, detectives found that in 1931 he had borrowed several thousand dollars to embark in a pie-baking business that later went bankrupt.

In April of 1934, a few weeks after Fisch's death, Hauptmann wrote to his family advising them that Isidor had left certain articles in his care. Hauptmann made no mention of a shoebox Fisch had left behind.

On Friday, September 21, Albert S. Osborn submitted a written questioned-documents report to Schwarzkopf. Based on his examination of Hauptmann's known writings, the handwriting sample he gave the police, and his signatures on the automobile license applications, Osborn concluded that Hauptmann had written all fifteen of the ransom documents.

Excerpts of Osborn's report were published on page one of the *New York Times*.[3]

On Friday, the newspapers were full of stories and articles about Hauptmann, his capture, and the discovery of the ransom money. The entire nation, indeed the world, had its eyes on the Lindbergh case. Aware of this, J. Edgar Hoover wanted to make sure his FBI was getting its share of the credit. With the Lindbergh kidnapper in custody, the FBI's role in the case was diminished. Indicting, extraditing, and trying Hauptmann were state matters. In a story published in the *New York Times* on Saturday, September 22, Hoover implied that the FBI, with the help of the local agencies, had broken the case.[4]

On Saturday, Hauptmann was back in the district attorney's office. This time he was wearing fresh clothes that his wife had brought him the day before. Foley grilled Hauptmann for eight hours without moving him off his original story. At ten o'clock, before being put back into his cell, Hauptmann was allowed a forty-five-minute visit with his wife.

Bruno was taken into a small office where a uniformed police officer stood behind his chair. A few minutes later, Mrs. Hauptmann, accompanied by a police guard, walked into the room. When she approached him he stood up and they embraced.

Anna was shocked by her husband's appearance.[5] He was pale, thin, and unshaven and his suit was badly rumpled. The two police officers took up positions at the door, giving the prisoner and his wife a little privacy. Anna noticed that Richard's eyes were puffy. "Richard, what happened?" she asked.

"Nothing," he replied curtly shrugging his shoulders. "I want to tell you about the money," he said. "And about Isidor Fisch."

Hauptmann spent the next thirty-five minutes explaining the money in the garage. He said he had felt justified in spending it because Isidor Fisch had owed him seven thousand dollars. He had been thinking about surprising her with a new house. That was why he hadn't said anything about the money. He then reminded Anna that on the night of the kidnapping, he had come to the bakery to pick her up. It was important that she remember that.

As Richard spoke, Anna examined his face. His eyes were swollen and black-and-blue. "Tell me, Richard," she pleaded, "what have they done to you?"

"Annie," he said, "they punched me and kicked me. The lights were out so I couldn't see who was hitting me. They strapped me to a chair and kicked me in the chest and stomach."[6]

After Bruno's visit with his wife, he was questioned in his cell by Leon Turrou. The interrogation had just gotten under way when Hauptmann asked, "If I made a confession, would it go easy on me?"

Trying not to appear surprised and overeager, Turrou responded with a casual, "It probably would go better for you."

"What kind of deal could I get?"

"Well, I'm not sure," the agent replied.

"Could the FBI guarantee an easy sentence?"

"The FBI couldn't do that," Turrou said. "We are not the prosecuting authority."

"There would be no guarantee?"

"Not from the FBI. But you could probably work something out with Schwarzkopf."

"I don't trust him," Hauptmann said. "Forget it."

"Look, I'm sure something can be worked out. It's always better to tell the truth. **221** Maybe you'd like to talk to Mr. Hoover?"

"I have nothing to confess. I was just curious."[7]

Shortly after Dr. Dudley Shoenfeld heard of Hauptmann's arrest, he got in touch with Lieutenant Finn to see if he could talk to the prisoner. Shoenfeld's psychiatric profile of the ransom-note writer had turned out to be remarkably close to Hauptmann.

Finn told Shoenfeld that Inspector Lyons wouldn't make Hauptmann available to anyone outside of law enforcement. Right now the police were trying to get a confession.

Shoenfeld said that he understood why Lyons didn't want outside interference at such a critical time, but he had a few suggestions on how to get Hauptmann to confess. For example, the interrogators should not get tough with a man like Hauptmann. The hard-nosed approach would only confirm his belief that he lived in a hostile world. If given the third degree, the prisoner would show his contempt and superiority by refusing to cooperate. The psychiatrist recommended that Hauptmann be questioned calmly by one or two men in a secluded and quiet place. Shoenfeld said that Hauptmann would be more receptive to the soft-sell. If the right interrogator used the correct technique, there was a good chance that Hauptmann would confess. The quiet and rational "what's-in-it-for-me" approach would be the best way to handle him.

Lieutenant Finn had a high regard for Dr. Shoenfeld's theories, but Shoenfeld didn't know the realities of police work. For one thing, even though Finn had handled the bulk of the investigation for the department, Hauptmann's interrogation was in the hands of his superiors—Chief Inspector Lyons and Deputy Chief Inspector Sweeney. The New Jersey State Police and the FBI were also involved in the interrogation. As a result, Finn had no say in how Hauptmann was to be handled.

On Saturday, Anna Hauptmann hired a qualified but obscure lawyer from Brooklyn named James M. Fawcett. Fawcett and Mrs. Hauptmann were distantly related through marriage.

One of Fawcett's first steps involved the handwriting evidence. Realizing that Schwarzkopf had lined up at least three handwriting experts who were going to say that Hauptmann had written the ransom notes, Fawcett took copies of the letters and samples of Hauptmann's handwriting to a respected Newark, New Jersey, documents examiner named J. Vreeland Haring. Like Albert S. Osborn, Haring had offices in New York City and a son who was in the questioned-documents business.

Haring looked at the evidence and reported that Hauptmann had indeed written all of the ransom notes. The lawyer thanked Haring for his time and said that he'd have no further need for his services. Fawcett began looking for another expert.

In the meantime, Bert C. Farrar, the Treasury Department's handwriting expert, submitted his report to Schwarzkopf. Farrar was in agreement with the Osborns and J. Vreeland Haring. He found that the first three ransom letters had been written at the same time and that the red portion of the kidnapper's symbol had been made by the cork of a red ink bottle. As for the holes punched through the three circles, Farrar said that they had been made simultaneously.

On Saturday night, the FBI released the drawing of "Cemetery John" by James T.

Berryman, the well-known political cartoonist. The next day, September 23, this portrait was published in *The New York Times* alongside a facial photograph of Hauptmann.[8] Berryman's rendition bore a striking resemblance to Hauptmann.

On Monday morning, Dr. Thurston H. Dexter, a New York City physician, came to the Bronx County Jail to give Hauptmann a physical examination. Dr. Dexter had come at Fawcett's request, and after examining the prisoner he wrote, "I conclude from this examination that Hauptmann had been subjected recently to a severe beating, all or mostly with blunt instruments. The injuries resulting from this are general and include the head, back, chest, abdomen and thighs."[9]

A few days earlier, just after the lineup at the Greenwich station, Dr. John H. Garlock, a New York City police surgeon, examined Hauptmann. Dr. Garlock reported, "Complete physical examination failed to reveal any evidence to suggest recent injury of any sort. Aside from the fact that this man was pale and suffered from loss of sleep, nothing was found. The heart was negative. All the joints of his body were normal. The head was normal, and there was no break in the skin. The patient's gait was normal."[10]

From the two medical reports, it seems that Hauptmann was beaten sometime between 9:30 Thursday night and Monday morning, the 23rd. Since he was questioned in the Bronx County District Attorney's office on Friday and then on Saturday morning, he was, in all probability, abused Saturday afternoon or early that evening.

In Hopewell, Hauptmann's arrest had led to speculation that the three New Jersey State troopers still guarding the vacated Lindbergh estate would be returning to regular duty.

The three officers who had been guarding the estate for the past thirty-one months were billeted in a small yellow shanty along the road leading to the mansion. The officers cooked their own meals, and when not on duty at the Lindbergh gate, maintained their living quarters. Each man was given three days off a month. Their primary responsibilities included keeping intruders off the premises and dealing with weekend and holiday sightseers. Traffic to the estate had become heavy since Hauptmann's arrest. Colonel Schwarzkopf had no intention of removing the guards; the investigation was still in progress and the estate, being the scene of the crime, had to be protected.[11]

On Sunday, a reporter for the *New York Daily News* got a tip through a Hauptmann acquaintance that Bruno had been treated for a leg injury early in 1933. Since it was believed that the kidnapper had fallen from the ladder, the reporter immediately passed this information on to the FBI.

The next day, Leon Turrou questioned Dr. Otto Meyer, the New York City physician who had treated Hauptmann's leg condition. Hauptmann had been under Dr. Meyer's care from January 3, 1933, to April 17. The Doctor said that Hauptmann had an aggravated case of chronic phlebitis, an ailment unquestionably caused by a sprain or fracture incurred sometime within the previous year. Doctor Meyer suggested that the Lindbergh investigators search for the physician who had treated Hauptmann's initial leg injury.

Dr. Meyer said, "I suggest that you X-ray Hauptmann's leg. The virulence of the affliction led me to believe at the time that the injury that caused the phlebitis probably resulted from a fall not more than a year previous. I asked him if his leg had been fractured but he ignored the question completely."[12]

Following up on Dr. Meyer's suggestion, the FBI arranged to have Hauptmann's ankles X-rayed in the Bronx County Jail. Meanwhile, detectives went to all of the hospitals in the area to see if Hauptmann had been treated for a leg injury shortly after the kidnapping. Hauptmann's X-rays were inconclusive and the police were unable to find the physician who had treated his injury. The investigators did turn up further evidence of a leg problem. An employee of the car dealership where Hauptmann bought his Dodge said that in March of 1932, when Hauptmann brought his car in for repairs, his left foot was in bandages.[13] It was very possible that Hauptmann had treated himself.

On Monday, September 24, Lewis E. Lawes, the warden of Sing Sing Prison, announced that since the Lindbergh kidnapping, the handwriting of every inmate in the penitentiary as well as those entering the prison had been checked against the ransom writings. The handwriting of about five thousand prisoners had been examined. Warden Lawes said that several other state and federal prisons had implemented similar programs in an attempt to identify the writer of the ransom notes.

In Leipzig, Germany, the authorities questioned Isidor Fisch's older brother Pinkus. Pinkus advised that shortly before Isidor died, he said that he had borrowed money from Hauptmann to pay for his trip to Germany. Pinkus said that Isidor was penniless.

"Isidor never gave a hint that he knew anything about the Lindbergh case," Pinkus said. The brother also stated that after Isidor died, his friends and associates from America and Germany sent letters demanding the repayment of loans that Isidor had incurred.[14]

Pinkus advised that his late brother was five to ten thousand dollars in debt at the time of his death. "I believe Hauptmann merely wants to shift the blame by involving others," he said. Pinkus's wife said that she and her husband had had to pay for Isidor's hospital bills and his tombstone. "Why would Hauptmann hide the money if he had received it in an honest way?" she asked.[15]

Sunday night, Colonel Schwarzkopf announced that the New Jersey authorities had enough evidence to extradite Hauptmann to New Jersey, where he would be tried for kidnapping and murder. When asked by a reporter if the New Jersey State Police would be able to prove that Hauptmann had been on the Lindbergh estate on the night of March 1, 1932, Schwarzkopf answered, "We have enough to bring him back and we want him."[16] Schwarzkopf said that he would be meeting the next day with New Jersey's attorney general to discuss the details of Hauptmann's extradition.

Richard, is there anything in or about your apartment that
you haven't told us about?
— S A M U E L J. F O L E Y ,
District Attorney of the Bronx

24 THE SECRETS OF THE HAUPTMANN HOUSE

ON MONDAY, SEPTEMBER 24, Hauptmann and his attorney stood before Magistrate Richard McKinery in the Bronx Supreme Court Building. The judge informed Hauptmann that he was accused of extorting fifty thousand dollars from Colonel Lindbergh and would be held without bail.

Following the arraignment, Fawcett issued the following statement to the press: "I am following certain clues which require much investigation, some of which are distant from New York. I have not completed my consultations with the defendant. They will be continued daily as my investigations progress. Mrs. Hauptmann will not make any further statements in this case. Any information will come from me." [1]

While Fawcett dealt with reporters in New York, Colonel Schwarzkopf, following his conference with the state attorney general in Trenton, addressed newsmen. Schwarzkopf refused to say whether he had witnesses who could place Hauptmann on the Lindbergh estate. He also wouldn't comment on the story that one of Hauptmann's shoes matched the footprint under the baby's window. When asked if Dr. Condon had positively picked Hauptmann out of the lineup, Schwarzkopf replied, "Ask Mr. Foley."

Earlier in the day, while the magistrate informed Hauptmann of the charge, three carpenters and a New York City detective were stripping Hauptmann's apartment. The detective was Insp. Henry D. Bruckman, head of the Bronx Detective Bureau.

In the nursery, Bruckman instructed a carpenter to take out the shelf and clothes bar in the baby's closet. When this was done, he backed into the closet and, with the aid of a flashlight, examined the door trim. Bruckman noticed a smudge and put on his glasses. Someone had written, in pencil, the following address: 2974 Decatur. Beneath it was a telephone number—3-7154. Following the number were the letters *SDG*. Bruckman knew the address—it was John Condon's, and so was the telephone number. It was the number he had at the time of the kidnapping. (Condon later got a private listing.) The letters *SDG* stood for Sedgwick, his exchange.

Instead of rushing to a telephone to report his find, Bruckman stayed in the closet and continued his search. A few moments later he came across writing on the back of the closet door. There, in pencil, someone had written:

$500

B0000 7162A

1928

B0000 9272A

Bruckman checked the ransom list to see if these serial numbers were on it. They weren't; they were not ransom bills. (The first number belonged to a $500 bill and the second to a $1,000 note.)

One of the carpenters pried off the trim board, exposing a hollowed-out place in the wall above the door. The board was loosely attached, suggesting that it had been frequently removed. Inspector Bruckman figured Hauptmann might have hidden some of the ransom money in this place.[2]

Bruckman telephoned Inspector Lyons, who instructed him to take the closet door and the five-foot eight-inch trim board to the district attorney's office.

The next day, Hauptmann was taken to Foley's office for questioning. The new evidence had renewed hopes of a confession.

With the usual party of officers looking on, Hauptmann was made comfortable in the big cushioned chair. Foley's private secretary, Benjamin Arac, was seated nearby. Arac was there to take down Foley's questions and Hauptmann's answers.[3] Hauptmann's attorney didn't know about the new evidence and wasn't present.

Foley got right to the point: "Hauptmann, I want to ask you some questions about this board." The prosecutor reached down and brought the piece of trim into view. "You know it is from your closet in your home, don't you?" Hauptmann's disheveled hair and groggy face revealed that he had been rousted from a nap.[4] "That is correct," he said.

"Your handwriting is on it."

"Yes, all over it," Hauptmann replied matter-of-factly.

Encouraged, Foley continued, "What did you write on that board? Read it to the stenographer." One of the detectives held the trim in front of Hauptmann.

"I can't read it," Hauptmann said.

"Can you read the address on it?" Foley asked.

"Two-nine-seven-four. I can't make out the first. I can read the number down below—three-seven-one-five-four."

Foley leaned forward in his chair, and with his elbows resting on the desk, asked, "What else can you read on that board that you wrote yourself?"

"I can't read; that's a *t—u—r;* another one I can't make out."

"That is Dr. Condon's address?" Foley snapped.

"I don't know," came the response.

"Why did you write it on the board?"

"I must have read it in the paper about the story. I was a little bit interest, and keep a little bit record of it and maybe I was just on the closet and was reading the paper and put down the address," Hauptmann stammered. He had suddenly lost control of his English.

"How did you come to put the telephone number on there?"

"I can't give you any explanations about the telephone number," Hauptmann replied in his nasal monotone.

Foley stared at Hauptmann then said, "Your only explanation for writing Dr. Condon's address on this board and telephone number is that you were probably reading the paper in the closet and you marked it down; is that correct?"

"It is possible that a shelf or two shelves in the closet and after a while put new papers on the closet and we just got the paper where this case was in and I followed the story of course I put the address on there?" Hauptmann replied. He was becoming incoherent.

"That is why you marked it on the door?"

"That is the only explanation I can give."

"Do you remember the day that you wrote this memorandum on the board?"

"No."

"But you remember that you wrote it?"

"I must write it, the figures; that's my writing."

"The writing is yours too, isn't it?" Foley was referring to Condon's address and telephone number.

"I hardly can read it."

"From what you see of it, it is your writing isn't it? It is your figures and your writing?"

"I really can't remember when I put it on," Hauptmann said.

"Regardless of *when* you put it on, it is your figures and your writing, isn't it?"

"The writing I can't make out so very clearly; I don't know."

"Do you know who rubbed it out or tried to rub it out?"

"No."

It was apparent that Hauptmann wasn't going to confess. His interrogators were disappointed but not surprised. They had gotten a typical Hauptmann response—implausible, matter-of-fact, and vague—and all of it carved in granite.

Foley was surprised that Hauptmann had admitted that some of the writing on the board was his. The evidence must have taken him by surprise; he had obviously forgotten that he had written it. Had he been given more time to think, he might have flatly denied that the writing was his. Instead, he had served up a rather silly explanation, one that would plague him later.

Foley asked Hauptmann to explain why he had jotted down the two serial numbers. Hauptmann said that they represented two large bills—either a five hundred-dollar bill or a thousand-dollar note. Isidor Fisch had given him this money to invest in the stock market. Hauptmann said he had hidden the bills in that hollowed-out place under the door trim.

Foley terminated the interview and ordered Hauptmann back to his cell. In a few hours the DA would start his extortion case before the Bronx Grand Jury. In New York, extortion carried a maximum sentence of twenty years.

Most of Foley's witnesses, thirty-two in all, would testify tomorrow. He was saving his star witnesses, Colonel Lindbergh and Hauptmann himself, for Wednesday, the final day.

On this Monday morning, Foley presented the testimony of Gregory Coleman, the city editor of the *Bronx Home News,* Dr. Condon, Joseph Perrone, the two attendants at the Warren-Quinlan gas station, Lieutenant Finn, and Captain Lamb.

At the conclusion of the first day's testimony, Foley told reporters that he would not summon Mrs. Lindbergh. "It would be a harrowing experience," he said.[5] A reporter asked Foley if Dr. Condon had strengthened his identification of Hauptmann as "Cemetery John." Foley said that he preferred not to comment about Condon at this time.

When Fawcett learned of Hauptmann's statements to Foley about the writing in his closet, he rushed to the Bronx and advised his client to stop talking to the authorities. He also promised that he would fight any attempt to extradite him to New Jersey.

On Tuesday, Foley ran twenty-one more witnesses before the grand jury. The first was Col. Henry Breckinridge, who was followed to the stand by the five detectives who were present when the ransom money was found in Hauptmann's garage. The next three witnesses were store clerks who had been given ransom bills. They were followed by the four employees of the J. P. Morgan Company who had assembled the ransom parcels. Then came Leon Turrou of the FBI, Frank Wilson of the IRS, Mrs. Cecile Barr, and Mrs. Pauline Rausch. Late in the afternoon, Albert S. Osborn and his son, Albert D., testified that Hauptmann had written all of the ransom documents.

The last witness of the day, and the most sensational, was Insp. Henry Bruckman. The tall, dark-haired thirty-five-year-old testified in a brusque, self-confident manner. His forceful and convincing testimony impressed the jury and guaranteed an indictment.

On this day, reporters questioned a man who had guided Hauptmann on a hunting trip in Maine six months after the kidnapping. According to the guide, Hauptmann had quipped: "Because it's a millionaire's son, they're making too much darn fuss about it."[6]

Mrs. Hauptmann spent the day conferring with Fawcett and visiting her husband in the Bronx County Jail. Late in the afternoon, she returned by taxi to her niece's home. She was met there by a Movietone camera crew, several hundred spectators, and a handful of uniformed policemen. Mrs. Hauptmann went into the house and a short time later came out carrying her son. Through her attorney, she had agreed to appear with Bubi on film. Fawcett wanted to arouse public sympathy for the Hauptmanns.

With the cameras turning and the crowd looking on, Mrs. Hauptmann set Bubi into his playpen. She ran her hand through his blond hair and called him pet names as he fondled a building block. Pointing to the camera, Mrs. Hauptmann asked Bubi if he could see his daddy. At the request of a cameraman, Mrs. Hauptmann sang a German cradle song, but before she could finish, she broke down and cried. The filming ended with Mrs. Hauptmann sobbing into Bubi's smiling face. It was a heartbreaking scene.

Four days after learning of Hauptmann's arrest, Charles and Anne Lindbergh, in their own aircraft, a two-seater monocoupe, took off from Santa Monica. Before nightfall, they landed on a remote airfield in the Texas panhandle near Spearman. Late in the afternoon of the following day, they arrived in Saint Louis, Missouri. On Tuesday, about the time Inspector Bruckman had found the writing in Hauptmann's closet, the Lindberghs landed in New York City.

The Lindberghs were met by Colonel Schwarzkopf, who drove them to his home in Lawrenceville, New Jersey, where Colonel Lindbergh was updated on the status of the case. Two hours later, the Lindberghs were driven to the Morrow estate in Englewood. Colonel Lindbergh was scheduled to appear before the grand jury the next day.

The following morning, New York City Detectives Maurice Tobin, Bill Wilson, and two carpenters showed up at the Hauptmann home. They were greeted by Lt. Lewis J. Bornmann of the New Jersey State Police. Bornmann had been recently promoted to the rank of lieutenant. He didn't spend his nights at the house, but he had been staying in the Hauptmann apartment to keep intruders out and to search for more ransom money.

The New York City officers and the carpenters had come to the apartment to assist Bornmann in his search. After they had searched the apartment again, the men climbed into the attic through the hatch in Hauptmann's linen closet. The Hauptmann attic was not completely floored. What flooring there was consisted of thirteen twenty-foot tongue-and-groove southern pine boards. Although he had been in the attic before, Bornmann noticed for the first time that a floor plank in the southwest corner of the room was shorter than the rest. About eight feet of this board had been sawed off and removed from the attic. In each of the four joists exposed because this board was shorter than the others, Bornmann found a nail hole where the missing plank had been secured to the attic.

As Bornmann and the others kneeled along the gap in the flooring, Bornmann thought about rail 16 and what Koehler had said about it. According to the wood expert, that board had been used somewhere else before it became part of the ladder. Was it possible that rail 16 had once filled this gap in Hauptmann's attic? Rail 16 was the right length, was southern pine, and contained four nail holes.

Bornmann telephoned his headquarters and asked to have rail 16 brought to the Bronx as quickly as possible. About an hour later, the plank was carried into the attic, where Bornmann laid it across the exposed crossbeams. The four nail holes in the rail lined up perfectly with the holes in the attic joists. To make sure they were in alignment, Bornmann inserted into them four eightpenny nails, the kind used in the attic. The nails dropped easily through the rail into the crossbeams. The nail holes in both boards had matching angles and were the right depth to bring the top of the nails flush to the plank.

Lieutenant Bornmann called Colonel Schwarzkopf, who in turn telephoned Arthur Koehler in Wisconsin. Koehler said he would get to the Bronx as soon as possible.

When FBI agents Sisk and Turrou learned of Bornmann's discovery they reacted with skepticism. In a series of memos to J. Edgar Hoover, they pointed out that at one time or another, thirty-seven police officers had been in Hauptmann's apartment looking for the origin of rail 16. The agents said that they couldn't understand why it had taken Lieutenant Bornmann six days to find this gap. According to Turrou, there had been nine searches of the attic since Hauptmann's arrest. Sisk noted that the space hadn't been discovered until *after* the FBI had been denied access to Hauptmann's apartment.

A few hours before he found the gap in Hauptmann's attic, Bornmann had written the following report: "This date [September 26, 1934] I was detailed by Captain Lamb to continue the search on the above-captioned home. Meeting Detective Tobin, two police carpenters, and Supt. Wilson on the premises at 9:00 AM, we immediately proceeded to make a thorough search of the attic. Nothing of value was found."[7]

The FBI agents had failed to mention that the searchers in the attic had been looking for the ransom money and not for the original site of rail 16.

While the Bornmann party was in Hauptmann's attic contemplating the gap in the flooring, Inspector Bruckman was outside with a crew of officers and carpenters dismantling Hauptmann's garage. One of the carpenters knocked down a short two-by-four that was wedged between two wall joists. When he examined this eight-inch piece of wood he found that it contained five wads of $10 gold notes. The bills were rolled up and stuffed into five holes that had been drilled into the board. All of the bills were listed as Lindbergh money. The first hole contained $190, the second $200, the third $150, and the fourth and fifth $200 each. The ransom cache totaled $840, bringing the total amount of Lindbergh money in Hauptmann's possession to $14,600.

That wasn't all. There was a sixth drilled-out area, which was larger than the others. This hole contained a tiny silver-colored pistol with a white plastic grip. The three-and-one-half inch gun, a German Liliput KAL 4.25 (.25 caliber), model 1926, was loaded with five rounds.

Bruckman took the board and its contents to Foley, who stepped out of the grand jury room to examine it. The jurors were then put on hold while Foley returned to his office with the evidence. He placed the money and the gun on a table and covered them with a newspaper. Hauptmann was brought into the office and seated in the big chair. "Richard," Foley said, "is there anything concealed in or about your apartment that you haven't told us about?"

"No." Hauptmann replied.

"Perhaps you didn't understand me. I will ask you again. Are there any things concealed in or about the premises connected with this case that you haven't told us about?"

"No."

The D.A. then peeled the newspaper off the table. "Well," he shouted, "how do you account for this?"

Hauptmann didn't respond.

"Does this belong to you?" Foley asked.

"Yes. It is from the shoebox. It belonged to Isidor Fisch."

"And what about the gun?"

"I got it a long time ago from a friend. It was a present."

"Who gave it to you?"

"I can't remember."

"Why were you hiding it?"

"Because I have no permit. I didn't want to get in trouble with the police."[8]

Hauptmann was taken back to his cell. Foley returned to the grand jury room, and Bruckman went back to the Hauptmann house, where the search continued for the ransom money. The wrecking crew was now tearing up Hauptmann's bathroom plumbing.

That evening, *The New York Times* reported that at one time Hauptmann had been worth fifty thousand dollars. Based upon data furnished by Foley's office, Hauptmann's assets were listed and identified as follows:

Credit bal. under his name with Steiner, Rouse & Co.	$886
Credit bal. with same firm under wife's maiden name	5,017
Deposit in joint acct. with wife in Central Savings Bank	2,578
Two mortgages on houses in Brooklyn	7,000
Ransom bank notes found in his garage	14,590
Two loans to Fisch, based on Hauptmann's assertion	7,500
Ransom money found already circulated and turned in	5,100
Lost in stock speculations	7,000
TOTAL	$49,671[9]

In Germany, New York City Det. Arthur Johnson was in Kamenz to question Hauptmann's mother. Mrs. Hauptmann wasn't home, so Johnson, with the help of a local locksmith, entered her apartment and searched it. If the old woman had any of the ransom money, it wasn't in her house.

On September 26, an official of the Nazi Propaganda Ministry in Berlin imposed a ban on the exportation of films depicting Hauptmann's hometown.

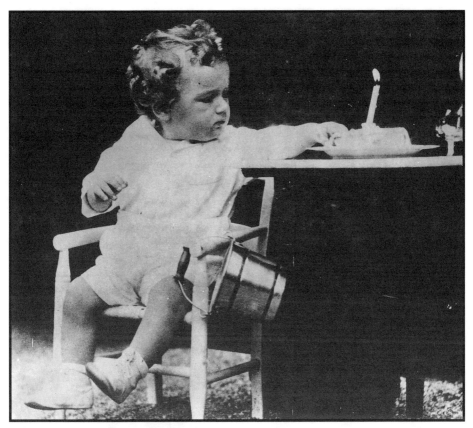

1 The baby on his first birthday. *NJSP.*

2 The ransom note demanding
$50,000 found in the baby's room on the night of
March 1, 1932. *NJSP.*

3 Corporal Kelly's crime scene photograph of the window used by the kidnapper to gain entry into the nursery. *NJSP.*

4 Kidnap ladder to the nursery window. The window below was to Colonel Lindbergh's den. The *X* marks the spot where the carpenter's chisel was found. *NJSP.*

5 The Reverend H. Dobson-Peacock and the Lindbergh case hoaxer, John Hughes Curtis.
International News Photos, Inc.

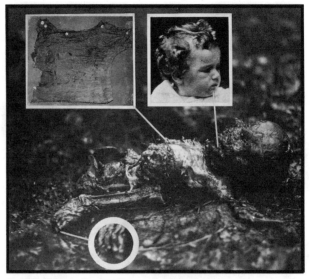

6 The baby's remains were discovered on May 12, 1932, in the woods two miles from his home. Three points of identity are featured. *NJSP.*

7 The baby's gravesite in the woods on Mount Rose Heights two miles from the Lindbergh estate along the Princeton-Hopewell road. *NJSP.*

8 The ten-dollar ransom bill passed by Hauptmann at the Warner-Quinlan gas station in upper Manhattan. One of the attendants penciled Hauptmann's license number—4U13-41—on the margin of the bill. This information broke the case and led to Hauptmann's arrest. *NJSP.*

9 A sample of Hauptmann's handwriting obtained from him at the Greenwich Street Police Station in lower Manhattan. Hauptmann spent many hours writing down what police officers dictated to him. Questioned documents experts would later find that Hauptmann's handwriting matched the ransom notes. *NJSP.*

10 Hauptmann was identified by several witnesses at a lineup held shortly after his arrest. *NJSP.*

11 (Top) A passport photograph of Hauptmann's wife, Anna. *NJSP.*
12 A search of Hauptmann's home in the Bronx turned up this insurance card
in his name. Like the writer of the ransom notes, Hauptmann hyphenated
"New York." *NJSP.*

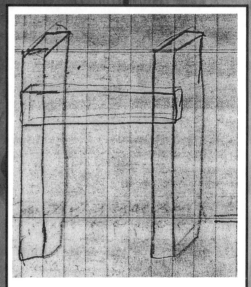

13 *(Inset)* Police found this sketch of a homemade ladder designed like the kidnap ladder in one of Hauptmann's notebooks. *NJSP.*

14 On September 26, 1934, the police found that a part of the kidnap ladder, rail 16, had been a floor plank in Hauptmann's attic. It is seen here in its former place. (Rail 16 is the board with the notch cut out of it.) The plank had been shortened and narrowed when fashioned into part of the ladder. *NJSP.*

15 Prosecutor David T. Wilentz (center) and his assistants, Joe Lanigan (left) and Anthony Hauck (right). *International News Photos, Inc.*

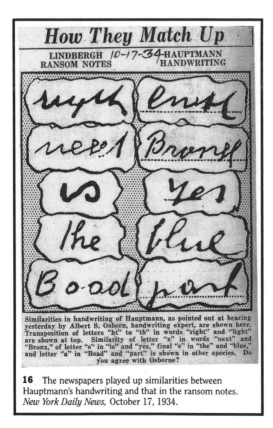

16 The newspapers played up similarities between Hauptmann's handwriting and that in the ransom notes. *New York Daily News,* October 17, 1934.

17 *(Opposite.)* Prosecutor David T. Wilentz (left) and his star witness, John F. Condon (Jafsie). *International News Photos, Inc.*

18 New Jersey State Police Superintendent H. Norman Schwarzkopf (left) and Charles A. Lindbergh. *International News Photos, Inc.*

19 Charles A. Lindbergh and his personal attorney, Henry Breckinridge. *International News Photos, Inc.*

20 Bruno Richard Hauptmann (right) conferring with his chief defense attorney, Edward Reilly. *International News Photos, Inc.*

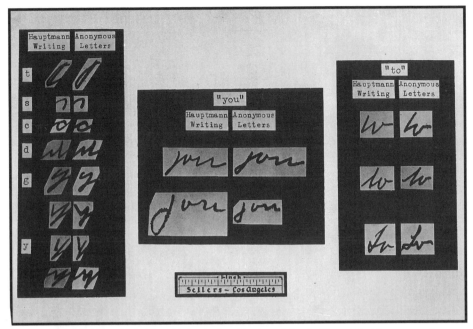

21 A typical handwriting exhibit at the trial showing how Hauptmann's handwriting matched the ransom notes. *International News Photos, Inc.*

22 The jury of eight men and four women found Hauptmann guilty of murder on February 14, 1935. Headlines in the *New York Daily News*.

DAILY NEWS, FRIDAY, DECEMBER 6, 1935

LINDBERGH HUNT REOPENED IN N. J.

23 Following Hauptmann's conviction, New Jersey Gov. Harold G. Hoffman reopened the Lindbergh case investigation. Headlines in the *New York Daily News*, December 6, 1935, tell of this baffling move.

Hoffman Visits Bruno in Prison; Ellis Parker Put on Trail

By ROBERT CONWAY.

Cryptic, newly revealed evidence indicating that Bruno Richard Hauptmann may be innocent of the murder of Charles A. Lindbergh Jr. led Gov. Harold G. Hoffman of New Jersey to visit the prisoner's death-house cell for an amazing and unprecedented mid-

Ellis Parker (left) famed sleuth is now working on a new clue in the Lindbergh case, Gov. Hoffman (right) of New Jersey declared yesterday, admitting he had secretly conferred with Bruno Richard Hauptmann (center) in Trenton, N. J., death cell on Oct. 15. The doomed carpenter pleaded his innocence. "He told me many things. I can't discuss the details," said Hoffman.

24 The U.S. Supreme Court refused to overturn Hauptmann's conviction. *New York Daily News*, January 16, 1936.

Vol. 17. No. 175   76 Pages   New York, Thursday, January 16, 1936   2 Cents

BRUNO'S FATE IN SUPREME COURT

Story on Page

25 Headlines in the *New York Daily News,* April 3, 1936, proclaiming Hauptmann's fate.

26 One of the many exhibits on display at the Lindbergh Case Archives housed at the New Jersey State Police Headquarters in West Trenton, N.J. The archives contain over two hundred thousand documents pertaining to the Lindbergh crime, investigation, and trial. *NJSP.*

HAUPTMANN
TELLS HIS OWN
STORY!

"I WAS a straggler!" cries Bruno Richard Hauptmann—convicted kidnaper and murderer of the Lindbergh baby...An unwanted child! The bitterness and tragedy of his youth creeps out in this, his life story he has written for the Daily Mirror. "Alone!" he sobs. As a child he was a solitary, shunned and jeered at by his playfellows because his mother dressed him in girl's clothes...Afraid of his father—who in a drunken rage struck him in front of a gaping tavern crowd, he hid in the woods...His brother left home, his sister went to America...The boy, Hauptmann, was left to help his mother eke out a precarious livelihood...Poverty gripped the household...He wore his wooden shoes only on Sunday...His only pet was a goat and that was slaughtered for food.

The Mirror assumes no responsibility for Hauptmann's assertions.

BY

Bruno Richard Hauptmann.

ONE of my daily jobs during the last three years of school was to carry lunch to my father. He still worked in the same quarry. While he ate his lunch, I ran around in the quarry and hunted blindworms among the stones. Often I looked for wild-tea roots on the slopes which led to the quarry. We called the plants Camonile and Hufflatsch (colt's foot), I am not certain whether the latter name is correct.

> I always have been a good father and husband. I hope I get cleared soon.
> — B R U N O   R I C H A R D   H A U P T M A N N

25   A TRUE BILL
IN NEW YORK

ON WEDNESDAY MORNING, about the time Lieutenant Bornmann and the others were climbing into Hauptmann's attic, Colonel Schwarzkopf pulled up to the Bronx County Courthouse with Colonel Lindbergh, who was about to testify before the grand jury. Lindbergh and Schwarzkopf stepped quickly from the car and walked briskly up the courthouse steps between a double line of policemen. As anticipated, a rather large crowd had gathered to see Colonel Lindbergh. Some of the bystanders cheered as Lindbergh, tan from his California vacation, climbed the stairs. Exhausted from his three-day flight across the country, and apprehensive about his grand jury appearance, the unsmiling hero chose to ignore his fans.

At the top of the steps, Lindbergh was met by a crowd of reporters, who bombarded him with questions like: "Will you be facing Hauptmann? Will you speak to the man who murdered your baby?" and so on.

"I have nothing to say," Lindbergh replied.

On the elevator, the operator stuck a pencil and pad into Lindbergh's face and asked him for an autograph. "Not now," Lindbergh said, "but on the way down."

Lindbergh conferred briefly with District Attorney Foley, then entered the grand jury chamber to testify. His appearance before the grand jury was more show than substance. There was very little he could add to the state's case. Nevertheless, Foley led the Colonel through the events of April 2, the night he drove John Condon to St. Raymond's Cemetery. Lindbergh said that as he sat in his car waiting for Jafsie to make contact with John, he heard a man's voice call out—"Hey, Doctor! Here, Doctor. Over here! Over here!" Lindbergh estimated that he had been sixty to eighty yards from the man who had spoken these words.

At the conclusion of Lindbergh's testimony, one of the jurors asked Foley to ask Lindbergh if he could recognize "Cemetery John's" voice if he heard it again.

Lindbergh thought this over for a moment then said, "It would be very difficult to sit here and say that I could pick a man by that voice."[1]

Having completed his testimony, Lindbergh was escorted from the chamber. He had been in the room for less than fifteen minutes. In the corridor, with Schwarzkopf and Inspector Lyons looking on, Foley told Lindbergh that he was intrigued by the juror's question. "Do you think sir, that you *could* recognize John's voice if you heard it again?"

"Maybe," Lindbergh replied.

"Well then, let me arrange something for tomorrow morning. Can you be in my office then?"

"What do you have in mind?" Lindbergh asked.

"Would you like to see the man who kidnapped your son?"

Lindbergh's face reddened a bit. He looked at Schwarzkopf, then back at Foley. "Yes, I would," he replied.

"Fine. I'll have him brought to my office in the morning. You'll be there too, but in disguise. We'll have him repeat the words."

"I'll be there," Lindbergh said.[2]

When he got back on the elevator, Lindbergh kept his promise to the operator and signed the autograph. "It isn't very often I do this," he said. A few minutes later he was being driven back to Englewood.

The next grand jury witness was Hauptmann himself. Looking pale and thin, Hauptmann said that he had come into possession of the shoebox in December of 1933 but didn't know what he had until August 1934, when he took the box out of the broom closet. Foley then got Hauptmann to admit that he had written Dr. Condon's address and phone number on the inside trim of his closet door. "Like everybody else," Hauptmann said, "I was interested in the case."

Hauptmann said he wasn't the man John Condon had delivered the money to in St. Raymond's Cemetery. Moreover, he had *not* quit his job at the Majestic Hotel on the day of the payoff. Contrary to what the records showed, he was at work that April second.

Hauptmann was followed to the stand by Foley's final witness, Charles Appel, Jr., a handwriting expert and the head of the FBI's brand new crime lab. Appel was questioned by Assistant District Attorney Edward F. Breslin.

Appel said that he had identified seven "peculiarities" common to all of the ransom notes, and he had found these handwriting peculiarities in Hauptmann's notebooks. There was one chance in a hundred million, he said, that some other person would exhibit the same handwriting characteristics. "You could tell," Appel continued, "that Hauptmann [in the ransom notes] had tried to change the natural slant of his writing, but the attempt was obvious to everyone who had seen the other samples of his hand. As a matter of fact," Appel said, "the later notes—the ones exchanged with Dr. Condon—show that Hauptmann had abandoned even that attempt at disguise."

Regarding some of the specific characteristics of Hauptmann's writing, Appel said, "The shape of the figure *2* in the notes indicates quite clearly that the writer was schooled abroad. Several of the letters were shaped in such a way that showed the influence of German script. In the 2's on Hauptmann's automobile registration card and in the 2's in the extortion notes, there is a very peculiar vertical or lengthened down-stroke and a most unusual print-form quirk in finishing the letter at the bottom."[3]

Appel went on to show the similarities between the letters *t, p,* and *o* in the ransom notes and Hauptmann's known writings. In the course of his Lindbergh case investigation, Appel said he had examined the handwriting of fifteen hundred people without finding any of the peculiarities contained in the ransom documents and Hauptmann's notebooks.

If there had been any doubts in the grand jurors' minds that Hauptmann was the Lindbergh extortionist, they had been swept away by the Osborns and Charles Appel.

As he left the courthouse, the FBI man stopped and talked to reporters. After repeating his testimony in surprising detail, Appel said, "It is inconceivable that anyone but Hauptmann could have written the ransom notes."[4]

Back in the courthouse, the twenty-three grand jurors voted unanimously to indict Hauptmann for extortion.

That afternoon, when Hauptmann was visited by his wife and child in Foley's office, he grabbed his little boy with the hand that wasn't shackled to his chair and cried, "Baby! Baby!" Speaking to Anna in a loud, clear voice, he said, "I hope the truth will get out. I always have been a good father and husband. I hope I get cleared soon."

On his way back to the cell, Hauptmann paused long enough to make the following statement to newsmen: "I wish to say to the people and to all German-Americans that I hope they believe my statements and help me. Seeing my wife and baby made me feel better."

At 9:30 the next morning, Hauptmann was back in Foley's office seated in the big chair. Lindbergh, with his face partially hidden behind a pair of sun glasses, was seated among a group of detectives. Hauptmann didn't know he was in the room.

"Now Richard," Foley said, "I want you to say—'Hey Doctor! Here Doctor! Over here!' Will you do that?"

"Yes, I will do that."

"All right then," Foley replied. "I want you to stand up and say that from various places in the room. Speak up so we can hear you."

Hauptmann got to his feet, and as though he was speaking to Foley, said, "Hey Doctor! Here Doctor! Over here!"

"No," Foley snapped. "Speak to those men over there. And put more life into it."

Hauptmann, like an actor under direction, turned stiffly around and repeated the phrases.

"Again," Foley said. "And this time louder."

Hauptmann said it again, and again, then repeated it several more times from other locations in the room. Lindbergh sat perfectly still, his eyes glued to Hauptmann.

Foley ordered Hauptmann back to his cell. The moment the prisoner was out of earshot, Lindbergh walked over to Foley's desk. "That is the voice I heard that night," he said. Lindbergh had removed the sunglasses and his face was grim.

Foley glanced at Schwarzkopf then back to Lindbergh. "Sir, are you perfectly sure?" "Yes, I am sure," Lindbergh replied.[5]

FBI agents Sisk and Turrou had witnessed the confrontation. The next day, Turrou wrote a memo to J. Edgar Hoover in which he questioned the trustworthiness of Lindbergh's identification. Turrou said that he didn't understand how Lindbergh could remember a voice he had heard from a distance of two hundred feet two and a half years ago. Hoover was also skeptical and said so, privately.

In Englewood, Lindbergh described Hauptmann to his wife, who listened uneasily. "He was a magnificent-looking man," Lindbergh said, "very well built. But his eyes were small—like the eyes of a wild boar—mean, shifty and cruel."[6]

On Thursday, September 27, Hauptmann, with his lawyer at his side, was arraigned before Judge Lester J. Patterson. The courtroom was packed with reporters, photographers, and newsreel cameramen. Standing before the bench, the prisoner looked forlorn in a double-breasted suit that was now too big for him. No one was surprised when Hauptmann pled not guilty and Fawcett asked to have the hundred thousand-dollar bail reduced to five thousand dollars. Judge Patterson denied the request, ordered Hauptmann bound over to trial, then called for the next case. Hauptmann was led back to his cell.

That afternoon, a dozen or so people were brought to the district attorney's office for questioning. The interviews were conducted by Assistant D.A. Breslin with the help of Lieutenant Keaten, Lieutenant Finn, and Agent Sisk. Most of those questioned were Hauptmann's friends and acquaintances.[7]

Mrs. Hauptmann was also questioned that afternoon. Before she and Fawcett reached Foley's office, they were surrounded in the corridor by newsmen. "When did you first know of the money in the garage?" a reporter asked.

Looking tired and speaking in a weak voice, Mrs. Hauptmann replied, "When the policemen took me down to the garage."

"What do you believe is your position in the case?"

"I am absolutely sure my husband is innocent," she said.

Fawcett declared that Hauptmann had only spent a few hundred dollars of the money after getting it from Isidor Fisch. The lawyer then expressed total confidence in his client's innocence.

"Is it true that the authorities in New Jersey are about to indict your client for murder?"

"You'll have to ask them. All I know is that Richard was not in New Jersey that night."

"What about the twenty-five thousand dollars your client had in a brokerage account?"

"I'll withhold comment on that until I look into it myself."

During the past week, nothing had been heard from Dr. Condon. Since his disappointing performance at the lineup, Condon had been under strict orders to keep a low profile. Feeling threatened by both the police and Hauptmann's accomplices, Condon hadn't ventured out of his house for a week, and he hadn't spoken to the press. But he was still hot news, and his name kept popping up in the tabloids. He was now the subject of a new wave of innuendos connecting him to the kidnapping. The *New York Times* and the *New York Daily News* carried stories about a man who supposedly saw Condon in a City Island restaurant frequented by Hauptmann. This so-called witness said that he had seen Jafsie there on the night of the ransom payoff. Since Condon had been with Colonel Lindbergh that night, the story was patently false.[8]

The fact that Condon's name was being dragged through the mud again infuriated Lindbergh, causing him to issue the following statement: "I had faith in Doctor Condon then and I have faith in him now. I trusted him then and I still trust him."[9]

Even Foley felt compelled to tell reporters that Condon was not under suspicion in the case.

On Friday, September 28, Hauptmann's day began as usual. At a quarter to eight a guard brought him breakfast on a tray. Today it was a dish of prunes, two pieces of bread, and a cup of coffee.

After breakfast, when the guard inventoried the contents of the food tray, he couldn't find the large pewter spoon. A few minutes later, Hauptmann was yanked out of his cell and strip-searched. Two guards checked out his cell while two others went through his clothing.

The guards couldn't find the spoon. Hauptmann looked on blankly, insisting matter-of-factly that the utensil had been on the tray when he returned it.

"We know you have it, where is it?" a guard asked.

"I do not have it," Hauptmann replied. "Why are you doing this to me?"

"I know it's here," the guard said. "Call the plumber."

The plumber came and dismantled the toilet and the sink. In the pipes beneath the toilet, the plumber found three pieces of the spoon. The largest fragment, the cup part and some of the stem, had been flattened into a crude knife. A fourth piece, most of the spoon's handle, was found in the sink drain. It had been bent into the shape of a hook.

Sheriff Hanley rushed to the jail. Taking Hauptmann aside, he asked, "What's going on here? What were you going to do with the spoon?"

"I don't know what you are talking about," Hauptmann replied.

Frustrated by Hauptmann's uncanny ability to look an interrogator straight in the eye and deny wrongdoing in the face of the most incriminating evidence, the sheriff, like so many before him, stalked off empty-handed.[10]

Following the spoon incident, Sheriff Hanley took added precautions against a suicide. Although the ordinary safeguards had been taken—the removal of Hauptmann's belt and tie—Hauptmann would be watched twenty-four hours a day. The once-an-hour peek through the little window in his cell door would no longer suffice.

Fawcett, in laying the groundwork for a possible insanity defense, decided to interpret the incident as an attempted suicide. He was thinking about having Hauptmann examined by a battery of psychiatrists.

Foley, Inspector Lyons, and Schwarzkopf discussed the incident and concluded that Hauptmann had been caught getting ready to escape. Hauptmann had broken out of jail in Germany, and, according to his friend Frank Talksdorf, Hauptmann had "cut his way out with a knife" when, as a stowaway, he was caught and locked in a ship's washroom.

The D.A. and the Lindbergh investigators believed that Hauptmann had been making a jail key out of the spoon's handle and a knife out of the other part. If the key hadn't worked, a guard might have gotten his throat slit.

Hauptmann's friends and acquaintances were still being interviewed in Foley's office. Among those questioned was Victor Schuessler, a fellow tenant of Hauptmann's. Mr. Schuessler said that he used to go into Hauptmann's garage a lot until Hauptmann, about a year ago, had padlocked the doors.

In Manhattan, police ballistics experts were finishing their examination of Hauptmann's Liliput pistol. Their findings added nothing to the case against Hauptmann.

In the Bronx, the police were still working at the Hauptmann house. Several laborers, under the supervision of Inspector Bruckman, were digging up Hauptmann's vegetable garden. Another crew was in the basement digging up the concrete floor to expose the subterranean plumbing. So far they hadn't turned up any more of the ransom money.

Hauptmann's entire garage had been dismantled and moved to the state police barracks in Wilburtha, New Jersey. Every piece of the neatly stacked lumber would soon be under the scrutiny of Arthur Koehler, the government wood expert. Schwarzkopf had set up a fully equipped lab for Koehler in the barracks. Also awaiting the expert's inspection were Hauptmann's nails, building supplies, and carpenter tools.

On Friday, the day of the spoon incident, Koehler arrived at the barracks and got down to work. He was eager to confirm Lieutenant Bornmann's theory that rail 16 had come from Hauptmann's attic. Shortly after his arrival, he and rail 16 were driven to the Bronx where Bornmann was waiting to greet him. Koehler followed Bornmann through the hatch into the attic. The wood expert examined the gap in the flooring, then carefully positioned rail 16 into the slot. He inserted the four nails Bornmann had taken from the attic floor into the rail 16 holes. Using his finger, he lightly tapped each nail through the rail into the joists. The nails sank easily into the holes, their heads ending up flush with the plank.

Koehler positioned rail 16 so that it lined up with the ends of the other floorboards, creating a one-and-one-quarter-inch gap where the rail faced up to the plank that had been cut short. Beneath this gap, on the lath-and-plaster ceiling, was a tiny pile of sawdust where rail 16 had been cut from the floor board. Koehler figured that after rail 16 had been removed from the attic, it had been shortened to fit the ladder, thus explaining the gap.

Even though there was a space between rail 16 and its parent board, Koehler could tell by looking at the grain that the planks had once been connected.

Koehler explained to Bornmann that every year a tree adds a new layer of wood, which shows up as rings, or grain when the tree is cut into boards. These rings indicate the tree's age and its rate of growth. The width, number and color of the growth rings in rail 16 and the floor board were identical.

Koehler noted that the grain pattern on the end of the attic plank was more distorted than the rings on the corresponding end of rail 16. Koehler said that this grain distortion was caused by a knot in the attic board. Even though a small piece of the wood was missing, Koehler could see the influence of this knot in the grain pattern of rail 16.

The evidence against Hauptmann was slowly piling up. Investigators and forensic scientists were closing in from all sides.

On October 5, Albert S. Osborn wrote to Foley requesting samples of Anna Hauptmann's handwriting: "If she [Mrs. Hauptmann] is examined again, I think it would be a good plan to have her do some writing, especially of figures."[11] Osborn was making sure that Mrs. Hauptmann hadn't had a hand in the ransom letters by writing the numerals. He and his son were making their final preparations for the upcoming grand jury deliberations in New Jersey.

On Saturday morning, October 6, Captain Lamb showed up at the Bronx courthouse with an eyewitness named Millard Whited.

The tall, gangling logger and part-time farmer had resided on a farm adjoining the Lindbergh property. The shanty in which he and his family had lived was about a mile from the Lindbergh mansion. The illiterate, wide-eyed, thirty-five-year-old had the face of a cadaver and wore a checkered hunting cap that was older than he was.

During the early hours of March 2, 1932, Colonel Lindbergh, Lieutenant Keaten, Trooper Wolf, and Captain Lamb had questioned the residents in the vicinity of the Lindbergh Estate. At three o'clock that morning they had knocked on Whited's door. According to Captain Lamb, Whited told the investigating party that on three occasions prior to the kidnapping he had spotted a strange man near the Lindbergh home. He said he had seen this person on February 18 and again on February 25 and 27. Whited's general description of the man fit Hauptmann.

Nine weeks later, Whited was questioned by Detectives Coar and Leon. Detective Coar asked Whited if he had seen any suspicious persons in the area: "Have you noticed any persons walking through the woods in the vicinity of the Lindbergh home before March 1, 1932—persons acting in a suspicious manner?"

"No, I have not," Whited replied.

"Have you heard anyone holding a conversation about the Lindbergh family or their baby?"

"No, I never did."[12]

Two and a half years later, when Hauptmann was arrested, Whited was on a logging trip in Pennsylvania. He therefore wasn't present at the Greenwich Station when the other eyewitnesses picked Hauptmann out of the lineup. When Whited returned from his trip, Captain Lamb and Corporal Wolf showed him two photographs of Hauptmann. Whited said that Hauptmann was the man he had seen wandering about the Lindbergh Estate in February 1932. At two o'clock in the afternoon, with ten police officers looking on, Whited picked Bruno Hauptmann out of Sheriff Hanley's lineup.[13]

As the only eyewitness who could place Hauptmann near the Lindbergh estate, Whited's testimony would be extremely valuable in New Jersey, where the Hunterdon County authorities were preparing to indict Hauptmann for murder.

While Hauptmann was being picked out of the lineup, his lawyer, unaware of Millard

254 Whited, was in Brooklyn announcing to the press that he had arranged for the services of his own handwriting expert.[14] He also said that he had retained the services of a Manhattan private investigator named William A. Martin.

After Whited picked Hauptmann out of the lineup, the prisoner was taken to Foley's office where he was told that Whited had seen him prowling around the Lindbergh estate shortly before the kidnapping.

"That man is a liar!" Hauptmann screamed. "I was never at the Lindbergh house— never! I will not confess. I am innocent of any crime!"

Foley knew that it would be a waste of time to pursue the issue, so he turned to other business. Arrangements had been made with the press to have Hauptmann and his wife photographed together. When Anna, followed by a crowd of jostling photographers, walked into the office, Hauptmann didn't like what he saw. "I want to go back to jail," he snapped. So back he went, leaving Anna Hauptmann without a visit and the photographers without a subject.

As Anna Hauptmann left the courthouse, she was swamped by reporters who wanted to know, among other things, why she hadn't brought her little boy to visit his father. "He has a bad cold," she said.

"Do you remember where your husband was the night the ransom money was passed?" a reporter asked.

"If I could only remember three years ago everything would be all right," she replied.[15]

That afternoon, Colonel Schwarzkopf called a press conference to announce that on Monday, October 8, a Hunterdon County grand jury would convene to hear evidence that could lead to a murder indictment. He said that twenty-three witnesses would testify against Hauptmann. Among these would be Colonel Lindbergh and the prosecution's newest eyewitness, Millard Whited.

. . . I can't understand why none of the guards will talk to me. I am lonesome and have nothing to read.

—BRUNO RICHARD HAUPTMANN
to his wife

26 AN INDICTMENT IN NEW JERSEY

THE EXTORTION INDICTMENT IN NEW YORK was a device to keep Hauptmann in custody until the authorities in New Jersey were ready to act. Contrary to what he had told the press, Foley had no intention of bringing Hauptmann to trial on the charge. The next step was to extradite him to New Jersey so that he could be brought to trial for murder. But first, the authorities in New Jersey had to indict him.

On October 8, 1934, twenty-three grand jurors were scheduled to meet in the Hunterdon County Courthouse in Flemington, New Jersey. They would decide if there was enough evidence to justify bringing Hauptmann to trial. By law, grand jury proceedings are secret, but it was common knowledge that the Hunterdon County grand jury was about to consider the Lindbergh case. As the twenty men and three women arrived in bunches at the steps of the old courthouse, they were greeted by a crowd of cheering, applauding townspeople.

The attorney general for the State of New Jersey, David T. Wilentz, had named himself chief prosecutor in the case. The district attorney of Hunterdon County would have normally taken the job, but the county couldn't afford the cost of trying Hauptmann. Since the trial would be paid for by the state, the job of prosecutor fell into the hands of the state's attorney general.

David Wilentz was thirty-eight, the father of three children, and a graduate of New York University Law School. When he was a year old, his parents, Russian Jews, brought him to America. He grew up in Perth Amboy, New Jersey, where he now resided. As a leading Democrat in Middlesex County, Wilentz had helped get Gov. A. Harry Moore elected by persuading his Republican friends to vote Democratic. In 1933, a year after he was elected, Moore appointed Wilentz attorney general. Wilentz had never tried a criminal case: The Hauptmann trial would be his first.

Short, thin, and dark, the dapper young prosecutor usually wore an off-white felt hat with half the brim turned down. He was often decked out in a Chesterfield coat and white silk scarf.

Wilentz's chief assistant was Anthony Hauck, Jr., the district attorney of Hunterdon County. Hauck had prosecuted John Hughes Curtis, the Lindbergh hoaxer. The balding thirty-five-year-old wasn't resentful that Wilentz was taking over; Hauck's only aim was to be a loyal, hardworking member of the prosecution team.

The third Hauptmann prosecutor was George K. Large, a Flemington attorney and former judge. A handsome fifty-year-old, he was the only member of the prosecution team from Flemington. Large was highly respected in the community, and most of the grand jurors knew him. The remaining three prosecutors, Joseph Lanigan, Robert Peacock and Richard Stockton III, worked out of the state attorney general's office.

Word had gotten out that Colonel Lindbergh would be in Flemington Monday morning to testify. When he arrived at the courthouse in the company of Colonel Schwarzkopf, he was greeted by a cheering crowd of spectators and newsmen.

After speaking briefly to the grand jury about the case, Wilentz called Colonel Lindbergh to the stand. Lindbergh told the jurors how he and Dr. Condon had driven to St. Raymond's Cemetery on the night of April 2, 1932, to deliver the ransom money.

"And what did you hear that night as you waited in the car while Dr. Condon went off to find the kidnapper?" Wilentz asked.

"I heard a voice," Lindbergh answered.

"Exactly what did you hear, sir?"

"I heard a man call out. He said, 'Hey, Doctor! Here, Doctor! Over here!'"

"Have you heard those words and that voice since that night?"

"I have."

"Would you tell the jurors when, and under what circumstances you heard that voice again?"

"Yes. I heard that voice in District Attorney Foley's office on September 28, 1934."

"Would you tell us, sir, who spoke those words to you on that occasion?"

"Bruno Richard Hauptmann."

The witness was excused.

Colonel Lindbergh was followed to the stand by Colonel Schwarzkopf. Following him, in quick succession were eight of his men, two FBI agents, an IRS man, and three officers from the New York City Police Department.

On Tuesday morning, Dr. Charles Mitchell, the Mercer County physician who was then believed to have performed the baby's autopsy, took the stand. Dr. Mitchell testified that the baby had died from a traumatic blow to the head, a wound received shortly after his abduction. Through the doctor's testimony, Wilentz established that the baby was killed in Hunterdon County—a jurisdictional necessity.

Wilentz had decided to charge Hauptmann with murder instead of kidnapping. Kidnapping in New Jersey carried a sentence of five to thirty years; murder I could bring a sentence of death.[1]

Under New Jersey law, if a death occurred in the commission of a felony, those committing the felony were as responsible for the death as the one who killed the victim. Even if the victim had been killed accidentally, everyone connected with the felony could be convicted of first-degree murder. Under this law, called the felony-murder doctrine, all Wilentz had to prove was that Hauptmann had entered the Lindbergh home to commit a theft and that in the course of this crime he had killed the baby—accidentally or otherwise. (In New Jersey, kidnapping itself was not a felony for purposes of the felony-murder doctrine. Wilentz would have to show that Hauptmann had entered the house to steal something—a crime that was a felony under this doctrine.)

While Dr. Mitchell described the autopsy, three state troopers carried the physical evidence into the courtroom. This included the ransom notes, Hauptmann's known handwriting, the chisel, some of Hauptmann's tools, the kidnap ladder, rail 16, and the floor plank from Hauptmann's attic.

Dr. Mitchell concluded his testimony without revealing that he hadn't touched a knife. If he hadn't broken the letter of the perjury law, he had certainly violated its spirit.

Dr. Mitchell was followed by the Osborns. The handwriting experts said that Hauptmann had written the ransom notes. Arthur Koehler testified that rail 16 had been a floorboard in Hauptmann's attic. And then came the eyewitnesses: Millard Whited, who placed Hauptmann on the Lindbergh grounds a week before the crime; Benjamin Lupica, the college student who had seen Hauptmann's car in the area; and Cecile Barr, the movie cashier who said Hauptmann had given her a ransom bill in November of 1933, long before Hauptmann supposedly got the money from Isidor Fisch.

By 1:30 Tuesday afternoon, Wilentz had presented his case. The grand jury had heard twenty-four witnesses. Although the evidence was circumstantial (there was no confession or witness who had seen the crime), much of it was physical, scientific, and very persuasive. The prosecutor was sure he had made enough of a case to cause an indictment; he didn't have to prove that Hauptmann was guilty, he merely had to show that there was enough evidence to justify a trial.

After deliberating less than thirty minutes, the grand jury voted unanimously to indict Hauptmann for the murder of the Lindbergh baby.

The next day, Wednesday, October 10, the press had three major stories to report: Hauptmann had been indicted for murder; Gov. A. Harry Moore had signed an extradition warrant that was on its way to Gov. Herbert Lehman of New York; and Colonel Lindbergh had testified that it was Hauptmann's voice he had heard that night in St. Raymond's Cemetery.

On October 10, the FBI officially withdrew from the case. In a memo written the next day, J. Edgar Hoover boasted that the bulk of the investigation had been carried out by his agents. He wrote that the New Jersey State Police "would probably find a situation which they could not handle," implying that Schwarzkopf and his men were in over their heads.[2] With the investigative phase of the case winding down, there was no need for the FBI. The case was now in the hands of the prosecutors in New Jersey.

On October 15, the day Hauptmann's extradiction hearing began, Colonel Schwarzkopf received a report from a lawyer, investigator, and private criminalist from Washington, D.C., named Robert W. Hicks. Hicks had conducted a series of experiments that led him to believe that the Lindbergh baby had been killed by a small-caliber bullet. Hicks had made a model skull out of plaster of paris and cement and had filled it with a brain-like solution. When he fired a .25 caliber bullet into the model it produced a wound similar to the baby's.

The criminalist theorized that the quarter-inch hole on the right side of the baby's head, located under his earlobe, hadn't been made by Inspector Walsh's stick, but by a bullet. Hicks figured that if the hole had been caused by a stick, its edges would have been ragged, but the edges of the hole in the baby's skull were smooth, typical of a small-caliber bullet wound. Hicks concluded that a bullet had penetrated the right side of the baby's head, passed through his brain, then came out the other side. The fracture on the left side of the skull, which, according to Dr. Charles Mitchell, was where the baby had been bludgeoned, was in Hicks's opinion an exit wound.[3] Hicks said that the baby might have been shot by the little gun found in Hauptmann's garage.[4]

Colonel Schwarzkopf dismissed Hick's gunshot theory as absurd. Where was the bullet? It wasn't in the baby's head and it hadn't been found at the gravesite. Schwarzkopf couldn't see any reason to challenge the accuracy of Dr. Mitchell's autopsy.[5]

Hauptmann's extradition hearing began on the morning of October 15. The man in charge of the proceeding was Judge Ernest E. L. Hammer.

Hauptmann was the first witness. Wearing the suit he had been arrested in, he took a seat in the leather-cushioned witness chair. Although pale and thin, he looked fresh and alert. He had just gotten a shave and a haircut from the jailhouse barber; his slicked-down hair was still moist and fragrant. He wore a freshly laundered shirt and a blue polka-dot tie. A sparkling white handkerchief shot smartly out of his coat pocket.

Hauptmann sat erect, and although his handcuffs had been removed, he folded his hands on his lap as though they were restrained. He gave no hint of being nervous or even a little apprehensive.

James Fawcett began his direct examination by establishing Hauptmann's alibi for the night of the crime. Speaking in a mildly contemptuous voice, Hauptmann said that on the evening of March 1, a Tuesday, he drove to Fredericksen's bakery-lunchroom at 3815 Dyre Avenue in the Bronx. He arrived there at six o'clock to pick up his wife. After eating dinner at the lunchroom, he and Anna drove back to their apartment on East 222nd Street.

Fawcett asked Hauptmann what he had done earlier in the day. Hauptmann wasn't sure: "Well, I can't exactly remember if I worked for the Majestic Hotel, but as far as I can remember, I took the subway and went down—I don't know if I went down Sixth Avenue looking for a job or I went to the Majestic Hotel."[6]

Fawcett led Hauptmann through the story of the ransom money. He had gotten it, unknowingly, from his friend and business associate, Isidor Fisch. It was given to him in a shoebox just before Christmas of 1933, prior to Fisch's departure for Germany. Hauptmann said that he discovered the bills in August of 1934, about a month before his arrest. He had spent some of it, yes, but he had no idea that it was Lindbergh money. He spent the gold notes because Isidor Fisch had owed him some money. As for the kidnapping, Hauptmann said he had nothing to do with it. He was not "Cemetery John," he was not the writer of the ransom notes, and he was not the person who had built the kidnap ladder. With that, Fawcett turned the witness over to Wilentz for cross-examination.

Wilentz had a variety of courtroom personalities. He could be courteous, gracious, and humble, or he could be brusque, sarcastic and aggressive. With Hauptmann, he started off courteous. He got Hauptmann to reiterate that he wasn't sure how he had spent the day of the crime, then pulled the rug: "Didn't you tell the police that you had been working that day at the Majestic?"

"Yes, I did."

"Why did you tell them that if you didn't know it as a fact?"

"They didn't give me any chance to think at all."

"You could just as well have said, 'I don't know,' couldn't you?"

Moving on to something else, Wilentz asked, "You are a carpenter? Isn't that right?"

"Yes."

"You never built a ladder?"

"Never."

A few questions later Wilentz turned aggressive and in a voice laced with venom asked, "Do you know how to build a ladder?"

"I guess every carpenter does know it."

"And isn't it a little bit unusual that you never built a ladder in all these years that you were a carpenter?"

Fawcett was on his feet objecting—the prosecutor was badgering his witness. Judge Hammer agreed, so Hauptmann didn't have to answer the question.

Wilentz stepped back from the witness chair. "On the occasion of your arrest, you had in your possession a twenty-dollar gold bill, did you not?"

"Yes."

"And you were asked where you got that twenty-dollar bill, were you not?"

"Yes."

"And you replied that the twenty-dollar bill was part of three hundred dollars you had saved up in gold certificates?"

"Yes."

"All right, sir. Why didn't you tell the truth about the twenty-dollar bill?"

"I was trying to hide this money," Hauptmann said.

After Hauptmann told how he had come to America illegally, Wilentz asked, "Were you convicted of any crime in Germany?"

"Yes." A little color came to Hauptmann's face.

"On June 3, 1919, were you convicted of grand larceny in Germany and sentenced to two years?"

"Yes."

"Sixteen days thereafter were you again convicted of a crime of robbery with a gun?"

"Yes."

"In June 1923, did you escape from jail and come to this country?"

Fawcett got to his feet, "Your Honor, I object to this line of questioning. It's immaterial and irrelevant."

"Sustained," the judge intoned.

The cross-examination continued for another forty minutes before Judge Hammer called a recess. Following this break, the questioning continued. Wilentz showed Hauptmann sixteen sheets of paper containing samples of his handwriting. These were the samples Hauptmann had given the police at the Greenwich Station. He identified these writings as well as the writing on the three vehicle registration applications as his. Wilentz was laying the groundwork for the testimony of Albert S. Osborn.[7]

Hauptmann was excused. The initial courtroom confrontation was over. The big battle, Hauptmann's life-and-death encounter with Wilentz, would come later. In the meantime, Hauptmann would lick his wounds and sharpen his story while Wilentz regrouped for another attack.

At three in the afternoon, Mrs. Hauptmann, wearing a black dress and a plain gray hat, took a seat in the witness chair. Fawcett had called her to corroborate her husband's alibi. She looked frightened but spoke out so everyone could hear.

Without getting up from the defense table, Fawcett asked, "Now, do you recollect that the first day of March, 1932 was a Tuesday?"

Clearing her throat, Mrs. Hauptmann answered, "Yes, I remember that."

"And do you remember whether your husband brought you down to the store in the morning of that day?"

"I can't remember if he brought me down, but he usually did bring me down every morning."

A few questions later, Fawcett got to the point: "On the night of March 1, 1932, did your husband call you at the store?"

"Yes he did."

"And take you home?"

"Yes."

"And about what time did he call for you at the store that night?"

"I can't remember exactly the time."

"Well, approximately?"

"Maybe he could be there seven o'clock, maybe six-thirty. I can't remember exactly the time when he came."

Having produced evidence that Hauptmann had not been in New Jersey on the night of the crime, Fawcett turned the witness over to Wilentz.

From his chair at the prosecution table, Wilentz, in his most courteous tone, asked, "Mrs. Hauptmann, you remember March 1 because it was a Tuesday, is that right?"

"Yes."

"And every Tuesday your husband called for you in the evenings?"

"Yes."

"And that is why you remember it?"

"Yes."

"You don't, of course, remember the Tuesday night of March 1 by itself, do you?"

"No, I didn't, I found out later it was on a Tuesday."

Wilentz had no more questions, he had made his point.

The defense called two more people to show that Hauptmann was not in New Jersey on the night of the crime. The witnesses were Mr. and Mrs. Christian Fredericksen, the owners of the bakery-lunchroom. Fawcett tried to get them to say that Hauptmann was in their store that night, but all he got was a feeble, "if it was a Tuesday, then Hauptmann must have called for his wife on the night of March first."

Wilentz called Albert S. Osborn to the stand. The dignified, elderly documents examiner took the chair and said that in his opinion, the ransom note found in the baby's room had been written by Hauptmann. Wilentz focused on the nursery note in order to connect Hauptmann to the scene of the crime.

Referring to this note, Osborn said, "The writing was that of a man who had originally learned to write in German, one who was somewhat illiterate, and also a writer who wrote what is known as the Latin script in an imperfect way."

Osborn called attention to the phrase *"passed red lihgt"* on Hauptmann's 1931 automobile license application, then compared it to the word "rihgt" in one of the ransom notes. Osborn said that Hauptmann spelled "the" as *hte* and formed the letter *X* as two small letter e's. The writer of the ransom letters did likewise. Osborn said that in his fifty years as a questioned-documents examiner he had never seen the letter *X* written that way. When Wilentz said he had no further questions, the expert gave the impression that he had much more to say. His face even dropped when Fawcett declined to cross-examine him.

Wilentz's next witness was Howard Knapp, the assistant treasurer of the Reliance Property Management Company, the firm that owned the Majestic Hotel in Manhattan where Hauptmann had worked as a carpenter. Knapp had brought a payroll timesheet that showed that Hauptmann didn't start work at the site until March 21, 1932. Knapp also brought Hauptmann's $36.67 paycheck, dated March 31, 1932, and covering eleven days of work. Wilentz used Knapp to counter the claim that Hauptmann was working in Manhattan on the day of the crime.

On cross-examination, Fawcett asked Knapp if he had the Majestic Hotel's payroll records for the first part of March 1932. Fawcett wanted to see for himself that Hauptmann didn't work on March first. Knapp replied that his company didn't have the payroll records covering the first half of March. "Our records do not indicate that any such record exists at this time—or at that time either," he said. Fawcett didn't understand. Was Knapp telling him that his company didn't start keeping payroll records until March 21, 1932? Knapp replied that he was telling him just that.

"Surely you don't expect me to believe that?" Fawcett snapped.

"It's the only explanation I have," the witness replied.

Fawcett turned to Wilentz, "I can think of another explanation—does the attorney general have these records?"

Wilentz replied, "I surely don't have them."

The witness was excused.[8]

Wilentz put Cpl. Frank Kelly, the fingerprint man, on the stand. Kelly was followed by Captain Lamb, Lieutenant Keaten, and Detective Leon. After Detective Leon, Wilentz called Millard Whited, his last witness. Before Whited was sworn in, Fawcett asked Judge Hammer to extend the hearing another day so that his handwriting witness, Aaron Lewis, could testify. Fawcett said that Lewis needed time to study the ransom notes and Hauptmann's known handwriting. Judge Hammer granted the request, then adjourned for the day.

The next morning, Judge Hammer advised Fawcett that the court was ready to hear his handwriting witness. Fawcett approached the bench and said that Mr. Lewis was not available. The attorney didn't say why and the judge didn't ask.

Wilentz called Millard Whited, Lindbergh's former neighbor. For the second time in a week, Whited testified that he had seen a strange man near the Lindbergh place a few days before the kidnapping. "Mr. Whited," Wilentz asked, "do you see that man in this courtroom?"

"Yes, sir, I do."

"Would you kindly walk over to this man and place your hand on his shoulder?"

"Yes, sir," Whited said as he rose from the witness chair. He walked to the defense table and touched the defendant lightly on the shoulder. As he walked back to the witness box Hauptmann leaned over and whispered something into Fawcett's ear.

Whited's identification had set the courtroom spectators buzzing, causing Judge Hammer to gavel them silent.

On cross-examination, Fawcett asked Whited if Captain Lamb had promised him some of the Lindbergh reward. Whited said that Lamb hadn't. Fawcett then got Whited to admit that prior to picking Hauptmann out of the lineup, Captain Lamb had shown him two photographs of the suspect.

Fawcett called one of Whited's cousins and two of his neighbors to the stand. When Fawcett asked the cousin, William Geltz, what kind of reputation Millard had, the witness said, "Not much." It took Judge Hammer five minutes to quiet the courtroom. Fawcett asked George J. Lentz, the neighbor, to describe Whited's reputation for honesty. The witness looked at Whited and shouted, "Bad!" The last character witness, an East Amwell Township farmer named William Deal, said that Whited's reputation was "Bad, yes, sir!"

Late in the afternoon, Judge Hammer announced his decision—Hauptmann would be extradited to New Jersey to stand trial for murder.

Fawcett asked that Hauptmann's move to New Jersey be delayed so he could appeal the decision. Judge Hammer said he'd delay the extradition for forty-eight hours.

On Wednesday morning, the day after the extradition hearing, Tom Cassidy, a reporter for the *New York Daily News,* questioned Joseph Furcht, Hauptmann's superintendent about when Hauptmann had worked at the Majestic Hotel. Furcht said that he remembered hiring Hauptmann and another carpenter named Gus Kassens through the Reliance Employment Agency. Furcht said that he had hired Hauptmann on February 27, and to the best of his recollection, he had started to work at the Majestic on March 1, working there from eight in the morning to five at night. Furcht took Cassidy to his office and showed him the files that verified the February hiring date. They could not find, however, any records showing when Hauptmann reported to work at the Majestic Hotel.[9]

The next day, October 18, at the suggestion of the reporter, Furcht called Fawcett and told him when Hauptmann had been hired. Furcht also told Fawcett that Hauptmann had started work on March 1. The lawyer hurried Furcht to a notary public, where the witness signed an affidavit to this effect.

While Fawcett was nailing down Furcht's statement, the *Daily News* published Cassidy's scoop along with two photographs of the records that showed Hauptmann was hired on February 27.

Later that day, Fawcett obtained permission from a judge to use this evidence in his extradition appeal.

Furcht's information had caught the prosecutors off guard. District Attorney Foley told reporters he had never heard of Furcht or the employment agency. Wilentz said that too much was being made of this business, that if Fawcett had introduced this evidence at the extradition hearing, the results would have been the same.

On Friday, a New York Appeals Court upheld Hauptmann's extradition. According to the court, the issue of his alibi was a matter to be resolved at his trial. Meanwhile, the *New York Daily News* carried the headline: "NEW WITNESS SUPPORTS ALIBI OF HAUPTMANN."

At eight o'clock Friday night, Hauptmann was taken from his cell and put into the back seat of a car between Captain Lamb and Lieutenant Keaten. He was going to Flemington. In front of Hauptmann's vehicle were three carloads of policemen, and behind it there were three more. The Hauptmann car was also flanked by a pair of motorcycles.

The seven-car, two-motorcycle caravan crossed the Hudson River and snaked its way through central New Jersey, roaring into Flemington shortly after ten o'clock. The little town was usually in bed by ten, but not tonight. Main Street and the area around the courthouse were brightly lit and teeming with people. At the rear of the courthouse, where the jail was located, flares outlined its roof.

Hauptmann and Captain Lamb, handcuffed together, struggled to get out of the car while the people lining the pathway to the jail strained their necks to get a peek at the famous prisoner. Flashbulbs exploded as Hauptmann, flanked by Lamb and Keaten, walked through the trooper-lined corridor to the jailhouse door. Hauptmann's face was hidden in the shadows of his wide-brim hat.

Sheriff John Curtiss of Hunterdon County greeted the party inside the building. Hauptmann would be his responsibility as long as he was a resident of the Flemington

264 Jail. The forty-eight-year-old sheriff, with a huge belly and round face, had gotten into the habit of distinguishing himself from the Lindbergh hoaxer—his name ended with a pair of s's, he would say.

The sheriff was getting a taste of what it would be like housing such a notorious prisoner. Hundreds of people—lawyers, reporters, photographers, novelists, columnists, professors, psychiatrists, politicians, and out-of-state police administrators had been requesting seats to the trial. They had been sending him letters and had been tying up his telephone. Since the Flemington courtroom held just a few hundred, Sheriff Curtiss had a problem. How would he decide who'd get in and who wouldn't? The upcoming event was already being billed as the trial of the century.

On the second floor, where Hauptmann would be housed, there were five tiny cells, each measuring seven by nine feet. The row of cells opened up to a long, narrow bullpen where the prisoners could mingle, exercise, and see visitors who came to the adjacent hallway on the other side of the bars. A fifty-foot bench ran the length of the bullpen.

The lobby area was perpendicular to the bullpen and the narrow cell range to which access was gained through a sliding prison door.[10]

Hauptmann was placed into cell number 5, the one closest to the lobby. He was assigned the lower bunk and would share the cell with a guard. A second guard would be seated at the table in the lobby and a third occupied cell number 4, the one next to Hauptmann's. The other three cells would remain vacant.

The entire range was brilliantly lit and would stay that way twenty-four hours a day; at no time would Hauptmann be watched by fewer than three guards. Sheriff Curtiss and Colonel Schwarzkopf were making sure that Hauptmann couldn't get a chance to repeat the Bronx County spoon act.

The men guarding Hauptmann, a combination of sheriff's deputies and New Jersey state troopers, were under orders not to converse with him.

The troopers who took turns watching Hauptmann from the adjacent cell had a very special assignment. Allen L. Smith and Trooper Hugo Stockberger were fluent in German and would monitor Hauptmann's activities and conversations with his visitors. They would submit daily reports to Colonel Schwarzkopf.[11] Although these troopers were in uniform and in full view, Hauptmann was not aware that his conversations could be heard and understood.[12]

On Monday morning, Hauptmann was examined by two physicians. He would see these doctors every day for the next four months. Hauptmann complained that he couldn't sleep with his head uncovered—every time he pulled the blanket over his face a guard would uncover him. He said that he couldn't sleep under the lights.

At ten o'clock, Fawcett, Wilentz, and Hauck met with Thomas W. Trenchard, the judge who had presided over the Hunterdon County grand jury hearings and who would sit at Hauptmann's trial. When the meeting broke up Wilentz announced that the trial would begin on January 2, 1935, and that Hauptmann would be arraigned next Wednesday at seven o'clock.

Later in the day, Fawcett announced that Hauptmann would be taking the stand in his own defense. As for the handwriting evidence, Fawcett said that he'd "match expert against expert." Fawcett also declared that he wasn't asking for a change of venue. "We will get a fair trial here," he said.[13]

At two o'clock, Anna Hauptmann came to the jail. "How are you being treated?" she asked.

"Fine, only I can't understand why none of the guards will talk to me. I am lonesome and have nothing to read."

While Hauptmann visited with his wife in Flemington, Fawcett was in Brooklyn huddling with his assistant, Harry Whitney. In Trenton, Wilentz met with Anthony Hauck, Colonel Schwarzkopf, and Captain Lamb. Wilentz said that he was troubled by two things—Joseph Furcht and John Condon. He asked Schwarzkopf to look into the Furcht business. He wanted to know, one way or another, if Hauptmann had been working in Manhattan on March 1, 1932. As for Condon, it was anybody's guess what he would say.

Sometimes I feel fine and other times I feel downhearted.
— BRUNO RICHARD HAUPTMANN
to his wife

27 GEARING UP FOR TRIAL

ON TUESDAY, OCTOBER 23, Lieutenants Keaten and Finn questioned Gus Kassens in Foley's office. Furcht had hired Kassens on February 27, 1932, the day he had hired Hauptmann. Kassens said that he and Hauptmann didn't begin work at the Majestic Hotel until sometime after March 1, 1932.

That afternoon, Keaten and Sergeant Haussling spoke to Joseph Furcht, who said that he had *guessed* that Hauptmann had started work on March 1 because Hauptmann had been hired two days before. Furcht signed a three-page affidavit to this effect.[1]

The next morning, Wilentz had John Condon brought to the Flemington jail to see Hauptmann. Wilentz hoped the confrontation would force the old man into a more positive identification.

Hauptmann was asleep on his cot when Condon took a seat on the long bench in the bullpen. A guard shook Hauptmann awake and led him to the bench, where the prisoner sat down heavily next to his visitor.

With several guards and police officers looking on, Condon broke the ice: "I'm not trying to harm you, John, won't you talk to me a while?"

Hauptmann looked blankly at Condon and shrugged his shoulders.

"I have been hounded, treated like a criminal, and accused," Condon said. "All the time you had the money that I handed you hidden in your garage."[2]

"I didn't know they treated you like that," Hauptmann replied.

"Have you thought about your mother?"

"Oh, yes," Hauptmann said solemnly.

"She does not know what to believe," Condon said. "Her heart would hold more peace if her son would speak, would tell the truth—even though the truth might be ugly. Do you want her to go on suffering, wondering what her boy had done and why he had done it? It would be better to speak now." When Condon reminded Hauptmann of his baby and the duty he owed his son to tell the truth, Hauptmann seemed more confused than moved.

266

An hour later, Condon led Hauptmann to his cell, where they spoke more privately. Shortly after that, the two men shook hands and Condon announced that he was ready to leave.[3]

Condon was driven straight to Wilentz's office for a top-secret conference with the attorney general and his assistants.

"Well," Wilentz asked, "is he the man in the cemetery?"

"I'm still not ready to declare my identification," Condon said. "I will do that at the trial."

"You'll do that right here and now!" Wilentz demanded loudly.

"A man's life is at stake."

"What are you afraid of, Doctor—Hauptmann's accomplices? There aren't any, but if there were, we'd protect you."

"I am not afraid, I just want to be sure. We're dealing with a man's life."

Wilentz jumped to his feet, "I have a mind to toss you in jail. Get him out of here."

As Condon was being driven back to the Bronx, Wilentz composed himself for the press. News of Condon's visit had leaked out, and the hallway outside Wilentz's office was crowded with reporters. Thirty minutes later, Wilentz, exuding confidence and flanked by Hauck and Captain Lamb, appeared in the corridor. When a reporter asked what had happened between Condon and Hauptmann, Wilentz said, "I'm not at liberty to make a statement about the meeting, but you can surmise what you please from the attitude in my office and at State Police Headquarters."[4]

The next day, the *New York Daily News* did just that with the following headline: "JAFSIE DAMNS HAUPTMANN AS RANSOM TAKER."

A few hours after Condon's visit, Hauptmann was taken before Judge Trenchard and arraigned on the murder charge. The defendant pled not guilty and the judge set the trial for January 2, 1935.

That night, under the bright lights, Hauptmann lay on his cot and wept.

As October wore on, the public heard less and less from James Fawcett and more and more from his mysterious assistant, Harry Whitney. Whitney had become the official spokesman for the Hauptmann defense, also functioning as the Hauptmanns' press agent and manager. For a price, Whitney would arrange interviews and photograph opportunities for the press and the newsreel companies, and to raise money for the defense fund, he was considering a vaudeville engagement for Mrs. Hauptmann.

Whitney had found an apartment in Flemington for Mrs. Hauptmann and had orchestrated a highly publicized birthday party for Bubi. Taking advantage of the public's insatiable appetite for news about the Lindbergh principals, Whitney presented the Hauptmanns as a pair of pathetic foreigners who were being mangled by an unfeeling and unjust government machine. At the same time, he was portraying Schwarzkopf and the New Jersey State Police as wicked, conspiratorial, and bungling.

Amid rumors of dissension between Fawcett and his client, the lawyer was struggling with the problem of how to mount a defense, and he still hadn't picked the New Jersey attorneys he'd need to assist him at the trial. Fawcett's problem was this: Hauptmann was maintaining his innocence in the face of evidence that suggested otherwise. Fawcett had raised the question of an insanity defense with Hauptmann and had considered using the spoon incident as a springboard. As an experienced trial attorney, Fawcett knew that he could find several psychiatrists who would testify that Hauptmann was crazy. Of course, the prosecution would find just as many to say that he wasn't—but at least he would have a defense. But Hauptmann wasn't interested in being insane, and he refused to discuss the spoon business. He said he had a defense—he was innocent.

While Fawcett vacillated over his defense strategy, the *New York Journal,* a paper owned by the Hearst Corporation, made Mrs. Hauptmann an interesting proposal. If Mrs. Hauptmann granted the *Journal* the exclusive rights to her story, up to and during the trial, the newspaper would help pay for Edward J. Reilly, the celebrated Brooklyn defense lawyer. This would mean of course that James Fawcett would have to be replaced. Mr. Fawcett was a very sound attorney, but he wasn't flamboyant and he wasn't well known. Mr. Reilly was both.[5]

After conferring with her husband, Mrs. Hauptmann accepted the deal—Fawcett was out and Reilly was in. On November 1, Mrs. Hauptmann went to Fawcett's office to give him the news. It was a jolt to his pride, but he took it well—he respected a defendant's right to select the lawyer he thought would do him the most good. Deep down, Fawcett might have been relieved; it is possible he never believed in Hauptmann's innocence and had no idea how he was going to defend the man.

On November 2, Edward J. Reilly publicly announced that James Fawcett had retired from the case. The fifty-two-year-old lawyer said that he would be taking over as Hauptmann's chief defense attorney.

Reilly was tall, thick-shouldered and florid-faced with a flabby neck that blended in with his chin. He combed his dark, thinning hair straight back. In court, Reilly wore cutaway coats, gray-striped trousers, and white spats. Before stepping into the courtroom he usually stuck a large white carnation into his lapel. Reilly's pince-nez gave him the look of a stern schoolmaster, an appearance that contradicted his ham-actor, sometimes clownish courtroom demeanor.

Although Reilly was only fifty-two, he was already past his prime. Three decades of heavy drinking, hard-living, and continuing domestic upheavals had worn him out. He was still colorful, professionally knowledgeable, and, in many ways, effective and impressive, but he was no longer reliable, and he was becoming more eccentric than flamboyant. Due to a recent string of courtroom defeats, he had picked up the unfortunate nickname "Death House."

At the height of his career, Reilly had another nickname. With over two thousand murder cases under his belt, he was called the "Bull of Brooklyn" and was one of the most successful and best-known trial attorneys in the city. When he was trying a case, young lawyers from all over town would flock to the courthouse to see him perform. He had successfully defended many of Prohibition's better-known gangsters, including the notorious Frankie Yale.

In his prime, Reilly had been a shrewd cross-examiner who quickly sensed a witness's soft spot, then zeroed in for the kill. An emotional man, he was prone to shouting, blustering, bluffing, and weeping. One moment he'd be sobbing pitifully; the next he'd be cold, sarcastic, even cruel. But Reilly's most potent weapon was his ability to appear triumphant in the face of total defeat. He had an uncanny ability to shrug off the most incriminating evidence in a way that would persuade a jury it didn't exist.

The news that Reilly had taken over Hauptmann's defense created considerable fanfare. Standing before a crowd of reporters, popping flashbulbs, and grinding newsreel cameras, Reilly dramatically announced that "a man must be considered innocent until he is proven guilty," proving that he still had the ability to turn a wornout cliche into a profound statement. He concluded his remarks by assuring everyone that he was certain beyond a shadow of doubt that his client was innocent.

On the day he was named to the Hauptmann case, Reilly had his own stationery printed up. For his special Hauptmann trial stationery, he had designed an incredibly tasteless logo. Running down the left-hand margin of the page, in red ink, was a drawing of the kidnap ladder. By doing this, Reilly had connected his client to what was essentially the murder weapon.

Reilly wasted no time in selecting the New Jersey lawyers who would assist him. As his chief assistant, he picked a Flemington attorney named C. Lloyd Fisher, the stocky, nice-looking thirty-eight-year-old who had defended John Hughes Curtis. Although Fisher was a competent attorney, he didn't have much experience in trying criminal cases, so Reilly didn't foresee a major role for him in the courtroom. When examining witnesses, Fisher asked relevant and pointed questions, but he was often tactless and had a tendency to lose his temper and become unduly sarcastic.

The second assistant was Frederick A. Pope, a short, bespectacled, square-faced lawyer from Somerville, New Jersey. Pope was a country lawyer about Reilly's age, with considerable legal experience. He was an outdoorsman who enjoyed woodworking, and as such was particularly interested in Arthur Koehler's work in the case. In court, Pope tended to be overly talkative and a little pompous. When objecting to an opponent's question, he would often become lost in his own rhetoric, and when overruled, he'd give the impression that the judge was wrong.

The final member of the defense team was Egbert Rosecrans of Blairstown, New Jersey. The forty-two-year-old Rosecrans had a chiseled, oblong face, a prominent nose, and narrow eyes. Always impeccably dressed, he had the bearing and look of an aristocrat. Reilly had brought Rosecrans into the case as an authority on consitutional law; therefore most of the motions would be drafted by him. In court, Rosecrans was formal and emotionless, but he would get angry when a reporter misspelled his name.

While the defense lawyers were getting organized, Wilentz was still chipping away at Hauptmann's alibi. On November 8, Lieutenant Finn and Corporal Horn questioned Edward Francis Morton, the timekeeper at the Majestic Hotel where Hauptmann had worked as a carpenter. Morton said his records showed that Hauptmann had started work on March 21, 1932, and on April 2, a Saturday (the day the ransom was paid) he didn't show up for work. Hauptmann was off on the third, a Sunday, then came back on Monday, which was his last day on the job.[6]

With the trial date fast approaching, there was a frantic demand for temporary living quarters in Flemington. The Union Hotel across from the courthouse, with only fifty rooms, could only accommodate a fraction of the reporters, radio broadcasters, witnesses, cameramen, columnists, photographers, and general spectators who'd be coming to town. One New York newspaper, in arranging to house and feed its reporters, special writers, and telegraph operators, had leased the local country club. Many of the local residents were becoming amateur innkeepers, and the reporters who couldn't find a car or empty pool table to sleep on would be driving back and forth between New York City and Flemington—a round trip of 120 miles.

In the midst of the scramble for quarters, Reilly announced to Lloyd Fisher that he was dissatisfied with his room at the Union Hotel. He needed more privacy, he said. Fisher responded by talking an old college friend and his wife into offering Reilly one of their bedrooms—free of course.

A few days later, Reilly's new hosts were awakened in the middle of the night by their doorbell. When they answered the call, they found themselves face to face with a tall, gorgeous young blonde wrapped in a mink coat. The young woman announced that she was there to take dictation. In case there was any doubt, she held up her notebook. During the next month and throughout the trial, Reilly would spend most of his evenings dictating to a bevy of secretaries. He also consumed a large quantity of liquor.

Wilentz was confident. Three truckloads of physical evidence, documents and courtroom exhibits had been shipped to Flemington from Trenton and New York City. The experts had filed their reports, and the witnesses were subpoenaed and ready.[7]

There had been only a handful of murder trials in Flemington's history. The first homicide in Hunterdon County took place in 1828. The defendant in that case was a black man accused of killing his employer. He was found guilty and hanged. One hundred and seven years later, the stately two-and-a-half story white stucco courthouse with its four Greek columns was about to become the site of what H. L. Mencken called the "biggest story since the Resurrection."

By New Year's Day, Flemington was swamped with seven hundred reporters, thousands of sightseers, and hundreds of communications technicians. Also in town for the big show were movie stars, big-time novelists, celebrity columnists, and famous radio commentators. Mingling with the common folk on Main Street and on the porch of the Union Hotel were people like Walter Winchell, Edna Ferber, Arthur Brisbane, Fannie Hurst, Damon Runyon, Kathleen Norris, Alexander Woollcott, Adela Rodgers St. John, Ford Madox Ford, Jack Benny, and Clifton Webb.

And there were the hucksters—the street entrepreneurs. One young vendor was selling models of the kidnap ladder, while another youngster sold locks of the "Lindbergh baby's hair." Sales were so brisk, the blond-headed boy was getting bald. Autographed photographs of Colonel and Mrs. Lindbergh were selling fast.

The carnival-like sounds from the streets filtered into Hauptmann's brightly lit cell. Lieutenant Smith, in his guard report for New Year's Day, remarked:

> The prisoner exhibited considerable nervousness in the last twenty-four hours. After starting to eat his supper he suddenly pushed same aside and commenced pacing cell. The prisoner has spent most of his waking hours for the last day and a half pacing up and down the bull pen. His reading has been confined to short periods, then the pacing would resume. He also has a worried expression.[8]

I have held the belief all along that the defendant would have as fair a trial in Flemington as he could get anywhere in the world.

— E D W A R D   J .   R E I L L Y

28 THE PROSECUTION BEGINS

ON A COLD BUT SUNNY JANUARY 2, the first day of the Hauptmann trial, the Hunterdon County Courthouse was packed with 150 prospective jurors, 100 reporters, 50 cameramen, 25 communications technicians, prosecution and defense lawyers, dozens of Lindbergh case investigators, 30 miscellaneous police and court officials, and 300 or so spectators who had fought their way into the courtroom. Outside, several hundred spectators were crowded on the courthouse steps and blocking traffic on Main Street. Countless faces, red from the cold, were mashed against the glass of the big courthouse windows, in the hope of seeing someone famous.[1]

The rush for courtroom seats had begun at nine that morning, when the courthouse doors were opened. Although reporters and trial officials had been issued tickets of admission, the public was seated on a first come, first serve basis.

Shortly before ten o'clock, the prosecution lawyers took their seats around the table nearest the jury box. A few minutes later, Reilly and his assistants sat down at the defense table.

The chief defense attorney was formally attired in his dark gray morning coat and gray striped trousers. One of Reilly's assistants, Frederick Pope, was also quite formal in his black swallow-tailed coat. The rest of the defense lawyers as well as Wilentz and his associates were dressed in business suits.

Shortly after ten o'clock, the court crier officially opened the trial with the familiar, "Oyez! Oyez! Oyez!" The crier brought the crowd to its feet by announcing the coming of the Honorable Thomas W. Trenchard of Trenton, New Jersey. The calm, white-haired judge in his flowing black robe emerged from his chambers and climbed the steps to his place at the bench.

After twenty-eight years on the bench, the seventy-one-year old jurist had built a reputation as a wise, patient, and compassionate judge. Lawyers who had practiced be-

272

fore him knew that Trenchard was a very considerate and courteous man who, in criminal cases, bent over backward for the defense. At times he seemed almost obsessed with the comfort and health of his lawyers and jurors, assuming the role of a benevolent patriarch. He had been known to make surprise visits to the jurors' living quarters to make certain they were comfortable, and if it were raining or snowing and the judge heard that a juror didn't have an umbrella, raincoat, or boots, he would see to the problem at once. A lawyer couldn't cough in the courtroom without the proceeding being stopped while the judge rummaged through his desk for a throat lozenge.

As soon as Judge Trenchard had settled into his high-backed chair, Hauptmann, followed by Deputy Sheriff Hovey Low and a New Jersey state trooper, entered the room through the door the judge had used. Anna Hauptmann smiled at Bruno, but he didn't see her as he walked slowly across the front of the courtroom. Hauptmann stopped at the defense table and said something to Reilly; then, with a faint smile on his lips, he slumped into a chair just inside the railing that separated the front of the courtroom from the spectators' benches. Hauptmann must have taken the wrong chair, because Hovey Low, with a look of exasperation, poked him on the arm and pointed to an adjoining seat. Hauptmann jumped to his feet and reseated himself at the appropriate place, while the two policemen sat down in the chairs on each side of him.

Obviously aware that he was the center of attention, Hauptmann sat erect and still in his oversized, double-breasted suit. Lloyd Fisher turned around in his chair at the defense table and shook Hauptmann's hand; the other defense lawyers greeted him with smiles and nods.

From her seat in the balcony, Kathleen Norris, the popular novelist, got her first look at the prisoner. She wrote:

> Bruno Richard Hauptmann in the flesh was a surprise to me; his entrance into the court was a surprise. Somehow one expects the suspected man still to be dragged into the court in the medieval manner; haggard, protesting, even in chains.
> . . . of Hauptmann we see a slender back with fine wide shoulders, a sleek head, a gray-brown suit. . . . we see the impressive face, not heavy or beastial, as so many of the pictures have made it; rather thin with deep-set eyes, wide forehead, and to my thinking at least, a stupid expression.[2]

When Colonel Lindbergh strode through the door, the spectators' heads swung from the defendant to the victim the way people watch a tennis match. If Hauptmann hadn't averted his eyes, he would have noticed that Lindbergh had carefully kept from looking at him. Wearing a lightweight gray suit, Lindbergh, flanked by Colonel Schwarzkopf and Hunterdon County Detective William Rittenhouse, was seated between the railing and the prosecution table. Wilentz spun around and greeted Lindbergh with a smile and a handshake.

Judge Trenchard, speaking loudly in order to be heard over the banging radiators and courtroom murmurings, ordered Sheriff Curtiss to draw 48 names from the box containing the names of 150 prospective jurors.

274   Wilentz dismissed the first potential juror, an elderly woman, because she said she opposed the death sentence. This woman was followed to the witness chair by a young farmhand who astonished everyone by declaring that he had never heard of the Lindbergh case or of Hauptmann. He was also dismissed.

Reilly rejected several would-be jurors who said they had been influenced by the radio commentaries and columns of Walter Winchell, the syndicated columnist for the *New York Daily Mirror.* Relying on information supplied by secret sources within the New York City Police Department and the FBI (Winchell and J. Edgar Hoover were close friends), Winchell had already tried and convicted Hauptmann. Since his writings and broadcasts reached everywhere, a change of venue was useless.

A few weeks earlier, someone had mailed 150 copies of a pamphlet entitled *No. 2310, Criminal File: Exposed! Aviator's Baby Was Never Kidnapped Or Murdered* to the homes of the members of the original Hauptmann jury panel. The booklet, a work of fiction with characters named Colonel Schweartupf and Elizabeth Gah, had been written in 1932 by a Chicago lawyer named Mary Belle Spencer. Spencer's story was predicated on the idea that instead of being kidnapped and murdered, the Lindbergh baby had wandered off on his own, gotten lost in the woods on Mt. Rose Heights, and was killed by wild animals. Since the book was absurd on its face and didn't in any way prejudice Hauptmann, it was simply ignored.[3]

The first prospective juror acceptable to both sides was a forty-year-old machinist from High Ridge named Charles A. Walton. A small, unsmiling former semiprofessional baseball player, he was, as the first juror picked, the foreman. Married and the father of two grown sons and a nine-year-old daughter, Walton was known to be fair but rigid once he had made up his mind.

The second juror selected was Mrs. Rosie Pill, a two-hundred-pound widow from Califon. Forty-five and the mother of a teenage son, Mrs. Pill looked overheated in her plain felt hat and heavy, full-length coat with a large fur collar. Mrs. Pill's full, friendly face seemed too large for the dark-rimmed, perfectly round eyeglasses perched on her tiny nose.

The next juror, another large woman in a bulky overcoat, was the 265-pound Verna Snyder, the thirty-six-year-old wife of a Centreville blacksmith. She told Wilentz that she wasn't sure how she felt about the death penalty but thought she could decide the case on the evidence. Wilentz replied that he couldn't ask for anything more than that.

Charles F. Snyder, no relation to Verna, a forty-seven-year-old farmer from Clinton Township, was the fourth juror to be picked. Fascinated if not spellbound by his closeness to the defendant, Snyder, a thin man with a grim face, never took his eyes off Hauptmann. Wilentz wondered how Snyder would have reacted had Hauptmann made a move toward him.

The next juror, Ethel Stockton, a legal stenographer in the offices of a former Hunterdon County district attorney, was a thirty-two-year-old brunette. She was married to a Patenburg machinist and the mother of a seven-year-old boy. When she took the stand her face was ghost white, but after a few questions she was able to flash the smile and display the dimples that would cause a reporter to call her the "Beauty in the Box." The most photographed and written-about juror, she was to become the darling of the press.

Juror number six was Elmer Smith, a nice-looking, smiling forty-two-year-old insurance salesman from Lambertville. Married and the father of a three-year-old boy, Smith was the most urbane member of the jury. With his slicked down hair parted in the middle and his friendly, open face, Smith looked like a man you'd buy insurance from.

Next came the youngest juror, Robert Cravatt, a twenty-eight-year-old high school teacher and recreation director at the High Bridge Civilian Conservation Corps Camp. Rather studious and somewhat stuffy, Cravatt was a bachelor who lived at home with his parents. The fact that he had been picked as a Lindbergh juror seemed to have depressed him.

Philip Hockenbury, a forty-eight-year-old truck driver for the Central Railroad of New Jersey, was juror number eight. The tall and tan father of three was from Annandale, New Jersey. He was as skinny as a stick and had a frosty white moustache that gave him an air of distinction.

George Voorhees, from Clinton Township, was the second farmer selected to the jury. Fifty-four and the father of three children, the tall, curly-haired Voorhees was a reclusive man who was uncomfortable in the limelight. He raised race horses on his farm.

The tenth and final juror to be picked that day was Mrs. Mary F. Brelsford, a thirty-eight-year-old mother of two, and the only juror from Flemington. The chubby, bespectacled electrician's wife was one of the town's busiest civic leaders and known for her hard work and efficiency.

Late in the afternoon, Judge Trenchard instructed two deputy sheriffs to escort the jurors to their quarters across the street on the third floor of the Union Hotel. Before filing out of the courtroom, the jurors were instructed not to discuss the case with outsiders, read about it in the press, or listen to news of it on the radio.

As the last juror disappeared through the door, the judge signaled Hovey Low and the state trooper to take the defendant back to his cell. With Hauptmann out of the room and en route to the jail, Judge Trenchard brought the first day to a close.

Outside the courthouse, Reilly spoke to reporters: "The jurors chosen were entirely satisfactory to the defense. I have held the belief all along that the defendant would have as fair a trial in Flemington as he could get anywhere in the world."[4]

In the Bronx, John Condon told a group of newsmen that he would be going to Flemington soon. He called his upcoming testimony a "dreadful ordeal" but said that it was a civic duty he had to perform. Condon said that if Hauptmann named his accomplices, he [Condon] would see President Franklin Roosevelt personally about clemency.[5]

When Wilentz read Condon's remarks he bit his cigar in two.

In spite of the elaborate communications system that had been installed to disseminate news of the trial, the worldwide interest in the case was so heavy that more equipment had to be brought in. Western Union, for example, had installed a special teletype printer that transmitted directly to London.

Every newspaper in the country carried a full account of the first day. Writing for the

New York Times, Kathleen Norris described Wilentz as "self-possessed, poised and brilliant." She wrote that Reilly "looks as if a magnificent priest might have been lost to the church when he turned to law."[6] The *Times* profiled the newly picked jurors individually, then characterized them as a group of middle-aged, hard-working, family people.

The next morning, January 3, the crowd outside the courthouse was even larger than the day before. A law student from Atlantic City had spent the night in the lobby of the Union Hotel. At six in the morning he got in line on the courthouse steps and three hours later, chilled to the bone, was among the throng that got inside the courtroom before the doors were closed.

There were two more jurors to be picked, so the questioning of potential jury members continued. The eleventh person to be seated in the jury box was Howard V. Biggs, a fifty-five-year-old unemployed bookkeeper from Annandale. Married and the father of two, Biggs was a frail man with a pinched face and quick, furtive gestures.

The last member to be named to the jury was Liscom C. Case, a retired carpenter and farm owner from Hamden. A widower without children, Case, at age sixty-two, was the oldest juror. When he told the court that he suffered from a chronic heart problem, a look of concern crossed Judge Trenchard's face.

When the hundred or so unpicked prospective jurors were dismissed from the courtroom, Sheriff Curtiss decided to let in a few more spectators to take their seats, but when one of his deputies opened the double doors, he was almost trampled. Several officers got the doors closed again, but before they did, 275 people had forced their way in. People were squeezed together on the benches, jammed in the aisles, lined up against the walls, perched in the window recesses, and packed into the balcony.

Wilentz rose to make his opening statement after Judge Trenchard announced that he was ready to hear the prosecution's case. The attorney general walked around the front of the prosecution table and approached the jury box. "This is my first criminal case," he said. "I came here because it was my duty as attorney general, not because I wanted to prosecute a man for murder."

Wilentz said that he would prove, by irrefutable evidence, that Hauptmann had kidnapped and murdered the Lindbergh baby, written the ransom notes, and received the money from John Condon.

The courtroom fell silent as Wilentz, in a lowered, dramatic voice, said that Hauptmann had parked his car on Featherbed Lane, then carried his homemade ladder to the southeast corner of the house. The jury sat spellbound as Wilentz described how Hauptmann, carrying a burlap bag, had climbed up the ladder into the baby's room. "Then as he went out the window," Wilentz said with a pained look on his face, "and down that ladder of his, the ladder broke! He had more weight going down than he had when he was coming up. And down he went with this child. In the commission of that burglary, the child was instantaneously killed when it received that first blow. It received a horrible fracture, the dimensions of which when you hear about it will convince you that death was instantaneous."

As Wilentz spoke to the jury, Anna Hauptmann kept an eye on her husband. Sitting there, Bruno looked bored and detached, like the last man in a dentist's waiting room. Anne Lindbergh sat frozen in her chair with her legs crossed, her hands folded on her knee and her eyes cast downward.

Wilentz continued: "Getting down there he took the ladder and about seventy feet away the load was too heavy. In the one hand he had the ladder and in the other he had this bundle, this dead package to him. The ladder was of no particular use to him. He abandoned that. Then he proceeded on his way until he had gotten about a half mile. The child was dead. Knowing it was dead, he wasn't a bit concerned about it and there, three thousand or more feet away and still on the Lindbergh estate, he yanked and ripped the sleeping garment of that child off its body. Though it was cold and raw, he yanked and ripped that sleeping garment off that child, because he didn't need the child, and we will show you, he needed the sleeping garment.

"Then, of course, at the very first convenient spot, some few miles away, he scooped up a hastily improvised and shallow grave and put the child in face downwards and went on his way to complete the rest of his plans in this horrible criminal endeavor."

Wilentz described the scene in the Lindbergh house following Betty Gow's discovery of the empty crib, then skipped to the finding of the infant corpse ten weeks later on Mount Rose Heights.

". . . pretty soon Colonel Lindbergh and Betty Gow and others had turned that body of that child face up, face up. The moisture in the ground had still preserved the face a little bit, so that it was white when it was turned up, and twenty minutes after the air struck it, it had turned black. (Wilentz was a little off his facts here—Colonel Lindbergh and Betty Gow didn't view the corpse at the gravesite, they saw it at the morgue.)

Wilentz was in total command; he had the jurors hanging on every word. Every so often Charles Snyder, the farmer from Clinton Township, would tear himself away from Wilentz to steal a look at Hauptmann. Wilentz was now describing the baby's corpse: "It was horribly decomposed; one leg had been eaten away and carried away, one hand had been taken away, a great part of its body had been eaten away, the rest of it decomposed, the skin, the flesh, rotted away, in that hole, that grave that Hauptmann had placed for it."

Wilentz had finally gotten to Hauptmann. The defendant jerked his head to one side then folded his arms across his chest. Colonel Lindbergh noticed that his wife's hands were trembling on her knee. Several of the jurors shifted uneasily in their chairs while Reilly took off his glasses and mopped his forehead with a handkerchief.

Wilentz assured the jurors that the corpse on Mount Rose Heights was baby Lindbergh's:

> . . . there was that little sleeping suit that Betty Gow had prepared and that Mrs. Lindbergh had helped her prepare that day; there was the forehead and the . . . curls and the . . . prominent forehead under the blond hair; there was that typical nose, and there were the toes overlapping, the overlapping toes of the Lindbergh child.
>
> Anybody that knew that child, any member of the family, would know right away that was the 'Little Eagle' and so of course they took the child and cremated the body and the ashes were delivered to Colonel Lindbergh.

278   Wilentz told the jury how the license number penciled on the ten-dollar ransom bill had led to Hauptmann's arrest, described the ransom cache found in his garage, and declared that a piece of the kidnap ladder had come from his attic.

Wilentz was coming to the end of his speech and was now talking softly. "We will be asking you to impose the death penalty, it is the only suitable punishment in this case. Thank you." [7]

As Wilentz returned to his chair, a few spectators, forgetting where they were, instinctively started to applaud. Judge Trenchard gaveled them back to reality.

The moment Wilentz sat down, Reilly got to his feet, "If your honor please," he said, "I move for a mistrial on the grounds that the impassioned appeal of the attorney general was not a proper opening. It was a summation intended to inflame the minds of this jury against this defendant before the trial starts."

Judge Trenchard denied the motion.

Reilly wasn't finished: "I ask now, most respectfully sir, that you will charge the jury at this time that the opening of the attorney general is merely what he intends to prove, that their minds are not to be prejudiced at this time, but they are to keep their minds free and open until the last word of this case."

"I suppose the jury already understands that," the judge replied. "Of course the jurors will keep their minds open until the last word has been said in this courtroom."

"May I make an exception to Your Honor's denial?" Reilly asked.

"An exception to what?" Trenchard replied. He couldn't see the point in the defense attorney's objection.

"I move for a mistrial . . . and Your Honor denied the motion at that time."

"I will give you an exception." [8]

Wilentz's first witness was Walter E. Roberts, a civil engineer and surveyor. Using several large maps, Roberts testified that the Lindbergh home was located in Hunterdon County, 870 feet from the Mercer County line. Roberts had been called to establish the court's jurisdiction over the crime.

The Lindberghs and the Schwarzkopfs were luncheon guests at the home of George Large, the local attorney on Wilentz's staff. Mrs. Lindbergh was too nervous to eat; in an hour or so she would be on the stand, a moment she had been dreading for months.

Back at the courthouse, the media people and the spectators waited. No one dared leave the courtroom for fear of losing their place.

Everybody was wondering how Mrs. Lindbergh would hold up under Reilly's cross-examination, and it was well-known that the Colonel carried a gun. It was rumored that if the "Bull of Brooklyn's" questions got too personal, Lindbergh would shoot him where he stood.

> I have an awful lot of questions to ask Colonel Lindbergh. . . .
>
> — E D W A R D   J .   R E I L L Y

29 THE LINDBERGHS TESTIFY

AFTER LUNCH, when the principals returned to the courtroom, Anna Hauptmann was given a seat at the defense table next to Lloyd Fisher. Bruno greeted her with a smile when he walked into the room. After the defendant was seated, Fisher turned in his chair and engaged him in a spirited conversation. Hauptmann appeared animated as he made a point by tapping his finger against Fisher's chest.

Judge Trenchard brought the afternoon session to order amid the sounds of the crowd outside and the noise in the room. The talking and rustling abruptly stopped when Wilentz called Anne Lindbergh to the stand. She hurried to the witness chair and sat down before the bailiff could administer the oath. When she realized what she had done, she stepped from the stand to be sworn in. She was smartly attired in a blue silk suit and black satin beret. Sitting perfectly straight with her legs crossed, she fixed her gaze on Wilentz, who was standing at his chair.

Wilentz, in his most gentle tone and manner, asked Mrs. Lindbergh to relate what she had done on the afternoon of March 1 up to the moment Betty Gow reached into the empty crib. Speaking clearly but without emotion, Mrs. Lindbergh retraced her activities on that day. After she had described the baby, Wilentz handed her a photograph of him, which she identified.

Wilentz next handed her, piece by piece, the various items of clothing her child had been wearing on the night he was kidnapped. She held each garment on her lap, fingering them gently and thoughtfully before identifying them. As she handled the two undershirts found on the corpse and the Dr. Denton sleeping suit delivered to Dr. Condon's house, Colonel Lindbergh looked on intently. The two heavy ladies in the jury box were on the verge of tears.

"You haven't seen that child since the first of March, 1932, have you?" Wilentz asked.

"No."

"And when it was realized that the child was missing, did you join with Colonel Lindbergh in an appeal to the person who had the child for its return?"

"What do you mean by that?"

"Did you make a statement asking the person who had your child to return it?"

"I joined with my husband."

When Wilentz asked Mrs. Lindbergh to describe the baby's bedclothing, she said that the blankets had been undisturbed and still secured to the mattress by the two large safety pins. She said there was a hole or pocket where the baby's body had been.

Wilentz asked a few more questions, then turned his witness over to Reilly for cross-examination, the part she had been dreading the most. The courtroom was perfectly still as he got to his feet.

"The defense feels that the grief of Mrs. Lindbergh needs no cross-examination," Reilly said in his most dramatic voice. He then sat down.

Virtually leaping out of the witness chair, Mrs. Lindbergh gave Reilly a grateful glance as she hurried back to her place in the courtroom next to Mrs. Schwarzkopf.

It was time for Colonel Lindbergh. When Wilentz called his name, the aviator eased his way clear of those sitting around him and strode to the witness box. Wearing a rumpled gray suit and blue tie, Lindbergh took the oath and seated himself in the witness box. He crossed his legs and rested his elbows on the arms of the witness chair. His hands were folded on his knee and he was bent slightly forward from the waist.

Wilentz began his direct examination by asking Lindbergh to tell the jury what had happened on the night of the kidnapping. Speaking confidently and in a manner that sounded a little rehearsed, Lindbergh said that at nine o'clock he heard what he thought was the slat of an orange box falling off a chair in the kitchen. About an hour later, when he was in his den, Miss Gow called to him in an excited voice and asked if he had the baby. He replied that he did not, then rushed to the nursery where he saw the empty crib.

Wilentz handed the nursery note to Lindbergh and asked him if this was the document he had found in the baby's room. The Colonel said that it was. The prosecutor took the ransom note from Lindbergh, then read it out loud to the jury, emphasizing the misspelled words by speaking them the way they had been written. When he got to the Germanic parts of the note, Wilentz spoke in a heavy German accent.

Wilentz led the witness through testimony already covered by Mrs. Lindbergh, then brought him to the morning after the crime: "I take it there was considerable confusion and walking in and about the premises?"

"Well, there was; and while the press was there, there was a great deal of walking around outside the house by the press, which was absolutely out of control as far as the vicinity was concerned."

"I suppose that included the taking of pictures and flashlights and things of that kind?"

"Yes, and walking around the house on the loose ground there."

"And during all that time you were doing what, Colonel?"

"During the first period I was around the house trying to familiarize the officials with what had happened."

"And go ahead, Colonel," Wilentz prompted.

"Later in the evening and during the early hours of the morning I was out on different parts, different places in the vicinity of the house with the group of police officers, visiting other houses."

At 4:30, Colonel Lindbergh was still on the stand, and since Wilentz wasn't close to finishing, Judge Trenchard decided to adjourn for the day. The judge thought the jury looked tired, and Wilentz could just as easily continue his direct examination in the morning. Judge Trenchard was pleased with the pace of the trial. In just two days he had seen a jury picked, the prosecution's opening speech, and three witnesses.

That night, over radio station WNEW in Trenton, Reilly declared that the Lindbergh crime had been an inside job committed by five people whose identities he'd rather not disclose. He said the baby hadn't been taken out a window and down a ladder, but had been brought to the first floor of the house by a member of the Lindbergh staff and handed to someone at the front door. Tomorrow he'd prove that the so-called ladder indentations in the mud beneath the baby's window were phony. "I have an awful lot of questions to ask Colonel Lindbergh, an awful lot of things I want answers to—an awful lot of questions," he said.

The jurors were quartered in eight rooms on the third floor of the Union Hotel where a partition had been placed across the corridor to segregate this area from the rest of the hotel. Before the jurors turned in for the night, they were taken on a closely supervised stroll up and down Main Street. The man in charge of the mile and a half walk was Odin Baggstrom, a police officer from Three Bridges. Judge Trenchard had made it clear that he wanted the jurors to get plenty of exercise during the trial.

The next morning, Wilentz resumed his direct examination of Colonel Lindbergh. "On the night of April 2, 1932, when you were in the vicinity of St. Raymond's Cemetery and prior to delivering the money to Dr. Condon, you heard a voice hollering, 'Hey, Doctor'?" I think. Since that time have you heard the same voice?"

"Yes, I have."

"Whose voice was it, Colonel, that you heard in the vicinity of St. Raymond's Cemetery that night, saying, 'Hey, Doctor'?"

"That was Hauptmann's voice," Lindbergh replied matter-of-factly.

Hauptmann straightened himself in his chair amid the commotion created by Lindbergh's identification. Anna turned around in her chair at the defense table to give him a reassuring smile, while Judge Trenchard banged his gavel to quiet the spectators. Lloyd Fisher was frantically taking notes.

Wilentz took Lindbergh through his identification of the baby's remains at Greenleaf's Funeral Parlor in Trenton and turned him over to the defense.

Reilly had a tough assignment; he had to poke holes in Lindbergh's testimony by testing his credibility, memory, and objectivity—without being disrespectful. He had to keep in mind that his witness was an international hero and a revered member of the community.

There was tension and electricity in the room as Reilly walked around the defense table to address Lindbergh. Judge Trenchard felt the excitement himself, but unlike the newsmen and most of the spectators, he hadn't heard the rumor about Reilly getting shot if he pushed too hard. The judge was therefore confused when Reilly asked Lindbergh if he was a police officer.

"No," the Colonel answered.

"Are you armed, Colonel?"

"No, I am not armed," Lindbergh said. He opened his suit jacket to show that he wasn't. Lindbergh had carried his gun the day before, but on this day, having been warned that Reilly might ask him this question, he had left his gun at home.[1]

Wilentz looked on in amazement as Reilly, in a bizarre line of questioning, suggested that Lindbergh's neighbors had kidnapped the baby because Lindbergh, in building his estate, had cut off access to their favorite hunting ground. Lindbergh replied that as far as he knew, none of his neighbors had been denied access to the forest because of his estate.

Wilentz couldn't believe what he was hearing—this fast-talking dandy from Brooklyn was standing before a jury of rural New Jersey residents and suggesting that some of their neighbors had kidnapped and murdered the Lindbergh baby. Lloyd Fisher, a local man himself, turned to the defendant to see how he was taking all of this. Hauptmann returned his glance and smiled.

Reilly charged ahead by pointing the finger of guilt at the Lindberghs' servants. "From what employment agency did you get the Whateleys?" he asked.

"I don't recall the name of the agency."

"What investigation did you make of Whateley before you hired him as your butler to take into your home?" (Oliver Whateley had died in 1933.)

"I talked to him."

"Beyond that, did you go any further?"

"Beyond that, I never go any further."

"You didn't know anything about his background?"

"I think that might have been looked into. Personally, I simply talked to Mr. and Mrs. Whateley for half an hour or an hour."

"The next person in the house on the night of the kidnapping was Miss Gow?"

"Yes."

"You say you obtained her services from somebody that you knew in the neighborhood?"

"She was recommended to us by one of the people who was working at Englewood in the Morrow home."

"Did you make any effort to learn her background?"

"I personally only talked to her. Mrs. Lindbergh may have looked into her background."

"Since then had you learned that Betty Gow had a brother who was in trouble in the state of New Jersey?"

"No."

"Have you learned that she has a brother in Canada?"

"I am not sure she has a brother at all." (Miss Gow did have two brothers, but neither one of them had ever been out of Scotland.)

"At the time of this kidnapping did you not want to find out the antecedents and backgrounds of everybody in the house?"

"That was thoroughly done by the police."

"By you?"

"I placed my confidence in the police organizations."

"Did you not make any effort as a father to find out the background of the people that were in the house the night your child was snatched away?"

Reilly was really pushing his luck—he was accusing the Colonel of being a negligent father. Wilentz looked at Judge Trenchard and thought he saw a scowl.

He then asked a series of questions about the family dog, implying that he hadn't barked that night because the kidnappers were not strangers.

Reilly next started laying the groundwork for his theory about a Lindbergh servant bringing the baby to an accomplice at the front door. "Colonel," he asked, "while you were in the dining room, if the front doorway of your home was opened by someone, anyone could have gone up the stairway of your house and taken the baby out of the crib, couldn't they?"

"I don't think so."

"It would have been physically possible, would it not?"

"I think it would be very improbable that could be done without our hearing it."

"Never mind whether it would be improbable or not, would it be physically possible?"

"I don't think so."

"Why?" Reilly asked.

"The door did not open easily. I don't think it could have been possible for someone to come in through that door without our knowing it."

"Then would it be possible," Reilly asked, "for someone in the house to take the baby out of the crib and bring it down the main stairs?"

"Answering your question directly, it might have been possible."

"If there was disloyalty in your home, would it be possible for a person acquainted with the home to take the baby out of the crib and descend the servants' staircase and hand it to someone in the yard while you were dining?"

"It would have been possible for someone in the house to take the baby out of the crib, as far as I know."

Leaving no stone unturned, Reilly brought up the subject of John Condon, implying that he too had something to do with the kidnapping. "Didn't you think it was strange that a man from the Bronx, a man you did not know, should call you up and tell you that he had a note with a symbol on it?" Reilly looked at the jury with a self-satisfied expression then realized, to his dismay, that none of the jurors were watching him. They were all looking at Colonel Lindbergh, and several of them seemed concerned.

"Not under those conditions, no; something like that had to happen," Lindbergh replied.

"When you contacted Rosner, did you give him a copy of the symbol?"

284   "No, I didn't, no, I don't know whether he had one or not. As a matter of fact, my recollection is that he had seen the symbol."

"He had seen it?" Reilly asked, again looking at the jury.

"That is my recollection at this time."

"Did it strike you as peculiar that an ad would be watched for and immediately answered by the kidnappers if it came from the *Bronx News*?"

Lindbergh replied, "Well, we considered all of those situations, but we also realized that after this circumstance had originally happened the sequence of the events would probably be peculiar, not according to the ordinary logic of life." The Colonel had been prepared for that one.

"Did it ever strike you that the master mind might insert an ad in the paper and answer it himself?"

"I think that is inconceivable from practically any practical standpoint."

"You think it is?" Reilly asked in feigned surprise.

"As a matter of fact, I tried to consider it with every individual who has been connected in any way with the case, exempting no one, whether there was any connection."

A few days later, in a letter to her mother-in-law, Anne Lindbergh boasted about her husband's courtroom performance: ". . . He was a wonderful witness—as he would be—natural, perfectly clear, and of course sure of the truth of his statements, which withstood any test of cross-examination. In fact, he made such a positive impression of integrity in the courthouse that one reporter remarked, 'I think *Reilly* withstood the cross-examination very well.'"[2]

Wilentz called his fourth witness, Charles E. Williamson of the Hopewell Police Department. Williamson took the stand and said that he had seen two indentations in the ground under the nursery window, impressions that matched up to the feet of the homemade ladder found seventy-five feet from the house.

Elsie Whateley took the stand and, over Reilly's strenuous objections, aroused the jury's sympathy by discussing, quite tenderly, the baby's playfulness on the day of the kidnapping. Then, in a calm and unemotional manner, she described how she, Mrs. Lindbergh, and Betty Gow searched the house while Colonel Lindbergh and her husband went outdoors to look for the kidnappers. She said that she and Betty Gow didn't get to bed until four that morning, while Mrs. Lindbergh stayed up all night.

On cross-examination, Reilly tried but failed to get Mrs. Whateley to admit that her husband had known Dr. Condon before the kidnapping. Reilly next tried to get the witness to say that she was well acquainted with Violet Sharpe. Mrs. Whateley replied that she knew Violet, but not very well. Reilly said that he was finished with the witness. Since it was late in the afternoon, Judge Trenchard adjourned for the weekend.

On Friday night, after Hauptmann had been returned to his cell, Lieutenant Smith made the following notation in his Guard Detail Report: "The prisoner appears more nervous as the trial progresses, and upon being returned to his cell, paces the bullpen continually."[3]

That weekend, with sixty thousand sightseers in town, Flemington was transformed into a theme park, the theme being the Hauptmann trial. With Sheriff John Curtiss and his deputies conducting tours, the main attractions were the jail that housed the prisoner, the Union Hotel, the home of the Hauptmann jurors and dozens of famous journalists, and the courthouse.

The courtroom was open to the public, and excited tourists waited their turn to sit in the chair marked "Lindy." A few of the bolder ones accepted the challenge of sitting in the defendant's chair. If one didn't mind waiting in line several hours, there was the thrill of having your photograph taken in Judge Trenchard's place. One souvenir hunter tried to steal the hundred-year-old witness chair, and another sightseer was caught carving his initials into the judge's bench.[4]

The newsmen in town were putting out a million words a day over 168 newly installed telephone lines—a communications network big enough to serve a city of a million. This was the largest telephone system ever set up to cover a news event.

On Monday morning, the fourth day of the trial, the prosecution called Betty Gow to the stand. Betty had sailed from Scotland under the name Bessie Galloway, arriving in New York City on Christmas Day. She had been staying at the Morrow estate.

Wilentz asked Betty to describe the events leading up to the kidnapping. He handed her a piece of flannel that she identified as the leftover cloth from the sleeveless undershirt she had made for the baby. Betty showed the jury how the remnant and the undershirt from the Mt. Rose gravesite fit together as one. She also identified the soiled, store-bought T-shirt and the sleeping suit that had been sent to Dr. Condon.

Wilentz concluded his examination by having Betty tell how she had identified the baby at the morgue. He thanked her and announced that Reilly had agreed to stipulate that the Lindbergh baby had been a normal and healthy child.

The mental and physical condition of the Lindbergh baby had become an issue shortly after the kidnapping, when rumors surfaced that the baby was physically deformed and retarded. A few weeks later, a Hearst reporter named Laura Vitray published a book called *The Great Lindbergh Hullaballo: An Unorthodox Account,* in which she theorized that the Lindberghs had orchestrated the kidnapping to remove a family embarrassment.[5]

As he began his cross-examination of Betty Gow, Reilly was extraordinarily polite, but he quickly turned aggressive and menacing as he badgered her about her former jobs, friends, and places of residence. Through his questions, Reilly was implying that Betty and some of her allegedly unsavory friends had been accomplices in the crime. Wilentz objected, and after a heated argument, Judge Trenchard ruled Reilly's questions irrelevant.

Reilly asked Betty about the phone call she had received from Red Johnson on the night of the kidnapping.

"Now, you certainly knew, did you not, that when Mrs. Lindbergh recalled you to Hopewell to take care of the sick child that you would not be able to keep any engagement with Red Johnson that night, didn't you?"

"I did know that."

"Why didn't you phone him then?"

"I did call the house; he wasn't there. I left a message where he could find me, that I had gone down to Hopewell."

"Now just what was the exact time that Red Johnson phoned you?"

"I should say, about eight-thirty."

"How long did you talk to him?"

"Oh, not more than five minutes."

Reilly's cross-examination seemed futile and without direction. Other than to harass the witness and to raise vague doubts about her character, his questions were purposeless. In his next line of questioning, he accused her of planting the baby's thumbguard on the driveway where she and Elsie Whateley had found it during a walk. Following an argument with Wilentz over the thumbguard questions, Reilly showed Betty photographs of three members of the notorious Purple Gang of Detroit and asked if she knew any of them. She said she did not. She also denied visiting Violet Sharpe on a yacht owned by Dr. Condon.

Reilly had no more questions, so Betty Gow was excused. As she walked back to her seat she fainted, but she was quickly revived and helped to her chair. Judge Trenchard, obviously worried about the witness, regarded Reilly with a sneer.[6]

Corporal Joseph Wolf of the New Jersey State Police took the stand and said that he had been one of the first officers to get to the Lindbergh house. He saw the ladder marks and the large footprint in the mud. He had compared the foot impression with his own shoe and guessed it to be a size nine or larger.

Under cross-examination, Wolf admitted that he should have measured the shoeprint more precisely. The officer had to admit that he didn't know if the print was a left or right shoe. His face was flushed when he stepped from the witness box.

Wolf was followed to the stand by Lt. Lewis J. Bornmann. Bornmann had arrived at the Lindbergh estate shortly after Wolf and had examined the ladder before it was taken into the house. Wilentz had Bornmann describe the ladder, then asked him if the ladder in the courtroom was the one he had seen lying seventy-five feet from the house. Bornmann said that it was, and Wilentz offered it into evidence.

Reilly jumped to his feet and objected, asserting the prosecution hadn't proven that the ladder had anything to do with the crime. Moreover, the ladder in the courtroom had been substantially altered since its recovery from the crime scene. It had been handled by many people and completely disassembled, tagged, and put back together again.

Judge Trenchard said that he'd make a ruling on the admissability of the ladder later and told Wilentz to make certain he'd be able to establish its chain of custody. The Judge said he would want to know who had handled the ladder, what they had done with it, and when they had it.

Lieutenant Bornmann was turned over to Reilly for cross-examination. Reilly went right to the throat: "What size shoe did the butler wear?"

"I never questioned him as to that," Bornmann said.

"Wasn't everybody in the house that night, with the exception of Colonel Lindbergh and his wife, under suspicion?"

"Naturally, they were."

"And you didn't measure the butler's shoe?" Reilly shouted. He looked at the jury to emphasize the question.

"I did not, no."

"Why?"

"Because the butler said he had not been outside that night."

"And you took his word for that?" Reilly screamed.

"Yes," Bornmann replied, glaring at the defense attorney.

"You came to the conclusion, didn't you, as a detective, that something had stood in the ground where there were two holes?"

"I did."

"You wanted to know whose footprint it was?"

"Naturally."

"You knew it wasn't the Colonel's, didn't you?"

"I knew it was none of the men that were there that night."

Having done his best to make Bornmann look ridiculous and incompetent, Reilly said he was finished with him. He plopped down heavily onto his chair while Bornmann, making no effort to hide his dislike of the defense attorney, stepped from the stand.[7]

Wilentz called Sgt. Frank Kelly, the fingerprint man and crime scene photographer, to the stand. Kelly related what he had done at the Lindbergh house that night, describing the nursery in great detail. He summarized his background and experience as a fingerprint man, then said that he hadn't found any latent prints in the baby's room, on the ransom note, or on the ladder. His crime-scene photographs were then admitted into evidence.

Wilentz turned the witness over to the defense, but before Reilly could get up to question him, Judge Trenchard brought the session to a close. It had been a busy Monday; nine witnesses had testified.

Wilentz was pleased. He felt that the first four days of the trial had gone well. Except for Troopers Wolf and Bornmann, all of his witnesses had been impressive. As for Reilly, he hadn't come off well against Colonel Lindbergh and the servants. His inside-job innuendoes were already wearing thin.

Shortly after Hauptmann was put into his cell he was visited by the county physician. (During the noon recess, Hauptmann had told one of the guards that he was suffering from a very bad cold.) The doctor looked at Hauptmann and proclaimed that there was nothing wrong with him except for a slightly dry and scratchy throat.[8]

Although things were going well for the prosecution, Wilentz had a few loose ends that were troubling him. He still had to get the ladder into evidence, and Condon's day in court was fast approaching.

In my experience I have never known a case where the witnesses
were so intelligent and impressive.

— D A V I D   T .   W I L E N T Z

30 JAFSIE AND THE POLICE WITNESSES

ON TUESDAY, JANUARY 8, the fifth day of the trial, Sergeant Kelly was back on the stand. Wilentz asked him a few questions, then turned him over to Reilly. Reilly wanted to portray the Lindbergh investigators, particularly the New Jersey officers, as bunglers. In his booming, ham-actor voice, Reilly asked, "Mr. Kelly, how much experience have you had in taking fingerprints?"

"Six years," Kelly replied without looking at his questioner.

"Where did you study?"

"While I have been in the department," the witness said, wiping the palms of his hands on his trousers.

"Under whom did you study?"

"I studied under Sergeant Jastrom, and I studied myself from various books that I have picked up."

"Various books? I see," Reilly said. "Do you use the Bertillon Method?"

"No, I use the Henry system. It is just as good."[1]

"Have you ever *heard* of the Bertillon system?"

"No," Kelly replied.

"Never heard of it?" Reilly asked in a voice full of shock and indignation. He looked at the jury as if to say, My God! This man is incompetent!

"No sir, I've never heard of it," Kelly answered weakly. Since Alphonse Bertillon's system of criminal identification didn't involve fingerprints, it is not surprising that Kelly didn't employ the method. Had Kelly been formally educated, he would have known of Bertillon and could have embarrassed Reilly.

Confident that he was making Kelly look bad, Reilly wanted to know why Kelly hadn't measured and taken a cast of the footprint beneath the baby's window. Becoming evasive and openly hostile, Kelly said that he thought Detective De Gaetano was doing that. The

288

witness volunteered that he had photographed the impression. Rolling back his eyes in a gesture of disgust, Reilly dismissed the fingerprint man, who glared at him as he stepped from the stand. Reilly acknowledged Kelly's stare with an expression of feigned surprise. Several of the jurors looked a little uncomfortable; they probably couldn't decide which they disliked most, a show off lawyer or an unprofessional police witness.

Detective Nuncio De Gaetano took the stand and covered much of the previous crime scene testimony. On cross-examination, Reilly tried to show how badly the New Jersey detective had botched his job. Referring to the large footprint under the window, Reilly asked, "Did you ever measure it with a tape?"

"No, sir."

"You have estimated that the impression was twelve inches long. Is that correct?"

"Yes sir."

"And you come by that accurately by laying your flashlight next to it?"

"Yes sir."

"Accurately?"

"Well, I had a five-cell Eveready flashlight, and that is fourteen and a half inches long. I measured it with the flashlight."

"Well then, you are giving us your best guess, isn't that it?"

"Yes, sir, just about it."

"And you don't know whose footprint it is, do you?"

"No sir, I don't."

Reilly indicated that he was finished with the witness and sauntered triumphantly back to the defense table. He was certain that the jury had been shocked by De Gaetano's unprofessionalism.

Reilly was making the police witnesses look bad, so Wilentz shifted gears and called Amandus Hochmuth, the frail, eighty-seven-year-old witness who lived on the corner of the Mercer County highway and Featherbed Lane, the road that led to the Lindbergh Estate. The old man sat erect in the witness chair with his hands folded on his lap. Hochmuth told the jury that on the morning of March 1, 1932, he saw a man in a green car with a ladder in it turn the corner in front of his house and proceed down Featherbed Lane toward the Lindbergh estate. Hochmuth said that the man in the car glared at him as he passed by. "And the man that you saw looking out of that automobile glaring at you, is he in this room?" Wilentz asked.

"Yes."

"Where is he?"

"Alongside the trooper there," Hochmuth said, pointing a trembling finger in Hauptmann's direction. As the old man had raised his arm to point, the courtroom lights went out.

"It's the Lord's wrath over a lying witness," Reilly boomed from the semidarkness. The remark brought down the house and infuriated Judge Trenchard, who had to restore order in a darkened courtroom.

When the lights popped on a few minutes later, Wilentz asked Hochmuth to go to the man he had seen in the green car. The witness stepped carefully from the chair, hobbled over to Hauptmann, then touched him on the knee. As he did so, Hauptmann shook his head, then leaned toward his wife and in German said, "The old one is crazy."

The prosecutor asked Hochmuth a few more questions in an effort to shore up his identification, then released him to Reilly.

Wilentz had caught Reilly off guard. The defense had been expecting Condon, not an eyewitness who placed Hauptmann near the Lindbergh house on the day of the crime. Although he wasn't prepared, Reilly realized that it was essential that he destroy this witness.

Before Wilentz got back to his chair, he said, "You say you are how old?"

"I am in my eighty-seventh year."

"Are you nearsighted or farsighted?"

"My eyes are all right."

"I didn't ask you that, mister," Reilly roared. "You are wearing glasses. Why do you wear glasses then—to see better?"

"At a distance, yes."

Referring to the man in the green car, Reilly asked, "How was he dressed?"

"Well, I think he had a dark shirt on."

"You think he had a dark shirt on?"

"You see, all I took in was the face and those glaring eyes."

Reilly could tell that Hochmuth wasn't going to budge, and since there was no use picking on an old man, he dismissed him.

Wilentz next brought Captain Lamb to the stand to round out the kidnap ladder's chain of custody up until the time the captain had turned it over to Arthur Koehler. Wilentz had already traced the ladder's custody from Lieutenant Bornmann to Sergeant Kelly, who had released it to Captain Lamb.

Arthur Koehler followed Captain Lamb to the stand and through him Wilentz offered the ladder into evidence. Reilly objected once again, on the grounds that the ladder had been altered and in the hands of people not identified by the prosecution. Speaking for the defense, Frederick Pope said, "There is absolutely no connection either by circumstance or by direct evidence between this ladder and the accused."

Judge Trenchard summoned Wilentz and Pope to the bench, "For the moment," he said, "I will defer the admission of this ladder in evidence." Having lost another skirmish over the ladder, Wilentz pulled Koehler off the stand and called Lt. John Sweeney of the Newark Police Department. Sweeney told the jury that on the day after the crime, when he had placed two sections of the homemade ladder against the Lindbergh house, the top of the ladder came to rest on two rubbed-off patches on the wall next to the baby's window, where splinters of wood were sticking to the stone. The legs of the ladder fit into a pair of indentations in the mud beneath the marks on the wall. Using one of Colonel Lindbergh's ladders, Sweeney, a man the size of the defendant, climbed in and out of the window several times.

When he concluded his examination, Wilentz was satisfied that he had established that the ladder found at the scene had been used by the kidnapper to gain entrance into the nursery.

Sweeney, aware that Reilly had a knack of turning cops into fools, braced himself as the attorney approached the witness chair. Reilly began his cross-examination by getting him to relate, in great detail, how he had gotten from the ladder into the baby's room, pointing out, time after time, that the job had required two hands. Reilly then forced Sweeney into admitting, much to his embarrassment, that the experiments had been conducted with the shutters open and the window up. If Sweeney had found it necessary to use both arms under these circumstances, how did the kidnapper manage it with the window and the shutters closed? Before Sweeney could answer, Reilly asked, "Did the trooper hold the ladder for you when you went up?"

"No, sir," Sweeney replied amid the laughter.

Reilly ridiculed Sweeney's experiment further by bringing out the fact that Sweeney hadn't climbed down the ladder with a bundle in his arms and hadn't carried the home-made ladder and the bundle to the place where the ladder was found seventy-five feet from the house.

Following a brief re-direct, which did little to revive the deflated officer, Sweeney was dismissed.

At the defense table, Fisher and Pope were smiling and congratulating each other— Reilly had made a fool out of another police witness.

Wilentz called Joseph Perrone to the stand. The cab driver with the slicked-down hair and delicate facial features climbed into the chair and said that on March 12, 1932, he had been given an envelope to deliver to Dr. Condon. Wilentz asked, "Who is the man that gave you that envelope?"

"Bruno Richard Hauptmann."

"Is he in the room?"

"Yes, sir."

"Come down and point him out, please."

The witness walked over to Hauptmann and placed a hand on his shoulder. "This is the man," he said.

"You're a liar," Hauptmann hissed. As Perrone walked back to the witness box, Lloyd Fisher turned around and said something to the defendant that made him smile.

When Wilentz released Perrone to Reilly, the witness, having been interrupted dozens of times by Reilly's objections, was a bundle of nerves. He responded to the defense attorney's questions in a whisper, and when he spoke he covered his mouth. Reilly had the witness thoroughly intimidated and seemed to relish attacking him. "You are on relief, aren't you?" he asked in a pompous tone.

"Yes, sir."

"You have a job with the CWA?"

"Yes."

"And you are living in the state troopers' barracks in West Trenton?"

"Yes, sir."

"Don't you know you secured your position with the CWA through the influence of people connected with this case?"

"No, sir, I didn't know that."

Reilly continued to badger Perrone, ridiculing his testimony, and implying that he had been bought and paid for by the prosecution. Reilly never let up on Perrone, beating him further and further into the ground.[2] When Reilly finally gave up, he hadn't gained a thing except to make everyone in the courtroom despise him for being a sadistic bully. Attorneys Fisher and Pope were no longer smiling, in fact, they looked rather grim.

The last four witnesses of the day were James J. O'Brien, another cab driver who had delivered a ransom message; Milton Gaglio and Max Rosenhain, the men who had accompanied Condon to Hopewell the night Jafsie was made an intermediary; and Al Reich, Condon's friend and the man who drove him to the Woodlawn Cemetery rendezvous. All gave accounts of their roles in the case.

At 4:30, in the middle of Wilentz's direct examination of Reich, Judge Trenchard adjourned for the day.

The next morning, as Al Reich testified, Judge Trenchard had to interrupt the examination several times to silence the spectators who were anticipating the Condon-Reilly confrontation, billed as the battle of the blustering bulls.

Reilly concluded his cross-examination of Reich, and the stage was set for Condon.

Jafsie walked slowly to the witness chair and solemnly took the oath. Wilentz placed a glass of water on the bench next to him. "I thank you," Condon said. "I don't need it yet."

When Wilentz asked the witness to state his age, Condon, fully aware that all eyes were on him, proudly announced that he was seventy-four and a lifelong resident of the Bronx—"The most beautiful borough in the world."

Lloyd Fisher brought down the house when, objecting to the witness stating an opinion, said, "Flemington, sir, is the most beautiful place in the world."

Condon told the jury that he had received a bachelor of arts from the College of the City of New York in 1882, a master of arts degree from Fordham University, and a doctor of pedagogy from New York University. He then launched into a lengthy explanation of why he deserved to be called "Doctor." Wilentz had to interrupt him to ask what he had done before he retired in 1932. Rather than stating simply that he had been a public school teacher, Condon began his life story, and when it became clear that he would go on indefinitely, Wilentz cut him off by asking how he and Colonel Lindbergh had happened to be at St. Raymond's Cemetery on the night of April 2, 1932. "Did you meet a man there?" Wilentz asked.

"I did."

"Did you have with you sometime or other that night a box of money?"

"The Colonel had the box of money with an extra package besides."

"Did you give some money in a box that night?"

"I did."

With great deliberation, Wilentz asked, "Who did you give that money to?" The moment of truth was finally at hand.

"I gave the money to John," Condon said.

"And who is John?"

"John is *Bruno Richard Hauptmann.*" Wilentz turned to the jury to make sure they had caught the significance of Condon's answer. This was hardly necessary—the courtroom was buzzing and dozens of news messengers were scrambling out of their chairs. Judge Trenchard was trying to restore order. Anna Hauptmann looked at her husband with obvious concern, and Lloyd Fisher reached back and grabbed the defendant by the shoulder. Hauptmann seemed dazed.

With the all-important identification out of the way and in the bank, Wilentz asked Condon to tell the jury how he happened to become the Lindbergh go-between. Following his explanation of that, Condon gave a full account of his meeting with John in Van Cortlandt Park. When he finished, Wilentz asked, "Who was this man in the park?"

"John," Condon replied. "John is Bruno Richard Hauptmann."

During the next hour, Wilentz took Condon through a step by step account of the ransom negotiations that led up to the payoff in St. Raymond's Cemetery. Wilentz read all of the ransom letters and the Jafsie ads to.the jury, then introduced them into evidence.

Condon recited the description of "Cemetery John" he had given the police after the ransom payoff and was handed over to Reilly for cross-examination.

This was the moment everyone had been waiting for, the thunderous clash of egos. According to rumors, Reilly had uncovered some dark secrets about Condon's past. Reilly, trying to appear at ease, asked Condon if he had taught schoolboys how to box. Always eager to talk about himself and to pontificate, Condon lectured the court on how to train athletes, the various weight classifications in boxing, and the Marquis of Queensberry rules.

"What am I, a heavyweight?" Reilly asked.

"You are a heavyweight? May I look?" Condon stepped from the witness chair and felt Reilly's bicep. "Am I hurting you?" he asked.

"No, not a particle," Reilly replied.

"Undoubtedly a heavyweight," Condon said as he settled back into the witness chair. The courtroom filled with laughter.

"And I take it you yourself are a heavyweight?"

"Yes."

"So we start even," Reilly said.

"Right—that is, physically," Condon quipped causing another round of laughter. Somewhat outdone, Reilly asked, "You're not angry?"

"Not a particle," Condon replied, again there was laughter.

When the giggling died down, Reilly asked, "Do you remember being in a town called Taunton [Massachusetts]?"

"Yes."

"Did you have a conversation with a druggist?"

"Yes."

"And did you at that time tell him you had not yet discovered 'John'?"

"No sir."

"And didn't you say to the druggist at that time, 'they haven't caught John yet; I'd give ten thousand dollars to find him'?"

"Finished?" Condon asked.

"Yes."

"No such thing," Condon snapped, shamelessly playing to the crowd that had burst into another round of laughter.

Reilly wasn't amused, "You make extravagant remarks, don't you?"

"No, sir."

"You are enjoying your day here before these people, your first day in court that you ever testified; you are enjoying it, aren't you?"

"No, sir, I feel sad over it." The courtroom suddenly grew quiet.

"Why, haven't you been preparing for weeks for this day in court by giving out statements to the press about what you were going to do to the cross-examiner?"

"I will tell you, because I found insidious snares in every single place that I went, in order to trap me and make fun of me and ridicule me and they haven't succeeded."

"Did the druggist in Taunton ridicule you?"

"He did not."

"What was his name?"

"I don't know."

"Well, would you know it if you heard it?"

"I would."

"Donegan?"

"That is the name."

Wilentz rose to his feet, "Just a minute. I have a letter from that gentleman which I would like to show to Mr. Reilly. Maybe it will help him in his examination."

"I don't want any assistance, Mr. Attorney General," Reilly bellowed.

"If Your Honor please," Wilentz said, "I present to the court an unsolicited letter from Mr. Donegan." (In his letter, Mr. Donegan denied that Condon had made any such remarks about "John.")

"Now I object to this—I object to it," Reilly screamed, his face turning red. "If this keeps up I move for a mistrial."

"I will withdraw the offer," Wilentz said with a smile. He had accomplished his purpose.

Wilentz's retreat didn't satisfy Lloyd Fisher. "Make the motion anyway," he said to Reilly.

"I move now for a mistrial," Reilly boomed. "I will ask Mr. Pope to argue the question of law."

Mr. Pope stood up and addressed the bench, "I don't think it needs any argument, your honor. The attorney general's announcement was so manifestly out of order, unfair, and prejudicial to the rights of this defendant that it requires no argument."

"Have you finished?" Judge Trenchard asked.

"Yes, sir."

"I will deny the motion but caution the jury to completely disregard everything about Mr. Wilentz's letter."

"You never once told any newspaperman that this defendant was John, did you?"

"Oh, I never did. I never mentioned his name to them. I made a distinction between *identification* and *declaration of identification.*"

"In other words, am I to understand that you split hairs in words?"

"No hairs at all. A man's life is at stake and I want to be honest about it."

"In the Greenwich Police Station, you said he was not the man, did you not?"

"No, sir. Get all the people that were there, I did not."

"You never said it was the man?"

"I never said it was or was not."

"Because you know you are not sure?"

"Because I make the distinction between declaration and identification. The identification meant what I knew mentally; the declaration meant what I said to others. There isn't a man who breathes has ever heard me say that that was the man."

"You were brought there for the purpose of identifying Hauptmann?"

"I was, yes sir."

"And you didn't identify him, did you?"

"No, sir. Beg pardon, there is that word *identification* again. When you begin to divide the identification and declaration and denial, you make it appear as though I were dishonest and I am not." Condon looked up at Judge Trenchard. "Is that too severe, Judge?"

Trying not to smile, the judge replied, "No."

"Come on, I can take it," Reilly said.

"That is good," Condon replied, again setting off the spectators. When the room quieted, Condon reiterated his identification–declaration of identification distinction.

"Do you know Judge Hammer in the Bronx?" Reilly asked.

"Very well, but I wasn't before him."

"Well, the State didn't call you, did they?"

Condon didn't respond. He seemed lost for words.

"Neither New York State nor Jersey called you, did they?"

"No."

"When Bruno Richard Hauptmann was on trial for extradition only two or three months ago, and you, with the secret locked in your heart—you were not called, were you?"

"Only by the jury—"

"I am talking about the extradition proceedings. Were you called?"

"No."

Through his next series of questions, Reilly wanted to cast doubt on Condon's motives for offering his services as an intermediary. "Why did you pick a local Bronx borough paper with a circulation of 150,000 with all of New York's six million people to insert your ad?"

"Because those papers all led to one poor miserable fellow that I thought was innocent. His name was Arthur "Red" Johnson."

Reilly pounded away for another hour. At 4:30 Judge Trenchard asked him if he were near the end of his cross-examination. Reilly said that he wasn't, so the judge adjourned for the day.

The next morning, Reilly had Condon tell of his March 12 meeting with Cemetery John on the Van Cortlandt Park bench. The questioning then got around to some remarks Reilly claimed Condon had made to various people about the kidnapping. Condon denied making any of these statements. Reilly's attack was losing its punch; he was now repeating himself and the jury was getting bored. As Reilly lost momentum, Condon became more confident, at times almost condescending. Just before noon, Reilly gave up and sat down. Following a few questions by Wilentz, Condon stepped triumphantly from the witness box with his eyes directed toward Hauptmann. Since the defendant was looking away, the two men did not exchange glances.

Following the noon recess, Wilentz called to the stand Henry Breckinridge, whose testimony about the ransom negotiations was mostly repetitious.

At five o'clock, Judge Trenchard brought the seventh day of the trial to a close. With Condon's testimony out of the way, Wilentz breathed a sigh of relief. Outside the courthouse, when confronted by the press, the prosecutor had this to say about his witnesses: "In my experience I have never known a case where the witnesses were so intelligent and impressive." He then said the following about a man he had once threatened to toss into jail: "It should be a source of great satisfaction to the thousands of people who have known Dr. Condon for years that the testimony has shown his only intention was to aid society and partly to aid Colonel and Mrs. Lindbergh. It would be well for some people to reflect before they direct ridicule at this man, or any other person, merely because of his age."[3]

Although he still hadn't gotten the ladder into evidence, Wilentz was pleased with the way things were going. The defense attorney's clumsy and shrill attempts to implicate Condon and the Lindbergh servants had backfired. Tomorrow, Wilentz was bringing out his handwriting experts.

> I wasn't present when Washington crossed the Delaware,
> but I've a pretty good idea he got over to the Jersey side.
>
> —*Handwriting expert Harry M. Cassidy when asked if he was present when*
> *Hauptmann gave his handwriting samples at the Greenwich Station*

31 THE HANDWRITING WITNESSES

ON FRIDAY MORNING, the eighth day of the trial, Agent Frank Wilson of the IRS Intelligence Unit took the stand and testified that he had directed the preparation of the $70,000 ransom package. Wilson said that after the ransom had been paid, the government printed and disseminated over 250,000 circulars containing the ransom bill list. The witness identified $14,600 in gold certificates, the bills taken from Hauptmann's garage as Lindbergh money. He said that since Hauptmann's arrest, not a single ransom bill had turned up.

Wilson's lengthy cross-examination was handled by Lloyd Fisher, whose questioning lacked direction and produced nothing interesting.

Colonel Schwarzkopf, dressed smartly in a well-fitting, well-pressed business suit, took the oath before identifying two handwriting specimens as being Hauptmann's. Questioned by George Large, Schwarzkopf said Hauptmann had voluntarily written the two samples at the dictation of Insp. John Lyons. Schwarzkopf made it clear that the spelling in the specimens was Hauptmann's and not the result of how the police had dictated the words to him.

On cross-examination, Fisher asked, "Were any promises made to Hauptmann in order to get him to do this writing?"

"No, sir."

"Was he threatened in order to compel him to do the writing?"

"No, sir. It was explained to him that we wanted a specimen of his handwriting and he willingly gave it to us."

Judge Trenchard leaned forward in his chair, "Now, Mr. Fisher, do you desire to present any proof upon the question of the voluntary or the involuntary character of this act of writing?"

"Not at this time, sir," Fisher replied. "I have no further questions for the witness."

Colonel Schwarzkopf stepped down and Wilentz introduced more handwriting documents, bringing the total number of handwriting exhibits to forty-five. Included in this material were the fifteen ransom notes, nine automobile registration applications containing Hauptmann's writing and signature, one insurance application bearing his signature, a promissory note written and signed by him, and seven of Albert Osborn's paragraphs dictated to Hauptmann at the Greenwich Police Station. Also included were six miscellaneous specimens of Hauptmann's handwriting and handprinting obtained that night and six of his notebooks and ledgers. Hauptmann's conceded writings, that is, the material written by him under natural conditions between 1931 and 1933, consisted of eleven signatures and hundreds of other words.

Having set the stage for the handwriting experts, Wilentz, following the noon recess, called Albert S. Osborn to the stand. The seventy-four-year-old expert was a tall, heavily built man with white hair and a white moustache. He was partly bald, had a large ruddy face, and wore small rimless eye glasses. In his dark suit and bright red necktie, he walked to the stand slowly, with his shoulders slightly stooped. Questioned by Joseph Lanigan, Osborn testified in the loud voice of a man who had trouble hearing.

Sounding like a learned college professor, Osborn presented a lengthy lecture on the science of handwriting identification. Using a large chart containing several enlarged photographs of key words from Hauptmann's known writings and the ransom notes, he pointed out numerous similarities between the two sets of words.[1]

After two hours of testimony, the jurors were showing signs of boredom. Sensing this, Lanigan prodded Osborn into a concise conclusion that Hauptmann had written all of the ransom notes.

As Osborn testified, the officers flanking Hauptmann noticed that his breathing had become labored. Trooper Smith thought that he detected a look of fear in the defendant's eyes.

At 4:30, before Albert Osborn had completed his testimony, Judge Trenchard, himself a little bored, adjourned for the weekend.

Aware of how badly his client had been hurt by Osborn's testimony, Reilly, in speaking to newsmen outside the courthouse, implied that Osborn's age had somehow impaired his judgment. Frederick Pope told reporters, "We can pick him [Osborn] up on his own words. There are many points to show that the old man was mistaken. The State seems to have some stuff which might possibly connect the defendant with extortion, but Osborn's testimony has many discrepancies." Pope went on to call Osborn's courtroom performance a "wonderfully tiresome lecture."

Standing nearby, Lloyd Fisher angrily corrected Pope by stating that as far as the defense was concerned, Hauptmann had no connection whatsoever with the extortion or any other aspect of the crime.

At 9:30 that night, Hauptmann was visited briefly by Fisher and Rosecrans. The prisoner retired at eleven but lay awake on his cot until two in the morning.[2] The next day the *New York Times* carried the following front-page headline: "EXPERT SAYS HAUPTMANN WROTE ALL RANSOM NOTES." The paper published, on four complete pages, the entire text of Osborn's testimony, including a photograph of his word charts.[3]

That Saturday, Reilly announced that he would be meeting in Trenton with eight handwriting experts who disagreed with Albert Osborn. Although he had already spent twelve thousand dollars of his own money on the case, Reilly said he had paid for the experts' travel expenses out of his own pocket. One of the examiners, he said, had come from Germany. Reilly denied receiving contributions from German and American Nazi organizations. "About fifteen experts have volunteered to help us, including one who is in the U.S. Navy," Reilly said.

Reilly's prospective witnesses were staying at the Hildebrecht Hotel in Trenton, where Wilentz and his assistants were headquartered. At noon that Saturday, Reilly and Frederick Pope led the experts to Wilentz's office on the third floor, where all of the handwriting exhibits, including Osborn's word charts and two of Isidor Fisch's letters, were spread out on several large tables. Several state troopers and Joseph Lanigan looked on as the handwriting people, five men and three women, studied the evidence for several hours.

The group Reilly had assembled consisted of Mrs. Charles Foster, Julia Farr, C. F. Goodspeed, and Hilda Braunlich from New York City; Arthur P. Meyers of Baltimore; Ruldolf Thielen from Germany; Samuel C. Malone from Washington, D.C.; and John N. Trendley from East St. Louis.

That afternoon in Flemington, Anna Hauptmann found her husband depressed and on edge. She assured him that the jury had not been impressed with Albert Osborn and that Reilly's handwriting witnesses would prove that he hadn't written the ransom notes. Anna was followed to the jail by Lloyd Fisher, who also tried to minimize Osborn's testimony. When Fisher left, Hauptmann was served his supper of baked beans, stewed fruit, and tea, after which he spent the remainder of the evening pacing back and forth in the bullpen.[4]

On Saturday, after the jurors had eaten lunch, they boarded a bus outside the Union Hotel that took them on a two-hour, fifty-mile pleasure ride through central New Jersey. Judge Trenchard had arranged the excursion to get the jurors out of the hotel over the weekend. The bus avoided the sights associated with the case and was followed by several carloads of troopers and reporters.

At a press conference on Sunday, Reilly refused to comment on his handwriting case but said that his client was penniless and unable to pay the four thousand-dollar bill Fawcett had submitted. This was a real problem, because Fawcett wouldn't release his files on the case until he was paid. (Two weeks earlier, a New Jersey Court had ruled that Fawcett could keep his papers until he was paid.) Reilly said that he had hired another lawyer, Maurice Edebaum, to look into the matter.[5]

Hauptmann may have been broke, but for Wilentz and the jurors, there were all sorts of money-making opportunities on the horizon. A vaudeville boxing agent had offered Wilentz thousands of dollars for his story, and at the conclusion of the trial, he was prepared to offer each juror three hundred dollars a week if they went on a tour of New England. Wilentz said that he wasn't interested—the jurors would have to make up their own minds later.

Monday morning, the trial opened with Joseph Lanigan taking Albert S. Osborn back over some of Friday's testimony to refresh the jury's recollection. Following the noon recess, Reilly, on cross-examination, asked Osborn about the holes in the ransom symbol: "And in your opinion they were made by a nail or some rough instrument?"

"Well, some rough instrument, I think. I couldn't say what."

"I take it that your testimony is that one person wrote all of these ransom notes."

"Yes."

Reilly tried but failed to get Osborn to admit that he had made mistakes in previous cases. When it became clear that Reilly wasn't going to get Osborn to modify or qualify his opinion about the ransom notes, and when he couldn't cite any cases where Osborn had been found wrong, Reilly abruptly terminated the examination. Reilly's failure to dent Osborn's testimony made him look foolish in the wake of his promises to do otherwise.

Concerned that one more questioned-documents examiner would put the jury to sleep, Wilentz switched gears and called to the stand Hildegard Olga Alexander, a surprise witness—and a beautiful one at that. When Miss Alexander stepped to the witness box even Judge Trenchard straightened in his chair.

The twenty-five-year-old blonde in the mink-trimmed coat and matching fur hat said she was a garment district fashion model from the Bronx who had known Dr. Condon since her childhood. In March of 1932, while the ransom negotiations were going on, she happened to be in the waiting room of a railroad station in the Fordham section of the Bronx when she saw Dr. Condon at the telegraph window arguing with the operator.

"Now, who else was in that station besides you and Dr. Condon?" Wilentz asked.

"I saw a man looking at Dr. Condon."

"How far away from Dr. Condon was this man?"

"About where I am sitting to where you are sitting, probably just a little bit farther."

"Now the man to whom you refer and who you saw in the station that night, did you see him again, madam?"

"Yes."

"Where?"

"He was walking at Fordham Road and Webster Avenue and he was turning the bend."

"Who was this man you saw in that station watching Dr. Condon on this night in March and whom you saw a few nights afterwards walking down Fordham road?"

Calmly and deliberately, the witness replied, "I say the man was Bruno Richard Hauptmann."

When the dust had settled from Wilentz's bomb, Reilly tried his best to minimize the impact of her testimony. When the witness held firm on her identification, Reilly attacked her character by asking if she were using the Hauptmann trial for a publicity gimmick. "Who knows," he said, "maybe you will land a movie contract."

Miss Alexander said that when she saw Hauptmann's picture in the paper she reported her sighting to the Bronx County district attorney's office. She insisted that she was not interested in publicity or a career in the movies.

Reilly's clumsy assault on the witness's character made him look desperate and inept and offended the jury.[6]

Miss Alexander was followed to the stand by Elbridge W. Stein, a sixty-two-year-old document examiner from Montclair, New Jersey. Aware that the jury was quickly bored by technical and repetitious testimony, Joseph Lanigan brought Stein quickly to the point of his testimony—that the defendant was the writer of the ransom notes.

Reilly, suffering from a cold and a sore throat, turned the cross-examination over to Lloyd Fisher, who suggested that the writer of the ransom notes had purposely misspelled many of the words. Stein replied that he didn't think so.

Fisher then launched into a prolonged, repetitious, and pointless cross-examination that infuriated Reilly. Judge Trenchard became so annoyed that he rebuked Fisher for delaying the trial with his irrelevant and purposeless questions. The judge could see that the jury was getting bored with the handwriting, and he wanted to spare them further tedium. But this was exactly what Fisher had wanted. He and the other defense attorneys, principally Pope and Rosecrans, wanted the jury to become so bored and fed up with the questioned-documents business they would ignore all of the prosecution's handwriting evidence. Reilly, on the other hand, felt that Fisher, by boring and irritating the jury, was turning them against the defendant.

Stein didn't get off the stand until four o'clock, and the moment he did, Judge Trenchard dismissed the weary jurors and gaveled the session to its inglorious end. The next morning, Tuesday, January 15, Joseph Lanigan put John F. Tyrrell on the stand. The veteran handwriting expert from Milwaukee, like Albert S. Osborn, was a pioneer in the field and one of the most respected criminalists in the world. The gray-haired, bespectacled witness, looking more like a kindly old bank clerk than a documents examiner, had testified in dozens of celebrated trials, including the 1924 Leopold and Loeb kidnap-murder case.[7]

During the past thirty-five years, Tyrrell and Albert S. Osborn had testified for the same side in over fifty trials.

Tyrrell placed a drawingboard in front of the jury box and, using a crayon, drew pictures of several letters from Hauptmann's writing and the ransom notes that had been formed in a consistently peculiar fashion. Tyrrell drew the letter x that looked like two e's, the letter t without a crossing, the letter y that looked more like a j, and the hyphenated New-York.

The handwriting expert then wrote out the address on the package that contained the sleeping suit that had been mailed to John Condon, then wrote down, on the same sheet of paper, a series of words taken from Hauptmann's writing and bearing obvious similarities.

On cross-examination, Frederick Pope got Tyrrell to acknowledge that there were some dissimilarities between Hauptmann's writings and the ransom notes. Using Tyrrell's crayon, Pope copied some of the letters from each set of writings that he thought were different. He and Tyrrell then got into a series of heated arguments over what was similar and what wasn't. When Tyrrell saw a similarity in two letters that Pope didn't, the lawyer said tartly, "Your eyes are better than mine," to which Tyrrell responded, "But my eyes are expert eyes."

After Tyrrell had been in the witness chair three hours he was starting to show the strain. It seemed that Pope had gotten all he could out of the witness and was finally finishing when, almost as an afterthought, he asked if Tyrrell had been a witness in a case against a man named Gordon Morgan ten years ago in Milwaukee.

"I don't recall it," Tyrrell replied.

"Morgan was charged with forging a document in a case in which you appeared as the handwriting expert for the State. Now do you recall it?"

"I remember a case of that description."

"Perhaps I can refresh your recollection. The particular case that I am referring to is this: This man was convicted and sentenced to prison and, after he was convicted upon your testimony, a man by the name of Herman Eckert confessed that he himself had written the checks, and the case was reopened and Morgan was discharged. And in that case you testified that the forged checks were in the hand of the defendant, didn't you?"

Wilentz rose to his feet, "I object. This gentleman's qualifications were admitted and conceded."

Judge Trenchard overruled the objection, pointing out that in Tyrrell's case, the defense had retained the right to question his qualifications.

Pope continued: "And the defendant was convicted, wasn't he?"

"Yes."

"And this man Eckert afterward confessed that he had forged the checks?"

"The next day."

"So that you made a serious mistake in that case, didn't you?"

"Well, I don't know. They were both confined in jail at the same time. There was always some little doubt in my mind."

"I see. That's all."

After lunch, Herbert J. Walter, a questioned-documents expert from Chicago whose testimony four years earlier had helped send Al Capone to the federal penitentiary, took the stand and testified that the ransom notes had been written by Hauptmann. He handled himself well under Rosecran's cross-examination and was excused after refusing to concede that the ransom notes could have been written by someone copying Hauptmann's handwriting style.

The last witness to testify that Tuesday was Morton C. Maish, the man who owned the company that made Baby Alice Thumb Guards, the brand the Lindbergh baby had worn the night he was kidnapped. Mr. Maish identified, as one of his, the thumb guard Betty Gow and Elsie Whateley had found on the Lindbergh driveway. The witness said his guards were rust-resistant, therefore one that had been exposed to the elements for several weeks would still be shiny. Wilentz was using Mr. Maish to counter Reilly's contention that the guard found by the servants was not one of the ones the baby had been wearing that night. This assertion was based on the premise that if it had been, it would have been rusty, not shiny like the one the women had found.

The location and the identity of the baby's thumb guard was important to Wilentz because it fit in with his theory that Hauptmann, while fleeing from the house, had ripped the sleeping suit off the baby's body, and in so doing, had torn off the guard that had been attached to the child's wrist by a string. The location of the thumb guard was evidence, albeit circumstantial, that the defendant had killed or was planning to kill the baby. According to this theory, Hauptmann wanted the sleeping suit so he could later prove that he had the child.

On cross-examination, Reilly got Maish to admit that he had never scientifically tested his product to determine the extent of its rust-resistance. He was excused and the court adjourned for the day.

That evening, when Albert S. Osborn was asked by a reporter what he thought about Reilly's claim that he had eight handwriting experts who would demolish the prosecution's case, the old man said that anyone who could not see that the handwriting in the ransom notes was Hauptmann's was "either incompetent or dishonest." [8]

Earlier in the day, two of Reilly's experts, Samuel C. Malone and Arthur P. Meyers, announced they no longer wished to be associated with the defense. According to a story published in a Philadelphia newspaper, Malone had withdrawn from the case because he was convinced that Hauptmann had written the ransom notes. When asked by a *New York Times* reporter why he had bailed out, he would only say that he had "very good reasons." [9] Arthur P. Meyers, the other defector, was more direct. He announced that he had backed out because his testimony "would have been adverse to the defense." [10]

The moment he learned of the defections, Reilly declared that the examiners had quit the case because he didn't have any money to pay them.

On Wednesday morning, the sixteenth, everyone in the courtroom, except the defendant and his supporters, got a delightful surprise in Lanigan's first witness, Harry M. Cassidy, a questioned-documents examiner employed by the Chesapeake and Ohio Railroad Company in Highland Park, Virginia. As soon as he began testifying, the handsome young expert, with his southern drawl and colorful, witty, and candid manner of speech, had everyone in the room hanging on his every word. After two days of tedious testimony, Cassidy was a breath of fresh air. Realizing this, Lanigan, who had intended a very brief direct examination, kept Cassidy going as long as he could.

When Lanigan asked Cassidy to explain his word charts, the witness said, "There wouldn't be a thing here that I can show you that hasn't already been shown. I have been in the courtroom part of the time, and my evidence has been shot to pieces. It has been absorbed."

After discussing eight words the ransom-note writer and Hauptmann had misspelled the same way, Cassidy said, "I should just like to remark here—I want to be conservative—at the same time I don't want to be mealy-mouthed."

"Go ahead."

"Now if this was one of those ordinary anonymous letter cases like I handle every few days down there in Virginia, I wouldn't hesitate to say the same person wrote both sets of writing. I wouldn't care if they had been written on a typewriter, because the same person—the possibility or probability of two people spelling all those words wrong in the same way is so impossible that I would say that it is entirely negligible, now that's my honest opinion and I am giving it to you; but this is a serious case here. It is too

304 important to decide it, I would say, just on that alone. I would decide an ordinary case on the strength of those eight misspelled words, but I don't feel like I should do it in a case of this importance. So if you will just bear and be patient with me for just one more illustration, I will get to it."

Lanigan said that he was sure the jury was interested in the witness's analysis, and encouraged him to proceed. Following a discussion of his two charts, which showed the similarities of Hauptmann's handwriting to the ransom notes, Cassidy said, "I have given careful consideration to all of these things, weighed them individually and collectively, and I hope weighed them in connection with each other. Regardless of the seriousness of this charge, I feel that I am obligated to say that the person who wrote those request writings is the same person who wrote all those ransom notes. Now, I don't see that this jury is required to have the patience to listen to me any further."

Lanigan thanked the witness and walked back to the prosecution table with a smile on his face. Judge Trenchard, looking very pleased himself, called for a brief recess.

When the trial resumed, Lloyd Fisher had the unpopular task of cross-examining Cassidy. In an effort to get the expert to admit that he had no way of knowing that Hauptmann hadn't been told how to spell certain words, had asked, "You weren't present when the test or request writings were written, were you?"

"I wasn't present when Washington crossed the Delaware, but I've a pretty good idea he got over to the Jersey side."

The courtroom exploded into laughter—even Reilly had to smile. Judge Trenchard, working to keep a straight face, said, "Now we have had quite enough confusion. The people must remain quiet if they are to remain here."

Having had enough, Fisher excused the witness.

Dr. Wilmer T. Souder, a documents examiner on the scientific staff of the U.S. Bureau of Standards and the chief of its identification laboratory, took the stand and said that he had been the first criminalist to examine the Lindbergh ransom notes. Following a discussion of his word charts and Souder's conclusion that Hauptmann was the ransom-note writer, Frederick Pope, on cross-examination, challenged Souder's credentials as an expert. The exchange quickly became heated and Judge Trenchard had to intercede. Trenchard and Pope got into a spirited argument over the witness's expertise, which the defense lawyer lost. Pope then set out on a long and fruitless cross-examination that bored if not irritated the jury.

By the time Dr. Souder stepped wearily from the stand, the courtroom was so damp and hot that the big windows were covered with mist and dripping water. It was so oppressive that Verna Snyder, the 265-pound wife of the blacksmith, removed her heavy fur-collared coat. Since it was the first time the juror had taken it off in the courtroom, the event was a topic of conversation among the lawyers.

Albert D. Osborn, the thirty-eight-year-old son of the prosecution's chief handwriting expert, was the day's third questioned documents witness. After making it clear that the younger Osborn wasn't in a direct partnership with his father, Lanigan led him to the conclusion that the defendant had written the ransom notes. Osborn was then turned over to Lloyd Fisher for cross-examination.

In response to questions regarding his qualifications, Osborn said that there was no such thing as a school for handwriting experts. (There still isn't.) Examiners were trained on the job and learned by reading books—principally his father's. Fisher also established that the witness and his father had adjoining offices in New York City. The attorney wondered out loud how young Osborn could have arrived at a conclusion independent of his father's influence. Osborn replied that he had made up his own mind in the case.

In response to a question regarding how many kidnapping suspects there had been prior to Hauptmann's arrest, Osborn said, "There were hundreds of people that were perfectly innocent. Finally they got the right man."

"Got the right man? That is your opinion?" Fisher asked.

"Absolutely."

"Yes, and it was your opinion up in Bergen County that they had the right woman in Mrs. Mowel?" (Mrs. Mowel was the defendant in the Von Moschzisker "poison pen case" in which Osborn testified for the state.)

"And it is still my opinion."

"But the jury disagreed with you, didn't they?"

"Oh, yes, I don't win every case I am in."

"No?"

"And neither do you."

"No. I didn't win with you on my side one day, did I? Due either to poor lawyering or poor experting, a case in which we were jointly involved was decided against us, wasn't it?"

"In that case Mr. Large was on the other side. After my testimony he had admitted that his client had written the letters. That is what I was there for. Then he went ahead and won the case anyway. I didn't feel that that was my fault."

The last witness of the day, and the final handwriting expert, was Clark Sellers, a noted documents examiner from Los Angeles. He had testified in numerous celebrated cases, including the Marian Parker kidnapping trial in 1927 and the Winnie Ruth Judd trunk murder case in 1931. He had also been a major witness in the suit over the legitimacy of Rudolf Valentino's will.

Sellers testified that Hauptmann's misspellings were due to his ignorance and the fact that he didn't understand the American sound of words. He said the defendant had tried to alter his writing but couldn't maintain the disguise. "He might as well have signed the notes with his own name," Sellers declared.[11]

Following Pope's brief and futile cross-examination, the witness was dismissed and the court adjourned.

Back at the prosecution's headquarters in Trenton, Wilentz and his men were jubilant. The testimony of the eight handwriting experts had lifted the burden of proof right off the shoulders of the prosecution and had dumped it on the lap of the defense. From this point on, Hauptmann would have to prove that he was innocent.

In a burst of lawyerly bravado, Reilly announced to the press that when it came time for him to put on his case, there'd be an imposing array of foreign and American handwriting experts to prove that Hauptmann hadn't written a single ransom note.

In the event that Reilly wasn't bluffing, Wilentz had four other handwriting experts waiting in the wings ready to testify in rebuttal.[12]

The prosecution was now in high gear, gaining speed and momentum as the trial progressed. If Reilly didn't come up with something to slow Wilentz down, Hauptmann would find himself on the wrong end of a verdict and headed straight for the electric chair.

I think it was a mighty good one.

— D R .   C H A R L E S   H .   M I T C H E L L
referring to his autopsy.

32 ATTACKING THE AUTOPSY

ON WEDNESDAY, as Hauptmann's lawyers battled with the prosecution's handwriting experts in Flemington, a group of FBI agents in Oklawaha, Florida, were shooting to death a couple of bank robbers and killers named Kate "Ma" Barker and her son, Fred.

Out in Illinois, in a town called Ottawa, a bank robber shot and killed a sheriff and a bank employee; then, when cornered by the police, shot himself in the head. On that day, a fifty-man posse chased four bank robbers to a farm near Leonore, Illinois. When the shooting stopped, one robber was wounded and another lay dead with four bullets in his chest.

In California on that Wednesday, four inmates at San Quentin Prison stormed the warden's house and beat him to death with clubs. When they were caught several hours later, three of the convicts were wounded and their leader fatally shot.

In Reilly's hometown of Brooklyn, a man being chased by the police commandeered a taxi and shot the cab driver in the head. Meanwhile, in Manhattan, when two patrolmen surprised four men robbing a leather goods store at Fifth Avenue and Forty-fifth Street, one of the holdup men killed one of the policemen by shooting him in the temple. The armed robbers were financing a trip to Florida.

On the Wednesday the four handwriting experts said that Bruno Richard Hauptmann had written all of the ransom notes, the American people were frightened and fed up with bank robbers, cop killers, and men who murdered babies.

That night, Sheriff Curtiss announced that the courtroom would be open to tourists on Sundays. Members of the local Rotary Club would be stationed in the building to prevent souvenir hunters from carrying the place away.

That day Reilly got some good news; an appeals court in Brooklyn ruled that James Fawcett would have to turn his Lindbergh case papers over to the Hauptmann defense.

On Thursday, January 17, the twelfth day of the trial, Robert Peacock of Wilentz's staff called William J. Allen to the stand. Allen was the truck driver who had stumbled upon the baby's remains on Mt. Rose Heights when he went into the woods to relieve himself.

Allen's driving partner, Orville Wilson, took the stand next and repeated much of Allen's testimony. Peacock then brought Det. Andrew Zapolsky of the state police to the witness chair. Following a brief questioning by Peacock, Zapolsky was turned over to Lloyd Fisher, who asked, "And you say that the body was in such condition that you could recognize it from the photographs of a living child; is that correct?"

"Yes, the features were there."

"Was there anything found around the body, by way of instruments or tools?"

"Not that I recall."

The next witness was Insp. Harry Walsh of Jersey City, who said that he had matched garments he had taken from the body with cloth remnants he had gotten from Betty Gow. Walsh said that when he moved the body he had accidentally poked a hole in its head with the stick he was using. On cross-examination, Fisher asked him about this: "Now did you report this matter of making a hole in the baby's head to the county physician?"

"No, I didn't have any occasion to make a report to the county physician."

"Did you make a survey of the scene?"

"Immediately surrounding the body, yes."

"Did you find anything there at all?"

"I found a sack."

"What kind?"

"A burlap bag."

Walsh was followed to the stand by Walter H. Swayze, the Mercer County coroner and the owner of the funeral home in Trenton that doubled as a county morgue. Swayze said that he had examined the corpse at the scene and had ordered its removal to his facility in Trenton where Dr. Mitchell later performed the autopsy. Swayze didn't mention that it was he and not the county physician who had performed the physical part of the autopsy. Following a brief and uneventful cross-examination by Reilly, Swayze was dismissed.

Dr. Charles H. Mitchell, the county physician whose testimony would establish the cause, manner, and time of the baby's death, was called to the stand. Addressing the physician, Wilentz asked, "When you saw the remains of this child, what have you to say as to whether it was recognizable?"

"The facial expression was quite good on this child. The facial muscles had not deteriorated, although the body generally was in a bad state of decomposition."

"Have you seen pictures of the Lindbergh child?"

"For that matter, we had a picture of the Lindbergh child produced at the morgue that evening, and I made a comparison, the best I could, between the picture and the facial expression of the child, and I was very much impressed with the fact that it was the same child."

"How many autopsies would you say you have performed in your experience?"

"Oh, probably a thousand."

"As the result of your autopsy, can you tell us what caused the death of this child?"

"There was no question as to the cause of death. The child died of a fractured skull."

"What was the nature of this fracture with reference to whether or not it was extensive?"

"It was quite extensive. The fracture extended from a point about an inch and half posterior to the left ear; it extended forward—well, probably three to four inches; it extended upward to one of the fontanels; it extended around the back of the head. In other words, it was a very extensive fracture." Dr. Mitchell looked at the jury to emphasize this point.

"Will you give us your opinion, doctor, based upon your experience, the experience which you have related, as to the time of death as related to the fracture?" This was a vital question. If the baby had been murdered in Hunterdon County, the blow to his head would have had to have been inflicted within minutes of the crime. Wilentz didn't want the defense arguing that the child had been killed in some other county a day or so later then taken to the site on Mt. Rose Heights. If that had been the case, then Hauptmann couldn't be tried for murder in the Hunterdon County Court.

Wilentz repeated his question and Dr. Mitchell said, "I would say definitely that death had occurred either instantaneous or within a very few minutes following the actual blow."

"There were some parts of the body missing when you performed this autopsy, were there not?"

"Quite a lot of them, yes, sir."

"Did that prevent you from ever ascertaining what in your judgment was the cause of death?"

"Not by any means. I came to my conclusions as to the fracture occurring during life by virtue of the fact that on the inner walls of the skull at the point of fracture there was still the remains of a blood clot. That blood clot could not come there if the child was dead when the fracture occurred. That fracture occurred on a living child. It bled. The clot was still there, or part of it. That indicates in my mind the blow was struck or the damage done, however it happened—I can't say—but it was done prior to the death of the child or at least sometime during its life."

The courtroom was silent and still as Wilentz turned Dr. Mitchell over to Reilly for cross-examination.

The defense attorney, in a voice dripping with hostility and contempt, asked the doctor a series of questions about his medical background. Answering calmly, in short, terse sentences, the doctor said he had been a physician for thirty-five years and during his eleven years as county physician had performed a thousand autopsies.

"How many autopsies have you performed on two-year-old children?"

"I can't say; I haven't any records here."

"Did you ever perform one before?"

"On a child of that age?"

"Yes."

"Oh yes."

"Now, doctor, in your opinion, how many causes of death are there?"

"Oh, Lord. There is a book full of them. There are several dozen."

"Yes. Well, repeat them for the jury please."

"Oh, it is an impossibility."

Reilly looked at the jury as if he couldn't believe what he had heard. "You can't repeat—"

"Cardiac conditions, kidney conditions, lung conditions, brain conditions—"

"All right," Reilly interrupted. "Wait. I will go down the list with you. Cardiac—heart, right?"

"Yes," Dr. Mitchell answered.

"Did you examine the heart of this child?"

"The heart was in such a condition it couldn't be examined."

"The liver, did you examine the liver of this child?"

"The liver was not in a condition to prove anything."

"All right, the stomach."

"No stomach there. There was no kidneys, bladder, or lungs either. The larynx was still present, but it was in a very much decomposed state."

"You made no effort to determine in your autopsy any cause of death from choking, did you?"

"We examined very carefully—"

"Did you?"

"We examined very carefully by opening the mouth, putting the finger down the throat, also opening the chest, looking at the various organs that were left. We examined the teeth, examined the tongue—the odor itself almost made it impossible for a man to work over the child."

"Then your examination of the child's body was rather perfunctory, was it not?"

"I wouldn't say so—I think it was a mighty good one, myself."

"How long did it take you to determine the cause of death?"

"How long?" Dr. Mitchell asked. Although he was still composed, beads of sweat had popped out on his forehead and there was a growing note of defensiveness in his voice.

"Yes," Reilly replied. "How long?"

"Well, I first made a general examination of the external portion of the body, made different measurements of the length of the body, examined the teeth, examined the condition of the muscles, which were in a badly decomposed state; then after that I made an effort to open up the scalp, to dissect it, but in dissecting, in cutting, it was in such a decomposed state, it brushed back. Then I found this marked fracture on the left side, extending upward to the frontal posterior occipital bone, the bone in the back of the head. There was no reason why there would be any external bleeding, because there was no opening in the scalp. But in taking the skin off the top of the skull, which I endeavored first to do, the bones separated and fell off. I did find a decomposed blood clot at the point of fracture."

Hauptmann sat frozen in his chair, the blood seemed to have drained from his face. His lips were drawn tight and the muscles of his neck twitched as his eyes shifted between the witness and the jury box.

Mrs. Hauptmann's fingers twisted convulsively on her lap as she watched her husband. Colonel Lindbergh, with only two men seated between him and the defendant, sat white-faced with his shoulders bowed. The Colonel had been in court every day; Mrs. Lindbergh had chosen not to return after her day on the stand. This was the first time the testimony had visibly affected the Colonel.

Everyone on the jury looked sullen and depressed. Charles Snyder, the farmer from Clinton Township, stared glumly at the defendant. Every once in a while Judge Trenchard would cast a worried glance at Liscom Case, the juror with the heart condition.

Reilly, still warming to the task, was so caught up in his attack on Dr. Mitchell that he was oblivious to the morbid aura hanging over the courtroom.

"Did you see this hole in the skull?"

"The one on the right side?"

"Yes."

"Yes, sir."

"Did you not determine the cause of death the first night to be a bullet hole until you found out a policeman had accidentally poked a stick in there?"

"I never determined the cause of death as a bullet wound at any time, anywhere. I made the statement in order to describe the hole, that it was rounded and irregular, like a bullet hole."

"On the evening you made the autopsy, did any other doctors assist you?"

"No, I had no other doctor," the witness replied. (Since Swayze was not a physician, Dr. Mitchell, in the strict sense of the word, had not lied.)

"Were you responsible for the Movietone people and the movie people making a picture of this child at the autopsy?"

"No. We didn't allow anyone to see that child. The coroner himself took special care to prevent people from getting in. We even called the police and asked them to keep everybody out. If there were any pictures made I didn't know it."

"There was no doubt in your mind but what you were examining was the Lindbergh baby, was there?"

"At the time I didn't know. I didn't know at that time whether it was the Lindbergh baby or whose baby. Of course we had our own ideas."

"I mean you hadn't been told when you came over there?"

"We were told that it was suspected to be the Lindbergh baby. I don't know at that time."

"You knew it was an important case?"

"We gave the case the same considerations that we give every case."

Reilly suddenly turned aggressive: "You didn't consider this case important enough to

312   call in some other doctor of standing in either Pennsylvania, New Jersey, or New York to join in the certification of the cause of death?"

"No, I didn't think I needed them."

"Now, I want to know whether or not you photographed the blood clot?"

"We did not."

"You did not?" Reilly exclaimed. The smell of blood brought a sneer to his lips.

"My memory still holds to me, just as I saw it on that occasion," Dr. Mitchell replied with some tightness creeping into his voice.

"Didn't you think it important enough to preserve the evidence by picture?"

"I felt my memory was just as good as the picture on that."

To heighten the intimidation, Reilly inched his bulk closer to the witness. "And did you take into consideration the fact that possibly before a suspect would be arrested you might die?"

"I didn't give that a thought," Dr. Mitchell said looking at Wilentz for moral support.

"Did you consider the fact that if you did die before an arrest was made no one could testify to the autopsy from a medical viewpoint?"

Wilentz got to his feet, "Well, now, I don't know that that is the fact, if Your Honor please."

Reilly swung around to face his adversary, "It is quite apparent it is the fact, sir."

Having given his witness a few moments to collect his thoughts, Wilentz said, "I will withdraw it and let him answer."

Dr. Mitchell cleared his throat and straightened in his chair. "I don't know the law, to tell you the truth. I don't know how you work it. You fellows would find some way to get around it." As the courtroom filled with laughter, Dr. Mitchell, obviously pleased with himself, smiled.

Enraged, Reilly roared, "Just a moment, doctor. You want it to appear now that you are ignorant of the law?"

"I am ignorant of some of the law. I really don't know what would happen if I'd die. All I know is I file a report. The report is accepted, I presume, as authentic. Now, if I should die—I don't know what would happen."

"Did anyone, Colonel Schwarzkopf, or any official connected with this case, suggest that it might be advisable to have another expert brought in?" By asking this question, Reilly was implying that the Lindbergh case had required real expertise, a forensic pathologist instead of a country doctor who didn't know enough to photograph the fatal wound in a murder case.

The message wasn't lost on Dr. Mitchell, who replied, "I don't recollect the Colonel speaking to me about that."

"So you came to your conclusion that because there was a clot on the brain and there were evidences of a cracked skull that the child died of a fractured skull?"

"Yes. I base my conclusions on those facts."

"On those facts?"

"On those facts, yes," Doctor Mitchell replied.

Wilentz waited for Reilly's punchline, but it never came. Instead, the cross-examination went on for a few more minutes before petering out.

Wilentz put Dr. Mitchell's autopsy report into evidence, then thanked the witness for his testimony. As Dr. Mitchell stepped from the stand, Judge Trenchard gaveled the morning session to a close.

All things considered, the county physician had emerged from Reilly's attack relatively unscathed. His secret was intact and that meant he could continue to draw a salary as county physician even though he had a mortician cut open his bodies for him. When he had testified directly about the autopsy, Dr. Mitchell had said *we* did this and *we* did that, keeping himself within the letter if not the spirit of the perjury law.

Wilentz and his men, in discussing Reilly's cross-examination over lunch, agreed that he had been laying the groundwork for some future attack, but they didn't know exactly what it would be. By raising questions about the cause of death, Reilly could have been getting ready to argue that the child's death and the extortion were not connected. Maybe he was going to assert that the ransom-note writer had nothing to do with the kidnapping—or that there hadn't been a kidnapping, or that the child's death had been caused by some unrelated event, an occurrence the extortionist had simply exploited. There was also the possibility that Reilly would attack the court's jurisdiction, claiming that the child had been killed several days after the abduction, somewhere outside Hunterdon County. He may have had this in mind when he asked questions about rigor mortis and when it set in. But in all probability, Reilly was going to argue that the body on Mt. Rose Heights wasn't the Lindbergh baby.

Although Wilentz was confident that Reilly wouldn't be able to make a convincing case on any of these points, it was a touchy issue since it involved the *corpus delecti* of their murder case. They could only wait and hope that the defense attorney didn't have something up his sleeve.

That night, after dining on scrambled eggs, bread, applesauce, two cookies, and tea, Hauptmann was visited by Lloyd Fisher and a stenographer from Fisher's office. The attorney left early, but the steno, Miss Apgar, stayed until 9:30. Since the beginning of the trial, Hauptmann had been, on and off, dictating his life story to her.

In his guard report that day, Lt. Allen Smith wrote: "He is becoming more nervous, reads less, paces the bullpen more, and cries oftener."[1]

> You are conceding Hauptmann to the electric chair.
> — L L O Y D   F I S H E R

33 REILLY'S CONCESSION

THE MOOD IN THE COURTROOM abruptly changed when, after the noon recess, ten employees of the J. P. Morgan Bank took the stand and testified about the preparation of the ransom package. The witnesses were all dismissed without cross-examination.

Wilentz next turned to the ten-dollar gold note Hauptmann had passed on September 15, 1934, at the Warren-Quinlan service station in upper Manhattan, the bill that had led to his arrest four days later. Two employees of the Corn Exchange Bank where the bill had been deposited took the stand. They were followed by Walter Lyle, the gas station employee who had penciled Hauptmann's license number on the ransom bill's margin.

When Wilentz, following his direct examination of Lyle, attempted to introduce the ten-dollar bill into evidence, Frederick Pope objected on the grounds that the bill, although evidence of extortion, had no connection to the case at hand. Sensing that Pope was about to launch into another lengthy, pompous speech, Judge Trenchard, in no mood for that, ordered the bill marked into evidence.

On cross-examination, Reilly asked Lyle one question: "You put in a claim for the reward, didn't you?"

"Yes, sir," Lyle replied as Reilly looked at the jury as though the witness had done something unpardonable.

FBI Agent William F. Seery took the stand and read a list of the ransom bills that had turned up since the first note had surfaced on April 5, 1932. He said that Hauptmann had admitted purchasing a pair of shoes for his wife with a twenty-dollar gold note. The ransom bill and the shoes, purchased on September 8, 1934, were admitted into evidence. Also placed into evidence, over Pope's strenuous objection, was the twenty-dollar bill that had been taken from Hauptmann's billfold when he was arrested. The bill had been folded into eight sections like several of the gold notes that had been passed before Isidor Fisch had sailed to Germany.

Just when everyone was getting thoroughly bored with the ransom testimony and Frederick Pope's longwinded objections, Reilly produced one of the biggest surprises of the trial. It occurred during the testimony of Elmira Dormer, the woman in charge of St. Michael's Orphanage located less than a mile from the site on Mount Rose Heights where the corpse had been found. Wilentz had put her on the stand to counter any claim that the body in the woods could have been one of her orphans. "How many children did you have in the orphanage on March 1, 1932?" Wilentz asked.

"Three hundred and six."

"Was there a child unaccounted for in that institution in February or March 1932?"

"None were missing. They were all accounted for."

"So in the year 1932 there were no children unaccounted for in your orphanage?"

"No, sir."

"Are those the books of attendance of your school?" Wilentz asked, referring to a ledger the witness held on her lap.

"Yes, sir."

Wilentz turned and faced Reilly, "If there is any dispute about the attendance I will offer the records. If there isn't, I won't."

"There is no dispute," Reilly replied.

"There is no claim that the child in the woods came from the orphanage?" Wilentz asked.

"No," said Frederick Pope.

Reilly then stunned everyone in the room; "I will say now that there has never been any claim but this was Colonel Lindbergh's child that was found there."

Lloyd Fisher jumped to his feet and cried, "You are conceding Hauptmann to the electric chair!" Fisher stormed out of the room.

Confused, and with a look of panic in his eyes, Hauptmann swung around in his chair and watched the only lawyer who cared about him stalk out of the courtroom.[1]

Having had his *corpus delecti* handed to him on a silver platter, Wilentz turned Mrs. Dormer over to the defense.[2] Reilly asked the woman a few questions, then excused her. In the meantime, Fisher had returned to the courtroom and was consoling Hauptmann, who was still visibly shaken.

The room was still buzzing when FBI Agent Thomas Sisk took the stand. After describing the defendant's arrest, the boyish-looking agent recalled the search of the Hauptmann apartment while the prisoner was being grilled in his bedroom.

"Did Hauptmann make any objection to the search?" Wilentz asked.

"No, he did not."

"What happened?"

"We had him sit down on a chair near the window and we were searching that same room—Corporal Horn and myself. While doing this I noticed that Hauptmann would get up a little from his chair and look out the window. He did that four or five times. I called Lieutenant Keaten and he observed it also. I then went over to Hauptmann and I said, 'What are you looking at when you are sneaking those looks out the window?' and he said, 'Nothing' so I tried to figure out what he was looking at, so I looked out myself."

"What did you see when you looked out?"

"Well, the garage. Then I said 'Is that where you have the money?' or some such remark, and he said, 'No, I have no money.'"

Hauptmann, his face flushed and his breathing labored, had been listening intently to Sisk's testimony. As the agent described the search of Hauptmann's garage, the defendant, in his high-pitched voice, screamed, "Mister, Mister, you stop lying! You are telling a story!" Hauptmann started to get out of his chair but was shoved down by the officer seated next to him. Several people, including Mrs. Hauptmann, had been startled by the outburst.[3]

Judge Trenchard surveyed the jury box to make certain everybody was all right, then declared, "One moment. Let me suggest to the defendant that he keep quiet. If he has any observations to make, let him make them quietly through counsel."

Following this mild reprimand, Wilentz turned Sisk over to Reilly, who making no effort to hide his hostility, asked, "Now, you are very much interested in this case, aren't you?"

Thinking a moment before answering, Sisk replied, "Yes, sir."

Reilly started to badger the witness, but when he realized that he wasn't getting anywhere, he relinquished him. It was almost 4:30, and Judge Trenchard brought the session to a close.

As Reilly left the courthouse, reporters asked him to comment on a story in *The New York Times* about a New York City private detective who said that Isidor Fisch had offered a man named Gustav Jukatis fifty thousand dollars in hot money. Reilly called the story bunk. He then said about his surprise concession: "At the present time the opinion of the defense is that Colonel Lindbergh identified the baby. We know of nothing to the contrary. Of course we have heard of many ridiculous stories that the child's body was two inches longer or shorter than the Lindbergh baby, but we believe that Colonel Lindbergh knew his own child."[4]

The next morning, Wilentz led off with Det. Sgt. John Wallace, one of the nine officers who had arrested Hauptmann. Fisher took over the questioning at ten, then subjected the jury to a two-hour cross-examination that was repetitious and fruitless. After lunch, Wilentz called a former Hauptmann neighbor, Mrs. Ella Achenbach, to the stand. As the plump, middle-aged housewife walked to the witness chair in her knit hat, Reilly looked at Fisher as if to say, "Who is she?"

"Where did you live in March 1932?" Wilentz asked.

"I lived at 1253 East 222nd Street."

"Did you know Mr. and Mrs. Hauptmann at that time?"

"I met Mrs. Hauptmann in 1927, when I took her into my employment as a waitress." (The witness's husband owned a restaurant.)

"Did you see Mr. Bruno Richard Hauptmann sometime in March 1932 after the Lindbergh kidnapping?"

"Yes, they came home from a trip."

"Where did you see him?"

"Anna Hauptmann came to my front porch and told me they had just come home."

Mrs. Hauptmann suddenly rose from her seat at the defense table and in a shrill voice shouted, "Mrs. Achenbach, you are lying!" She then sat down.

The courtroom buzzed as Wilentz, Fisher, and Reilly hurried to the bench. The prosecutor spoke first. "If Your Honor please, we object to these demonstrations, whether they are staged or otherwise." Fisher started to say something, but Judge Trenchard interrupted him, "One moment. Who said that?"

"Mrs. Hauptmann," Wilentz replied.

Speaking to Mrs. Hauptmann in a loud, stern voice, Judge Trenchard asked, "Well, madam, don't you see the impropriety of your interrupting this trial in an outburst of this kind."

Mrs. Hauptmann, who had been sitting with her head bowed, jumped to her feet when addressed by the judge. Speaking in a voice that sounded as though she were weeping, she said, "I am sorry, Your Honor, but I couldn't help it."

Wilentz turned to the judge, "I object to the lady making an address in the courtroom!"

Waving the prosecutor aside with the sweep of his hand, Trenchard said, "I am asking her whether or not she does not see the impropriety of that thing." Fixing his gaze on Mrs. Hauptmann the judge asked, "Now you see that it was wrong for you to make that outburst, don't you?"

Mrs. Hauptmann, still on her feet, replied, "Yes, I see but—"

"You see that it was wrong, do you not?" Trenchard interrupted.

"Yes, sir, Your Honor."

"Now will you promise me and these lawyers here and the jury that you won't offend in that respect again?"

"Well, I will try to do so," Mrs. Hauptmann replied, "but sometimes I can't help it."

"But I am asking now whether or not you will promise to keep quiet." The judge was getting angry.

"I will," Mrs. Hauptmann replied quite meekly. She then sat down with her eyes lowered.

Turning his attention to Bruno Hauptmann, the judge asked, "And I think we have in effect that kind of promise out of the defendant, haven't we?"

Bruno nodded his head in the affirmative, then started to get up to say something when his guards pushed him back into his chair. Speaking on the defendant's behalf, Reilly said, "Yes, sir. In fact, Mr. Hauptmann wanted to address the court yesterday, but I wouldn't permit it because I didn't want anything interrupted, but he wanted to apologize to Your Honor for his outburst."

"Well," Judge Trenchard said with a sigh, "we'll have to proceed."

Wilentz resumed his direct examination of Mrs. Achenbach: "Mrs. Hauptmann came to the porch that day?"

"We were talking about ten minutes about her trip."

"Did Mr. Hauptmann come?"

"Yes."

"Did you observe anything about him?"

"Before they went home Mrs. Hauptmann said, 'Oh, another thing happened to Richard; he hurt his leg.'"

"Was he there?"

"Of course he was there. He said he sprained his ankle pretty bad."

"How did he walk when he went down the steps?"

"When he went down my front steps he kind of supported himself on the side of the stoop."

"Did he walk with a limp?"

"He was walking with a limp on the left leg."

As Mrs. Achenbach testified, Hauptmann and his wife, both flushed with anger, exchanged scornful smiles. Mrs. Hauptmann was heard muttering, "Lies, lies—all lies!" [5]

The defendant looked on in disgust, with his arms and legs crossed. At one point, Egbert Rosecrans turned and patted him on the knee, silently cautioning him to remain quiet. Hauptmann waved him off with the motion of his hand.

Mrs. Achenbach was briefly cross-examined by Reilly, who wasn't able to shake her testimony.

Wilentz next called five police witnesses from New York City and New Jersey who in one way or another had participated in the discovery of the ransom money in Hauptmann's garage.

Following Reilly's cross-examination of the fifth officer, Insp. Henry D. Bruckman climbed into the chair and told the jury how he had found Dr. Condon's address written on the trim inside Hauptmann's closet. After Wilentz had placed the board into evidence and Reilly had finished with Bruckman, Benjamin Arac, the stenographer who had been in District Attorney Foley's office when Hauptmann admitted that the writing on the door trim was his, faced the jury. Arac's notes were marked into evidence over Pope's objection. Then the witness was excused after a brief but heated cross-examination by Lloyd Fisher.

The last four witnesses of the day were bankers and stockbrokers who had specific knowledge of Hauptmann's financial dealings. Individually their testimony was insignificant, but taken as a whole Wilentz was able to show that Hauptmann, an unemployed carpenter, had accumulated a considerable amount of money.

That night, Hauptmann was visited by his wife and Lloyd Fisher, who tried to reassure him that things would look up when the defense put on its case. After his visitors had left, Hauptmann paced the bullpen for several hours, then hurled himself onto his cot where he cried himself to sleep.

On Saturday morning, the jury took a stroll; in the afternoon they were taken on a bus ride to Frenchtown, New Jersey. That evening, the jurors celebrated Ethel Stockton's birthday with chocolate cake and ice cream.

On Monday morning, Wilentz led off with William Frank of the IRS, who said that he had analyzed Hauptmann's bank and brokerage accounts as well as his other financial assets. The witness said that the defendant's total assets, from the date of the ransom payment to the time of his arrest, amounted to $44,486.00. Taking the stand next was Edward F. Morton, the timekeeper at the Majestic Hotel, who said that Hauptmann did not work at the hotel on the day of the crime or on the day the ransom money exchanged hands.

During Reilly's unproductive cross-examination of Morton, he coughed constantly, frequently stopping to sip from a glass of water. When the timekeeper stepped from the witness chair, Judge Trenchard held up a small box and said, "Mr. Reilly, try these for your cough." Reilly took a coughdrop from the box and popped it into his mouth. He thanked the judge and returned to the defense table to await Wilentz's next witness—Mrs. Cecile Barr, the cashier at the Loew's Sheridan Theater in Greenwich Village.

The shy woman with the birdlike face took the stand and identified Hauptmann as the man who had rudely tossed her the folded five-dollar gold note on the night of November 26, 1933, a full month before Isidor Fisch had sailed for Germany.

Reilly, still bothered by a persistent cough, challenged the reliability of Mrs. Barr's identification: "I suppose you can remember everybody that you saw go into the theater?"

"No, sir."

"And everybody that went in in 1933?"

"No, sir."

"How many five-dollar bills do you suppose you took during 1933?"

"I couldn't account for them."

Reilly, in a dramatic move, then asked a clerk from his office to stand up. Pointing him out to the witness, Reilly said, "This is Mr. Rao, my clerk. Do you see him?"

"Yes."

"Have you seen him at your window during the past three weeks?"

"No."

"That is all, Mr. Rao," Reilly said, smiling at the jury in a way that suggested that Mr. Rao had been to the theater when in fact he had not.

Mrs. Barr was dismissed, and, following the testimony of a bank employee, the court was adjourned.

Tuesday morning, Wilentz made his third attempt to get the kidnap ladder into evidence by calling Lt. Lewis J. Bornmann to the stand. The New Jersey detective said that the ladder in the courtroom was the one found seventy-five feet from the Lindbergh house on the night of the crime. Once again Frederick Pope objected on the grounds that the ladder had been altered and that there was no proof that it had ever been in the defendant's possession. Judge Trenchard reminded Pope that Amandus Hochmuth had said that he had seen the defendant with a ladder in his car. With that, the kidnap ladder was admitted into evidence over Pope's strenuous objection.

FBI Agent Thomas Sisk was called back to the stand to be cross-examined by Reilly, who asked him about a recording Dr. Condon had made in which he had imitated Cemetery John's voice. Sisk acknowledged its existence but said he didn't have it; it was in Washington D.C. Reilly then asked Sisk to produce the plaster cast made from the footprint in St. Raymond's Cemetery. Sisk, in a hostile and evasive manner, told Reilly that he could not produce the recording or the cast without the approval of the U.S. attorney general. Reilly used the occasion to imply that the federal government was withholding evidence that would have been helpful to the defense.

Wilentz's next witness was Millard Whited, the logger who had lived in a shanty about a mile from the Lindbergh house. Whited said that in late February, 1932, he had seen Hauptmann, on two separate occasions, prowling in the vicinity of the Lindbergh estate.

Lloyd Fisher, making it clear that he had doubts regarding Whited's character and memory, aggressively cross-examined him without shaking his testimony.

The next man in the witness chair was Charles B. Rossiter, a surprise witness. The traveling salesman said that he was driving on Route 31 on his way to Philadelphia when he saw Hauptmann changing a tire at the side of the road near the Princeton airport. Rossiter said he had stopped and asked Hauptmann if he wanted a hand. It was eight o'clock Saturday night, three days before the kidnapping.

"What did he say?" Wilentz asked.

"He said he was all right; he didn't need any help."

"Did you proceed on your way?"

"No, I stood there and looked the man over pretty well."

"What sort of hat was he wearing?"

"A slouch hat."

"Now, when was the next time that you saw this man or a picture of him?"

"The next time I saw a picture of him was the day after his arrest, September twentieth."

"And when you saw that picture did you call it to the attention of the authorities?"

"I called them two days later."

On cross-examination, Rossiter admitted to Reilly that his memory wasn't perfect, but as far as Hauptmann was concerned, he wasn't mistaken.

The last five witnesses of the day consisted of the owner of Hauptmann's house, two employees of the National Lumber and Mill Work Company, a representative of the J. J. Dorn Lumber Mill, and a bookkeeper for the Halligan and McClelland Lumber Company. Through these witnesses, Wilentz set the stage for the testimony of Arthur Koehler, the wood expert from Madison, Wisconsin.

On Wednesday morning, Wilentz called Lt. Lewis J. Bornmann back to the stand. Bornmann said that on September 26, 1934, he and three other policemen were in Hauptmann's attic searching for the ransom money. Wilentz handed Bornmann a photograph and said, "Show the jury the condition you found in that attic."

"Well, this is the southwest corner, this is the south side, and this is the west side and the end board, approximately eight foot of it had been removed."

"Well, there was no board, there, was there?"

"There was no board, and upon examining it further I found there were nail holes still in the beams, and between the seventh and eighth beam there was a small quantity of sawdust; there was also on this adjoining board a small indentation made by a saw where, when this board had been sawed off, the saw went into it."

"Now, were you at the same place on October ninth with Mr. Koehler?"

"Yes sir."

"What did you do when you and Mr. Koehler arrived there?"

"We checked the nail holes in the beams with nail holes in what we know as rail 16 in the ladder."

"I show you a photograph with rail 16 on the floor; is that correct?"

"Yes, sir, it is."

"Now, did you check the nails?"

"Yes, sir."

"In the holes through rail 16 to the holes in the joists?"

"We placed four cut nails in this rail 16 and placed it upon the beams. Those nails fitted perfectly into the holes that were still in the beams here."

"What was the slant of those nails?"

"They were on a slight angle, sort of toed in."

"Was it necessary to pound the nails in or could you push them in with your finger?"

"We pushed them in with our finger."

Wilentz placed rail 16 into evidence, then turned the witness over to Frederick Pope, who took Bornmann over much of his earlier testimony before asking him a series of technical questions about wood that the detective said he wasn't qualified to answer. The witness was excused after Pope got him to say that after Hauptmann's arrest he had moved into the defendant's apartment.

The two New York City police carpenters who had been in Hauptmann's attic took the stand and corroborated Bornmann's testimony. Following their brief cross-examinations, Arthur Koehler climbed into the witness box. Through Koehler, Wilentz hoped to hang the kidnap ladder right around Hauptmann's neck.

Wilentz asked the balding, forty-seven-year-old technocrat a series of questions to establish his credentials as an expert witness. After Koehler had carefully summarized his education and experience in the field, Frederick Pope stood up and objected: "We say there is no such animal known among men as an expert on wood; that is not a science that has been recognized in court; that is not in a class with handwriting experts, with fingerprint experts, or with ballistic experts."

Judge Trenchard replied, "I think the witness is qualified as an expert upon the subject matter."

The jury seemed impressed as Koehler explained how he had traced the origins of a board in the kidnap ladder from its place of milling to a lumber store in the Bronx. Koehler also stated that one of Hauptmann's wood chisels could have been used in the construction of the ladder.

Wilentz handed Koehler the section of the ladder that had rail 16 and said, "Show the jury the part of the ladder where the nail holes are."

"This rail here, rail 16, you can see one nail hole there."

"Indicating one nail hole near the first rung of the ladder, as you are holding it up; is that it?" Wilentz asked.

"Yes, sir; near the top rung, yes. Another one there, and two of them over here."

"All right, what about them?"

"I took some nails which I had removed from a joist in the attic and placed them into the nail holes in this rail, and the nails fit perfectly. They also fit exactly into the four nail holes which were in the exposed joist."

"All right, tell us what your opinion is."

"In my opinion, rail 16 had at one time been nailed down there on these joists, because it would be inconceivable to think—"

"Well, what is your reason for the opinion?"

"There are four nail holes a certain distance apart and a certain direction from each other and in my opinion it wouldn't be possible that there would have been another board with cut nail holes in them, spaced exactly like these nail holes are in the joist, the same distance apart, the same direction from each other."

Following the noon recess, Koehler asked Judge Trenchard if he could attach clamps to his bench so he could demonstrate why he had concluded that the ladder rung had been planed by a tool found in Hauptmann's garage. With the judge's permission, the witness took a sample piece of wood and placed a sheet of paper over the edge he was to plane. With a pencil, he took an impression of the edge of the board on the paper. Putting the impression aside, he used a plane from Hauptmann's garage and used it on the surface of the wood. He took a second impression of the wood on another piece of paper then made a third from one of the ladder rungs. He showed the three sheets of paper to the jury, directing their attention to the fact that the first impression did not show ridges similar to the other two impressions. When he compared impressions of the edge he planed in the courtroom with that of the ladder rung, the two impressions were identical. Koehler said that his demonstration proved conclusively that the plane found in Hauptmann's garage had been used to plane the rung of the kidnap ladder.

Koehler spent the remainder of the afternoon discussing his study of the grain patterns in rail 16 and the sawed-off board in Hauptmann's attic. When he had finished, Wilentz felt certain the jury was convinced the two boards had at one time been joined.

Late in the afternoon, Judge Trenchard interrupted Koehler's testimony by adjourning for the day.

On Thursday morning, Koehler spent an hour discussing how he had been able to find the mill that had planed the ladder rungs. Using several charts and diagrams showing how a machine planer operates, Koehler demonstrated how he had identified the defective knife in the revolving cutting head that had planed the boards used in the kidnap ladder.

Before turning Koehler over to the defense, Wilentz placed a photograph of Hauptmann's car into evidence. Referring to the photograph Wilentz asked, "Now, did you take this ladder and attempt to fit it into that car?"

"I did."

"Did it fit in the car?"

"Yes. When I took the three sections and nested them together, they fit in on top of the front and rear seats, and there were several inches to spare."

Frederick Pope's cross-examination of Koehler was disastrous for the defense. The more Pope pressed, the more impressive Koehler became. Realizing that he was hurting his own cause, Pope wisely called it quits.

As Koehler stepped from the stand, Wilentz rose to his feet and said, "The State rests."[6]

Reilly had his work cut out for him. Wilentz had buried his client in evidence.

"What Bruno needs is a second act."

— J A C K   B E N N Y

34 THE DEFENSE CALLS
BRUNO RICHARD HAUPTMANN

AFTER LUNCH, Egbert Rosecrans for the defense moved for a directed verdict on the grounds that the State had not proven that the baby had been killed in Hunterdon County. There was also no proof, he said, that a burglary had been committed pursuant to the felony-murder doctrine.

After Wilentz's rebuttal, Judge Trenchard denied the motion and ordered Reilly to proceed with his defense.

Lloyd Fisher, the only local man on Reilly's staff, gave the opening speech. Addressing the jury in a casual conversational tone, he said the defense would provide an alibi for the defendant on all of the key dates. As for the handwriting evidence, he said:

> We will produce competent handwriting experts who will take the very exhibits put in evidence by the State of New Jersey and show you clearly and, I am convinced, to a point where there can't be a doubt in any of your minds that that is not the handwriting of Bruno Richard Hauptmann. . . . We will prove it by witnesses who are competent, and I am sure you will agree with me that they are when you hear them testify.

Fisher said the defense would explain Hauptmann's wealth, then attack the prosecution's eyewitnesses. Fisher charged that Amandus Hochmuth was a crazy old man and that Millard Whited was a well-known liar. He then laced into the New Jersey State Police: "We believe we will be able to show that no case in all of history was as badly handled or as badly mangled as this case . . ."

At the conclusion of Fisher's speech, Reilly, at nine minutes after three, called the defendant to the stand. One of Hauptmann's guards took a position directly behind him in the witness chair. There was a breathless silence in the room as Reilly approached his client. Colonel Lindbergh, sitting fifteen feet away, had his eyes glued on Hauptmann.

The defendant's unhealthy pallor and his carefully pressed but poorly fitting double-breasted suit gave him the look of an inmate dressed up for court. He rested his left elbow on the chair and leaned forward from the waist. In a thin, nasal monotone, Hauptmann told of his hard life in Germany and his early days in America when he and Anna had worked hard and had saved their money. Occasionally struggling with his English, Hauptmann spoke slowly and every so often, as though silently coached by Reilly, looked into the jury box. As he spoke, he made an obvious effort not to look in Colonel Lindbergh's direction.

Through Reilly's skillful questioning, Hauptmann accounted for himself on March 1 and April 2, 1932, and told how his relationship with Isidor Fisch had led to his possession of the ransom money. Reilly then showed Hauptmann one by one, the ransom notes, and each time the defendant, after a moment of deliberation, said that he had not written it. Just before Judge Trenchard gaveled the session closed, Hauptmann denied any connection to the kidnap ladder and said he did not pass the five-dollar ransom bill at the Loew's Sheridan Theater in Greenwich Village.

Although central New Jersey had been hit by a major snowstorm Thursday night that had closed many of the roads, the courtroom was packed Friday morning. People were standing six deep in the aisles and squeezed into the window recesses to watch Hauptmann fight for his life. Colonel Lindbergh had arrived at the courthouse with Schwarzkopf and Breckinridge after having spent the night in Trenton at the Hildebrecht Hotel. Mrs. Hauptmann was there in her familiar blue dress and tiny black hat.

The defendant walked slowly to the witness chair and seated himself in front of his guard. The spectators, many of whom were standing on their chairs to get a better view, saw Reilly bring forward the baby's sleeping suit and show it to Hauptmann. Taking care not to touch it, Hauptmann, in a raised voice, said, "I have never seen it." Reilly then held out the baby's thumb guard, which Hauptmann also denied having seen before.

Reilly next guided Hauptmann through a complicated and at times confusing discussion of his financial dealings. As Hauptmann spoke casually of his freewheeling business transactions involving large sums of money, Wilentz kept an eye on the jury. From their reactions, the prosecutor concluded that Hauptmann's discussion of his stock market speculations may have been a mistake.

Following the mid-morning recess, Hauptmann told the jury about his arrest and treatment at the Greenwich Police Station. Reilly then asked, "Now, in the station the first night, what did they do to you, if anything?"

"The first night they required the requested writings."

"Yes. Now, in writing, did you spell the words of your own free will or did they tell you how to spell the words?"

"Some of them words they spell it to me."

"How do you spell 'not'?"

"*N-O-T.*"

"Did they ask you to spell it, *N-O-T-E?*"

"I remember very well they put an *e* on it."

"How do you spell 'signature'?"

"*S-I-G-N-U-T-U-R-E.*"

"Did they tell you to spell it '*S-I-N-G—*'?"

"They did." (The word "signature" was not in any of the material dictated to Hauptmann by the police. It had been purposely omitted because of the publicity that had been given its misspelling.)

"So when they were dictating the spelling, that was not your own free will in spelling?"

"It was not."

"How many hours did they make you write?"

"I can't remember exactly the time but I know real well it was late; it was really late in nighttime, probably after twelve o'clock. I refuse to write."

Reilly questioned Hauptmann for another fifteen minutes, then turned him over to Wilentz for cross-examination. Judge Trenchard, thinking this was a good time to break, adjourned for lunch.

Huddling with his staff at the prosecution table, Wilentz whispered that he had expected better from the defendant. Not only wasn't he believable or sympathetic, he was boring. Wilentz thought that one of the jurors, Rosie Pill, was actually dozing during his testimony.

After lunch, the courtroom bristled with anticipation as Wilentz opened his cross-examination by asking the defendant about his criminal record in Germany. The defendant said that he had served almost four years in prison on a burglary conviction. With considerable prompting, Hauptmann admitted that following his release from custody, he was arrested again for another crime then escaped from jail. When pressed further, Hauptmann conceded that the burglary was a second-story job involving a ladder, and that he and another man had robbed two women at gun point.

Having established that the defendant was a convicted felon, Wilentz walked back to the prosecution table and picked up one of the ledgers that had been taken from Hauptmann's apartment. The book, covering the year 1931, contained Hauptmann's handwriting. "Now, tell me," Wilentz asked, "How do you spell 'boat.'"

"*B-O-A-T.*"

Holding up the ledger, Wilentz asked, "Why did you spell it '*B-O-A-D*'?"

"Now listen. I can't remember I put it in there." Hauptmann's legs were crossed and he was pumping his foot vigorously. His face was quite flushed, and he was leaning forward in his chair. Mrs. Hauptmann, with a solemn look on her face, sat clutching the leather purse on her lap.

"Will you please look at this one word," Wilentz said as he opened the book under Hauptmann's eyes.

"Some handwriting I can't even make out," Hauptmann said, finally looking at the page.

"But the word 'boad' is there, you won't say that it is not in your handwriting, will you?"

"I wouldn't say yes either."

"You don't say yes or no?"

"I don't say yes or no because I can't remember ever putting it in."

"The reason you don't say yes or no is because you know you wrote 'boad' when you got the fifty thousand from Condon; isn't that right?"

"No, sir."

"You come from Saxony in Germany, don't you? In Saxony they use the *d* instead of the *t*, don't they? All the words are 'boad' instead of 'boat' and things like that; isn't that a fact?"

"Some of them, yes."

Wilentz hammered away until ten to five, when Judge Trenchard, much to the defendant's relief, put a stop to the onslaught by adjourning for the weekend.

Friday night, Verna Snyder, the 265-pound juror from Centreville, New Jersey, reported that she wasn't feeling well. After a steak-and-mashed-potato dinner topped off by two pieces of pie, three cups of coffee, and fifteen rolls, she had danced to the strains of "Casey Jones" on a borrowed phonograph. She had been suffering from a cold and because of her size had been unable to put on the golashes Judge Trenchard had wanted her to wear. Not feeling well Saturday morning, she breakfasted in bed.

Saturday afternoon, Liscom Case, the juror with the weak heart, was examined by a physician after he had complained of chest pains. Mr. Case said that all of the stair climbing at the Union Hotel was getting to him.

Because Judge Trenchard had decided that the streets were too slushy for their daily walk, the jurors spent Saturday cooped up in the hotel.

Amid speculation that he was about to crack, Hauptmann issued the following statement through Lloyd Fisher: "I was tired yesterday, yes, after six hours as a witness, but I was telling the whole truth every minute, to the best of my recollection. To make up reports about a confession is very unfair to me, because I have confessed all there is to confess."[1]

Reilly was busy that Saturday rounding up alibi witnesses in New York City. He told reporters that he had found a surprise witness who would swear that he had spoken to Hauptmann on the night of the kidnapping. "This witness," Reilly said, "will say that on the night of March one he saw Hauptmann in front of a gasoline station in the Bronx holding a police dog."[2] Reilly announced that he would call two or three carpenters who would say that boards of North Carolina pine often have identical grain patterns.

New Jersey Governor Hoffman announced on Saturday that the Hauptmann trial would probably cost the state $250,000. Twenty-eight rooms at the Hildebrecht Hotel in Trenton had been turned over to Wilentz, his staff, and the prosecution's witnesses at a cost of $700 a day. A chartered bus was used to carry the witnesses back and forth between Trenton and Flemington every day, a round trip of forty-four miles. Hoffman said that it had cost $10,000 just to transport four·of Isidor Fisch's relatives from Germany.

On Sunday morning, when Lloyd Fisher was at the jail visiting Hauptmann, the fire whistle sounded. "I hope that's Dr. Condon's house," Hauptmann quipped.

That Sunday, when a reporter asked Jack Benny, a regular courtroom spectator, what he thought of the trial, the comedian replied, "What Bruno needs is a second act."[3]

At ten o'clock Monday morning, the nineteenth day of the trial, Hauptmann walked to the witness stand with an air of confidence. Wilentz asked him a few questions about his finances, then handed him a canceled check he had made out. "How much is the amount of that check?"

"Seventy-four dollars," Hauptmann replied.

"How do you spell 'seventy'?"

"Seventy? I guess—"

"Well, read it from the check you wrote. Read it. Nice and loud, please."

"S-E-N—"

"You have an *n* in there, haven't you?"

"Yes."

"All right. The same *n* as you have in 'singnature.' Isn't that right? Didn't you place the *n* in 'senvety' just like you placed the *n* in 'singnature' and for the same reason?"

"No."

Wilentz then began pointing out misspellings in Hauptmann's notebooks and ledgers, comparing them to corresponding misspellings in the ransom documents. Every so often he'd take a ledger and a ransom note over to the jury and let them look at a similarity.

Wilentz picked up a small black notebook and turned to a page containing a pencil drawing of a window and a sketch of part of a ladder that resembled the kidnap ladder. "There are some drawings there," Wilentz said, showing the page to Hauptmann. "Are they yours?"

"No, they are not mine."

"How about the picture of that window—that isn't yours? The drawing of that window?"

After showing the jury the drawings, Wilentz addressed the subjects of Hauptmann's finances, his life of leisure after the ransom had been paid, and Isidor Fisch. He then got Hauptmann to admit that prior to April 1932, he didn't have much success in the stock market. Wilentz next showed Hauptmann the trim taken from inside his closet.

"Do you know what this is, Mr. Defendant?" Wilentz asked.

"A piece of board, yes."

"From your house?"

"I really don't know if it's from my house. Trimming from every house looks the same."

"That is your handwriting on it, isn't it?"

"No."

"What?"

"No, sir."

"That is not your handwriting?"

"No."

"Do you remember District Attorney Foley asking you, 'Why did you write it on the board?' Do you remember that?"

"I can't make out your question."

"Now, do you remember this answer to that question: 'I must have read it in the paper about the story. I was a little bit interest and keep a little bit of a record of it and maybe I was just in the closet and was reading the paper and put down the address.'"

"Not exactly, I—"

"Are you saying you didn't write Condon's phone number and address?"

"I don't want to say that, I didn't—"

"You didn't want to say yes or no."

"I guess I told him something about it."

"Now, Mr. Hauptmann, what you mean then is this: That you had the habit of writing down telephone numbers and addresses of things that are interesting; isn't that right?"

"Yes."

"And you must have read this in the paper and you were near the closet, so you wrote it down; that is what you mean, isn't it?"

"There is a possibility, but I can't remember."

"Well, you know you wrote on the board. You remember that?"

"But I am positively sure that I wouldn't write anything in the inside of a closet."

"Well, didn't you say in the Bronx that you wrote the numbers on?"

"I said it looks like that."

"Did you tell the district attorney the truth?"

"Well—"

"Why don't you answer the question, Mr. Defendant?"

"Well, anybody can show me a piece of wood like that; you find it in every house."

"Did you tell the district attorney the truth when he spoke to you about this board? You might just as well answer it because I'm going to stay here until you do."

"The truth; well, I told him—"

"Did you tell him the truth?"

"I told him the truth, yes."

Hauptmann finally said that he hadn't written Condon's phone number and address on the door trim. In an effort to explain something he himself didn't understand, he had given Foley the only explanation he could think of at the time—so it really wasn't a lie, not exactly.

The defendant did admit writing the serial numbers of a five hundred- and a thousand-dollar bill on the back of the closet door. Wilentz hoped the jury would assume that if Hauptmann had jotted down the serial numbers, he had also written the Condon data on the door trim.

After lunch, Wilentz launched a blistering attack on the defendant, who was showing some signs of wear. Every so often a tight, nervous smile crossed Hauptmann's lips. Annoyed by this, Wilentz said, "You are having a lot of fun with me, aren't you?"

"No."

"Well, you are doing very well. You are smiling at me every five minutes."

"No."

"You think you are a big shot don't you?"

"No. Should I cry?"

"No, certainly you shouldn't. You think you are bigger than everybody, don't you?"

"No, but I know I am innocent."

"Lying when you swear to God that you will tell the truth. Telling lies doesn't mean anything."

"Stop that!" Hauptmann snapped in a shrill voice.

"When you were arrested with this Lindbergh money, and you had a twenty-dollar bill, Lindbergh ransom money, did they ask you where you got it? Did they ask you?"

"They did."

"Did you lie to them or did you tell them the truth?"

"I said not the truth."

"You lied, didn't you?"

"Yes."

"Lies, lies, lies about Lindbergh ransom money, isn't that right?"

"Well, you lied to me too."

"Yes? Where and when?"

"Right in this courtroom here."

"We will let the jury decide about that. In this courtroom."

At this point Judge Trenchard decided to cool things off with a short recess. When the proceeding resumed, in a somewhat calmer atmosphere, Hauptmann testified that he had been to his attic many times but never noticed a board missing from the flooring. He then stated that he had told John F. O'Ryan, the police commissioner of New York City, that the ransom money was in his garage before the police had found it.

The questioning then swung back to Hauptmann's financial dealings with Isidor Fisch. Hauptmann said that he had written to Fisch's relatives after the fur trader's death but didn't mention the money Fisch had left behind. "And when you did find the money, you forgot to tell them, isn't that right?"

"Oh well, no. I was—"

"You were saving the secret for them?"

"No."

"You were not going to keep the money?"

"I was going to keep my share."

Fifteen minutes later, Judge Trenchard took advantage of a good place to break and adjourned for the day.

Thirty minutes after the adjournment, Mrs. Hauptmann stopped by the jail to have a word with her husband. Having observed the visit, Lieutenant Allen Smith wrote: "During the interview between prisoner and his wife at 5:02 P.M., it was noticed that she seemed unusually worried, and seemed about to cry."[4]

The next day, Tuesday, Wilentz spent most of the morning grilling Hauptmann about his business transactions. That afternoon he pressed the defendant about Isidor Fisch and the ransom money. "Why did you hide the money in the garage?" he asked.

"If somebody comes in, he takes it away."

"You had a bank account. You had a vault."

"Yes."

"You didn't put it there?"

"No."

"When you had $4,200 of your own to hide, that you wanted to hide from your wife, you didn't hide it in the garage?"

"No."

"As a matter of fact, you knew that you were planning to go to Germany right at that time, weren't you?"

"Oh, that is planned for a year already."

"For a year already," Wilentz said, looking at the jury.

"Yes."

"You said 'that is planned for a year already,' didn't you?"

"Yes."

"And that is what you said in the ransom note—'this kidnapping was *prepared for a year already!*'"

"I did not write any ransom note," Hauptmann replied.

Before the court adjourned for the day, a translator read into the record two letters Hauptmann had written, in German, to Isidor Fisch's brother after Isidor's death.

The next day, before the noon recess, Wilentz was winding up his cross-examination by once again quizzing Hauptmann about Condon's phone number and address in his closet. Hauptmann explained his admission to District Attorney Foley by saying that he was confused and couldn't think. Wilentz's response was sarcastic: "You have a very good mind, haven't you?"

"Well, I don't think so, not so good," Hauptmann said dejectedly.

"Oh, you really do think so, don't you?"

Hauptmann, looked disheartened, made no reply.

"That is all," Wilentz snapped as he stepped away from the witness box. Hauptmann jumped up from the chair, stretched, and walked quickly back to his seat in the courtroom. Before he sat down he looked at the jury and smiled.

On the stand for seventeen hours, Hauptmann had been cross-examined, at times savagely, for eleven. Although he had survived the ordeal without cracking, Reilly and his assistants couldn't have been pleased. Hauptmann's expressionless face, his metallic, whining voice, superior attitude, and outbursts of rage had made him a rather unattractive, hard-to-believe, and unsympathetic witness.[5]

Jack Benny was right—Hauptmann needed a second act.

Who wouldn't trust their husband?

— A N N A H A U P T M A N N

35 ANNA AND THE ALIBI WITNESSES

AFTER LUNCH, Reilly called Mrs. Hauptmann to the stand. She was flushed and looked nervous as she settled into the witness chair. Around her neck she wore a white medallion on a black ribbon, and on the fingers of her left hand were her gold wedding and engagement rings.

Annoyed by the rustling, coughing, and whispering that was going on, Judge Trenchard abruptly ordered everybody who didn't have a seat out of the sweltering courtroom. Once the complaining standees were ushered out of the room by the deputy sheriffs, Reilly, in his most sincere and sympathetic voice, questioned Mrs. Hauptmann about her early life with the defendant.

Anna said that when she met her future husband in January 1924, she had only been in the country three months. Two years later they were married. She worked first as a housekeeper, then, in June 1929, got a job as a waitress at Fredericksen's Bakery-Lunchroom in the Bronx, where she earned, in wages and tips, eighteen dollars a week. Richard was at that time bringing home sixty-six dollars a month as a carpenter.

In 1928 and in the summer of 1932, she had traveled to Germany. The first trip was to visit her parents, the second to see if Richard, as she called him, could return to his homeland without being arrested. An attorney in Germany told Anna that it would be a few more years before her husband could come home.

Reilly took Mrs. Hauptmann back to March 1, 1932, when, according to her testimony, Richard had called for her at the bakery at seven o'clock that evening. He had hung around the place until 9:30, then drove them back to their apartment on 222nd Street.

On April 2, 1932, the night the ransom money changed hands at St. Raymond's Cemetery, Anna remembered that Richard was at home entertaining his friend Hans Kloppenburg. On Sunday, November 26, 1933, the night the five-dollar ransom bill was passed at the theater in Greenwich Village, Richard was celebrating his birthday with

Paul Vetterle and Isidor Fisch. Mrs. Hauptmann's niece, Mrs. Mueller, was also at the apartment that night.

In his cross-examination of the defendant Wilentz had implied that Bruno had had an affair with the beautiful Gerta Henkel. Just in case there were any doubts about his client's marital fidelity, Reilly asked, "When was it, Mrs. Hauptmann, that you first met Mrs. Henkel?"

"It was in 1932 after I came back from Germany, I believe, in October."

"Where did you meet her?"

"In our house."

"Who took you there to meet her?"

"My husband."

"Had he met her while you were in Europe?"

"Yes."

"You saw her many times after that?"

"Oh, yes; she came in my house often."

"Now, Mrs. Hauptmann, from anything you saw or anything you heard in connection with Mrs. Henkel and your husband, have you ever entertained the slightest suspicion concerning your husband's infidelity toward you?"

"Mrs. Henkel was not only a friend of my husband, she was my friend too."

"Did you ever entertain any thoughts or opinions that your husband was untrue to you?"

"Never."

Mrs. Hauptmann testified further that she had first met Isidor Fisch at the Henkel home after she had returned from Germany. Late in November 1933, about four days before Isidor sailed for Germany, the Hauptmanns gave him a farewell party. A week before that, Isidor had brought to their apartment a suitcase, several cardboard boxes full of furs, and a valise containing books. Mrs. Hauptmann described her kitchen broom closet and said that because of a leak in the roof, things stored in there often got wet. She said she never saw the shoebox Richard had put on the top shelf of that closet because it was beyond her reach and above her view.

During her marriage, Mrs. Hauptmann said that she had earned about seven thousand dollars, which she had deposited in a bank account she shared with her husband. Reilly asked her if she had trusted Richard enough to put all that money in his control. Seemingly shocked and a little offended that Reilly would ask such a question, she replied, "Sure."

Rising to his feet, Wilentz objected to the question because it called for a conclusion. He asked to have the question and Mrs. Hauptmann's answer stricken from the record.

When Reilly reframed the question, Mrs. Hauptmann said, "Who wouldn't trust their husband?"

Reilly looked at Wilentz and quipped, "That speaks well for some of us. The witness is yours, General."

Mrs. Hauptmann braced herself as Wilentz approached the witness chair. This was, after all, the man who had savagely attacked her husband for eleven hours, the man who was trying to put him in the electric chair. Reilly had warned Anna that the prosecutor would try to demolish her alibi testimony—she would have to stand firm, not give an inch. Her husband's life depended on it.

Speaking softly and in a respectful tone, Wilentz asked, "You put your money in the bank; the money that you saved as the result of your hard work, you put in the bank, didn't you?"

"Yes, I did."

"And then finally your husband started to gamble in the stock market, is that right?"

"Yes."

"And then he lost some money, is that so?"

"I guess so."

"When Mr. Fisch died, and you got word, and you went down to look at the valises and the trunks, or whatever it was he had, what happened to them?"

"My husband went down to the garage and brought them up."

"Brought them up to the house?"

"To the front room."

"And what happened to them?"

"We opened them, looked it over, what was in it."

"Yes. And when you found out what was in it, what did you do with it?"

"Took them to the garage."

"What did you do with the furs?"

"They were still in the room, in the baby's closet."

Wilentz brought the witness to the subject of Isidor Fisch's shoebox and the closet Bruno said he had put it in. "Now, this broom closet we talked about, it was in the kitchen, wasn't it?"

"Yes."

"And it was the closet to which you went everyday, wasn't it?"

"Yes."

"Everyday you went to that closet, and you never saw any shoebox on the top shelf, did you?"

"I didn't know what was on the top shelf."

"You never saw a shoebox there, madam, did you?"

"I didn't."

"No. From December 1933, the month and the day that Mr. Fisch was last at your home, until September 1934, you never saw a strange box on the top shelf of that closet, did you?"

"I never had anything to do with the top shelf. I didn't use it for myself."

With the friendly tone slipping from his voice, Wilentz handed Mrs. Hauptmann a photograph of the broom closet, directing her attention to an apron hanging on the hook on the back of the closet door. "Is that your apron?"

"Yes."

"And could you hang it on the back like that with ease?"

"Yes."

"You had no problem reaching the hook?"

"No."

Moving in for the kill, Wilentz asked, "So you had no trouble reaching above the top shelf of the closet to hang up your apron?"

"I had no trouble reaching it."

"And you know if you stand a few feet away from it you could see everything on that top shelf?"

"Why should I stay away a few feet and look up there?"

"I know that, but if the closet door was open and you stood a few feet from it, if you looked at it you could see everything on the top shelf?"

"I didn't stay away a few feet; when I went to the closet I went over, opened the door, and got whatever I needed from the closet."

"I don't want to argue with you, madam. I would like to have you answer the question. If you don't want to answer it, I will stop asking it. Will you please tell me if it is not a fact that if you stepped away from the closet a few feet, that, beginning a few feet away from the closet, that as you looked at it, if the door was open, you could see everything on the top shelf of that closet, couldn't you?"

"I don't think so," Mrs. Hauptmann said. Her cheeks were flushed as she shifted uneasily in the chair.

"You were the lady of the house and I take it you did your own cleaning, Mrs. Hauptmann?"

"I did."

"And of course you cleaned the closet too, once in a while?"

"I do clean closets," Mrs. Hauptmann snapped.

"How often do you clean this closet—once a month, once in six months?"

"Almost every week."

"Did you ever clean the shelves?"

"I did."

"Did you ever clean the top shelf?"

"No, I didn't."

"Never cleaned the top shelf?"

"No."

"You cleaned the first shelf, didn't you?"

"I had to clean the first and second because I had my stuff there."

"So you cleaned the first shelf and you cleaned the second shelf, but you never cleaned the top shelf?"

"No, I didn't use it."

But Wilentz persisted, "Didn't you tell Mr. Reilly that you kept some shelf trimming on that top shelf?"

"Yes. My niece had given me the shelf paper, but I couldn't use it so I stored it on the top shelf."

"Of course it wasn't dirty up there, was it?"

"What should I do up there? I put that stuff up there and I left it there."

"Now won't you just try for a minute, please, and see if you can't remember whether you kept something else on there besides the shelf trimmings?"

Mrs. Hauptmann didn't respond.

"Well, maybe I can help refresh your recollection. You used to have a tin box up there, didn't you?"

"Yes, a box I had up there."

"And in that tin box you used to keep coupons, didn't you?"

"Yes, I did."

"You used to keep the coupons you got from soap?"

"Yes."

"And you kept that up on the top shelf, and every time you bought soap and you got coupons from the soap, you would save them, wouldn't you?"

"I saved them, yes."

"So, after you would save a certain number of coupons, you would take them and put them in the tin box?"

"No, I would get the box down."

"Then when you went to take the tin box down, that would happen how often, about once a month, two months, three months?"

"Once every three months, four months."

"From December 1933 until September 1934, I suppose that you took that box down at least two or three times, didn't you?"

"Maybe I did."

"Now, when you went to take that box down, that tin box down, you had to reach into the closet, didn't you?"

"Yes."

"And into that top shelf?"

"Yes."

"You didn't see any shoebox there, did you?"

"Well, that—"

"Please answer the question, madam."

"No, I didn't."

Wilentz paused, glanced at the jury to punctuate the answer, then turned and looked at the defendant, who sat there glumly. The prosecutor had made a vital point. If the shoebox containing the ransom money had been in the broom closet as the defendant had said it was, Mrs. Hauptmann would have seen it. She didn't see it because it wasn't there, and it wasn't there because the business about Isidor Fisch was bunk.[1]

Wilentz next reminded Mrs. Hauptmann that in October 1934, when Insp. Henry Bruckman of the Bronx had asked her if she could recall what her husband had been doing on March 1, 1932, she had said that she couldn't remember what he was doing on that particular day. Did she say that? Yes, she replied in a flat, dead voice, she had said that.

Wilentz asked a few more questions, then backed away from the witness chair. He was finished with Mrs. Hauptmann. Reilly, on re-direct, tried to breathe some life back into his deflated witness. He wound up his examination by getting her to say that there was no doubt in her mind that the defendant was with her on the night of March 1, 1932.

Mrs. Hauptmann got up from the witness chair and walked heavily back to her seat at the defense table. None of the defense attorneys bothered to speak to her or even look her way—it was as though she had betrayed them. For Wilentz, it was total victory, and for Reilly, one of the lowest points of the trial.[2]

The next witness was Elvert Carlstrom, a tall young Swede. Speaking in a heavy accent, Carlstrom said that at 8:30 on the night of March 1, 1932, which happened to be his birthday, he was sitting in Fredericksen's Bakery in the Bronx. He had planned to call on a girlfriend that night but had gotten into town too late for that.

Reilly asked the witness if he had seen anyone in the bakery that night who was now in the courtroom. Carlstrom said yes. Reilly pointed toward the defendant and asked him to stand up so the witness could get a better look at him. Yes, that was the man, Carlstrom said. The witness said that when he saw Hauptmann's photographs in the papers following his arrest, he realized he had seen that face in the bakery.

On cross-examination, Wilentz got the witness to say there were four or five other customers in the bakery that night. When Wilentz asked the witness to describe these people, he couldn't. Wilentz then asked Carlstrom how he had been able to remember Hauptmann so well. The witness said that he remembered Hauptmann because the defendant had made him angry that evening—Hauptmann had laughed at his broken English when he ordered a meal from the waitress—Mrs. Hauptmann.

Wilentz asked Carlstrom to describe Hauptmann's face, and when the witness tried to look at the defendant, Wilentz blocked his view. Completely flustered in his attempts to describe Hauptmann, the witness became evasive and hostile. Under Wilentz's prodding, the witness described a feature of Hauptmann's face, then changed his mind. After several minutes of this, it was obvious that he could not describe the defendant. Judge Trenchard called a five-minute recess.

When the court got back into session, Wilentz asked the witness to account for his activities after he left the bakery. Carlstrom said he went to a movie, then drove to Brooklyn. But when Wilentz asked him what he had done in Brooklyn that night, the witness wouldn't answer. Wilentz kept pressing until Carlstrom said that if he answered that question he'd incriminate himself.

On that note, Judge Trenchard adjourned for the day.

The next morning, armed with data dug up overnight by his investigators, Wilentz tore Carlstrom apart. It seemed that Reilly's alibi witness was a petty thief and a former bootlegger with a history of mental instability. By the time Wilentz was finished with him, not even Hauptmann took Carlstrom seriously. On re-direct, Reilly tried to salvage what he could out of Carlstrom's testimony but ended up making the witness appear even more unstable.[3]

The next alibi witness was a thirty-five-year-old Hungarian-American from Manhattan named Louis Kiss. He spoke so softly no one could hear him. Asked by Reilly to speak a little louder, he said he was a "silk painter artist."

"What is that?" Judge Trenchard asked. "I don't get it."

"I paint on silk—wall decorations," the witness explained. With that cleared up, Kiss said that he was in Fredericksen's Bakery on the night of March 1, 1932, having a cup of coffee when Hauptmann came into the place accompanied by a police dog. Kiss was sure this took place on March 1, because one week earlier, on Washington's birthday, he had taken his seven-year-old son who was suffering from a kidney ailment to the emergency room at Bellevue Hospital. Reilly finished his direct examination and Judge Trenchard called for a short recess.

After Wilentz reminded Kiss how he had fixed the day he had seen Hauptmann at the bakery, he showed him a calendar and pointed out that 1932 was a leap year. Therefore, in 1932, one week after Washington's birthday was February 29, not March 1.

Wilentz asked Kiss what he had been doing in the Bronx that night. "Delivering two pints of whisky to a friend," Kiss said nonchalantly.

"Where did you buy it?"

"I made it."

"Did you manufacture rum at the time?" (In 1932, Prohibition was still in effect.)

"No, I bought alcohol on Second Avenue and I put in the flavor."

"How long did it take you to make the rum?"

"Ten minutes."

"How much did you sell the rum for?"

"Dollar and a quarter a pint."

When the giggling stopped, Wilentz concluded his cross-examination by asking Kiss if he had been drinking his own rum the night he saw Hauptmann and the police dog. Kiss made everyone laugh when he said, "I only drink rum in the morning—at night I drink wine."

August Van Henke, the owner of a Manhattan restaurant, took the stand and said that on the night of March 1, 1932, he was at a gas station near Fredericksen's Bakery when he saw a man with a police dog. Since Rex, his own police dog, was missing, Van Henke approached the man to inquire about the dog, which turned out not to be Rex. The man Van Henke spoke to was Bruno Richard Hauptmann. Later that night, the witness said he heard about the Lindbergh kidnapping over the radio. Two and a half years later, when Hauptmann was arrested and his pictures appeared in the newspapers, Van Henke wrote a letter to James Fawcett informing him of the defendant's whereabouts on the night of the crime.

Obviously pleased with his witness, Reilly turned him over to Wilentz for cross-examination.

Van Henke, sitting back comfortably in the witness chair, was jolted to attention by one of Wilentz's more savage attacks: "What is your name, sir?"

"August Van Henke."

"Who is August Wunstorf?"

"That is me."

"I thought your name was Van Henke?"

"Yes."

Under further questioning, the witness admitted he had once used the name Wunstorf because of "family trouble." He also said his restaurant had been a speakeasy. Leaning forward in the chair with a menacing look on his face, the witness denied that he also owned a restaurant in Harlem where white men and black women co-mingled in rented rooms upstairs. "Dot's a lie," he snarled. Van Henke then said his true name was August Marhenke.

"You told us before that Van Henke was your right name," Wilentz said in feigned exasperation.

Reilly's next witness was a tall, broad-shouldered, young ditchdigger from Trenton named Lou Harding. In contrast to the last three witnesses, who wore business suits, Harding was wearing tattered, baggy work trousers and a red checkered shirt with a tear in one sleeve from the elbow to the cuff.

Harding testified that on the morning of March 1, 1932, while he was repairing a sidewalk in Princeton, a blue sedan occupied by two men pulled up to him at the curb. One of the men in the car asked Harding for directions to the Lindbergh estate, and while the witness was telling them how to get there, he saw a ladder and a brown pasteboard box in the back seat. Bruno Richard Hauptmann, Harding said, was not one of these men. Harding said that he had reported the incident to the Princeton police, who took him to the Lindbergh house. There he was questioned by two detectives, who showed him the kidnap ladder, which he identified as the one he had seen in the blue car.

Under Wilentz's blistering cross-examination, Harding admitted that he had served time in Rahway Prison. "Well," Wilentz asked, "weren't you convicted a second time?"

"I was convicted of assault and battery, yes."

Wilentz asked Harding if the detectives who had questioned him at the Lindbergh house were in the courtroom. The witness said yes and pointed to Trooper William Kelly (not to be confused with Frank Kelly, the fingerprint man).

"Don't you know, as a matter of fact, that William Kelly never spent one minute on the Lindbergh case?" Wilentz said.

"Well, I don't know who spent any minutes on it."

"Weren't you convicted of another crime of assault and battery on a woman?"

"Yes, I was convicted of a crime, yes."

"An attack on a woman, wasn't it?"

"No, I did not."

"Well, that is what you were convicted of."

"My lawyer told me to plead not guilty to it."

"To the charge of—"

"Carnal abuse."

Wilentz next got Harding to admit that he had served two thirty-day drunk-and-

340   disorderly sentences in the Mercer County Workhouse. When asked to describe the ladder in the car, Harding said it was ten feet long, then said each section was eight feet long, then said he wasn't sure how long it was. He couldn't say how it was made, recall its color, or say how it was designed. Finally, Harding said that he had only gotten a "glance" at the ladder.

On re-direct, Reilly tried to prop up his sagging witness, but it was too late.

Hauptmann leaned over to Lloyd Fisher and whispered that Harding and the others were poor witnesses. As Hauptmann complained about his witnesses, the relative silence of the courtroom was broken by a resounding crash. The commotion had come from the press section, where a bench holding several reporters and a fat man had collapsed. A few minutes later, the huge spectator demolished a chair. A deputy sheriff helped the unfortunate man to his feet, then escorted him out of the room. Judge Trenchard, ignoring the destruction of his courtroom, adjourned for lunch.

When Wilentz looked over at the defense table, he saw something he hadn't seen before, the defendant was consoling his wife. In the past it had been the other way around.

Where are they getting these witnesses? They're killing me!

— B R U N O   R I C H A R D   H A U P T M A N N

36 THE PHANTOM EXPERTS

WHEN THE COURT RECONVENED at one o'clock Thursday afternoon, Reilly called to the stand John Trendley, a sixty-seven-year-old documents examiner from St. Louis, Missouri, who had volunteered his services to the defense six weeks ago.

On the day before the trial, Trendley had told a reporter from the *St. Louis Globe-Democrat* that he would testify that Isidor Fisch had written the ransom notes.[1] He said that some of the *d*'s in the ransom documents looked like the letter *d* in Fisch's signature. Trendley had formulated this opinion even though the only known handwriting he had seen of Fisch's was a newspaper photograph of his signature, which he had compared to newspaper photographs of two of the ransom notes. Trendley was one of the eight handwriting people who, on January 12, had examined the documents evidence for Reilly at the Hildebrecht Hotel in Trenton. Shortly thereafter, two experts, Samuel C. Malone and Arthur P. Meyers, announced that they would not be able to testify on Hauptmann's behalf.

Before Trendley could state his opinion about who wrote the ransom notes, Reilly had to get him qualified as an expert witness. (Wilentz hadn't followed this procedure because Reilly had conceded the expertise of the prosecution's witnesses.) In outlining his qualifications, Trendley said that during the past forty years he had testified as an expert in four hundred murder, fraud, and forgery trials. He had made, he said, a specialty of imitating or forging people's handwriting, a skill he had used to fool other documents examiners, including Albert S. Osborn and John Tyrrell, who had opposed him in past cases.[2]

Reilly relinquished his witness to Joseph Lanigan, whose cross-examination was intended to show that Trendley was not a bonafide questioned documents expert. Regarding one of Trendley's earlier cases, Lanigan asked, "Do you recall going on the witness stand as an expert and being shown a document that you said was genuine and then going out to lunch and coming back and under oath testifying that the document you swore in the morning was genuine was a forgery?"

"No," Trendley replied.

"You don't?" Lanigan asked as though he were surprised by the denial.

"No."

Lanigan pressed Trendley until he said that he did recall testifying in a case involving a man named Olmer. From the transcript of that trial, Lanigan read to the jury the part where Trendley had admitted that in a previous case, he had told the defendant that the signature was genuine, and then, without realizing it, he gave the plaintiff the opinion that it was a forgery. Lanigan got Trendley to concede that the statement was true and that he had also changed his testimony in the Olmer trial.

Lanigan concluded his very successful cross-examination and moved to have Trendley disqualified as a questioned-documents expert. Judge Trenchard deliberated for a moment before ruling that the witness could testify as an expert, which meant that, unlike ordinary witnesses, Trendley could express his opinion. The judge said the jury could decide if Trendley's conclusions had any validity.

With the witness qualified as an expert, Reilly proceeded with his direct examination by asking Trendley if he had been in the courtroom when the prosecution's experts had testified. Trendley said that he had, and that he had taken the opportunity to study their word charts carefully. Since it was late in the afternoon and Judge Trenchard didn't want to interrupt Trendley's testimony at a crucial point, he adjourned for the day.

That evening, several New York City newspapers published an interview with Hauptmann's seventy-year-old mother, Pauline. Mrs. Hauptmann said that she had been following the trial in the German newspapers and was disappointed with the way it was going for her son. She recalled that after Richard's father had died in 1917, the boy had no strong hand to control him. "I was often too weak and let him have his own way," she said. "When he was sometimes a little good-for-nothing, that was simply a fault of his temperament." Referring to Richard's criminal activities after the war, Mrs. Hauptmann said that those years had brought her "a great deal of sorrow and trouble."[3]

Knowing that Reilly was always good for a story, reporters that night asked him to comment on the trial. Gesturing wildly with his arms, the defense attorney said that seven of his witnesses had been frightened off by "plug uglies" who said they were members of the New Jersey State Police. He claimed that several of his potential witnesses had been threatened with arrest if they took the stand on Hauptmann's behalf.

Meanwhile, investigators checking into the stories of Hauptmann's alibi witnesses had located a house painter named Arthur Larsen who said that on the night of the kidnapping, Elvert Carlstrom had spent the night with him at a house in Dunellen, New Jersey. The owner of the house, Oscar Christiansen, corroborated Larsen's story.

On Friday morning, before John Trendley resumed his handwriting testimony, Wilentz put into evidence a record from Bellevue Hospital that showed that Louis Kiss's seven-year-old boy had entered the hospital at 1:30 A.M. on February 22, not February 23 as claimed by the defense.

Under Reilly's direct examination, Trendley said that although he had spent "day and night" going over photographs of the ransom note, he had only looked at the originals for two and half hours at the Hildebrecht Hotel. Regarding Albert S. Osborn's word charts, Trendley said that Osborn had not included all of the letters needed to form the phrase, "Dear Sir," the beginning of the note found in the nursery. Trendley had also noticed that the figure "$50,000" did not appear on any of Osborn's charts.

Trendley testified that Hauptmann's known writings showed that his y's were made with four strokes, or at least three, while the writer of the ransom letters had made his y's with just two strokes, using a downward and an upward motion. At this point, Reilly asked, "So then, is it not a fact that, beginning 'Dear Sir', line one, 'Have 50,000$ redy', to the end of line five, you cannot find on Mr. Osborn's chart any symbol, letter, or word taken from those five lines?"

"I cannot."

Reilly's handling of Trendley had been masterful. By casting doubt on Hauptmann's authorship of the nursery note, Reilly was hitting the prosecution in its most vulnerable spot. If Hauptmann had written all of the notes except the one in the nursery, he would have been an extortionist but not necessarily the abductor and killer of the child. If there was one area of proof where the prosecution was a little thin, it was in placing Hauptmann inside the Lindbergh house.

Reilly had also done a marvelous job of making Trendley sound qualified and credible. Instead of asking the expert to state his conclusions, then explain his reasons, the customary way of questioning an expert, Reilly had incorporated the conclusions in the questions so that Trendley merely had to agree.

On cross-examination, Joseph Lanigan asked Trendley about the day he and the others studied the original handwriting evidence at the Hildebrecht Hotel: "Now you examined fifty documents in two and a half hours?"

"No, I told you we just looked them over casually; they were shuffling them up and passing them around."

Lanigan asked Trendley how he accounted for the fact that Hauptmann and the ransom note writer had misspelled many of the words in the same way. Trendley disregarded this aspect of the handwriting evidence, stating that because the request writings had been acquired under the supervision of the police, they were suspect and therefore not worthy of consideration.

"If somebody was imitating Hauptmann's handwriting," Lanigan asked, "Wouldn't he have to be familiar with his misspellings?"

"I thought he might have been told to spell them that way."

"Wouldn't he have to be thoroughly familiar with his grammar?"

"Yes. I noticed there were some mistakes."

Lanigan was finished, so Trendley, looking sullen and a little less confident, stepped from the stand. A few minutes later, the court broke for lunch.

Following the break, Wilentz was surprised to hear Reilly call a man named Peter H. Sommer to the witness box. Wilentz had been expecting more handwriting experts be-

344 cause Reilly had said that there would be at least eight of them. After Lloyd Fisher's opening speech, Wilentz assumed that Reilly didn't have eight, but surely he had more than one.

Peter Sommer seated himself comfortably in the witness chair and said that on the night of the crime he was crossing the Hudson River on the Forty-second Street ferry. He said that Isidor Fisch, in the company of another man, was sitting on the bench across from him. When the boat docked on the Manhattan side, shortly after midnight, Sommer saw Fisch and the other man get onto a trolley car with a young woman who had a baby in her arms. The baby was wrapped in a blanket and whenever the woman shifted the bundle in her arms, Sommer could see that it was blond, dressed in a "one-piece nighty," and perhaps two years old.

"And who was this woman?" Reilly asked quite dramatically.

"The woman was Violet Sharpe," Sommer replied, setting the courtroom abuzz.

The witness said that he reported all of this the next day to Detective Mulrooney in Brooklyn, and a few days after that had put it all down in a letter to the New Jersey State Police in Trenton. He said his letter wasn't answered, and no one from the State Police came to see him. Then, two weeks ago, Sommer wrote to Mr. Reilly.

Reilly thanked Mr. Sommer, and knowing that he had caught Wilentz by surprise, smiled at the prosecutor and said, "The witness is yours."

Wilentz asked the witness if he had reported his ferry boat story to Hauptmann's initial attorney, James Fawcett. The witness said that he hadn't, prompting Wilentz to ask sarcastically if Sommer were as keenly interested in justice in September 1934 as he was now. Seemingly oblivious to Wilentz's sarcasm, the witness said that he was, yes.

Next, Wilentz wanted to know exactly when Sommer first noticed each man, what they had looked like and where they had gone after they got off the trolley car. Sommer seemed a little confused and was losing some of his composure. "What happened to the tall man so far as you know?" Wilentz asked.

"Why, he assisted this woman on the trolley car."

"So that the short man didn't assist her, did he?"

"This picture [a photograph of Isidor Fisch] that I identified, yes."

"Well, the short man you didn't see on the trolley car?"

"The one, the short—"

"Just a minute now," Wilentz snapped.

"Please, don't puzzle me up," the witness pleaded.

"I am not going to puzzle you up," Wilentz replied.

"And I am not going to be puzzled. I am stating that the short man that came—"

"Just one minute now. You are going to answer the questions," Wilentz blared.

"All right, I am going to answer them."

"Yes sir."

"But I am not going to be puzzled by anybody."

Wilentz kept pressing the witness about the two men and Sommer kept complaining that the prosecution was trying to confuse him. Wilentz showed Sommer a photograph of Isidor Fisch and one of Violet Sharpe and asked if these were the people he had seen that night. The witness refused to say, claiming that the photographs were too blurred to identify. By the time Judge Trenchard had adjourned for the weekend, the cross-examination had degenerated into a pointless argument. Wilentz announced that on Monday he would have more questions for Mr. Sommer.

That evening, Reilly was back on the radio talking about the trial, assuring his listeners that within a few days his client would be walking the streets of Flemington a free man. Reilly concluded his broadcast by appealing to anyone who had information about the case to come forward.

Following the broadcast, Reilly told reporters that the New Jersey State Police were still harassing and intimidating his witnesses. He claimed that the only reason Wilentz had kept Peter Sommer on the stand until the court adjourned was to give his detectives a chance to investigate the witness over the weekend.

The previous night, Judge Trenchard was shocked to learn that newsreel films of the trial were showing in several theaters in New York City and New Jersey. The next morning, the judge discovered that a motion picture camera, housed in a special box to deaden its noise, had been set up in the balcony. The witnesses' voices had been picked up by a directional beam microphone installed on a windowsill thirty-five feet from the stand. The mike was partially hidden by an electric fan that didn't work.

Friday evening, Wilentz and the representatives of five motion picture companies conferred in the judge's chambers. When the meeting broke up, Wilentz told the press that the motion picture companies had violated a gentlemen's agreement not to film the proceedings. The prosecutor said that he had sent a message to the companies involved—Universal Pictures, Fox Movietone, Pathé News, Paramount Pictures, and Hearst Metrotone News—asking them not to show the films until the trial was over. The camera had been operated, Wilentz said, without the knowledge of the judge, the prosecution, the defense, or Sheriff John Curtiss. Wilentz then lashed out at the executives of these companies: "These cheap tricksters sit in their offices in New York and Hollywood and think that nothing is superior to the movies and the dollar. They give their word of honor through their representatives—and it was violated."[4]

Fox, Paramount, and Hearst agreed to withhold their films, but Universal and Pathé did not. As Wilentz spoke, newsreels of the trial were playing in moviehouses all over New York City and New Jersey.

Truman Talley, the editor of Fox Movietone News, stood next to Wilentz, and when the prosecutor finished speaking, Talley said that Judge Trenchard, Wilentz, and the defense counsel knew about the camera. "Why, they had a state trooper stationed next to the camera to make sure it wasn't making any noticeable noise," he said.

On Saturday morning, Lloyd Fisher, suffering from a bad cold, visited Hauptmann and found him surly and depressed. On Friday, the defendant had been in such a peevish mood he had complained to his guards that his chair was dusty. Hauptmann told Fisher he didn't like the way Reilly was handling his defense. "Where are they getting these witnesses?" he asked. "They're killing me!"

Fisher was also critical of Reilly, but he didn't want Hauptmann to know this. Instead of poking holes in the State's evidence and building reasonable doubt, Reilly was trying to prove not one but several alternative theories of the case. He was doing this with lunatic witnesses who were embarrassing Hauptmann with their farfetched, fantastic stories. Fisher also disapproved of soliciting witnesses over the radio. By doing this, Reilly was inviting every charlatan in New York, New Jersey, and Pennsylvania to join in the fun. Moreover, it made the defense look desperate.

On that Saturday, one of Reilly's original eight handwriting experts, Hilda Braunlich, a thirty-seven-year-old examiner from Wuertzburgh, Germany, said that she was prepared to testify for Hauptmann. Braunlich, a portrait painter by trade, had immigrated to America in 1931. She lived in New York City and had been recommended to Reilly by a German-American physician from Queens. Reilly had asked another one of his handwriting people, C. F. Goodspeed of Brooklyn, to determine if she was a competent questioned-documents examiner. To do this, Goodspeed had shown her sixteen checks containing fifteen genuine signatures and asked her to identify the one that was forged. (This is a skill most students can learn in five minutes.) Hilda had picked out the forged document and Goodspeed reported to Reilly that she was legitimate.[5]

The prospect of another handwriting expert telling the jury that Hauptmann hadn't written the ransom notes delighted Reilly. He was therefore very much interested in how she had arrived at her conclusion. When she stated her findings, Reilly was shocked, dismayed, and then angered. She was ready to testify that after Hauptmann's arrest, someone had altered—tampered with—all of the ransom notes to make the handwriting in them similar to the defendant's. This theory was so absurd that even Reilly considered it too preposterous to use.[6]

Reilly told Miss Braunlich that he didn't want her anywhere near the courthouse. "Tell people you are sick," he said. Worried that some reporter would hear of her theory, Reilly told her to leave Flemington. That night, wearing a disguise, Hilda Braunlich slipped out of town.

The next day, when Reilly met with Julia Farr and C. F. Goodspeed, two of his remaining four handwriting experts, they agreed with Braunlich that the ransom notes had been tampered with. A few hours later, Reilly's handwriting case went up in smoke when Mrs. Charles Foster and Rudolph Thielen, his last two examiners, told him that they couldn't take the stand on the defendant's behalf. Meanwhile, John Trendley complained to reporters that Reilly hadn't asked him the right questions.

Sunday morning, as Hauptmann paced the bullpen waiting for Anna and their son, he could hear, from the floor below, a choir made up of twelve short-termers singing, "What a friend we have in Jesus."

Anna arrived at 2:30 and was allowed to take Bubi into the bullpen so his father could hold him. The little boy was dressed up in a white knit jacket, blue shirt, and blue knee-length knickers. Bruno, in a rare show of emotion, held the child at arm's length and admired his size and beauty. Mrs. Hauptmann was smiling but had tears in her eyes. Ten minutes later, the two visitors were gone and Bruno was sitting on his cot with his face in his hands.[7]

Mrs. Hauptmann's departure from the jail created a commotion that attracted the attention of the jurors, who were stretching their legs on the second-story porch of the Union Hotel. Crowding to the railing, they watched as newsmen swarmed around Anna and Bubi as they got into a car that took them away.

That afternoon, over three thousand tourists, led by members of the local American Legion, flocked to the courtroom. In the hallway outside, the sightseers could buy picture postcards of the courthouse and the Union Hotel, photographs of the Lindbergh family, and copies of the local newspaper, the *Hunterdon County Democrat*.

Speaking to reporters that Sunday evening, Wilentz said that Peter Sommer, the witness he had been cross-examining at the close of business Friday, was in for a hard time on Monday. Lieutenant Keaten's investigators had learned that Sommer had testified for a fee, or a reward, in dozens of civil and criminal trials, including the celebrated Hall-Mills murder case in 1926. He was a professional witness.

You've never been convicted of a crime? You've never been
in a lunatic asylum? I can't use you!

— E D W A R D   J .   R E I L L Y
to a person who volunteered his services as a defense witness

37 TRAGIC BURLESQUE

PETER SOMMER CLIMBED INTO THE WITNESS chair a little after ten o'clock on Monday.
He was still being cross-examined by Wilentz who asked, "You are a professional witness,
aren't you, Mr. Sommer?"

Caught off guard by the question and thinking that Wilentz meant expert witness
rather than one who testifies for anyone who pays, Sommer replied, "Well, I don't
qualify as a professional witness."

"Did you not testify in court for a price?"

"Why, I haven't spoken about any price."

Wilentz named four cases and Sommer admitted that he had been a witness in each
trial. He then denied changing his testimony in one case because he wasn't paid. He said
he had made an error in that instance and had corrected it later by affidavit.

"But isn't it a fact that you only had it corrected because you weren't paid the
money?"

"No, sir."

"Isn't it a fact that you threatened to go to the district attorney and tell him about
it?"

"I said I would go to the district attorney and tell, because this fellow wanted me to
be in court."

"And when he paid you fifteen dollars, you didn't go to the district attorney; isn't that
right?"

"Why, I was going to—the case was coming up again."

"Yes, and then he paid you the fifteen dollars, didn't he?"

"That was my expenses."

"But you did threaten to go to the district attorney if he didn't pay you?"

"I did, yes."

Wilentz showed Sommer a photograph and asked him if it depicted the woman he
had seen with the baby that night. "I won't say yes and I won't say no," the witness said.
The photograph was of Violet Sharpe.

The defense called Benjamin Lupica, the Princeton prep school student who had reported that at 6:00 P.M. on the evening of the crime he had seen a man and a ladder in a car near the Lindbergh estate. Lupica had been subpoenaed by the State but Wilentz didn't call him because his description of the man's car didn't tally with Hauptmann's vehicle. In addition, Lupica had sold his story to a newspaper, thus destroying his credibility as a witness, in Wilentz's opinion.

Questioned by Lloyd Fisher, Lupica described the man's car as a 1929 Dodge with New Jersey plates beginning with the letter "L." (Hauptmann owned a 1931 Dodge with New York plates.) "Have you at any time said to anybody that you can *definitely* recognize the defendant, Hauptmann, as the man in that car?" Fisher asked.

"No," the young man replied.

"Can you identify Bruno Richard Hauptmann as the man you saw in the car that night?"

"I cannot."

On cross-examination, Wilentz, in a fatherly tone, asked, "You have always said that the man in the car resembled Hauptmann, haven't you?"

"Yes, it is the truth."

At 11:30, following a five-minute recess, Hauptmann's friend Hans Kloppenburg took the stand and said that he had been at the defendant's apartment on the night of April 2, 1932. The witness knew this because he and the defendant regularly got together on the first Saturday of the month. "I came up to his house about seven o'clock," Kloppenburg said. "Then we played some music, played cards, had some coffee and cake, and between eleven and twelve o'clock he drove me to the White Plains Avenue subway." He said that he had also attended the farewell party the Hauptmanns had thrown for Isidor Fisch in December 1933. Referring to Isidor Fisch, Reilly asked, "Did you notice whether or not he had any packages or bundles with him that night?"

"Yes, he carried a package in his arm. It was about, I would say, five to six inches high, and seven wide, and the length was about fourteen inches."

"And when was the last time you saw Fisch with that package in Hauptmann's house?"

"The last time both went together through the hall in the kitchen."[1]

On cross-examination, Kloppenburg told Wilentz that he didn't remember seeing Fisch leave the apartment when the farewell party was over. He therefore couldn't say that he saw Isidor Fisch leave the apartment without the package. Before the witness was dismissed, he admitted that shortly after Hauptmann was arrested, he told District Attorney Foley that he couldn't remember what day in April he had seen Hauptmann in 1932. He had told Foley that it was "too long ago." After lunch, Anna Bonesteel, the owner of a restaurant in Yonkers near the ferry to Alpine, New Jersey, told Reilly that two or three months before the kidnapping Violet Sharpe and another girl had come into her lunchroom. Reilly then asked, "On March first, did you see her?"

"Yes sir. She came into our restaurant that evening at seven-thirty. She stayed until half-past eight or a quarter to nine."

"Now, what was she doing in your restaurant?"

"She came in; she had a gray blanket in her arm; she was very nervous; she says: 'I am waiting for someone.' She kept looking out and opening the door and I kept watching her and several times I said, 'Gee, she looks like a hen on a hot griddle. Why don't she stop that?'"

"And when she left, what did she do, and in what direction did she go?"

"She left when she saw a car come down; she put her hand up to it and the car stopped about two hundred feet away from the restaurant—she ran up to the car, and she got into it, and the car drove away."

When it came time for Wilentz to question the witness, he informed her that Violet Sharpe had not left the Morrow house that night until eight or eight-thirty. "So you've made an error, haven't you?"

"I have not!" The witness exclaimed angrily.

"Miss Sharpe couldn't have been in your restaurant at seven-thirty. You have made a mistake, haven't you?"

"She was in the restaurant at seven-thirty," the witness replied, making no effort to conceal her hostility.

"Is this the girl who was with Violet when she came into your restaurant three months before the kidnapping?" Wilentz asked, handing Miss Bonesteel a photograph.

"No it isn't," the witness snapped, handing the picture back to Wilentz.

"Please, madam, take a good look," Wilentz said, handing the photograph back to her.

"It is not the girl."

"Then who is it?" Wilentz asked.

"I don't know."

"You don't know?"

"I said I don't know."

"Yes. Well let me tell you who it is—it is Violet Sharpe!"

The witness looked surprised, then defiant. "That isn't Violet Sharpe," she growled.

"That is Violet Sharpe, the person you said was in your restaurant at seven-thirty on the night of the crime," Wilentz replied, looking at the jury with a boyish grin.

"If it is, I can't—her face—"

"Look at the photograph again," Wilentz said.

The witness studied the photograph then said, "It does and it doesn't—yes, it does."

"Is that Violet Sharpe or isn't it?" Wilentz demanded.

"I think it is—I am sure that's Violet Sharpe."

Reilly called Capt. Russell A. Snook, the head of the New Jersey State Police Bureau of Identification, to the stand and asked him about the latent fingerprints Dr. Erastus Hudson, the independent fingerprint expert, had gotten off the kidnap ladder. Captain Snook said that most of the latents Dr. Hudson had developed through his silver nitrate method were smudges left by people who had handled the ladder after the kidnapping. Captain Snook denied that all but twenty or thirty of five hundred latents had been identified.

Colonel Schwarzkopf was recalled to the stand and asked about the experiments he had made with the duplicate kidnap ladder. Reilly then brought up the fingerprints, or lack of them, "Now, is it a fact that Trooper Kelly didn't bring back from the kidnap room a single readable fingerprint?"

"There were a number of smudges and the lines and marks in them were such that they would not be of any value for identification purposes."

"At no time was the fingerprint of Bruno Richard Hauptmann identified as being on the ladder?"

"Not that I have any knowledge of."

Reilly asked a few more questions, then brought up the subject of Morris Rosner. "Now, did you display to Rosner the original ransom note [the nursery note]?"

"I did not."

"Did he ever see it?"

"I don't know."

Following Wilentz's brief cross-examination, Colonel Schwarzkopf was excused. It was four o'clock and too early to quit for the day, but five of Reilly's witnesses hadn't shown up, so he had to ask for an early adjournment.

Reilly led off Tuesday morning with an unemployed cab driver, dancer, actor, and former newsstand employee named Philip Moses. From the witness chair Moses unraveled a confusing and vague tale of four men he had seen around a stalled car near St. Raymond's Cemetery shortly after eight o'clock on the night of April 2, 1932.

The next three witnesses, Marie Mueller, Louise Wollenburg, and her husband Otto, confirmed earlier testimony regarding Bruno's birthday get-together and Isidor Fisch's farewell party.

Following the alibi witnesses, Reilly brought on Bertha Hoff, a meek, middle-aged woman who said that in November 1933 a farmer she knew came to her house in New York City with a man she didn't know but later identified by photograph as Isidor Fisch. When Reilly started asking the witness about a package she said Fisch had wanted to leave with her, Wilentz objected on the grounds that the testimony was absurd. "Why would a man the witness didn't know come to her house and ask her to keep a box containing fifty thousand dollars?" Wilentz asked.

Reilly's face turned purple. "Now, if the Court please, we might just as well face the issue. During the day I am prepared to prove, if my witnesses come from New York, that the man who had jumped over the cemetery wall was Isidor Fisch and that Fisch from that day on approached many persons in New York trying to dispose of this money. I'm going to trace every connection of Isidor Fisch with this money until he left on the steamer."

Judge Trenchard ruled in Wilentz's favor and Reilly withdrew his questions about Isidor Fisch's package. Much to the relief of Fisher and the other defense attorneys, Reilly dismissed the witness.

Just before lunch, FBI Agent John E. Seykora testified that following the ransom payment, he had questioned Dr. Condon several times. Through Seykora, Reilly tried to cast doubt on Condon's character and mental stability. Reilly wanted to know if the FBI had Condon examined by an alienist and if the government thought the old man was eccentric. Seykora said that he wasn't qualified to make judgments on such matters, and as far as he knew, Condon was never examined by an alienist (the term used for psychiatrists at the time).

On cross-examination, Wilentz portrayed Condon as a community leader who was active in the Boy Scouts, the Girl Scouts, and other civic groups in the Bronx. On redirect, Reilly asked the agent if there were FBI reports that contained information that Condon sometimes paraded about his neighborhood dressed as a woman. Reilly also wanted to know if certain parents had objected to Condon's involvement with the scouting groups. Seemingly surprised by these questions, the agent said he had no knowledge of these things. Reilly's questioning of the FBI agent seemed to have embarrassed everyone in the courtroom.

After lunch, Victor Schussler, a tenant at 1279 East 222nd Street when the Hauptmanns lived there, said that he had been present at Isidor Fisch's farewell party. He also testified that after the defendant's arrest, some of his (Schussler's) tools had disappeared from the basement. Schussler said that Hauptmann was a kind and loving husband and a devoted father.

Wilentz took over the questioning and got Schussler to say that he didn't own a handplane, and the chisel that had been introduced into evidence was not his.

The next two witnesses were people who had attended the farewell party thrown for Fisch; a restaurant cashier named Benjamin Heier followed them. The twenty-four-year-old restaurant employee said that on the night of April 2, 1932, while seated in a car, he saw a man jump from the wall bordering St. Raymond's Cemetery. Since the man had leaped into his headlight beams, the witness had gotten a good view of him. When the Hauptmann trial had gotten underway, Heier had seen photographs of Isidor Fisch in the papers and realized that he was the man he had seen coming out of the cemetery that night. Reilly showed Heier a photograph of Isidor Fisch and the witness said, "There is a strong resemblance."

Under Wilentz's aggressive cross-examination, Heier reluctantly admitted that he had been convicted of a crime and that he was with a woman the night he saw Isidor Fisch leap out of the cemetery. When Wilentz asked the witness to name his companion that night, Heier refused because she had since died and he didn't want to embarrass her family. Referring to Oliver Whately, Violet Sharpe, and Isidor Fisch, Wilentz said, "Nobody else who has died in this case has been spared."

When Heier restated his direct testimony for Wilentz, he said that he had seen the man between 10:45 and 11. (The ransom payment had been made at nine o'clock.) This contradicted his statement to Reilly that he had seen Isidor Fisch jump off the wall between 9 and 9:30. When confronted with the conflicting times, the witness, much to Wilentz's amazement and delight, stuck to his later answer, thus demolishing the value of his testimony to the defense.

Heier was dismissed and Judge Trenchard called a five-minute recess. During the break, Heier walked over to the defense table and handed Hauptmann a pen and a postcard and asked him for his autograph. As Hauptmann reached for the pen, Heier was waved away by a guard. A few minutes later, when Hauptmann tried to get up to talk to Reilly and Fisher, one of the troopers grabbed him by the arm and yanked him back into his chair. "I'm not going to run away," he snarled.[2]

The final witness of the day was the steamship agent who, on November 14, 1933, had sold Isidor Fisch and Henry Uhlig tickets to Germany on the S.S. *Manhattan*.

It was a little past four when the steamship agent stepped from the stand. Instead of calling another witness, Reilly asked the court for an early adjournment. He said that five of his witnesses were snowbound in Trenton. Judge Trenchard granted the request. Outside the courthouse, Reilly told reporters that he had two surprise witnesses who would "blow the roof off the courthouse." These witnesses, he said, had seen Isidor Fisch with the ransom money.

On Wednesday morning, before the first witness was sworn in, Judge Trenchard stepped from the bench and walked over to the jury box to see if Mrs. Verna Snyder was getting over her cold. The juror smiled at him and said that she was feeling much better, thank you.[3]

At ten o'clock, a man in his mid-thirties named Sam Streppone said that in May 1932, a man he later identified as Isidor Fisch came to his repair shop in the Bronx to have his radio fixed. Fisch left the radio and a shoebox in the shop, picking them up six hours later. The witness said he didn't look into the shoebox, so he had no idea what was in it. Reilly wanted the jury to think the box had contained the ransom money.

When Reilly had finished with Streppone, Wilentz, wondering if this was one of the witnesses who would "blow the roof off the courthouse," asked, "You were adjudged insane some years ago, were you not?"

"In 1928; discharged with no psychosis," Streppone replied softly. (At the time of his discharge, Streppone was classified as a psychopathic who had "peculiar hallucinations.")

"How many times were you in the institution for mental disorders?"

"A few times."

"Eight times, six times, seven times?"

"I will make it about five times." (Four times in the psychopathic ward at Bellevue, and one time at the State Hospital for the Insane at Central Islip, Long Island.)

"Was one of the times due to the fact that you threatened harm to a woman member of a charity organization?"

"Yes, sir." (The witness had also shot his wife in the leg and had threatened to shoot a district attorney.)

"One of the times you were put away for writing filthy letters to this woman?"

Objecting to the term "filthy letters," the witness answered, "Abusive language, yes, sir."

Lloyd Fisher exchanged glances with Hauptmann, who was shaking his head in disgust. Anna Hauptmann, with a concerned look on her face, was whispering something to Frederick Pope.

Lt. E. Paul Sjostrom, the assistant supervisor of the New Jersey State Bureau of Identification, was called to the witness stand to remind the jury that Hauptmann's fingerprints were not in the nursery, on any of the ransom notes, or on the kidnap ladder. When Reilly turned the witness over to Wilentz, the prosecutor asked, "If this defendant, Mr. Hauptmann, wore gloves when he was handling the ladder, would his fingerprints show?"

"No, sir."

"Is it not a fact, Lieutenant, that your experience shows to you that men who are experienced in crimes wear gloves?"

"Yes, sir."

On re-direct, Fisher asked, "Your experience is, Lieutenant, that mothers in putting children to bed and nurses putting children to bed don't wear gloves, do they?"

"That is not my experience. I don't know."

On re-cross-examination, Wilentz asked, "You have never been a nurse, have you?"

"No."

On re-direct, Fisher quipped, "Nor a mother, I take it?"

"No, sir," the witness said amid the laughter.

The next witness, Sgt. Louis Kubler, a member of the New Jersey State Bureau of Identification, testified that he had helped Dr. Erastus Hudson process the kidnap ladder for prints. Next Reilly called Sgt. Frank A. Kelly (he had been promoted) back to the stand. The fingerprint man testified that although it was windy on the night of the crime, the ransom note on the windowsill had not been weighted down by anything to keep it from blowing away. Kelly also said that in the recess of that open window, off to one side, was an eight-inch beer stein. Although none of the crime scene photographs of the room showed the stein, it was depicted in a newspaper photograph of the nursery.

Wilentz, in his cross-examination, used the courtroom window to demonstrate how the nursery window had looked with the beer stein in it. Wilentz got Kelly to say that someone coming through the window would not have disturbed the mug.

By revealing the existence of the beer stein, the defense was implying that it could have been used to hold down the ransom note, further implying that the police, in handling it, had destroyed the kidnapper's fingerprints. The second, more radical implication was that the kidnapper couldn't have come through the window without disturbing the stein, proof that the baby had been taken out some other way.

At 12:10 Oscar John Bruchman, a New York City cab driver, testified that in May 1933 he had met Isidor Fisch by chance in lower Manhattan. On that occasion, the witness said that Fisch had flashed a large roll of "yellowback" bills (gold certificates). When Wilentz objected to the line of questioning, Reilly said, "We are offering this witness to show that after April 1932, down to the time Fisch sailed for Europe, he exhibited to many people large sums of money and that is as far as I will go with this witness."

Judge Trenchard overruled Wilentz and told the witness to proceed. Bruchman said that Fisch had given him a five-dollar bill as cab fare and told him to keep the change.

It was twelve-thirty, and when Wilentz said he had no questions for the witness, the court recessed for lunch.

During the noon break, as was their custom, the trial correspondents and the defense lawyers crossed the street to the Union Hotel for lunch. As Reilly sat at his table sipping his third orange blossom from his coffee cup, he was approached by a small, middle-aged man in a tattered shirt who said that he had information about the case. The man said he would testify for the defense. Reilly spoke to him briefly, ordered another drink, then bellowed, "You've never been convicted of a crime? You've never been in a lunatic asylum? I can't use you!"[4]

After lunch, Reilly put a plumber on the stand, who, in August 1934, had fixed a leak in one of Hauptmann's closets. The workman, Gustave Miller, said he had spent six or seven minutes in Hauptmann's attic and didn't see any floorboards missing.

Reilly's next witness, Theron J. Main, identified a photograph of Isidor Fisch as the man he had seen on August 2, 1933, in a Manhattan restaurant playing a slot machine. According to Main, Fisch gave the bartender a twenty-dollar gold note.

On cross-examination, the witness's testimony collapsed when he described Fisch's twenty-dollar bill as being yellow on one side. Wilentz asked, "Haven't you read in every paper in this country that the gold bills didn't have any yellow backs or gold backs to them?"

"I did not."

"Don't you know the only reference to gold is a little seal saying it was a gold certificate and it wasn't yellow or wasn't gold at all?"

"I did not."

"But you are sure that you saw that yellowish gold on the back?"

"Yes."

Reilly questioned the witness briefly on re-direct, then thanked him.

"You have the thanks of both sides," Wilentz added.

The jury perked up when Reilly called Gerta Henkel to the stand. Gerta was the slender, dark-haired beauty Hauptmann had met in July 1932 when his wife was in Germany. This was the woman Hauptmann had stopped to have coffee with two or three mornings a week on his way to his broker's office. He had, in fact, enjoyed Gerta's coffee on the Saturday morning preceding his arrest.

As Gerta strode casually to the witness chair, she popped a stick of chewing gum into her mouth.[5]

Under Reilly's questioning, the witness said that she had gone to school with Isidor Fisch in Leipzig, and that before her marriage, her husband, Fisch, and Henry Uhlig had lived together. Reilly then asked, "Was there anything at any time in Mr. Hauptmann's conduct toward you ungentlemanly or dishonorable?"

"Certainly not."

Wilentz began his cross-examination by asking Gerta about her relationship with the defendant. "Now there were mornings when he came to your home, weren't there?"

"Sure," Gerta answered. She looked at the jury and smiled.

"And he used to have coffee at your home?"

"Yes; I like my coffee."

"While Hauptmann was at your house, in July or August of 1932, he was introduced to Isidor Fisch?"

"But they knew each other before that."

"When? A couple of years ago?"

"Yep."

"You knew, did you not, and you have known right along, Mrs. Henkel, that it has been an important matter as to when Fisch was introduced to Hauptmann?"

"I didn't know it was important."

"He brought you a present, didn't he?"

"Uh-huh. Got a nice slip, I got—I mean from Mrs. Hauptmann and some, oh—"

"From *Mrs.* Hauptmann?"

"That's right."

It was 3:30 when Mrs. Henkel, following Wilentz's cross-examination and Reilly's re-direct, stepped from the stand. Her face was flushed and Mrs. Hauptmann looked glum. Lloyd Fisher doodled on his legal pad.[6]

Dr. Erastus Mead Hudson, the New York City physician who had been working with fingerprints for fifteen years, took the stand, and under Frederick Pope's direction, explained his silver nitrate method of developing latent fingerprints. Dr. Hudson said that on March 13, 1932, at the request of the New Jersey State Police, he went to the Lindbergh estate where he processed some of the baby's toys and the kidnap ladder for latent fingerprints. From the toys he had developed thirteen latents that he presumed to be the child's, and from the ladder, he had brought out five hundred fingermarks. He didn't say how many of the five hundred prints were clear and complete enough to be identifiable. In speaking about the kidnap ladder, Dr. Hudson said that when he examined it, he noticed that rail 16 had one nail hole, not four. By saying this he was discrediting the testimony of Lt. Lewis Bornmann and Arthur Koehler. He was also implying that rail 16 had been altered to match the holes in the cross-beams in Hauptmann's attic.

Frederick Pope finished with the witness at 4:30 and Judge Trenchard adjourned for the day.

On Thursday morning, Wilentz got Dr. Hudson to concede that the latents he had developed on the ladder probably belonged to people who had handled it after the kidnapping. Dr. Hudson then admitted that his notes on the case didn't indicate that rail 16 contained just one nail hole. Wilentz handed him a photograph of rail 16 that had been taken shortly after the crime. The photo clearly showed the four nail holes. "Will you admit then, Doctor, that you were mistaken in your testimony and your recollection?"

"Well," the witness replied, "I would say yes."

Worried that the jury would think that the New Jersey State Police had been out of date because they didn't use Dr. Hudson's silver nitrate process, Wilentz had Dr. Hudson point out that there wasn't a police department in the country using this method.[7]

Before Judge Trenchard adjourned for lunch, Reilly put on six witnesses. The first three were people who knew Millard Whited, the logger who had lived in a shack near the Lindbergh estate, and who had testified that he had seen Hauptmann in the area a few days before the crime. All three of the witnesses swore that Whited had a well-earned reputation in the community as a liar.

Gerta Henkel's mother-in-law, Mrs. Augusta Hile, testified that in 1925 she had lent Isidor Fisch $4,300, money he had invested in a pie-baking company that went bankrupt. She was never repaid.

Karl Henkel, Gerta's husband took the stand. When asked how he felt about Hauptmann's coffee-drinking sessions with his wife, the witness mopped his flushed face with his handkerchief and said, "I trust my wife." There wasn't a soul in the courtroom who believed him.

The last witness before the lunch break was Henry Uhlig, Fisch's best friend. Uhlig said that he had lent Fisch $400 which he didn't get back. The money went into the pie-baking company.

After lunch, a forty-five-year-old painter named Walter Manley testified that he had seen Hauptmann at Fredricksen's Bakery at 8:15 on the night of the kidnapping. On cross-examination, the witness said that he hadn't told anyone of this until a few days ago. Weary of these so-called alibi witnesses, Wilentz let Manley off with a light cross-examination.

Frederick Pope next questioned a pattern maker who said that the same wood plane could leave different marks on a piece of wood. When he demonstrated this on two wooden surfaces, Wilentz was able to point out similarities in the two cutting patterns.

The next witness, an architect from Brockton, Massachusetts, took the stand as an expert on wood, then astounded everyone by saying that he was only qualified as an expert about things that were common knowledge.

The day's final witness was Charles J. DeBisschop, a general contractor, boat builder, house wrecker, and lumberjack from Waterbury, Connecticut, who said he had thirty years experience with wood. When Frederick Pope tried to get him qualified as an expert, Wilentz launched a savage attack that resulted in Judge Trenchard allowing the witness to testify not as an expert but as a "practical lumberman."[8]

The rough-round-the-edges Yankee with the stubby fingers showed the jury two boards from different trees and pointed out the similarity of their grain patterns. Following a lecture on wood that confused everyone in the courtroom, DeBisschop said that rail 16 had not come from Hauptmann's attic.

On Friday morning, February 8, the twenty-eighth day of the trial, with Arthur Koehler sitting at the prosecution table as a consultant, Wilentz tore into Charles De-Bisschop. By the time he had finished, it was obvious that the witness was in over his head. His testimony was an embarrassment to the defense.

Frederick Pope next put William Bolmer on the stand. Bolmer said that early in the afternoon of March 1, 1932, a light green Ford coupe with a ladder attached to it stopped at his gas station on the Somerville-Princeton road. The witness said he got a good look at the driver of the car and it wasn't the defendant. There was also a woman in the vehicle, but the witness didn't see enough of her to make an identification. In describing the ladder, Bolmer called it, "poor looking" and pointed to the kidnap ladder and said, "It was that one, but it wasn't extended."

Wilentz asked Bolmer if he had reported his March 1 sighting to the police and the witness said that he hadn't.

Shortly after eleven o'clock, Pope questioned Ewald Mielke, a pattern maker, millwright, and carpenter from Lindenhurst, Long Island, who said that rail 16 had not been cut from the board in Hauptmann's attic. On cross-examination, Mielke stated that he hadn't compared the grain patterns on the two boards, but had based his conclusion on the fact that the board in the attic came from the upper part of a tree and rail 16 the lower. He said he could tell this from the spacing of the knots. "Now," Wilentz said, "you have stated that the attic board was from the top of the tree?"

"Yes."

"Did you hear the other wood witness, Mr. DeBisschop, say that because the attic board had more knots it was from the *bottom* part of the tree?"

"I did not."

The witness stepped from the stand and Judge Trenchard called a recess. When the court reconvened, Reilly stood up and declared, "The defense rests." Reilly's announcement took everybody by surprise. He had created certain expectations that were never realized. What happened to the witnesses who were going to prove that Hauptmann had been framed? Where were the people who were going to name the real kidnappers? The defense had just fizzled out—Reilly had merely left the jury with Hauptmann's Fisch story and a few doubts about the State's eyewitnesses. Even if the eyewitnesses were not to be believed, Wilentz had produced more than enough evidence to convict the defendant. Where did all those handwriting experts go—the people who were going to say that Hauptmann *hadn't* written the ransom notes?

Instead of real experts, Reilly had brought in a man who forged people's signatures, a millwright, and a lumberjack. He had also produced, as alibi witnesses, a pathetic assortment of criminals, charlatans, and lunatics.

Not having any credible witnesses or a theory of the crime that made any sense, Reilly's strategy should have involved poking holes in the State's evidence, questioning the identity of the corpse, and raising questions regarding the court's jurisdiction in the case. Instead, Reilly had insulted Colonel Lindbergh, conceded the baby's identity, and conjured up fantastic images of John Condon, Betty Gow, and the late Isidor Fisch, Violet Sharpe, and Oliver Whateley pulling off the crime.

Before the case went to the jury, Hauptmann would have to face even more bad news—Wilentz had lined up over twenty rebuttal witnesses. Edward Reilly was hungover and defeated; Hauptmann wilted and glum; Lloyd Fisher confused and disgusted; and the jury, having already made up its mind, wanted to do its job and go home.

> Either this man is the filthiest and vilest snake that ever
> crawled through the grass, or he is entitled to an acquittal.
>
> — D A V I D   T.   W I L E N T Z

38 SUMMING UP

BEFORE THE JURY HAD A CHANCE to get used to the idea that the defense had rested, Wilentz put Joseph L. Farber, the State's first rebuttal witness, on the stand.

Farber, an insurance agent, said that at ten o'clock on the night of April 2, 1932, when alibi witness Benjamin Heier said that he had seen Isidor Fisch come out of St. Raymond's Cemetery, Farber's car and a vehicle driven by Heier collided in Manhattan on Sixth Avenue between Fifty-fourth and Fifty-fifth streets. The accident occurred nine miles from St. Raymond's Cemetery.

In his half-hearted cross-examination, Reilly questioned Farber without seriously challenging his testimony. Since Heier couldn't have been at two places at once, he obviously hadn't seen Isidor Fisch coming out of St. Raymond's Cemetery shortly after the ransom money was paid. If Benjamin Heier had intentionally lied, he had committed perjury.

Next, a middle-aged housepainter named Arthur Larson took the stand and swore that Elvert Carlstrom, another alibi witness, couldn't have been in Fredericksen's Bakery on March 1, 1932, because Carlstrom was with him that night in Dunellen, New Jersey. When Reilly couldn't shake the witness on cross-examination, he released him. As Larson stepped from the stand, Hauptmann turned to the United States correspondent seated behind him and said, "I don't feel so good about this thing."[1]

Following the lunch recess, Cpl. George G. Wilton of the New Jersey State Police identified several photographs he had taken of rail 16 on March 8, 1932, which showed the four nail holes. Two of these photographs were marked exhibits 302 and 303 and admitted into evidence. Wilentz next called a U.S. Forest Service employee named Betts who said that he had examined the kidnap ladder on June 1, 1932, and found that it contained the four holes.

The next three rebuttal witnesses testified that Isidor Fisch, on the night of March 1, 1932, was at the home of Henry Jung, a resident of the Bronx. By showing that Fisch was not at the scene of the crime, Wilentz was disassociating him with the kidnapping, and in so doing, weakening Hauptmann's claim that Fisch had given him the ransom money.

Isidor Fisch's sister, Hannah, took the stand and through an interpreter testified that after Isidor had returned to Leipzig, Germany, he lived with her. She said that Isidor had come home with two suits, six shirts, a woolen shawl, two pairs of shoes, a few ties and 1,500 marks (about $500 in American currency). He entered the hospital on March 27, 1934, and two days later died of tuberculosis.

Wilentz next called John F. O'Ryan, New York City's police commissioner at the time of Hauptmann's arrest. Addressing this witness, Wilentz said, "It was testified here by this defendant that before certain moneys were found in his garage, that he told you where these moneys were; is that correct?"

"No, that is not correct."

"The moneys were discovered without any information from him?"

"Oh, yes. The money had been found before he told me about where the money could be found."

Mrs. Selma Kohl, Isidor Fisch's landlady from April 1932 until he left the country in December 1933, took the stand and said that Fisch could barely afford his $3.50-a-week room.

The final witness of the day was Princeton Police Officer William Konietsko who said that he had taken Lou Harding to the Lindbergh estate on the day after the kidnapping. Harding had testified that a man and a woman in a car with the kidnap ladder attached to it had asked him directions to the Lindbergh home. "At any time did he mention a ladder being in the automobile which he described to you?" Wilentz asked.

"Not at all."

"Did he mention seeing a woman in the car?"

"No, sir."

Reilly asked the officer a few token questions and the court was adjourned for the day.

That night, Reilly was upset when he heard that Judge Trenchard might invoke an old state law that would prohibit the jury from eating or sleeping until they reached a verdict. "I will protest vigorously against such attempt on the part of the prosecution to starve the jury into submission," he declared.[2]

Speaking to reporters, Lloyd Fisher said that Hauptmann was more impressed with his wood expert, Charles DeBisschop, than with Arthur Koehler. Fisher quoted the defendant as saying that "any man who works for thirty years in the wood business has got more brains in his head than a man from Washington."[3]

In order to speed things along, Judge Trenchard had authorized a special Saturday session. So, on the morning of February 9, Wilentz recalled Lt. Lewis J. Bornmann to the stand. Bornmann corroborated his previous testimony about finding the gap in Hauptmann's attic that corresponded to rail 16. Bornmann was followed to the stand by Arthur Koehler, who contradicted the testimony of Charles DeBisschop and the other lumber people put on by Reilly.

Following two inconsequential witnesses, Wilentz put four people on the stand who said that on the night of the crime, Violet Sharpe hadn't left the Morrow house in Englewood until eight o'clock. This discredited the testimony of Anna Bonesteel, who had said she had seen Violet in Yonkers that night at 7:30.

The final testimony of the day, and the State's last rebuttal witness, was Mrs. Elizabeth Morrow, Anne Lindbergh's mother. Mrs. Morrow, in the company of her daughter, had arrived at the courthouse that morning just before eleven. Although Colonel Lindbergh hadn't missed a day, Mrs. Lindbergh hadn't been back to court since the day she had testified.

Regarding Violet Sharpe's activities on the evening of the crime, Wilentz asked, "Now, Mrs. Morrow, will you tell us about what time you saw her that evening?"

"She served dinner at seven, then left the house at a quarter to eight."

"And you saw her again before twelve?"

"It was much earlier than that."

On cross-examination, Reilly, speaking softly and with obvious respect, asked a few questions then said, "I think that is all, Mrs. Morrow."

Wilentz stood up and said, "The State rests."

Since the defense had no sur-rebuttal, Reilly stated, "We rest."

It was almost over. After 29 court sessions, 162 witnesses and 381 exhibits, all that remained were the summation speeches and the judge's instructions. Wilentz had lined up four new handwriting experts who, on rebuttal, would have testified that Hauptmann had written the ransom notes, but he didn't call them. Had the defense put on any kind of handwriting case, they would have been used, but as things turned out, they weren't needed.

Since it was too late in the day to begin the summations, Judge Trenchard adjourned until Monday morning.

That night, Anne Lindbergh put her impressions of the day into her diary: "We go through cameras the back way to the courtroom. I sat about in same place. I felt as if I'd been sitting there forever. The crowded rows, the slat chairs, the fat bored-looking woman opposite me in the jury, the high windows behind; outside the red bricks of an old building, lit by the sun."[4]

That evening, speaking to reporters in Englewood, Colonel Lindbergh stated that in his opinion the State had done all it could to obtain Hauptmann's conviction. He then said: "I am satisfied with their conduct of the case. As they conclude, I feel there's no possibility of a mistake in the outcome, I feel so, not only because of my own opinion that Hauptmann is guilty, but because, to my mind the defense has produced nothing of sufficient importance to outweigh the prosecution's evidence that he committed the crime."[5]

Saturday night, the turmoil and conflict within the Hauptmann camp broke out into the open when Lloyd Fisher announced that Hauptmann had asked him to deliver the closing speech before the jury. When Reilly came out of the jail after a short visit with Hauptmann, he was asked if Fisher was doing the honors. "I'm running this show and I'll do the talking," he snapped.

An hour or so later, Fisher emerged from the jail and quoted Hauptmann as follows:

"I think a New Jersey lawyer ought to take part in the summation. The best evidence on my side has been presented by the local lawyers. I have tried to get Mr. Reilly to agree with my wishes, and I will ask him again Monday morning."[6]

Fisher told reporters that he was on his way to Brooklyn to ask Reilly to consider letting him or one of the other local attorneys address the jury. Fisher said that Hauptmann had expressed a desire to speak to the jury himself, but that was out of the question.

On Monday morning, Judge Trenchard announced that Anthony Hauck of the prosecution would be addressing the jury first. Edward Reilly would have his turn then Wilentz would be given the last word.

As the slender, easygoing Hunterdon County prosecutor addressed the jury in his matter-of-fact tone, Reilly looked surprised when Hauck announced that the prosecution had abandoned the felony-murder doctrine in favor of the theory that Hauptmann had murdered the Lindbergh child in cold blood. Hauck looked at the defendant then back at the jury, and said, "We have shown you that the infant child was forcibly taken from his crib. Miss Gow testified that the covers were pinned to the mattress. Further, we have the fact that it was a very short distance from the top of the blankets to the head of the crib which was proof that the baby must have been yanked from the crib. When Colonel Lindbergh went into the room after the baby was taken, the covers still bore the impression of that little body."

Hauck's speech, lasting only ten minutes, was well organized and clearly presented, but it lacked emotion. It was now Reilly's turn.

The flashy, red-faced defense attorney was Hauck's opposite. Hauck was cool and conservative, Reilly was emotional and unpredictable. Formally attired, with his hair slicked back and the diamond on his pinky finger sparkling, Reilly hurled himself at the jury. "I don't care about handwriting," he bellowed. "I don't care about the wood, nor do I care about the ransom money."

Undaunted in his belief that he could ram the inside-job theory down the jurors' throats, Reilly pointed the finger of guilt at the Lindbergh servants: "Colonel Lindbergh was stabbed in the back by the disloyalty of those who worked for him. A man can't come up to a strange house with a ladder and stack it against the wall and run up the ladder, push open a shutter, and walk into a room that he has never been in before. I say that ladder was a plant: that ladder was never up against the side of that house that night. Oh, it was so well planned by disloyal people, so well planned!"

This was Reilly at his best, while standing knee-deep in prosecution evidence, he was boldly serving up his own tray of suspects. The jurors looked on with reluctant fascination.

Reilly turned to another theme—bungling police: "They didn't even find fingerprints on the glass that Betty Gow had handled when she gave the child the physic." Going one step further, Reilly implied that the police had destroyed the evidence: "Now who rubbed those prints off the glass? Who rubbed them out?"

Reilly removed his glasses and wiped them clean with his silk handkerchief. "Now, they must prove the cause of death by direct evidence. So they call in the coroner's physician. You saw him—a big, swaggering, blustering individual who says he is a doctor. 'Are you connected to any hospital?' I asked. 'No,' he replied. Now, you and I know from our experience that every respectable, high-standing professional man is always connected with some hospital if he is a physician.''

Referring to Inspector Walsh's handling of the corpse at the gravesite, Reilly said, "As a result of his picking up the head with the sharp stick, he punctured a hole in this little child's skull. The pressure of that stick on the little baby's skull was sufficient to crack it open. The cracks the doctor found in the skull are no indication that the baby in life received a blow.''

Returning to his favorite theme, Reilly said, "The pressure of that stick by that police officer, careless and clumsy, more bungling, punctured the skull. That little child should have been treated with the greatest reverence in the world; it was easy to allow the little baby's body to stay there until some trained mortician came with a little basket, and who knew how to gather up the child, and then you wouldn't have this careless bungling of a great big copper with a stick, unfortunately puncturing the head and the skull of this child, and of course there was force enough for that undoubtedly to cause the little skull to crack, and that was the condition Doctor Mitchell found it in.''

Although he had gone to great lengths to line up his own expert witnesses, Reilly reminded the jurors that experts were not to be taken seriously. "Expert evidence," he said, "is nothing more nor less than opinion evidence.''

Dr. Condon was the next target. "Then we come to the picture of what General Wilentz describes as a 'patriotic gentlemen of the old school.' Well, General Wilentz, you are entitled to your opinion. Condon stands behind something in this case that is unholy. Now, I don't care anything about this man, but he stands out in this case, and Condon is always doing things alone, alone.''

Violet Sharpe then came under attack. "Now, a girl who is as sophisticated and worldly enough as Violet Sharpe to go out on the road and flirt with a fellow—that may be harmless—doesn't commit suicide because she fears she might lose her job. Life is too sweet. But the net is closing in; the net is closing in. Sharpe has said something; Sharpe has given a clue. . . . Suddenly, suddenly detectives come back and they say, 'Bring Violet down here again.' And a poison which is never permitted in any house— cyanide of potassium I think it was—this girl drained when she knows Inspector Walsh and the police have checked up and found something. She didn't do it because she feared she would lose her job. She did it because a woman from Yonkers, Mrs. Bonesteel, told the truth. Violet was at a ferry with a blanket, with a child, and that child was the Colonel's. . . . I don't think Mrs. Morrow remembers correctly when she saw Violet Sharpe.''

With that, Reilly was asking the jury to believe that in addition to Isidor Fisch, the kidnapping had been committed by John Condon, Betty Gow, the Whateleys, and Violet Sharpe. Reilly didn't bother to explain how these people had come together, who had done what, why Isidor Fisch had ended up with all the ransom money. The jury could put all of that together themselves. Reilly didn't bother with details—he painted with a big brush.

As for Arthur Koehler, the man who had connected the kidnap ladder to Hauptmann's attic, Reilly said, "Well, Mr. Koehler comes in, and we come back again to expert evidence against horse sense. I don't know why he got into the case. I assumed that the importance of the case compelled those in Washington at the time to send him up. He is nothing more or less than what we call a 'lumber cruiser.' He goes around the country spotting groves of trees to see what they are good for and reports down to Washington. . . . Now, he'd have you believe by his testimony—and I don't see how he can sleep at night after giving that testimony where a man's life is at stake—that this carpenter went out and got two or three different kinds of wood to make the ladder. Do you believe the defendant said to himself, 'My goodness, I am short a piece of lumber! What am I going to do?' There is a lumber yard around the corner. So he crawls up into his attic and tears up a board and saws it lengthwise and crosswise and every other wise to make this side of a ladder."

Referring to his own witnesses, Reilly said, "Well, we can't go out and pick these people out of colleges."

It was a little past twelve, so when Reilly paused long enough for the judge to get in a word, the court broke for lunch.

There were so many people in Flemington that day that several state troopers had to clear a path to the Union Hotel for the jury. The jurors walked single file to the hotel dining room through a crowd that was festive and a little loud, but nothing like the ugly mob the newspapers described.

A small restaurant on Main Street was advertising a "Special Trial Lunch," featuring Writer's Cramp Soup, Lindbergh Steak, Hauptmann Beans, Trenchard Roast, Jafsie Chops, and Gow Goulash. The dessert menu included such delights as Jury Pie and Reilly Pudding.

After lunch, Reilly was a different man: He looked haggard and his speech had lost its punch. He was repeating himself, relying on cliches, and at times rambling. Maybe he was tired, maybe it was the four drinks he had had over lunch, or maybe he had simply gotten tired of hearing himself talk.[7]

By 2:30, it was obvious that the jury had lost interest. Even Hauptmann was staring blankly at his shoes. With the sounds of the crowd outside filtering into the courtroom, those inside felt that all the excitement was out in the street.

Finally, at three o'clock, Reilly, on a maudlin note that embarrassed everyone in the room, concluded his summation this way: "May I say to Colonel Lindbergh, in passing, that he has my profound respect, and I feel sorry for him in his deep grief, and I am quite sure that all of you agree with me, his lovely son is now within the gates of heaven."

Reilly walked heavily to the defense table, and without looking at the defendant, sank onto his chair. None of the other defense attorneys greeted him. They were all busy doing other things or looking away. Nobody was smiling.

The next morning, Wilentz, wearing a dark blue double-breasted suit, a white starched shirt, and a blue striped tie, approached the jury. Talking to the jurors as though they were guests in his living room, he asked, "What type of man would murder the child of

Charles A. Lindbergh and Anne Morrow?" Hitching his leg over the edge of the small, round table that sat in front of the jury box, Wilentz said, "He wouldn't be an American. No American gangster ever sank to the level of killing babies. Aah no! An American gangster who wanted to participate in a kidnapping wouldn't pick out Colonel Lindbergh. There are many wealthy people in the city of New York, much more wealthy than Colonel Lindbergh."

Wilentz pulled out the white linen handkerchief that had been folded into his breast pocket and dabbed his lips. Then he turned to Hauptmann with his finger pointed. "Oh no! It had to be a fellow that had ice water in his veins. It had to be a fellow who had a peculiar mental makeup, who thought he was bigger than Lindy. It had to be a fellow that was an egomaniac, who thought he was omnipotent. It had to be a secretive fellow. It had to be a fellow that wouldn't tell his wife about his money. It had to be a fellow that could undergo hardship; it had to be the kind of fellow that would stow away on a boat and travel three thousand miles to sneak into the country and when caught would go back and try again. It had to be the sort of man that, when he did break and enter a home, he would go through the window of the mayor's home in Germany, not the ordinary citizen; not because the mayor was a rich man, but because the mayor was a respected man. Yes, it would have to be the type of man that would hold up women at the point of a gun."

Hauptmann, having been told by Fisher to maintain a calm, detached manner, did his best to conceal his fury. But his flushed face and blinking eyes gave him away.

Gesturing before the jury like a bandleader before his musicians, Wilentz raised his voice in scorn, "And let me tell you, the state of New Jersey and the state of New York and the federal authorities have found that animal—an animal lower than the lowest form in the animal kingdom, Public Enemy Number 1 of this world—Bruno Richard Hauptmann; we have found him and he is here for your judgment!"

Wilentz took everyone by surprise when he swung around, and facing the courtroom, shouted, "Schwarzkopf, please stand up!"

Colonel Schwarzkopf, wearing a well-pressed business suit, got to his feet. "Jury," the prosecutor cried out, "look at Colonel Schwarzkopf. Take a look at his eyes. Does he look like a crook? A graduate of the United States Military Academy, a man who served his nation against his Fatherland on the fronts of Europe. Does he look like a crook? Don't you suppose he is sorry for a German? He has German blood running through his veins. Do you imagine Colonel Schwarzkopf is going to frame this fellow up?"

The colonel sat down, a little flushed from the attention. No sooner had he been seated when Wilentz said, "Inspector Bruckman, will you do me the honor to stand up, please!"

The big, dark-haired detective rose from his chair. "Jurors, look at Inspector Bruckman—one of the highest commanding officials in the New York Police Department. He became an inspector after twenty-seven years, risking his life many days and many nights, with an invalid wife at home. He has to listen over the radio that he is a crook.

366   He is also a German—the man they say who wrote on the door trim, writing that the
defendant had admitted was his."

Wilentz next reviewed the wood evidence then turned to the handwriting: "Did they
tell you about their handwriting experts? I don't remember the names—they are in the
record—Malone, Meyers, and others four or five more, and only one man, all the way
from East St. Louis, only one man would dare walk in this courtroom to say it wasn't
Hauptmann."

Wilentz next pointed out numerous inconsistencies, contradictions, and implausi-
bilities in the testimony of Reilly's alibi witnesses. Then he defended John Condon's character. At this point, Judge Trenchard interrupted Wilentz's summation to break for
lunch.

The jurors had to make their way to lunch through the five thousand people who
were in town for the verdict. As the jurors snaked their way behind the troopers, someone yelled, "Kill Hauptmann." But it was, on the whole, a good-natured crowd.

The hotel dining room was also noisier than usual and jammed with excited people.
All of the noise and humanity was too much for Verna Snyder, the 265-pound juror from
Centreville. She said she couldn't eat and asked one of the women jury guards to accom-
pany her back to her room.

When the court got back into session at 1:30, Wilentz, still intense, crisp, and animated, immediately took command. Holding onto the railing with both hands and leaning into the jury box, he said, "But let me tell you this: This fellow took no chance on
the child awakening. He crushed that child right in the room, into insensibility. He
smothered and choked that child right in that room. That child never cried, never gave
an outcry, certainly not. The little voice was stilled right in that room. He wasn't interested in the child. Life meant nothing to him. That's the type of man I told you about
before—Public Enemy Number 1 of the World! That's what we are dealing with. You are
not dealing with a fellow who does not know what he's doing."

Wilentz turned away from the jurors and pointed toward Hauptmann. "Take a look at
him as he sits there. Look at him as he walks out of the room, pantherlike, gloating,
feeling good!"

Wilentz stepped back from the jury box, took a deep breath, then launched into a
sixty-minute interpretation of the testimony of several key witnesses. Next, he tore into
the Fisch story, then came back to John Condon: "Now, what did Condon do? Condon
risked his life, risked his life for Colonel Lindbergh, just as millions of people would.
Colonel Lindbergh thinks Condon is all right. Colonel Breckenridge, a member of President Wilson's cabinet, thinks he is all right. He must have been all right."

Now facing Hauptmann, the prosecutor, his voice saturated with emotion, said, "Mr.
Defendant here wanted to show you he didn't write 'Singnature' with the *n* in it. He said
they dictated it to him that way—remember? I asked him, How do you spell 'Signature'?
And he said, 'S-I-G-N-A-T-U-R-E.' That was in court. You remember it. Did they tell you to
spell it 'S-I-N-G-N-A-T-U-R-E?' I asked. They did, he said. But you can take the request
writings. You can go through every one of those misspelled writings, and there isn't the

word 'singnature' on one of them to show that we asked him to spell it, right or wrong. What do you think of that? And here he is in this courtroom. He knew the importance of that 'signature.'"

Several of the jurors cast furtive glances at Hauptmann whose flushed face bore no expression. The prosecutor was now talking about Isidor Fisch: "We found no gold notes in his possession, either in this country or elsewhere, and during all this time there hasn't been one ransom bill that turned up in Germany, not one, not a single, solitary one—all in the Bronx."

Wilentz ridiculed the defense's lumber witnesses, talked about Hauptmann's bank accounts, reminded the jury that the word 'boad' was written in one of Hauptmann's notebooks, then said, "Now, men and women, don't be weak. Don't be weak! If he got that sleeping garment from somebody else he had a chance to tell it to you. If he wrote those notes for somebody else he had the chance to tell it. He hasn't told his lawyer a thing. He hasn't told this court a thing. He didn't tell the judge a thing—he has got nothing to tell!"

Wilentz was approaching the end of his speech and was finishing strong. He wanted more than a guilty verdict, he wanted a first-degree murder conviction, and he wanted it without a recommendation of mercy that would automatically lead to a life sentence. Wilentz wanted death. "Now, men and women, as I told you before, there are some cases in which a recommendation of mercy might do, but not this one, not this one. Either this man is the filthiest and vilest snake that ever crawled through the grass, or he is entitled to an acquittal. If you bring in a recommendation of mercy, a wishy-washy decision, yes, it is your province, I will not say a word about it. I will not say another word. But it seems to me that you have the courage. If you are convinced, as all of us are—you must find him guilty of murder in the first degree."

The testimony and the speeches were over. Wilentz had held his audience spellbound for five hours. His summation had been scathing, emotional, purposeful, powerful— and effective. Wilentz took his seat, and Judge Trenchard was about to say something when one of the spectators cried out, "If it please Your Honor, I have a confession that was made to me by the man who committed the crime!" Before the man could say anything more, a detective clamped a hand over his mouth, then, with the help of two deputy sheriffs, hauled him out of the room. The speaker, dressed in a cleric's outfit, was the Reverend Vincent G. Burns of Palisades, New Jersey.[8]

Wilentz and Reilly rushed to the bench. "Did he say anything?" Wilentz asked.

"He shouted something," Reilly replied.

"If he did, it would be in your favor," Wilentz snapped.

"No, it wouldn't," Reilly growled.

"Did he say anything? I didn't hear anything." Wilentz said.

Judge Trenchard spoke. "I don't know whether he did or whether he didn't. I didn't hear anything myself except 'Your Honor.'"

"I think he ought to be committed to an insane asylum," Reilly said. "He came to me once and I threw him out. He was here the first day, dressed that way, and I had the troopers throw him out. They tell me he is the rector of a small church up on the banks of the Hudson here, more of a mission."

"I think he ought to be put in jail," Wilentz murmured.

"So do I," said Reilly.

Judge Trenchard turned to the jury and said, "Ladies and gentlemen of the jury, it is very unfortunate that this scene had to occur. I don't imagine that you heard anything that this man said, except his exclamations that he wanted to address the court; but if you did hear anything, my instruction to you is, at the request of counsel on both sides, that you utterly and entirely disregard anything that you heard and forget the scene."

Judge Trenchard looked at his watch and said, "Now, I had rather hoped to charge you this afternoon but the hour is now late. I think it is better for us to take an adjournment; it is better for you to get a good night's sleep and take the case in the morning with a fresh mind. The court is adjourned."

That night, Dr. Barclay S. Fuhrmann, the Hunterdon County Physician, examined Verna Snyder and reported that the crowd, the noise, the rigid confinement, and the pressure of the trial had given her a "case of the nerves." The doctor advised her not to eat so much and to go to bed early.

> The trial is over. We must start our life again. . . .
> — A N N E   M O R R O W   L I N D B E R G H

39 WEDNESDAY THE THIRTEENTH

FEBRUARY 13 WAS A WEDNESDAY, the thirty-second and final day of the trial. That morning, at 9:55, Hauptmann entered the courtroom in his usual manner. With his head bowed and his eyes downcast, the defendant walked to his seat in the row of chairs just inside the rail that cut off the public part of the courtroom. The moment he sat down he raised his eyes and looked about the room. His face was very white, and his cheekbones appeared more prominent than ever. A reporter sitting behind him leaned over his shoulder and asked, "How do you feel, Bruno?"

"I feel fine," Hauptmann replied, not bothering to turn around.

"What do you think the verdict will be?"

"Your guess is as good as mine."

Reilly came into the room and took his place at the defense table without speaking to or looking at his client. Fisher and Pope came in and greeted the defendant warmly. Mrs. Hauptmann took a seat two chairs from her husband and spoke to him solemnly across the knees of a trooper and a deputy sheriff.

At ten o'clock, Judge Trenchard, his gray hair rumpled and his black robe flowing loosely from his shoulders, mounted the bench. He was carrying a sheaf of papers and a yellow pencil. Despite the fact that streams of sunlight poured through the big side windows, all of the lights in the room were burning. The jurors were seated in the jury box beneath the huge American flag on the wall above and behind them.

The court was brought to order and Judge Trenchard, addressing the jury, said, "It now becomes your duty to render a verdict upon the question of the defendant's guilt or his innocence and upon the degree of his guilt." The judge next told the jury that they were the evaluators of the evidence, then explained that the State had the burden of proving the defendant guilty beyond a reasonable doubt. The judge covered the basic facts of the crime, then addressed the crucial subject of where the baby had been killed:

"The fact that the child's body was found in Mercer County raises a presumption that the death occurred there; but that, of course, is a rebuttable presumption, and may be overcome by circumstantial evidence. In the present case, the State contends that the uncontradicted evidence of Colonel Lindbergh and Dr. Mitchell, and other evidence, justifies the reasonable inference that the felonious stroke occurred in Hunterdon County, when the child was seized and carried out the nursery window and down the ladder by the defendant, and that death was instantaneous."

Judge Trenchard reviewed Dr. Condon's role in the case, then said, "If you find that the defendant was the man to whom the ransom money was delivered, as a result of the directions in the ransom notes, bearing symbols like those on the nursery note, the question is pertinent: Was not the defendant the man who left the ransom note on the windowsill of the nursery, and who took the child from its crib?" The judge next summarized Reilly's theory of the case: "It is argued by the defendant's counsel that the kidnapping and murder was done by a gang, and not by the defendant, and that the defendant was in nowise concerned therein. The argument was to the effect that it was done by a gang, with the help or connivance of one or more servants of the Lindbergh or Morrow households. Now do you believe that? Is there any evidence in this case whatsoever to support any such conclusion?"

Addressing the state's handwriting case, Trenchard said, "Numerous experts in handwriting have testified, after exhaustive examination of the ransom letters, and comparison with genuine writings of the defendant, that the defendant Hauptmann wrote every one of the ransom notes. On the other hand, the defendant denies that he wrote them, and a handwriting expert, called by him, so testified. And so the fact becomes one for your determination."

Following a discussion of the ransom money found in Hauptmann's garage, the Judge said, "The defendant says that these ransom bills were left with him by one Fisch, a man now dead. Do you believe that?"

Referring to Isidor Fisch's shoebox, the container Hauptmann said he had placed into his broom closet, Judge Trenchard said, "Mrs. Hauptmann, as I recall, said that she never saw it; and I do not recall that any witness excepting the defendant testified that they ever saw the shoebox there."

Except for Verna Snyder who at times had her eyes closed, the jury seemed attentive and interested in what the judge was saying. Trenchard next summarized the defendant's testimony and reminded the jurors that several alibi witnesses had testified that Hauptmann was in the Bronx on the night of the crime. Regarding these witnesses, the judge said, "You should consider the fact, where it is the fact, that several of the witnesses have been convicted of crimes, and to determine whether or not their credibility has been affected thereby; and where it appears that witnesses have made contradictory statements, you should consider the fact and determine the credibility."

The judge said that the State's case was completely circumstantial—no one had seen Hauptmann steal or murder the baby. "If the State has not satisfied you by evidence beyond a reasonable doubt that the death of the child was caused by the act of the defendant, he must be acquitted."

Regarding the felony-murder doctrine, Trenchard said, "Now, our statute declares: Murder, which shall be committed in perpetrating a burglary, shall be Murder in the First Degree. . . . If you find that the murder was committed in perpetrating a burglary, it is murder in the first degree, even though the killing was unintentional." He was nearing the end of his charge when he brought up the subject of New Jersey's death penalty. "If you find the defendant guilty of murder in the first degree, you may, if you see fit, recommend imprisonment at hard labor for life. If you should return a verdict of murder in the first degree *and nothing else, the punishment on that verdict would be death."*

It was 11:13 when Judge Trenchard finished instructing the jury. He called the three men and three women whose duty it would be to guard the jury during their deliberations to come forward and be sworn in by the court clerk. When that was done, the judge asked the jurors to remain in their seats for a few minutes while the room they would be deliberating in was readied. FBI agents were making a last-minute check to make sure the room hadn't been bugged.

Sheriff John Curtiss came into the courtroom at 11:21 and announced that the twelve- by twenty-foot witness room directly above Hauptmann's cell was ready for the jury. "The jury may retire," the judge declared.

The jurors gathered up their hats and coats and walked single file across the room, passing between the judge on their right and Hauptmann on their left. Although they passed within a few feet of the defendant and his wife, none of the jurors looked in their direction. Colonel Lindbergh watched until the last juror was out of the room, then turned and said something to Colonel Schwarzkopf.

When the jurors were out of earshot, Frederick Pope got to his feet and moved for a mistrial on the grounds that Judge Trenchard's charge to the jury was heavily opinioned and patently biased in favor of the State. Pope declared that the judge's remarks had seriously prejudiced the defendant. Pope also complained that Trenchard's charge had left the jury no room for a verdict of second-degree murder or manslaughter. Judge Trenchard overruled Pope's objections and cleared the spectators out of the courtroom.

Sheriff Curtiss walked over to Hauptmann to take him back to his cell. The defendant got up, gave his wife a half-smile and a slight nod, then followed the sheriff to the door. Fisher patted Hauptmann on the shoulder as he passed by, but Reilly ignored him.

Colonels Lindbergh, Breckinridge, and Schwarzkopf drove to Attorney George K. Large's house for lunch.

At three o'clock, the jury asked for a magnifying glass so they could closely examine the ransom notes and the handwriting on the closet door trim.

At six o'clock, the jail warden's wife brought the jurors a home-cooked meal—hamburger steak, green peas, fried potatoes, a large cake, and several pots of hot coffee.

At 7:45, the jury was still out, so Judge Trenchard sent for Odem Baggstrom, the head of the jury guard. The Judge told Baggstrom that the jury would not leave the courthouse until they reached a verdict. The judge was prepared to lock the jury in all night and all the next day.

At nine o'clock, the jurors sent out for cigarettes.

372   Directly below the jury room, Hauptmann paced the bullpen. At 6:30, after leaving most of his dinner untouched, he called for Lloyd Fisher. The jury had been out seven hours and Hauptmann wanted to know if that was good or bad. Fisher sent word that under New Jersey law he was not permitted to visit the defendant while the jury was out. Mrs. Hauptmann had wanted to wait in a room in the courthouse but was told that she was not allowed on the premises. She was therefore waiting at her Flemington boarding house with her landlords, her son, and Gerta Henkel.

Back in the courtroom amid the tobacco smoke and the litter—bottles, sandwich boxes, napkins, coffee cups and wastepaper—the lawyers, policemen, and reporters waited. At 10:28, Sheriff Curtiss ordered a deputy to mount the stairs to the cupola on the courthouse roof and ring the 125-year-old bell. This was the signal that a verdict had been reached. Curtiss then entered the courtroom and announced that the jury would be returning.

An Associated Press reporter who had been waiting in the courtroom rushed to a secluded spot where he opened his brief case and muttered a code word into a shortwave radio microphone. The message was received by another AP reporter stationed in the courthouse attic. This was exactly what Sheriff Curtiss had wanted to prevent—he had instructed his men to be particularly vigilant at this point, to make certain that reporters, among other things, weren't sending hand signals out the courtroom windows.

The AP reporter in the courtroom had a code signifying that the jury was coming in and a set of codes designating the verdict of the sentence. In all of the excitement, he got his codes mixed up and instead of indicating the jury's return, he signaled that Hauptmann had been found guilty of first-degree murder and sentenced to life. Radio Press News picked up the inaccurate news bulletin and passed it on to all of the broadcasting networks.

Mrs. Hauptmann, her face waxen, entered the room with Reilly. She took her regular seat and smiled halfheartedly at Edward Reilly, who regarded her blankly.

Wilentz turned to Reilly and whispered, "We won't accept anything but a first degree conviction."

"Well," Reilly replied, "we are game, let it come."

Lloyd Fisher suddenly got out of his chair and went to Mrs. Hauptmann. Putting his arm around her shoulder, he said, "This is only the beginning. Don't show a sign, because, if you do, it will count against us." The attorney patted Mrs. Hauptmann's shoulder, then returned to his chair.

At 10:30 the jury, led by Sheriff Curtiss, Odem Baggstrom, and the foreman, Charles Walton, filed into the room. The jurors looked grave as they took their places in the jury box. None of them had looked in the direction of Hauptmann and his wife. Mrs. Snyder was biting her lip, fighting back tears. Ethel Stockton, the most jovial of the jurors, looked as though she was about to faint. Elmer Smith, the forty-two-year-old insurance salesman, was breathing heavily and was unable to control his hands, which twitched as though they were on a string. Once seated, the jurors kept their faces down and fidgeted on their rubber-padded chairs. It seemed that no one could get comfortable.

At 10:31 Hauptmann, preceded by Sheriff Curtiss and five state troopers, came through the door. His feet were manacled and his right wrist was handcuffed to a state trooper. His eyes were lowered, and when he raised his head to look for his wife, his face was pasty and sallow and his eyes were afraid.[1]

Hauptmann stole a peek at the jury box, then quickly looked away, no doubt disturbed by what he saw.

Elmer "Pop" Hann, the court crier, came into the room and climbed the steps to the bench, where he cleared away some of the debris—paper, cigarette butts, and paper plates. Above the courthouse, the bell in the cupola was tolling, and outside, the crowd was getting excited and louder.

It was 10:40 when Judge Trenchard emerged from his chambers. The court crier intoned, "Oyez! Oyez!" and everybody rose. The judge took his seat and everyone sat down; with a wave of his hand, Judge Trenchard said, "The jury will rise."

The jurors virtually jumped to their feet.

"Let the defendant stand," Judge Trenchard said.

Hauptmann and his two guards stood up. The defendant was still handcuffed to the state trooper, and his head was bowed.

"Members of the jury," said the court clerk, "have you agreed upon a verdict?"

"We have," came the joint reply.

"Who shall speak for you?"

"The foreman."

"Mr. Foreman, what say you: Do you find the defendant guilty or not guilty?"

Charles Walton, the foreman, reading slowly from a slip of paper, said, "Guilty. We find the defendant, Bruno Richard Hauptmann, guilty of murder in the first degree." Walton's hands were trembling so badly he almost tore the paper he was holding in two.

The moment the verdict was read, several messenger boys scrambled to the door with their press bulletins. Before they could get out, Judge Trenchard ordered that no one could leave the courtroom.

Hauptmann, white as a sheet, looked stoically into space, then sank onto his chair without looking at his wife.

The court clerk said, "Members of the jury, you have heard the verdict—that you find the defendant, Bruno Richard Hauptmann, guilty of murder in the first degree—and so say you all?"

"We do," the jurors replied in chorus.

"The defendant may stand," Judge Trenchard said in his sternest voice. "Bruno Richard Hauptmann, you have been convicted of murder in the first degree. The sentence of the court is that you suffer death at the time and place, and in the manner provided by law. And the court will hand to the sheriff a warrant appointing the week beginning Monday, the eighteenth of March, 1935, as the week within which such sentence must be executed. You are now remanded to the custody of the sheriff."

It was 10:50 when Hauptmann headed toward the courtroom door. As the defendant shuffled by Lloyd Fisher, the attorney said something to him, but Hauptmann, as if in a stupor, merely nodded.

Judge Trenchard looked at the jury, "Thank you most sincerely for the service you have rendered in the performance of this jury duty. You are now excused."

The jurors picked up their hats and coats and filed out of the jury box. Led by Sheriff Curtiss, they walked back to the hotel along the path cut into the crowd by the double line of state troopers.

Back in the courtroom, Mrs. Hauptmann was still in her chair. Suddenly her shoulders shook and the tears started to come. She reached into her purse for the tiny blue handkerchief—the one that matched her dress.

The last juror stepped out of the room at eleven o'clock, and Judge Trenchard banged his gavel, bringing the thirty-two-day-old trial to an end.

Wilentz, flushed with victory, followed Judge Trenchard into his chambers to sign the warrant of execution.

Seven thousand people were jammed into the area between the courthouse and the Union Hotel and flares from the moving-picture and sound-reel trucks lit up the night.

Mrs. Hauptmann sat alone in the littered, smoke-filled courtroom where the chairs were still warm and the air hot and heavy. John Walters, the Flemington chief of police, happened to pass through the vacant courtroom. He saw Mrs. Hauptmann and stopped to see if he could escort her back to the boarding house. She sat there for a moment, then got to her feet. As they walked toward the big double doors, Mrs. Hauptmann took hold of the policeman's arm.

When Hauptmann was taken back to his cell following the verdict, his body slumped the moment he stepped out of the courtroom. He had to be half-carried the rest of the way.[2] When he got to his cell, he collapsed face down onto his cot. His muffled, hysterical sobs and German mutterings could be heard throughout the jail.[3]

At midnight, several reporters called the Morrow home to get the Lindbergh reaction to the verdict. A spokesman at the house said that Colonel Lindbergh had "no statement nor comment on the case whatsoever."

A dozen or so reporters gathered in front of John Condon's home in the Bronx, but Jafsie wouldn't come to the door. Mrs. Condon, speaking for her husband, made the following statement: "We heard the verdict over the radio and we have no comment to make on it. The family feels that we have been in the public eye long enough."

Wilentz publicly thanked all the investigators who had worked on the case, his witnesses, and the jury. Speaking of the jurors, he said, "The nation is indebted to these courageous men and women."

Colonel Schwarzkopf gave credit to the New York City Police and the FBI, then thanked his own investigators, mentioning Captain Lamb and Lieutenant Keaten by name. "I hope that this verdict will act as a crime preventive throughout the nation and that the security and sanctity of the American home may be materially enhanced," he said.

Edward Reilly, looking tired and slightly disoriented, said that an appeal to the New

Jersey Court of Errors and Appeals would be made within the thirty-day deadline. "Although the jury has rendered a verdict on the facts, we still believe a great many errors of law were committed which will ultimately mean the reversal of this judgement," he said.

Lloyd Fisher, looking tired and crestfallen, said that he preferred not to make a statement. Fisher, having anticipated the verdict, had been thinking about the appeal for several days. The defense had no money and it would cost ten thousand dollars just to have the trial transcript typed—an absolute must for the appeal. Fisher would have to petition the state to pay for that expense.

The next day, Anne Lindbergh sat before her diary and wrote the last thing she would ever write on the case: "The trial is over. We must start our life again, try to build it securely—C. and Jon and I. . . ."[4]

Lawyers must be paid. Whether Anna likes it or not,
she is going to pay and pay through the nose.
            — E D W A R D   J .   R E I L L Y

40 MOVING TO
THE DEATH HOUSE

HAUPTMAN HAD CRIED ALL NIGHT, and in the morning was physically exhausted and emotionally drained. Just before noon, Anna came to the jail to cheer him up, but she was clearly upset and only added to his grief. Later, Reilly came to the jail to tell his client that it was time for him to confess everything. Reilly said that if he came clean, his sentence would be commuted to life. Hauptmann, in his whining emotionless voice, said that he had nothing to tell.

Outside the jail, standing before a group of reporters, Reilly quoted Hauptmann as saying, "How could anyone believe that a father of a baby like Mannfried could kill any other man's baby."[1]

"I am still convinced of Hauptmann's innocence," Reilly said. "We are appealing to the people of the United States for contributions to carry on our fight."

That afternoon, Lloyd Fisher, with the approval of Sheriff Curtiss and Warden Henry McCrea, brought two reporters to the jail to interview Hauptmann. The reporters stood in the hallway outside the bull pen and talked to Hauptmann through the bars. The prisoner, wearing an undershirt, a pair of old gray trousers, and wornout shoes without laces, said, "I am innocent and I know I will win my appeal, but I guess I have to depend on the public for money, because I haven't got any."

"Not a dollar?" one of the reporters asked?

"No, not a dollar. The government has tied up all of my money and all my wife's money. I know there must be a lot of people in the United States who do not believe that I am guilty, and who would like to help me."

"There have been reports that you've been offered a lot of money to make a confession: To tell the whole story of the crime."

"If I had anything to confess, I'd have done so right after I was arrested, to spare my wife and mother all they have gone through."

"Do you think you got a good defense?"

"As far as they could go, it was all right," Hauptmann replied, looking at Fisher. "I am a common man, not a lawyer, but it seems to me that Judge Trenchard favored the State too much in his charge to the jury."

"Some of your witnesses made a bad impression on the jury, didn't they?"

"I am not responsible for my witnesses. I guess some of them came here because they wanted publicity or something out of the case."

"What do you think about Attorney General Wilentz?"

"Sometimes he made me wise guy, sometimes a dumbbell. But I'm just a common man."

"Did the appearance of Colonel Lindbergh in court every day hurt your case?"

"I guess it was bad for me, all right. Such a big man naturally has got to affect the jury."

"What about rail 16 and your attic?"

"That was the most ridiculous thing—I got so many boards in my garage I don't know why I should go to the attic."

"Are you afraid of the electric chair, Bruno?"

"You can imagine how I feel when I think of my wife and child, but I have no fear for myself because I know that I am innocent. If I have to go to the chair in the end, I will go like a man, and like an innocent man." Hauptmann's face sagged a bit, and he turned away. He quickly regained his composure, turned back to the reporters, and said, "I hear from the newspapers that I am not religious, but that is not so. I am probably more religious than most people who go to church. I am a friend of nature. I have always been a Lutheran—I pray in my heart. I don't want to make myself any angel, but when they went searching my life history it was only for them black spots. They didn't mention at all that I saved three lives in Germany. There were two drownings and one man, he was sliding down into a quarry when I caught him just at the edge 100 feet down. I put my life at stake then. Now I come to America and the State wants to take my life for nothing."[2]

After the interview, Fisher told the reporters who were waiting outside that contributions to Hauptmann's defense fund could be sent to the Flemington Bank and Trust Company. Fisher said that so far the fund had received a pair of two-dollar bills.

On that Thursday, the day following the verdict, the Morrow estate was under siege. The roads in the area were traffic-clogged and hundreds of tourists were lined along the iron fence surrounding the grounds hoping to catch a glimpse of the Lindberghs.

In Kamenz, Germany, the prisoner's mother, Pauline, told the press that "In America the rich can do anything. I know my son is not guilty, but Lindbergh wanted it so and therefore everything came that way." She said she had just written a letter to President Roosevelt asking him to pardon her son. (The President's pardoning authority only extends to persons convicted in the federal courts.)

Sheriff Curtiss announced that evening that Hauptmann would be transferred to the New Jersey State Prison in Trenton on Saturday and would be placed into a cell in the death house.

On Friday morning, Charles Walton, the jury foreman, punched a newsreel man in the face when the newsman approached him for an interview. Walton said that he and the other jurors had agreed not to tell their stories until later. But as Walton spoke, the *New York Daily News* published an exclusive interview of Howard V. Biggs, juror number twelve.[3]

That same day, several of the jury guards were telling reporters how the voting had unfolded. *The New York Times* reported that five ballots had been taken.[4] On the first count, only seven of the jurors had voted for the death sentence. The minority favoring life consisted of Rosie Pill, Verna Snyder, Elmer Smith, Robert Cravatt, and Philip Hockenbury. On the second ballot, the two women switched to the majority; on the third, Philip Hockenbury went over. It was then ten to two for death. When the fourth vote was counted, only one juror held out for life—Robert Cravatt, at twenty-eight, the youngest member of the jury. On the fifth and final ballot, Cravatt joined the others.

Juror Biggs, in his *New York Daily News* interview, indicated that he had been impressed by Hauptmann's sudden wealth and the improbability of the Fisch story. "Hauptmann spent $400 on a radio shortly after the ransom was paid," the juror said. "He could have got a fine radio for less than a hundred. Any man who would keep records of small outlays of money in a little notebook as Hauptmann did is pretty tight with his money. Is it reasonable to think he suddenly spent $400 for a radio?" Biggs was also impressed by Charles Lindbergh: "Colonel Lindbergh is a level-headed, upright man. He'd have no reason to identify Hauptmann unless he was sure he was right."

Later that day, with the code of silence broken, several other jurors made statements. Charles Walton said, "Edward J. Reilly showed his contempt for us from the start. Our state police could have closed the book by pinning the whole thing on poor, dead Violet Sharpe. That would have been easy. We knew, though, that this theory had been found false, and discarded."

Charles F. Snyder liked Dr. Condon. "Doctor Condon," he said, "made a fine witness, we were impressed by his sincerity and we believed what he said." The juror also thought a lot of Betty Gow. "She made a hit with all of us even though the defense tried to implicate her in the crime." Snyder added that the handwriting experts were "a treat" and that Arthur Koehler was "a man who had learned his subject from A to Z."

Philip Hockenbury commented about how the defendant and his wife had created a scene during the testimony of FBI Agent Sisk and Mrs. Achenbach: "Some of us thought such behavior was natural with the Hauptmanns. Others thought it was all an act. My own idea was that the Hauptmanns deliberately acted that way to impress the court and the jury . . . business of outraged innocence."

According to juror George L. Voorhees, "Reilly came down from Broadway to us hicks to show off his tricks. We all thought he was a big bluff, all dressed up like a clothing model. We have known Lloyd Fisher for a long time, he did the best he could. Mr. Wilentz handled himself in a masterly style."[5]

Hauptmann had a lot of visitors on Friday. From three o'clock to four, two women reporters from the Hearst Corporation questioned him, and when they left, Fisher brought in a newsreel crew from Paramount News.[6]

While Hauptmann was being interviewed and filmed in his cell, Betty Gow boarded a ship for Scotland, and Dr. Condon, accompanied by his daughter Myra, sailed from the Hamilton Avenue Pier in Brooklyn on the Grace liner *Santa Maria*. Betty was going home and Dr. Condon was on a seventeen-day vacation to Panama. Attorney General Wilentz, having left for Florida the day before, was also on a holiday.

Betty Gow, while looking for her stateroom on the Cunard White Star Line's S. S. *Berengaria* was recognized by a group of passengers, who immediately surrounded her. One woman grabbed her by the arm and said, "Let's have a look at you." The nursemaid screamed, slapped the woman in the face, then fled to her cabin. Although she had assured the Lindberghs that she would be returning to their household in six weeks, Betty Gow never came back to America.

Dr. Condon, having been recognized on the pier, was followed to his stateroom by a crowd of autograph seekers. Unlike Betty Gow, Condon enjoyed the attention, affably giving his autograph to all who asked.

On Saturday morning, the sixteenth, Hauptmann, dressed up in his double-breasted suit and fedora hat, embarked upon a trip of his own. After living 116 days in the Hunterdon County Jail, Hauptmann was being moved to the state penitentiary in Trenton. He was handcuffed to Trooper Allen Smith and Warden McCrea, and at 9:30 was placed into the back seat of a Buick sedan. The unmarked car, wedged between two police cruisers and flanked by a pair of motorcycles, made the twenty-three-mile trip in an hour. In Trenton, the motorcade was greeted by an orderly crowd of fifteen hundred people gathered at the prison gates.

Hauptmann and his party were met at the big steel doors to the main building by the warden, who led the group to the intake center where Hauptmann was to be fingerprinted, photographed, issued his prison garb, and given the number 17,400. As the group passed through the mess hall en route to the processing center, Hauptmann was immediately recognized by six hundred inmates, who stopped eating long enough to boo him soundly.

At the intake center, Hauptmann and his escorts from Hunterdon County parted company. After being strip-searched, fingerprinted, photographed, and outfitted in his prison clothes, Hauptmann, on the verge of tears, was marched across the open yard to the little brick death house where he was installed in cell number 9 just eight feet from the electric chair.

Besides the death chamber, the little red building contained eighteen cells in two tiers of nine cells each. Although Hauptmann was the only occupant of the lower range, the top tier housed five men who were waiting to be electrocuted.

Hauptmann would no longer have the benefit of a bullpen to exercise and pace, and his ten by nine-foot cell was much smaller than the one he had occupied in Flemington. He would be watched around the clock by two guards, and a light would be constantly lit in his cell. He would be allowed frequent visits with his wife and lawyers but only one visit a month from relatives other than his wife. He could read books but not newspapers, and, unlike his arrangement in Flemington, he could talk to his guards. He was told that he could mail two letters a month and receive up to six, and if

380   the guards were willing, he would be allowed to play cards or checkers with them through the bars.

Back in Flemmington, representatives of the two local banks announced that their institutions would not handle contributions to Hauptmann's defense fund.

On Sunday, Lloyd Fisher told reporters that Hauptmann had taken the pauper's oath, which meant that the defense could petition Judge Trenchard to have the State pay for the typing of the trial transcript.

Fisher, Pope, and Rosecrans had been diligently preparing a written brief that contained their legal arguments for a new trial. Reilly, on the other hand, had been so busy giving speeches he hadn't been involved in the mechanics of the appeal. On Monday, Fisher telephoned Reilly and said that he and the others were eager to file Hauptmann's appeal. Reilly told Fisher to relax, there was no use doing anything until Wilentz returned from Florida. Fisher protested, and Reilly had to remind him who was boss. Incensed, Fisher drove to the Bronx and tried to talk Mrs. Hauptmann into firing Reilly. Reilly had lost the trial and he was now holding up the appeal.[7]

Mrs. Hauptmann found herself in a dilemma—she needed Fisher, since he was the only lawyer who believed that her husband was innocent, and she needed Reilly, because he was a celebrity and an exciting speaker who was going to be featured at several of her fund-raising rallies.

The next day, concerned about the internal bickering and the effect it could have on her husband, Mrs. Hauptmann arranged a four-hour meeting between Reilly and the New Jersey attorneys. The conference was held at the Hildebrecht Hotel in Trenton, and although there was plenty of shouting, name-calling, and finger-pointing, Mrs. Hauptmann was able to engineer a temporary truce.

The day after that, Judge Trenchard ordered the State to pay for the typing of the 1,600,000-word trial transcript. The judge announced that because of the forthcoming appeal, Hauptmann would not be executed before June of that year.

On February 22, Mrs. Eleanor Roosevelt, the President's wife, was in Atlantic City to give a speech before some women's group. When she had finished her talk, a reporter asked, "What do you think of the Hauptmann trial and do you think it will deter kidnapping and crime?"

She replied, "I thought from what I read that the verdict was based entirely upon circumstantial evidence and, while not in sympathy with Hauptmann, I was a little perturbed at the thought of what might happen to any innocent person in a similar situation. The entire trial left me with a question in my mind and I certainly was glad that I did not have to sit on that jury."[8]

Although it wasn't her intention, Mrs. Roosevelt had given the Hauptmann defense a boost. The next day, Lloyd Fisher told the press that he and the other defense attorneys were in total agreement with the First Lady.

Five days after Mrs. Roosevelt's speech, Reilly, speaking about the trial at a Lions Club luncheon in New York City, said: "We would have stood no more chance in Flemington if John the Baptist had taken the stand for the defense." When the laughter had faded,

Reilly said, "The State of New Jersey paid $600,000 on the Lindbergh case, and the taxpayers had to be shown some return for their money."[9]

Reilly had his figures right—the Lindbergh investigation and trial had been expensive. The New York City Police Department had spent a quarter of a million dollars on the investigation, and Schwarzkopf's investigation had cost the state of New Jersey twice that much. The trial itself had cost $650,000, $50,000 of it going to the eight handwriting experts. Arthur Koehler's bill had been $10,000 and the court stenographer's $8,000. There was also a lot of money spent by the FBI and the IRS.

The first Hauptmann Defense Fund rally, held in the heavily German Yorkville section of Manhattan on February 27, was a huge success. Twenty-five hundred people, mostly German-Americans, paid twenty-five cents apiece to hear speeches by Mrs. Hauptmann, Edward Reilly, and several others.

Before the meeting was adjourned, Mrs. Hauptmann's helpers went into the audience and collected $750, bringing the total take to $1,350.

Four days after the Yorkville fundraiser, the second Hauptmann rally, held at the Turn Hall in Passaic, New Jersey, and sponsored by a number of German-American societies, drew another overflow crowd. Over a thousand people squeezed into the hall to hear Mrs. Hauptmann say, "When I heard the verdict I went home and wept with my child." Over the sobs of the women in the audience, Mrs. Hauptmann continued, "Help me get a new trial for my husband. Whatever you will give will help him and me and our baby."[10]

Besides paying for admissions tickets, Mrs. Hauptmann's audience donated another nine hundred dollars, bringing the total take that night to twelve hundred dollars.

While Mrs. Hauptmann was breaking hearts in Passaic, Ed Reilly was in a Brooklyn hospital. Following a frantic call from his mother, four men in white had come to the house to put the ranting attorney in a straitjacket. A spokesman from Reilly's office said that he was suffering from "exhaustion" and would be back on the job in ten days.

Meanwhile, in the Bronx, Hauptmann's old apartment had become a tourist attraction, drawing a thousand people a day. Mrs. Rauch, the landlady, told reporters that some promoter had suggested making the place into a museum with photographs and exhibits of the trial.

On March 4, the Reverend D. G. Werner drove Mrs. Hauptmann, Gerta Henkel, and Mannfried to Trenton, where Mrs. Hauptmann spent an hour with her husband. Mrs. Henkel took care of Mannfried while Anna told Richard of her money-raising activities. When she returned to the car at four o'clock, a reporter asked her why she hadn't taken the baby in to see his father. She replied, "I will never take my baby into the death house." Mrs. Hauptmann said that her husband was "serene and eating well."

On March 6, the day Dr. Condon and Wilentz returned from their vacations, a third defense fund rally, this one held in the Bronx, was attended by fifteen hundred supporters. Once again, forty men wearing green armbands went into the audience to collect money, this time gathering one thousand dollars for the fund.

One of the rally's speakers, a lawyer and leader of the American Nazi support group, Friends of the New Germany, worked the crowd into a frenzy by attacking Wilentz, whom he called Wilensky. When the red-faced speaker finished his thinly veiled anti-Semitic speech, he was given a standing ovation.

On March 8, following another fundraiser in Brooklyn, the Welfare Commissioner of New York City announced that because the Hauptmann Defense Fund did not have a permit to solicit funds in public, they had been ordered to gather up their public collection boxes and stop holding public meetings.

Meanwhile, ingenious autograph hunters were getting Hauptmann's signature by sending him one-dollar checks that he would endorse.

Reilly got out of the hospital on March 12 and announced that Mrs. Hauptmann would be making a multi-city fund-raising tour. He said she would speak in Detroit, Chicago, and Milwaukee.

Mrs. Hauptmann returned to New York City on March 31 after having raised fifteen thousand dollars on her midwestern tour. As soon as she got back, she sent Reilly a check for five thousand dollars, a sum she felt adequate since he had already been paid twenty-five thousand dollars by the *New York Journal.*

Thinking that Mrs. Hauptmann had raised forty thousand dollars on her trip, Reilly, on April 1, sent her a bill for twenty-five thousand dollars. The next day, she hurried to Trenton to consult with her husband. When he saw the bill, he shouted, "Don't pay it Annie, Reilly must go. I've never liked him, and I know he doesn't like me. If Lloyd Fisher had been in charge of the trial I wouldn't be in here. You're the one who wanted to keep him, remember?"

The coffers of the Hauptmann Defense Fund were full and Reilly was no longer needed as a fundraiser, so Mrs. Hauptmann saw no reason to keep him around. She had no intention of squandering the hard-earned nickels and dimes of Bruno's supporters on a drunken, greedy lawyer. As for the appeal, Lloyd Fisher was taking care of that.

On April 3, Anna sent Reilly a registered letter notifying him that his "services would not be required henceforth." The next day, calling Reilly's legal bill exorbitant, Anna publicly announced his dismissal, naming Lloyd Fisher as the new chief defense counsel. Frederick Pope and Egbert Rosecrans would continue to assist the defense.

That night, Reilly said that he was surprised the Hauptmanns considered his fee exorbitant. "If I had been trying this case in New York, my fee would have been $100,000."[11] Reilly reminded the newsmen that he had worked thirteen weeks on the case and had spent five thousand dollars of his own money. "I went into this case purely from a business standpoint and presented my bill in a businesslike transaction," he said. He then announced that he was turning the matter over to *his* lawyer, who would initiate a breach of contract suit if the Hauptmanns didn't pay. On April 5, in yet another speech before another service club, Reilly said, "Lawyers must be paid, whether Anna likes it or not, she is going to pay and pay through the nose."[12]

On the day Reilly was threatening to make his former client pay through the nose, one of his trial witnesses, Benjamin Heier, was indicted for perjury by the Hunterdon County grand jury. Heier was the one who had said he had seen Isidor Fisch running out of St. Raymond's Cemetery on the night the ransom was paid. Now that he was indicted, Heier would get the chance to explain how he had managed to be in the Bronx at the same time he was having an automobile accident in Manhattan.

On April 30, a spokesman for the Hauptmann jury announced that the group was writing a book that would reveal each juror's most intimate impressions of the trial. Each juror was contributing a chapter to the book, which was scheduled for publication in June. (This project never became a book. It did, however, become a twelve-part article that was published in installments in the *New York Daily News*.)

On May 10, Fisher and his colleagues filed Hauptmann's appeal, citing 193 points of law justifying a reversal of his conviction and a new trial. The defense lawyers charged that Wilentz, in his closing remarks, had gone far beyond the evidence by suggesting that the baby had been killed in the nursery instead of being dropped from the ladder. The prosecutor was also criticized for his inflammatory summation in which he had called the defendant, among other things, a snake, and the "Public Enemy Number One of this World."

In their brief, Fisher and his colleagues argued that the excessive and harmful pre-trial publicity, the circuslike atmosphere in Flemington, and Colonel Lindbergh's daily presence at the trial had unduly prejudiced the defendant, thereby denying him a fair trial under the Fourteenth Amendment of the U.S. Constitution. Judge Trenchard's charge to the jury, characterized by the appellants as heavily biased in favor of the State, was also cited as grounds for a new trial.

On June 20, in Trenton, Wilentz and the defense attorneys made their oral arguments before the New Jersey Court of Errors and Appeals, the state's highest court. The case was heard by fourteen judges seated in two rows of high-backed leather-cushioned chairs in a purple-carpeted room on the fourth floor of the new State House Annex. The judges, elderly and somber-looking in their black robes, heard Egbert Rosecrans's three-hour address. Rosecrans charged that Judge Trenchard had improperly admitted the homemade ladder into evidence, and he argued, among other things, that the prosecution had failed to prove that a burglary had been committed, an element vital to the establishment of the felony-murder doctrine. In concluding, Rosecrans said, "The question is not whether Hauptmann is guilty or innocent, it is whether he had received a fair trial."

At two o'clock, Wilentz, having been allotted one hour to make his case, argued for the State. Because only legal issues, or points of law, were being considered, the proceeding did not include a jury, witnesses, or the general public. The only nonlegal persons allowed in the room were a handful of reporters. Even the Hauptmanns were excluded.

The court adjourned at four o'clock and the judges returned to their chambers with their notes on the oral arguments and the written briefs from both sides. Fisher went directly to the prison to explain to Hauptmann how the appellate system worked. Under New Jersey law, he said, at least eight judges would have to vote in his favor in order to reverse the conviction and stay the execution. A seven-to-seven vote would sustain the conviction and move him one step closer to the death chamber. Fisher said that it would be four months before the court rendered its decision. He told his client he was confident they would win.

On July 23, Fisher announced that a few weeks earlier Hauptmann had completed a short autobiography called *The Story of My Life*. The authorities of the prison, however,

384   were not letting Hauptmann send the manuscript to a publisher. Fisher said that because the defense had been counting on the money from the sale of the book, this was a serious problem. The Hauptmann Defense Fund was already broke.

Late in August, the case took a bizarre turn when Fisher announced that his investigators had located a baby on Long Island who was probably the missing Lindbergh child. [13]

Fisher asked Colonel Schwarzkopf about fingerprints and was told that although the Lindbergh baby had never been printed, the Long Island baby's prints could be checked against the latent prints Dr. Hudson had taken off of the Lindbergh baby's toys. Fisher wasn't interested in making such a comparison because there was no way to be certain that the latents on the toys were the baby's. "Yes, but what if they match?" Schwarzkopf asked. "If you are sure you have young Lindbergh, why don't you see if his prints are on the toys?"

Fisher still wasn't interested.

Colonel Lindbergh declined Fisher's invitation to go to Long Island and look over the baby. Having seen the little corpse in the Trenton Morgue, the Colonel knew that his son was dead. The last thing Lindbergh wanted was to give his wife false hopes by humoring Lloyd Fisher.

In September, the new prison warden, Mark O. Kimberling, a former officer of the New Jersey State police, announced that Hauptmann's manuscript would not be released by the prison until after the appeals court reached its decision. It seemed that while Lloyd Fisher was trying to get the autobiography into print, the state of New Jersey was doing its best to keep Hauptmann's life story a short one.

Would I kill a baby? I am a man. Would I build that ladder?
I am a carpenter.
— B R U N O   R I C H A R D   H A U P T M A N N
to Gov. Harold G. Hoffman

41 STEPPING CLOSER TO THE CHAIR

THE FOURTEEN JUDGES on New Jersey's Court of Errors and Appeals had voted unanimously on October 9 to affirm Hauptmann's first-degree murder conviction. Justice Charles W. Parker wrote the forty-five page opinion and summarized the Court's rationale as follows:

> Our conclusion is that the verdict is not only not contrary to the weight of the evidence, but one to which the evidence inescapably led. From three different and, in the main, unrelated sources the proofs point unerringly to guilt, viz: (a) possession and use of the ransom money; (b) handwriting of the ransom notes; and (c) wood used in the construction of the ladder.[1]

A few hours after the appeals court decision became public, an Associated Press reporter telephoned Mrs. Hauptmann to get her reaction. Anna was living in a small apartment in the Bronx with Bubi. She hadn't gotten the news and was therefore stunned when the reporter broke it to her. "I just saw him yesterday," she said, fighting back the tears. "He was so cheerful. We don't talk about the appeal, but I could tell he expected the court to find him innocent."[2]

Colonel Lindbergh was in Baltimore that day witnessing the test flight of a new clipper plane, and Mrs. Lindbergh was vacationing at the Morrow summer home in North Beach, Maine. Newsmen were unable to reach the Colonel and Mrs. Lindbergh had no comment.

Ed Reilly, always available to the press, said, "I still believe that Hauptmann is not guilty, and if at any time I can be of service to his cause, I am at the defendant's command."

Now that the Appeals Court had made its decision, Fisher was no longer barred from selling Hauptmann's life story. Since the defense fund had dried up, Fisher was eager to get the manuscript published. He was also preparing a writ of certiorari to get the case before the United States Supreme Court.

Two days after the appeals court had handed down its decision, Hauptmann, desperate and frantic with worry, told Warden Mark Kimberling that he wanted to talk to New Jersey's governor, Harold G. Hoffman. Kimberling, thinking that Hauptmann was ready to confess in return for a life sentence, said he'd pass the message on to the governor.

When the Lindbergh baby was kidnapped in March 1932, Harold G. Hoffman was head of New Jersey's Motor Vehicle Commission. The thirty-seven-year-old bureaucrat had been born and raised in South Amboy, New Jersey, not far from Perth Amboy, David Wilentz's hometown. Although Hoffman and Wilentz were members of different political parties, they had been good friends since childhood. Wilentz, in fact, had helped Hoffman become governor.

At the end of World War I, Captain Hoffman returned to New Jersey to get into politics. Having more than his share of ambition, street smarts, and energy, along with a back-slapping, good-old-boy personality, Hoffman was destined to succeed. Named head of the Republican party in Middlesex County in 1920, he next became city treasurer of South Amboy in 1922 and mayor in 1925. While rising through the political ranks, Hoffman also pursued a career in finance, becoming treasurer, vice-president, then president of one of South Amboy's largest banks.

Following his four-year term as South Amboy's mayor, Hoffman ran for and won a seat in the U.S. House of Representatives. After serving two terms in Congress, he was appointed head of the State's Motor Vehicle Department, a steppingstone to the governor's office.

Hoffman was married, had three daughters, and belonged to virtually every service club in South Amboy—Rotary, Elks, Masons, Shriners, Odd Fellows. Hoffman's favorite club, the Order of Circus Saints and Sinners, gave him the opportunity to make people laugh, something he loved to do. He liked nothing better than to dress up and hit other clowns over the head with brooms and balloons.

Although many considered Hoffman a real-life saint, others called him a loud-mouthed buffoon. What nobody knew was that Harold G. Hoffman, family man, clown, civic leader, was also a very active thief. Over the past ten years he had been embezzling money from the bank he had helped start. He had taken three hundred thousand dollars in government funds that had come into his hands as city treasurer and later as head of the motor vehicle commission. He had pocketed this money instead of depositing it in his bank. The money had been used to finance his various political campaigns and to support a luxurious lifestyle he couldn't afford on his salary.[3]

Hoffman, the dynamic politician, after-dinner speaker, practical joker, and embezzler, was elected governor of New Jersey six weeks after Hauptmann's arrest. He was sworn in on the day the Hauptmann trial began and was the youngest governor in America.

Kimberling passed Hauptmann's message on to Hoffman, who said he'd think about the prisoner's request to see him. As a member of the eight-man court of pardons, Hoffman was already officially involved in the case. But his real interest in Hauptmann was unofficial, and based upon his long-time personal and political association with Ellis Parker, the flamboyant Burlington County detective who, because he had been on the political outs with former Governor A. Harry Moore, had been denied access to the inner circles of the Lindbergh investigation.

Parker, the "small-town detective with the world-wide reputation," had been trying to make life difficult for Schwarzkopf from the very beginning. Fuming with jealousy and rage over his role as an outcast, and desperately trying to get into the Lindbergh limelight, Parker had tried to get attention by claiming that the corpse on Mount Rose Heights wasn't the Lindbergh baby. He was now convinced that Hauptmann had been railroaded, and was investigating the case, on county time, for the Hauptmann defense. It seemed that the taxpayers of Burlington County had paid Schwarzkopf and Wilentz to investigate and prosecute Hauptmann and were now paying their chief detective to get him off. Influenced by Parker's views on the case, the governor believed that Hauptmann might have been the ransom note writer but not the one who had actually kidnapped and murdered the baby.

Like many politicians, Hoffman couldn't resist free publicity, and Hauptmann was still news. The 1936 National Republican Convention was less than a year away and Hoffman had his eye on the vice-presidential nomination.

On the night of October 16, one week after the appeals court had handed down its decision, Governor Hoffman went to see the prisoner. The last-minute cancellation of a social function gave him the opportunity to slip over to the death house. From his suite of rooms at the Hildebrecht Hotel, Hoffman called Kimberling and arranged to meet him at his home on the prison grounds. The governor then telephoned Anna Bading, Ellis Parker's secretary, and asked her to meet him at Kimberling's house at ten o'clock. Besides being fluent in German, Mrs. Bading was a skilled stenographer and would be useful in the event Hauptmann was in the mood to confess.

When they got to the death house, the secretary was asked to take a seat on the little iron bench in the death chamber. There, sitting a few feet from the electric chair, now covered by a sheet, she tried not to think of the real-life horrors that had been played out in that room. If Hauptmann had a statement to make, she would be called into his cell. If not, she'd have to wait it out in that awful place.

"Richard, the governor wants to see you," Kimberling announced as he unlocked the door to cell number 9. The prisoner, wearing an open-necked blue-gray shirt and dark blue trousers, stood up from his cot and extended his hand.

"Thank you for coming, sir," Hauptmann said as Kimberling closed the door, locking the governor into the cell.

"I'll be down the hall, call when you need me," Kimberling said as the governor, and the prisoner sat down on the cot.

This was a new experience for Hoffman; he had never been in a prison cell. He was surprised that it was so small and dimly lit. Besides the normal prison plumbing, there was a stand with a water pitcher and a drinking cup on it and a small table holding photographs of Anna and Bubi, a Bible, and the eleven-volume transcript of the trial.

"Governor, why does your state do this to me? Why do they want my life for something somebody else has done?" Hauptmann asked in his whining voice.[4]

"Because you have been found guilty in our court—by the jury," the governor replied.

"Lies! Lies! All lies," Hauptmann cried. "Would I kill a baby? I am a man. Would I build that ladder? I am a carpenter."

So much for a confession, Hoffman thought.

"Why don't they use the lie detector on me?" Hauptmann asked. "And Dr. Condon, too. They have some kind of drug—why don't they use that on us?"

Hauptmann complained that he hadn't been properly represented by Edward Reilly. "Could a man do for dollars what Reilly has done to me? Only once, for about five minutes, did I have a chance to explain my case to him. Sometimes he came to see me, not often, for a few minutes. How could I talk to him?"

Hauptmann then spoke of the police and charged that they had withheld exculpatory evidence: "I can only think that they had fingerprints, but they are not like mine, so they say they have none. But they invent another story. They say I had worn gloves. Is this not a worthless lie? Why would the jury believe Koehler?" Hauptmann asked, after telling the governor that Charles DeBisschop, the lumberjack, had been a better, more qualified wood expert.

"But Richard," Hoffman said, "Surely you don't deny writing the ransom notes? How could all of those experts be wrong?"

"They admitted that many times they had been wrong in important cases. Sometimes they are hired by one side and again by another in a case. Sometimes these experts oppose each other; one says the handwriting is right, the other says it's wrong for the person accused. Lloyd Fisher has told me that the state had spent more money for handwriting experts alone than we had for our whole defense. So, when it is a question of sending me to the electric chair, right away the state, with· many thousands of dollars, gets all the experts who are well-known in the country and have them on their side against me."

"All right," Governor Hoffman answered. "But you hid the ransom money in your garage and the jury didn't believe that you got it from Isidor Fisch."

"The Saturday before Isidor left for Germany, my wife and I gave for him a farewell party. He brought along, in his arm, a cardboard box, and he asked me to put it in the closet for him and to keep it until he comes back from Germany. I thought maybe in the box were some things he forgot to put in the satchel, maybe papers and letters. Fisch had told me once that he had bank accounts and a safe-deposit box and that he also got ten thousand dollars in some company that bakes pies; also lots of furs. When I look into the box three weeks before I got arrested, I find it is full of money. Oh, I say to myself, that is where Isidor's money has gone. What he has saved he has put in gold certificates to be safe. I did not put it in the bank because with gold certificates I think I should have trouble. Could I have known that the money was the Lindbergh money? No! How could any sensible person think that?"

When the governor asked Hauptmann to explain how Dr. Condon's phone number and address happened to be written in his closet, Hauptmann said, "If I had committed this crime, would I have marked down in my house this number? Because in the Bronx I had no telephone and must go some distance to call. What good would it have been to me to have a number written inside my closet which is very small and dark?"

Referring to Dr. Condon, Hauptmann asked, "Even after he had seen me in what they call the police lineup, why would he keep going around all over the country trying to find 'John'?"

Regarding another prosecution eyewitness, the governor said, "The cashier at the theater in Greenwich Village, she said you passed a ransom bill long before you got the shoe box from Fisch. How do you explain that?"

"Can anyone believe that on the night of my birthday—November 26, 1933—I would go from my home on 222nd Street way downtown to Greenwich Village to see a moving picture? Or that for over a year a cashier who must wait on thousands of people would remember one man who bought from her a ticket?"

Hauptmann said that when he was arrested, he thought he was being stopped for speeding. He said he had been beaten by the police at the station in lower Manhattan: "They showed me a hammer and then they put out the lights and started to beat me on the shoulders, the back of the head, and the arm. Then, too, they kicked my legs with their feet and kept yelling, 'Where is the money? Where is the baby? We'll knock your brains out!'"

Governor Hoffman decided that it was time to leave. It was getting late, and it was obvious that Hauptmann wasn't going to confess. The governor remembered that poor Mrs. Bading was still keeping company with the electric chair. He got up from the cot and called for the warden, then shook Hauptmann's hand and said, "It's been an interesting night."

Warden Kimberling came and the governor was let out of the cell. Before the two men snatched the stenographer from the jaws of death, Hauptmann said, "The poor child has been kidnapped and murdered, so somebody must die for it. For is the parent not the great flyer? And if somebody does not die for the death of the child, then always the police will be monkeys. So I am the one who is picked out to die."

The day after Governor Hoffman's death house visit, Edward Reilly, looking haggard, hungover, and harried, announced that he had decided not to sue the Hauptmanns for his legal fees.[5] Reilly had fallen off the wagon, his third ex-wife was suing him for back alimony, and he was being dunned by his own lawyer, who was reminding him that "lawyers must be paid." Reilly figured that since the defense fund was broke and Hauptmann was about to be electrocuted, there was nothing to sue.

Only a handful of people knew that the governor had been to the death house to visit the prisoner. Those who didn't know of the governor's meeting with Hauptmann, people

390   like Wilentz, Schwarzkopf, Breckinridge, and Colonel Lindbergh, felt that as the execution date drew near, Hauptmann, in order to save his life, would confess.

Lloyd Fisher and his colleagues were elated over Governor Hoffman's personal interest in Hauptmann. They rejoiced over the fact that the governor had taken the trouble to hear Hauptmann's side of the story. Fisher had not spoken directly to Hoffman, but he had learned through Ellis Parker that the governor had been very impressed, indeed moved, by Hauptmann. It was a good sign.

Fisher had his problems, however. There was no money, so he had been desperately trying to peddle Hauptmann's manuscript—but the story was so sugary, self-serving, and corny no book publisher wanted it. Late in November, having nowhere else to turn, Fisher sold the story for peanuts to the *Daily Mirror,* a New York City tabloid.

On December 3, 1935, the *Mirror* published the first installment, Chapter One, under the massive, front-page headline: "HAUPTMANN'S OWN STORY!" The byline, "Bruno Richard Hauptmann," in the form of Hauptmann's signature, ironically bore, even to the untrained eye, similarities to the handwriting in the ransom notes.

Hauptmann's life story was a ploy to arouse sympathy. The introduction to the next day's installment, typical of what was to follow, read:

> "I was a straggler!" cries Bruno Richard Hauptmann—convicted kidnapper and murderer of the Lindbergh baby. . . . An unwanted child! The bitterness and tragedy of his youth creeps out in this, his life story he has written for the *Daily Mirror.* "Alone" he sobs. As a child he was a solitary, shunned and jeered at by his playfellows because his mother dressed him in girl's clothes . . . Afraid of his father—who in a drunken rage struck him in front of a gaping tavern crowd, he hid in the woods . . . His brother left home, his sister went to America . . . The boy Hauptmann was left to help his mother eke out a precarious livlihood . . . Poverty gripped the household . . . He wore his wooden shoes only on Sunday . . . His only pet was a goat and that was slaughtered for food.[6]

On Thursday, December 5, the day the *Daily Mirror* ran Chapter Three of Hauptmann's story, Governor Hoffman was in New York City watching the six-day bicycle races in Madison Square Garden. The governor watched the cyclists for a while then went into the pressroom to meet some of the reporters. One of the newsmen mentioned that he had covered the Hauptmann trial and said that he thought that some of the State's evidence had been phony. Hoffman replied that Ellis Parker shared this view. The reporter asked if Parker was still investigating the case and Hoffman said that he was.

The next morning, the *New York Daily News* carried the story on a back page under the headline: "LINDBERGH CASE REOPENED." The writer of the piece implied that Parker was looking into the case on the governor's behalf.

Later that day, following a luncheon speech at the New York Advertising Club, Hoffman was surrounded by reporters who fired questions at him about the Lindbergh case. Hoffman explained that Ellis Parker had been working on the case from the beginning and that he had therefore not been engaged by him to reopen the investigation. An Associated Press reporter named Pat McGrady then asked, "Governor, have you ever seen Hauptmann?"

"Yes, once."

"Where? And when?"

"Six or seven weeks ago, at the state prison."

The governor's reply sent the reporters scrambling for the telephones, and by the time Hoffman got back to New Jersey that night, the story of his visit to the death house and his doubts about Hauptmann's guilt was on the front page of every newspaper in New Jersey and New York City.

An editor for the *Perth Amboy Evening News* called the governor's visit with Hauptmann shocking, stealthy, and inappropriate. The next day, in a prepared statement, Hoffman denied that he was interfering with the orderly processes of law, challenging "Jersey justice," or trying to save a convicted murderer.[7]

When Wilentz found out about Hoffman's meeting with Hauptmann, he called Warden Kimberling to see if it were true. Kimberling said that it was and if the attorney general had any complaints, he should take them up with the governor himself. Wilentz said that he would do that, and on the night of December 7, he was at the Hildebrecht Hotel sitting in the governor's living room.

Wilentz knew that Hauptmann would not confess as long as he thought that Hoffman believed he was innocent. He would never confess if he thought the governor would save his life. Moreover, Hoffman's interference on behalf of a convicted man would harm him politically. Hoffman replied, "Look, all I'm after is the truth. The people of this state are entitled to it, and Hauptmann has a right to live if he didn't murder the Lindbergh baby."[8]

On December 9, the United States Supreme Court, in a terse, twelve-word statement, announced that it had decided not to review the constitutionality of Hauptmann's trial, thus moving the prisoner one step closer to the death chamber.

With his appellate remedies apparently exhausted, it became clear to Hauptmann that his life was in the hands of Governor Hoffman and the New Jersey Court of Pardons. So, three days after the Supreme Court's announcement, and without the knowledge of his lawyers, Hauptmann wrote the governor a letter asking him to arrange a lie-detection test.[9]

On December 13, the day Governor Hoffman read Hauptmann's letter, Judge Trenchard set the execution for Friday, January 17, 1936.

On December 22, 1935, a Sunday, the Lindberghs, Charles, Anne, and their three-year-old son, Jon, boarded the freighter *American Importer* for Liverpool, England. Having been frightened by a small army of lunatics who were constantly threatening to kidnap and murder their son, and imprisoned by newsmen who besieged them twenty-four hours a day, the Lindberghs were escaping to England, where they hoped to live a normal life in peace and security. To a friend, Lindbergh had said, "We Americans are a primitive people. We do not have discipline. Our moral standards are low. . . . It shows in the newspapers, the morbid curiosity over crimes and murder trials. Americans seem to have little respect for law, or the rights of others."[10]

In describing how his life had been in America, Lindbergh said: "It was impossible for me or my family to lead a normal life because of the tremendous public hysteria—we couldn't go to a theater, a store, or even for a stroll without being surrounded, stared at and harassed. We came to the conclusion that it would be best to take a trip abroad for a time until the events had been forgotten and we could return to ordinary life." [11] (The Lindberghs lived in England for two years then, in 1938, moved to France. In 1939 they returned to America to escape the war in Europe.)

Two months earlier, when Jon's teacher was driving him to school, a black sedan forced them off the road. Several men leaped out of the car and jumped on to the teacher's runningboard. The teacher, believing that she and the boy were being kidnapped, was terrified. As it turned out, the men were reporters and newsreel cameramen. The next day, close-up photographs of the terrified teacher and her little student appeared in the papers. From that day on, Jon was kept at home under armed guard.

Since only a handful of people knew of the Lindberghs' plans to flee the country, their sudden departure shocked the nation. The next day, the following headline was on the front page of the *New York Times:* "LINDBERGH FAMILY SAILS FOR ENGLAND TO SEEK A SAFE, SECLUDED RESIDENCE; THREATS ON SON'S LIFE FORCE DECISION."

On December 23, the day after the Lindberghs sailed for England, Lloyd Fisher filed Hauptmann's appeal before the New Jersey Court of Pardons.

Liscom C. Case, the juror with the bad heart, died on December 29, not quite a year from the day he was selected to the Hauptmann jury. The sixty-year-old retired carpenter was buried near his home in Hamden, New Jersey. His physician said that the strain of the trial had been bad for his heart and might have hastened his death.

On New Year's Day, 1936, the *New York Daily Mirror* published the last installment of Hauptmann's life story. In the final chapter, Hauptmann said that although most of what had been written and said about him was untrue, he did not hate anyone, not even David Wilentz, "the man who had used the lowest type of language against me."

On January 7, with the execution just ten days away, Warden Kimberling, following the procedures outlined by New Jersey law, issued execution invitations to eighteen witnesses. Kimberling also acquired the services of Robert G. Elliott, the country's most active and famous executioner. The sixty-four-year-old Long Island resident, owner of a New York City electrical firm, had been electrocuting people for forty-six years. In 1927 he had executed Sacco and Vanzetti, and a year later Ruth Snyder and Judd Gray. The fee for Elliott's service was $150. His assistant would get $50.

Meanwhile, Fisher and his colleagues were frantically preparing for their court of pardons presentation. The hearing would be held in four days. They had lined up several witnesses who would appear on Hauptmann's behalf. Warden Kimberling would be saying that in all of his talks with Hauptmann the prisoner had never said anything but that he was innocent. The Reverend John Matthiesen, the pastor of the Trinity Lutheran Church, had visited Hauptmann in the death house fifteen times and was going to plead for his life. Fisher was also planning to read a heartbreaking letter Hauptmann had received from his mother.

The defense had received a letter from a "penman" who said that he would appear before the court of pardons and testify that Hauptmann had not written any of the ransom notes. Fisher questioned this person, a man named Samuel Small, and decided not to use him.

At eleven o'clock Saturday morning, January 11, the New Jersey Court of Pardons met in Trenton to hear Fisher's argument for clemency. Wilentz, accompanied by Colonel Schwarzkopf, was present to speak on behalf of the State and to defend the decision of the jury. There were no reporters in the room, and the members of the panel, made up of Governor Hoffman, Chancellor Luther A. Campbell of the Court of Errors and Appeals, four other appellate judges, and two laymen, a publisher and a retired butcher, would not be hearing from Hauptmann or his wife. Fisher had invited the panel to the death house, and when that idea was rejected, had asked if he could bring Hauptmann into the courtroom. That request had been denied as well.

Wilentz led off the proceeding with a short review of the trial, then turned the floor over to Colonel Schwarzkopf, who summarized the investigation and the evidence that had led to Hauptmann's arrest. When it came Fisher's turn, he presented his witnesses, then begged the court to spare Hauptmann's life. The hearing was over, and Fisher looked confident and pleased as the eight panelists filed out of the room to make their decision.

Following a short deliberation, the panel returned to the courtroom and announced that the vote had gone seven-to-one against the prisoner. Hauptmann would be executed. Governor Hoffman had been the lone dissenter.

Fisher was crushed. Fighting to maintain his composure, he went straight to the death house to break the news to his client.

If the prisoner goes to the electric chair he cannot blame
his counsel, because they have done all that capable, earnest,
industrious counsel can do.

— J U D G E   J.   W A R R E N   D A V I S
of the Federal Court of Appeals in Trenton

42 BUYING TIME

ON MONDAY MORNING, Anna found her husband listless and despondent, emotionally drained and losing hope. That day the *New York Daily Mirror* ran an installment of her life story in which she said, "I cannot sit here and watch this terrible thing happen to Richard but I do not know what to do."

While Mrs. Hauptmann was trying to revive Richard, the newest addition to the defense team, a pair of constitutional lawyers named Nugent Dodds and Neil Burkinshaw, petitioned a federal appeals court in Trenton for a writ of habeas corpus. Since the U.S. Supreme Court had already decided not to review the Hauptmann trial, there was little chance that a lower appellate court would consider the constitutionality of the case. The action was a desperate, last-ditch effort to stay the execution—to buy a little time.

On Tuesday, Anna moved into the Stacy-Trent Hotel in Trenton to be nearer her husband. That afternoon, Judge J. Warren Davis of the circuit court of appeals in Trenton surprised no one when he refused to issue the writ of habeas corpus. He announced his decision in open court before the two lawyers who had drafted and filed Hauptmann's petition.

The next day, while Richard talked to Anna through the bars of his cell, a technician on the other side of the wall tested the electric chair. Richard was telling Anna that he had just refused an offer to sell the "inside story of the crime" to the *New York Evening Journal* for seventy-five thousand dollars. The paper wanted to publish the story the day after his execution. He was now wondering if he had done the right thing; it was a lot of money. Anna was shocked that he was having second thoughts about the offer—of course he had made the right decision. She and Bubi didn't want to spend the rest of their lives as the wife and son of a confessed baby killer!

While Anna was in Trenton trying to console her husband, Governor Hoffman and Wilentz were in New York City attending a law enforcement convention. That night, Hoffman called Wilentz to his hotel room to tell him that he was meeting with Mrs. Hauptmann in the morning. The governor wanted to offer the prisoner this deal—if he confessed, the governor and the attorney general would ask the court of pardons to commute his sentence to life. Would Wilentz go along with this—even if Hauptmann admitted killing the baby in cold blood? Yes, Wilentz said, he'd join the governor in asking for a life sentence—even if Hauptmann confessed to that. Governor Hoffman said he'd ask Mrs. Hauptmann to convey the deal to Richard, and if necessary, talk him into it. The governor felt that Mrs. Hauptmann would jump at the chance to save her husband, and that she would make him open up.

Thursday morning, Hoffman used a back door and a service elevator to get to Mrs. Hauptmann's room without being seen by the reporters camped out in the lobby.

Since he wanted to speak confidentially, the governor asked Miss Jean Adams, a reporter for the *New York Evening Journal* and Anna's constant companion over the past several weeks, to leave the room. Once they were alone, Hoffman took a seat in one of the overstuffed chairs. Mrs. Hauptmann sat straight and tense on the edge of the sofa. The governor was struck by how drab, disheveled and tired she looked. Her face had lost its color and her eyes were swollen and red.[1]

"Mrs. Hauptmann," the governor said, "your husband is going to die tomorrow and there is nothing I can do. But there is a way to save his life."

"What way is that?" Mrs. Hauptmann asked dabbing her sore eyes with the handkerchief.

"He has to tell the truth."

"But he didn't do it!" Mrs. Hauptmann screamed. "He didn't! He didn't! I tell you—he couldn't do it!"

"I know that's what you believe, Mrs. Hauptmann, but you'll have to face reality. Richard's life is at stake. If we don't do something bold and dramatic Richard will be electrocuted—tomorrow night. Let him know that you *want* him to confess because if he *doesn't,* he'll be killed and you and Bubi will be left alone in this world."

"My husband has only a few hours to live! Could I do that to him—make him think that I, like the judge, like that jury—believe too that he would kill a baby? Would I make Richard think I too have believed those lying witnesses who for money would send a good man to die? No! No! Never would I do that even to save Richard's life!" Mrs. Hauptmann got to her feet and walked over to the window and looked out. She wiped her eyes with the handkerchief and turned to Hoffman and said, "How could he do a thing like that without me—his wife—knowing he was doing it? How could he cut from the attic floor a board and take it out to make a ladder? No! Without me he couldn't commit this! If Richard is guilty I must be guilty—I too should go to the electric chair." Collapsing onto the sofa, Anna sobbed, "He is not guilty, my Richard—I swear it!"

"Please understand that I'm trying to save your husband's life. He's been tried and convicted, his appeals have failed, and the court of pardons has said, 'Go ahead and execute!' Now we must save his life. How could he be totally innocent of this thing—he must know something. What is it? All he has to do is tell! He will do this if you ask him to—I know he will."

"Do you want him to make up lies—to say he did it—just to save his life? No! Bubi and I would always be sorry he said such a thing—even to save his life! For the rest of Mannfried's life people would point to him with their fingers and say that his father was a kidnapper and a murderer. So too they will say of me, 'She is the wife of Hauptmann, who killed a baby.'"

The governor had made a major miscalculation. He wasn't talking to a politician, lawyer, or police officer, he was speaking to a simple, hardworking woman. Richard had told her that he was innocent, so he was. This was a woman who could never understand or forgive a husband who had committed such a crime. This was a woman who would be maddened by the idea that her clothes, her furniture, and Bubi's things had been purchased with money stained in baby Lindbergh's blood. The governor, with all of his good and bad intentions and complicated political motives, had asked this wide-eyed, wild-haired woman to give up the only things she had left—her memories, her pride, her beliefs, and her sanity.

"All right. Will you do this, Mrs. Hauptmann—go down and see Richard, ask him if he will talk to the attorney general and me?"

"That I will do," Mrs. Hauptmann replied. "Richard has always said that gladly he will answer questions that anybody wants to ask him. But, I will not say to him—his wife—that at last he should tell the truth when always I know that he has told the truth."

About an hour later, Mrs. Hauptmann phoned to say that Richard would be glad to see anyone, but his story would be the same. The governor hung up and immediately called Wilentz, "Hauptmann will talk to us, but he insists that he has nothing to add to his story."

With his Save Hauptmann plan up in smoke, the governor returned to the State House, where he was met by more bad news. Hauptmann's petition to the U.S. Supreme Court to overrule the lower court's refusal to issue a writ of habeas corpus had been denied. If the court had held otherwise, it would, in essence, have overruled its decision a week earlier not to review the constitutionality of the case.

With Hauptmann's legal remedies exhausted, there was nothing between him and the electric chair. He had less than thirty hours to live.

That afternoon, Governor Hoffman made the most important decision of his political life. At four o'clock, he called a press conference and announced that he was granting Hauptmann a thirty-day reprieve. Hoffman had asked Wilentz and Anthony Hauck to come to the Executive Suite and stand with him when he made his announcement. The prosecutors' grim faces made it clear that although they were standing next to the governor, they weren't standing with him.

Hoffman declared that he had doubts that "complete justice" had been done in the Hauptmann case. "A shocking crime was committed," he said, "and, in the interest of society, it must be completely solved. A human life is at stake. As governor of New Jersey I have a duty to perform. It is my heart, my conscience, my job—and this is my decision."

Hoffman said that he needed more time to complete his independent investigation of the crime. He declared that under New Jersey's constitution, the governor was allowed only one reprieve, but if his investigators turned up information that convinced the attorney general that another stay was called for, he would grant it.

In New Jersey, once the execution date that had been set by the judge had passed, the prisoner had to be resentenced. That meant that the earliest date Hauptmann could be electrocuted would be the week of March 16, 1936. If Judge Trenchard didn't get around to resentencing Hauptmann until sometime after the thirty-day reprieve had passed, the prisoner's execution wouldn't be scheduled until later. In response to a reporter's question regarding how he felt about the governor's action, the unsmiling Wilentz said that he'd ask the judge to resentence Hauptmann as soon as possible.

When Mrs. Hauptmann got the news, she cried, "God be thanked!" and fell across the bed and wept. An hour later she was in the hotel lobby with Bubi posing for pictures.

Lloyd Fisher rushed to the prison to tell Hauptmann that he had been reprieved. The prisoner, looking weary and detached, took the news with surprising calm.

The response to Hoffman's action was immediate, broad-based, and intense. People were stunned, confused, and infuriated. The governor of the state, a public servant, a politician, was second-guessing the police, the prosecution, the judge, the jury, three appeals courts, and his own court of pardons. The *Trenton Times* carried a front-page editorial under the heading "Impeach Hoffman." The writer of the editorial declared that the governor had "dishonored himself, disgraced the state, and converted New Jersey into international laughing stock." The incensed editor then called for Hoffman's removal from office.

If Hoffman had wanted headlines, he had certainly gotten them. He had also incurred the wrath of millions, something he apparently hadn't counted on. He was genuinely shocked and angered by the savage criticism being leveled against him.

On Thursday, the seventeenth, Hoffman issued a statement that offended many journalists, insulted the state police, and enraged Wilentz. The governor seemed to be declaring war on his own state:

> I have never expressed an opinion upon the guilt or innocence of Hauptmann. I do, however, share with hundreds of thousands of our people the doubt as to the value of the evidence that placed him in the Lindbergh nursery on the night of the crime; I do wonder what part passion and prejudice played in the conviction of a man who was previously tried and convicted in the columns of many of our newspapers. I do, on the basis of evidence that is in my hands, question the truthfulness and mental competency of some of the chief witnesses for the state; I do doubt that this crime could have been committed by any one man, and I am worried about the eagerness of some of our law enforcement agencies to bring about the death of this one man so that the books can be closed in the thought that another great crime mystery had been successfully solved.[2]

Following his visit with Hauptmann in the death house, Hoffman had been conducting his own Lindbergh case investigation. His principal investigator had been Ellis Parker. In early December, after Hoffman's views on the case had become public, a motley group of Lindbergh case outsiders and dissenters, like Ellis Parker, had emerged from the woodwork. One such person was Dr. Erastus Hudson, the physician-fingerprint man who had processed the kidnap ladder and the baby's toys with his silver nitrate solution. Dr. Hudson believed that Hauptmann was innocent because his fingerprints weren't found on the ladder, the ransom notes, or in the nursery. The doctor didn't think that Hauptmann had been in the Lindbergh house.

The governor shared Hudson's thesis and was somewhat receptive to Parker's notion that the baby found at the Mount Rose gravesite was not baby Lindbergh. For that reason, he was interested in the fingerprints Dr. Hudson had developed off the child's toys. In the event the Lindbergh child turned up someday, the boy could be identified by these latents.

On January 3, a week before the court of pardons had met to consider Hauptmann's plea for clemency, Hoffman had written a letter to Schwarzkopf requesting numerous documents, exhibits, and articles of evidence connected with the case. Among the items the governor wanted were: "A set of the fingerprints of Charles Augustus Lindbergh, Jr., made by Dr. Erastus M. Hudson, or any other fingerprints taken from the child's toys."[3]

On Friday, two days after he had announced the reprieve, Hoffman met with his investigators at the State House. Dr. Hudson reported that sometime between the kidnapping and the time Trooper Kelly processed the nursery for fingerprints, someone in the Lindbergh household had carefully wiped the room clean of latents. It was ludicrous, he said, to imagine that the kidnapper had gone down the ramshackle ladder with a pail of water and a rag in one hand and the baby in the other.[4] According to Dr. Hudson, Trooper Kelly and Captain Lamb, after Hauptmann's arrest, had asked him if latent fingerprints could be counterfeited. The doctor told the officers that they couldn't, that any expert could tell the difference between real and fake fingerprints. Once informed of this, Kelly and Lamb suddenly lost interest in the subject, Doctor Hudson said.

Robert W. Hicks, the Washington lawyer and part-time criminalist who had submitted a ballistics report to Colonel Schwarzkopf a few weeks after Hauptmann's arrest, was among the group in the governor's office that day. In his October 1934 report to Schwarzkopf, Hicks had theorized that the Lindbergh baby had been shot through the head by a small-caliber bullet fired by the Liliput handgun found in Hauptmann's garage. Since no bullets were ever found, and Dr. Mitchell's autopsy said that the child had died from a fractured skull, Hicks and his report were ignored. It was therefore ironic that Hicks was now working to free the man he had once said had shot the Lindbergh baby through the head.

Robert Hicks was being paid by another Lindbergh case enthusiast, Mrs. Evalyn McLean, the Washington socialite who had been swindled by Gaston Means, the private investigator who had taken one hundred thousand dollars of her money to pay a gang of phantom kidnappers. Means was in a federal prison, and Mrs. McLean, with more money and good intentions than things to occupy her time, was back into the case. Hicks was also receiving money from Paul G. Clancey, the editor of a magazine called *American Astrology*.

No one knew why Mrs. McLean was now using her money to free the man convicted of killing the baby she had once tried to ransom. Paul Clancey's motives and interest in the case were also unknown. Maybe Hauptmann's astrological data indicated that he was innocent, or Hicks was going to write an article about the case for the magazine.

Hicks had written a report for Governor Hoffman, a document that he said raised serious questions about the identity of the body at the Mount Rose Heights gravesite. Hicks informed Hoffman that he could prove that Hauptmann hadn't kidnapped the baby and had no part in the extortion. He said he had found Hauptmann's "double," a man named Robert Scanian. He claimed that Scanian had been seen near the Lindbergh property on the day of the crime. Hicks had also studied the ransom notes and reported that he was convinced that they had been written by Isidor Fisch.[5] Hicks said he would be living in Trenton until he was finished with his investigation.

Another member of the governor's team was Samuel Small, the "penman" who had offered to appear before the court of pardons to say that Hauptmann had not written the ransom notes. A graduate of the Palmer-Zaner College of Penmanship, Small had spent many years studying types and styles of handwriting. "Look," he said, pointing to several enlarged photographs of the ransom notes and Hauptmann's known writings, "the shadings are different—so are the downstrokes and the upstrokes. Every letter has different characteristics—they are started in different places. It isn't a question *if* Hauptmann had penned these letters, it is a question of whether he *could* have written them. I tell you Governor, that if you went to the prison and said to Hauptmann, 'I will let you free if you can write a single sentence the way it is written in the ransom letters,' Hauptmann would have to stay in prison the rest of his life. Any expert who has studied types and methods of handwriting will tell you that."

Besides Ellis Parker, Dr. Hudson, Robert Hicks, and Samuel Small, Governor Hoffman's Lindbergh squad consisted of three private detectives. William Pelletreau, a private eye from Jersey City, had brought several exhibits that he said illustrated that Hauptmann was not the writer of the ransom notes. George Foster, an investigator who had been employed by James Fawcett when Fawcett was Hauptmann's attorney, and Harold Keeves, a private eye who had done work for Mrs. Hauptmann when the defense fund had money, rounded out the governor's crew.

On Sunday, the nineteenth, Hauptmann learned that Lieutenant Keaten and his detectives were monitoring the progress of his investigators. Whenever possible, Keaten's men were double-checking their leads. The governor declared that he was shocked by this behavior and said that he had ordered it stopped.

Meanwhile, the governor was getting hundreds of angry letters protesting the reprieve. His home in South Amboy was placed under round-the-clock guard, and the leaders of the state's Republican party were meeting to consider dropping him as a delegate to the National Convention.

On January 21, Robert Hicks moved into Hauptmann's old apartment in the Bronx. The last person to occupy the place had been Lt. Lewis J. Bornmann of the New Jersey State Police. Hicks said that he would be conducting a "scientific examination" of the Hauptmann attic to determine if rail 16 had once been part of its flooring.

400 Governor Hoffman believed that if he could get Hauptmann to submit to a lie detector, the truth would finally come out. By asking the right questions, a polygraph examiner could find out if Hauptmann was telling the truth when he claimed complete innocence. Maybe he had just lied about not writing the ransom notes, or perhaps he had lied about not kidnapping and murdering the baby. If Hauptmann had conspired with others to commit the crime, the polygraph could be used to find out who these people were. Hoffman wondered what the machine would say when Hauptmann was asked about John Condon, Violet Sharpe, Isidor Fisch, Betty Gow, and Oliver Whateley.

Hauptmann had asked to be tested on the lie detector back in October when the governor had talked to him in his cell. In his December 12 letter to Hoffman, he had again asked to be tested. Since Anna was also eager to have Richard cleared on the polygraph, she was willing to travel to Chicago to meet with Leonarde Keeler, the country's most famous polygraph examiner. Keeler, on the staff of Northwestern University Law School's Scientific Crime Detection Laboratory, had offered his services to Colonel Schwarzkopf in 1932 when the police were trying to eliminate suspects. Schwarzkopf had been interested, but Colonel Lindbergh hadn't wanted to humiliate and insult the Lindbergh-Morrow servants by questioning their honesty. Because of this, Keeler and his polygraph weren't brought into the case.

Early in January, about a week before the Court of Pardons had heard Hauptmann's plea for clemency, Anna Hauptmann boarded a train for Chicago.

Although Keeler didn't invent the polygraph (it had been fashioned in 1921 by Keeler's mentor, Dr. John Larsen), he had refined and improved the instrument. Something of a showman and publicity-hound, Keeler was a legitimate pioneer in the field and scientific lie detection's most prominent practitioner. While Dr. John Larsen,the polygraph's inventor, was still conducting polygraph research, Keeler was thinking about commercializing the process—selling his lie-detection services to banks, retailers, and industrial corporations. He therefore jumped at the chance to bring himself and his lie detector into the Lindbergh case limelight. (In 1938, Keeler opened the country's first private polygraph firm, and by 1941, he was a millionaire.)

In order to convince Mrs. Hauptmann that the polygraph worked, Keeler conducted several demonstrations in which she was a subject. By using his "peak of tension" test, he said, he could determine her age. Keeler read off a list of ages, including hers, and when he mentioned the correct number, the instrument recorded a change in Anna's blood pressure, pulse rate, and breathing pattern that gave her away.

Back in Trenton, Mrs. Hauptmann told Richard and the governor that she was impressed with Keeler and his lie detection device. She said that Keeler would come to New Jersey to test Richard, without charge. Keeler had also promised not to make his involvement in the case public. The governor was pleased and said that he'd make the necessary arrangements to get Keeler into the death house.

In the meantime, Keeler leaked the story to the press, and the next day several newspapers were reporting that the famous detector of lies had tested Mrs. Hauptmann and was about to examine the condemned man himself. In one of these articles, the reporter had implied that once Mrs. Hauptmann realized that the polygraph worked, she decided against having the instrument used on her husband. By jumping the gun on the publicity, Keeler had killed his chance to perform what would have been one of the most celebrated polygraph tests in history.

On Janaury 23, with the first week of the reprieve already past, William Marston, a Boston attorney and lie-detection pioneer, arrived in Trenton to discuss using his lie-detection technique on Hauptmann. Marston's method, based solely on changes in the subject's blood pressure, was not nearly as sophisticated and reliable as Keeler's. Nevertheless, Governor Hoffman was impressed with Marston, who set his fee at a hundred dollars a day. The lawyer said that his examination would take at least two weeks.[6]

Marston had agreed not to divulge the results of his tests to the press, Wilentz or Schwarzkopf. Any clues derived from his examination could then be checked by the governor's investigators without interference from the state police.

When Governor Hoffman started to arrange Marston's visit to the death house, he ran into a problem. Under New Jersey law, the only people allowed to visit an inmate on death row were his relatives and lawyers. Exceptions to this rule had to be in the form of a special order from the trial judge. Hoffman promptly requested permission from Judge Trenchard, who just as promptly denied it.

The only way Marston could get in to see Hauptmann was to be appointed associate counsel for the defense. The governor considered asking Lloyd Fisher to make the appointment, but changed his mind when he realized that as one of Hauptmann's attorneys, Marston would lose his objectivity and credibility as a lie-detection expert. His findings would be rendered invalid and therefore useless.

Marston returned to Boston, and the idea of unlocking Hauptmann's mind through scientific lie detection was dropped for good.[7]

When John Condon was asked to take a polygraph test by one of Hoffman's investigators, he replied, "I'll take a test if Hauptmann will bring back the Lindbergh baby."[8]

Politically, the governor of New Jersey was in a fix. If he couldn't justify his reprieve by proving that Hauptmann was just an extortionist, or by identifying more kidnappers, or by showing that the condemned man had been railroaded by the police and the prosecution, he would look like a headline-grabbing fool. So far, his motley crew of unemployed private eyes and self-designated experts hadn't come up with anything concrete. They were spending most of their time sitting around swapping theories. With his back to the wall, his bridges burning, and the clock running, Hoffman needed to uncover something earthshaking—something really big. If he didn't, his political career would be sitting on Hauptmann's lap when they threw the switch.

The Lindbergh matter is quite generally referred to as the most bungled case in police history.

—GOVERNOR HAROLD G. HOFFMAN

43 THE HOFFMAN WARS

LIEUTENANT KEATEN WAS SEATED IN THE CHAIR facing Colonel Schwarzkopf. The colonel picked up a sheet of paper from his desk and said, "This is from the governor."

"What is it now?" Keaten asked. It was the last day of January 1936; in a month the lieutenant would be starting his fifth year as the main Lindbergh case investigator. The jury's verdict should have closed the files on the investigation, but Governor Hoffman's eleventh-hour intrusion into the case had changed all of that. During the past six weeks, Keaten and four of his detectives—Horn, Bornmann, Wallace, and De Gaetano—had been monitoring the activities and progress of Ellis Parker, Robert Hicks, and the other Hoffman investigators.

Colonel Schwarzkopf let the governor's letter drop onto his desk. "We've been told to reopen the case—officially. He wants us to identify Hauptmann's accomplices—it's the same old story—maybe Bruno is not the one who actually took the baby."

Governor Hoffman's letter contained a dozen or so questions, accusations really, that Schwarzkopf was supposed to answer. Hoffman wrote that he was concerned about Dr. John Condon. Was it true the police had threatened to indict Condon as an accessory if he didn't make a courtroom identification of Hauptmann? Did Detective Bornmann plant a board in Hauptmann's attic that later became rail 16? Hoffman also wanted to know about Violet Sharpe, and he was calling for a full review of the handwriting evidence.[1]

Schwarzkopf put the letter aside and called Attorney General Wilentz, who said that he had gotten one, too. "How do you respond to something like this?" Schwarzkopf asked.

"You don't," Wilentz replied. "Hauptmann has been tried and convicted and he's exhausted his appeals. As far as I'm concerned, the governor's investigation is irrelevant."

"But he wants a weekly report—on our progress."

"All right. So you look around and what do you find?"

"Nothing."

"So that's what you report."

On February 6, Evalyn McLean met with Sam Leibowitz, a famous New York City defense attorney. Mrs. McLean figured that if Hauptmann could be helped, Sam Leibowitz was the man. Leibowitz had kept dozens of gangsters out of prison and had successfully defended Al Capone against a charge of triple murder.

Excited by the smell of money and the prospect of national publicity, the forty-three-year-old lawyer had rushed to Mrs. McLean's Washington, D.C., mansion, where he had agreed to talk to Hauptmann. Mrs. McLean and Leibowitz agreed that he would be paid a retainer of ten thousand dollars, and if he could get Hauptmann to identify his accomplices or to say anything that would save his life, the lawyer would get a bonus of fifteen thousand dollars. Mrs. McLean said that she'd have Robert Hicks talk to Mrs. Hauptmann about bringing Leibowitz into the case. Before Leibowitz could get into the death house to see Hauptmann, he'd have to be named as a defense counsel. Mrs. McLean said that no one was to be told about her plan, not even Governor Hoffman or any of Hauptmann's attorneys.

Mrs. McLean didn't seem put off by the fact that Leibowitz was sure that Hauptmann was guilty. In the column he wrote for the *New York Evening Journal,* he had expressed his feelings about the case quite clearly. He had also referred to Hauptmann's guilt when discussing the case several times over the radio. Leibowitz did not believe, however, that Hauptmann had committed the crime by himself.

The day following Leibowitz's meeting with Mrs. McLean, Hicks met secretly with Mrs. Hauptmann at the Stacy-Trent Hotel in Trenton. Anna said that she would discuss the matter of Sam Leibowitz with Richard later that day.

Governor Hoffman received Colonel Schwarzkopf's first weekly progress report on February 8 and was disappointed by its lack of substance. He complained to an aide that Schwarzkopf and his men were just going through the motions. Frustrated by what he called foot-dragging by his own state police, Hoffman called New York City Police Commissioner Lewis J. Valentine and asked him to reopen New York's case and to reassign Lieutenant Finn and his men to the investigation. The commissioner applauded the governor's eagerness to get at the truth and promised to give the matter some thought, but he had no intention of reopening the Lindbergh investigation.

Hoffman next got in touch with J. Edgar Hoover of the FBI. Although Hoover was convinced of Hauptmann's guilt, he still considered Schwarzkopf a rival and therefore took delight in the colonel's problems with the governor.[2] Because Hoover was still smarting over what he considered Schwarzkopf's uncooperative attitude toward the FBI and was jealous of Schwarzkopf's success in the Lindbergh investigation, he was willing to discredit Schwarzkopf by indicating that he hadn't been impressed by many of the eyewitnesses in the case. Hoover then added fuel to the governor's suspicions by saying that he was suspicious of the authenticity of the rail 16 evidence.[3] But that was as far as Hoover would go. He said that he wasn't interested in reopening the Bureau's Lindbergh investigation.

404   While the governor was conversing with Hoover, Anna Hauptmann was at the death house visiting her husband to persuade him to see Samuel Leibowitz. The next day, February 11, in a letter to Warden Kimberling, Hauptmann wrote:

> I do not care to see Lloyd Fisher or any of my other attorneys until I notify you personally in writing at a near future date. I wish to thank you in advance for your co-operation in this matter. For your information I am very desirous of seeing Mr. Samuel Leibowitz. It is my definite understanding that arrangements have been made by my wife for such an interview.[4]

Two days later, with Anna looking on hopefully, Hauptmann and the celebrated trial lawyer shook hands through the bars to cell 9. "I only want to get the truth," Leibowitz said. "You ought to know that whatever you tell me will be reported to Mrs. McLean and to Governor Hoffman, and to anybody else that I think ought to know."

"Sure, sure," Hauptmann replied. "My wife told me. There is nothing that I say that I do not want the world to know. I am an innocent man and I shouldn't be in this place."

"We'll talk about that later," Leibowitz said. He then asked Hauptmann how the prison authorities were treating him and Hauptmann responded with a lengthy, detailed description of his prison routine. When he had finished, Leibowitz said, "You must think about the kidnapping a great deal."

"I never think on that at all," Hauptmann snapped. "I didn't do it, so why should I be interested?"

"But you've been cooped up here in this cell a whole year, with no one but your thoughts to keep you company. Surely you must have turned it over in your mind a thousand times. You must have said to yourself, 'Here's how the crime must have been committed. It wasn't done the way Wilentz says.'"

Hauptmann didn't respond. He looked at his wife and shrugged his shoulders indifferently.

"Well, I'll come to see you again in a few days," Leibowitz said. "Think it over. Let me know then, how you think the child was taken from the house."

The next evening, Leibowitz, referred to as the Great Defender by his admirers, telephoned Hoffman at the governor's home in South Amboy. By that time, Leibowitz's involvement in the Hauptmann case was no longer a secret. He was being portrayed as the only man who had any chance of saving the condemned prisoner.

The next day, February 14, Leibowitz unveiled his plan: "Governor, I know that I can crack this fellow. But I need your help."

"What makes you think you can do it—nobody else has. I tried, and couldn't."

"He's guilty as hell, but Lloyd Fisher keeps telling him that he's innocent. Fisher also tells him that the governor won't let an innocent man go to the chair. He thinks you'll save him."

"But what if he is innocent?"

"He's guilty. I know it and so do you. Maybe there were accomplices, but we'll never know these things until he confesses."

"But nobody has broken him."

"That's because of Lloyd Fisher. I want you to ask Fisher to come with me to the prison. I want Fisher to look Hauptmann straight in the eye and tell him that he's guilty as hell and that everybody knows it. I want Fisher to tell Hauptmann that the governor knows that he's guilty, too, and that he won't save him."

"I don't think Lloyd will like that idea."

"I don't care if he likes it or not. What do you think?"

"Well—"

"There isn't a man alive who won't confess if he's certain that a confession will keep him out of the electric chair. If Fisher does what I want him to do, I'll have Hauptmann crying for help. It's the only way to save his life and get the full story."[5]

Two days later, Governor Hoffman was in the State House listening to a livid Lloyd Fisher. "Your man Hicks and Mrs. McLean worked on poor Mrs. Hauptmann until she was convinced that Leibowitz could save Richard. She then talked Richard into pushing me out of the case! Leibowitz didn't even have the decency to tell me he was taking over."

"Sam says that Richard hasn't confessed because you keep telling him that he's innocent. If he doesn't open up he'll be electrocuted. You must tell him that I won't be granting any more stays. There is nothing more I can do for him—he'll have to save himself."

"He knows that," Fisher replied.

"Sam is going to the prison again, and he wants you to come along. He wants you to pull the rug on Richard—tell him that *you* think he's guilty. Will you do that?"

"No! Richard *is* innocent, and I'm not going to lie to him. Besides, I'm no longer his lawyer, I'm out of the case."

"Lloyd, be reasonable, *please.* There is no other way to save this man! Once his life is spared, you can tell him how you really feel."

"I don't like it, but I guess there's no other choice."[6]

At two o'clock, Monday, February 17, the day Hauptmann's reprieve expired and the day on which Judge Trenchard was to set the new execution date, Sam Leibowitz went to the death house to question Hauptmann privately. Leibowitz figured that if he didn't get a confession that afternoon he'd get one the next day when he returned with Lloyd Fisher. If nothing else, he'd soften up Hauptmann for the final blitz.

Leibowitz broke the ice by asking the prisoner about his family. Hauptmann, with tears in his eyes, talked freely and at great length about little Mannfried.[7] He told the lawyer that he hated the thought of his son growing up with the stigma of his father's conviction upon him. When Hauptmann fell silent, Leibowitz asked, "Do you remember that you promised to tell me how you think the crime was committed?"

"I'll show you," Hauptmann replied. He had constructed a cardboard replica of the east side of the Lindbergh house. "The kidnapper used the ladder to enter the nursery here," he said, pointing to the southeast window of the baby's room. "He took the child from the crib and carried him out of the house by going down the stairs and out the front door."

"But Colonel Lindbergh was sitting in his study that opened just off the front hall. He would have heard the kidnapper coming down the stairs. He would have heard the howling wind when the front door was opened."

"I tell only the truth," Hauptmann snapped. He set the cardboard box on the table, then leaned back on his cot with a sullen expression on his face.

"Let's take your story of Isidor Fisch," Leibowitz said. "Suppose you were on the jury, would you have believed the story you told? You tell me that Fisch was a pretty smart fellow. He had a safety deposit box. Why wouldn't he put the money into that box, instead of taking all these chances by leaving it with you? And isn't that exactly how the jury felt?"

"The story about Fisch didn't sound so good," Hauptmann allowed, "but it is the truth."

Leibowitz, trying hard to keep his tone friendly and conversational, continued to point out what he considered absurdities in Hauptmann's story. This went on for three hours with the prisoner shrugging his shoulders and saying things like "that was bad" and "that evidence hurt." Realizing that he was doing most of the talking, Leibowitz decided to call it quits.

Outside the prison gates, Leibowitz was surrounded by reporters. "My client and I are making progress," he announced.

"Has Bruno confessed?" a reporter asked.

"No."

"Do you believe that he's innocent?"

"No. I've said all along that he is guilty."

"Did you just say that you believe your client is guilty?" the reporter asked.

"Yes. It's my job to get him to confess. It's the only way to save his life."

That night, when Mrs. Hauptmann read in the papers that Leibowitz was telling the world that her husband had kidnapped and murdered the Lindbergh baby, she almost went into shock. Frightened, confused and angry, she telephoned Robert Hicks and screamed, "Get rid of that man! He's killing Richard!"

Hicks agreed that there had been a terrible miscalculation. Leibowitz was out of control—he was reading the wrong script. "Call Fisher," he said. "He'll know what to do."

Mrs. Hauptmann reached Fisher at his home in Flemington. He had seen the papers and he was upset and worried, too. The distraught woman, after apologizing for having thought that someone else could do more for Richard, asked Fisher to meet her and Hicks the next morning in Trenton.

Earlier that afternoon, while Leibowitz was at the prison cross-examining Hauptmann, Judge Trenchard set the new execution date for the week of March 30. Warden Kimberling then fixed the electrocution for the evening of March 31, a Tuesday. Hauptmann had forty days to live.

Early the next day, Fisher went to the Stacy-Trent Hotel in Trenton, where he found a worried Mrs. Hauptmann and a contrite Robert Hicks. "Let's go to the prison and get Richard to sign a letter dismissing Leibowitz," Mrs. Hauptmann said.

"No, Anna, that's not a good idea," Fisher replied. "It would look bad—people would think that Richard was about to confess and is now afraid to be questioned by Leibowitz. No, we'll let the 'Great Defender' play out his hand."[8]

That night, the governor, Leibowitz, and Fisher met at the Hotel Towers in Brooklyn. The governor's chief aide, Andrew Dutch, and Leibowitz's assistant, John Terry, were also present.[9] Fisher, not known for his even-tempered ways, started things off by tearing into Leibowitz, accusing him of muscling into the case at the last minute just for the publicity.

"You've got a lot of nerve," Leibowitz roared. "What in the hell have you done for Hauptmann—except stand there with your self-righteous finger up your ass watching him drift closer and closer to the electric chair. Is there something wonderful about being a small town, hick lawyer?"

"Gentlemen—*please*," Governor Hoffman shouted. "This isn't doing Richard any good." Turning to Fisher, the Governor said, "You agreed to hear Sam out—he thinks he can get Richard to confess. That will save his life. Please Lloyd, you told me you'd go along, for Richard's sake."

"We all want to get at the truth," Leibowitz said, "whether it's that Hauptmann is the lone criminal, is an innocent man, or whether others were involved in the crime." Addressing Fisher, he said, "This fellow would have confessed long ago but for you. You are his prop—his crutch. He is leaning on you to save his life. By telling him that he's innocent, you are bolstering his courage."

"He *is innocent*," Fisher blared, "and you know it!"

"He'll never confess while you are in his corner. You must tell this man that the jig is up—if he expects to beat the chair he must open up and talk. I want you to go with me to the prison tomorrow and tell Richard that you believe that he is guilty. If you say that, I'm sure he'll confess."

"I want you to promise me that if he doesn't, you will announce to the press that you believe him innocent, that you've changed your mind. Agreed?"

"Yes," Leibowitz said, "I agree to that. But when I'm done with him tomorrow he'll be crying for mercy."

"We'll see," Fisher said.

The next day, at two o'clock, Fisher and Leibowitz paid Hauptmann a surprise visit. Fisher told the prisoner that Judge Trenchard had reset the execution date for March 31. Hauptmann took the news calmly. "I see," he said.

Pointing in the direction of the death chamber, Leibowitz said, "In thirty-nine days you will be walking into that room. As a defense lawyer, I've only lost one man to the electric chair, and I still remember how his flesh smelled when it burned. Oh, it was a terrible thing to see. They will put a hood over you—so the people watching won't have to see your face get all twisted. The hood will be especially tight around the eyeballs because that much juice can pop them right out of their sockets. It's true. If the executioner does it right, your body temperature will jump up to 140 degrees and your skin will turn the color of beets—but if he does it wrong—shoots in too much juice—well, you will catch on fire. And if he hits the switch when you got some air in your lungs, you'll make a loud gurgling sound and scare a few witnesses." Hauptmann glanced up at Lloyd Fisher, then down at his shoes. "When they strapped that man into that seat the man wept—he begged for his life. 'I want to live! I want to live—please God, I want to live!' he screamed. But Richard—it was too late for that poor soul. Once he was in that room, no one could help him. Oh, he fought that chair, he fought against death. The first jolt, about 2000 volts, didn't kill him, but it almost did. He kicked and heaved against the straps. He even broke a bone in his leg—you could hear it. But that man didn't care about his leg—he was fighting for his life. He had already confessed, but he was strapped into the chair anyway. There was nothing he could do. 'I'll be a better man' he screamed, 'let me live in the prison. I will do anything! Please let me live.' Well, they killed him. It's different with you, Richard—you can save your life, feel little Manfried's arms around your neck, watch him grow to be a handsome young man. You have a chance! Isn't that true, Lloyd?"

Fisher cleared his throat, "Yes," he said.

Leibowitz pounded away, frequently picking up Hauptmann's copy of the trial transcript to point out discrepancies in his testimony. But Hauptmann didn't budge. Three hours later, Leibowitz was still going at it, he was perspiring heavily and his tie had been pulled away from his shirt collar. "You must not care about your son, little Bubi," he said in a rasping voice, "or your sweet wife."

"I do, I do," Hauptmann cried. "Annie knows that I'm innocent."

"Guilty!" Leibowitz shouted. "Lloyd Fisher told me that he thinks you are guilty as hell! He knows that if you don't come clean they'll be scraping the charred skin from your ass off the seat of that electric chair! The one right over there!"

"How could they kill an innocent man?" Hauptmann asked, matter-of-factly.[10]

Outside the prison, when confronted by the press, the bedraggled Leibowitz ignored the gentlemen's agreement that he had made with Fisher and announced that as far as he was concerned, Hauptmann was guilty. He said that he was withdrawing from the case.

Fisher wasn't surprised, and he wasn't really angry—at least not at the moment. All he could think about was Hauptmann and his loneliness, his love for his family and his courage. He knew that Hauptmann felt betrayed—that his own lawyer was a traitor. Fisher suddenly broke away from the crowd. Before the day was over, he'd go back to the prison and explain to Hauptmann that he wasn't a traitor.

Two days after Sam Leibowitz's sudden and inglorious departure from the Hauptmann case, a guard at the prison reported that the notes Hauptmann had been giving him, mainly requests and messages to the warden, contained handwriting that looked like the writing in the ransom notes. He reported his observations to Warden Kimberling, who said that he was not concerned with such matters.[11]

On February 22, Governor Hoffman had Millard Whited brought to the State House for questioning. Whited was the impoverished logger who had lived in a shack near the Lindbergh estate. Whited had been taken to the Bronx after Hauptmann's arrest to identify him as the prowler he had seen, on two occasions, near the estate a few days before the crime. Questioned by Lloyd Fisher in the presence of Governor Hoffman and

Prosecutor Anthony Hauck of Hunterdon County, Whited admitted that when questioned by the police two months after the crime, he had said that he had not seen any
suspicious person in the vicinity. Whited also said that he had received $150 for his
expenses and that the police had promised him a share of the reward money. But
he refused to back off his identification of Hauptmann and insisted that his testimony
at the trial was not perjured. After being yelled at for an hour or so by Lloyd Fisher, he
was released.

Colonel Schwarzkopf, in his fourth weekly progress report, submitted to the governor on February 28, one day shy of the fourth anniversary of the kidnapping, charged
that officials from Hoffman's office had tried to get some of his men to say that they had
helped frame Hauptmann by fabricating the rail 16 evidence. Lieutenant Bornmann and
Detectives Wallace and Horn were told that if they cooperated with the governor by telling him how they had fabricated the evidence, they would keep their positions on the
force after Schwarzkopf had been replaced by the new Hoffman appointee. If they didn't
come clean, they'd be demoted and transferred. Sergeant Kelly, the state fingerprint
man, was also approached and told that if he didn't tell how the latent fingerprints had
disappeared from the nursery, he would lose his job. (In 1936, the New Jersey State Police force was not under civil service.)

In his report, Colonel Schwarzkopf didn't have anything to offer in the way of new
developments or leads in the investigation.

Frustrated by the lack of progress in the investigation, and angered by Schwarzkopf's
sandbagging, the governor wrote a letter, dated March 1, telling the colonel not to
bother sending him any more of his so-called progress reports:

> I am not interested in receiving further weekly reports simply indicating that the usual
> conferences are being held. If you feel that the Lindbergh case has been completely
> solved and that no persons other than Hauptmann were involved, it is your duty to so
> advise me.
> The Lindbergh matter is quite generally referred to as the most bungled case in police
> history, and it is to your interest and to the interest of all members of your organization
> as well as in the public interest, to work sincerely and effectively to bring about its com-
> plete solution.[12]

The gloves were off—it was all-out war. The governor, fighting desperately to save his
future in politics, was preparing a major attack on the prosecution's stronghold—the
wood evidence.

In March, with the last day of the month designated as Hauptmann's last day of life,
Governor Hoffman's investigation centered on rail 16 and Hauptmann's attic. If the governor could prove that the wood evidence had been planted, that the police had taken a
plank of southern pine, cut it in two, put one section in the attic and the other on the
ladder as rail 16, he would, in one bold stroke, break Schwarzkopf's back and save
Hauptmann's life. He'd also be a hero and that much closer to the vice-presidency. If he
failed, he'd probably be unemployed when his term ran out in 1938.

To get the proof he needed, Hoffman was counting on Robert Hicks, who had rented Hauptmann's old apartment and was working with a so-called wood expert named Arch W. Loney, an employee of the Public Works Administration. During the trial, Edward Reilly had asked Loney to look at rail 16 on behalf of the defense, but Loney had declined, explaining that Reilly hadn't given him enough time to study the evidence. Hicks and Loney had been conducting experiments in the apartment to determine if rail 16 had really come from Hauptmann's attic.

On March 1, Paul G. Clancey, the editor of *American Astrology,* announced that he had discharged Hicks for "disobeying orders." [13] He said that Mrs. McLean was withdrawing her support as well. Neither Clancey nor Mrs. McLean would say why they had dropped Hicks. Shortly thereafter, Hicks moved out of the house, leaving Loney to work there alone.

A week following Hicks's departure, Loney reported to Governor Hoffman that he could prove that rail 16 and the board it had been cut from had been planted in Hauptmann's attic. The excited governor immediately called Wilentz to arrange a confrontation between Loney and Arthur Koehler, the Department of Agriculture wood expert and one of the prosecution's star witnesses. Wilentz said that it would take a little time to get Koehler from Madison, Wisconsin, to the Bronx.

On Thursday morning, March 26, six men were gathered in Hauptmann's attic—Governor Hoffman, Arch Loney, Wilentz, Koehler, Anthony Hauck, and Lt. Lewis J. Bornmann, who had discovered the shortened floor board. The governor had carried rail 16 into the attic himself.

Pointing to the shortened board, Loney said, "This plank has twenty-five nails in it, the other floorboards are held to the joists by seven nails" (implying that the board from which rail 16 had been cut had been planted). [14]

"I imagine," Koehler said, "that this was the first board to be nailed down. That's why it's secured better than the others."

"But there's something else," Loney said. "That board there is one-sixteenth of an inch thicker than the rest of the floor boards. It's an imposter."

"This is an unfinished attic, uneven flooring is to be expected," Koehler replied.

"All right. When I count the boards from the center of the attic, I get thirteen on that side and fourteen planks on this side. There seems to be an extra one that doesn't belong—this one," Loney said touching the disputed board.

"I noticed that myself," Koehler said. "The floor is only partially covered, so I don't see any relevance to the fact that the builder put more boards on one side than on the other. He probably used what lumber he had."

"Look at the end of the board," Loney said with a touch of frustration creeping into his voice. "It has been sawed straight, but rail 16 has been cut at an angle."

"Yes," Koehler said, "but after rail 16 had been cut from the floor, it was sawed again, at an angle. We all know there is a one and one-quarter inch chunk missing from between the two boards."

Anthony Hauck, whispering to Wilentz in a voice loud enough to be heard by everyone, said, "I can't believe they brought Koehler all the way from Wisconsin for this!"

"I'll show you why we've asked Mr. Koehler to come to the Bronx," the governor said. Hoffman picked up rail 16 and laid it in the gap, carefully lining up its four nail holes with the holes in the four cross-beams. Taking four nails from Loney, the governor tapped each one through rail 16 into the joists. "Look here," he said, "they don't go down! They are sticking up a quarter of an inch! You see, the board that had originally been in this place was thicker than what you got here. How do you explain *that?*"

Koehler and Bornmann were stunned. When they had tapped the nails into those exact holes, the nails had sunk flush to the surface of rail 16. Both of them had testified to this at the trial. Neither man spoke.

Anthony Hauck, the Hunterdon County prosecutor and Wilentz's chief assistant at the trial, wasn't at a loss for words. He had been in Hauptmann's attic just before the trial and had dropped those same nails into those same holes, and when he had done it, they had sunk all the way in. "Something is fishy here," he snorted. "Someone has tampered with these nail holes!"

"I got an idea," Wilentz said. "Let's get a carpenter up here and have him cut out the sections of cross-beams that contain the nail holes. Loney and Koehler can take the sections over to the physics lab at Columbia where they can be examined to see if they have been tampered with."

"No one has tampered with these nail holes," the governor said. "But let's have them examined. What we're going to discover is that some people have committed perjury!"

"Who are you calling a liar!" Bornmann screamed.

"Wait a minute," Wilentz shouted. "Let's have none of that! We can discuss this downstairs—privately."

While Hoffman, Wilentz, and Bornmann repaired to Hauptmann's old bedroom, Loney and Koehler arranged to have a carpenter cut out sections of the joist containing the questioned nail holes.

Wilentz closed the bedroom door and said, "Now, we can talk."

"Lewis," the governor said, putting his hand on the detective's shoulder, "tell me about that strange board."

"I don't know what you are talking about," Bornmann replied.

"Come on, don't play dumb—you know what I mean. That board up there was planted. I want to know about that."

"No one put any board in that attic," Bornmann said fighting to control his anger.

"Lewis, if you cooperate with me there's a lot I can do for you. Just tell me about that board and how it got there."

"With all due respect, sir," Bornmann said, "I told the truth and I wouldn't change it for no son-of-a-bitch!"

Wilentz grabbed Bornmann by the arm and said, "Hey—you're talking to the governor."

"That son-of-a-bitch is trying to make me commit perjury," Bornmann shouted.

"He's just upset," Wilentz said to the governor as he pushed Bornmann to a corner of

412 the room. "I want you to shut up," he hissed at the red-faced detective. "That man over there is the governor! What's wrong with you?" Wilentz turned to say something to Hoffman, but the governor was walking out the door.[15]

That afternoon, Dr. Lincoln T. Work, a physics professor at Columbia, examined the four sections of wood that Loney and Koehler had taken to his laboratory. The professor exposed the nail holes by dissecting the joist and found wooden plugs on the bottom of each hole. When these plugs, consisting of sawdust, were removed, the nails sank through rail 16 into the joists the way they had gone in when tested by Koehler, Bornmann, and Hauck. It was obvious that someone had tampered with the nail holes to make it appear that rail 16 did not belong in Hauptmann's attic.

That evening, Wilentz and Hauck confronted Hoffman with Professor Work's findings. The governor was devastated by the revelation. Deflated, defeated, and suddenly meek, Hoffman said that one of his investigators must have tampered with the nail holes. He promised to look into the matter and was forced to concede that rail 16 had come from Hauptmann's attic. He was very tired, he said, and a little depressed.

The next morning, Hoffman held a press conference in his office. He gave a rambling, vague, and confusing statement in which he described the five-hour confrontation in Hauptmann's attic. In a burst of transparent bravado, Hoffman insisted that although he couldn't prove it, he still had doubts about rail 16. He didn't mention the plugs in the nail holes.

Although Wilentz's comments were brief—he called the attic confrontation "Nonsensical and ridiculous"—Anthony Hauck had plenty to say:

> I feel he has made laughing stock of the courts which have passed upon the legal questions involved in this case. I think the legislature of this State of New Jersey should take cognizance of his actions in the cause of common decency.
>
> I am getting sick and tired of the Governor's action in this case. Yesterday's incident has brought it to the limit.
>
> So far he has shown us nothing whatever of importance to lead to the belief that Hauptmann is innocent or that others are involved.[16]

Although Governor Hoffman would continue to pay lip service to the Hauptmann defense, he was no longer interested in the case. He had lost his credibility with the press, had angered the public, and had made a fool of himself politically. The promise of fame and glory had turned to disgrace and humiliation. Hauptmann was scheduled to die on Tuesday, and the governor wasn't going to interfere.

Just when it seemed that all of the politicians, investigators, and pseudo-experts had bowed out of the case, Ellis Parker surfaced with one of the wildest developments in the case.

Mr. Willenz, whit my dying breath, I swear to God that you convicted an innocent man. Once you will stand before the same judge, to whom I go in a few hours. You know you has done wrong on me, you not only take my life, but you also all the happiness of my family. God will be judge between me and you.

— BRUNO RICHARD HAUPTMANN
in a letter to Governor Hoffman March 31, 1936

44 THE CONFESSION

ON FRIDAY, MARCH 27, all eight members of the New Jersey Court of Pardons received a strange document in the mail. The court of pardons would be reconvening on Monday to hear Hauptmann's last-minute plea for clemency. If the court decided not to commute Hauptmann's sentence to life, he would be executed the following evening at eight o'clock.

The document received by the members of the court was a twenty-five page, type-written statement signed by a man named Paul H. Wendel. According to Wendel's confession, he had kidnapped the Lindbergh baby. Although the sender of the document was not identified, Wendel had confessed to Burlington County Detective Ellis Parker.

Immediately after reading his copy of the confession, Governor Hoffman called Wilentz, who said that he had not received a copy.

The governor's next call was to Lloyd Fisher, who was also in the dark about the confession and eager to see a copy of it. Ellis Parker was a well-respected detective in Fisher's eyes, so if he were involved, there must be something to it.

In the meantime, Wilentz had asked Colonel Schwarzkopf to identify Paul Wendel and to find out where Ellis Parker was holding him.

As Wilentz read Wendel's statement, he was reminded of the other phony Lindbergh confessions he had seen over the past few years. There had been dozens of them. In this one, Wendel said that he had constructed the kidnap ladder. Wearing heavy socks over his shoes, Wendel said that he had used the ladder to climb into the Lindbergh house through the baby's window. The ladder, having been poorly made, had split when Wendel started up it. After applying paregoric to the baby's lips to keep him sleeping, Wendel put the child into a laundry bag which he hung around his neck by its string. Because the ladder had broken, Wendel, with the bag hanging around his neck, crept down the stairs and out the front door. Although Colonel Lindbergh was sitting in his den at the time, the carpeting on the stairway and Wendel's padded feet kept the Colonel from hearing the intruder make off with the child.

Wendel soon realized that he couldn't manage both the ladder and the baby so he

414 abandoned the ladder about seventy-five feet from the house and proceeded to Feather-bed Lane where his car was parked. According to the confession, Wendel drove the child to his residence, a tenement in the slums of Trenton, where he, his wife, and their two children would care for the child in a room in the attic.

The story continued: A few days after the kidnapping, the baby's cold had worsened and the child became seriously ill. Wendel wanted to take the baby to a doctor but didn't because it was too risky. It seemed that everyone in the country was on the lookout for the child. A week or so later, when Wendel went to the attic to check on the baby, he found it lying dead on the floor next to its bed. The child had fallen out of the makeshift crib and had fractured his skull. On this rainy day in May, Wendel put the child's body in a burlap bag and drove it back to Hunterdon County where he buried it in the woods on Mount Rose Heights, just two miles from its home.

Wilentz found the burial part of Wendel's statement ironic because Ellis Parker, the man who had gotten the so-called confession, had been the first one to assert that the remains along the Princeton-Hopewell Road were not the Lindbergh baby's. Finding that idea no longer useful, Parker had apparently disregarded it for the prosecution's theory.

In the statement, Wendel said that he was the real Cemetery John and the one who had written all of the ransom notes. He said he had committed the crime without ac-complices. A few months after the baby's body was found, Wendel, an ex-lawyer, made a deal with a former client of his named Isidor Fisch. For a fee, the little German narcotics smuggler would launder twenty thousand dollars of what Wendel said was counterfeit money. But Fisch was no fool. When he saw all of those gold notes he put two and two together and figured that it was part of the Lindbergh money. The moment Fisch real-ized what he had, he decided to keep the money. What was Wendel going to do—report him to the police?

Wendel said that the twenty thousand dollars Fisch had stolen from him was the money Fisch had left with Hauptmann when he returned to Germany in December 1933. Wendel said that he had spent the balance of the ransom money.

So far, the New Jersey State Police investigation into Wendel's background revealed that sixteen years earlier, when Paul Wendel was a successful thirty-four-year-old Tren-ton attorney, he was convicted of perjury, served nine months in jail, and was disbarred. His friend Ellis Parker had tried but failed to get the bar association to reinstate him. From that point on, Wendel's life and career went steadily downhill. He ended up spend-ing time in the state insane asylum, and in 1931 was indicted for passing worthless checks and embezzling money from an estate that had been entrusted to him. He had since dropped out of sight; even his family in Trenton said that they hadn't seen him for years. Because his whereabouts were unknown, his bad-check and theft warrants were still waiting to be served.

On Saturday morning, Schwarzkopf sent Parker a telegram commanding him to turn Wendel over to the New Jersey State Police in Trenton or to the Mercer County Sheriff's Office. Schwarzkopf assumed that Paul Wendel was in Mount Holly, New Jersey, locked up in the Burlington County Jail. Mount Holly, a quiet Quaker community of seven thousand, was the county seat and the site of the 140-year-old yellow brick courthouse that housed the jail and Ellis Parker's office.

That Saturday, Parker was on the second floor of the courthouse working in the office he had occupied for forty-four years. Paul Wendel, however, was not in the Burlington County Jail. Parker had him squirreled away in a place where nobody could find him.

Parker's office was small and cluttered with loose papers, case files, books, old court exhibits, trial transcripts, and crime scene photographs—the by-products and souvenirs of several hundred investigations. In a corner of the room, sitting very erect and wearing a gray fedora hat with a small feather, was a human skeleton, no doubt an unidentified murder victim no one had wanted. Parker himself was thin, of average height, and except for the patches of short, white hair above his ears, he was bald. His head, jutting lower jaw, and corncob pipe gave him a remarkable likeness to Popeye.

When he received Schwarzkopf's telegram, Parker telephoned Detective James Kirkham of Mercer County and informed him that he would deliver Paul Wendel to him. Kirkham, having no idea that Wendel had confessed to the Lindbergh kidnapping, assumed that the ex-lawyer had been arrested on the old embezzlement warrants. Without telling Kirkham about the Lindbergh business, Parker arranged to turn his prisoner over to Kirkham that night at the county line near White Horse.

At eleven o'clock that night, after Parker had delivered the prisoner to Kirkham, Wendel handed the Mercer County detective a copy of his Lindbergh confession. Shocked and somewhat confused by this revelation, Kirkham took Wendel before Justice of the Peace Charles Mulford who arraigned the prisoner on the charge of murder. Kirkham then turned Wendel over to Sheriff Walter Bradley, who locked him up in Trenton's Mercer County Jail.

That night, Wilentz, Anthony Hauck, Schwarzkopf, Captain Lamb, and Lieutenant Keaten were gathered at the Stacy-Trent Hotel in Trenton awaiting Parker's reply to Schwarzkopf's telegram. At midnight, Sheriff Bradley called the hotel and told Wilentz that Paul Wendel was in the Mercer County Jail.

Since news of Wendel's Lindbergh confession and arrest had already leaked out, there was a small crowd of reporters, photographers, and spectators outside the entrance to the Mercer County Courthouse. An hour after the sheriff's call, Wilentz and his party entered the building through a rear door.

Paul Wendel was seated in the sheriff's office wearing a rumpled three-piece brown suit, a bow tie, and a battered fedora hat. He was tall, husky, and bald except for the hair around his ears. When introduced to Wilentz, he smiled and said, "Gee, but I'm glad to see you."

"Your confession," Wilentz said, "is it true?"

"False," Wendel replied. "I was forced to make that confession. Lookie here," he said rolling up his trousers to his knees, "look at the bruises and welts, they go all the way up my legs."

"Go ahead," Wilentz replied, "let's hear it."[1]

"It started outside my hotel in Manhattan when four men forced me into their car at gunpoint. They put me into a black sedan and drove me to a house in Brooklyn."

"So you did confess?"

"Yes, eventually. I said I'd write anything they wanted. So, one of the men, a guy who called himself Harry Spidella, dictated a confession to me which I wrote down and signed. The next day, Harry came back and said that changes would have to be made. The next day, Harry came back and said the revised confession was okay. He said they'd be taking me out of the basement in the morning. He also had my suit, which had been laundered. In the morning they put me into the black car and drove me to Mount Holly, New Jersey. But before I left the house I scratched my initials, PHW, into the cellar floor. I also saved the laundry tag from my suit." Wendel handed the tag to Wilentz. It read 907-3XU.

Wilentz passed the laundry tag to Schwarzkopf. "You said you were taken to Mount Holly?"

"That's right. I was driven right up to a house I knew very well—Ellis Parker's place."

"What happened when you got to Parker's house?"

"Spidella pointed a gun at me and said, 'You go right up to that house and don't run away or I'll blow your brains out.' So I went up to the house and rang the bell. When Parker's son, Ellis Junior, came to the door, the black car pulled away."

"Was Ellis Senior at home?"

"Oh, yes. I told him what had happened and asked him to call the police. I figured they could still catch the kidnappers before they got back to the city."

"What did Parker say to that?"

"He wasn't interested in calling the police. He said that I had fallen into the hands of the Mafia, that it would be too dangerous for me to call the police. He had a better idea, he said he'd hide me somewhere until the whole thing blew over. He figured the mob might try to kidnap me again. The next morning Parker drove me to New Lisbon Colony, about ten miles from his house."

"You mean the asylum, the institution for mental defectives?"

"Yes. We went straight to the superintendent's office. The man in charge was a Dr. Carroll James. He said I could live in one of the bungalows. From then on I was guarded, they said protected, by one or more detectives from Burlington County. Later on I was guarded by two, then at night three, detectives. I signed a paper that said I had voluntarily committed myself into the sanitarium."

"This is incredible," Wilentz said.

"It's all true. So now I'm living in this little house with my guards and Ellis Parker is checking in on me every so often. About the third or fourth day, he comes and says, 'You know, Paul, maybe it would be a good idea if you *did* confess to the kidnapping.' I couldn't believe what I had just heard. 'You're joking,' I said. 'No, I'm serious,' he said. 'There would be definite advantages.'"

"What kind of advantages?" Wilentz asked.

"Mostly money. He said I could sell my story for a million dollars. Then I'd plead guilty and say that I had been temporarily insane. Ellis said that because he was tight with the governor he could guarantee me a commuted sentence."

"So you went along with the plan?"

"Not at first. I was shocked that Ellis Parker had even suggested the idea. When I said I wasn't interested, Ellis told me to think it over."

"So what made you change your mind," Wilentz asked.

"They kept me prisoner at the institution three weeks, and every day Ellis and his son came to work on me. Toward the end, Ellis was threatening to put me into a real insane asylum if I didn't confess. I finally agreed to go along and signed the twenty-five page confession Parker had composed. It was the only way I could get out of that place. After that, one of Parker's detectives drove me to the county line and turned me over to Detective Kirkham. I was then taken before a judge and brought here."[2]

At three in the morning Wendel finished writing and signing the statement repudiating his confession and accusing Ellis Parker, his son, and the four other men, of kidnapping.

That afternoon, while Governor Hoffman was publicly denying charges that he was the force behind Wendel's confession, New York City Police Commissioner Lewis Valentine and Brooklyn District Attorney William F. X. Geoghan announced that they'd be opening investigations on the Wendel kidnapping. Since Wendel alleged that his abductors had taken him from New York to New Jersey, J. Edgar Hoover said that the FBI had jurisdiction on the case.[3]

On Monday morning at eleven o'clock, March 30, the court of pardons met in Trenton to hear Hauptmann's final plea for clemency. In his petition, Lloyd Fisher asked the court to " . . . pass on these facts and matters with cool and calm deliberation—with deliberation that is not incited by the cry of the mob, nor by an overwhelming desire on the part of police officials to clear from their records a matter which has been baffling and embarrassing."[4]

Fisher argued that because serious questions had been raised about the rail 16 evidence as well as the credibility of the prosecution's eyewitnesses, Hauptmann's life should be spared. Fisher asserted that it would be highly improper and unwise to execute Hauptmann when Paul Wendel was being held in jail on the charge of killing the baby. Fisher pointed out that the prosecution had claimed all along that one person had committed the crime—and now the state had two men in custody for the kidnapping and murder. "How could the State," Fisher asked, "under these perplexing circumstances, electrocute Mr. Hauptmann?"

Wilentz and Anthony Hauck presented the State's case, and when they were finished, at four o'clock, the eight-member panel filed out of the courtroom to deliberate. An hour later, the board returned with their decision—Hauptmann's plea for clemency was denied. Governor Hoffman, having voted this time with the majority, announced that he would not grant Hauptmann another reprieve. It was a severe blow to the defense,

Hauptmann was scheduled to die the following evening at eight o'clock and it seemed that there was nothing Fisher could do to stop it.

That night, Fisher broke the news to Hauptmann, who sat on his cot and cried. By the time Anna got to the prison at 8:30, he had pulled himself together. They held hands through the bars and Anna assured him that Governor Hoffman would change his mind and grant a reprieve. After all, a man had confessed to the crime, how could the governor not delay the execution? As they spoke, Bruno could hear, in the background, a hum he had heard before. Someone was testing the generators in the death chamber, the power source to the electric chair. The first time Hauptmann had heard that noise he had asked a guard about it. The guard told him about the dynamos, then explained that when a prisoner was electrocuted, the lights in the death house never dimmed like they did in the movies. "The chair has got its own juice," he said.

On Tuesday morning, the day of the execution, Hauptmann refused to eat his breakfast. One hour later he was issued a blue shirt and a pair of khaki trousers with a dark stripe running up the legs. This was the outfit he'd be wearing when they put him into the electric chair. When he put on the trousers Hauptmann noticed that they had been slit at his right calf. He asked one of the guards about this. The guard hesitated a moment, then told Hauptmann about the electrodes, how one would be attached to the crown of his head and the other to his right leg. As Hauptmann contemplated the workings of the electric chair, the prison barber came into his cell to shave his head. Bruno didn't have to ask what that was all about.

That morning, Lloyd Fisher was in Judge Trenchard's chambers pleading for a postponement of the electrocution until the Paul Wendel matter was cleared up. The judge read Wendel's confession, then declared that he could see no reason to delay the execution. "If executions were put off," he said, "every time some nut made a last-minute confession, the business of the state would never be carried out according to the law and the instructions and wishes of the jury."[5]

Hauptmann didn't touch his lunch, the knowledge that he'd be dead in eight hours had killed his appetite. At two o'clock, Bruno was rocked by the news that he was being moved across the corridor to cell number 8. His guards said that this was standard procedure; the idea was to prevent a prisoner from using some device he had hidden in his cell to kill himself. "We wouldn't want that," a guard said. So, to ensure that the prisoner would be alive when he was placed onto the electric chair, Hauptmann was taken from the place that had been his home for the past fourteen months and put into a cell that had no furniture except for a stool.

Dressed and groomed for his electrocution, the condemned man, perched on the lonely stool, whimpered, prayed out loud, and cried. The death row guards, having seen more men inch their way to the electric chair than they cared to recall, paid little attention to Hauptmann as they systematically searched his old cell just in case a last-minute call from the governor delayed the event.

At 1:30, Warden Kimberling stopped by the cell to encourage Hauptmann to eat. The warden told Hauptmann he could have any food that he wanted. "I'm not hungry," Hauptmann said. "But there is something you can do for me."

"Good, what is it?" Kimberling asked.

"I am innocent and I want to make a plea to the American people. I want to speak to them over the radio—from my cell."

"I'm sorry, Richard, I can't do that. We can't let prisoners make radio broadcasts from their cells. I'm sorry."

Kimberling left the death house, closing the door on Hauptmann's sobs. He felt stupid having offered the prisoner a big meal when he knew Hauptmann wouldn't be living long enough to digest it.[6]

At the State House, Wilentz received the call from Erwin Marshall, the Mercer County Prosecutor, who reported that the Mercer County grand jury had insisted that morning on considering the Wendel matter. When the prosecutor told the grand jurors that Wendel had nothing to do with the Lindbergh case, he was asked to leave the room. The jury foreman, Allyne Freeman, a close friend and political ally of Governor Hoffman's, said the jury would be subpoenaing Ellis Parker, his son, and Ellis's secretary, Anna Bading, in an effort to determine if Wendel's confession was legitimate. If there was any chance that it was, Wendel would be indicted for the murder of the Lindbergh baby.

"I've never seen anything like it," Marshall exclaimed. "I've lost control of my own grand jury! If they indict Wendel tomorrow, what effect will it have on Hauptmann's execution?"

"I don't know," Wilentz replied. "The whole thing is illegal. They don't have jurisdiction over the Lindbergh case—the baby was kidnapped in Hunterdon County."

"But according to Wendel's confession, the child died in Mercer County," Marshall said. "What will happen if they indict?"

"Governor Hoffman would think seriously about a reprieve—there'd be another delay," Wilentz said.[7]

That afternoon, Hauptmann's lawyers, Fisher, Pope and Rosecrans, stopped by the death house. Hauptmann was still upset about having been moved out of his old cell. He wanted to look at his photographs of Anna and Bubi. "I have been a good prisoner," he said to Fisher, "I have never made anybody any trouble. I've never broken a rule. Why should they do this to me?"

"You'll be moving back to your old cell soon," Fisher said. "The grand jury is about to indict Paul Wendel for the kidnapping. That means there will be a reprieve. Don't upset yourself, Richard, everything will be okay."

"They didn't move the other man, they let him stay in his cell!" (Another death row prisoner, Charles Zeid, was also scheduled for execution that evening.)

"Richard, please."

"Why should I be pushed around when this is my last day to live?"

At four o'clock, a few minutes after the lawyers left, Hauptmann's two spiritual advisors, the Reverend John Matthiesen and the Reverend D. G. Werner, came to console him. The Reverend Mr. Werner stayed an hour, and at six, the Reverend Mr. Matthiesen had to leave. Sitting on the stool under the watchful eyes of his two guards, Hauptmann cried, "Gott. Gott. Gott."

By seven that evening, the invited witnesses to Hauptmann's execution started show-

420   ing up at the prison. Thirty minutes later, all forty-five of them were crowded into War-den Kimberling's office. The group consisted of police administrators and detectives from the New Jersey State Police, the New York City Police Department, and the FBI; a number of reporters, columnists, and newsreel journalists; county and state prose-cutors from New Jersey and New York; politicians from both states; a variety of federal, state, and local bureaucrats; and members of Hauptmann's defense team. The group was quiet, tense, and fidgety.

At 7:45, the official spectators were still waiting to be ushered into the death cham-ber. Warden Kimberling was beside himself with worry and indecision—Hauptmann was scheduled to die in fifteen minutes and there was still no word from the Mercer County grand jury. The executioner and his assistant were in the death chamber making their final preparations, the two guards who would escort the prisoner to the electric chair were standing by, and Hauptmann, sitting on his stool, silent and expressionless, stared into space as the two ministers, who had returned to the cell a few minutes ear-lier, recited passages from their Bibles.

Anna Hauptmann, wearing the black dress she had purchased that morning, was stretched across her bed at the Stacy-Trent Hotel. Her matching black hat and veil were lying nearby on the night stand. She was being attended by a physician who had just given her a sedative. She was also being consoled by her friend Miss Adams, the reporter for the *New York Journal,* and Robert Hicks.

Robert Elliott, the executioner, had carefully examined the squat, three-legged, bolted-down electric chair, with its extra-wide arms, heavily insulated wiring, and leather straps, and found it in good working order. This particular chair, typical of most, had been built twenty years earlier by an electrical engineer from Trenton. Unlike most people, Mr. Elliott didn't consider the electric chair a horrifying and grotesque killer of men; to him it was an instrument that if properly operated, did the job it was designed to do—quickly and efficiently. He had operated this very chair many times and had never encountered a problem. The entire process only took three minutes, one minute to strap the man in and two to electrocute him. Elliott would be giving Hauptmann two thou-sand volts for sixty seconds, then, during the final minute, one thousand more for good measure. From his experience, Elliott knew that Hauptmann wouldn't present any prob-lems—that is, cause a delay, embarrass the prison officials, or create a scene that would offend the witnesses. The executioner had never seen a condemned man fight his guards or resist being put into the chair. They had all been docile—either in a state of physical collapse or religious exaltation. In his forty-six years behind the electric chair, Elliott had never heard a long farewell speech or last-minute wisecracking. If there was a prob-lem, it usually involved a nervous guard fumbling with the straps, the hood, or some-thing like that. Elliott had never experienced a snafu in Trenton—the New Jersey death house was a busy place and the guards there were well-practiced.

Another Trenton death row prisoner would be following Hauptmann to the chair that night. Mr. Elliott would be handling that execution as well, pocketing three hundred dollars for one night's work. A perfectionist by nature, as well as a professional, Elliott would make sure the electric chair had cooled before the second man was brought in. There was nothing he could do, however, about the lingering odor. The executioner was ready.

Warden Kimberling, however, wasn't so ready—he couldn't decide what to do.

A crowd of eight thousand had gathered outside the prison gates. Although the group, made up of newsmen and curious onlookers, was quiet and orderly, ninety New Jersey state troopers were on hand to maintain order. Nearby, out of sight, stood two fire companies ready to deploy their water hoses in the event of a riot.

At five to eight, Kimberling called Erwin Marshall who advised that the grand jurors were still deliberating on the Wendel matter.

"What if I go ahead with this thing," Kimberling said, "and the grand jury indicts Wendel for the murder? I need some guidance—and fast. I'm not sure what to do!"

"I don't know what to tell you, Mark. It's your decision."

"I'm really stumped."

"What does the governor say?"

"He won't step in, and neither will the judge."

"Then I guess you'll just have to go ahead with it."

"But what if Wendel is indicted? How would that look?"

"The Wendel thing is a farce, it really doesn't have anything to do with Hauptmann."

"I don't see it that way—it's a terrible complication," the Warden exclaimed.

It was eight o'clock, the appointed time, and everybody was in place and waiting. Although he was acting against his better judgment, the warden signaled one of the keepers to lead the witnesses into the death chamber. But before the guard started for the door, the telephone rang. Kimberling waved off the keeper and picked up the phone. The caller was Allyne Freeman, the foreman of the Mercer County grand jury. "We would like you to postpone the execution forty-eight hours," he said, "until we can get this Wendel business straightened out."

This was all Kimberling needed. He called the death house and ordered Hauptmann back into his old cell. A guard was dispatched to the death chamber to inform Robert Elliott that he would only be executing one prisoner that night.

Judge Trenchard had set Hauptmann's execution for the week of March 30, 1936. It was Kimberling who had scheduled it for Tuesday, March 31. Since the day of the week had been left to the warden's discretion, he had the authority to make such an adjustment. But unless the governor or the judge ordered otherwise, Hauptmann would have to be executed before the week was out, regardless of what the Mercer County grand jury decided or didn't decide.

Addressing the forty-five witnesses waiting in his office, Kimberling said, "There's not going to be anything tonight. I've postponed the execution until eight o'clock, Friday, April 3. If the grand jury is still deliberating then I'll set it back two more days."

Lloyd Fisher ran from Kimberling's office to the death house. When he got there the guards were moving Hauptmann back into cell number 9. "They've put it off for three days," Fisher shouted.

Hauptmann wasn't jubilant, he had already learned of the postponement and was taking it calmly. "I think this means better things for me," he said.

Using the phone in the death house, Fisher called Mrs. Hauptmann's room at the Stacy-Trent. He spoke to Robert Hicks, who gave Anna the good news. "I knew it!" she cried. "I told you so." No longer drowsy from the sedative, Mrs. Hauptmann changed out of her black dress.

That night, in the relative comfort of his old cell, surrounded by his books, papers, and the photographs of his family, Hauptmann, in his own hand, wrote a letter to Governor Hoffman, which in part read:

> Your Excellence:
>
> My writing is not for fear of losing my life, this is in the hands of God, it is His will. I will go gladly, it means the end of my tremendous suffering. Only in thinking of my wife and my little boy, that is breaking my heart. I know untill this terrible crime is solvet, they will have to suffer unter the weight of my unfair conviction.
>
> I beg you, Attorney General, believe at least a dying man. Please investigate, because the case is not solvet, it only adds another death to the Lindbergh case.
>
> I thank your Excellence, from the bottom of my heart, and may God bless you,
> Respectfully,
> Bruno Richard Hauptmann

The next morning, Wednesday, April 1, the *Trenton Times* carried a front-page editorial accusing Governor Hoffman, Ellis Parker, and Grand Jury Foreman Allyne Freeman of conspiring to interfere with the orderly process of law. Once again, the newspaper called for Governor Hoffman's impeachment.

That day, the Mercer County grand jury heard three witnesses—Ellis Parker, Paul Wendel's son, and his daughter. Wendel's children testified that they did not help their father care for the Lindbergh baby as alleged in his confession. They said they hadn't had any contact with their father for several years.

The grand jurors, before adjourning at midnight, voted to ask Erwin Marshall, the Mercer County Prosecutor, back into the fold. It was dawning on the jurors that Wendel's confession was worthless.

It was on that Wednesday that Hauptmann's mother Pauline, still living alone in Kamenz, Germany, received a letter Bruno had written to her two weeks earlier. In it, Hauptmann had written: " . . . Human hypocrisy may go far, but I still have so much confidence in humanity that I believe it will shy from murdering an innocent."[8]

On Thursday morning, April 2, the Mercer County grand jury reconvened at 9:30, and shortly thereafter heard Paul Wendel's story of how he had been kidnapped and beaten, then taken to a mental institution where he was held until he signed the twenty-five page Lindbergh confession.

Wendel was followed to the stand by Governor Hoffman and Attorney General Wilentz, who brought copies of the ransom notes and samples of Wendel's handwriting to show that Wendel had not written any of the ransom documents. After the jurors had examined this evidence, they agreed that Wendel could not have been the ransom note writer.

Just before midnight, the Mercer County grand jury voted to drop the Wendel case.

At five that afternoon, Governor Hoffman called Wilentz and asked him to come to the Executive Suite. A few minutes later, the two men were alone in the governor's office. "Dave," the Governor said, "I'm thinking about another reprieve. Will you back me?"

"You've got to be kidding! Hal, for Christ's sake, get ahold of yourself. If you interfere again, they'll impeach you."

"If we wait he might still confess."

"He's had plenty of time for that. Hauptmann will never confess. The police couldn't get him to, none of the prosecutors could, his lawyers couldn't, you couldn't, and Leibowitz couldn't. Hauptmann won't come clean because his wife won't let him. She doesn't want to live the rest of her life as the widow of a confessed baby killer. He knows that. If he confessed, even to the extortion part, she would turn her back on him. He's made his choice, and so must you. It's time to put this case behind us—to get it over with!"

"What about the possibility of accomplices?"

"If there were accomplices—and there weren't—but if there were, he'd never tell us because he'd have to first incriminate himself. He'll never do that."

"I guess you're right. I got a letter from him the other day, and everytime I read it I get second thoughts."[9]

Wilentz left the Governor's office at five o'clock that afternoon with the knowledge that the path to the electric chair had finally been cleared. In three hours, Robert Elliott, the electrician from Long Island, would be back in New Jersey.

> I am glad that my life in a world which has not understood me has ended.
> —BRUNO RICHARD HAUPTMANN

45 THE EXECUTION

THAT AFTERNOON, on the day of the execution, Lloyd Fisher went to the death house to tell Hauptmann there was no word from the State House regarding a reprieve. The prisoner had been moved back into cell number 8 and Fisher could tell that he had been crying. Hauptmann told Fisher that he'd been writing a final statement to be released after his execution.

At 5:30, Fisher told Hauptmann that he had to leave because he had an appointment with the governor and he didn't want to be late. "There is still a good chance for a reprieve," he said before departing.

"Don't tell Annie I'm in a strange cell," Hauptmann replied.

"I'll be back—and I'll have good news," Fisher promised.

Governor Hoffman had just wound up his conference with Wilentz when Fisher entered the Executive Suite. The governor let Fisher state the defense's position one more time, and when the attorney had finished, the governor said that he was in sympathy with Hauptmann—everybody knew that—but there was nothing more he could do. "Lloyd," he said, "my hands are tied."

It was 6:30, and outside the prison spectators and newsmen were gathering. There were about five hundred of them standing about, just a fraction of the crowd that had gathered there at this time last Tuesday. It was a clear night, with the sky filled with stars, but it was bitter cold and blustery and this had kept the crowd small.

Gabriel Heatter, the famous radio newscaster, had been on the air since six o'clock commenting on the upcoming execution. He was telling his listeners that if there were any last-minute developments such as a confession or stay of execution, they would be getting all of the details.

Fisher returned to the death house at 7:30 to say good-bye. Hauptmann, bald and pasty-white, was perched on the stool amid his spiritual advisors. The Reverend John Gourley, the prison chaplain, the Reverend John Matthiesen, and the Reverend D. G. Werner were there.

"What does the governor say?" Hauptmann asked in a weak and quivering voice.

424

Fighting to keep his emotions in check, Fisher replied, "Richard—tell me something that will save your life."

"Lloyd, there isn't anything I can say."

The Reverend Mr. Matthiesen handed Fisher a sheet of paper, "This is Richard's final statement," he said.

Fisher looked at the paper but couldn't read it because it was in German. It read:

> I am glad that my life in a world which has not understood me has ended. Soon I will be at home with my Lord, so I am dying an innocent man. Should, however, my death serve for the purpose of abolishing capital punishment—such a punishment being arrived at only by circumstantial evidence—I feel that my death has not been in vain. I am at peace with God. I repeat, I protest my innocence of the crime for which I was convicted. However, I die with no malice or hatred in my heart. The love of Christ has filled my soul and I am happy in Him.[1]

Fisher said good-bye, and with tears in his eyes, stepped away from the cell. He had to be in Kimberling's office where the other people who would be watching his client die were grouping. As Fisher walked away, Hauptmann called him back, and in a somber voice said, "Lloyd, I want to say goodbye to you again. You have been very kind to me."

Fisher reached into the cell between the bars and shook Hauptmann's hand. The two men then broke into tears.

Over at the State House, one of Governor Hoffman's aides came out of the Executive Suite and read the following statement to the reporters who were crowded in the hallway: "I am now without power, under the New Jersey Constitution, to grant another reprieve."

The governor's announcement sent the reporters running for the telephones. Could this be it—was this the night that Hauptmann was really going to die?

In the death chamber, Executioner Elliott, stern-faced and thin and wearing a gray suit and a brightly patterned tie that was perhaps too festive for the occasion, had just completed his final tests of the equipment. He was standing by with his assistant. It was twenty minutes past the appointed hour.

The death room, with its smudged, whitewashed brick walls, harsh lighting, high ceiling, and scuffed, linoleum floor, was cold and ugly. Besides the heavy, three-legged chair and the large metal cabinet behind it, containing the gauges, dials, and the big wheel that controlled the flow of electricity, the room contained a small porcelain sink, a radiator, an iron bench, three rows of wooden card chairs for the witnesses, and three doors. The door behind the electric chair and off to its side opened into the small autopsy room. Since New Jersey law no longer mandated the autopsy of electrocuted prisoners, this room would not be used for Hauptmann. The door on the wall facing the electric chair opened into the prison yard and would be the one entered by the witnesses. The remaining passageway, secured by a barred jail door, was the one Hauptmann would be coming through. The electric chair would be on his left when he stepped or was carried into the chamber.

The fifty-five execution witnesses were crowded into Warden Kimberling's office. The group included thirty newsmen, six physicians, and a variety of politicians, bureaucrats, and policemen. Colonel Schwartzkopf, Captain Lamb, and Lieutenant Keaten were there representing the New Jersey State Police. Before leading the group out of his office, Kimberling made sure that everyone had signed the affidavit in which they swore that they had not brought any deadly weapons, cameras, drugs, or contraband into the prison. All of the witnesses had been frisked before entering the administration building.

It was 8:25 when the witnesses, led by Kimberling, moved out of the warden's office en route to the death chamber. Formed into a double, one-hundred-foot line, the witnesses marched out of the administration building, through the iron-barred gates into the middle cell block, through the dimly lighted mess hall and kitchen corridors, and out into the open prison yard. The witnesses trekked across the prison yard to the little brick building that contained death row and the electric chair. Just before entering the death chamber, each man was searched again.

Once inside the room, the witnesses took their seats in the three rows of wooden chairs that faced the electric chair. The chairs were behind a three-foot-high divider made of canvas sheets draped over a chain strung across the room.

The warden, standing between the witnesses and the electric chair, instructed them to keep their overcoats buttoned and warned them not to place their hands into their pockets. This was a precaution against one of the newsmen snapping a clandestine photograph of Hauptmann in his final moments. Five years earlier, a reporter using a cleverly rigged camera strapped to his leg had photographed Ruth Snyder, the convicted murderess, as she was being electrocuted. "If Hauptmann wants to say anything," Kimberling said, "I'm warden of this prison and I will handle it. No police officer, no press and no one else will have anything to do with it but listen to it. Everybody is to remain seated until the execution is over. If there is any demonstration, the person making it will be removed from the chamber."[2]

Kimberling turned to one of the guards and said, "See if there is any message for us." The guard nodded then walked briskly out of the death chamber and down the corridor past cell number 8, where Hauptmann and his ministers were praying. Using the telephone at the other end of death row, the guard called the governor's office to see if Hoffman had any last-minute instructions. An aide in the Executive Suite picked up the phone and said that the governor had nothing to say. The guard hung up, then walked quickly back to the death chamber where he said calmly, "No message."

"Bring in the prisoner," Kimberling ordered.

At 8:41, Hauptmann stepped out of cell number 8 to begin the very short walk to the electric chair. He was flanked by two guards and followed by the three ministers, who were dressed in black and reading out loud from their Bibles. Walking behind the religious men were two more guards.

Hauptmann, wearing bedroom slippers, entered the death chamber slightly ahead of his two keepers. The bright lights in the room reflected yellow off his shaved head, which was tilted slightly to one side. Hauptmann's eyes found the electric chair the moment he entered the room. He shuffled over to it, and without hesitation sat down on it, seizing both arms with his hands. He appeared composed, above it all—and maybe a bit defiant. Sitting in that chair, he looked very much the way he had when he sat in the witness box at the trial. His ministers were standing nearby, still reading out loud from their Bibles.

A guard stepped forward and began fastening Hauptmann's arms to the chair. John Bloom, the executioner's assistant, attached the first electrode to Hauptmann's right calf at the place where his khaki trousers had been slit. Elliott himself slipped the leather, cuplike skull cap onto Hauptmann's head. It contained the other electrode and was wet from having just been dipped into a pail of salt water. Elliott adjusted the chin strap on the cap, then carefully squared it on Hauptmann's head. Hauptmann didn't move a muscle or utter a word. He stared blankly ahead in the direction of the witnesses, who sat frozen in their wooden card chairs. As Elliott tied the black mask over Hauptmann's face, his assistant strapped the prisoner's legs to the chair. The executioner and his helper worked quickly and efficiently. This was not a job for amateurs.

Some of the reporters in the room held pencils in their hands just in case Hauptmann had a last-minute message—a good-bye or perhaps a confession. A guard stood near the chair holding up a large clock that Elliott would use to time his electrical charges.

It was 8:44 when Warden Kimberling, still wearing his hat and overcoat, and looking a bit pale, signaled Elliott to turn on the electricity. The lanky executioner, standing behind the chair with his back to Hauptmann and the witnesses, rotated the wheel in the control panel. The generator made a whining sound and there was a sudden creaking of the leather straps. A tiny wisp of smoke shot from the top of Hauptmann's head and the trunk of his body slumped forward. A minute later Elliott cut the voltage in half and held it there for another sixty seconds.

The executioner cut the electricity and one of the guards hurried to Hauptmann and unfastened him from the chair. He was followed by the prison physician, Dr. Howard Wiesler, who placed his stethoscope on Hauptmann's chest and said, "This man is dead."

It was 8:47, and the ministers were still reading in German from their Bibles. One of the reporters cried out, "It's terrible!"

Two guards cleared the straps from Hauptmann's body, then carried him, by his head and knees, into the little room behind the chair.

Another guard opened the door to the prison yard and the witnesses filed out. The newsmen in the group hurried ahead to call in their stories. Gabriel Heatter, after three hours, was finally able to tell his radio audience that Hauptmann was dead.

At nine o'clock, Warden Kimberling sent an aide outside the prison to tell the small group gathered at the main gate that the electrocution had taken place. There were a few halfhearted cheers, but most of the people, shivering from the cold, seemed more interested in getting back to their cars. In minutes the crowd had melted into the night.

Lloyd Fisher was surrounded by reporters the moment he walked through the prison gates. "This is the greatest tragedy in the history of New Jersey," he said. "Time will never wash it away." He climbed into a waiting car.

A mile and a half from the prison, Laura Apgar, Lloyd Fisher's secretary, was knocking on Mrs. Hauptmann's door at the Stacy-Trent Hotel. "I'm sorry—it's all over," she said to Miss Adams, the Hearst reporter who had answered the door.

Mrs. Hauptmann was lying face-down across her bed, crying hysterically. She was being consoled by her physician and Robert Hicks. "It is done," the doctor said.

Mrs. Hauptmann sat up suddenly and cried, "Oh, God, why did they do it? Oh, Bubi!" She then scampered into the bathroom and locked the door.

Lloyd Fisher and the Reverend Mr. Matthiesen arrived at Anna's room to find Miss Apgar and the others standing at the bathroom door pleading with Mrs. Hauptmann to come out. Matthiesen spoke softly to Mrs. Hauptmann in German, and after fifteen minutes, she bolted out of the bathroom and threw herself back onto the bed. Meanwhile, a dozen or so reporters and cameramen had forced themselves into the room. Flashbulbs were popping and newsmen were firing questions at Mrs. Hauptmann. Lloyd Fisher angrily cleared the newsmen out of the room, then tried to console Mrs. Hauptmann. Fifteen minutes later the lawyer left the hotel to see Governor Hoffman at the Hildebrecht.

Following the electrocution, Lieutenant Keaten headed straight for his home in Morristown, New Jersey, where a group of his friends had gathered to help him celebrate the final closing of the Lindbergh investigation. The execution marked the culmination of four years of stress, frustration, tedium, and hard work. He could now have a drink and relax with his friends. The Lindbergh case had dominated his life for four years. It was finally over.

The lieutenant got home at 9:30 and was greeted at the door by his wife and his guests. When he had removed his coat and hat someone stuck a glass into his hand. Keaten handed the drink to his wife, muttered something to his friends, then climbed the stairs to his bedroom. The celebration that night would go on without him. The detective was exhausted and had wanted to sleep—and he wanted to get Hauptmann's image out of his mind.[3]

At 11:30, four New Jersey state troopers and two New York City detectives escorted Anna Hauptmann out of her hotel room. The party used a freight elevator to avoid the reporters and cameramen who were camped out in the hotel lobby. The distraught woman was ushered into a car that was parked behind the building. She had no further use of her room in Trenton and was being driven back to her apartment in the Bronx.

In Kamenz, Germany that night, when Pauline Hauptmann was told of her son's death, she said, "My son was my only hope. What have they done to my boy? Oh, God, how could it happen?"[4]

The next morning, Governor Hoffman, his interest in the Lindbergh case suddenly renewed, announced that he would be asking the New Jersey legislature to authorize an investigation into the activities of the New Jersey State Police and the attorney general's office.

While Governor Hoffman was declaring another war on New Jersey law enforcement, a pair of district attorneys from Brooklyn were in Mount Holly, New Jersey, questioning Ellis Parker and his son about the alleged kidnapping of Paul Wendel.

That afternoon, at four o'clock, Lloyd Fisher arrived at the prison to claim Hauptmann's body. Accompanying him were the Reverend D. G. Werner and Henry Stolzenberger, an undertaker from the Bronx. Fisher was also at the prison to pick up Hauptmann's personal things—his toiletries, a few books, photographs of his family, and a bundle of letters. Before Hauptmann's body was removed, Warden Kimberling handed the mortician a document stating that pursuant to New Jersey law, no religious services could be held over the remains of an executed prisoner. Since that law only applied in New Jersey, it had no effect on the services planned for Hauptmann in New York City.

The black hearse containing Hauptmann's body pulled away from the prison at 5:30. Six hundred people were at the gate to watch the hearse and its police escort go by. As it passed no one spoke and some of the men in the crowd removed their hats.

That Saturday, Hauptmann's execution made the front pages of every paper in the country. The *Pittsburgh Post-Gazette,* in huge front-page headlines, declared: "HAUPTMANN DIES IN CHAIR REMAINS SILENT UNTIL END."

The execution was also big news in Great Britain and in Europe. An editor for the *London Daily Telegraph* was critical of the way in which the American authorities had played "cat and mouse" with Hauptmann while delaying his execution so many times. This criticism was echoed in a French paper, which called Hauptmann's stays of execution "judicial inquisition." In Vienna, the *Neue Freie Press* declared, "Hauptmann's fate was fulfilled after senseless torturing postponements. What has happened in America was a travesty of every conception of justice. The way in which they played with the life of this man was a world scandal."[5]

Hauptmann's funeral services were held at one o'clock on Monday afternoon, April 6, at the Fresh Pond Crematory in Middle Village, Queens. His two ministers, D. G. Werner and John Matthiesen, officiated. The service was attended by thirty people—members of the defense team, a few of Mrs. Hauptmann's relatives, and a dozen or so of Hauptmann's friends, including Hans Kloppenburg, Henry Uhlig, and Gerta Henkel. Governor Hoffman wasn't there, but he sent an aide. Outside, fifty New York City policemen were positioned around the building to keep an eye on the thousand or so people who had been drawn, for one reason or another, to the service.

At 1:45, Hauptmann's body, like the remains of the Lindbergh baby, was cremated. At two o'clock, someone from the crematorium went outside and announced to the crowd that Hauptmann's body had been cremated. With that the crowd started to disperse and within five minutes the place was deserted.

NOTES

CHAPTER 1 "THE CRIME"

1 Lieutenant Dunn's reaction to Lindbergh's call on the night of March 1, 1932 is one of the anecdotes told by retired Det. Lewis J. Bornmann in an interview conducted by Det. Sgt. Cornel D. Plebani of the New Jersey State Police on June 28, 1983. The audio tape of this interview is part of the Lindbergh Case Archives, New Jersey State Police Headquarters, West Trenton, N.J.

2 Although the Lindbergh house is located two and a half miles from Hopewell, N.J., it will, for the sake of convenience, be referred to as the Hopewell estate.

CHAPTER 2 "THE CRIME SCENE"

1 The information regarding Colonel Schwarzkopf's early years, and the formation of the New Jersey State Police, is from Leo J. Coakley, *Jersey Troopers* (New Brunswick, N.J.: Rutgers University Press, 1971). Coakley was a New Jersey State Police officer.

2 The information about Lt. Arthur T. Keaten was obtained from his wife, Lydia, in an interview at her home conducted by the author and Det. Sgt. Cornel D. Plebani of the New Jersey State Police.

3 Critics of the Lindbergh investigation find it hard to believe that Cpl. Frank Kelly did not find any clear fingerprints at the scene of the crime. Anthony Scaduto, in *Scapegoat: The Lonesome Death of Bruno Richard Hauptmann* (New York: G. P. Putnam's Sons, 1976), asserts that the kidnapper had somehow managed to wipe clean every surface in the nursery. Scaduto reaches the conclusion that the absence of Hauptmann's fingerprints at the scene is evidence of his innocence.

Alan Hynd, in the "Why the Lindbergh Case was Never Solved" chapter of *Murder, Mayhem and Mystery* (New York: A. S. Barnes, 1958), also had a problem with the absence of fingerprints in the baby's room. Hynd writes: "Cu-riously, there was not a single fingerprint found in the nursery—on the crib, on the walls, and on the window woodwork, on other articles of furniture, or anywhere else. 'I'm damned,' said one cop, 'if I don't think somebody washed everything in that nursery before the print men got there.'" (p. 17).

The missing fingerprint analysis is considered by Prof. James W. Osterburg in his text, *The Crime Laboratory: Case Studies of Scientific Criminal Investigation* (New York: Clark Boardman, 1982). Osterburg makes the point that when a person touches something, an identifiable latent is not automatically left on the object. The thing touched must have the kind of surface that will accept a print. If the object is held too tightly or released in the wrong way, the latent will be smudged and therefore useless. Thus, the fact that latent fingerprints are not found on an object does not necessarily mean that it wasn't touched or that it had been wiped clean. And it doesn't automatically suggest that the person processing the objects for prints was inept.

4 Lindbergh Case Archives, New Jersey State Police Headquarters, West Trenton, N.J. Corporal Wolf saw two sets of footprints leading from the Lindbergh house to the kidnap ladder. Harold G. Hoffman, governor of New Jersey from 1935 to 1939, wrote a fourteen-part article about the case for *Liberty Magazine*. In Part B of the series, called "The Crime—The Case—The Challenge," published on March 19, 1938, Hoffman quotes this portion of Wolf's report as follows: "Apparently two members of the party proceeded on foot to the east side of the Lindbergh residence and assembled a three-piece homemade extension ladder . . . two sets of fresh footprints leading off in a southeast direction. . ."

Modern-day writers have made the argument that two or more persons were involved in the kidnapping.

5 One of the myths of the Lindbergh case is that the police had trampled valuable crime scene evidence as they approached the Lind-

432 bergh estate. The following quote from Henry Morton Robinson's 1935 book, *Science Versus Crime* (Indianapolis: Bobbs-Merrill) helped establish the myth: "To summon up a ghostly remembrance of police conduct, bend your glance backward to the opening chapter of the Lindbergh case. Do you remember—could anyone forget—the foaming and senseless cataract of gorgeously uniformed state troopers that descended on the Lindbergh home in motorcycles, roared up and down the road, trampling every available clue into the March mud, systematically covering with impenetrable layers of stupidity every fingerprint, footprint, dust trace on the estate" (p. 286).

6 On April 5, all of the letters that had been received by the Lindberghs up to that date dealing with the kidnapping were sorted into categories. The mail, according to content, broke down as follows: dreams, 12,000; sympathy, 11,500; suggestions, 9,500; and cranks, 5,000.

et (New York: Vanguard, 1932), pp. 230–231.

4 Sidney B. Whipple, *The Lindbergh Crime* (New York, Blue Ribbon Books, 1935), p. 43.

5 Gaston B. Means, *The Strange Death of President Harding*, as told to Mary Dixon Thacker (New York: Guild Publishing, 1930).

6 George Waller, *Kidnap: The Story of the Lindberg Case* (New York: Dial, 1961), p. 28.

7 Whipple, *The Lindbergh Crime*, p. 55.

8 Sullivan, *The Snatch Racket*, p. 220.

9 Theories about Al Capone's involvement in the Lindbergh case persist. One of these holds that Al Capone's gang had kidnapped the child as a lesson to airmail pilots who were spotting stills and reporting the bootleggers to the U.S. Treasury Department.

10 Leonard Katz, *Uncle Frank: The Biography of Frank Costello* (New York: Drake, 1973), p. 250.

11 The incidents involving Colonel Lindbergh and the interference with his private telephone are reported in Sullivan, *The Snatch Racket*, pp. 211–212.

CHAPTER 3 "THE INITIAL INVESTIGATION"

1 Since neither Lindbergh, Schwarzkopf, Keaten, Breckinridge, nor Rosner published anything about the case, I do not have a direct written source for Schwarzkopf's and Keaten's feelings about Rosner getting a copy of the ransom note. However, based upon the writings of John Condon, Elmer Irey, Harry Walsh, Harold Hoffman, and others closely associated with the investigation, it is clear Keaten and Schwarzkopf disapproved of this action. As far as I know, neither Keaton nor Schwarzkopf openly criticized this action in any of their letters, memos, or reports on file at the Lindbergh Case Archives, New Jersey State Police Headquarters, West Trenton, N.J. Given their relationship to Colonel Lindbergh, their tact is understandable.

2 Betty Gow's statement to Lieutenant Keaten is on file at the Lindbergh Case Archives.

3 Edward Dean Sullivan, *The Snatch Rack-

CHAPTER 4 "THE GO-BETWEENS"

1 Dr. Condon retired in 1932. He had been allowed to work beyond the mandatory retirement age of seventy.

2 Edward Dean Sullivan, *The Snatch Racket*, (New York: Vanguard, 1932), pp. 221–222.

3 According to Ludovic Kennedy, Robert Thayer, Colonel Lindbergh's private secretary has said that he was the only person Dr. Condon talked to that night. The account of the Condon-Lindbergh telephone conversation in this book is based upon Condon's re-creation of it in *Jafsie Tells All!* (New York: Jonathan Lee, 1936).

4 Condon, *Jafsie Tells All!*, p. 59.

5 C. Lloyd Fisher, "The Case New Jersey Would Like to Forget," *Liberty*, August 1, 1936, p. 8.

6 Sidney B. Whipple, *The Lindbergh Crime* (New York: Blue Ribbon, 1935), p. 34.

7 *New York Times,* March 13, 1932, p. 1.

CHAPTER 5 "JAFSIE AND THE RANSOM NEGOTIATIONS"

1 John F. Condon, *Jafsie Tells All!* (New York: Jonathan Lee, 1936), p. 72.

2 The Condon-"Cemetery John" park bench conversation is reported in Condon's book. I have excerpted parts of this conversation in re-creating what took place.

3 In 1916, Frederick Kuhn published a book called *The Finger Print Instructor.* Published by Munn and Company, it was America's first authoritative text on the subject. Kuhn's book was based on the English system of fingerprint classification and filing devised by Sir Edward Richard Henry in 1901. In 1904, America's first fingerprint bureau was established by the St. Louis Police Department. The first American book on fingerprinting, called *Brayley's Arrangement of Finger Prints,* was written by Frederick A. Brayley and published in Boston by the Worcester Press in 1910.

4 Hans Gross (1847–1915), an Austrian lawyer, judge, and professor of criminology at the University of Prague, published *Handbuch für Untersuchungsgerichter* in 1893 (Munich). In 1906, as *Criminal Investigation,* it was published in London by Sweet and Maxwell. The book has been reprinted and revised many times. Gross is considered the other father of scientific crime detection.

5 The data regarding the number and condition of the latent fingerprints developed on the kidnap ladder by Dr. Hudson using his silver nitrate solution are from an interview of Det. Sgt. Cornel D. Plebani on July 16, 1984, at the Lindbergh Case Archives, New Jersey State Police Headquarters, West Trenton, N.J.

6 Plebani interview, July 16, 1984.

7 News stories and articles about the argument over the existence of the ransom note can be found in the March 8, 1932, editions of the *New York Daily Mirror* and the *New York Daily News.*

8 *New York Times,* March 14, 1932, p. 6.

9 In *Jafsie Tells All!* Condon mistakenly describes the baby's sleeping suit as twenty-four inches long. The error is picked up by George Waller in *Kidnap: The Story of the Lindbergh Case* (New York: Dial, 1961). I measured the suit at the Lindbergh Case Archives in West Trenton. It is twenty-eight inches long.

10 Some writers have suggested that the sleeping suit sent to Dr. Condon was not the one the Lindbergh baby was wearing on the night he was kidnapped. In an unpublished article on file at the Lindbergh Case Archives, entitled "The Prosecution of Bruno Richard Hauptmann: An Imitation of Falconry," James E. Starrs, professor of law and forensic sciences at George Washington University, notes that Dr. Denton type suits were commonplace in the 1930's. He also notes that the suit sent to Condon differed from the regular Dr. Denton suits in two ways: first, the one received by Condon had a pocket in the upper front portion, and second, the one mailed to Condon was made of wool while other Dr. Denton suits were made of wool and cotton. Starrs makes the point that these discrepancies were not thrashed out at the trial, where Colonel and Mrs. Lindbergh identified the sleeping suit as the baby's.

It should be noted, however, that the Lindberghs never said that the sleeping suit their son was wearing that night was identical to any particular type of Dr. Denton garment. These discrepancies do not, therefore, by themselves offer any proof of misidentification. The baby's sleeping suit was later sent to two private laboratories for analysis. In 1934, the Albert E. Edel Chemical and Toxicological Laboratory in Newark reported that a piece of the garment at the collar had been cut before it had been received by the lab. Professor Starrs notes that the missing piece of collar was never explained by the Hauptmann prosecution at the trial.

11 The New Jersey State Police later sent the sleeping suit to the E. R. Squibb Laboratories at New Brunswick, N.J. On May 27, 1932, the lab reported that the sleeping suit had been "freshly laundered" by someone outside the Lindbergh household.

12 Colonel Lindbergh's words have been

434   taken from Condon's book, *Jafsie Tells All!*, p. 109.

13   Ibid.
14   Ibid., p. 11.
15   Ibid, p. 127.

CHAPTER 6   "THE PAYOFF"

1   Lloyd Fisher, "The Case New Jersey Would Like to Forget," Part 1, *Liberty*, August 1, 1936, p. 9.
2   *New York Daily News*, March 25, 1932, p. 2.
3   *New York Daily News*, March 25, 1932, p. 4.
4   *New York Daily News*, March 26, 1932, p. 3.
5   *New York Daily News*, March 25, 1932, p. 4.
6   John F. Condon, *Jafsie Tells All!* (New York: Jonathan Lee, 1936), p. 135.
7   *New York Daily News*, April 2, 1932, p. 8.
8   George Waller, *Kidnap: The Story of the Lindbergh Case* (New York: Dial, 1961), pp. 70–71.
9   Fisher, "The Case New Jersey Would Like to Forget," Part 2, *Liberty*, August 8, 1936, p. 32.
10   Condon, *Jafsie Tells All!*, p. 148.
11   Ibid.
12   Ibid., pp. 155, 156, 158.

CHAPTER 7   "THE 'BOAD' NELLY"

1   George Waller, *Kidnap: The Story of the Lindbergh Case* (New York: Dial, 1961), p. 79.
2   Later, Lieutenant Finn of the New York City Police Department publicly criticized Condon for holding back the twenty thousand dollars. Finn said that if Condon hadn't done that, the case might have been solved sooner. In *Jafsie Tells All!* (New York: Jonathan Lee, 1936), Condon refers twice to this criticism. In explaining why he withheld the money, Condon writes: "It was because of my deep respect for his [Lindbergh's] courage and dignity and the brave, quiet way in which he raised seventy thousand dollars for cash—a task which most of those who read these words would find enormous—that I tried, later, to help him salvage some of that money. For this act, sharp criticism, even suspicion, were to fasten upon me" (p. 141).

Regarding Finn's criticism, Condon said: "I do not wish to cast disparagement on Lieutenant Finn's estimable qualities as a present-day Sherlock Holmes, but I do wish to say that, given the same set of circumstances, I would do again exactly what I did that night—I would save Colonel Lindbergh every possible penny" (p. 156).
3   John F. Condon, *Jafsie Tells All!* (New York: Jonathan Lee, 1936), pp. 170–172.
4   *New York Daily News*, April 4, 1932, pp. 3–4.
4   *New York Daily News*, April 5, 1932, p. 3.
6   Anne Morrow Lindbergh, *Hour of Gold, Hour of Lead: Diaries and Letters of Anne Morrow Lindbergh, 1929–1932* (New York: Harcourt Brace Jovanovich, 1973), p. 238.
7   *New York Times*, April 10, 1932, p. 1.
8   Lindbergh, *Hour of Gold, Hour of Lead*, pp. 238–239.
9   This account of how *The New York Times* found out who Jafsie was is the one given by Condon himself in *Jafsie Tells All!* George Waller disagrees. According to Waller, the *Bronx Home News* had Condon's permission to break the story of his role in the Lindbergh case (*Kidnap*, p. 85).
10   Condon, *Jafsie Tells All!*, p. 181.
11   Violet Sharpe's two-page statement of April 13, 1932, in question-and-answer form, is on file at the Lindbergh Case Archives, New Jersey State Police Headquarters, West Trenton, N.J. The statement does not indicate where the Peanut Grill is located and contains no information about what Violet and her companions did there. In *Kidnap*, George Waller says Violet told Walsh that the Peanut Grill was in Orangeburg, New York, and that while there she only drank coffee (p. 134). These things may be true, but they are not in Violet's April 13 statement.
12   This is according to the statement Violet gave to Inspector Walsh. According to George

Waller in *Kidnap*, Violet told Inspector Walsh that she didn't go out with Ernie on that day because it was raining too hard and she preferred to stay in. (p. 134).

13 Lindbergh, *Hour of Gold, Hour of Lead*, p. 239.

14 Edwin Hoyt, *Spectacular Rogue* (Indianapolis: Bobbs-Merrill, 1963), pp. 307–308.

15 Ibid., pp. 240–241.

CHAPTER 8 "LINDBERGH GOES TO SEA"

1 The description of the gang members, as provided by John Curtis, is taken from Part 2 of a seven-part series of articles by C. Lloyd Fisher, published in *Liberty* magazine from August 1, 1936, to September 12, 1936, entitled "The Case New Jersey Would Like to Forget." The gang-member descriptions appear on p. 33 of the August 8, 1936 issue.

2 Ibid.

3 Ibid, p. 31.

4 Ibid., Part 3 (August 15, 1933), p. 15.

5 Anne Morrow Lindbergh, *Hour of Gold, Hour of Lead: Diaries and Letters of Anne Morrow Lindbergh, 1928–1932* (New York: Harcourt Brace Jovanovich, 1973), pp. 242–243.

6 Fisher, "The Case New Jersey Would Like to Forget," Part 4, *Liberty*, August 22, 1936, p. 21.

7 Lindbergh, *Hour of Gold, Hour of Lead*, pp. 246–247.

CHAPTER 9 "THE BABY IN THE WOODS"

1 The activities of Fitzgerald and Zapolsky on Mount Rose Heights are documented in a one-page report, which they filed jointly dated May 12, 1932. This document is on file at the Lindbergh Case Archives, New Jersey State Police Headquarters, West Trenton, New Jersey.

2 Corp. Frank Kelly's May 12, 1932, grave-site report is on file at the Lindbergh Case Archives.

3 Harry W. Walsh, as told to E. Collins, "Hunt for the Kidnappers: Inside Story of the Lindbergh Case," *Jersey Journal*, November 18, 1932, p. 20, Part 4 of 8.

4 A photograph showing how the homemade nightshirt and the flannel remnant fit together is on display at the Lindbergh Case Archives.

5 A photograph of B. Altman woolen T-shirts, one from the grave and the other from a batch of ten purchased for the Lindbergh baby, was one of the Hauptmann prosecution's trial exhibits. A photograph of these shirts, shown side by side, is on display at the Lindbergh Case Archives.

6 Almost two years after the baby was found, the New Jersey State Police sent three groups of hair samples to the Edel Laboratory, a private, industrial facility owned by Albert Edel. The facility was located in Newark, New Jersey. In 1932, there were only a handful of major police labs in the United States. The only scientists making hair comparisons at the time were two private criminalists working on the West Coast (Oscar Heinrich and Luke S. May). The FBI crime lab did not exist in 1932. It wasn't operational until 1933 and didn't do hair-comparison work until several years later. As of 1968 there were only one hundred police crime labs in the United States.

To the Edel lab, the state police sent samples of hair from the corpse and hair taken from inside the burlap bag. Schwarzkopf asked that these two groups of hair be compared with known samples of the Lindbergh baby's hair. These known samples had been obtained from Mrs. Dwight Morrow, the child's grandmother, who had cut his hair on February 23, 1932. On December 31, 1934, the Edel Laboratory reported that all three groups of hair looked the same under a microscope. Since hair can't be individualized as fingerprints can, that is the closest identification possible with this type of evidence.

7 Inspector Walsh and Lieutenant Keaten filed a joint one-page report, dated May 12, 1932, regarding the finding of the body on Mount Rose Heights. This report is on file at the Lindbergh Case Archives.

8 The scene describing how Colonel

436

Schwarzkopf broke the news to Mrs. Lindbergh and her reaction to it is based upon a statement Schwarzkopf gave to the press at 6:45 P.M. on May 12, 1932, and reportage of the story on p. 1 of *The New York Times* on May 13, 1932.

9 The items found in the ten containers of gravesite debris were packaged and preserved in five glass vials sealed by corks. One vial contained a toenail. The second a heel bone, the third a piece of wool from the baby's shirt, the fourth an unidentified bone, and the fifth the four metatarsal bones. These bones were sent to the Albert E. Edel Chemical and Toxicological Lab in Newark on January 30, 1934. About a year later the lab reported that these bones were consistent with the skeletal remains of a twenty-month-old child.

The New Jersey State Police had also preserved, from the gravesite area, two pint-sized jars of leaves and hair that had been inside the burlap bag. And inside a small container about the size of a baby food jar was a piece of paper that had been found inside the burlap bag. This material was also subjected to laboratory analysis at the Edel facility. These eight jars still contain the material gathered from the gravesite and are available for inspection at the Lindbergh Case Archives.

10 Anne Morrow Lindbergh, *Hour of Gold, Hour of Lead: Diaries and Letters of Anne Morrow Lindbergh, 1929–1932,* (New York: Harcourt Brace Jovanovich, 1973), pp. 246–247.

11 In his statement, Colonel Schwarzkopf said: "The skull had a hole in it about the size of a quarter, just above the forehead." That was incorrect. The hole in the baby's head was smaller and located beneath the right earlobe. Schwarzkopf was probably referring to the hole made by Inspector Walsh when he poked the baby's head with a stick. Walsh had reported this mishap to Schwarzkopf, but for some reason, there was confusion over its size and location. Apparently Schwarzkopf had not examined the body himself—at least not carefully, and the autopsy had not yet been performed by Dr. Mitchell.

12 Betty Gow's identification of the Lindbergh baby is the subject of a one-page report dated May 12, 1932 by Det. Robert Coar and Samuel Leon. This report is on file at the Lindbergh Case Archives.

13 There has been considerable debate over whether Dr. Philip Van Ingen, the Lindbergh pediatrician, identified the remains in the morgue as the Lindbergh baby. According to a September 19, 1977, interview of Walter H. Swayze, the Mercer County coroner, when Dr. Van Ingen examined the body he identified the corpse as young Charles Lindbergh. The audio tape of this interview, conducted by Det. Sgt. Cornel D. Plebani, is part of the Lindbergh case files in West Trenton. At the time of the interview Swayze was seventy-four and suffering from lung cancer. He died less than a year later.

One of the first to argue that Dr. Van Ingen didn't identify the infant corpse was Harold G. Hoffman, the man who succeeded A. Harry Moore as governor of New Jersey. In 1938, almost two years after Bruno Hauptmann was executed for the Lindbergh crime, Hoffman published his series of articles about the case in *Liberty* magazine. In Part 12 of the series, published in the April 11, 1938, edition of the magazine, Hoffman wrote:

> Dr. Van Ingen, who, you will recall, made the examination of the child within two weeks prior to the crime, viewed the body at the morgue of County Coroner Walter H. Swayze, in Trenton on May 13, and refused to identify the body as being that of the Lindbergh child. He states (and I have the letter, in Dr. Van Ingen's handwriting, in my possession): *"The condition of the body is such that positive identification by me is impossible."* [p. 58, italics mine].

The argument that Dr. Van Ingen didn't identify the corpse was also advanced by crime writer Alan Hynd, who in 1949 wrote an article about the case, "Everyone Wanted to Get into the Act." In this article, first published in the March, 1949, edition of *True* magazine, Hynd wrote:

> The baby's doctor—Dr. Philip Van Ingen of New York—who had examined little

Charles only a couple of weeks before the kidnapping—took a long professional look at the body. "If someone were to come in here and offer me ten million dollars," he said to the coroner, "I simply wouldn't be able to identify these remains."

At Hauptmann's trial, the chief defense attorney conceded that the remains were those of the Lindbergh baby. As a result, the matter was not fully litigated and Dr. Van Ingen did not testify.

According to Detective Sergeant Plebani, the New Jersey State Police files on the case do not include any documentation from Dr. Van Ingen regarding his examination of the corpse.

14   At the time of the Lindbergh crime, only two jurisdictions in the U.S. had replaced the coroner system with a modern, more efficient medical examiner operation. New York City had formed the nation's first medical examiner's office in 1918. The other medical examiner's office, formed in 1926, was located in Newark, New Jersey, and was headed by Dr. Harrison S. Martland.

15   At Hauptmann's trial, Dr. Mitchell was asked if he knew of Dr. Gettler. Dr. Mitchell answered that he had never heard of him. This is indeed surprising.

16   Although Dr. Mitchell didn't know it, there was evidence that Dr. Van Ingen's measurement of the Lindbergh baby was inaccurate. The Dr. Denton sleeping suit the baby was wearing on the night of the kidnapping was twenty-eight inches long. Assuming that the garment was a proper fit and that the child's neck and head extended six or seven inches out of the garment, it's reasonable to estimate that the child was in fact much taller than Dr. Van Ingen's twenty-nine inches. From this it would seem that before he was killed, the Lindbergh baby was closer in height to Dr. Mitchell's rather than Dr. Van Ingen's measurements.

17   That Dr. Mitchell did not physically perform the autopsy on the Lindbergh baby has been a well-kept secret. Almost three years after the autopsy, Dr. Mitchell and Walter Swayze testified at Hauptmann's trial. There is nothing in their testimony that even hints of

the fact Dr. Mitchell talked Swayze through the operation.

The cat was let out of the bag in 1977 when the seventy-four-year-old Swayze was interviewed by Detective Sergeant Plebani. The results of this interview have not been published until now. The audio tape of this interview is on file at the Lindbergh Case Archives. According to Plebani, there are no documents written by Dr. Van Ingen or Dr. Mitchell in the Lindbergh files that confirm Swayze's story. Plebani knows of no other document that corroborates the fact that Dr. Mitchell did not physically perform the autopsy.

18   The conversation in the autopsy room has been drawn from the audio-taped interview of Coroner Walter Swayze carried out in 1977. Swayze's account is the only one, it is the only source relied upon. To fill out the scene, I had to infer what words were actually spoken, and by whom.

19   Although Dr. Mitchell had determined that the baby had not choked to death, he did not rule out asphyxia as a general cause of death. Asphyxia involves any death caused by lack of oxygen. Choking is just one type of asphyxia. Among other things, asphyxia can be brought on by drowning, strangulation, suffocation, and carbon monoxide poisoning. Dr. Mitchell did not rule out any of the above causes of death. He didn't, for example, examine the child's hyoid, which is a small bone located at the base of the neck. In cases of strangulation, this bone is usually broken.

20   In 1983, Dr. Mitchell's autopsy was reviewed by Dr. Michael M. Baden, Deputy Chief Medical Examiner, Suffolk County, Hauppauge, New York. Dr. Baden found Dr. Mitchell's autopsy lacking in many respects. Besides failing to rule out strangulation and suffocation as causes of death, Dr. Mitchell did not exclude the possibility that the baby had been shot through the head with a small-caliber firearm. Dr. Baden believes that it is highly unlikely that the child's skull could have been perforated by a stick. (Inspector Walsh's mishap). Dr. Baden also noted that skull fractures in themselves do not cause death. The cause of death in the Lindbergh case would have involved some kind of trauma to the brain, as evidenced by the blood clot beneath the skull fracture.

Dr. Baden presented his findings at the Plenary Session, 35th Annual Meeting of the American Academy of Forensic Sciences, held on February 15–19, 1983, at Cincinnati, Ohio. Part of Dr. Baden's presentation was published in the form of an article, "The Lindbergh Kidnapping: Review of the Autopsy," *Journal of Forensic Science*, October 1983.

21 In May 1932, the New Jersey State Police sent the baby's sleeping suit, the one that had been returned to the Lindberghs two weeks after the crime, to the E. R. Squibb Laboratory in New Brunswick, New Jersey. On May 27, 1932, the lab reported that there were no bloodstains on the garment. It was also determined that the sleeping suit had been laundered by someone other than Mrs. Lindbergh.

22 The absence of blood issue was raised by an attorney named Richard A. Knight in "Trial by Fury," *Forum Magazine*, January 1936. Knight pointed out that the lack of blood in the nursery proved that Bruno Hauptmann could not have struck the Lindbergh baby with a blunt instrument before taking him out of the window.

Knight's article, essentially an argument that Hauptmann had been unfairly tried, brought several responses from physicians who took issue with the lawyer's assumption that a violent blow to the head would leave bloodstains. In their letters to the editor, published in the February 1936 edition of *Forum,* the doctors pointed out that infant skull fractures seldom cause external bleeding. A Boston surgeon named Frederic J. Cotton wrote: "It just so happens that a baby's skull is a gristly, fibrous vault easily dented or crushed . . . So, it seems that the absence of bloodstains in the nursery does not, by itself, rule out the possibility that the Lindbergh child was beaten over the head in his crib."

23 After the sleeping suit was sent to the Squibb Laboratory, it was sent, on April 30, 1934, to the Albert E. Edel Chemical and Toxicological Laboratory in Newark. The suit was described at the Edel Lab as showing wear. A button was missing from the rear and another

button had a loose thread. In addition, bluish-purple marks were found on the garment. The Edel report does not elaborate further on these marks. There is no indication, however, that these marks were bloodstains.

24 In his 1938 article in *Liberty* magazine, Gov. Harold G. Hoffman included an excerpt from Dr. Mitchell's testimony at Gaston Means's June 8, 1932, swindling trial, Regarding the baby's skull, Dr. Mitchell said:

> It had an unclosed fontanelle. In other words, to make it clear to you, it is what is commonly known as the soft spot on the top of a child's head after birth, which usually closes within the first year, but in this case *the fontanelle was still open.* I made a measurement of the fontanelle, which was larger than normally should be present [The italics are Hoffman's. Harold G. Hoffman, "The Case—The Crime—The Challenge," Part 12, *Liberty* magazine, April 11, 1938, p. 58].

Dr. Mitchell's testimony was cited by Hoffman to prove that the body in the woods was too young to be the Lindbergh baby—further evidence of a misidentification.

CHAPTER 10 "A NEW BALLGAME"

1 The scene in which Colonel Lindbergh is given the news of his son's death has been fashioned from the following sources: Sidney B. Whipple, *The Lindbergh Crime* (New York: Blue Ribbon, 1935), pp. 98–99; George Waller, *Kidnap: The Story of the Lindbergh Case* (New York: Dial, 1961), p. 104; and Walter Ross, *The Last Hero: Charles A. Lindbergh,* rev. and enlarged ed. (New York: Harper and Row, 1976), chap. 17, "The Hauptmann Case."

2 C. Lloyd Fisher, "The Case New Jersey Would Like to Forget," Part 4, *Liberty,* August 22, 1936, p. 24.

3 Walter S. Ross, in *The Last Hero,* cites the morgue break-in as one of the reasons Colonel Lindbergh hated the press. Ross writes: "The most ghoulish incident took place when they [reporters] made into the Trenton morgue and pried up the lid of the baby's coffin to take pictures" (p. 227). In the original 1968 edition of the biography, Ross quotes the following Lindbergh response to a person who had defended the reporters on the case by saying that they were just doing their job: "Yes, and they were only doing their job when they pried the lid off my son's coffin to take pictures in the morgue." (p. 227). Since this quote did not appear in the revised edition of Ross' book, it is possible that Lindbergh, when he listed the errors in the first book and sent the list to Ross, denied making that statement. Lindbergh, in his own book, *Autobiography of Values* (edited and published by Harcourt Brace Jovanovich in 1977 following the Colonel's death in 1974), wrote: ". . . the child's body was found, not far from the roadside, in a wood only a mile or two from our house. It had been taken to a morgue in Trenton. I returned to New Jersey immediately. While I was en route, newspaper photographers broke in through a window of the morgue to take pictures of the child's remains" (p. 140).

The break-in was brought up at Hauptmann's trial during defense attorney Reilly's cross-examination of Dr. Mitchell. A photograph of a decomposed infant, lying in what appears to be a coffin, has appeared in several recent books on the Lindbergh case. Since the only New Jersey State Police photographs of the child were taken by Cpl. Frank Kelly at the gravesite, (there were no official autopsy photographs), this photograph was taken by an intruder. The corpse in this photograph is without a left leg from the knee down. The body is also without hands.

4 *New York Times,* May 14, 1932, p. 2.

CHAPTER 11 "CRITICISM"

1 Schwarzkopf's reason for not using bloodhounds was reported by former New Jersey Gov. Harold G. Hoffman in Part 8 of his article, "The Crime—The Case—The Challenge," *Liberty,* March 19, 1938, p. 54. According to Hoffman, Schwarzkopf stated these reasons in a letter to C. A. Norton, a Boston, Massachusetts City Councilman.

2 It is interesting to speculate on how the Lindbergh case would have turned out if the baby's body had been found before the ransom money had been paid. Since it was the passage of the ransom money that eventually led to the identification and capture of the kidnapper, it is possible that if the ransom money had not been paid, the case would never have been solved.

3 *New York Times,* May 14, 1932, p. 3.

4 Ibid.

5 Ibid.

6 John Henry Wigmore's *Treatise on Evidence* was first published in 1905. The second edition was published in five volumes in 1923; the third edition appeared in 1940 when he was seventy-seven. The third edition comprised ten volumes. This work has gained recognition as the standard in the legal field and is cited more than any work of its kind. Wigmore wrote several other books and, with August Vollmer, helped organize the Scientific Crime Detection Laboratory in Chicago in 1929. He and Vollmer were tireless crusaders for fingerprint technology, ballistics, questioned documents, the polygraph, and other forms of scientific crime detection.

7 Dunlap's article was published in the September 1932 edition of *The Detective.* It has been reprinted in Donald C. Dilworth, ed., *Silent Witness: The Emergence of Scientific Criminal Investigation* (Gaithersburg, Md.: International Association of Chiefs of Police, 1977), pp. 153–158.

CHAPTER 12 "THE HOAX"

1 Anne Morrow Lindbergh, *Hour of Gold, Hour of Lead* (New York: Harcourt Brace Jovanovich, 1973), p. 249.

2 C. Lloyd Fisher, "The Case New Jersey Would Like to Forget," Part 5, *Liberty,* August 29, 1936, p. 28.

3 Curtis's account of the interrogation and confession is in the series of articles by his attorney, C. Lloyd Fisher: "The Case New Jersey Would Like to Forget." This seven-part series was published by *Liberty* magazine in 1936. In Part 5, published on August 29, 1936, Curtis tells how the police promised not to publish any confession he made.

4 The Curtis statement is on file at the Lindbergh Case Archives, New Jersey State Police Headquarters, West Trenton, New Jersey. It was also published in full in the May 18, 1932 edition of the *New York Times,* p. 16. According to Curtis's account of the confession in Part 5 of Fisher's article, he repudiated the confession immediately after he wrote it. He is quoted in this article as saying: "There it is. It's a lie, but if it will serve your purposes and get me free, I am glad to give it to you."

5 In "The Case New Jersey Would Like to Forget," Fisher writes that Curtis said the following to Schwarzkopf and Keaten outside the Lindbergh house that morning: "We talked about my supposed confession, and I stated that I regretted that I had signed it—not only because if it was ever published I would be a ruined man, but because I hated to do it since it wasn't true."

6 One of Dobson-Peacock's stories to the press that Curtis claimed to be false was his claim that he had been held up by gangsters on the eighth floor of a New York City hotel on a visit to that city to meet Curtis.

7 *New York Daily News,* May 18, 1932, p. 8.

8 Fisher, "The Case New Jersey Would Like to Forget," Part 5, p. 29.

CHAPTER 13   "THE EXPERTS"

1 *New York Times,* May 19, 1932, p. 16.

2 John F. Condon, *Jafsie Tells All!* (New York: Jonathan Lee, 1936), p. 188; *New York Times,* May 21, 1932, pp. 1 and 16.

3 *New York Times,* May 17, 1932, p. 14.

4 Ibid.

5 *New York Times,* May 20, 1932, p. 9.

6 *New York Times,* May 21, 1932, p. 16.

7 Ibid.

8 The second edition of Albert S. Osborn's *Questioned Documents,* published in 1929 by the book's original publisher, Lawyer's Cooperative Publishing Company in Rochester,

N.Y., is still a standard in the field. As a vocation, questioned documents should be distinguished from graphology. Document examiners, unlike graphologists, do not determine personality traits from handwriting. Some graphologists, however, claim to be questioned documents examiners and are hired in questioned documents cases. Graphologists do not, however, have the necessary credentials for this type of work and are not generally recognized as questioned documents experts. In *Kidnap: The Story of the Lindbergh Case* (New York: Dial, 1961), George Waller refers to Albert S. Osborn as a graphologist (p. 141). Mr. Osborn is no doubt turning in his grave over this.

9 In 1947, Clark Sellers, a well-known West Coast questioned-documents examiner, wrote this about Albert S. Osborn: "Through his scientific procedures, which he disseminated widely, Osborn was the guiding light in making a recognized profession out of the questioned documents work. His leadership kept the United States in the forefront in scientific document investigation" ("Albert S. Osborn, *Journal of Criminal Law, Criminology and Police Science,* May–June, 1947, p. 76).

10 From June 1932 to September 1934, Albert S. Osborn gave his handwriting test to over three hundred people whose handwriting and spelling were compared with that in the fifteen ransom notes. None of these samples came close to matching the questioned writing.

CHAPTER 14   "VIOLET SHARPE"

1 The medical data concerning Violet Sharpe are based upon a statement given by her surgeon, Dr. Walter Philips, on June 16, 1932, at Alpine, NJ. This statement is on file at the Lindbergh Case Archives, New Jersey State Police Headquarters, West Trenton, N.J.

2 Italics mine. This letter is also on file at the Lindbergh Case Archives.

3 Harry W. Walsh, "Hunt for the Kidnappers: Inside Story of the Lindbergh Case, *Jersey Journal,* November 17, 1932, pp. 1, 10.

4 A copy of Violet Sharpe's thirteen-page

statement, dated May 23, 1932, is on file at the Lindbergh Case archives. This statement was also published, in full, in the June 12, 1932, edition of *The New York Times*.

5 Colonel Lindbergh's defense of Violet Sharpe and the lawmen's skepticism are based on the following sources: Harry W. Walsh, "Hunt for the Kidnappers: Inside Story of the Lindbergh Case," *New York Times*, November 17, 1932, pp. 1, 10; "Morrow Maid Ends Life; Suspected in Kidnapping," *New York Times*, June 11, 1932, p. 1. The actual dialogue used on this occasion is not known.

6 Violet Sharpe's letter to her friend, Fan Simons, dated June 7, 1932, is on file at the Lindbergh Case Archives. Her letter had not been altered except to add punctuation for clarity.

7 On the day following Violet Sharpe's suicide, Laura Hughes told the police about Violet's smile and wink following her identification of Ernest Brinkert's photograph. This portion of her statement was published on page 3 of the June 12, 1932, edition of *The New York Times*.

CHAPTER 15 "THE SUICIDE AND ITS AFTERMATH"

1 George Waller, *Kidnap: The Story of the Lindbergh Case* (New York, Dial, 1961), p. 150.

2 Harry W. Walsh, "Hunt for the Kidnappers: Inside Story of the Lindbergh Case," *Jersey Journal*, November 17, 1932, pp. 1, 10; *New York Times*, June 11, 1932, p. 1; and Waller, *Kidnap*, p. 150.

3 Violet Sharpe's familiarity with cyanide of potassium is explained by the fact that she had worked in the home of a silversmith in England.

4 Brinkert's comments regarding his fears about being beaten up by the New Jersey State Police were reported in the *White Plains Daily Reporter*, June 13, 1932, p. 3.

5 Walsh, "Hunt," p. 10.

6 "Brinkert Supported in Kidnapping Alibi; Next Figure in Case," *New York Times*, June 12, 1932, p. 1.

7 Walsh, "Hunt," p. 10.

8 Emily Sharpe's statements to the British press were reported on page 3 of the June 12 edition of the *New York Times*.

9 *New York Daily News*, June 13, 1932, p. 1.

10 *Manchester Guardian*, June 13, 1932, p. 1.

11 Sydney, Whipple, The Lindbergh Crime, (New York: Blue Ribbon Books, 1961), p. 138.

12 *New York Times*, June 12, 1932, p. 1.

13 *White Plains Daily Reporter*, June 13, 1932, p. 3.

14 Ibid.

15 The inventory of the things found in Violet Sharpe's room is on file at the Lindbergh Case Archives, New Jersey State Police Headquarters, West Trenton, N.J.

16 Anne Morrow Lindbergh, *Hour of Gold, Hour of Lead, Diaries and Letters of Anne Morrow Lindbergh, 1929–1932* (New York: Harcourt Brace Jovanovich, 1973), p. 272.

17 A year later, the FBI arrested Mean's accomplice, a disbarred lawyer and car thief named Norman Whitaker. He and Means were tried for conspiracy in connection with the additional thirty-five thousand they had tried to swindle out of Mrs. McLean. Means took the stand and unraveled a fantastic tale of his dealings with the kidnappers. The jury found Means and Whitaker guilty of trying to squeeze another thirty-five thousand out of Mrs. McLean. They were sentenced to two years each. Means's penalty was tacked onto the stretch he was already serving in the federal penitentiary.

18 George Payne's statement, dated June 17, 1932, is on file at the Lindbergh Case Archives.

19 *London Times*, June 30, 1932.

20 Sgt. A. E. Norman's February 10, 1936, report about Violet Sharpe and her relationship with William O'Brien is on file at the Lindbergh Case Archives. On August 1, 1984, in an interview of Det. Sgt. Cornel D. Plebani at the New Jersey State Police Headquarters in West Trenton, it was confirmed that the Lindbergh files show that Violet had been sexually intimate with five men during a period prior to the kidnapping.

CHAPTER 16 "A FLOUNDERING INVESTIGATION"

1 Walsh's statement about Condon at this press conference is quoted in Part 9 of Harold G. Hoffman's article, "The Crime—The Case—The Challenge," *Liberty* magazine, March 26, 1938. The press conference was held on May 18, 1932.

2 This description of Walsh's interrogation of Condon is based upon Condon's account of the incident in *Jafsie Tells All!* (New York: Jonathon Lee, 1936), pp. 190–200.

3 Fisher's seven-part article, "The Case New Jersey Would Like to Forget," is a detailed account of the John Hughes Curtis affair. The article appeared in the August and September 1938 editions of *Liberty* magazine. In 1935 and 1936 Fisher played a vital role in the defense of Bruno Richard Hauptmann.

4 In 1935 and 1936 Anthony Hauck and Joseph Lanigan were members of the team that prosecuted Bruno Richard Hauptmann. Both men had been born and raised in Flemington.

5 As late as November 1933, the police were investigating people Condon telephoned. On November 23, 1933, Sgt. E. A. Haussling of the New Jersey State Police received a report from the New York Telephone Company listing Condon's toll calls for the past six months. Condon had called thirteen people and they were checked.

6 Scotland Yard's interpretation of the ransom note's symbols was brought out at Hauptmann's trial by Prosecutor David Wilentz. Since Hauptmann didn't confess, it was never determined if he had intended to convey this secret meaning through his symbols. Hauptmann denied such an intention, claiming merely coincidence. Speaking of coincidence, on page 43 of the May 14, 1932, issue of *Time* magazine, there is a photograph of a German dramatist named Gerhart Hauptmann. Opposite this photograph, on page 42, is the story of the May 12 discovery of the Lindbergh baby's remains. Two and a half years later a Hauptmann would be arrested for the crime.

There is another possible connection between Hauptmann, a World War I machine gunner in the German Army, and the symbols on the ransom notes. The symbol of three interlocking circles is very similar to the rifle qualifications target for the German Army. The German target was made up of two solid black circles with a red circle, the bull's eye, overlaid in the middle.

7 Dr. Dudley Shoenfeld's November 10, 1932, memo is set out in his book, *The Crime and the Criminal: A Psychiatric Study of the Lindbergh Case* (New York: Covici, Friede, 1936), pp. 53–58.

CHAPTER 17 "TRACKING THE LADDER"

1 A year and a half later, in the summer of 1934, a few months before Bruno Hauptmann was arrested, Lieutenant Finn was promoted to First Grade Detective upon the recommendation of Deputy Inspector Sullivan. At the time Lewis Valentine was New York City's police commissioner.

2 The substance of Koehler's report is included in his article, "Technique Used in Tracing The Lindbergh Ladder," *Journal of Criminal Law and Criminology* 27, no. 5 (1937):712–724. Another detailed and technical account of Koehler's work with the ladder is: Skip, Palenik, "Microscopic Trace Evidence—The Overlooked Clue—Part IV Arthur Koehler—Wood Detective," *The Microscope,* First Quarter, 1983, pp. 1–14. This article includes many excellent photographs of Koehler's trial exhibits. Other accounts of Koehler's role in the Lindbergh case are found in: Henry Morton Robinson, *Science Catches the Criminal* (Indianopolis: Bobbs-Merrill, 1935), chapter 8, "Clues in the Woods"; and Edward D. Radin, *12 Against Crime,* (New York, G. P. Putnam's Sons, 1950), chapter 10, "Sawdust Trail."

3 Condon's viewing of Arthur Barry at Newark Police Department is chronicled on pages 210–211 of *Jafsie Tells All!* (New York: Jonathon Lee, 1936).

4 Harold G. Hoffman, "The Crime—The Case—The Challenge," Part 9, *Liberty,* March 26, 1938, p. 59.

5 Mrs. Lindbergh's book, *North to The Ori-*

ent, was published in 1935 by Harcourt, Brace and Company. Colonel Lindbergh drew the maps for it. The book became a best-seller.

6   John F. Condon, *Jafsie Tells All!* (New York: Jonathan Lee, 1936), p. 213.

7   FBI Agent Larimer's memo of the conference contains his view of how Lindbergh felt about Condon:

> Colonel Lindbergh made the remark that were Doctor Condon a younger man he would be immediately suspicious of him, but that in spite of Condon's age there were several little things that raised doubts as to Condon's sincerity. The Colonel was suspicious of Al Reich, who claimed that he had observed John jump the fence and . . . Lindbergh was not impressed with the arrangement whereby Condon and Al Reich were to make the contact (with the kidnapper) and deliver the money.

The text of Special Agent Larimer's memo regarding Colonel Lindbergh's view of John Condon is in Part 9 of Harold G. Hoffman's article, "The Crime—The Case—The Challenge," in the March 26, 1938, edition of *Liberty* magazine.

8   Harry W. Walsh, as told to E. Collins, "Hunt for The Kidnapper: The Inside Story of the Lindbergh Case," *Jersey Journal,* November 15, 16, 17, 19, 21, 22, 23, 1932.

9   Walsh wrote, "I believe that if the usual police procedures had been followed and the police taken in confidence to St. Raymond's Cemetery in the Bronx at the time Jafsie paid the ransom there, the arrest of the kidnappers would have been accomplished' (*Jersey Journal,* November 22, 1932).

10   In his article, Walsh wrote the following regarding Violet Sharpe: "I believe that if Violet Sharpe had been arrested because of the very strong suspicion that surrounded her, and held without bail or in bail so high it would have been difficult for her to raise the price of her release from detention, information of her knowledge, if she had any, would have been possible and her suicide would have been avoided" (*Jersey Journal,* November 17, 1932, p. 10).

Walsh noted that "Cemetery John" had told Condon that there were five kidnappers in the gang—three men and two women. Walsh wrote: "In my mind was the suspicion that one of the women in the second group might be Violet Sharpe" (*Jersey Journal,* November 17, 1932).

11   In 1935 Insp. Harry Walsh-became chief of the Jersey City Police Department.

12   In his 1976 book *Scapegoat,* Anthony Scaduto says that Leigh Matteson's idea was carried out by Lieutenant Finn. According to Scaduto, Finn and his men, after looking at all the motor vehicle cards in the Bronx that contained German names, ended up with forty-eight possible handwriting matches. Finn and his detectives then ran background checks on these forty-eight suspects. Scaduto says that although Bruno Richard Hauptmann's card would have been pulled, he was not one of the forty-eight investigated. If this were true, it illustrates that Finn should have listened to Albert S. Osborn.

According to Cornel D. Plebani, the official Lindbergh case archivist for the New Jersey State Police, nothing in the Lindbergh case files indicates that Matteson's idea was put into action. George Waller (*Kidnap: The Story of the Lindbergh Case* [New York: Dial, 1961], p. 238) and Dudley Shoenfeld(*The Crime and the Criminal: A Psychiatric Study of the Lindbergh Case* [New York: Covici-Friede, 1936], p. 34) agree with Plebani.

CHAPTER 18   "THE GOLD NOTE TRAIL"

1   The first ten-dollar gold note to be identified as part of the ransom money turned up in June 1932 in New Castle, Pennsylvania. After Hauptmann's arrest, when the $13,700 in ransom money had been found in his garage, it was determined that the farthest from New York City that any ransom bill was picked up was Chicago. This particular bill had come from a small town in Michigan. Later, several towns along the Mohawk and Cherry valleys in upstate New York reported the passage of ransom bills. Although rumor had it otherwise,

444

none of the ransom money surfaced outside the U.S. All together, excluding $2,000 worth of bills deposited in a New York City bank by a man using the name J. J. Faulkner, a person never identified, only fifty ransom bills were pulled out of circulation. About $1,000 worth of gold certificates, all in fives and tens, were passed in the New York City area between April 1932 and September 1934.

2   Subsequent handwriting analysis of the J. J. Faulkner deposit slip showed that the writing was not in the hand of Hauptmann, Isidor Fisch (the man Hauptmann claimed had given him the gold notes found in Hauptmann's garage), or any other person connected to the Lindbergh investigation. It was an investigation loose end that was never tied up.

3   According to Ludovic Kennedy, the author of *The Airman and the Carpenter* (New York: Viking, 1985), FBI Agent Sisk did not have a very high opinion of Lt. Arthur Keaten or Keaten's immediate supervisor, Capt. John J. Lamb.

4   A detailed account of the ransom bill passing incident at the Loew's Sheridan Theatre in Greenwich Village on November 26, 1933 can be found in: Alan Hynd, "The Real Story Behind The Lindbergh Capture," *True Detective Mysteries,* January, 1935, pp. 6–13, 96–100.

5   This is according to Andrew K. Dutch, the author of *Hysteria: Lindbergh Kidnap Case* (Philadelphia: Dorrance, 1975), p. 47.

6   According to some accounts of the case, a sales clerk who had seen the man tender the ten-dollar gold certificate and then abruptly leave the lumber store jotted down the license number of the man's car. Six months later, after Bruno Richard Hauptmann's arrest, this clerk looked up the license number and found it belonged to Hauptmann.

7   This was the second time in the Lindbergh investigation that the press had consented, in the interest of the police, to suppress the news. The first time was when they had halted further publication of the ransom bills' serial numbers that had been leaked to a paper that had printed them. In that incident a reporter for the *Newark Evening News* had obtained the list of several numbers from a bank employee.

This happened before the Lindbergh baby was found dead. After that, the serial numbers were made public.

8   This description of Condon's spotting of John is based upon his account of the incident in *Jafsie Tells All!* (New York: Jonathan Lee, 1936), pp. 215–218.

9   John Condon would continue to embarrass those associated with the Lindbergh investigation. After Hauptmann's conviction Condon would lecture church and civic groups on the case. Following that, he announced a hundred city vaudeville tour, billing himself as "The Most Enigmatic, and Colorful Personality in America." Condon's show-business career never got off the ground. After two appearances in New Jersey, a third was cancelled because of protests by the local clergy. In defense of Condon's venture into the entertainment world, Condon said that he was just recouping some of the thousands of dollars he had spent in his quest for the kidnapper.

10   Kennedy, *The Airman and the Carpenter,* pp. 159–160.

11   According to Ludovic Kennedy, Capt. John J. Lamb of the New Jersey State Police resented having to cooperate with the FBI and the New York City Police Department.

CHAPTER 19   "THE ARREST"

1   The original ransom bills circular was so cumbersome that the FBI had devised a simplified form for bank clerks and merchants, which was printed on a card.

2   It has been written in many places that Hauptmann, some time after the kidnapping, had his car repainted. This is not true. In April of 1932, Hauptmann had his car's taillight repaired and the rear springs reset. The Dodge's mudguards were painted at this time. This is how the story got started that Hauptmann's Dodge had been repainted after the crime.

3   On June 5, 1984, Det. Sgt. Cornel D. Plebani, with the author in the car, retraced the route taken by Bruno Richard Hauptmann from his house to the point of his arrest on the morning of September 19, 1934. That aspect of this account of Hauptmann's arrest is based upon that experience.

4 Besides Finn, Keaten, and Sisk, the arresting party consisted of New Jersey officers Dennis Duerr, William Horn, and John Wallace; New York officers William Wallace and Chester Cronin; and FBI agent William Seery.

5 The fact that the ransom bill found on Hauptmann was folded into eight sections would later become an extremely important point. This is because Hauptmann would later assert that he had no knowledge of the ransom money prior to August 1934. The fact that the twenty in his wallet was folded just like the bill passed prior to August 1934 tends to contradict his assertion.

Those who argue Hauptmann's innocence like to emphasize that the bill taken from Hauptmann at the time of his arrest was not folded like the ones passed in 1933 and early 1934. When asked about this in the summer of 1984, Det. Sgt. Plebani, the official Lindbergh archivist with the New Jersey State Police, stated emphatically that the twenty in Hauptmann's wallet was folded just like the one that had been passed in November 1933 at the Loew's Sheridan Theater in Greenwich Village.

6 "Hauptmann Alibi Offered by Wife," *New York Times,* September 23, 1934, p. 1.

7 This account of Hauptmann's explanation to his wife that he was under arrest because of gambling problems is based upon information received in the summer of 1984 from Det. Sgt. Cornel Plebani.

8 It was later determined that Hauptmann had, prior to 1932, hunted on a chicken farm near Flemington, New Jersey. This site was only a few miles from the Lindbergh estate.

9 The fact that Hauptmann had been in possession of a ransom note in December 1933 was important because he would later say that he had not touched the money until August 1934. The police questioned Miss Rauch's daughter, Mrs. Laura Uruant, and she confirmed that Hauptmann had paid his rent with gold notes (*New York Times,* September 28, 1934, p. 8).

10 Ibid.

11 This account of how Agent Sisk noticed

Hauptmann looking out his bedroom windows is based upon Sisk's January 17, 1935, testimony at Hauptmann's trial.

12 George Waller, *Kidnap: The Story of the Lindbergh Case* (New York: Dial, 1961), p. 223.

CHAPTER 20 "THE INTERROGATION"

1 The Lindberghs' reaction to the news of Hauptmann's arrest is chronicled in Leonard Mosley, *Lindbergh: A Biography* (Garden City, N.Y.: Doubleday, 1976), p. 185.

2 About three months after Hauptmann's arrest, Schwarzkopf sent sweepings from his car trunk to the Edel Laboratory in Newark. A few weeks later the laboratory reported they had found nothing in Hauptmann's car that linked him to either the Lindbergh estate or the baby. Since the crime had been committed two and a half years before Hauptmann's car was searched, it was not surprising that the vehicle contained no evidence. On January 7, 1935, the New Jersey State Police sent Hauptmann's coat, shoes, and several other garments to the Edel Lab. Again, the results were negative.

3 Excerpts from Hauptmann's interrogation have been taken from the transcripts of his interview dated September 19, 1934. A copy of this transcript is on file at the Lindbergh Case Archives, New Jersey State Police Headquarters, West Trenton, N.J. It should be noted that I have taken the liberty of tightening some of the excerpted parts of Hauptmann's interrogation by removing repetitious questions and answers and by deleting certain questions and responses that were not particularly relevent. The order of the questions and their answers has not been changed, and the questions and answers themselves have not been altered in any way.

4 Albert S. Osborn's test handwriting paragraph reads:

We were not near Smith Hall where the robbery took place, between 6 and 12 by our time. During all the time I was out of the house, but later came home. Did you not write letters to New York sending back anything that was stolen from Dr. Conway? Please keep those letters and papers, they will be good for something later maybe. One of the letters said, Dr. Sir, Thank you for the bills and your money. We will send back the bills later perhaps. Where shall we send them, the address we lost? Be at home every night so you will hear from us. You cannot tell when that will be.

5 Regarding the missing chisel from Hauptmann's tool chest, Anthony Scaduto, the author of *Scapegoat,* writes that Hauptmann owned two or three three-quarter- inch chisels at the time of his arrest. Scaduto suspects that the police took a three-quarter-inch chisel from Hauptmann's tool chest and removed two others this size from his garage so that when Arthur Koehler, the wood expert, later examined the evidence he would find a three-quarter-inch chisel missing from Hauptmann's tool supply. Scaduto knows that the crime scene chisel was a Bucks Brothers brand, while all of the chisels possessed by Hauptmann were either Stanley or National Tool brand. According to Koehler, however, Hauptmann, at the time of his arrest, possessed a quarter inch Bucks Brothers chisel. (Koehler, "Technique Used in Tracing the Lindbergh Ladder," *Journal of Criminal Law and Criminology,* January– February, 1937, p. 717).

6 This conversation is based upon a FBI memo written by Special Agent Thomas Sisk. According to Ludovic Kennedy, Perrone had previously identified a man named Chetel and various others as the man who had handed him the note for Condon. Kennedy also asserts that even Colonel Schwarzkopf considered Perrone an unbelievable witness (Kennedy, *The Airman and the Carpenter: The Lindbergh Kidnapping and the Framing of Bruno Richard Hauptmann* [New York: Viking, 1985], p. 176).

7 The following officers witnessed Perrone's identification of Hauptmann at the Greenwich Police Station: Colonel Schwarzkopf, Capt. John J. Lamb, Thomas Sisk, Arthur Keaten,

William Wallace (New York City Police Department), John Wallace (New Jersey State Police), Sam Leon, Leon Turrou, Captain Bennet, William Seery, William Horn, John Duane, and Sylvester McCaskety.

8 The following officers witnessed the taking of Hauptmann's handwriting samples and their signatures appear on the samples themselves: Sgt. Thomas G. Ritchie, Colonel Schwarzkopf, Det. William Horn, Thomas Sisk, Insp. John Lyons, Detective Finn, Det. James Cashman, and Det. Phillip Cremar.

9 Turrou's account of the Lindbergh case is reprinted in *Crusade Against Crime* Jerry D. Lewis, ed. (New York: Bernard Geis Associates, 1962), "The Lindbergh Tragedy," pp. 156–157. Regarding Hauptmann's handwriting samples sent to the FBI lab, Turrou writes: "At 8:30 the next morning, Charlie Appel, Head of the FBI Laboratory called. 'Congratulations,' he said, simply. 'It checks.'"

10 In 1921, the U.S. Treasury Department became the first federal agency to create a crime laboratory and the position of Document Examiner. Bert C. Farrar was the department's first questioned documents expert. Farrar was not one of the eight document examiners who testified at Hauptmann's trial, and as such is not usually associated with the Lindbergh case. Farrar was held back with three other handwriting experts as a possible rebuttal witness. His testimony was not needed.

11 On the night the body of the Lindbergh baby was discovered, Bruno Richard Hauptmann was with some of his friends. The subject of the Lindbergh case came up and one of the group remarked, "Now they [the police] will arrest the person responsible." Hauptmann than replied, "If the one who kidnapped the child doesn't talk, how will they arrest him?"

This anecdote was told by John Wallace, a retired New Jersey state police officer who had played an active role in the Lindbergh case. Wallace told the story to Det. Cornel D. Plebani, who interviewed him in June, 1981, when Wallace was eighty years old. Wallace said that the story was told to him by Hauptmann's best friend, Hans Kloppenburg. I reviewed a tape of this interview on July 31, 1984. It is on file at the Lindbergh Case Archives, New Jersey State Police Headquarters, West Trenton, New Jersey. Wallace died, following a stroke, in September 1985 at the age of eighty-four.

CHAPTER 21 "THE FISCH STORY"

1 The date, generally, when Hauptmann wired his garage is according to Laura Uruant, the daughter of Hauptmann's landlady. Mrs. Uruant's comments about Hauptmann's garage-lighting system were published in the September 28, 1934 edition of *The New York Times*, p. 8.

2 The questions and answers in this section have been excerpted from the official transcript of Hauptmann's interrogation, which is on file at the Lindbergh Case Archives, New Jersey State Police Headquarters, West Trenton, N.J.

3 The fact that the discovery of the ransom money in Hauptmann's garage was staged for Mrs. Hauptmann was never made part of the official Lindbergh case record. This information was disclosed in June 1981 when John Wallace, then eighty years old, was interviewed by Cornel Plebani. An audio tape of this interview is on file at the Lindbergh Case Archives. Wallace retired from the New Jersey State Police as a captain in 1952. Wallace was one of the men who arrested Hauptmann in Manhattan and was in the garage when the $11,930 in ransom money was discovered.

4 In his book, *Secrecy and Power: The Life of J. Edgar Hoover* (New York: The Free Press, 1987), Richard Gid Powers writes:

> Hoover rushed to New York so he could stand beside New York Commissioner John F. O'Ryan . . . during the announcement of the Hauptmann arrest. He was also able to pose for photographs shaking hands with Special Agent T. H. Sisk and the other two agents on the New York Lindbergh squad. . . . The *Washington Star*'s caption with this picture was that Hoover and his men were the "Justice

Board of Strategy in Lindbergh Case." Rex Collier's story credited the "Sherlocks of the Justice Department" with trapping Hauptmann, and said that Hoover had supervised the interrogation. "The coolest customer I've ever seen," was Hoover's analysis of Hauptmann's character. (p. 194)

5 This is according to a memo authored by FBI Agent Leon G. Turrou, who reported that after hanging up the telephone, Schwarzkopf turned to the other officers in the room and said, "It doesn't look so good. He [Albert D.] says that when he first looked at the specimens [the known handwriting samples and the ransom notes] he thought they were the same [all written by Hauptmann], and that there were some striking similarities, but after examining them for a while, he found a lot of dissimilarities, which outweighed the similarities, and is convinced he (Hauptmann) did not write the ransom notes." The text of this FBI memo, discovered in 1982, is excerpted in an article by Tom Zito entitled, "Did the Evidence Fit the Crime?" *Life Magazine*, March, 1982, pp. 48–49.)

According to the above memo, when the younger Osborn learned that a large portion of the ransom money had been found in Hauptmann's garage, he changed his mind. Turrou wrote: "Within an hour Mr. Osborn [Albert S.] called the undercover squad headquarters. . . and advised that he and his son had positively decided that Hauptmann wrote the ransom letters."

Agent Turrou concludes his memo by writing that "There was. . . laughing [apparently among the police officers present] as to the ability of handwriting experts, it being pointed out that the Osborns did not make the identification until after the money was found."

In *The Airmen and the Carpenter*, pp. 178–182, Ludovic Kennedy also asserts that Albert D. Osborn at first didn't think that Hauptmann had written the ransom notes. According to Kennedy, Albert D. changed his mind after his father decided that Hauptmann was the ransom note writer.

    CHAPTER 22 "THE LINEUP"

1 The conversations and actions that took place at the Condon-Hauptmann lineup confrontation are based upon the official New York City Police Department transcript of the event.

2 Ludovic Kennedy, *The Airman and the Carpenter: The Lindbergh Kidnapping and the Framing of Bruno Richard Hauptmann* (New York: Viking, 1985), p. 190.

3 John F. Condon, *Jafsie Tells All!* (New York: Jonathan Lee, 1936), p. 220.

4 Ibid, p. 221.

5 Ibid., pp. 221–224.

6 Inspector Lyon's impatience with Condon at the lineup is reflected in the accounts of the incident by Condon himself and by FBI agent Leon G. Turrou, who was present. Turrou writes: "Instead of trying to identify the suspect, Condon got into squabbles with Inspector Lyons, of the New York City police, and others" ("The Lindbergh Tragedy," in *Crusade Against Crime,* ed. Jerry D. Lewis, [New York: Bernard Geis, 1962], p. 157.)

7 Condon, *Jafsie Tells All!,* p. 224.

8 There are several theories why Condon equivocated at the lineup. His own explanation is as follows:

> Hauptmann, from the moment of his arrest, was being tried in the newspapers. Because I happened to be the one man who had met and talked with him face to face during the ransom negotiations, I had no desire to add to the crushing weight of my testimony at the time.
>
> At the proper time—and only at the proper time—would I declare my identification. The proper time, in my opinion, would be when I stepped upon the witness stand, under oath at his trial. Condon, *Jafsie Tells All!,* (p. 226)

The problem with this explanation is that at the time Condon was not "declaring his identification," the newspapers were not crucifying Hauptmann. The press was, at this time, just learning of his arrest and the discovery of the money in his garage. It seems odd that Condon would take it upon himself to be so protective of Hauptmann, the man who was accused of kidnapping and presumably killing the son of his hero, Colonel Lindbergh.

Another theory is that Condon, ham that he was, was simply milking his part. His refusal to identify Hauptmann until the trial was, according to this theory, a supreme act of showmanship.

There is also the theory, expressed by Dr. Dudley Shoenfeld, the New York City psychiatrist, that Dr. Condon's refusal to declare his identification of Cemetery John was his revenge against the New Jersey and New York City police who had treated him roughly. Dudley D. Shoenfeld, *The Crime and the Criminal: A Psychiatric Study of the Lindbergh Case* [New York: Covici-Friede, 1936], p. 40).

Finally, there were many who believed that Condon had looked at so many lineups and mugshots over the two-and-a-half-year period that he was virtually useless as a credible eyewitness. Because he wasn't sure in his own mind Hauptmann was Cemetery John, he couldn't, in good conscience, positively identify him at the lineup. This theory holds that Condon came through for the Hauptmann prosecution at the trial because if he hadn't, he would have been charged as Hauptmann's accomplice.

There is of course, the possibility that Condon's actions were based upon a mixture of some or all of these motivations.

9 The conversation between Condon and Turrou after the lineup is excerpted from Turrou's September 21, 1934, FBI memo, numbered 62-3057. A copy of this two-page document is on file at the Lindbergh Case Archives. It is interesting to note that Condon did not refer to this conversation in *Jafsie Tells All!*

10 Hauptmann's arrest record is on file in the Lindbergh Case Archives.

CHAPTER 23 "THE THIRD DEGREE"

1 *New York Daily News,* September 22, 1934, p. 6.

2 *New York Times,* September 28, 1934, p. 8.

3 *New York Times,* September 22, 1934, p. 1. A complete copy of Albert S. Osborn's report is on file at the Lindbergh Case Archives, New Jersey State Police Headquarters, West Trenton, N.J.

4 Ibid., p. 4.

5 "Hauptmann Alibi Offered by Wife," *New York Times,* September 23, 1934, p. 1.

6 Hauptmann's comments to his wife about being beaten are based upon the statements Mrs. Hauptmann made to Anthony Scaduto in 1975 when he was writing *Scapegoat: The Lonesome Death of Bruno Richard Hauptmann* (New York: G. P. Putnam's Sons, 1976). Mrs. Hauptmann's statements about the beatings are on p. 442.

7 This invented dialogue revealing Hauptmann's apparent interest in trading a confession for leniency is based upon two letters from Leon G. Turrou to Harold R. Olson dated January 24 and March 21, 1977. In the March 21 letter Turrou writes:

> During the many interviews I had with him [Hauptmann] when he was imprisoned in the Bronx County Jail, he once asked me what leniency he would get if he would confess. I told him that I had no right to make such a promise to him, because it was not, at that time, a federal offense. However, I told him, I would bring this to the attention of the State prosecutor and because of his confession he might receive leniency. That shut him up as a clam and during the entire investigation he refused to answer any questions.

Copies of these letters are on file at the Lindbergh Case Archives.

8 *New York Times,* September 23, 1934, p. 26. James T. Berryman was a political cartoonist for the *Washington Star.*

9 In 1936, after Hauptmann was convicted but before he was executed, Governor Hoffman took it upon himself to reinvestigate the kidnapping/murder. Pursuant to his inquiry, he asked the New Jersey State Police to supply his office with a variety of material, including numerous reports, associated with the investigation. Since he was obviously in possession of Dr. Dexter's medical report in 1938 when he wrote his article, it is not surprising that the document is not with the other Lindbergh Case material still in the hands of the New Jersey State Police. (Governor Hoffman's papers, twenty-one thousand documents, were found in the fall of 1985 and turned over to the New Jersey State Police. Dr. Dexter's report was among this data.)

10 A copy of Dr. John H. Garlock's report, dated September 22, 1934, is on file at the Lindbergh Case Archives.

11 The New Jersey State Police officers assigned to guard the Lindbergh estate were William Sawyer, Joseph Wolf, and John Gens.

12 *New York Daily News,* September 24, 1934. *The New York Times* reported Dr. Meyer's story in a slightly different way. According to the *Times* account, Dr. Meyer saw Hauptmann's photograph in the paper and recognized him as a former patient. He then checked his files and called the police.

13 *New York Times,* September 25, 1934, p. 2.

14 *New York Times,* September 24, 1934, p. 2.

15 Ibid.

16 *New York Times,* September 24, 1934, p. 1.

CHAPTER 24   "THE SECRETS OF THE HAUPTMANN HOUSE"

1 *The New York Times,* September 25, 1934, p. 3.

2 Inspector Bruckman's motive for having the trim board removed is documented in his January 18, 1935, testimony at Hauptmann's trial.

3 The account of the Foley-Hauptmann interrogation is excerpted from Benjamin Arac's notes.

4 Hauptmann's appearance in Foley's office is based upon my observations of photographs of him taken just after he left the office.

5 *New York Times,* September 25, 1934, p. 3.

6 *New York Times,* September 26, 1934, p. 2.

7 Lieutenant Bornmann's September 26, 1934, memo is on file at the Lindbergh Case Archives.

8 This exchange was recorded by Benjamin Arac.

9 "Suspect Assets, Losses and Ransom Bills So Far Traced Reach Nearly $50,000 Total" *New York Times,* September 27, 1934, p. 2. For a more detailed breakdown of Hauptmann's financial transactions, see: Sidney B. Whipple, *The Trial of Bruno Richard Hauptmann: Edited with a History of the Case,* New York: Doubleday Doran, 1937), pp. 58–59.

CHAPTER 25   "A TRUE BILL IN NEW YORK"

1 Lindbergh's statement to Foley about recognizing John's voice is taken from the transcript of the Bronx grand jury hearing, September 26, 1934.

2 Walter S. Ross, *The Last Hero: Charles A. Lindbergh,* rev. and expanded ed. (New York: Harper and Row, 1976), p. 215.

3 *New York Times,* September 27, 1934, p. 2.

4 Ibid, p. 1.

5 Lindbergh's statements in Foley's office regarding the identification of Hauptmann's voice have been taken from Benjamin Arac's notes of the meeting. On January 3, 1935, Colonel Lindbergh repeated this identification in his testimony at Hauptmann's trial.

6 Ross, *The Last Hero,* p. 215.

7 Two of the people questioned in Foley's office on September 27, 1934, were John Braue, a clerk at the Radio City Doughnut Shop, and Miss Anita Lutzenberg, a saleswoman at Oppenheim, Collins, and Company. Braue and Lutzenberg had canoed with Hauptmann at Hunter's Island.

8 *New York Times,* September 28, 1934,

p. 8: *New York Daily News,* September 28, 1934, p. 3.

9 *New York Times,* September 28, 1934, p. 8.

10 The conversation among the guard, Sheriff Hanley, and Hauptmann is based upon detailed reportage of the incident in *The New York Times:* "Blade Made by Hauptmann Found Hidden in His Cell," September 29, 1934, p. 1. The exact words in the text reflect my reconstruction of what was said.

11 Albert S. Osborn's October 5, 1934, letter to District Attorney Foley is on file at the Lindbergh Case Archives. In *Scapegoat: The Lonesome Death of Bruno Richard Hauptmann* (New York: G. P. Putnam's Sons, 1976), Anthony Scaduto asserts that the Osborns were taking an active role in the Hauptmann investigation. They were, in Scaduto's opinion, therefore diminishing their roles and credibility as independent scientists.

12 Whited's responses to Detective Coar's questions are contained in his report dated April 26, 1932. This document is on file at the Lindbergh Case Archives, New Jersey State Police Headquarters, West Trenton, N.J.

13 The names of the other ten men in Hauptmann's lineup and the officers who had witnessed Whited's identification are in a New York City Police Department report dated October 6, 1934. It is on file at the Lindbergh Case Archives.

14 Fawcett's questioned-documents investigator was Aaron R. Lewis. Fawcett was replaced as Hauptmann's attorney a month later. Although other handwriting experts would look at the ransom notes on behalf of the defense, it is not known if Aaron R. Lewis was one of them. It should be remembered that the first questioned-documents examiner approached by Fawcett, J. Vreland Haring, looked at the writings and declared that the ransom notes had been written by Hauptmann. Haring then offered his services to the prosecution and Fawcett looked for another expert.

15 *New York Times,* October 7, 1934, p. 28.

CHAPTER 26 "AN INDICTMENT IN NEW JERSEY"

1 In New York, a fairly representative state, the sentence for kidnapping was ten to fifty years. In nine states, it was punishable by life imprisonment.

2 In *Scapegoat: The Lonesome Death of Bruno Richard Hauptmann* (New York: G. P. Putman's Sons, 1976), Anthony Scaduto takes the position that the FBI pulled out of the case as a gesture of disgust over the manner in which Hauptmann was being framed by the New Jersey State Police and David Wilentz.

3 In 1983, the possibility that the Lindbergh baby had been shot through the head was considered by Dr. Michael M. Baden, the deputy chief medical examiner of Suffolk County, New York. According to Dr. Baden, death by gunshot to the head was not ruled out by Dr. Charles Mitchell, the Mercer County physician. In Dr. Baden's opinion, Dr. Mitchell's autopsy was so incomplete that the cause of the baby's death was never really established.

4 Robert Hicks's October 15, 1934, report and his cover letter to Colonel Schwarzkopf, as well as a drawing of his model skull, are on file in the Lindbergh Case Archives, New Jersey State Police Headquarters, West Trenton, N.J.

5 This was not the last Schwarzkopf would hear of Robert Hicks. A year later he would be back into the case, this time on behalf of the Hauptmann defense.

6 The direct quotes from Hauptmann's extradition hearing have been taken from transcripts in the October 16, 1934, editions of the *New York Times* (p. 18) and the *New York Herald Tribune* (pp. 14 and 15).

7 *New York Herald Tribune* (October 16, 1934) p. 15.

8 Anthony Scaduto and Ludovic Kennedy believe that the Reliance Property Management Company had payroll records for the first half of March 1932, and that these records proved that Hauptmann had worked at the Majestic Apartments from 8:00 A.M., to 5:00 P.M. on March 1, 1932. In *The Airman and the Carpenter: The Lindbergh Kidnapping and the Framing of Richard Hauptmann* (New York: Viking, 1985) Kennedy charges that this evidence was suppressed by the Bronx district attorney's office with Wilentz's knowledge. Kennedy says that the timesheets were in a safe in Assistant District Attorney Breslin's office. Both authors assert that the records produced by Howard Knapp were altered to show that Hauptmann began work on March 21, 1932.

9 In *The Airman and the Carpenter,* Kennedy implies that the records of the Reliance Property Management Company show that Hauptmann started work at the Majestic on March 1. Photographs of these records, published in the October 18, 1934, edition of the *New York Daily News,* only show that Hauptmann was hired on February 27, 1934.

10 The description of the interior of the Flemington Jail is based upon a series of slides of the facility I viewed at the Lindbergh Case Archives on July 17, 1984. These slides were presented by Det. Cornel D. Plebani, who offered additional details about the jail and Hauptmann's stay there.

11 The Daily Guard Detail Memos written by Stockberger and Smith from October 20, 1934, to February 16, 1935, are on file at the Lindbergh Case Archives.

12 Shortly after New Jersey's Lindbergh files were opened to the public in 1981, and the existence of the daily guard detail memos discovered, a reporter for the *New York Times* wrote, "Hauptmann, his wife and attorneys apparently had no idea they were being overheard, although they sometimes voiced suspicions. The clandestine monitoring was done by officers fluent in German, the language Hauptmann and his wife usually used" (*New York Times,* December 6, 1981, p. 61).

The Hauptmanns later became suspicious of the state troopers: "Do not talk so loud," Mrs. Hauptmann said. "I read in a German paper that our conversations were being overheard." Lieutenant Allen would later be assigned a seat at Hauptmann's trial next to the defendant, where he could overhear conversations between Hauptmann and his wife.

13 *New York Times,* October 20, 1934, p. 1.

CHAPTER 27   "GEARING UP FOR TRIAL"

1   Joseph Furcht's three-page affidavit, dated October 23, 1934, is on file at the Lindbergh Case Archives.

2   There are two firsthand accounts of the Condon-Hauptmann confrontation at the Hunterdon County Jail. One is found in Hauptmann's unpublished autobiography, as discussed in Scaduto's *Scapegoat*, pp. 450–452. The other is Condon's account, published in *Jafsie Tells All!* (New York: Jonathan Lee, 1936), pp. 230–236. The meeting was also reported in the October 25, 1934, edition of the *New York Daily News*. Since Condon's book and Hauptmann's autobiography are both self-serving, they tell two different accounts of the meeting. Hauptmann says that Anthony Hauck was present; Condon has Wilentz on the scene. Except for some minor modifications, the account related here is based upon Condon's version of the visit.

3   According to Hauptmann's account of his visit with John Condon, Condon had shouted, "No! I cannot testify against this man! I will not testify against him!" It should be noted that in Governor Hoffman's account of the visit, an account biased in favor of Hauptmann, there is no mention of such an exclamation. (Harold Hoffman, "The Crime—The Case—The Challenge," *Liberty Magazine*, February 12, 1938, p. 24.

4   *New York Daily News*, October 25, 1934.

5   Mrs. Hauptmann's dealings with the *New York Journal* were through reporters Jeanette Smith and Jacob Clements.

6   Edward Francis Morton's two-page statement, dated November 8, 1934, is on file at the Lindbergh Case Archives. Scaduto, Kennedy, and others claim that Morton's timekeeper records had been fudged to show that Hauptmann did not work on April 2, 1932. They believe that he was on the job that day.

7   In a letter to August Vollmer, the progressive chief of the Berkeley Police Department, Albert S. Osborn wrote, ". . . The handwriting evidence is very strong indeed, one of the most positive cases that I had ever had. There are, of course, fourteen documents with plenty of standard writing" (Albert S. Osborn to August Vollmer, November 16, 1934; Bancroft Library, University of California at Berkeley).

The other five questioned-documents examiners lined up to testify against Hauptmann were Albert D. Osborn, J. Vreeland Haring, and J. Howard Haring of Newark; Bert C. Farrar of the Treasury Department; and Wilmer T. Souder of the National Bureau of Standards.

8   Lieutenant Smith's Guard Detail Memo of January 1, 1935, on file at Lindbergh Case Archives, New Jersey State Police Headquarters, West Trenton, N.J.

CHAPTER 28   "THE PROSECUTION BEGINS"

1   In describing the first few days of the trial, I have relied heavily upon newspaper articles by Special Correspondent Russell B. Porter of the *New York Times*.

2   *New York Times*, January 3, 1935, p. 4.

3   When Mrs. Spencer was questioned by the FBI on December 23, 1934, she claimed that she had no idea who had mailed her book to the 150 prospective jurors. She said that 250 of the 26,000 books in print had been sent to a man named Colonel Hutchinson in New York City a year before the trial. "The whole thing was just a satire," she said. "It was entirely fictional, all the characters and incidents, and was intended merely to be funny" (*New York Times*, December 24, 1934, p. 4).

4   *New York Times*, January 3, 1935, p. 5.

5   *New York Times*, January 4, 1935, p. 6.

6   *New York Times*, January 3, 1935, p. 3.

7   Sidney B. Whipple, *The Trial of Bruno Richard Hauptmann: Edited with a History of the Case* (New York: Doubleday, Doran, 1937), pp. 95–103.

8   In *Get Me Geisler* (New York: Belmont Books, 1962), John Roeburts notes that courtroom dialogue is unique. He says, "Questions are repetitious, trite, put in child's primer form. And the smallest detail is patiently (and exasperatingly) explored—that idiot trivia that writers thrust out of mind, or if they write it down blue-pencil—or erase" (p. 37).

The trial testimony that appears in this book has been condensed. Although some material has been deleted, nothing has been changed or added: all quotations are exactly as they appear in the official transcript of the trial. A copy of the transcript is on file at the Lindbergh Case Archives, New Jersey State Police Headquarters, West Trenton, N.J.

CHAPTER 29   "THE LINDBERGHS TESTIFY"

1 For a complete discussion of Colonel Lindbergh's gun, see "Lindy's Little Lifesaver," *Guns and Ammo Magazine*, September 1982, pp. 80–81, 110.

2 Anne Morrow Lindbergh, *Locked Rooms and Open Doors: Diaries and Letters of Anne Morrow Lindbergh, 1933–1935* (New York: Harcourt Brace Jovanovich, 1974), p. 235.

3 Lt. Allen Smith's Guard Detail Memo of January 9, 1935, Lindbergh Case Archives, New Jersey State Police Headquarters, West Trenton, N.J.

4 My description of the scene in Flemington is based on David Davidson, "The Story of the Century," *American Heritage*, February 1976, pp. 23–24. Davidson covered the trial for the *New York Evening Post*.

5 Vitray's 190-page book, published by William Faro, Inc., is dedicated to William Randolph Hearst, who "fired me for writing it. . . ."

6 *New York Times*, January 8, 1935, p. 1.

7 The hostility between Bornmann and Reilly is described by Dr. Dudley D. Shoenfeld in his book, *The Crime and the Criminal: A Psychiatric Study of the Lindbergh Case* (New York: Covici-Friede, 1936), p. 131. Dr. Shoenfeld was in attendance in the courtroom every day of the trial, paying particular attention to the demeanor of the principals.

8 Lieutenant Smith's Guard Detail Memo of January 7, 1935.

CHAPTER 30   "JAFSIE AND THE POLICE WITNESSES"

1 In 1901 Sir Edward Richard Henry published *Classification and Uses of Fingerprints*, the book that contained the method of fingerprint classification eventually adopted in every English-speaking country in the world. The system was first used in America in 1904 by the St. Louis Police Department. In 1910 it was adopted by the police in New York City.

2 Reilly's harsh treatment of Perrone is noted in *The New York Times* reportage of the trial as well as by Dr. Dudley D. Shoenfeld in his book, *The Crime and the Criminal: A Psychiatric Study of the Lindbergh Case* (New York: Covici-Friede, 1936, p. 147).

3 *New York Times*, January 12, 1935, p. 30.

CHAPTER 31   "THE HANDWRITING WITNESSES"

1 "Expert Says Hauptmann Wrote All Ransom Notes," *New York Times*, January 12, 1935, p. 1.

2 Lt. Allen L. Smith's Guard Detail Memo of January 11, 1935, Lindbergh Case Archives, New Jersey State Police Headquarters, West Trenton, N.J.

3 *New York Times*, January 12, 1935, p. 1.

4 Lieutenant Smith's Guard Detail Memo of January 11, 1935.

5 *New York Times*, January 12, 1935, p. 1.

6 Dudley D. Shoenfeld, *The Crime and the Criminal: A Psychiatric Study of the Lindbergh Case* (New York: Covici-Friede, 1936), p. 205.

7 For an account of John Tyrrell's work in the Leopold-Loeb case, see Hyland J. Barnes, "Document Detective," *True Detective*, March 1944, pp. 42–46, 103–106.

8 *New York Times*, January 15, 1935, p. 1.

9 *New York Times*, January 16, 1935, p. 1.

10 Ibid.

11 For a complete discussion of Clark Sellers' analysis of the handwriting evidence, see his article, "The Handwriting Evidence Against Hauptmann," *Journal of Police Science*, March, 1937, pp. 874–886.

454

12 The prosecution's four rebuttal witnesses were Joseph Schulfhafer, Bert C. Farrar, J. Vreeland Haring, and J. Howard Haring. All together, at least twenty-one questioned-documents experts have concluded that Hauptmann was the ransom-note writer. In addition to the eight prosecution witnesses and the four rebuttal witnesses, Arthur P. Meyers, Samuel C. Malone, and Charles Appel of the FBI concluded this. At least six modern handwriting experts agree. They are Bill Burke, Donald F. Doud, Paul Osborn, Richard Tidey, Paul Batan, and John P. Osborn. When he examined the handwriting evidence in 1977, Richard Tidey was a questioned documents examiner for the New Jersey State Police. The other experts were in private practice at the time they examined the evidence. Bill Burke and the Osborns practiced in New York City, and Donald E. Doud works in Milwaukee.

CHAPTER 32 "ATTACKING THE AUTOPSY"

1 Lt. Allen L. Smith's Guard Detail memo of January 16, 1935, Lindbergh Case Archives, New Jersey, Trenton State Police Headquarters, West Trenton, N.J.

CHAPTER 33 "REILLY'S CONCESSION"

1 Dr. Dudley D. Shoenfeld, *The Crime and the Criminal: A Psychiatric Study of the Lindbergh Case* (New York: Covici-Friede, 1936), p. 217.

2 On December 5, 1972, Harold Olson, one of the people claiming to be young Charles Lindbergh, discussed the Lindbergh case with Wilentz in his law offices in Perth Amboy, New Jersey. According to Olson, Wilentz had said, "The defense should have used the lack of true identity in defense of Hauptmann, but the defense never did" (cited in Theon Wright, *In Search of the Lindbergh Baby* [New York: Tower, 1981], p. 148).

3 Shoenfeld, the psychiatrist from Mt. Sinai Hospital who was brought into the case by Lieutenant Finn of the New York police department, was in the courtroom when Hauptmann shouted at Sisk. Shoenfeld had been watching Hauptmann closely, and in *The Crime and the Criminal,* he states that in his opinion the outburst had nothing to do with Sisk's testimony. According to Dr. Shoenfeld, Hauptmann had been outraged by Reilly's concession and the emotional tension had built up since then. Shoenfeld noted, however, that he had been told by Gov. Harold Hoffman, a short time before Hauptmann's execution, that the defendant had told the governor that immediately after his arrest, he told the police how much of the ransom money he had and exactly where it was hidden. If this were true, then Hauptmann's outburst would have been in protest of Sisk's testimony. (*The Crime and the Criminal,* p. 220).

4 *New York Times,* January 17, 1935, p. 12.

5 Russell B. Porter, "Woman Says Hauptmann Limped After Kidnapping; 'You're Lying,' Wife Cries," *New York Times,* January 19, 1935, pp. 1, 7.

6 In February of 1983, the prestigious American Academy of Forensic Sciences, at its Thirty-fifth Annual Convention held that year in Cincinnati, sponsored a plenary session entitled, "The Lindbergh Kidnapping Revisited: Forensic Sciences Then and Now." The seven experts who presented papers at the Lindbergh Plenary Session were: Dr. Michael Baden ("The Autopsy"); Paul A. Osborn ("Questioned Documents"); Lucien Haag ("The Wood Evidence"); Dr. Emanuel Tanay ("Psychiatric Evidence"); James E. Starrs ("Legal Aspects"), and Jim Horan ("The General Investigation"). Paul A. Osborn is the son of Albert S. Osborn; John P. Osborn is his son. The entire session was recorded on video tape, which is on file at the Lindbergh Case Archives. It is also discussed in an article by Dr. Baden published in the October 1983 edition of the *American Journal of Forensic Science.* Except for the quality of Dr. Mitchell's autopsy, all of the experts agreed that the Lindbergh investigation is a high point in the history of criminal investigation and forensic science.

Col. Clinton Pagano, the superintendent of the New Jersey State Police, in 1977 asked Alan T. Lane, senior forensic chemist, for the state police, to compare samples of the Lindbergh baby's hair with the hair follicles in the burlap bag found near the Mount Rose gravesite. Mr. Lane's microscopic examination of the two sets of hair led him to the conclusion that the hair in the burlap bag was the same size, color, and texture as the baby's. Mr. Lane also compared the store-bought undershirt taken from the corpse with one of the shirts purchased by Mrs. Lindbergh. He concluded that the two garments matched in the following ways: labeling, size, style, cloth, weave pattern, stitching, and placement of patches. Mr. Lane studied the homemade flannel shirt found on the baby's body and found it had been cut from Betty Gow's remnant. He compared the blue thread that had been in the nursemaid's possession and found that it matched the thread that had been used to make the gravesite garment. Mr. Lane's testing of the Dr. Denton sleeping suit, the two undershirts, and the burlap bag for traces of human blood were negative. Mr. Lane's reports are on file at the Lindbergh Case Archives, New Jersey State Police Headquarters, West Trenton, N.J.

CHAPTER 34 "THE DEFENSE CALLS BRUNO RICHARD HAUPTMANN"

1 *New York Daily News*, January 25, 1935, p. 27.

2 *New York Daily News*, January 26, 1935 p. 20.

3 *New York Times*, January 27, 1935, p. 16.

4 Lt. Allen L. Smith's Guard Detail Memo of January 28, 1935, Lindbergh Case Archives, New Jersey State Police Headquarters, West Trenton, N.J.

5 Hauptmann had been watched closely by Dr. Dudley D. Shoenfeld, the psychiatrist who had worked with the New York City Police Department on the case. Shoenfeld was fascinated by Hauptmann's impassive face and his apparent lack of emotion. Seated in the court-

room every day since the trial began, Shoenfeld noticed that Hauptmann hadn't seemed bothered by questions that ordinarily would be quite disrupting. When asked directly by Reilly if he had kidnapped the Lindbergh baby, Hauptmann's denial was objective and impersonal. When the defense attorney asked him if he had ever seen the Lindbergh child, the defendant had tersely replied, "Never saw it." Since these questions were asked by Hauptmann's own lawyer, the defendant, assuming that he was innocent, had let an opportunity pass to express his outrage at such an allegation. Shoenfeld noted that even a guilty person's denial would normally be emotional, reflecting feelings of guilt and sorrow. The absence of what Shoenfeld called Hauptmann's "feeling tone," his complete control of his emotions regarding the commission of the crime, struck the psychiatrist as quite strange.

Shoenfeld was even more fascinated by the fact that when questioned about his own abilities and powers, Hauptmann's reaction had been markedly different. When answering these questions, Hauptmann had responded in a rather aggressive way. In particular, when asked if he had constructed the kidnap ladder, Hauptmann immediately defended himself, and without waiting to deny that he had made it, replied, "I am a carpenter," in a voice shaking with emotion. Hauptmann had been also touchy and emotional when responding to questions about his financial affairs. Dr. Shoenfeld thought it odd that Hauptmann was more worried about being perceived as a hack carpenter than he was of being painted as a kidnapper.

From these and other courtroom observations of Hauptmann, Dr. Shoenfeld concluded that the defendant was the type of person who was capable of committing the most atrocious crime without having feelings of remorse.

After watching and listening to the defendant's testimony, it was quite possible the jury shared Dr. Shoenfeld's conclusion *(The Crime and the Criminal: A Psychiatric Study of the Lindbergh Case* (New York: Covici-Friede, 1936), pp. 403–404.

CHAPTER 35 "ANNA AND THE ALIBI WITNESSES"

1 In Anthony Scaduto's *Scapegoat: The Lonesome Death of Bruno Richard Hauptmann* (New York: G. P. Putman's Sons, 1976), Mrs. Hauptmann recalled her testimony about the broom closet. She remembered that Wilentz had shown her a photograph of the closet with her apron hanging on the hook inside the door. When she examined the photograph she noted that the apron was higher than the top shelf. According to Mrs. Hauptmann, after her testimony, she and a group of reporters visited her old apartment to look at the closet. Something was different—she had no problem reaching the top shelf. The mystery was solved when a reporter discovered that the interior of the closet had been repainted. There were several layers of paint everywhere except where the shelves used to be. In these areas, there was only one coat of paint. It was obvious to Mrs. Hauptmann that someone had lowered the shelves about a foot so that her apron, when photographed, was higher than the top shelf. (p. 469).

2 Dr. Dudley D. Shoenfeld, *The Crime and the Criminal: A Psychiatric Study of the Lindbergh Case* (New York: Covici-Friede, 1936), p. 314.

3 Ibid, p. 315.

CHAPTER 36 "THE PHANTOM EXPERTS"

1 *St. Louis Globe-Democrat*, January 1, 1935, p. 1.

2 John Trendley claimed that he had fooled Albert S. Osborn this way thirty-five years earlier in the celebrated Patrick-Rice murder case. In that case, after the millionaire Rice was murdered, two conflicting wills were offered at probate. One of the wills left everything to Rice's nurse-valet and the other to what became Rice University. Osborn had testified that the latter will was genuine; Trendley had taken the opposite view. The verdict in that trial was consistent with Osborn's findings. If Osborn had been tricked by a Trendley forgery, the judge and jury in the Rice case must not have been impressed.

3 *New York Times*, February 1, 1935, p. 13.

4 Ibid., p. 1.

5 Hilda Braunlich's background and role in the Lindbergh case are part of an article about the defense's handwriting case published in the *New York Times* on April 4, 1977, p. 21. When this article was published, Miss Braunlich (married name Schaffer) was living in Clearwater, Florida.

Braunlich noted that Hauptmann's writing was characterized by a pattern of pressure points found in such letters as *a, b, g,* and a Germanic *h.* According to her analysis, the ransom notes were originally written smoothly, but an examination of the writing under a magnifying glass disclosed a thickening of the lines and a different blend or hue of ink.

6 In the second edition of his book, *Questioned Documents*, Albert S. Osborn devotes an entire chapter to inks and questioned documents. In this chapter he notes that in 1928 three classes of black ink were in use. Although these inks look alike on paper, differences can be revealed when the proper chemical tests or visual examinations are made. According to Osborn, it is possible to show that the ink on one document is fresher or younger than the ink on another. Moreover, ink lines on paper made by different inks of the same class can usually be distinguished from each other. If the ransom notes had been written over in places as Braunlich claimed, there would have been more to indicate this than a thickening of the lines. The ink used by the forger would not have matched the original ink. Also, the forger's ink would have been considerably fresher than the kidnapper's. Had this been the case, Osborn and the other questioned-documents examiners would have noted this on the ransom notes when they compared them to Hauptmann's known handwriting. The defense experts didn't have the time or the equipment to make scientific tests to prove or disprove their allegations.

7 George Waller, *Kidnap: The Story of the Lindbergh Case* (New York: Dial, 1961), pp. 442–443.

CHAPTER 37 "TRAGIC BURLESQUE"

1 Anthony Scaduto, in *Scapegoat: The Lonesome Death of Bruno Richard Hauptmann* (New York: G. P. Putman's Sons, 1976), says Kloppenburg complained to him that Reilly didn't ask him the right questions about Fisch, the shoebox, and the fact that Fisch was a crook. Kloppenburg also claimed that, a few days before he was to testify, Wilentz threatened to arrest him if he testified that he had seen Fisch bring the shoebox to Hauptmann's apartment (p. 447).
2 *New York Times*, February 6, 1935, p. 12.
3 *New York Times*, February 7, 1935, p. 14.
4 David Davidson. "The Story of the Century," *American Heritage*, February 1976, p. 28.
5 *New York Times*, February 7, 1935, p. 1.
6 Ibid., p. 14.
7 The first American textbook on scientific crime detection, *Modern Crime Investigation*, appeared in 1935, the year of the Lindbergh trial. This book, written by Dr. Harry Soderman and John J. O'Connell, doesn't mention silver nitrate. Silver nitrate wasn't mentioned in an American criminalistics text until it appeared in B. C. Bridge's *Practical Fingerprinting* (New York: Funk and Wagnalls, 1942). Silver nitrate is used today and so is dusting, which is still the most common way to process a crime scene for latents.
8 *New York Times*, February 8, 1935, p. 15.

CHAPTER 38 "SUMMING UP"

1 *New York Daily News*, February 8, 1935, p. 3.
2 Ibid., p. 1.
3 Ibid., p. 14.
4 Anne Morrow Lindbergh, *Locked Rooms and Open Doors: Diaries and Letters of Anne Morrow Lindbergh, 1933–1935* (New York: Harcourt Brace Jovanovich, 1974), pp. 246–247.
5 Grace Robinson, "Lindbergh Sure of Bruno's Guilt," *New York Daily News*, February 9, 1935, p. 4.
6 *New York American*, February 9, 1935, p. 8.
7 Reilly's appearance and demeanor following the lunch break are noted in Russell B. Porter's reportage of the trial in the *New York Times*, February 12, 1935. Reilly's lunchtime drinking during the trial is noted in several accounts of the case. In his article, "Why the Lindbergh Case Was Never Solved," Alan Hynd writes: "He [Reilly] was never fully awake until after lunch, when he drank eight or ten orange blossoms out of a coffee cup in a hotel across the street" in Alan Hynd's *Murder, Mayhem and Mystery* [New York, A. S. Banes, 1950] p. 37.
8 "Ejected Pastor Reticent on Story," *New York Times*, February 13, 1935, p. 15.

CHAPTER 39 "WEDNESDAY THE THIRTEENTH"

1 The descriptions of Hauptmann and the jury returning to the courtoom are based upon Russell B. Porter's reportage in the February 14, 1935, edition of *The New York Times*, pp. 1 and 12.
2 Craig Thompson, "Both Prepared for Worst," *New York Times*, February 14, 1935, p. 11.
3 Lt. Allen L. Smith's Guard Detail Memo, February 14, 1935, Lindbergh Case Archives, New Jersey State Police Headquarters, West Trenton, N. J.
4 Anne Morrow Lindbergh, *Locked Rooms and Open Doors: Diaries of Anne Morrow Lindbergh, 1933–1935*. (New York: Harcourt Brace Jovanovich, 1974), p. 249.

458

CHAPTER 40 "MOVING TO THE DEATH HOUSE"

1 *New York Times,* February 15, 1935, p. 5.

2 The Hauptmann jail interview appeared on p. 6 of the February 15, 1936, edition of *The New York Times.*

3 *New York Daily News,* February 15, 1935, p. 2.

4 *New York Times,* February 15, 1935, p. 6.

5 The statements of Walton, Snyder, Hockenbury, and Voorhees initially appeared in the February 15, 1935, edition of the *New York Evening Journal,* which on June 24, 1935, began a series of articles about the jurors and their feelings about the trial.

6 Lt. Allen L. Smith's Guard Detail Memo of February 15, 1935, Lindbergh Case Archives, New Jersey State Police Headquarters, West Trenton, N.J.

7 George Waller, *Kidnap: The Story of the Lindbergh Case* (New York: Dial, 1961), p. 502.

8 *New York Times,* February 23, 1935, p. 1.

9 *New York Times,* February 27, 1935, p. 14.

10 *New York Times,* March 4, 1935, p. 36.

11 *New York Times,* April 6, 1935, p. 15.

12 Ibid.

13 *New York Times,* August 30, 1935, p. 38.

CHAPTER 41 "STEPPING CLOSER TO THE CHAIR"

1 *New Jersey v. Hauptmann,* 180 A. 806 (1935).

2 *New York Times,* October 10, 1935, p. 21.

3 On June 5, 1954, Hoffman was found dead on the floor beside his bed in the Blake Hotel in Manhattan. The fifty-nine-year-old politician had died of a heart attack. Hoffman had found it increasingly difficult to hide his earlier thefts, and in 1950, when it looked as if his defalcations might come to light, he sought help from another state official, who, instead of helping him, blackmailed him for $150,000. (Hoffman was being investigated by Schwarzkopf, who at the time was the director of the

New Jersey Department of Law and Public Safety. By March 1954 Schwarzkopf had dug up enough evidence to get Hoffman fired.) Ten days after Hoffman's funeral, New Jersey governor Robert B. Meyner announced that Hoffman had given his daughter Ada an envelope to be opened at his death. Inside was a full confession of his thefts. Ada had shown the letter to two people and then had destroyed it. On June 15, 1954, in a sworn affidavit, Ada recited, to her best recollection, the substance of her father's confession. For more on Governor Hoffman's embezzlements, and his confession, see: George Cable Wright, "Hoffman's Theft of $300,000 Bared in Letter He Left," *New York Times,* June 15, 1954, pp. 1, 20, 21; George Cable Wright, "Hoffman Story: Politics, Payoffs," *New York Times,* June 27, 1954, pp. 4, 8; Leo J. Coakley, *Jersey Troopers* (New Brunswick, N.J.: Rutgers University Press, 1971), pp. 189–190.

4 This account of the Hoffman-Hauptmann meeting is based upon Hoffman's account of it, published in Parts 2 and 3 of his fourteen-part article, "The Crime—The Case—The Challenge." Part 2 and Part 3 are in the February 5 and February 12 editions of *Liberty Magazine.*

5 "Drops Hauptmann Suit," *New York Times,* October 17, 1935, p. 48.

6 *New York Daily Mirror,* December 4, 1935, p. 4.

7 *New York Times,* December 7, 1935, p. 4.

8 The substance of the Hoffman-Wilentz conversation is drawn from Hoffman's article, "The Crime—the Case—the Challenge," Part 4, *Liberty,* February 19, 1938.

9 Hauptmann's December 12 letter to Governor Hoffman is on file at the Lindbergh Case Archives, New Jersey State Police Headquarters, West Trenton, N.J. Following Hauptmann's execution, J. Vreeland Haring, the well-known handwriting expert from Newark, compared this "mercy letter" and another one written by Hauptmann the following March to the ransom note left in the nursery. Haring declared that his examination of these writings provided further proof that Hauptmann had written the nursery note. Haring's Lindbergh case findings are in *The Hand of Hauptmann: The Hand-writing Expert Tells the Story of the Lindbergh Case* (Plainview, N.J.: Hamer, 1937).

10 Walter S. Ross, *The Last Hero: Charles A. Lindbergh*, rev. ed. (New York: Harper and Row, 1976), p. 223.

11 Ibid., p. 226.

CHAPTER 42 "BUYING TIME"

1 The account of Governor Hoffman's visit with Mrs. Hauptmann is very close to Part 5 of his *Liberty Magazine* series, "The Crime—The Case—The Challenge," published on February 26, 1938.

2 *New York Times,* January 18, 1936, p. 1.

3 Hoffman's January 3, 1936, letter to Schwartzkopf is on file at the Lindbergh Case Archives. The documents, exhibits and pieces of evidence sent to Governor Hoffman by the New Jersey State Police were recovered, among other Lindbergh case papers, from Hoffman's garage in the fall of 1985 following the death of his wife. The baby's latent fingerprints were found with this material and, when compared to the prints of a man who claimed to be the Lindbergh baby, did not match.

4 Dr. Hudson's views are expressed in Part 5, Hoffman, "The Crime—The Case—The Challenge."

5 The details of Robert Hicks's report were reported in *The New York Times,* January 17, 1936, p. 2.

6 William Marston's visit to Trenton was reported by the *New York Times,* on January 23, 1936 (p. 40) and the *New York Daily News,* which referred to him as Dr. Marson, a "consultant-psychologist and mechanical lietester manipulator" (p. 22).

7 The story of Marston's involvement in the Lindbergh case is in his book, *The Lie Detector Test* (New York: Richard R. Smith, 1938), chapter 6, "Legal Obstacles—The Hauptmann Case."

8 Ibid., p. 86.

CHAPTER 43 "THE HOFFMAN WARS"

1 Hoffman's letter to Schwarzkopf, dated January 30, 1936, is on file at the Lindbergh Case Archives, New Jersey State Police Headquarters, West Trenton, N.J.

2 In an FBI memo dated November 21, 1966 (on file at the Lindbergh Case Archives), Hoover strongly denied an alleged 1936 remark that he had doubts regarding Hauptmann's guilt.

3 In an FBI memo dated March 28, 1936 (on file at the Lindbergh Case Archives), Hoover tells of how his agents were ordered out of Hauptmann's apartment just prior to the discovery of the gap in Hauptmann's attic. In this memo, Hoover implies that the New Jersey police had fabricated the wood evidence.

4 Hauptmann's letter to Warden Kimberling, dated February 11, 1936, is reproduced in Hoffman, "The Crime—The Case—The Challenge," Part 6, *Liberty,* March 5, 1938.

5 The February 13, 1936, Leibowitz-Hauptmann conversation is set out in Quentin Reynolds, *Courtroom: The Story of Samuel Leibowitz* (New York: Farrar, Straus, 1950) pp. 328–329. The substance of the Leibowitz-Hoffman conversation the next day is reported in Hoffman, "The Crime—the Case—the Challenge," Part 6; and in *The New York Times,* February 14, 1936.

6 The Hoffman-Fisher conversation is excerpted from Hoffman, "The Crime—the Case—the Challenge," Part 6.

7 Leibowitz's second visit with Hauptmann on February 17, 1936, is chronicled in Reynolds, *Courtroom,* pp. 330–333.

8 Hoffman, "The Crime—the Case—the Challenge," Part 6.

9 Accounts of the Hoffman-Fisher-Leibowitz meeting in Brooklyn on February 18, 1936, can be found in Reynolds, *Courtroom,* pp. 333–334; Andrew Dutch, *Hysteria: Lindbergh Kidnap Case* (Philadelphia: Dorrance, 1975), pp. 129–131; and Part 6 of Hoffman's *Liberty Magazine* article, March 5, 1938. Leibowitz's statements have been excerpted from

460 Dutch's book, but the remainder of the dialogue in the Hoffman-Leibowitz-Fisher meeting in the Hotel Towers reflects the author's idea of what was said and by whom.

10 Reynolds, *Courtroom,* p. 333; Hoffman, "The Crime—the Case—the Challenge," Part 6.

11 The prison guard's observation regarding Bruno Richard Hauptmann's handwriting was reported in the *New York Times,* February 21, 1936, p. 36.

12 Hoffman's letter is on file at the Lindbergh Case Archives.

13 *New York Times,* March 2, 1936, p. 15.

14 The substance of the following re-creation of the Wilentz-Hauck-Koehler-Bornmann-Loney-Hoffman confrontation in Hauptmann's attic on March 26, 1936, is based upon statements given to the press by Hoffman and Hauck following the meeting. George Waller, in *Kidnap: The Story of the Lindbergh Case* (New York: Dial, 1961), describes the scene on pp. 552–553. Most of the dialogue reflects my idea of what was said.

15 Lewis Bornmann's account of his confrontation with the governor is on an audio tape of his interview by Det. Sgt. Cornel Plebani and David Holwerda on June 28, 1983. This tape is on file at the Lindbergh Case Archives.

16 *New York Times,* March 27, 1936, p. 3.

CHAPTER 44 "THE CONFESSION"

1 George Waller, *Kidnap: The Story of the Lindbergh Case* (New York: Dial, 1961), p. 563.

2 Wendel first wrote of his kidnapping and confession in "Wendel Tells All—'My 44 Days of Kidnapping, Torture, and Hell in the Lindbergh Case,'" serialized in *Liberty Magazine.* The first installment appeared in the November 28, 1936, issue. In 1940, Wendel published *The Lindbergh-Hauptmann Aftermath* (Brooklyn: Loft).

3 Hauptmann had been dead eight days when, on April 11, 1936, the New York City police identified Martin Schlossman as one of the men who had kidnapped Paul Wendel. On April 20, four days after the Mercer County murder charges against Wendel had been dropped, the police arrested Schlossman at his home in Brooklyn.

Schlossman confessed to his role in the kidnapping and implicated five other men, including Ellis Parker and his son. According to Schlossman, Ellis Parker, Sr., had been the brains behind the scheme. The dirty work had been handled by his son and another father and son team, Harry and Murray Bleefeld. Harry, the father, owned the house in Brooklyn where Wendel had been beaten and confined. The remaining abductor was Harry Weiss, also of Brooklyn.

On April 24, Brooklyn District Attorney William F. X. Geoghan brought the Wendel case before the Kings County Grand Jury, which promptly indicted Schlossman, Weiss, the Bleefelds, and Ellis Parker, Jr., for kidnapping. Five days later the police arrested Harry Weiss in Youngstown, Ohio. In New York, the police collared Murray Bleefeld, and three days later they arrested his father, Harry, as he lay suffering from a kidney ailment in a Brooklyn hospital. Later that month the elder Bleefeld died.

The Kings County grand jury indicted Ellis Parker, Sr., on June 3, and three hours later, Lt. Lewis Bornmann of the New Jersey State Police arrested him as he walked out of the Mount Holly Elks Club. The next day, Governor Hoffman announced that he would not extradite Parker to New York. On July 8, police arrested Ellis Parker, Jr. Following young Parker's arrest in Mount Holly, Governor Hoffman made it clear that he wouldn't be extraditing him either.

Realizing that Parker and his son could not be brought to justice as long as Hoffman was governor, D.A. Geoghan turned the case over to the FBI. The fact that Wendel had been taken across a state line made the offense federal under the four-year-old Lindbergh law. In October 1936 the Parkers were indicted by a federal grand jury pursuant to the statute created by the crime they said their victim had committed.

In the spring of 1937, the Parkers were brought to trial in the federal district court in

Newark. Several weeks later, following the testimony of Paul Wendel, Murray Bleefeld, and Harry Weiss, they were found guilty of violating the Lindbergh law. Ellis Parker was sentenced to six years and his son three.

4   Lloyd Fisher's petition, filed March 30, 1936 before the court of pardons, is on file at the Lindbergh Case Archives, New Jersey State Police Headquarters, West Trenton, N.J.

5   Judge Trenchard's statement regarding Wendel's confession was taken from Harold Hoffman's article, "The Crime—the Case—the Challenge," Part 7, *Liberty*, March 12, 1938, p. 31. In *Kidnap*, Waller quotes the judge differently, but the meaning is the same.

6   Waller, *Kidnap*, p. 575.

7   Wilentz's statement was quoted by E. E. Marshall in the April 4, 1936, edition of *The New York Times*. See "Reprieve Denied at Last Minute by Hoffman after 2-Hour Parlay," p. 1.

8   Letter on file at Lindbergh Case Archives.

9   Harold Hoffman, "The Crime—the Case—the Challenge," Part 6, *Liberty*, March 5, 1938, p. 56.

CHAPTER 45   "THE EXECUTION"

1   George Waller, *Kidnap: The Story of the Lindbergh Case* (New York: Dial, 1961), p. 587.

2   *New York Times*, April 4, 1936, p. 2.

3   The account of Lieutenant Keaten's reaction to Hauptmann's execution is based upon an interview with his wife Lydia in the presence of Det. Sgt. Cornel Plebani on July 18, 1984, at her home in Morristown, N. J.

4   *New York Times*, April 3, 1936, p. 3.

5   The reaction of the world press was reported in the April 4, 1936, edition of *The New York Times*.

SOURCES AND ACKNOWLEDGMENTS

I am grateful to Det. Sgt. Cornel D. Plebani of the New Jersey State Police. Detective Plebani is in charge of the Lindbergh Case Archives housed at the New Jersey State Police Headquarters in West Trenton, New Jersey. Without his help and cooperation I would not have been able to write a true and thorough account of the Lindbergh story.

In 1981, pursuant to an executive order issued by Gov. Brendan T. Byrne, all of the Lindbergh case documents, photographs, trial exhibits, and physical evidence became permanently available to public inspection. It took Detective Plebani and Lt. Tom Barna (now deceased) five years to catalogue, file and index the two hundred thousand documents related to the case.

On my first visit to the Lindbergh Case Archives on June 4, 5, and 6, 1984, I examined the following pieces of physical evidence: The fifteen ransom documents, samples of Hauptmann's requested and conceded handwriting, his tool box, the three-piece kidnap ladder, the attic board from which rail 16 had been cut, the garments found on the Lindbergh baby's corpse, a notebook belonging to Hauptmann containing a sketch of a section of a ladder and a window, the door to Hauptmann's closet that contains Dr. John Condon's phone number and address, the baby's thumb guard, the drilled-out two by four in which ransom bills and Hauptmann's gun were hidden, and the 4.25 Liliput pistol itself. I also viewed a video account of the Lindbergh Case called "Men in Crisis," by Alan Landsburg. Narrated by Edmund O'Brien, it tells the story through hundreds of Fox Movietone news clips.

On the June 1984 trip to West Trenton, I accompanied Detective Plebani to the following places of interest in the case: The spot on Mount Rose Heights where the baby's body was found, the Hunterdon County courthouse and jail in Flemington, the Lindbergh estate at Hopewell, and the home of prosecution witness Amandus Hochmuth. In the Bronx, we visited St. Raymond's Cemetery, Woodlawn Cemetery, John Condon's home, and the Hauptmann

apartment in the house on East 222nd Street. Detective Plebani and I also traced the route Hauptmann took from his home to the place in Manhattan where he was taken out of his car and arrested.

On my second visit to the Lindbergh Archives, on July 16, 17, and 18, 1984, I viewed a four-hour video tape of the February 1983 Academy of Forensic Sciences Plenary Session entitled, "The Lindbergh Kidnapping Revisited: Forensic Science Then and Now." This program, held in Cincinnati, Ohio at the 35th Annual meeting of the Academy of Forensic Sciences, was a review of the Lindbergh evidence fifty years after the crime.

On this second visit to West Trenton I listened to several taped interviews of persons who had played vital roles in the Lindbergh investigation and trial. I also reviewed numerous documents, including parts of the 32-volume, 7,587-page transcript of the Hauptmann trial, and examined many of the exhibits introduced by the prosecution.

On my third trip to the New Jersey State Police Headquarters, on July 31 and August 1, 1984, I studied several more Lindbergh case documents including numerous files pertaining to Violet Sharpe. I also had the pleasure of discussing the case briefly with Col. Clinton C. Pagano, the superintendent of the New Jersey State Police and the man most responsible for the existence of the Lindbergh Case Archives.

In the course of my research I had hundreds of Lindbergh case documents duplicated at the archives. Among other data, this material included twenty-seven *Liberty Magazine* articles written by C. Lloyd Fisher and Harold G. Hoffman and published in 1936 and 1938; Trooper A. L. Smith's guard memos reporting Hauptmann's conversations and activities during his incarceration in the Flemington Jail from October 10, 1934, to February 15, 1935 (224 pages); and 195 pages, in question-and-answer form, of Hauptmann's interrogations by the New York City Police, the New Jersey State Police, and the FBI. The other material included dozens of memos, police reports, letters, state-

464 ments, affidavits, and portions of the official trial transcript.

In April 1986 I returned to the Lindbergh Case Archives to study the documents that had been recovered in the fall of 1985, material that had been in the possession of Governor Harold G. Hoffman. I reviewed these papers to satisfy myself that there was nothing in these documents that contradicted my earlier findings and beliefs about the case. On this occasion the New Jersey State Police made available several photographs for use in the book.

I am deeply indebted to my friend and fellow criminal justice Professor, E. Ernest Wood. Professor Wood painstakingly went over the manuscript and in the process discovered many errors and several major mistakes and defects, which he helped correct. He also acted as a sounding board and advisor and was a continuing source of encouragement. Had Mr. Wood not expended so much effort and talent on the book, the product would not have come out as well as it did. I cannot thank him enough or overstate the value of his contribution.

Typing the manuscript was a huge undertaking, and I am grateful for the work of Gail Glenn and her daughter Sue, who between them typed half of the book. Craig McConnell typed the bulk of the other thousand pages, with Peggy McConnell typing the rest. I am fortunate to have had such competent and dedicated assistance.

Thanks to Dr. Roy Brant, the chairman of the Political Science Department at Edinboro University, I didn't have to make my own copies of the manuscript. Dr. Brant arranged to have the school's duplicating office handle this enormous task. I am therefore grateful to Dr. Brant and the school.

The following criminal justice students at Edinboro University made copies of hundreds of microfilmed articles from *The New York Times:* Harry Franks, Robert Daugherty, David Seretti, and Craig McConnell. On March 12, 1984, Harry Franks visited the Lindbergh Archives on my behalf and on that occasion photographed, under Detective Plebani's supervision, much of the physical evidence and many of the trial exhibits.

I would also like to thank Sue Hennip at Edinboro's Baron-Forness Library for the books and articles she obtained for me through interlibrary loan system.

Through the efforts of Patterson Smith, the well-known antiquarian bookseller and publisher from Montclair, New Jersey, I was able to purchase six hard-to-get books on the Lindbergh case as well as three large scrapbooks containing hundreds of Lindbergh case clippings from four New York City newspapers.

My friend Dick Ballantine, the owner of a used bookstore in Grove City, Pennsylvania, supplied me with many out-of-print books and magazines containing articles about the case. For his interest and help, I am very grateful.

I am also grateful to Jean Calhoun and Helen Thompson of New Wilmington, Pennsylvania, for each giving me a collection of old newspapers containing Lindbergh case reportage. Russell and Claire Wood gave me old copies of the *Erie Dispatch-Herald*, which were also helpful in writing the book.

In the course of my research, I interviewed the following people, to whom I am indebted: *Mrs. Lydia Keaten.* Mrs. Keaten is the widow of Lt. Arthur T. Keaten, one of the principal Lindbergh case investigators for the New Jersey State Police. I talked to Mrs. Keaten at her home on July 18, 1984, in the presence of Detective Cornel Plebani, who kindly arranged the interview.

Alan T. Lane. Mr. Lane is the senior forensic chemist at the New Jersey State Police Crime Laboratory. He was interviewed at the crime lab on June 4, 1984. Detective Plebani arranged this interview as well.

Mr. Albert Axelrod. Mr. Axelrod is the superintendent of Highfields, a home for teenage boys. Highfields was formerly the Lindbergh Estate. Mr. Axelrod was questioned at Highfields, which was at the time temporarily closed because of fire. Detective Plebani was present during the interview.

Det. Sgt. Cornel D. Plebani. On each of my four visits to the Lindbergh Archives, I questioned Detective Plebani at length about various aspects of the Lindbergh Case. He answered more questions on October 24 and 25, 1984, when he spoke about the case at Edinboro University. Detective Plebani also responded to dozens of my telephonic inquiries in 1985 and 1986.

Audio-taped interviews of the following key figures in the Lindbergh case, conducted by Detective Plebani, were reviewed by me in the summer of 1984:

Walter H. Swayze. Mr. Swayze was the Mercer County Coroner. He was interviewed on September 19, 1977, when he was seventy-four. This tape reveals that Dr. Mitchell talked Swayze through the baby's autopsy.

John Wallace. Mr. Wallace was an officer with the New Jersey State Police. Mr. Wallace, who died in September 1985, was interviewed in June 1981.

Lewis Bornmann. Mr. Bornmann was the New Jersey State Police officer who found the gap in Hauptmann's attic that corresponded to rail 16 of the kidnap ladder. He was interviewed in June 1983 by Detective Plebani and David Holwerda. Mr. Bornmann also appears in the 1982 PBS television documentary, *Who Killed the Lindbergh Baby?*

NEWSPAPERS CONSULTED

From March 1, 1932 to April 4, 1936, millions of words about the Lindbergh case were published in *The New York Times*. The *New York Times* Index and the microfilm collections at Edinboro University and Westminister College gave me access to all of this material. I am especially indebted to *New York Times* correspondents Russell B. Porter and Craig Thompson whose coverage of the Hauptmann trial was particularly helpful.

Ethel Stockton, one of the Hauptmann jurors, put together a large scrapbook of the trial, containing clippings from several newspapers. A copy of these clippings was made available by Detective Plebani. This collection was very helpful and contained pieces from the following newspapers:

Hunterdon County Democrat

New York American

New York Evening Journal

New York Daily News

Detective Plebani also made available a copy of a newspaper clipping file that had been collected by Insp. Harry Walsh of the Jersey City Police Department. Inspector Walsh was one of the key Lindbergh case investigators. His scrapbook contained clippings from the *New York Daily News* from March 3, 1932 to May 27, 1932.

The three scrapbooks obtained from Patterson Smith included clippings from the following newspapers:

New York Daily Mirror (Correspondent James Whittaker)

New York Daily News (Staff Correspondents Russ Symontowne, Jack Alexander, and Robert Conway)

New York Evening Journal

New York Herald Tribune

Other newspapers I consulted are:

Erie Dispatch-Herald

Erie Daily Times

Erie Morning News

Jersey Journal

Johnstown Tribune

New Castle News

Pittsburgh Post-Gazette

Pittsburgh Sun Telegraph

The Bronx Home News

The White Plains Daily Reporter

Youngstown Vindicator

BIBLIOGRAPHY OF BOOKS AND ARTICLES ABOUT THE LINDBERGH CASE

Note: Some of the books and articles listed below are more useful than others. The most valuable are those written by Sidney B. Whipple, George Waller, John F. Condon, J. Vreeland

466 Haring, and Dudley D. Shoenfeld. The published diaries and letters of Anne Morrow Lindbergh are also very valuable sources. The most significant articles are those by C. Lloyd Fisher, Harold G. Hoffman, Alan Hynd, Arthur Koehler, and Tom Zito.

BOOKS:

Ahlgren, Gregory, and Stephen Monier. *Crime of the Century: The Lindbergh Kidnapping Hoax.* Boston: Branden Books, 1993.

Battan, David. *Handwriting Analysis.* San Luis Obispo, Calif.: Padre Productions, 1984. Chapter 17, "Document Examination: The Lindbergh Case."

Behn, Noel. *Lindbergh, The Crime.* Boston: Atlantic Monthly Press, 1993.

Brant, John, and Edith Renaud. *True Story of the Lindbergh Kidnapping.* New York: Kroy Wen, 1932.

Busch, Francis X. *Prisoners at the Bar.* London: Arco, 1957. "The Trial of Bruno Hauptmann for the Murder of Charles Lindbergh, Jr. 1935."

Coakley, Leo J. *Jersey Troopers.* New Brunswick, N.J.: Rutgers University Press, 1971. Chapter 6, "The Lindbergh Kidnapping."

Collins, Max Allen. *Stolen Away: A Novel of the Lindbergh Kidnapping.* New York: Bantam, 1991.

Condon, John F. *Jafsie Tells All!* New York: Jonathan Lee, 1936.

Davis, Kenneth. *The Hero: Charles A. Lindbergh and the American Dream.* Garden City, N.Y.: Doubleday, 1954. Chapter 12, "Blood Sacrifice."

Dearden, Harold. *Aspects of Murder.* London: Staples Press, 1951. "The Ladder."

Demaris, Ovid. *The Lindbergh Kidnapping Case: The True Story of the Crime that Shocked the World.* Derby, Conn.: Monarch Books, 1961.

Dutch, Andrew K. *Hysteria: The Lindbergh Kidnap Case.* Philadelphia: Dorrance, 1975.

Elliott, Robert G., with Albert R. Beatty. *Agent of Death: The Memoirs of an Executioner.* New York: E. P. Dutton, 1940. "Hauptmann Execution."

Haldeman-Julius, Marcet. *The Lindbergh-Hauptmann Kidnap-Murder Case.* Girard, Kans.: Haldeman-Julius Publications, 1937.

Haring, John Vreeland. *The Hand of Hauptmann: The Handwriting Expert Tells the Story of the Lindbergh Case.* Plainfield, N.J.: Hamer, 1937.

Herrmann, Dorothy. *Anne Morrow Lindbergh: A Gift for Life.* New York: Ticknor & Fields, 1993.

Hoyt, Edwin. *Spectacular Rogue: Gaston B. Means.* Indianapolis: Bobbs-Merrill, 1963. Chapter 14.

Hynd, Alan. *Murder, Mayhem, and Mystery.* New York: A. S. Barnes, 1958, "Why the Lindbergh Case was Never Solved."

———. *The Giant Killers.* New York: Robert M. McBride, 1945. "The Intelligence Unit Encounters Murder."

Irey, Elmer L., told to William J. Slocum. *The Tax Dodgers.* New York: Greenberg: 1948. Chapter 3, "The Crime of the Century."

Kennedy, Ludovic. *The Airman and the Carpenter: The Lindbergh Kidnapping and the Framing of Richard Hauptmann.* New York: Viking, 1985.

Leighton, Isabel, ed. *The Aspirin Age: 1919–1941.* New York: Simon and Schuster, 1949. "The Lindbergh Legends," by John Lardner.

Lewis, Jerry D. ed. *Crusade Against Crime.* New York: Bernard Geis Associates, 1962. "The Lindbergh Tragedy," by Leon G. Turrou.

Lindbergh, Anne Morrow. *Hour of Gold, Hour of Lead: Diaries and Letters of Anne Morrow Lindbergh, 1929–1932.* New York: Harcourt Brace Jovanovich, 1973.

———. *Locked Rooms and Open Doors: Diaries and Letters of Anne Morrow Lindbergh, 1933–1935.* New York: Harcourt Brace Jovanovich, 1974.

Lindbergh, Charles A. *Autobiography of Values.* Edited by William Jovanovich and Judith A. Schiff. New York: Harcourt Brace Jovanovich, 1977.

———. *The Wartime Journals of Charles A. Lindbergh.* New York: Harcourt Brace Jovanovich, 1970.

Marston, William M., *The Lie Detector Test.* New York: Richard B. Smith, 1938. Chapter 6, "Legal Obstacles—The Hauptmann Case."

Milton, Joyce. *Loss of Eden: A Biography of Charles and Anne Morrow Lindbergh.* New York: HarperCollins, 1993.

Mosley, Leonard. *Lindbergh: A Biography.* Garden City, N.Y.: Doubleday, 1976. Chapter 13 "The Fat Lamb is Stolen."

Mott, Frank Luther, ed. *Headlining America.* Boston: Houghton Mifflin, 1937. "Hauptmann Execution," by Damon Runyon; "Scientist Lindbergh," by Jack Alexander and Ellwood Douglas; and "The Lindberghs Leave America," by Lauren D. Lyman.

Nicolson, Nigel ed. *Harold Nicolson: Diaries and Letters 1930–1939.* New York: Atheneum, 1966.

O'Brien, P. J. *The Lindberghs: The Story of a Distinguished Family.* New York: International Press, 1935.

Osborn, Albert D. *Questioned Documents Problems.* Albany, N.Y.: Boyd Printing, 1944.

Osterburg, James W. *The Crime Laboratory: Case Studies of Scientific Criminal Investigation, 2nd ed.* New York: Clark Boardman, 1982. "Hauptmann-Lindbergh Case."

Pearson, Edmund. *Studies in Murder.* New York: Random House, Modern Library Edition, 1938. "Hauptmann and Circumstantial Evidence."

Pease, Frank. *The "Hole" in the Hauptmann Case?* New York: Frank Pease, 1936.

Powers, Richard Gid. *Secrecy and Power: The Life of J. Edgar Hoover.* New York: The Free Press, 1987.

Radelet, Michael L. et al. *In Spite of Innocence: Erroneous Convictions in Capital Cases.* Boston: Northeastern University Press, 1992.

Radin, Edward D. *12 Against Crime.* New York: G. P. Putnam's Sons, 1950. Chapter 10, "Sawdust Trail."

Reynolds, Quentin. *Courtroom: The Story of Samuel S. Leibowitz.* New York: Farrar, Straus, 1950.

Robinson, Henry. *Science Catches the Criminal.* Indianapolis: Bobbs-Merrill, 1935. Chapter 8, "Clues in Wood"

Ross, Walter. *The Last Hero: Charles A. Lindbergh, revised and enlarged ed.* New York: Harper & Row, 1976. Chapter 17, "The Hauptmann Case."

Scaduto, Anthony. *Scapegoat: The Lonesome Death of Bruno Richard Hauptmann.* New York: G. P. Putnam's Sons, 1976.

Sheridan, Leo W. *I Killed for the Law.* New York: Stackpole Sons, 1938. Chapter 9, "Bruno Richard Hauptmann."

Shoenfeld, Dudley David. *The Crime and the Criminal: A Psychiatric Study of the Lindbergh Case.* New York: Covici-Friede, 1936.

Spencer, Mary Belle. *No. 2310, Criminal File Exposed! Aviator's Baby was Never Kidnapped or Murdered.* Chicago: Confidential News Syndicate, 1933.

Still, Charles. *Styles in Crime.* Philadelphia: J. B. Lippincott, 1938. Chapter 15, "The Lindbergh Case and Kidnap Laws."

Sullivan, Edward Dean. *The Snatch Racket.* New York: The Vanguard Press, 1932. Chapter 12, "The Snatch Racket Reaches its Climax: The Lindbergh Case."

Tully, Andrew. *Treasury Agent: The Inside Story.* New York: Simon and Schuster, 1958. Chapter 18, "A Baby Named Lindbergh."

Turrou, Leon G. *Where My Shadow Falls,* Garden City, N.Y. Doubleday, 1949. Chapter 6, "The Lindbergh Tragedy."

Vernon, John. *Lindbergh's Son.* New York: Viking, 1987 (novel).

Vitray, Laura. *The Great Lindbergh Hullabaloo: An Unorthodox Account.* New York: William Faro, 1932

Waller, George. *Kidnap: The Story of the Lindbergh Case.* New York: Dial Press, 1961.

Wendel, Paul H. *The Lindbergh-Hauptmann Aftermath.* New York: Loft, 1940.

Whipple, Sidney B. *The Lindbergh Crime.* New York, Blue Ribbon Books, 1935.

Whipple, Sidney B. ed. *The Trial of Bruno Richard Hauptmann: Edited with a History of the Case.* Garden City, N.Y.: Doubleday, Doran, 1937.

Wilson, Frank J., and Beth Day. *Special Agent: A Quarter Century with the Treasury Department and the Secret Service.* New York: Holt, Rinehart, and Winston, 1956. Chapter 4.

Wright, Theon. *In Search of the Lindbergh Baby.* New York: Tower Books, 1981.

468   ARTICLES

Adams, Jean. "The Untold Truth about Haupt-mann's Wife." *True Detective Mysteries,* September 1936.

Allen, Neal. "They Called It the Crime of the Century." *Woman's World,* March 6, 1990.

Allhoff, Fred. "What Happened to Ellis Parker?" *Liberty Magazine,* 8 parts beginning May 7, 1938.

Badin, Michael M. "The Lindbergh Kidnapping: Review of the Autopsy Evidence." *Journal of Forensic Science,* October 1983.

Barnes, Harry E. "The Deeper Lesson of the Lindbergh Kidnapping." *Survey,* April 1, 1932.

Bedau, Hugo A., and Michael L. Radelet. "Miscarriages of Justice in Potentially Capital Cases." *Stanford Law Review,* November 1987.

Blackman, Samuel G. "The Case That Shook the World." *The Milwaukee Journal,* February 3, 1992.

———. "Hauptmann Trial Gripped the U.S. Half Century Ago." *Youngstown (Ohio) Vindicator,* February 10, 1985.

———. "Lindbergh Kidnapping: 'Crime of the Century.'" *Youngstown (Ohio) Vindicator,* February 21, 1982.

Boehn, Sid. "Hauptmann—A Jersey Industry." *Easy Money,* June 1936.

Carnes, Cecil. "Let's Finish the Lindbergh Case." *Bluebook Magazine,* August, 1952.

Christensen, Donna J. "Lindbergh Kidnapping: The Ladder Link." *Forest and People* 27(1977).

Collins, Frederick L. "What Will Happen Next in the Lindbergh Case?" *Liberty,* November 7, 1936.

Condon, John F. "Jafsie Tells All!" 10 parts. *Liberty,* January 18, 1936–March 21, 1936.

Curtin, D. Thomas. "What Hauptmann Did with the Missing Money." *Liberty,* May 9, 1936.

Curtin, D. Thomas, and James J. Finn. "How I Captured Hauptmann." *Liberty,* October 12, 19, 26, November 2, 9, 16, 23, 1935.

Davidson, David D. "The Story of the Century." *American Heritage,* February 1976.

DeWan, George. The Lindbergh Case Just Won't Go Away." *Newsday,* December 15, 1987.

Doud, Donald F. "Literary Retrials of Notable Forensic Science Cases—Convoluted History for Sale." *Journal of Forensic Sciences,* January 1988.

———. "A Review of *The Lindbergh Case.*" *Journal of Forensic Sciences,* January 1989.

Duncan, Gerald. "Unsolved Mysteries of the Lindbergh Case." *New York Daily News,* November 29, 1935.

Dunlap, Al. "Was the Body of the Lindbergh Baby Really Found?" *Startling Detective,* May 1932.

———. "Why No Lie Detector for the Lindbergh Case?" *The Detective,* September 1932. Reprinted in *Silent Witness,* edited by Donald C. Dilworth (Gaithersburg, Md.: International Association of Chiefs of Police, 1977).

Earle, Robert. "Find the Lindy Killers!" *Startling Detective,* August 1932.

Elliot, Robert G., as told to Albert R. Beatty. "And May God Have Mercy on Your Soul." *Collier's,* September 24, 1938.

Feld, Rose C. "Circumstantial Evidence: How Strong?" *New York Times Magazine,* June 16, 1935.

Fiedler, Cheryl. "The Lindbergh Case." 35-part article. *Flemington, Clinton Family News,* January 26, 1988–November 1, 1988.

Fisher, C. Lloyd. "The Case New Jersey Would Like to Forget." *Liberty,* August 1, 8, 15, 22, 29, September 5, 12, 1936.

Fisher, Jim. "How Can Such a Guilty Kidnapper Be So Innocent?" *The Chief of Police,* November/December 1988.

Haag, Lucien C. "The Lindbergh Case Revisited: A Review of the Criminalistics Evidence." *Journal of Forensic Sciences,* October 1983.

Hauptmann, Bruno Richard. "Hauptmann's Own Story." *New York Daily Mirror,* December 3–10, 1935.

———. "Why Did You Kill Me?" *Liberty,* May 2, 1936. Reprinted in *America: An Illustrated Diary of its Most Exciting Years* (New York: Stonehouse Press, 1972).

Hoffman, Harold G. "The Crime, The Case, The Challenge." *Liberty*, January 29, February 5, 12, 19, 26, March 5, 12, 19, 26, April 2, 9, 16, 23, 30, 1938.

———. "Things I Forgot." *Liberty*, July 2, 9, 1938.

Horan, James J. "The Investigation of the Lindbergh Kidnapping Case." *Journal of Forensic Sciences*, October 1983.

Hudson, Erastus M. "A Scientific Verdict on the Lindbergh-Hauptmann Riddle." *Liberty*, April 3, 1937.

Hynd, Alan. "Everyone Wanted to Get Into the Act." *True Magazine*, March 1949. Reprinted in Alan Hynd, *Violence in the Night* (New York: Fawcett, 1955) and *A Treasury of True* (New York: A. S. Barnes, 1956).

———. "The Real Story Behind the Lindbergh Capture." *True Detective Mysteries*, January, March 1935.

———. "Unrevealed Secrets That Torture Gaston Means." Nine parts, *True Detective Mysteries*, September–December, 1936 and January–May 1937.

———. "Untold Facts in the Lindbergh Kidnapping." Seven parts, *True Detective Mysteries*, November, December 1932; January, February, March, April, and May 1933.

Keenan, John F. "The Lindbergh Kidnapping Revisited." *Michigan Law Review*, February–April 1986.

Keith, Stanley R. "Identification of the Lindbergh Ladder Nails." *Iron Age*, October 17, 1935.

Knight, Richard A. "Trial by Fury." *Forum*, January 1936.

Koehler, Arthur. "Techniques Used in Tracing the Lindbergh Kidnapping Ladder." *Journal of Criminal Law and Criminology*, January–February 1937. Also published in *Police Journal* (London, July 1937).

———. "Wood Expert." *South Dakota Bar Journal*, July 1935.

———. "Who Made That Ladder?" *Saturday Evening Post*, April 20, 1935.

MacKaye, Milton. "For the Defense." *The New Yorker*, January 12, 1935.

McLean, Evalyn Walsh, with Alan Hynd. "Why I Am Still Investigating the Lindbergh Case." Ten parts. *Liberty*, beginning July 23, 1938.

Matteson, Leigh. "I Could Have Broken the Lindbergh Case Two Years Ago." *Today*, October 27, 1934.

Mefford, Arthur L. "Did Hauptmann Work Alone?" *Real Detective*, August 1935.

Mitchell, Charles H., as told to Fenton Mallory. "Did Hauptmann Die in the Chair?" *Daring Detective*, June 1936.

Moseley, Seth H. "The Night the Lindbergh Baby Disappeared." *Yankee Magazine*, March 1982.

Oursler, Fulton. "Jafsie in Panama Discusses New Evidence." *Liberty*, March 28, 1936.

Palenik, Skip. "Microscopic Trace Evidence— The Overlooked Clue." *The Microscope*, First Quarter, 1983.

Prescott, Peter S. "Cobbling Up Conviction." *Newsweek*, June 24, 1985.

Prosser, William. "The Lindbergh Case Revisited: George Waller's 'Kidnap.'" *Minnesota Law Review* 46 (1961).

Reilly, Edward J. "Will Lindbergh Save Hauptmann?" *Liberty*, October 5, 1935.

Resinger, D. Michael, et al. "Exorcism of Ignorance as a Proxy for Rational Knowledge: The Lessons of Handwriting Identification 'Expertise.'" *University of Pennsylvania Law Review* 137 (1989).

Robbins, Albert H. "The Hauptmann Trial in the Light of English Criminal Procedure." *American Bar Association Journal*, May 1935.

Sanders, Paul H. "Scientific and Procedural Aspects of the Hauptmann Trial." *American Bar Association Journal*, May 1935.

Seidman, Louis M. "The Trial and Execution of Bruno Hauptmann: Still Another Case That Will Not Die." *Georgetown Law Journal*, October 1977.

Sellers, Clark. "The Handwriting Evidence Against Hauptmann." *Journal of Police Science*, January 1937.

Smith, Patterson. "The Literature of Ransom Kidnapping in America." *AB Bookmans Weekly*, April 23, 1990.

———. "Puzzles of True Crime Literature: The Lindbergh Case." *AB Bookmans Weekly*, April 25, 1983.

470 Smits, Jeanette. "How Much Did Hauptmann Tell His Wife?" *True Detective Mysteries,* November 1935.

Starrs, James E. "The Prosecution of Bruno Richard Hauptmann: An Imitation of Falconry." *Journal of Forensic Sciences,* October 1983.

Tanay, Emanuel. "The Lindbergh Kidnapping—A Psychiatric View." *Journal of Forensic Sciences,* Ocrober 1981.

Taylor, Becky. "Hauptmann Placed at Kidnap Scene." *Sunday Times Advertiser* (Trenton), November 14, 1976.

Thompson, Craig. "Did They Really Solve the Lindbergh Case?" *Saturday Evening Post,* March 8, 1952.

Walsh, Harry W., as told to E. Collins. "Hunt for the Kidnappers: Inside Story of the Lindbergh Case." *Jersey Journal,* November 15, 16, 17, 18, 19, 21, 22, 23, 1932.

Wedemer, Lou. "50 Unanswered Questions in the Hauptmann Case: A Searching Survey of the Doubts and 'Sinister Suggestions' That Still Shadow the Famous Crime." *Liberty,* January 4, 1936.

Wendel, Paul H. "Wendel Tells All—'My 44 Days of Kidnapping, Torture, and Hell in the Lindbergh Case.'" *Liberty,* Multi-part series starting November 28, 1936.

Werner, D. G., as told to Avery Hale. "What Hauptmann Revealed Just Before He Died." *True Detective Mysteries,* October 1936.

Wilson, P. W. "The Lindbergh Case." *North American Review,* January 1934.

Wixen, Joan Saunders. "I Covered the Lindbergh Kidnapping." *Modern Maturity,* April–May 1982.

Yagoda, Ben. "Legacy of a Kidnapping." *New Jersey Monthly,* August 1981.

Yerkes, Peter. "Did Bruno Hauptmann Really Do It?" *Today, The Inquirer Magazine,* April 9, 1978.

Zito, Tom. "Did the Evidence Fit the Crime?" *Life Magazine,* March 1982.

INDEX